MW00648927

Radical Friend

Radical Friend

Amy Kirby Post and Her Activist Worlds

NANCY A. HEWITT

The University of North Carolina Press Chapel Hill

© 2018 The University of North Carolina Press
All rights reserved
Set in Charis and Lato by Westchester Publishing Services
Manufactured in the United States of America

The University of North Carolina Press has been a member of the
Green Press Initiative since 2003.

Library of Congress Cataloging-in-Publication Data
Names: Hewitt, Nancy A., 1951– author.
Title: Radical friend : Amy Kirby Post and her activist worlds /
    Nancy A. Hewitt.
Description: Chapel Hill : University of North Carolina Press, [2018] |
    Includes bibliographical references and index.
Identifiers: LCCN 2017044377 | ISBN 9781469640327 (cloth : alk. paper) |
    ISBN 9781469640334 (ebook)
Subjects: LCSH: Post, Amy Kirby, 1802– | Quaker women—New York
    (State)—Biography. | Social reformers—New York (State)—Biography. |
    Women radicals—New York (State)—Biography. | Social movements—
    United States—History—19th century.
Classification: LCC BX7795.P65 H49 2018 | DDC 289.6092 [B]—dc23
    LC record available at https://lccn.loc.gov/2017044377

For Mary M. Huth, who inspired me to begin

For Irene Hewitt, Will Hewitt, and Neerja Bhatnager, who cheered me on

&

For Steven F. Lawson, who sustained me to the end

Contents

A gallery of illustrations follows page 192

Map

City of Rochester, 1851, 90

Cast of Characters

Jericho and Westbury Family and F/friends

Amy Kirby (AK), b. 1802, d. 1889
Mary Seaman Kirby, AK's mother, d. 1854
Jacob Kirby, AK's father, d. 1859
Mary W. Kirby, AK's sister, b. 1791
    m. John Willis
Hannah Kirby, AK's sister, b. 1799, d. 1827
    m. Isaac Post, 1821; daughter Mary, b. 1823; son Edmund, b. 1825
Elizabeth Kirby, AK's sister, b. 1814
    m. James Mott
Sarah Kirby, AK's sister, b. 1818
Esther Seaman and Willet Robbins, AK's aunt and uncle
Mary Robbins, b. 1806, AK's first cousin and confidante
    m. Joseph Post 1828, Isaac Post's brother
John and Rebecca Ketcham, AK's cousins
Jemima Seaman, Mary Seaman Kirby's cousin
    m. Elias Hicks 1771, Quaker minister and antislavery advocate
Isaac Post, b. 1798, d. 1872, Westbury, N.Y.; moves to Ledyard, N.Y., after
    marrying Hannah Kirby in 1821
Phebe Post Willis and Lydia Post Rushmore, Isaac Post's married sisters
Edmund and Joseph Post, Isaac Post's brothers
Charles Willets, Isaac Post's first cousin and AK's fiancé, d. 1826
Amy Willis and Anna Greene, AK's childhood friends

Society of Friends Traveling Ministers and Visitors

Elias Hicks, advocate of reforming Quaker practices and leader of Hicksite
    faction
Lucretia and James Mott, Kirby cousins and weighty Philadelphia Hicksite
    Friends
Anna Braithewaite, English Friend opposed to Elias Hicks's views
Priscilla Coffin Hunt Cadwalader, Hicksite minister

Joseph John Gurney, English reform-minded minister, visited central N.Y. late 1830s

Rachel Hicks and George White, Hicksite ministers opposed to worldly activism

Isaac Hopper, prominent Hicksite, disowned for exciting discord over worldly activism

Thomas and Mary Ann M'Clintock, Philadelphia Hicksites, moved to Waterloo, N.Y.

Charles Townsend, Hicksite visitor to Genesee Yearly Meeting 1835

Ledyard and Central New York Family and F/friends

Amy Kirby m. Isaac Post, 1828 in Ledyard

Stepchildren: Mary and Edmund (d. 1830); sons Jacob (b. 1829), Joseph (b. 1832), Henry (b. 1834)

Sarah Kirby, Amy Kirby Post's (AKP) sister, b. 1818, spends extended time in central N.Y.

Phebe Post Willis, stayed with Posts after traveling with Lucretia Mott

Rhoda and Elias DeGarmo, Post F/friends, moved to Rochester in 1834

Sarah and Benjamin Fish, Post F/riends, moved to Rochester c. 1829

Anna Greene, F/friend of AKP

Benjamin and Mary Howland, Orthodox Quaker neighbors of the Posts

Lydia and Abigail Mott, AKP cousins, Abolitionists (Ab)

Sarah and Phebe Thayer, AKP cousin and her daughter, Ab

Esther and Frances Titus, AKP cousin and daughter, Ab, later Freedmen's Aid

Susan White, Post F/friend, m. Elias Doty 1833, Ab

Hannah Willets, F/friend of AKP

Rochester, N.Y., Family Members

Amy and Isaac Post, move to Rochester in 1836

Children: Mary Post m. William Hallowell 1843; Jacob Post m. Jennie Curtis 1857; Joseph Post m. Mary Jane (Mate) Ashley 1854; Henry, b. 1834, d. 1837; Mathilda, b. 1840, d. 1844; Willet, b. 1847, m. Josephine Wheeler 1877

Sarah Kirby, m. Jeffries Hallowell 1838, moves to Rochester; Hallowell, d. 1844

m. Edmund Willis 1853, Isaac's nephew, moves to Rochester in 1838

George and Ann Willets, Isaac Post cousins, move to Rochester c. 1848

Post Servants

Sarah Birney, Irish servant, hired 1847

Bridget Head, Irish servant, hired c. 1848

Mary Dale (Johnson), English servant, hired 1849; boards with AKP, 1870–80

Henry Van Auken, hired boy, c. 1876–80

Activists Living with Posts

William C. Nell, lives with Posts 1847–49 and 1851–52

Frances Nell, William Nell's sister, lives with Posts 1848

Harriet Jacobs, lives with Posts 1849–50; later works in contraband camps in Alexandria, Va.

Mary Ann Pitkin, c. 1850–56

Sojourner Truth, 1851 and intermittently in 1866–68, 1878

Jay Chaapel, c. 1880–84

Rochester Coworkers of the Posts

Asa and Huldah Anthony, F/friends and Abolitionists (Ab)

Daniel and Lucy Anthony and daughters Mary and Susan B. Anthony, F/friends and Ab, Women's Rights (WRts)/Suffrage, Women's Loyal National League (WLNL)

Sarah Anthony and Lewis Burtis, F/friends, Ab, Communitarians (Comms)

William C. Bloss, evangelical and Ab

Abigail and Henry Bush, ex-evangelicals and Ab, WRts, move to California c. 1850

Lucy Colman, Ab, WRts, later works in contraband camps in Washington, D.C., Freedmen's Aid

Sarah and Silas Cornell, Orthodox Friends and Ab

Rhoda and Elias DeGarmo, F/friends and Ab, WRts/Suffrage

Frederick Douglass, Ab and WRts/Suffrage

Anna and Rosetta Douglass, Frederick Douglass's wife and daughter, Ab

Sarah and Benjamin Fish, F/friends and Ab, WRts, Comms

Catherine Fish, daughter of Sarah and Benjamin, Ab, WRts/Suffrage, Freedmen's Aid

    m. Giles Stebbins, Ab, and moves to Michigan 1849

Mary and Isaac Gibbs, AME Zion Church members and Ab

Julia Griffiths, British supporter of Douglass's work, lives in Rochester 1849–55

Mary Hebard, Unitarian, WRts/Suffrage

Rev. Thomas James, minister of AME Zion Church, Ab

Lemira and John Kedzie, ex-evangelicals and Ab, WRts

Mrs. Newton (Eliza) Mann, Unitarian, Suffrage

Abigail Mott and Lindley M. Moore, Orthodox Friends and Ab

Sara C. Owen, ex-evangelical and Ab, WRts/Suffrage, moves to Michigan 1849

Susan and Samuel D. Porter, evangelicals and Ab

Laura and Murray Ramsdell, Ab, WRts/Suffrage, Comms

Mrs. L. C. Smith, Unitarian, moral reform, suffrage

Austin Steward, Ab

Julia Wilbur, Orthodox Friend, teacher, Ab, works in contraband camps in Washington, D.C., and Alexandria, Va., Suffrage

Western and Central New York and Midwestern Coworkers

Betsey Mix Cowles, Ohio, Ab, WRts, WLNL

Joseph and Ruth Dugdale, Ohio, Ab

Joseph Hathaway and sister Phebe Hathaway, Orthodox Friends and Ab

Sallie Holley, Ab, Freedmen's Aid

Emily Howland, Orthodox Friend and Ab, WLNL, Freedmen's Aid

Sarah and John Hurn, Hicksite Friends and Ab, Comms

Reverend Samuel J. May, Syracuse, N.Y., Unitarian minister and Ab, WRts/Suffrage

Mary Ann and Thomas M'Clintock, Hicksite Friends and Ab, WRts/Suffrage

Nathaniel Potter, Buffalo, Hicksite Friend and Ab

Gerrit Smith, philanthropist, political Ab

Elizabeth Cady Stanton, Ab, WRts/Suffrage, WLNL

Esek and Maria Wilbur, Hicksite and Orthodox Quaker, respectively; Ab, WRts

Martha Coffin Wright, Ab, WRts/Suffrage, Freedmen's Aid

National Activists, Lecturers, and Friends of the Posts
(date indicates the first time individuals met the Posts and
* indicates those who stayed at the Post home)

Lucretia Mott, 1828 or earlier
*Frederick Douglass, 1842
*Abby Kelley (Foster), 1842
*William Lloyd Garrison, 1842
*William Wells Brown, 1843
*Charles Lenox Remond, c. 1843
*William C. Nell, 1847
Elizabeth Cady Stanton, 1848
Amelia Bloomer, c. 1848–49
*Harriet Jacobs, 1849
John S. Jacobs, 1849
Wendell Phillips, 1849 or earlier
*Sarah Parker Remond, c. 1849
Susan B. Anthony, 1849
Ernestine Rose, 1849
*Lucy Stone, 1849
Rev. Antoinette Brown Blackwell, c. 1849–50
*Oliver and Mary Ann Johnson, c. 1850
George Thompson, 1851
*Sojourner Truth, 1851
Aaron Powell, c. 1853
Josephine Griffing, 1865
Matilda Joslyn Gage, c. 1867
*Belva Lockwood, c. 1878

Spiritualists, Free Thinkers, and the National Liberal League

Asa and Huldah Anthony, Spiritualist (Sp)
D. M. Bennett, publisher of *Truth Seeker*, a Free Thinker (FT) newspaper,
    and member of the National Liberal League (NLL)
Jay Chaapel, FT, NLL
Lucy Colman, FT, NLL
Cora Hatch Daniels, Sp
Andrew Jackson and Mary (Fenn Love) Davis, Sp
Dr. Fred C. Farlin, Sp, FT
Sarah and Benjamin Fish, Sp, FT

Kate and Margaretta Fox, founders of Sp
Leah Fox Fish, Kate and Margaretta Fox's older sister, Sp
Mrs. Cornelia Gardner, Sp, FT
Sallie Holley, NLL
Harriet Jacobs, Sp
Reuben T. Jones, Rochester editor and Sp, FT
Lemira and John Kedzie, Sp
William C. Nell, Sp
Dorius and Nettie Fox Pease, Midwestern Sp
A. L. Rawson, NLL president
Dr. Aurelia Raymond (Lucy Colman's sister), FT
Horace Seaver, editor of *Boston Investigator*, FT, NLL
Elizabeth Cady Stanton, FT, NLL
Giles B. Stebbins, FT
Sarah Thayer, AKP cousin, Sp
Dr. A. E. Tilden, Rochester physician, FT, NLL
Frances Titus, Sojourner Truth assistant and AKP cousin, NLL
Sojourner Truth, Sp
George and Ann Willets, Sp

Introduction

• •

Amy Kirby Post, a married mother of four, epitomizes radical activism in nineteenth-century America. She advocated a wide range of causes and worked earnestly to orchestrate ties between issues, individuals, and movements. Her activist worlds demonstrate the significance of egalitarian, interracial, and mixed-sex movements for social change across the nineteenth century; and her contributions illustrate the central role that radical Quakers played as both public advocates for and role models of a just society.

In the 1840s, Amy Kirby Post became a force in local, regional, and national movements for social change. Post circulated temperance and anti-slavery petitions in her hometown of Rochester, New York; sought to ensure the sovereignty of Seneca Indians; became a leader in the interracial and mixed-sex Western New York Anti-Slavery Society; served as a confidante of Frederick Douglass and his *North Star* coeditor William C. Nell; organized dozens of fund-raising fairs; and hid fugitive slaves in her home. She also opposed the U.S. war with Mexico, fearing it would expand slave territory, and applauded revolutionary developments in France, including the emancipation of slaves in the French West Indies. In 1848, at the age of forty-five, she joined Douglass at the first woman's rights convention in Seneca Falls and helped organize the second, coordinating it with Rochester's annual Emancipation Day celebration. In the aftermath of these groundbreaking events, she cofounded the local Working Women's Protective Union and promoted health reform as an important aspect of women's empowerment. This inveterate activist pursued these public labors while overseeing a household filled, sometimes to overflowing, with children, friends, visitors, boarders, and servants.

Amy Post and her husband Isaac—a farmer-turned-pharmacist—held religious views that contributed to their shared political vision. They were birthright Quakers, who sided with the Hicksites in the separation of Friends that occurred in 1828. In 1845, however, they withdrew from the Hicksites to protest restrictions on members' participation in "worldly" movements for social justice. Neither, however, left Quakerism or faith behind. Three years later, they joined a group of dissident Hicksites to form the Yearly

Meeting of Congregational Friends—later known as Progressive Friends—whose members advocated racial and economic justice, women's rights, interracialism, and internationalism. At the same time, the Posts experimented with another religious innovation—spiritualism—that allowed women and men to communicate directly with the spirits of those who had passed beyond an earthly existence. As with her diverse political commitments, Post embraced a multifaceted religiosity—considering Progressive Friends, spiritualists, and later Unitarians as sharing fundamental ideas and values.

While Amy Kirby Post was unusual in the range of issues and movements she embraced, she was not unique. She was, however, different in three crucial ways from the women who have received the bulk of attention in historical analyses of antebellum reform. First, scholars have long credited evangelical Protestants with being the motivating force behind moral reform, temperance, abolition, and other social movements in antebellum America. Evangelical revivals did inspire thousands of wives, mothers, and sisters to extend their efforts at social improvement beyond home and church through single-sex organizations and institutions.[1] Post, however, illuminates a more radical world of activism, rooted in Friends' testimonies against war, slavery, and intemperance; their recognition of women's equality in education and the ministry; and their early embrace of interracial and mixed-sex movements.

Second, Post was committed not only to a radical vision of social transformation but also to a radical form of organizing that prefigured participatory democracy. As Temma Kaplan defines the term, "Participatory democracy entails people forming committees and holding public meetings to govern themselves. It includes speaking out and perhaps suffering the consequences." Those engaged in this work believed "that democracy involves commitments to social justice, equality and ethical behavior carried out through popular initiatives and verbal arguments. . . . In the course of resisting unjust authorities," they, like Post and her allies, "forged entirely new communities."[2]

Third, Amy Post's career reveals a crucial layer of activists who forged ties between national leaders and far-flung followers. Many studies of nineteenth-century activism highlight national leaders, such as Elizabeth Cady Stanton, Susan B. Anthony, Lucy Stone, Abby Kelley Foster, and Lucretia Mott. The extensive attention these women receive often overshadows the efforts of lesser-known activists. Carol Faulkner's recent biography of Mott takes a different tack however, locating the famed Quaker minister in wider circles of activists who promoted abolition, women's rights, Indian rights, peace, and religious liberty. Mott preached that "all these subjects of reform are kindred in their nature" and encouraged younger women like Post to raise the banner of social justice in their own communities.[3] While Mott labored to connect with diverse groups of activists, her experiences and the challenges she faced were distinct from those who remained more deeply embedded in local and regional efforts. Still, she inspired women such as Post, who then served as a critical connection between national leaders and local activists without the resources to attend numerous conventions, subscribe to multiple newspapers, or participate in urban hives of activity.

Post's activism, like Mott's, was embedded in the Quaker communities of her youth. In the nineteenth-century United States, the Society of Friends offered an important template for democratic communities. More egalitarian than most religious denominations, especially in its recognition of women's authority in spiritual and business affairs, the Society was founded on principles of discussion and consensus. All members of a meeting, whatever sex or age, were free to express their views; and through their "inner light," all "had access to divine revelation."[4] There were limits to individual authority among Friends, especially women; and meetings were overwhelmingly white, although a few African Americans joined the Society. In addition, most Quakers believed that members should testify against social ills only within the confines of their own meetings rather than in "worldly" or "popular" associations. Still, the emphasis on discussion, consensus, and inner light inspired some women and men to carry Friends' testimonies against slavery, intemperance, war, and other social ills into the wider society. These Quakers, some of whom eventually withdrew or were dismissed from the Society of Friends, were drawn to organizations that were open to everyone who embraced a cause and that advocated freedom of speech and conscience. An emphasis on ethical behavior and practical righteousness led many to live out testimonies on a daily basis—rejecting titles of privilege and status, refusing to serve alcohol in their homes, boycotting slave-produced goods, assisting fugitive slaves, and socializing as well as organizing alongside activists of different races and classes.

Scholars have recognized the critical role of Friends in animating a wide range of social movements, particularly peace campaigns. Historians of women's rights and abolition, too, have documented the outsized role of Friends and thereby challenged the standard narrative of those movements. Moreover, because many Friends embraced a range of emancipatory efforts—Indian rights, abolition, women's rights, peace—scholars of Quaker activism are spurred to highlight the connections among movements often treated as distinct. In the process, they have illuminated the long history of social justice campaigns by linking eighteenth-century appeals for abolition and women's equality within Friends meetings to society-wide movements to achieve racial and gender equality in the nineteenth and twentieth centuries.[5]

Numerous Friends in Post's hometown of Jericho, New York, considered social justice a natural outgrowth of their faith, as did many of her Quaker neighbors in central New York, where she lived after her marriage to Isaac Post. Once she and Isaac moved to Rochester in 1836, they joined other radical Quakers as well as fugitive slaves, free blacks, ex-evangelicals, spiritualists, Unitarians, and English and Irish immigrants to forge overlapping movements for abolition, racial equality, women's rights, religious liberty, and economic justice. Some of these activists joined utopian communities, while others, including Amy Post, created new social and political configurations in the midst of the general populace. Post's most well-known coworkers included Lucretia Mott, Frederick Douglass, William C. Nell, Harriet Jacobs, Lucy Stone, Sojourner Truth, Elizabeth Cady Stanton, and Susan B. Anthony. While Post befriended many leading radicals, she also sustained close ties with a vast network of lesser-known (and unknown) activists across New York, the Midwest, and Upper Canada. Her public labors reached across both time and issues. She advocated abolition, women's rights, Indian rights, and temperance before the Civil War; joined the Women's Loyal National League and supported work in contraband camps during the war; and participated in campaigns for civil rights, universal suffrage, free speech, and religious liberty in its aftermath.[6]

Belinda Robnett's concept of "bridge women" captures important aspects of the vital work done by activists like Post who occupy an "intermediate layer of leadership." They build bridges between emerging campaigns and potential recruits, between movement organizations and local people, and between political beliefs and strategic actions.[7] Post brought family members, friends, and neighbors into her activist worlds, encouraging those who were like-minded and urging the more hesitant to attend a meeting, sign a petition, or give up slave-produced sugar. She insisted that progressive Friends act on their beliefs in the wider society and urged secular associations to embrace Quaker testimonies against slavery and other injustices. Over time, she nurtured connections between local reformers and national leaders; Friends and those of other faiths; women and men; African Americans and whites; and working-class and middle-class women.

Yet Post went beyond the work of most bridge leaders by forging ties not only within but across causes: abolition, women's rights, religious liberty, Indian rights, racial justice, temperance, and health reform. In this sense, she served more as a conductor than a bridge, orchestrating movements of people and resources and transmitting ideas and tactics from one campaign to another.[8] Barely five feet tall and slightly built, with a gentle voice but a fierce spirit, Post persisted in the face of disagreement and hostility and, with her husband, defied the law against aiding fugitive slaves. She believed she could turn skeptics into allies through the power of collective action and her own moral example. Although she did not convert everyone to her vision, she did forge deep and lasting friendships with people from widely different backgrounds. These personal bonds undergirded Post's success as a conductor, allowing her to create coalitions, mediate conflicts, organize events, and communicate ideas across disparate factions and movements.

Still, activist commitments and personal compassion could not overcome every obstacle, nor was Post willing to compromise certain fundamental principles. She insisted on the interdependent character of movements for racial and gender justice and religious liberty, and she sought out organizations built on a foundation of participatory democracy and free speech. Those principles sometimes interfered with Post's efforts as a conductor. Thus, even though Amy Post devoted enormous time and energy to raising funds for Frederick Douglass's *North Star*, she refused to join forces with Julia Griffiths, an equally committed British abolitionist who moved to Rochester in 1849. Post admired Griffiths's fund-raising abilities and never questioned her friendship with Douglass, but she disliked her authoritative style as much as her dismissal of women's rights and her support for partisan politics.[9] Post's refusal to orchestrate a union between her radical coworkers and the more moderate reformers Griffiths recruited ensured the division of Rochester's abolitionist women into rival organizations as well as a painful, if temporary, rupture with Douglass.

Even if Post had been willing to forge an alliance with Griffiths, not all of her coworkers would have readily followed. Many were suspicious of the British abolitionist's motives and condemnatory of her relationship with Douglass. Perhaps the greatest obstacle to Post and Griffiths working together, however, was their different approaches to race. While Griffiths befriended Douglass and lived in his household for an extended period, she was not an advocate of interracial organizing. When she founded the single-sex Rochester Ladies' Anti-Slavery Society, she invited white women, most from well-to-do families, to join. Post, on the other hand, was active in the

Western New York Anti-Slavery Society, an interracial and mixed-sex organization that attracted people from diverse economic backgrounds.

The insistence of Post and her allies on forging interracial circles was unusual even among abolitionists. From the beginning, Amy Kirby Post's activist endeavors were grounded in personal friendships. Many, especially in her early years, were also Friends in a religious sense, including an expansive network of family members. Over time, however, she created and sustained intimate ties with activists of other faiths and no faith, with men and women, and with blacks and whites. Historian Cassandra Good argues that the veneration of friendship in the early American republic arose from its egalitarian, rational, and dispassionate qualities. She notes, however, that friendships that crossed gender lines were more suspect because they might slip into seduction or romance. Still, Good demonstrates that mixed-sex relationships occurred with some frequency.[10] The likelihood increased among Quakers, who recognized women's spiritual equality with men, embraced female ministers, and established coeducational schools. Yet even among this group, true friendships between women and men of different races were rare.[11]

For the Posts, moving to an urban environment was crucial. Only when they relocated to the boomtown city of Rochester did it become possible to build an extensive network of relationships outside the Society of Friends and across racial lines. In 1836, the young Quaker couple and their growing family entered a vortex of religious, reform, and radical activities. The pace of change and the cacophony of competing movements and organizations accelerated rapidly in the 1830s and 1840s as the Erie Canal and expanding railroad and telegraph lines brought itinerant lecturers, conventions, and the reform and radical press to the city. Events that might have unfolded over a number of years on Long Island or in central New York now rushed together. From fall 1847 to late 1848 alone, meetings, conventions, religious upheavals, protests, fund-raising fairs, and visiting lecturers produced a whirlwind of activity in which Amy Post eagerly participated, with an infant on her hip. Indeed, the necessity of combining public and domestic labors ensured that the Post home on 36 Sophia Street became a hub of such activity.[12]

In Rochester, Post explored relationships with evangelicals, ex-evangelicals, and Unitarians; with Irish immigrants and urban working women; and with significant numbers of black activists. Although some of her Long Island relatives were deeply concerned about what they considered her promiscuous ties, Post considered interdenominational and interracial friendships fundamental to her activist labors. She formed a valued friendship with Harriet Jacobs, who fled slavery in North Carolina and lived with the Posts in 1849 and 1850. Jacobs revealed to her host the sexual abuse she had confronted while enslaved, and Post encouraged her to write her life story as a testament to slavery's brutality and black women's courage. Post also befriended Sojourner Truth, who stayed with the Posts for several months in 1851 and many times thereafter. Truth reinforced Amy's and Isaac's views on abolition, racial equality, and women's rights, and embraced spiritualism and the Progressive Friends. Even more unusual, given race and gender norms, were the close friendships Amy Post nurtured with Frederick Douglass and William C. Nell, the former staying with the Posts on his first visit to Rochester and the latter living with them for more than a year while helping to launch the *North Star.* Charles Lenox Remond and William Wells Brown also considered Post a trusted confidante. These friendships endured for decades amid dramatic social, political, and personal transformations. In the era of abolition and emancipation, few whites—male or female—matched the dense and enduring bonds Post forged with a significant circle of black activists.[13]

Moving to Rochester expanded the Posts' interactions not only with black activists but also with white reformers from different religious and ethnic backgrounds. Black and white evangelicals and Unitarians labored along- side Hicksite and Orthodox Friends in the Underground Railroad; and self- emancipated blacks, white Quakers, and ex-evangelicals joined forces in the Western New York Anti-Slavery Society and in efforts to promote women's rights. Through these activities, the Posts met William Lloyd Garrison, Abby Kelley, and other national leaders and itinerant lecturers, many of whom stayed at 36 Sophia Street. Postal services and telegraph networks that quickened the exchange of news ensured that Amy and Isaac remained bound to coworkers who moved further west as well as to family and F/friends on Long Island.[14] These and other innovations in communication and transportation nurtured bonds among hundreds of like-minded activ- ists in New York, Pennsylvania, New England, the Midwest, Canada, Ireland, and Britain. In this environment, Hicksite constraints on participating in "worldly"—that is, non-Quaker—organizations proved far weaker than the Posts' desire to transform society.

Even as Amy and Isaac became enmeshed in socially and religiously di- verse movements, continued reliance on one's "inner light" inspired them to live out their political beliefs in both personal and public ways. Follow- ing Quaker traditions, they maintained simplicity in dress, speech, and domestic arrangements and refused to use slave-produced goods or serve alcohol in their home. The couple shared decision making and child rearing and treated all who lived in their household—from children and siblings to boarders, guests, and servants—as part of the family circle. On small issues and large—having their sons sign temperance pledges at age twelve, extending familial assistance to domestic servants, hosting interracial dinners, harboring fugitive slaves—they practiced what they preached. The concept of separate spheres, so often wielded by scholars to distinguish between the private and public lives of nineteenth-century women, barely existed for Amy Post. Instead, personal, familial, and communal forms of activism were deeply enmeshed, allowing her to fulfill her social commitments as she cared for a growing family, including four children by the mid-1840s.

After 1845, when the Posts freed themselves from the strictures of the Hicksite meeting, Amy emerged more fully as a conductor among increasingly diverse circles of activists. While campaigning for social justice alongside Progressive Friends, she forged ever closer bonds with black activists, with evangelical women who had been excommunicated for their reform activities, and with white working-class women. Post developed intimate friendships with several of the English and Irish women who labored in her household. She shared medical knowledge and an interest in spiritualism with some of these women, who joined familial as well as activist gatherings at the Post home. Over time, Post became a crucial contact for dozens of women—friends and friends of friends—who suffered from physical ailments, emotional turmoil, or spousal abuse.

The wide range of Post's activism and the diversity of her radical friends challenge scholars' tendency to focus studies on a single movement or to insist on the primacy of one over another. Even when noting the importance of earlier campaigns in inspiring supposedly later ones—antislavery for woman's rights—many historians quickly move on to the primary object of their research: antislavery *or* woman's rights. Indeed, volumes have been written about a single strand of activism—Garrisonian abolitionism or the National Woman Suffrage Association—providing rich and detailed analyses of one crucial dimension of a larger struggle. While syntheses of antebellum activism analyze multiple issues, they, too, generally divide movements into separate chapters that suggest the distinctive character of each.[15]

In recent years, however, equally important insights have been gained by scholars attending to the ways that movements intersect, converge, and continually reshape one another. Bruce Dorsey's *Reforming Men and Women*, Martha Jones's *All Bound Up Together*, Carol Faulkner's *Lucretia Mott's Heresy*, and Stephen Kantrowitz's *More Than Freedom* provide penetrating examples of this approach. Dorsey brings diverse activists and causes into dialogue with each other in antebellum Philadelphia while Jones and Faulkner highlight the battle for women's rights within other social movements. They along with Kantrowitz also cross the standard chronological divide between pre- and post-Civil War activism. In *The Slave's Cause*, Manisha Sinha focuses on abolition but illuminates its deep connections to other battles against inequality and injustice. She also traces the cause back to the American Revolution, when egalitarian impulses moved blacks and their white allies, mainly Quakers, to push for emancipation across the North. Amy Kirby Post labored on the complex terrain these historians illuminate.

Post's commitment to universal or holistic reform—that is, to simultaneous efforts to achieve race, class, and gender equality; spiritual and physical health; religious liberty and political democracy; peace and social justice—highlights the continual but shifting connections among activist movements, ideologies, and strategies across the nineteenth century. For Post and many other radical activists, no single campaign—not even abolition—could fully transform American society. For them, women's rights were deeply enmeshed with, indeed embedded in, efforts to achieve racial equality. Similarly, attempts to eliminate war were fully entangled with movements to eradicate slavery, the exploitation of Indians, and capital punishment. Thralldom to religious orthodoxy was viewed as an especially serious constraint on social change of all kinds. Thus, Post embraced vital aspects of radical Quakerism, spiritualism, Unitarianism, and free thought and insisted that religious liberty was central to social transformation.

Moreover, Post's life focuses our attention on the ways that ordinary people advanced a radical vision of social change. That vision is manifest as much in the household Post managed, the marriage she forged, the child-rearing practices she championed, and the friendships she sustained as in the religious commitments she embraced, the conventions and fairs she organized, the petitions she circulated, and the fugitives she hid. When challenges and setbacks threatened to overwhelm her, like-minded friends and family came to the rescue. At mid-century, amid upheavals among Friends and abolitionists, her first cousin and sister-in-law Mary Robbins Post reminded her, "We rejoice in commotion for it gives signs of vitality."

Certainly, Post never retreated for long. In the 1880s, a leading advocate of religious liberty noted Post's "firmness in the defense and advocacy of truth, and the wisdom of her counsels."[16]

It was in pursuit of a universalist vision that Post honed her skills as a conductor. To manage diverse efforts, she meshed private and public activities, orchestrated introductions and conventions, and circulated ideas and tactics among activist circles with distinct priorities. Corresponding with a wide array of reformers, radicals, and skeptics provided one critical means of sustaining friendships, initiating connections, and transmitting light. A constant stream of letters bound Post to reformers and radicals across the country, including those who, by dint of economic or geographical location, lived on the margins of her activist worlds. Many of the recipients read the same antislavery newspapers, reform pamphlets, religious treatises, and books, and Post often referenced these materials as shorthand for longer discussions.[17] As with other nineteenth-century epistolary networks, members of Post's circle read missives aloud, passed them on to friends and relatives, quoted comments from one correspondent to another, and sometimes published excerpts or whole letters in the reform press.

Written at dining tables or small desks, by sunlight, candlelight, or oil lamp, with a quill pen on rag or wood pulp paper, the letters are layered with family news, medical diagnoses, weather reports, business updates, shared confidences, convention notes, fair schedules, and political analyses, as well as commentaries on friends, visitors, books, speakers, activist developments, and religious visions. Unfortunately, only a small percentage of Amy Post's side of these exchanges survives, fewer than sixty handwritten letters over more than six decades.[18] We know she wrote many more. She and William Nell exchanged dozens of letters between 1849 and at least 1869, but only his side of the correspondence survives. Similarly, there are far more extant epistles from relatives than to them. Still, many of the letters sent to Post mirror her reports and opinions by quoting or commenting on her latest missive.[19] Her character and vision, and the frustrations and challenges she faced, come alive in the dense lines of thready script that fill page after page and often race crosshatched along the last sheet or fill the borders of a page where sentences once had room to breathe. Interwoven with the many references to Post in the extensive print culture of the period, these letters reveal the inveterate radical and the activist worlds in which she labored over six decades.

Scholars of nineteenth-century Britain and the United States have wielded family correspondence to trace bonds among kith and kin that created the environment and the resources to achieve economic security, even prosperity. These bonds were equally important to advancing social change, especially for women and blacks, whose access to funds, time, and information was often limited.[20] For African American activists, especially those who were self-emancipated, extrafamilial relations were often critical to sustaining themselves and their communities. Post's friendships with Douglass, Nell, Jacobs, and Truth lasted decades and provided all four with material and emotional support at key moments. In turn, Post received powerful insights on race and gender relations that deepened her sense of purpose and inspired her to rethink cherished ideals. It is noteworthy that three of Post's friendships—with Douglass, Nell, and Jacobs—preceded what have often been viewed as the "unprecedented" bonds fashioned among men such as Frederick Douglass, Gerrit Smith, John Brown, and James McCune Smith.[21] Such interracial bonds were unusual, yet they were neither unique nor confined to men.

Amy Post's ability to forge friendships with black women and men, expand her activist circles and labors, and juggle domestic and political commitments was rooted in her marriage to Isaac Post.[22] Partners in political as well as domestic ventures, the two shared views on religious liberty, abolition, Indian rights, and women's rights. Isaac, who was four years older than Amy, led the way in the 1820s and 1830s, participating in the Friends Joint Committee on Indian Affairs and in early, often all-male, antislavery meetings. After moving to Rochester, both signed antislavery petitions, assisted fugitive slaves, joined the interracial and mixed-sex Western New York Anti-Slavery Society (WNYASS), hosted itinerant lecturers in their home, and befriended Douglass and Nell. In the late 1840s and 1850s, however, Isaac's apothecary business demanded more of his time, and he turned more of his activist attention to spiritualism. As a result, Amy increasingly took the lead in abolitionist efforts, organizing fund-raising fairs for the *North Star* and attending annual meetings of the American Anti-Slavery Society. Building on her battles for gender equality in Friends' meetings and antislavery societies, she embraced the newly-launched movement for woman's rights, attending and organizing conventions, circulating petitions, and joining working women in demanding economic justice. Even in the promotion of spiritualism, with Isaac the more ardent exponent, Amy provided significant support to Kate and Margaretta Fox and other female mediums.

The importance of Amy Post's alliances with individual activists and movements was abundantly clear in the nineteenth century. Frederick

Douglass launched his antislavery paper, the *North Star*, in Rochester in part because of the welcome he had received from the Posts during early visits to the city. Once in Rochester, WNYASS fund-raising fairs led by Amy provided crucial funds, and it was her hospitality to Nell that allowed him to spend more than a year as Douglass's fellow editor. After Nell's return to Boston, he proclaimed the Posts' "Sophia Street Circle" an oasis of hope and succor. Harriet Jacobs credited Amy with inspiring her to write *Incidents in the Life of a Slave Girl* and assisting her throughout the long process of publication. Indeed, she asked Post to write the preface for the book, "as there is no one whose name I would prefer to Yours." Dr. A. E. Tilden, a well-known advocate of religious liberty, declared Post "the Mother of Modern Spiritualism." And Susan B. Anthony relied on Post to circulate petitions, host visiting lecturers, and organize conventions.[23]

Some of these correspondents were also crucial to Post's increasingly internationalist perspective. Activists such as Douglass, Mott, and Ernestine Rose not only befriended Post but also brought her into the transatlantic worlds they inhabited. So, too, did the reform press.[24] Thus, even as Post remained geographically rooted in the United States, she eagerly followed issues and events in other parts of the world. The *Liberator*, the *National Anti-Slavery Standard*, the *North Star*, and *The Anti-Slavery Bugle* brought the U.S. war with Mexico, famine in Ireland, revolutions in Europe, and emancipation celebrations in the British and French West Indies into Post's living room. Like other radicals, she linked these developments to domestic campaigns against slavery, racism, and class exploitation and for American Indian sovereignty, religious freedom, and women's rights.[25]

Not only did Amy Post expand and transform her radical vision over time, but she also remained an ardent activist throughout her life. In the 1850s, when she was in her fifties, Post added the campaign against capital punishment to her already overflowing agenda. During the Civil War, she and many of her coworkers focused their efforts on ensuring that the conflict would end with emancipation, organizing, advocating, and petitioning on behalf of those who remained enslaved.[26] At the same time, she focused on the immediate needs of freed people, raising funds and awareness about Southern blacks living in contraband camps behind Union lines. The harrowing reports of inadequate food, housing, and health care circulated by Harriet Jacobs and Julia Wilbur, who labored together in Alexandria, Virginia, inspired Post and other radical activists to deliver clothes, bedding, food, and other necessities to so-called contrabands living in Washington, D.C., and Alexandria, Virginia. In December 1863, the sixty-year-old Post visited the camps to see conditions for herself.

When the war ended, Post continued to battle racial inequities as she and Isaac joined Sojourner Truth in her efforts to provide the newly freed with jobs, homes, and other necessities in the North. At the same time, Post joined the fight for universal suffrage launched by the American Equal Rights Association. Dismayed by the deep divisions that erupted between advocates of woman's suffrage and black male suffrage, she—along with Lucretia Mott, Sojourner Truth, and a few others—insisted that universal suffrage was the only legitimate goal. Initially unwilling to ally herself fully with either the American or the National Woman Suffrage Association, she was gradually drawn into the efforts of the latter and participated in its effort to create test cases by attempting to register and vote in the 1870s. Even after the Supreme Court ruled against such efforts, Post continued to battle for school and municipal suffrage while enjoying a new celebrity status as one of the pioneers of the woman's rights campaign.

Still, Post neither rested on her laurels nor restricted herself to a single cause. In the 1870s and 1880s, she continued to promote spiritualism and religious liberty through the Progressive Friends as well as through spiritualist and free religious associations. Even after her beloved Isaac died in 1872, Amy expanded her activist ventures. She was among the founders of the National Liberal League, which carried on the fight for religious liberty and freedom of conscience. Into the 1880s, Post served as a league leader while urging the organization to be more attentive to women's rights and leadership. She also participated in the Sovereigns of Industry—a branch of the Grange that focused on organizing working people—and in Thomas Paine birthday celebrations, in which economic democracy was intertwined with religious liberty. In March 1888, Post attended her last public event— the International Council of Women, in Washington, D.C.—less than nine months before her death at age eighty-one.

In the numerous obituaries that appeared, Amy Kirby Post was remembered for her friendship with Douglass, her involvement in the Underground Railroad, and her support for woman's suffrage. While some obituaries captured her understanding of these movements as being deeply intertwined and interdependent, others highlighted her work as either an abolitionist or a suffragist. A few even portrayed her as a follower, rather than a leader, of the women's rights movement. Her younger coworkers, including stepdaughter Mary Hallowell and sister Sarah Willis, generally embraced more moderate demands and emphasized suffrage and institution building rather than a universalist vision. In doing so, they may have contributed to the waning recognition of Post's universalism. Indeed, from the 1920s until the 1970s, when the gift of the Post Family Papers to the University of Rochester revived interest in the pioneering radical, Amy Post faded from public memory. Moreover, only a few photographs and a couple of paintings give us a glimpse of this passionate activist, and then only in her sixties and seventies, after several bouts of illness. Still, the activist worlds she helped create and sustain did not disappear but reemerged in new forms as later generations of activists took on the challenges of transforming, not simply reforming, society.

Those who seek models of transformative social movements would do well to look back to Amy Post and her activist worlds. In a time of deep political and social divisions, white Quakers, free and fugitive blacks, ex-evangelicals, and agrarian and émigré radicals sustained a democratic vision of social justice across the nineteenth century. From Philadelphia and Chester, Pennsylvania, to Jericho, Westbury, Farmington, and Rochester, New York; Vineland, New Jersey; Battle Creek, Michigan; Salem, Ohio; and Upper Canada, black and white women and men joined forces to promote racial justice, religious liberty, and economic democracy, as well as the rights of Indians, prisoners, workers, and women. Amy Post highlighted the connections among these issues and movements. She was a valued ally to black and white, working-class and middle-class, agrarian and urban activists. The efforts of Post and her coworkers sparked outrage from opponents and heated debates among allies, yet never achieved their ultimate goal of a democratic and egalitarian society. They did, however, contribute mightily to the abolition of slavery, the mobilization of women, and the acknowledgment that racial and gender justice were deeply American values.

1 Family and Faith, 1790–1828

· ·

Before she was conscious of the world around her, Amy Kirby was enveloped in radical possibilities. Born in 1802 in a Long Island farming community, Amy was preceded by generations of English Friends who established farms, built meetinghouses, and testified against war and slavery. Some of these families had migrated to Westbury in the late seventeenth century, joining one of the first Quaker communities in what is now Nassau County. In the early eighteenth century, the Kirbys and a few other families ventured eastward along an old Indian trail and built homes at a place known as Lusum, later Jericho.[1] For decades, Jericho Friends worshiped in Westbury, creating an intimate community on the eastern edge of New York Yearly Meeting. Members helped one another clear land, build houses, and harvest crops. They shared tools and produce, sewed clothing and quilts, exchanged cheese and preserves, attended births and laid out bodies. Young people courted, married, and raised children, forging dense layers of kinship and friendship.

Friends established tight-knit communities rooted in family and faith, but they also interacted with Dutch and English settlers of other faiths and with indigenous communities. European pioneers were attracted by Long Island's rich farmland, freshwater springs, extended network of streams and bays, and easy access to the sea. The newcomers claimed they purchased land from local Indians, though the two groups no doubt understood property ownership differently.[2] While Quakers testified against the exploitation of Indians, their settlements nonetheless posed a threat to native inhabitants.

When Friends began settling Long Island in the 1650s, indigenous groups such as the Shinnecock, Massapequa, and other Lenape and Pequot peoples were already far smaller than they had been just forty years earlier. Eager to trade with the Dutch in the 1610s and 1620s, Indians were devastated by European diseases, forced onto smaller parcels of land, and slaughtered in attacks launched by Dutch governor Willem Kieft in the early 1640s. In 1650, the English gained authority over lands east of Oyster Bay and fourteen years later wrested control of all of New Amsterdam from the Dutch. But the transfer of power changed little for native inhabitants. English taxes were as burdensome as the Dutch, and epidemic diseases continued to kill large numbers of Indians on Long Island as elsewhere.[3]

English Presbyterians had preceded the Friends, establishing their first major community in 1642, just as Kieft launched his war against the Indians. Forty Presbyterian families from Connecticut settled on an extensive tract of land purchased from the Massapequa. The settlers then obtained a land patent from the Dutch for the area, which they named Hempstead. In 1648, Englishman Robert Williams purchased nine square miles of adjacent land that stretched to the north shore of Long Island.[4]

Some Quakers reached Long Island directly from England, as they fled religious persecution and sought to extend their spiritual mission. The Religious Society of Friends was founded in 1652 by George Fox in northwestern England. He and his spiritual partner, Margaret Fell, sparked a religious awakening in the region, attracting thousands of men and women to the new faith. Their followers met outdoors or in farmhouses and barns "to remake their lives under the probing 'Light of Christ within' them." Faith in this inward knowledge of the divine—or inner light—led Friends to deny the need for ministers as intermediaries with God. They also believed "that God's Truth, Grace, or Light was reborn on earth with the birth of every individual," thus making perfection in this world possible.[5] These tenets profoundly challenged the structure and beliefs of the Church of England as well as Calvinist claims for original sin.

Quakers developed a distinctive form of worship in which members gathered in silence and spoke only when moved to do so by the Spirit of God. Condemned in England along with other "separatist" groups as blasphemers and heretics, Friends were denigrated as well for the "outward quaking" they experienced as they struggled to accept "the inner 'leadings' of conscience." Among Quakers, however, these leadings formed the core of the group's ethical norms, "which they called 'testimonies': truth and honesty in all business dealings; simplicity in dress and life; equality that humbled all classes and both sexes equally; and the emerging Peace Testimony."[6] The efforts of English Friends to live out these testimonies, particularly amid the political and religious upheavals of the 1650s and 1660s, met with censure, beatings, imprisonment, and even death by Anglican and English authorities.

Like the Puritans, Friends sought to extend their teachings to Holland and North America. The largest number of Friends migrated to Pennsylvania, but smaller communities appeared in New England and New Amsterdam. On Long Island, the more scattered population allowed significant religious autonomy, and Friends forged thriving settlements there.[7] English land speculators had paved the way, including Robert Williams and John Seaman, an English sea captain. Little is known about Williams, but Seaman left Connecticut in the 1650s to join the Presbyterian community in Hempstead. Quakers Edmund Titus and Henry Willis purchased land from Seaman and named their settlement Westbury after Willis's English birthplace. Around the same time, Captain Seaman and his wife joined the Society of Friends.[8]

Meanwhile, Robert Williams had settled with his family a few miles to the east near a spring-fed pond in Lusum. He and his wife, Sarah Washburne Williams, resided on his estate, the Plantation, with two sons. His widowed sister-in-law, Mary Washburne Willets, and at least two of her children built a small house nearby in 1672. Several Quaker families purchased land from Williams, drawn to the area by the large freshwater pond, fertile fields, and abundant pasture for cattle grazing. Other Friends soon followed. When the Anglican-born Mary Washburne Willets converted to Quakerism in 1683, she began holding religious meetings in her home. Like other Friends, she was penalized by English authorities for "non payment of Ministers' and Church Rates."[9]

By 1692, Quakers dominated the community and renamed the village Jericho, the biblical town where Jesus restored the sight of a beggar. When Friends in Westbury built a formal meetinghouse in 1700, Jericho residents traveled there for worship services and business meetings. By that time, a latticework of Quaker families bound the villages together. For instance, Edmund Titus of Westbury married Martha Washburne of Jericho, a sister of Mary Washburne Willets and Sarah Washburne Williams. A fourth sister, Agnes Washburne, married Robert Jackson, a large landowner in the area. A generation later, their daughter Elizabeth married one of Captain John Seaman's sons. Another of Seaman's sons married Robert Williams's granddaughter Hannah, who joined him in the Society of Friends. Other Seaman children and grandchildren married into the Kirby, Hicks, Titus, and Jackson families, creating a complex web of in-laws, aunts, uncles, and cousins that stretched across the region.[10]

Still, Jericho and Westbury were not exclusively Quaker communities. Landowners who supported the Presbyterian, Dutch Reformed, and Anglican churches lived in the area, as did the remnants of Indian nations and a growing number of Africans and African Americans.[11] Many Friends felt kindlier toward the remaining Indians than did their fellow Christians, who spurned them, or the British colonial government, which imposed taxes and sustained its authority through military might. Beginning in the late 1600s, some Quakers also criticized the institution of slavery, not only writing epistles against its brutalities but also urging the faithful to free those they held in bondage. Their views were at odds with those of most English and Dutch neighbors and with British policies.

Early on, the Dutch had imported Africans as laborers into New Amsterdam, and by the 1640s, enslaved Africans were clearing land, planting crops, raising cattle, and performing domestic labor for dozens of Long Island families. When the English took control of New Amsterdam in 1664, they continued importing Africans. Although leading Friends—including George Fox and Irishman William Edmondson, both of whom visited Long Island in the 1670s—questioned the right of Quakers to enslave Africans, many Friends did so. While most held only a few bondsmen or bondswomen, their participation in the slave trade boosted the overall number of blacks on the island. By 1720, the ratio of slaves to white settlers was about 1:10 on Long Island. Two years later in Hempstead, it reached 1:5.[12]

Not all blacks on Long Island were enslaved, however. In 1664, just before the Dutch lost control of New Amsterdam, they freed enslaved Africans "who had been in loyal service and demonstrated good behavior."[13] In 1685, following challenges from Fox and Edmondson, a few Friends at Oyster Bay freed their slaves, but hardly anyone else followed suit. Three decades later, in 1716, a number of Friends at New York Yearly Meeting "declared that they were fully satisfied in their consciences that yet set practice was not Rite [sic]." Others, however, argued that as long as they provided enslaved workers with decent food, shelter, clothing, and a basic education, the institution was acceptable.[14]

A turning point came in 1749, when John Woolman, a respected Philadelphia Friend, visited Long Island and spoke forcefully against the right of any person to enslave another. In his pamphlet *Considerations on the Keeping of Negroes*, he argued that holding slaves was against the principles of the Society of Friends. A year later, New York Yearly Meeting agreed that no member could import slaves but left open the question of whether owners had to free those they already owned. Some owners claimed that such emancipations would leave freed blacks indigent and isolated. By 1767, Friends in Flushing, a town twenty miles west of Jericho, formally adopted an antislavery resolution, condemning the practice as unchristian. Four years later, some New York area meetings disowned members who refused to manumit their slaves. Benjamin Lay, a Pennsylvania Friend who visited

Long Island, furthered this movement by denouncing slavery and circulating his pamphlet *All Slave-Keepers that keep the Innocent in Bondage, Apostates* in 1773.[15]

That same year, Elias Hicks publicly voiced his opposition to human bondage at New York Yearly Meeting. Even though his father, brother, and father-in-law all owned slaves, he insisted that the Society should disown members who continued to buy or sell slaves or to hold in bondage any person reaching adulthood. Hicks had been born to Quaker parents in Hempstead in 1748 but did not embrace the faith with any enthusiasm until his twenties. Then, while teaching school and training as a carpenter and surveyor, he began reading the Bible more closely. In 1771, he married Jemima Seaman, the granddaughter of Captain John Seaman, and moved to her family's farm in Jericho. There he was appointed to various Friends committees, including a committee to persuade area Friends to free their bondsmen and bondswomen.[16]

Each yearly meeting of Friends oversaw local and regional meetings for worship and business, and each of these meetings appointed committees to carry out specific tasks. The most local gathering was a preparative meeting, where Friends usually gathered twice a week for worship and once to conduct business. All business meetings—preparative, monthly, quarterly, and yearly—were carried out separately by women and men, with representatives of the women's meetings then presenting any issues that required concurrence to the men's meeting. Monthly meetings, which might include two or more preparative meetings, were authorized to approve and host marriages, receive and disown members, and purchase property. Participants in monthly meetings also selected representatives to quarterly and yearly meetings, which dealt with doctrinal and organizational issues. While any member of affiliated monthly meetings could attend these larger gatherings, certain individuals were appointed to represent and report back to the men's and women's meetings. Some members of monthly meetings were recognized as "weighty" or "select" leaders, most often ministers and elders. In 1774, when the twenty-six-year-old Hicks experienced "deep openings in the visions of light," he was certified to minister to other meetings. Thereafter, he participated in select meetings, where ministers and elders gathered to discuss critical issues.[17] A separate meeting for sufferings, equivalent to an executive committee, was authorized to act on cases or issues that could not be delayed until the following yearly meeting.[18]

As a weighty member in the 1770s, Hicks urged New York Yearly Meeting to move more quickly to abolish slavery among its members. In addition to insisting that those who freed young, aged, or sick slaves provide for their care, the meeting in 1776 forbade owners to break up families and required them to get approval from the meeting to sell individual slaves. Still, many Quakers on Long Island felt an urgency regarding emancipation that their counterparts in New York City, a center for southern trade, did not.[19] Nonetheless, the antislavery forces among Friends gradually gained ground. Some of Hicks's family members manumitted their slaves in the 1770s, as did members of other prominent families. Most either hired these newly freed people for wages or assisted those who wished to move elsewhere.[20] From 1775 on, the patriotic rhetoric of liberty that fueled the American Revolution reinforced Quaker efforts and stoked emancipationist arguments among colonists of many faiths.[21] Still, these sentiments were voiced more strongly in areas where slavery was less central to the economy. And on Long Island, once war erupted, the British occupation of the region curtailed Quakers' abolitionist efforts.

Long Island's diverse population ensured significant divisions during the Revolution. Many Dutch and some wealthy English families favored the British, many small farmers supported the Patriots, and most Quakers refused to fight or give aid to either side. At the same time, Long Island was vulnerable to British attack with nearly five hundred British warships carrying some forty thousand British and Hessian troops anchored in New York harbor by August 1776. On 22 August, the Battle of Long Island, which took place mainly in Brooklyn, nearly ended the Revolution. While General George Washington managed to save the Continental Army by retreating into New Jersey, the inhabitants of New York City and Long Island were left under British control.[22]

For seven long years, from 1776 to 1783, British authorities ruled Jericho and other Long Island towns. They imposed martial law and required residents to quarter troops in their homes and provide them with food and equipment. When provisions proved insufficient, soldiers simply confiscated hogs, horses, produce, tools, and other items. Troops camped in local churches and on farmland and disgraced the Flushing Friends Meetinghouse by using it first as a barracks, then as a jail, a hospital, and a storehouse. Quakers, being pacifists, were sometimes allowed to travel more freely than other groups, but they were required to assist the British in numerous ways. Soldiers were quartered in the homes of several Jericho Friends, including those of Elias and Jemima Hicks and of Amy Kirby's grandparents. Amy's parents—Mary Seaman and Jacob Kirby—born in 1774 and 1765, respectively, grew up amid the presence of British and Hessian troops.[23] Their parents may have warned them to stay away from Lieuten-ant Colonel Banastre Tarleton, a dashing but cruel cavalryman headquar-tered in the area in 1778 and 1779, and Jacob was old enough to understand the privations caused by British troops confiscating butter, cheese, geese, turkey, cows, hogs, oats, and cider from local residents.[24]

The situation changed dramatically in 1781, when General Charles Corn-wallis surrendered to Continental troops at Yorktown, Virginia. Between then and 1783, when the Treaty of Paris officially ended the war, Loyalists on Long Island were subject to vicious reprisals by Patriots, as were some Quakers for their refusal to fight. Thousands of Loyalists eventually left the island for England, Canada, or the West Indies, and a few dozen Quaker families relocated to Canada as well. Gradually, however, life in Jericho re-turned to normal, and efforts to end slavery reemerged. Black advocates of abolition spoke at New York Yearly Meeting, and many Friends, including Jacob Kirby's mother, taught their children passages from Phillis Wheatley's 1773 volume, *Poems on Various Subjects, Religious and Moral*.[25] In addition, Elias Hicks and Gideon Seaman—both cousins of Amy's mother, Mary Seaman—renewed their mission to abolish slavery in the region. Although it is not known whether the Kirbys held, or manumitted, any slaves, Friends in Westbury, Jericho, and throughout Queens County freed 154 slaves by 1791, the vast majority of those owned.[26]

These and other developments in the postwar period profoundly affected the lives of those born in the early years of the new republic. Perhaps most importantly, by the time Amy Kirby was born in 1802, the rising number of emancipations had fueled the creation of free black communities in the region, and the existence of such communities led fugitive slaves to seek shelter there. Some freed people continued to live and work on the farms of their former owners; others established separate households and neighborhoods, though some contracted their children to farmers or arti-sans to learn a trade. This allowed fugitives to hide in plain sight, either laboring for Quaker families or working among clusters of free black households.

In 1794, Jericho and Westbury Friends established a Charity Society, whose members sought to "help improve the poor among the African people by educating their children."[27] But free blacks also developed their own in-stitutions. Thus, when the Charity Society offered to educate black children alongside Quaker boys and girls in private homes, black parents made it clear that they preferred to educate their sons and daughters in their own community. In the 1810s, the Charity Society finally opened three schools for black children, including one in Jericho.[28] The schools provided additional classes for black adults on First Day (Sunday), after worship services.

Residents of Westbury, home to the local meetinghouse, generally led in these religious and educational efforts until Jericho was approved to hold its own preparative meeting in 1787. The next year, Jericho Quakers constructed a meetinghouse on Oyster Bay Road.[29] Its design, which diverged significantly from its English counterparts, was increasingly popular among American Friends.[30] English meetinghouses and those built in colonial North America were typically designed with one large room for worship and men's business meetings and a smaller room for women's business meetings. Separate men's and women's meetings for business had been instituted in England in the 1650s at the behest of Margaret Fell and with the support of George Fox. At these meetings, Friends discussed the issues of the day, such as war or slavery; wrote epistles on important topics to other meetings; and settled disciplinary matters. By the late 1660s, English Friends began criticizing separate meetings and the authority they granted women; but women's meetings were established with little controversy in North America, and men "generally respected the decisions" of their sisters on marriage proposals and other issues.[31]

Indeed, women's business meetings gained increased importance in the young nation in the late eighteenth century as part of a wider reformation within the Society. Concerned about growing complacency among worshippers, Philadelphia Yearly Meeting was especially worried that "marrying out of meeting"—that is, marrying non-Quakers—was on the rise. Fearing for the integrity of the Society, Philadelphia Yearly Meeting officially changed its Discipline in 1762, declaring marriage to non-Quakers grounds for expulsion.[32] Other yearly meetings followed suit.

Since women's meetings were in charge of approving marriage proposals, the new Discipline enhanced the role of female Friends and, in turn, influenced the design of meetinghouses. In 1768, Friends in Buckingham, Pennsylvania, introduced a new style—a meetinghouse with one large room designed for worship that could be partitioned into two equal sections for men's and women's meetings for business. During the 1770s and 1780s, this plan became standard among Friends in much of the eastern United States. The design furthered the distinction between male and female Quakers in another way. Early on, all Friends sat together in one large room for worship before women moved to their own room for business. Now, however, they often separated on entry, with women and young children on one side of the partition and men on the other. This made it easier to simply lower the partition between the two sides of the room for business.

In 1788, Jericho Friends entered their new meetinghouse, a perfect example of the Buckingham design. Two doors on the long side of the rectangular building opened into meeting rooms for men and women. The outside was covered with hand-hewn cedar shingles, and a porch was later added to protect worshippers from inclement weather. Inside, local Friends looked up to a high ceiling, below which a gallery projected out over two-thirds of the room. There was no altar or communion table; instead, the whole room was filled with benches, with men and women sitting on opposite sides of a low partition. While Friends did not believe in elevating preachers above worshippers, a "facing bench" allowed ministers and other weighty members to gaze at their fellow congregants. A second raised bench provided some of these members with a good view of the upper gallery, where many young people preferred to sit. Wooden shutters on the north windows helped keep out cold winds in winter, while a wood-burning stove warmed the interior. When worship ended and it was time for business meetings, held on the third First Day of each month in Jericho, the top part of the partition was lowered from the attic to divide the meeting space in two.[33]

Since many Friends traveled to meeting in horse-drawn wagons, wagon sheds eighty feet long were constructed by the side of the road. On the opposite side of the meetinghouse, land was set aside for a cemetery. And five years later, in 1793, a school was constructed adjacent to the wagon sheds.[34] Amy Kirby would spend many hours of her young life in this Quaker complex.

Inside the meetinghouse, members followed the quietist tradition of worship, sitting in silent contemplation unless moved to speak by their inner light. Those so moved, male or female, delivered their thoughts on diverse topics. While some declaimed on the nature of divinity, the evils of slavery, or individual responsibility for God's work in the world, others offered concise comments on religious education or charitable work. In business meetings, Friends also mingled social issues with spiritual concerns, writing epistles on war, temperance, and slavery while considering marriage proposals, appointing committees to visit absent members, and discussing changes to the Discipline.

In the early eighteenth century, Enlightenment thinkers in Europe began influencing Americans, challenging diverse religious traditions by emphasizing reasoned discourse and scientific thought. Some Quakers embraced the Enlightenment, but by mid-century, leading Friends John Woolman, Anthony Benezet, and John Churchman urged their co-worshippers "to 'dig deep' to find the 'pure springs' of God's will" in the face of rationalization, self-will, and fears of persecution, which could muddy individual " 'leadings to act or speak.' " As supporters of the French Revolution continued to gain currency in the following decades and even religious groups like the Unitarians touted the age of reason, many Friends became more insistent on the purity of conscience and inner light.[35]

In the midst of these transformations, in June 1790, sixteen-year-old Mary Seaman and twenty-five-year-old Jacob Kirby exchanged promises of love and faithfulness in the Jericho Meetinghouse, with those in attendance serving as witnesses. Although female Friends did not promise obedience to their husbands, they did take their last names.[36] As Seamans intermarried with Hickses, Robbinses, Willetses, and Tituses, relatives and neighbors kept track of lineages through family histories and Friends meetings. Thus, local Quakers were well aware that Mary Seaman and her older brother, David, married siblings Jacob and Sarah Kirby, the children of Willets and Hannah Kirby. These relationships were particularly complicated. Hannah Kirby had died in 1784; and three years later, Willets married Mary Jackson Seaman, the widow of William Seaman and the mother of David and Mary. Thus, when Jacob Kirby and Mary Seaman wed and chose to live in the Kirby homestead, they each lived with a surviving parent. Indeed, by 1787 thirteen-year-old Mary Seaman and her younger sisters Hannah and Esther were already ensconced in the Kirby Lane farm, having moved there with their mother.

The Kirby family farm sat on a rise in an area known as Locust Grove, walking distance to the Jericho Meetinghouse. It was said that on a clear day "you could see as many as 40 sails on the ocean" from its porch.[37] The house was likely built of wood on a stone foundation and enlarged over time. In 1790, it was commodious enough to house Willets and Mary Jackson Seaman Kirby, Willets's daughters Sarah and Phebe, Mary's daughters Hannah and Esther, and newlyweds Jacob and Mary Seaman Kirby. The extended family welcomed Mary and Jacob's first child, also named Mary, thirteen months after the wedding. Soon after, Sarah Kirby left the farm upon her marriage to David Seaman. Over the next decade, Mary and Jacob Kirby became parents to four more children, including Amy, born in 1802. Three years later, twenty-six-year-old Esther Seaman, Amy's aunt, married Willet Robbins and moved across the road and down the hill from the Kirby homestead.[38]

The Kirbys' nearest neighbors were Thomas and Phebe Willis, whose far smaller family lived on a five-hundred-acre farm, the largest in the area. Yet Mary Seaman Kirby and her mother were probably too busy with household chores and children to spend much time visiting neighbors, while Jacob and his father likely devoted whatever leisure hours they had to discussions with other small farmers, who shared their concerns and obligations.

Despite their different responsibilities, Mary's and Jacob's roles were not as distinct as the terms *household labor* and *farmwork* might suggest. Following the model set by their own parents, the younger Kirbys likely took on more of the chores as their father and mother aged. Mary's domestic responsibilities would have included feeding chickens, gathering eggs, churning butter, and other "light" aspects of farmwork. And Jacob would have chopped wood, built fires, and milked cows, tasks that aided Mary as she laundered and cooked.[39] Quakers were unusual in their day in considering husbands and wives as partners, each assisting and respecting the other. Women were often seen as spiritual authorities in the household, reminding husbands of and training children in Friends' practices and testimonies. While not all Friends' marriages reflected the relative equality of the ideal partnership, Mary and Jacob Kirby—despite their nine-year age difference—seem to have mirrored it well.[40]

The Kirbys certainly had many couples to set good examples for them, including their own parents and cousins Jemima and Elias Hicks, who had been married almost twenty years by 1790. Indeed, they had children nearly ready to wed themselves. When the Hickses' eleven children did marry, they extended family ties into the Willet, Titus, and Underhill families, ensuring that Mary and Jacob Kirby's children were raised in a thicket of family and F/friends whose religious beliefs and moral principles profoundly shaped their vision of faith, community, and social justice.

Growing up in the opening decades of the nineteenth century, Amy Kirby and her siblings were acutely aware of one of the most important principles—the right of all persons to be free from bondage. Amy attended the Jericho Friends School with black children until 1817, when the Charity Society established a school in the African American community. She also encountered African Americans working on neighboring farms and in local households, including her own. Blacks visited Jericho shops, carried jugs of fresh water from Spring Pond, and collected wood and other necessities from the surrounding fields and forests. The simple presence of blacks did not necessarily induce discussions about freedom, but Elias and Jemima Hicks were among the most outspoken Friends on the issue. And they practiced what they preached, hiding fugitive slaves in their home, as did several other Jericho Quakers. While that effort was likely kept secret from the children, issues related to abolition were debated at family gatherings. When Amy was nine years old, those debates swirled around Hicks's *Observations on the Slavery of Africans and Their Descendants*. In this pamphlet, Elias decried not only the institution of bondage but also whites' use of slave-produced goods, like cotton and sugar.[41]

Sometimes discussions about slavery and abolition took place at monthly meetings, which the Kirbys regularly attended. Although neither Mary nor Jacob served as clerks or were designated as elders or ministers, they were related to a number of Quaker preachers, including Hicks and Lucretia Mott.[42] The Society of Friends did not support a distinct class of ministers, but some women and men were recognized for the quality of their spiritual expressions. However, even acknowledged ministers did not have specific training, were not paid, and did not receive formal ordination. Individuals wanting to minister to Friends in other locales required the approval of their monthly meeting. Some of these "Public Friends" traveled only to neighboring meetings, but others, such as Woolman, Hicks, and Mott, visited meetings far and wide. Public Friends were especially significant in the late eighteenth and early nineteenth centuries, traveling throughout the United States and across the Atlantic Ocean to help sustain small or declining meetings and to provide refreshing "convincements" to meetings that had grown complacent.[43]

Long Island attracted hundreds of traveling Friends to their meetings. At least 830 visited the island between 1732 and 1827, including such leading Quakers as Woolman and Mott of Philadelphia and Anna Braithwaite of England. Some visited every preparative and monthly meeting in the region; others, only a few. More than half traveled from Philadelphia Yearly Meeting; about a fifth from other parts of New York Yearly Meeting; and the rest from elsewhere in the United States, Canada, England, Ireland, and the West Indies. Approximately a third of the traveling Quakers were women, many of whom forged close friendships with other female ministers or with the women who housed and fed them on their visits.[44] Even in well-attended meetings, like those at Jericho and Westbury, these Friends might raise ideas or questions that members had not previously considered. Some travelers brought news of family and friends from other places, adding to the pleasure of their visits; others agitated local meetings by objecting to certain practices or beliefs.

While traveling ministers added excitement to Friends' normal routine, Mary Seaman Kirby may have barely noticed, occupied as she was with managing a busy and growing household. Mary Kirby's first child, Mary, was born in 1791. More births followed every few years over the next two and a half decades. William, born in 1795, died at age two, but was followed two years later by Hannah. Then, in 1802, Amy was born, followed by Willets four years later and then Edmund in 1808. Amy may have been too young to fully understand pregnancy and childbearing when her brothers were born, but she was certainly aware of the anxiety and joy when her forty-year-old mother safely bore Elizabeth in 1814 and her last child, Sarah, four years later. Throughout their youth, Amy and her sisters were surrounded as well by pregnant aunts, cousins, and neighbors, who gave birth, miscarried, and buried stillborn babies. Their mother's younger sister Esther Robbins was especially close to the Kirby sisters; and her first child, another Mary, was born just a month before Amy's fourth birthday.[45]

In 1820, the Kirby siblings ranged in age from two to twenty-nine and likely spent as much time with cousins and other relatives their own age as with one another. Indeed, Amy's closest childhood friend was her cousin Mary Robbins. Despite the four-year age gap, Amy spent endless hours with Mary, first helping to care for the infant and later sharing secrets, exploring nearby woods and streams, and sitting together in Friends meetings.[46]

The two young Friends learned how to behave, worship, and interact with the world under the tutelage of their mothers and Amy's older sisters. Like their parents, siblings, and cousins, Amy Kirby and Mary Robbins dressed plainly. The gray cotton, linen, and wool dresses worn by most Quaker women met Society dictates and the realities of farm life. Their clothes were handmade, just as most of their food was raised on their farm or bought locally. While rural Friends were not averse to buying imported goods, they were not likely to purchase fancy items for personal or domestic use.

By the early 1800s, those most deeply committed to ending slavery, including Elias and Jemima Hicks and Willet and Esther Robbins, refused to consume slave-produced goods, such as West Indian sugar and southern cotton.[47] Quaker testimonies on temperance ensured that most members never imbibed rum, a crucial item in the trade between New York merchants and Caribbean planters. In 1807, Willet Robbins joined several family members in the New York Manumission Society, founded twenty-two years earlier to promote emancipation and assist the enslaved who had gained their freedom. A majority of members were Friends, but other prominent New Yorkers, including John Jay and Alexander Hamilton, helped found the society. By 1812, Willet Robbins chaired a standing committee and served as a delegate to the American Convention for Promoting the Abolition of Slavery, held in Philadelphia. Numerous other Kirby relatives worked alongside Willet in the New York Manumission Society and the larger antislavery movement.[48]

Jacob Kirby was not listed among the early members of the New York Manumission Society, but as a young man, he saw Paul Cuffee speak at New York Yearly Meeting. Cuffee was one of the rare African American Quakers, and he promoted Sierra Leone as a haven for his people among Friends. At age ninety, Kirby still recalled the black activist's visit as well as his mother "repeating some lines of phillis wheatley's poetry" to him just before she died in 1784.[49] The power of these memories and Jacob and Mary's close bonds with the Hickses and the Robbinses indicate that they shared their antislavery views.

With a growing family and a plain lifestyle, the Kirbys likely embraced free produce as well. They had little money to spend on imported goods, fancy cloth, or ornamental items, and they did not consume alcohol—except perhaps for medicinal purposes. Amy and her siblings were taught to use plain speech, replacing *you, we,* and *yours* with *thy, thee, thou,* and *thine.* The use of these singular personal pronouns emerged from and shaped Quaker thinking in two ways: the forms were already archaic in the 1650s, so their use identified Friends as a distinctive group; and the rejection of plural forms when addressing individuals or groups was intended to demonstrate the equality of all people, regardless of station or wealth.[50] Friends also refused to use titles of rank and often referred to co-worshippers, neighbors, and in-laws simply as brothers and sisters.

The Kirby and Robbins children were instilled with Quaker values not only at home but also at the local Friends school. Concerned that their children not learn "the corrupt ways, manners, fashions, and languages of the world," Friends organized their own educational institutions. By the late eighteenth century, New York Yearly Meeting had established seminaries and boarding schools for families who could afford to send their children away from home.[51] Monthly meetings, like those in Jericho and Westbury, built schools to meet the needs of children who remained in the community. The education of girls and boys was considered equally important, and Amy and her sisters attended the Jericho Friends School alongside their brothers.

Young people also imbibed spiritual and practical lessons at First Day (Sunday) and Fourth Day (Thursday) meetings.[52] Sitting among the women, Amy experienced a rich female world of faith, family, and friendship. She and her friends observed growing bellies, squirming babies, and grieving relatives at close range. The meetings also ensured that Amy and her sisters saw nothing unusual in women speaking out or overseeing their own business. The ordinariness of female Friends' participation certainly shaped girls' assumptions about the capacities of their sex. Still, this did not mean that they were unaware of women's legal and economic disabilities. Girls must have heard whispers about wives abused by their husbands or known women left destitute as widows, and they learned soon enough that young women had to wait on the initiatives of young men to find a life partner. Nonetheless, Quaker girls—in domestic circles, classrooms, and meetinghouses—experienced a fuller appreciation of female abilities and rights than their counterparts in most American communities at the time.

Assumptions about women's capabilities may have been reinforced by the predominant community of non-Quakers with whom Amy and her friends had meaningful contact: free and fugitive blacks. African Americans residing on central Long Island maintained close ties with many Friends while living separately from them. In establishing churches, supporting families, and organizing social events, black women played crucial roles. A few even became preachers, though this role was still highly contested in most African American churches. In addition, black women regularly worked alongside their husbands on farms and in shops, earned wages as laundresses and domestic servants, and attended births and deaths. When families like the Kirbys hired black girls to help with household chores, they often performed the same tasks assigned to Amy and her sisters.[53]

Still, Quaker women held a unique place in the meetinghouse. Despite the importance of black women in establishing and sustaining churches, they were only rarely granted the right to preach and never held the kind of authority over discipline, marriages, and other matters that female Friends wielded.[54] Quaker girls probably started attending women's business meetings in their teens and observed female members serving as clerks. Chosen by her sisters, the clerk stood at the front of the meeting, took notes, and summarized the concerns voiced and decisions reached by the group. Other women testified on spiritual and social issues, considered marriage proposals, and appointed committees to visit sisters who had strayed from disciplinary admonitions. Women were also selected to present their concerns to the men's meeting and to draft epistles—letters to other meetings—voicing their views on peace, slavery, temperance, and other concerns. Others were appointed representatives to monthly or quarterly meetings and reported back to their Jericho sisters.[55]

Just when Amy Kirby was old enough to participate more fully in women's meetings, Friends confronted a range of controversies. The passionate pleas that characterized monthly, quarterly, and yearly meetings in the 1820s offered Amy and her F/friends a different sense of Quaker ways of being than those born a generation earlier. Although debates over slavery certainly broke the quiet of Long Island meetings in the late eighteenth and early nineteenth centuries, the most outspoken advocates of emancipation were men. But the religious controversies that swept through the Society as Amy came of age affected both sexes with equal force. Whether at home with parents and siblings or spending time with their cousins, the Kirby children must have felt the tension between simplicity and quietism on the one hand, and ardent contestation on the other.

Beginning in the late 1810s, Friends across the country engaged in increasingly tense discussions over the authority of the Bible and the Discipline, the centrality of inner light, the role of ministers and elders, and the divinity of Christ.[56] While these differences were sometimes aggravated by growing distinctions between urban and rural or wealthy and middling Friends, Quakers were never isolated from developments at other meetings. Instead, traveling Friends stirred debate by carrying news and discussions from community to community. These disagreements occurred mainly among American Quakers, but traveling ministers from England also riled the waters, many supporting the more evangelical wing of the Society of Friends, which put more faith in the Bible, the Discipline, the authority of ministers and elders, and Christ's divinity. Although all Quakers considered Jesus divine, some believed he was born divine and others that he achieved divinity through his perfect reflection of the inner light. For the latter, his saintly life rather than his death led to salvation.[57]

As neighbors, relatives, and ministers voiced their views in meetings, on porches, and around fireplaces and kitchen tables, young Quakers listened and sometimes chimed in. Jericho Friends were especially passionate about these concerns because Elias Hicks led the challenge against those he thought too dependent on the printed word and the advice of ministers and elders. In the late 1700s and early 1800s, Hicks traveled widely, insisting on the need for all Friends to return to the founding principles of the Society. "Tall and spare," he often dressed in a plain suit and a "very plain round crowned White Hat."[58] Although Hicks questioned the authority granted ministers and elders, he generally sat in the "Minister's gallery." He quoted liberally from the Bible and accepted the miracles performed by Jesus while denying that Christ was born divine. And he repeated a core theme: "When we centre down into a state of self-abasement and nothingness—when the . . . temple of the heart is emptied of every thing of self, . . . it can become a fit receptacle for the King of glory to . . . make himself known there."[59] Silent worship, freeing oneself from worldly concerns, emptying one's mind and soul—these were the prerequisites of opening one's heart to God's light.

Hicks's views were widely challenged, and some detractors even accused him of heresy. Many of his critics belonged to meetings that organized Bible and missionary societies and embraced other evangelical efforts. Even in Jericho, more evangelically minded Friends, such as Thomas and Phebe Willis, disagreed with Hicks. Although they voiced their concerns mainly in personal letters, Hicks sometimes responded to their criticisms publicly. The Willises and other Friends felt aggrieved when their private correspondence suddenly appeared in print, fueling bitter pamphlet wars. English Quakers such as Anna Braithwaite joined the fray, challenging Hicks's views in person and in print.[60] But neither Elias nor his followers, known as Hicksites, backed down. Indeed, they became more outspoken as the attacks intensified.

While the Kirbys supported Hicks's views, other urgent matters pressed on them as well. In farming communities like Jericho, spiritual crises converged with financial and familial upheavals. A scarcity of land and economic opportunity inspired many young men to migrate to central New York and other frontier areas. Most were eager to take a wife to help establish new homes and new meetings. In their teens and early twenties, Amy and her friends joked about "the marrying fever" and exchanged the latest news about who was pursuing whom.[61] Yet they were also anxious lest marriage, even to the best of Friends, take them far from home.

Amy's sister Hannah was among those who left family behind after her marriage to Isaac Post in February 1821. Isaac, who lived in Westbury, could trace his American lineage to Richard Post, who had arrived in Long Island via New England in the 1650s. The family of Isaac's mother, Catherine Willets, also had deep roots on Long Island, migrating to Oyster Bay from Wiltshire, England, in 1676.[62] By the 1820s, Westbury families had become so intertwined that numerous names were repeated across generations. Marys, Sarahs, Elizabeths, Phebes, and Catherines regularly married Johns, Roberts, Jacobs, Isaacs, and Edmunds. And both Willet and Willets, initially last names, became favored first names in some families. Some married women used their maiden names as middle names—for example, Isaac's sister, Phebe Post Willis—to distinguish one family line from another.

Isaac planned to leave these family ties behind to take advantage of cheap and fertile land in Ledyard, a town some 270 miles northwest of Jericho. He may have chosen Ledyard because an uncle and his family had migrated to nearby Skaneateles, but Hannah had no relatives in the area and was far more anxious about leaving Long Island. Almost immediately after settling into her new home, she felt homesick and begged her sister Amy, just three years younger, to visit. When Amy finally agreed, a friend used her imminent departure to encourage a young man who was "very interested" in the younger Kirby daughter to press his case. After all, Amy was twenty years old and might find a beau in Ledyard.[63]

Amy Kirby was barely five feet tall and slim, with long dark hair and an oval face. She considered herself plain—noting late in life, perhaps jokingly, that she would rather be "anybody better and handsomer." Most of her life, she wore simple linen or wool dresses and a bonnet, though she sometimes added a frilled collar and, later in life, enjoyed more high-quality fabrics. Despite her somber dress, Amy was lively, attracted a wide circle of devoted friends, and enjoyed dancing as well as knitting. Perhaps most importantly, she was not afraid to express her opinions on religion or other matters. One friend considered her outspoken enough to be courted by a law school teacher.[64]

Speculating about courtship was fun, but marriage was a more serious matter. Quaker women and men were allowed to choose their own partners in the sense that every marriage was supposed to be rooted in love. Thus, relationships were often initiated by young people rather than by their parents. Still, once interested in each other, a young couple had to gain the assent of their parents to court. If they decided to marry, the couple announced their intentions before the men's and women's monthly meetings, and the women's meeting sent a committee to "investigate the 'clearness' from prior ties and particularly the 'conversation' [mutual feelings] of the man and the woman."[65] The committee might visit with potential spouses and talk to friends or family members to ensure that they had not made promises to anyone else and had conducted themselves appropriately. Its decision was generally announced to the couple at the next monthly meeting. If the man and woman attended different monthly meetings, each had to investigate the prospective spouses and come to a mutual agreement. Even after clearance was granted, couples who engaged in sexual relations risked disownment. But Friends did not expect young people to delay marriage for long. Usually a month or two after gaining the meeting's approval, the couple married at the bride's monthly meeting, exchanging vows of love and faithfulness in front of those gathered for regular worship. The Friends witnessing the vows then signed a certificate, a copy of which would later be taken to local authorities to ensure the marriage was recognized by law.

While much of the process was in women's hands, potential brides faced many challenges, as Amy learned in her teens. First, men initiated the marriage proposal. Second, in tight-knit Quaker communities, private matters easily became public. Before Hannah married Isaac, their courtship was troubled. She initially refused Isaac's marriage proposal, perhaps because she knew about his plans to move west. Then, apparently after he "plac[ed] his affections on another," she changed her mind. Mary Kirby Willis, the oldest of the Kirby siblings and the longest married, thought Isaac should "have nothing to do with Ha[nnah] now since trying and being refused." Isaac proved more forgiving. Still, his decision caused distress for the woman he had begun "addressing" and upset many F/friends and neighbors.[66]

Given the circumstances, gaining approval for the marriage from both sets of parents and Jericho and Westbury Monthly Meetings must have been difficult. The women's meetings were apparently sympathetic to Hannah's concerns, since they granted the couple clearance to wed. Mary and Jacob Kirby approved as well, but they were undoubtedly relieved when a severe winter kept Hannah and Isaac on Long Island through the spring of 1822. Once rivers and roads were passable, however, the newlyweds headed to their new home amid the Finger Lakes of central New York. Their farm sat along a high ridge in the recently established town of Ledyard. From their house on Poplar Ridge Road, Hannah and Isaac gazed on panoramic views of fertile fields, budding trees along the shore of shimmering Lake Cayuga, and forested hills beyond.[67]

Hannah, however, barely noticed the gorgeous scenery, instead grieving over her lonely life. "My lot is cast in a distant land," she wrote Amy, "and my time much taken up with the cares of the world."[68] In early 1823, she happily returned to Jericho to await the birth of her first child, a daughter—also named Mary—born on 20 February. Two months later, about to return to Ledyard, Hannah received a consoling letter from Isaac's cousin Maria Willets, who also lived in central New York. Recognizing how difficult it was to leave loved ones behind, she reminded Hannah that they shared "a solitary blessing few can find[;] . . . we are blessed with kind affectionate husbands—ready to share with us whatever may attend us through life."[69]

Although many women faced anxieties about leaving home, it did not slow the pace of migration. Hundreds of Revolutionary War soldiers, who accepted land in lieu of pay, had settled in central New York in the 1780s and 1790s. General Benjamin Ledyard arrived in 1793 and named the growing community along Lake Cayuga Aurora, for the goddess of dawn. Other towns and villages sprang up nearby and along the neighboring Finger Lakes. Pioneers were amazed at the ease of growing crops in the rich soil. The area's fertility had earlier attracted Seneca, Onondaga, and Cayuga Indians, who tilled the land for generations. But many of them had sided with the British during the American Revolution and were driven west by Patriot troops. General Sullivan had employed a scorched-earth policy in the region to force Indian Loyalists to flee, but the abundant orchards and fertile fields they had cultivated returned under the labor of pioneer settlers.[70] By the early 1800s, older settlements grew quickly and new towns sprouted regularly as newlyweds and young families from New England, Pennsylvania, and eastern New York migrated to the region.

Quakers were drawn to Ledyard, neighboring Scipio and the village of Aurora, as well as to Farmington fifty miles to the west. In 1789, a group of Friends in North Adams, Massachusetts, bought some 25,000 acres in the vast Phelps and Gorham Purchase in central New York and were disowned by their meeting for such a "rash action."[71] The first families, led by Nathan Comstock, migrated the next year and established the town of Farmington. They hosted meetings for worship in their homes until 1796, when sufficient settlers arrived to build a log meetinghouse. Two years earlier, a major treaty was signed between the Six Nations of the Iroquois, or Haudenosaunee, and the U.S. government at nearby Canandaigua. The Haudenosaunee had invited Friends from Philadelphia Yearly Meeting to serve as witnesses, and Quakers later established a school at Alleghany for Seneca settled there. By 1816, the growing settlement of Quaker families constructed a two-story meetinghouse, and quarterly meetings for the region were often held at Farmington. Isaac Post and other Friends from Ledyard, Scipio, and Aurora made the long journey over country roads to attend these meetings until 1825, when Scipio was granted its own quarterly meeting.[72]

While Hannah and baby Mary did not join Isaac on trips to Farmington, they did attend local meetings. It helped that they could easily walk to the meetinghouse on Poplar Ridge Road. The couple served on various committees for the men's and women's meetings, and Hannah was periodically appointed to report to the men's meeting on education and other issues.[73]

The Poplar Ridge Meetinghouse was an important site for socializing as well, especially for the many mothers caring for young children.

Isaac, Hannah, and Mary also visited Isaac's uncle William Willets— brother of his mother Catherine Willets Post. He had moved his family to Skaneateles, seventeen miles northeast of Ledyard, around 1820.[74] Located at the head of Skaneateles Lake, the town sat along a major road, whose route paralleled the Erie Canal. By the mid-1820s, with completion of the canal, the region was booming, with workshops and stores supplying goods to the rural hinterland and providing farmers with access to markets from Buffalo to New York City. The thriving village of Auburn was even closer to Ledyard than Skaneateles was, though it was farther from the canal. Lying at the northern tip of Lake Owasco, it served as the county seat and was home to a theological seminary and a model state prison. Quakers were scattered across these communities, forming an expanding network bound together by kinship, friendship, and faith. Still, they were surrounded by a wide range of ethnic and religious groups, including former Continental soldiers as well as Irish, German, and Dutch immigrants. To ensure their distinctiveness, most Friends retained their characteristic dress, speech, and forms of worship.

Despite the booming economy and growing population in the region, Hannah Post continued to feel isolated. Soon after returning to Ledyard, she again begged Amy to visit: "I feel I could not be satisfyed [sic] to pass this summer alone."[75] Her neighbors Benjamin and Mary Howland, whose home sat on the crest of Poplar Ridge, might have been surprised to hear her laments. Their farms offered stunning views of fields and woods falling away to the crystalline lake below. Lake Cayuga was only three-fourths of a mile wide, but it was eleven miles long, offering opportunities for fishing, sailing, and picnicking along its shores. Bright with new crops and budding flowers in spring, rich with birds and orchards in summer, bathed in gold and red leaves in fall, and frosted for sleighs and sleds in winter, the area boasted well-traveled roads, boat rides on the lake, abundant fruits and vegetables, and thriving Quaker communities.

Hannah, however, spent a great deal of time alone with baby Mary. Isaac, like most of his neighbors, worked the family farm, but as his mother-in-law noted, "He ha[d] so many ways to go to look for nessary [sic] things, and work of [various] kinds crowding in." She hoped her son-in-law would "not get overdone" and clearly worried about the effect his frequent absence had on Hannah.[76] Isaac also regularly attended yearly meetings in

New York City, after which he often visited family on Long Island. When away from home, he assured his "dear Hannah" that "I often think of thee and thy lonely situation."[77] She, in turn, felt his absence keenly and invited women friends to stay with her. They helped with housework, and some, she reported, were "kind enough to sleep with me."[78] Still, she longed for Amy's company.

If Amy's decision to visit Ledyard in spring 1823 thrilled her sister, it dismayed their parents. The arduous journey from Jericho to Ledyard took at least three days if there were no delays from bad weather or mechanical problems. That May, the Kirbys had seen Hannah, Isaac, and baby Mary off at New York harbor, where they boarded the steamboat *Constitution* for the trip to Albany. From there, they probably traveled by coach to Ledyard. The Kirbys did not hear of their safe arrival until ten days later, by which time Amy was on her way to Ledyard. When a relative later related the travails that Amy faced along the route, Mary Kirby thanked her daughter for "not telling us more" about the difficulties because it would have only caused greater anxiety.[79] It must have been both exciting and frightening for a young woman who had rarely ventured beyond Jericho.

Once Mary Kirby was sure all were safely settled in Ledyard, she wrote "her dear children" that she and Jacob had "endeavoured to keep still, and abide in the quiet," knowing that such separations "must, must be submitted to." Still, she missed her daughters' company, and also their labor. Although Amy tried to do all the heaviest housework before she left, her mother had to hire "a little black girl who works very well" to take on some of the chores. Her parents also worried that Amy, at twenty years old, still needed their guidance. Mary Kirby thus insisted that Isaac provide "not only a brother's, but a father's, care of her."[80]

More often, however, it was Amy who cared for Hannah. She immediately took on some of the domestic chores and within a couple of weeks had nearly the whole of the house under her management when Hannah and baby Mary fell ill. Amy nursed them back to health, and once the crisis passed, she assured her mother that they all "lived very comfortably together." Amy noted that their "cousin J[oseph] Loines serves as a doctor here," so she could call on him for advice if needed. Increasingly impressed with the challenges of frontier living, Amy admired the fact that Isaac never got discouraged.[81] Of course, life was not all work and illness. Amy and Hannah enjoyed long hours reminiscing about home and speculating on their futures, and often visited Abraham Willets and his wife, cousins of Isaac who had recently moved from Skaneateles to Ledyard. Amy also made friends with other young Quaker migrants to central New York and reconnected with Anna Greene, a former class-mate and close friend of Mary Robbins.[82]

Amy saw her new friends at Scipio Monthly Meeting, where she came to appreciate Quaker concerns about the exploitation of Indians. The Society of Friends had long sought to assist American Indians in their relations with the U.S. government and land speculators. While few Indians survived on Long Island, expanded settlement in central New York in the early nine-teenth century—including by Friends—intensified difficulties for the On-ondaga and Seneca Nations there. While most Seneca had been driven from the shores of Lake Cayuga during the American Revolution, they retained large tracts of land farther west. In battling with land speculators, most no-tably Phelps and Gorham and the Holland Land Company, and dealing with government officials pressing for new treaties, native leaders often turned to Quakers for support. Farmington Quarterly Meeting willingly addressed the concerns of the Seneca, and leading members of that tribe visited local Quakers in the 1820s. Chief Red King of the Onondaga also attended Farmington Quarterly Meeting in spring 1823, just before Amy arrived, and seemed "much pleased" with their manner of doing business.[83]

When Amy accompanied Isaac to the next Quarterly Meeting in June 1823, she focused more on the conflicts among Friends than the plight of the Sen-eca. She reported to her mother that there were "several valuable friends there . . . but no strict disciplinarians like cousin Elias."[84] Still, Amy's in-terest in Indian affairs was apparently sparked. After she returned home in winter 1824, Anna Greene wrote her concerning a powerful sermon by Adin T. Corey, a Quaker Indian rights advocate. Corey, she noted, takes an interest "in instructing the Indians (*for whose civilization thou too feels solicitous*)."[85]

While Amy Kirby enjoyed new experiences in Ledyard, F/friends back home worried that she might decide to stay. Amy Willis, with whom she shared many a private thought, felt "lonely & dejected" in summer 1823 "without one female friend to whom I could unbosom my feelings." She vis-ited Mary Kirby, hoping for news of her daughters, and wrote to Amy after-ward: "It really seemed strange to be there without seeing either of you which led me to view how uncertain it was where our lot might be cast." Still, Willis joked that several eligible beaus were suddenly thinking of vis-iting central New York now that Amy was there.[86]

Meanwhile, Amy Kirby discovered that there were plenty of eligible beaus already living in central New York. The most attentive was thirty-year-old Charles Willets, the son of William Willets, who had grown up in

Westbury and then migrated with his family to Skaneateles. He likely met Amy when Isaac took her to visit his uncle William's family. The two might have renewed their acquaintance at a quarterly meeting in Farmington, which Amy attended on at least two occasions, or Charles might have visited Abraham Willets in Ledyard. In either case, Amy and Charles would have socialized among unmarried Friends who gathered for hikes along the lake, tea at someone's home, or—once winter arrived—skating parties. It is not clear when their relationship became more serious, but by the time Amy returned to Jericho in January 1824, Charles was ready to enter into an understanding.[87]

Amy appeared more ambivalent, perhaps fearing to commit herself to a man living so far from Jericho and worrying about the challenges of carrying on a long-distance courtship in tight-knit Quaker communities. Amy Willis's experience certainly reinforced her concerns. Shortly before Amy Kirby's journey to Ledyard in spring 1823, Townsend Rushmore secretly began courting Willis. By fall, rumors of their relationship reached Amy and Hannah in Ledyard.[88] When the couple's "intentions" were "made publick" late that year, Willis "said she felt as though she could not move in it, without my Amy."[89] Perhaps she anticipated trouble even though the women's monthly meeting approved the match. Soon thereafter, a letter circulated among Friends suggesting that another young man had a claim on Willis's affections, and the bride-to-be felt disgraced by the revelations.[90] In December, Willis revealed her troubles to Amy in an anguished letter: "I have long wished to acquaint thee with [my plans to marry]," she wrote, "and the last night I slept with thee I was several times upon the point of [telling thee] but diffidence forbade me." Afterward, she feared "putting any such thing on paper." She realized now how Hannah must have felt "to be talked about" before her marriage. "I used to pity her," but now "it has come home to myself."[91]

Despite the turmoil, the wedding was scheduled for January 1824, and Amy desperately wanted to attend. Isaac agreed to accompany her to Jericho, but the trip proved nearly disastrous. As Amy reported to Charles Willets, "I suffered with little or nothing on our way, except with fear and anxiety, we were many times in iminant [sic] danger of *upsetting* or *running* off the banks into *high* precipices." When Amy finally made it to Jericho, too late for the wedding, she found the Rushmores "mutually happy."[92] Fortunately, Townsend soon accompanied Elias Hicks on his ministry, giving the two Amys plenty of time to share confidences.

In these precious days together, Amy Kirby likely confided her own dilemma regarding Charles Willets. She had sent "a message of love" to him via Hannah but was stunned when his reply included a marriage proposal.[93] Amy responded almost immediately. She had enjoyed the "many favours" received at his "kind hands" and admitted, "I cannot affect to feel an indifference towards thee, but I must, I must decline." Hoping that "resentment on thy part will not destroy the tie of friendship," Amy ended the letter with newsy accounts of her travels to Jericho, her conversations with Amy Willis, and her hopes that Charles might still visit her on Long Island.[94]

Undeterred, Willets continued to woo Amy Kirby. While Amy admitted that she thought of him often, she could not "announce a dedication of heart, without the knowledge of my parents." When she finally raised the issue with them, she "found their approbation unattainable" and begged Charles to "relinquish the idea, for it [is] my duty to obey, and thine to submit." Hoping to assuage his "pang of disappointment," Amy concluded, "think not that thou art the only sufferer."[95] That statement was apparently sufficient for Willets to persist in his efforts. When Charles visited Long Island in September 1824, Isaac's brother Joseph reported that his visits to family in Westbury were limited: he "spent most of this time at Jericho . . . I suppose on particular business."[96]

A month later, Mary and Jacob Kirby visited Hannah and Isaac in Ledyard, and Charles again made his case. Although the meeting did not go smoothly—each later apologized to the other for some of their "expressions"—the Kirbys were ultimately persuaded that Charles would make a suitable husband. During the visit, Hannah may have announced that she was pregnant again, leading her parents to realize that Amy would be returning to Ledyard anyway, making their opposition more difficult to justify.[97] In addition, Isaac was involved in establishing a new mail and passenger coach line for central and western New York, which meant he would be away more than ever.

On 1 January 1825, when Hannah was seven months pregnant, Isaac Post, his F/friend Isaac Mott, who ran a Hudson River coach line, and two additional partners announced a new line of "Daily Post Coaches" in newspapers throughout the region. Proclaiming the advantages of "direct communication between the city of N. York and the western part of the state," the advertisement detailed the routes offered and the various points at which they intersected with coaches to Albany, Utica, Rochester, Buffalo, Pittsburgh, Philadelphia, and New York City.[98] Isaac's interest in the coach business likely led to his appointment that year as an overseer of highways in Ledyard, a position he held from 1825 to 1829. Homeowners were expected to maintain the roads that ran along their property; the overseer ensured that they did so and arranged for leveling, snow removal, and other work when needed. Isaac supervised District 22, covering Poplar Ridge Road and the surrounding area. Especially after storms, he was out inspecting the roads for problems that endangered travel.[99] At the same time, Isaac and his younger brother Joseph, along with Ledyard neighbors Humphrey Howland and Joseph Frost, invested in a "Full-Blooded English Horse" to be stabled on Poplar Ridge and available for stud service.[100] Isaac's entrepreneurial spirit ensured his family's financial future but meant lonely days and nights for Hannah, Mary, and baby Edmund, born in March 1825.

Mary and Jacob Kirby's acceptance of Willets as a suitor for Amy not only raised Hannah's hopes but also recast the young couple's correspondence. Addressing Charles in October 1824 "under very *different*" and "far happier prospects," Amy still noted one concern: "I cannot help shuddering at the idea of being so very widely severed from my most precious, yes the best of all parents, dear brothers and sisters and many much loved friends, together with this delightful spot of earth, to which I am so strongly attached." She could not become a "Willets," she claimed, until convinced that she could be as happy in Skaneateles as in Locust Grove. Seeking to avoid rumors about her intentions, Amy sent her letters via Isaac, "as Jericho folks are very watchful at the post office." Meanwhile, Charles sent her copies of local newspapers to introduce her to the many delights of Skaneateles.[101]

Over the ensuing months, Amy regularly covered three pages with her spidery script and added another paragraph or two crosshatched on the last sheet. In winter 1825, Charles again visited Long Island, much to Amy's delight. Afterward, she discussed more intimate matters in her correspondence. She noted in her very next letter that when he visited, "thee thought I was quite as fleshy as when I left Scipio, but I think thou was mistaken, as my weight the week after was 92, and it is now 103. I should be glad to hear thee gained as much." Anxious about his well-being, Amy constantly worried that he weakened his health by applying himself so "constantly and closely to business." She also offered her views on the propriety of Charles attending a wedding at which he would encounter a Friend who had once hoped to become his wife. As Amy finished her letter, her mother came into the room, sending "love to thee" but also "insist[ing] on seeing thy letter," saying "how will I come to love him" otherwise.[102] Carrying on a long-distance relationship amid familial and community oversight required delicacy as well as patience.

While personal concerns dominated the couple's letters, Amy readily expressed her opinions on religious matters as well. First, she criticized a letter to Friends written by Anna Braithwaite that critiqued "the anti-christian doctrine professed by Elias Hicks" and later complained that "Ann Shipley comes out with another printed letter, affirming to the truth of A. B. statement after Elias has contradicted it."[103] The exchange of published letters focused on Hicks's refusal to acknowledge the original divinity of Jesus, but other issues swirled just below the surface. Anna Braithwaite; her husband, Isaac; and other English Friends had denounced Hicks's doctrines on several visits to the United States between 1822 and 1826. Hicks's supporters printed the attacks with lengthy replies and circulated transcripts of Hicks's sermons. Throughout this period, dissension between evangelical and Hicksite Friends escalated in a number of yearly meetings.[104]

Many Friends chose or felt forced to choose sides. The Post and Kirby families were engrossed in the debates, with most embracing Hicks's views, as did many rural and small-town Quakers across the North. Mary Kirby, her daughter Mary W. Willis, and cousin Lydia Mott, along with Isaac's sisters Phebe Post Willis and Lydia Post Rushmore, regularly exchanged news of Hicks's meetings, his sermons, and his responses to critics.[105] Isaac's parents were not initially among Hicks's supporters, but Lydia assured her brother in fall 1826 that "father[']s and mother[']s ideas respecting Dear Elias Hicks are much favourable than when I wrote last."[106] While some Jericho Friends thought the conflict unseemly, Amy did not. Noting that Anna Braithwaite was again coming to America in spring 1825, she told Charles that "most folks are very sorry but for my part I am rather glad that she is coming," for "I have little doubt but what she herself will be sorry, for the truth apprehend[ed] will this time be told on her certificates."[107] Clearly, Amy was willing to let the conflict escalate if it meant alerting more Friends to Braithwaite's "errors" and Hicks's "truth."

In May 1825, Amy wrote Charles that his latest letter had arrived while she was sick, "bolstered up in an easy chair, and cousin Elias Hicks by my side." She insisted it was his letter, rather than Hicks's presence, that "cheered my drooping spirits."[108] By then, Amy was anxious to return to Ledyard. The birth of Hannah and Isaac's son, Edmund, heightened her desire to see them, and the fact that both baby and mother were ill only intensified that feeling. Still, Amy hesitated, hoping to return as Willets's wife.

Despite delays in setting a wedding date, Amy poured out her hopes and fears to Charles. She recognized that it was inappropriate to say too much;

it is "a very delicate thing for a girl to acknowledge that she loves" someone. "My dear cousin Mary Robbins is my only confidant[e]," but that bond also fueled her hesitation. "Oh my Charles thou little knows how often we have wept together at the prospect that at some future day it will be our lot to dwell remote from each other." In the next breath, Amy urged Charles to return to Long Island, insisting that "this more southern air" would help cure that "absurdly sorrowful cough of thine."[109]

In mid-May, while Amy was awaiting Charles's visit, his parents stopped by the Kirbys' with their two younger sons and assured their future daughter-in-law that they enthusiastically approved the marriage. Hannah and Isaac arrived the next day with Mary and Edmund, allowing Amy to talk at length about plans she had yet to share with anyone but Mary Robbins. As soon as Charles arrived, they could "acknowledge the truth" publicly and ask the women's monthly meeting for permission to wed. In anticipation, Amy allowed herself more epistolary freedom, recalling a ride she and Charles took "with all its thrilling sensations the evening previous to my leaving Scipio . . . even the pressure of thy hand is indelibly stampt on my heart."[110]

Instead of a loving reply, however, Amy received word that Charles was seriously ill. Then, on 19 June, his uncle arrived at the Kirby home with letters from Charles's brother and father, detailing symptoms of a serious respiratory disease. Mary Kirby escorted Amy upstairs and read the letters to her "as she lay on the bed." The news, her mother reported, "affected her very sensibly and deeply, only the evening before we were looking & hoping to open up our door to him." When Amy could not sleep, "Dear Mary Robbins staid with us nights mostly, and when she can't, Sister Phebe sleeps with her." Two days later, a letter arrived from Charles's brother-in-law, reporting that Amy's "esteemed friend" had died. As her mother read the letter aloud by candlelight, Amy sat "perfectly still, so that I looked to [see] whether she *did* breath[e]." Since that day, Mary wrote Hannah, "there has been an [easy] shower of tears, many days we have laid in the bed together, sweetly conversing and communing together."[111]

Letters of sympathy and grief poured in, and Isaac personally carried "the last we shall receive from [Charles's] dear hand" to Jericho. Amy poured out her despair to Hannah. "I have been unwise, and was not sufficiently prepared with fortitude to meet this poignant arrow of disappointment." Confident in Charles as "the only source of my earthly happiness and comfort, I had almost forgotten, that I was resting upon anything mortal, but now alas; alas, these anticipated years of bliss where are they."[112] Even when writing to Charles's parents, Amy could barely restrain her anguish. She described "the sense of love and gratitude with which my feelings glow towards you"; but, she continued, "I have frequently been ready to cry out O my God, my God, why hast thou afflicted me." A devastated Amy closed, "Now I might very consonantly with my feelings subscribe myself your affectionate daughter, for I feel myself nothing less than the widow of your affectionate son."[113]

Amy could not bear to return to central New York that fall, so Hannah and Isaac traveled to Jericho, where the sisters reveled in each other's company even as they mourned Amy's blighted hopes. On returning to Ledyard, the Posts hosted Elias Hicks, who was holding meetings in the area. Hannah enjoyed conversing with him about maternal responsibilities and children's education but worried that dissent was growing in the local meeting. Isaac wondered if the yearly meeting might divide.[114] Eager to discuss these issues, Hannah urged Amy to spend the winter of 1826 in Ledyard, while Charles's sister invited her to Skaneateles, where there will be "sorrow mingled with that pleasure when we recollect what our prospects once were."[115] When Amy had not arrived by late January, Hannah sent her a gloomy letter, dwelling on Isaac's absence on business, the death of a close friend, and the abuse of another by her alcoholic husband. She also noted that she had been diagnosed with rheumatism following "a violent cold" and needed to be "very careful" of her health. She may, in fact, have been suffering from rheumatic fever, which can develop as a complication from a strep infection. The only development that engendered any enthusiasm in Hannah was the possibility of establishing a yearly meeting "in the western country."[116]

Despite her sister's pleas, Amy did not visit Ledyard until a year later. By then, Hannah was desperate for her company, insisting that she and Isaac needed the change Amy's presence would bring. In an earlier letter she had admitted that "living as we now do renders it unpleasant. . . . I am so foolish, sometimes there is nothing that looks much pleasant here to me, and I believe my Isaac is tired of always trying to pleas[e] as I am. . . . He tries to be as quiet as he can but says he feels but little courage to go on with the work &c."[117] Shortly after Amy arrived in February 1827, Hannah and two-year-old Edmund took ill. In late March, Anna Greene urged Amy to notify her mother, certain that she would want to be with her daughters.[118] But it was already too late. Hannah died at 3:00 A.M. on 4 April. Both Amy and Isaac were devastated, though caring for Mary and Edmund kept them from collapsing under their grief. A F/friend hoped that by looking to God, Amy would "be sustained in this, as in a former bereavement."[119] Still, it must have seemed doubly cruel to lose both her fiancé and her sister in such a short time.

In late April, Amy and Isaac took the children to Long Island to visit their families, after which Amy returned to Ledyard to care for Mary and Edmund. That fall, she brought the children back to Jericho to visit her still grieving parents. After the harvest, Isaac joined them and then visited Westbury, where Amy remained with the children when Isaac returned to the farm. Finally, in November, Amy returned to Ledyard with her niece and nephew.[120]

In the midst of their personal anguish, the Kirbys and Posts also had to confront what they long anticipated—a schism in the Society of Friends. In February 1827, Lucretia Mott, a cousin by marriage to the Kirbys and the Posts, wrote her mother-in-law Anne about "the state of the Jericho M[eetin]g," where disputes between Hicks, his supporters, and his detractors intensified. She saw no hope of resolution "when we see those of unblemished lives repeatedly arraigned before their [monthly meeting] tribunal."[121] By April, as condolence letters and mournful conversations consumed Hannah's family and friends, conflict erupted in Philadelphia Yearly Meeting when opposing groups sought to take control. When neither evangelicals nor Hicksites succeeded, the latter adjourned to the Green Street Meetinghouse and drew up a framework for a separate Philadelphia Yearly Meeting.

In the following months, other yearly, quarterly, and monthly meetings suffered divisions, fueled in part by debates over whether to send epistles and queries to the old or new Philadelphia Yearly Meeting. Although Hicks had hoped to convince his detractors of the truth of his views, he finally accepted that the rupture was irreversible. In spring 1828, he attended the new Philadelphia Yearly Meeting and gave his reluctant blessing to the separation.[122]

Hicks's presence immediately afterward at New York Yearly Meeting heightened ongoing tensions, but there it was his opponents, now called Orthodox, who left to establish a separate meeting. In Jericho and Westbury, Hicksites significantly outnumbered the Orthodox, but conflicts still erupted among relatives and neighbors. Most of Amy's family and friends continued to worship, as Hicksites, at the original meetinghouses. Valentine Willets, Thomas and Phebe Willis, and other local evangelicals then established an Orthodox meeting for Westbury and Jericho combined. In Farmington, too, Hicksites controlled the existing meetinghouse, built in 1816, while the Orthodox returned to the smaller 1804 meetinghouse across the road. And in Scipio, the Poplar Ridge Meetinghouse was retained by Hicksites.[123]

The separation had numerous consequences, including battles over minute books, financial resources, schools, and cemeteries, each revealing or reinforcing religious fissures. The division was also deeply personal. Adam Mott, Anne's husband, was visiting Rochester, New York, during the separation. Years later, he recalled seeing "tears in the eyes of the venerable Friends who stood in front" of the meetinghouse "from which they had just withdrawn."[124] Still, in the end, the 1828 separation into Hicksite and Orthodox Friends allowed most Quakers to find a more comfortable spiritual home and to refocus on outpourings of divine truth rather than doctrinal and disciplinary disputes.

Amy Kirby was aware of the spreading conflict, but it likely seemed less important than Hannah's death. Fortunately, there was no doubt where Amy's sympathies lay, and she lived in areas—Jericho and Ledyard—where Hicksites controlled the existing meetings. Although she did not consider siding with Hicks a radical act, Orthodox Friends believed Hicksites' elevation of inner light over the Bible and Friends' Discipline undermined the fundamental basis of their belief. As the schism unfolded, Amy Kirby must have wondered what lay in store for her as an unmarried, twenty-five-year-old woman traveling between the home of her parents and her brother-in-law, as an aunt with obligations to her niece and nephew, and as a devout Friend with responsibilities to the new Hicksite meeting.

2 Frontier Friends, 1828–1836

Throughout the spring and summer of 1828, Amy Kirby traveled back and forth between the upstart town of Ledyard and the established village of Jericho. While in central New York, she cared for her niece and nephew and deepened her friendships with Hannah Willets and Anna Greene. At the Poplar Ridge Meetinghouse, close to Isaac's home, Amy found solace in the quiet contemplation of First and Third Day meetings with like-minded Hicksites. She probably took Mary and Edmund with her on occasion and sat with the mothers who had known Hannah. Back in Jericho, Amy basked in the company of her parents, siblings, and oldest friends. She shared domestic tasks with her mother and "baby" Sarah, now ten years old; visited her married sisters and other relatives; and carried news to Isaac's family in Westbury.

Amy spent a good deal of time with Mary Robbins, her sole confidante about Charles Willets and her mainstay after his unexpected death. Mary, who was being courted by Isaac's younger brother, Joseph, was probably the first to hear that Amy's relationship with Isaac had taken a significant turn. By summer 1828, Amy was considering a crucial change in status, from Mary and Edmund's favorite aunt to their stepmother. She and Isaac had developed a special bond, sharing childcare and daily chores as they mourned. Still, the transition from sister-in-law to wife would be difficult. Was it possible, little more than a year after Hannah's death, for Amy to imagine marrying Isaac?[1] How would their parents and siblings and other F/friends on Long Island respond?

When Amy first visited Ledyard in 1823, Mary Kirby insisted that Isaac care for her as a father while Amy addressed him as "Brother Isaac," just as Joseph Post called his sister-in-law "Sister Hannah." Amy and Isaac knew that their existing familial bonds would arouse deep concern over their marriage. The Society of Friends opposed marriages between "persons of too near kin," which included "a man and his deceased wife's half-sister" or sister. Indeed, the Discipline proclaimed that when "any person of degree of kindred as near as these shall intermarry, they shall be disowned."[2] At the time, a number of other Protestant denominations also refused to recognize marriages between widowers and sisters-in-law, considering it a form of incest.[3]

Yet united by grief and affection, Amy and Isaac fell in love and, in so doing, defied the Friends Discipline. No record remains of how family members responded to the news, though some must have been wary, nor do any letters between the couple survive for this period. Still, the circumstances that drew them together are clear. Isaac had already proven himself a devoted husband and father and a good provider. He appears as well to have been a dapper fellow, about five feet six inches tall, with a well-trimmed beard, lean figure, and cordial demeanor. He was eager to better himself and his family but also concerned about the welfare of others, including African Americans and Indians. And Amy, although as firmly bound to Jericho as Hannah, turned out to be more adventurous than her sister. Or perhaps she was simply more willing to take chances after experiencing the sudden loss of Charles and Hannah. Caring for Mary and Edmund brought Amy joy, and the children were young enough—five and three—to transfer their affection from Hannah to her. Amy was eager as well to join in Hicksite testimonies on the rights of blacks and Indians, a concern she shared with Isaac and other members of the Scipio Monthly Meeting.

Thus, on September 4, 1828, Amy Kirby and Isaac Post took one of the first of many unconventional paths they would travel together. They chose to marry at Scipio Monthly Meeting rather than at Amy's home meeting in Jericho. Perhaps concerned about the response of Long Island F/friends and family, they exchanged vows before others could object. After announcing their intentions and receiving approval from the Scipio women's meeting, Amy and Isaac wed before co-worshippers and a few close F/friends from Long Island.

While some Scipio Quakers, aware of the sorrows each had suffered, willingly overlooked the Discipline and witnessed the marriage, others voiced their disapproval. Not long after the ceremony, a committee of men from Scipio Monthly Meeting visited Isaac and raised the prospect of disownment.[4] The transgression was at least as serious on Amy's part in that she should have asked the women's meeting at Jericho for clearance to wed. Members of that meeting expressed their concerns, as did Jericho men, who investigated the propriety of members of their meeting attending the Scipio ceremony.[5] No immediate family members were included in this investigation, suggesting either that none had traveled to Scipio or that the meeting viewed their participation more sympathetically.

Despite the cloud hanging over their nuptials, Amy and Isaac visited Long Island just three weeks later to witness the vows of Amy's cousin Mary Robbins and Isaac's brother Joseph Post. Once the joyous occasion was over, however, a committee of Jericho women questioned Amy about her defiance of the Discipline. The issue remained unresolved for months, and Amy seemed unwilling to compromise her principles to reach an amicable settlement. Then, in February 1829, just when it seemed that Amy might be disowned, she wrote a penitent letter to the women's meeting. Isaac's sister Lydia Rushmore was "much pleased with what sister Amy offered." Although she did not "either justif[y] the discipline or sa[y] that thou wast sorry for being married," Amy explained her decision in a way that eased the minds of her critics.[6] On 3 March, the women's meeting asked that her transgression be "passed by." The men's meeting concurred, and in June Amy was granted a certificate of removal to Scipio Monthly Meeting. Isaac, who remained under investigation in Scipio, was apparently even less willing to finesse his position. Nonetheless, by fall 1829, Isaac regained his standing as well, and the couple resumed their position among local Hicksites.[7]

While Isaac and Amy's challenge to the Discipline was under scrutiny, some of their F/friends faced questions as well. In January 1829, John Ketcham, who was a cousin and neighbor of the Kirbys and a close friend of the Posts, wrote Isaac that he was happy to learn that "the stream of *connubial* happiness glides smoothly along its verdant banks, bearing to its votarys [devotees] the choice treasures of domestic felicity." This, he joked, despite the match being "the *fruits* of *disobedience*."[8] By then, Ketcham and three others had been investigated by Jericho Monthly Meeting for attending the wedding. When asked to explain his transgression, Ketcham replied that he did not think the literal word of the Discipline had been transgressed. But even if it had, "there were *good* and *sufficient* reasons for doing what I did"; and "under all the attendant circumstances, I thought I should feel better satisfied to go than to omit it." He believed that the Friends Discipline is "probably the best *written* code in existence," but considering ourselves bound to "*unconditional* obedience to all its requirements . . . would prove a snare to us rather than a preservation." Ketcham was singled out for refusing to admit his transgressions, but he was not disowned and believed that the frank discussion his actions inspired "has been quite *refreshing*."

At the same time, Ketcham dropped "a friendly hint" to cousin Amy, noting that her recent letters included "one or two expressions . . . a little too *tart* to go down with some quite as well as could be wished."[9] Admitting that she had a right to be upset, he yet observed that "people who stand in our predicament" must "endeavour to be clothed with that charity which thinketh no evil." While supportive, Ketcham clearly worried that Amy's lack of humility might fuel calls for her disownment. A few weeks later, Amy wrote the letter that persuaded Jericho Women's Meeting to let her transgression pass. We will never know whether Amy's epistle was heartfelt, strategic, or some combination of the two, but it was effective.

The fact that Amy and Isaac married amid the upheavals of the Hicksite–Orthodox separation both complicated and eased matters. On the one hand, Hicksites in Jericho and Scipio had retained control of the original meetinghouses, so the Posts were being examined by longtime F/friends who shared their religious commitments. Moreover, most Hicksites considered the inner light, rather than the printed Discipline or the Bible, the ultimate basis for action. Still, Hicksites did not want their Orthodox opponents to claim that they failed to enforce the fundamental rules of the Society. Moreover, many Friends suffered from strained relations with neighbors and family members who had made choices different from their own. In Ledyard, Benjamin and Mary Howland—next-door neighbors who had befriended Isaac, Hannah, and Amy—joined the Orthodox meeting, as did the Kirbys' Jericho neighbors, Thomas and Phebe Willis. A few other families with close ties to the Posts and Kirbys also broke with the Hicksites. Perhaps criticisms from Orthodox Friends induced Scipio Hicksites to threaten Isaac with disownment after they had allowed the irregular marriage to take place.

Tensions among Scipio Friends over the 1828 schism continued to rankle for months afterward. In February 1829, the Hicksite meeting at Poplar Ridge bemoaned "the unexampled and truly awful state" into which "the body of [F]riends of this yearly meeting is plunged." In response, both women's and men's meetings established committees—of seventy women and forty-six men—to visit with members so that Friends "may sympathize with each other in their conflict and administer such council and assistance as through faithfulness they may be mercifully enlightened and enabled to do."[10] The size of the committees suggests the difficulties of reestablishing neighborly ties among Quakers whose shared labor, friendship, and kinship had been sorely tested by prolonged religious disputes. Neither Amy nor Isaac—still under the pall of disciplinary hearings—were appointed to these committees, but several cousins and close friends were, including Lydia Mott, Rachel Seaman, and Sarah Fish. Five weeks later, the preparative meeting at Poplar Ridge reported, "All our meetings for religious worship and discipline are attended but not as fully by all as is desired."[11]

Despite the general travails among Quakers and their own disciplinary problems, Isaac and Amy settled happily into their new life. Having spent prolonged periods in Ledyard since 1823, Amy was surrounded by supportive F/friends as well as extended kin from the Seaman, Hicks, Mott, and Willets families. The newlyweds had also made friends among neighboring farmers and co-worshippers, notably Susan White and brothers George and Elias Doty, who had moved to central New York as children in the 1800s. Susan's parents, Peleg and Eunice White, had migrated from Massachusetts to Cayuga County in 1810, the same year that pioneer Quakers built the large meetinghouse at Poplar Ridge. Despite the rural environs and the scattered clusters of households along Lake Cayuga, those pioneers raised a substantial two-story frame structure. Its double doors, facing the road, were flanked by windows on each side, and four more windows ran along the second floor. The building must have impressed migrants like those from Jericho, who had worshipped in a smaller meetinghouse.[12] In 1816, the Whites built a home in Ledyard, just west of the meetinghouse and next door to Jethro Wood, a farmer and inventor who developed the cast iron plow in 1814. Isaac Post's farm lay near the Wood and White homesteads, and Susan White befriended both Hannah and Amy.

In 1828, Susan and Amy both married at the Poplar Ridge Meetinghouse. However, Susan's husband George Doty died in 1831, and when the widow married brother Elias Doty two years later, she surely turned to Amy for advice and support. The two women, often pregnant at the same time, also bonded over domestic concerns and their shared commitment to Hicksite principles.[13]

Walking to and from the meetinghouse with their children, the Posts and Whites strolled under maple, walnut, and poplar trees that shaded the roads and paths. Along the way, fruit blossomed in yards and orchards—peach, pear, plum, apple, and sweet and sour cherries. Mary turned six in February 1829, and by the next summer, she may have helped Amy can fruit and bake pies. Vegetables, too, grew in abundance. The soil—"a highly productive sandy and gravelly loam, intermixed with clay"—ensured fertile fields. So, too, did the long history of Indian settlement, as generations of Cayuga and Seneca had cultivated the land and fertilized the soil with fish heads and other organic materials. From June on, the curly green leaves of corn stalks slowly sprouted alongside rows of tomatoes, peas, beans, and squash, while strawberry plants shot out tendrils along the ground and thorny bushes sprouted red and black raspberries.[14]

As Amy surveyed the agricultural fecundity in spring 1829, she realized she was bearing fruit as well. By summer, her pregnancy was visible, and her mother hoped that Amy would return to Jericho for the birth. Instead, she bore her first child in Ledyard on 27 November 1829, fourteen months after her marriage. She and Isaac named their new son Jacob, after Amy's father. Sarah Kirby, now eleven, likely spent part of the fall with Amy, assisting with childcare and housework. Just five years older than her niece Mary, Sarah could easily have been mistaken for the young girl's sister. Joseph and Mary Robbins Post, still childless, probably also visited that summer, joining in farmwork, domestic chores, neighborly visits, and Friends' meetings. John and Rebecca Ketcham, who had family in central New York, returned as well; and in spring 1830, Isaac's older sister Phebe Post Willis arrived, helping to sustain family ties over the hundreds of miles that separated Long Island and Lake Cayuga.[15]

Despite the joys of a happy marriage and a new baby, the Posts remained acutely aware of how quickly tragedy could strike. On September 7, 1830, five-year-old Edmund was killed instantly by a lever while driving horses attached to a threshing machine. Despite the long journey, Mary Kirby rushed to Ledyard and helped care for Mary and Jacob, who was not yet a year old. Edmund's death aroused sad memories for the entire family, but especially for Isaac. Realizing the depth of his grief, Mary Kirby thanked her son-in-law for his many kindnesses during her stay.[16]

Of course, illness and death were regular occurrences in the early nineteenth century. Rarely did a letter arrive from Long Island without news of ailments—common and life threatening—among family and friends. On the fourth anniversary of Hannah's death—4 April 1831—Amy's mother began a long letter to her daughter.[17] Mary Kirby did not mention the significance of the date but reported on Aunt Phebe's problems with rheumatism and the various doctors and remedies tried—or refused—by her. Sarah, now thirteen, was helping to nurse her aunt, and Mary was clearly proud that another of her daughters was acquiring medical skills. She also noted the appearance of scarlet fever on Long Island, which had earlier appeared in Ledyard, lamenting the death of a friend's infant son. Mary Robbins Post, too, fell ill that spring.

Concerned by the constant news of ailing relatives, Isaac visited Jericho and Westbury in late April with his daughter, Mary. Amy, who had suffered problems with her breast since Jacob's birth, did not join them. Distressed by the news from Isaac, Mary Kirby took up the letter begun early that month. She warned her daughter to "try to be carefull not [to] put thyself in d[anger] taking cold. I feel much for thee in being left so long without Isaac." Perhaps hoping Isaac would read the letter he carried home, Mary continued, "Had not he better be encouraged to narrow up his business so as to be more in his home business, and with his family?"[18] But the post coach venture was thriving, necessitating meetings with co-owners in towns from Long Island to Albany, which, along with his farmwork, kept him busy day and night. At least he had relinquished his position as overseer of highways, his one concession to domestic obligations.

Isaac also sought to ease Amy's burdens by leaving eight-year-old Mary with her grandparents in Jericho. Despite some misgivings, the Kirbys promised "to do the best we could with her[. T]he prospect seams pleasant to Sarah," wrote Mary Kirby, but "I feel most too old a Woman to nurture to [the] dear little girl as she ought to be."[19] Nonetheless, they embraced the chance to have Hannah's daughter with them and registered her at the local Friends school.

The following year, illness and other problems continued to plague the Post and Kirby families on Long Island. A seventeen-year-old black youth, working as an indentured servant on the Kirby farm, had absconded in October 1831 and was still missing in January 1832. That winter, Amy's older sister, Mary Willis, fell seriously ill but ultimately recovered. Isaac's older brother, Edmund, only thirty-nine, was not so fortunate. On 30 June, he felt unwell. Three days later, his wife called in two doctors, but Edmund did not improve. His family and close friends were alerted so that they might "endeavor to bring their minds into a state of resignation."[20] The next evening, 4 July, he died in a "quiet peaceful state of mind"; however, he left behind a widow and five children. Isaac received the shocking news a few days later in a letter from cousin Amos Willets, who had been at Edmund's bedside the day of his death. He assured Isaac that Edmund "did not appear to suffer much" and noted that "much simpathy is felt & express'd for thee in thy being separated from thy friends at this time."[21] When Willets's letter arrived, Edmund had already been buried in a plain coffin.

The demands of farmwork and Amy's second pregnancy kept the Posts from returning to Long Island after Edmund's death. At some point that summer, a family member brought Isaac's daughter back to Ledyard, which cheered her stepmother considerably. Perhaps Edmund's unexpected death led Amy and Isaac to want their children at home. Certainly, Mary and her younger brother, Jacob, lightened the mood as Isaac grieved the loss of his brother, and Amy navigated her pregnancy while nursing Anna Greene, who was "an invalid" throughout that summer and fall.[22]

Amy had honed her nursing skills in Jericho but was tested more fully in the rural environs of central New York. Given concerns about "heroic" methods employed by medical professionals, such as bleeding and purging, many families were willing to try less invasive treatments offered by knowledgeable friends and neighbors. It is likely that Amy gained experience in the healing arts from her mother and aunts and recognized that she had a special skill in applying them. She would have been introduced to herbal and other traditional remedies growing up in Jericho, some of which were probably passed on to pioneer Friends by Long Island's native inhabitants. Indian remedies circulated through central New York as well, as did treatments carried by settlers from New England and the Hudson River valley. Amy may also have obtained copies of Nicholas Culpeper's *Complete Herbal*, a seventeenth-century book reprinted many times in North America, or E. Smith's *The Compleat Housewife; or, Accomplish'd Gentlewoman's Companion*, first published in the early eighteenth century. Such books contained recipes for salves and medications and were often handed down from generation to generation.[23]

Amy cultivated her medical skills in her early twenties while nursing Hannah, Mary, and Edmund. She likely shared information with F/friends and neighbors, adding to her knowledge of illnesses and injuries common to children as well as female complaints. Among favored treatments in the Scipio area was an "All Healing Ointment" developed by Peleg White, the father of Amy's good friend Susan White Doty. It was used to treat "Burns, Scalds, Cuts, Bruises, . . . Piles, Erysipelas, Tetter, Salt Rheum, Boils, [and] Carbuncles." Peleg and his wife, Eunice, produced, packaged, and sold the salve from their home in Ledyard. It was sufficiently effective that it was eventually sold in apothecary shops across the Northeast.[24]

Amy also had to look after herself, since she was once again pregnant, giving birth to a son, Joseph, in October 1832. Fortunately, she recovered more quickly this time and was soon back to nursing others. Her patients included traveling Friend Priscilla Cadwalader, who had preached in the Scipio area throughout that summer and fall. Local Quakers were "deeply impressed with Cadwalader's devotion and purity of purpose" and concerned when they learned in December that she suffered from a "severe indisposition." Confined to bed near Farmington, Cadwalader was finally well enough to travel in February 1833, when she moved to the Post home.[25]

For the next seven months, Amy and her sister-in-law Phebe Post Willis served as Cadwalader's "constant attendants."[26] In the early 1830s, Willis had accompanied Lucretia Mott as she ministered to Friends in New York State and Upper Canada and probably met Cadwalader then, if not earlier. Both Amy and Phebe found nursing the Quaker preacher uplifting. As Amy later wrote, while Cadwalader experienced "great suffering, sometimes very acute pain," her "spirit was always beautifully serene and quiet." Reserved with strangers, she proved "cheerful and instructive" in their family circle.[27]

Still, hosting Cadwalader was complicated by the controversy that swirled around both her preaching and her private life. She was born to Matthew Coffin and Hannah Mendenhall in Guilford County, North Carolina, in 1786. Her mother died when Priscilla was young, and her father remarried. A few years later, Priscilla wed Jabez Hunt, the son of a prominent Friend. When he died just a year and half later, Priscilla and her infant daughter migrated with her father and stepmother to Indiana, where new Quaker settlements were increasing rapidly. It was in Indiana in 1815, at the age of twenty-nine, that Priscilla began her ministries.[28]

Priscilla Hunt visited Philadelphia in the early 1820s, where she met Lucretia Mott, a distant cousin of her father. Having embraced Hicks's views concerning the primacy of inner light over biblical authority and the role of ministers and elders, Hunt was not demure in critiquing her adversaries. Philadelphia Hicksite Thomas M'Clintock was convinced that she was "divinely commissioned" to "thresh the mountains of formality with a sharp threshing instrument."[29] During the 1827–28 separation, Priscilla espoused the Hicksite cause and was at the center of the schism in Indiana, though Hicksites were far less numerous there than in Pennsylvania. In July 1827, she married fellow minister Joseph Cadwalader, a widower with six children. A decade later, she became as well known for the dissolution of that marriage as for her preaching. In June 1837, Joseph filed for divorce. Although Priscilla's confidantes claimed that Joseph was unkind at best and "licentious and brutal" at worst, her husband insisted that his wife's years-long absence served as evidence of desertion.[30]

The Cadwaladers had indeed spent little of their married life together. Shortly after they wed, Joseph spent several months traveling to Friends' meetings near and far while his new wife cared for her daughter and six stepchildren. But Priscilla refused to be confined to domestic labors. She organized her own extensive ministerial journey for fall 1829 and remained away from home for nearly eight years. Traveling to meetings in Ohio, North Carolina, Pennsylvania, New England, Canada, and New York State, she

combined a powerful ministry with periods of illness. Despite being received warmly at many meetings, her travels were plagued by rumors of
scandal, some spread by Orthodox adversaries and others by concerned
Hicksites.

Amid claims and counterclaims, the Posts nursed Priscilla on at least two
occasions. While Amy managed Priscilla's physical care, Isaac corresponded
with midwestern F/friends about her spiritual well-being. In company with
Noah Haines, an Ohio Hicksite, Isaac sought to quash questions about her
moral character.[31] Many Hicksites shared the Posts' faith in the Indiana
Friend. Indeed, while Priscilla was being invited to numerous meetings in
the 1830s, her husband's ministry and his standing in the Society of Friends
diminished. After recovering her health, Priscilla continued preaching in
Canada and western New York, returning to Farmington in June 1835 for the
first anniversary of the founding of Genesee Yearly Meeting.

Two years earlier, New York Yearly Meeting acknowledged that the rapid
growth of Friends in central New York, the Midwest, and Upper Canada necessitated the creation of a new assembly. Genesee Yearly Meeting (GYM),
encompassing twenty-five monthly meetings, was formed in 1834, and the
inaugural gathering was held in Farmington that June. Unfortunately, Amy
was forced to remain at home, where she gave birth to her third son, Henry,
on 14 July. Amy's cousin Lydia P. Mott, who served as clerk of the women's
meeting, passed on news, as did many other F/friends and neighbors.[32]

Amy and Isaac were excited to be part of this new venture, but relatives
on Long Island worried that New York Yearly Meeting would no longer
beckon them home. Family crises, however, still drew them back. In January 1834, for example, the Posts and their children returned to Long Island
when Lydia Rushmore, Isaac's sister, fell gravely ill. While family members
remained anxious about Lydia, they were overjoyed to see Amy, Isaac, Mary,
Jacob, and one-year-old Joseph. As relatives gathered around Lydia's bedside and family fireplaces, they likely discussed the continuing migration
of Long Island Friends to central and western New York. By the end of February, with Lydia on the mend, Amy, Isaac, and the children bid farewell
and made the long trek back to Ledyard, where Amy soon realized she was
once again pregnant.[33]

In June 1835, the Posts happily traveled the fifty miles to Farmington to
join some four hundred Friends for the second GYM. Whether they left the
children behind with relatives or neighbors or brought Sarah Kirby with
them to assist with childcare, there was no thought that Amy should miss out
on another GYM. She and Anna Greene were appointed to the committee

responding to epistles from other yearly meetings, and Amy attended numerous meetings for both business and worship. At the weeklong event, she and Isaac met F/friends from other meetings in the region as well as two dozen or so traveling ministers from other yearly meetings. Many ate meals communally, and some may have camped out, since there were not enough local Friends to host participants.[34]

The Farmington Hicksite Meetinghouse provided the spacious venue required for yearly meetings, and it was readily accessible by carriage and canal boat. Accommodations, however, were another matter. Friends who lived relatively close—in Macedon (6 miles), Palmyra (10), Rochester (22), or even Waterloo (27)—might travel back and forth each day, though that could be exhausting since meetings were held morning, afternoon, and evening. Many local Quakers invited friends and relatives for tea, dinner, or a night's rest. Charles Townsend of Philadelphia, who made the trip with his wife and a friend, recorded the complicated arrangements necessary to meet the needs of participants. The Townsends stayed with F/friends Brice and Huldah Aldridge, who had lived in the Farmington area since the early 1800s. The first morning, they awakened to a wet and chilly day, so Brice drove a group of men to the meetinghouse in his wagon and then returned for the women. At least six more visitors stayed with the Aldridges that night, and Charles noted that throughout the meeting, "nearly as many staid as our kind friends could accommodate." On Fifth Day, some forty Quakers enjoyed tea at the home of a neighbor. There, amid "social conversation," Elizabeth Thomas "broke out in sweet expression of desire for the continuance of Love & Unity." Amy and Isaac, too, enjoyed social conversation and spiritual renewal in these informal settings. Still, providing room and board for shifting numbers of adults and children meant crowded quarters and well-coordinated schedules.[35]

Friends from other yearly meetings who attended GYM generally participated only in meetings for worship, not those for business. Traveling Friends were eager to speak at these large gatherings, and the 1835 GYM gladly accepted certificates for Priscilla Cadwalader, Lucretia Mott, and a number of other ministers.[36] Members of GYM packed the gatherings for worship, seeking inspiration in an atmosphere simultaneously festive and solemn. One day, meetings for worship were held at South Farmington, Palmyra, Macedon, and Farmington so that more Friends could participate. Amy felt fortunate to find a seat at the Farmington Meetinghouse, where Mott and Cadwalader spoke. Three decades later, Post recalled Cadwalader's stirring critique of slavery and her prescience about the dangers it posed:

"She predicted our present national conflict, saying, 'I hear the cannon's roar and the beating of drums, and I see the horse and his rider amid the clash of arms and pools of human blood. . . . Slavery will go down sooner or later, and I entreat *you* to wash your hands in innocency.' "[37]

Significant business was also conducted at these annual gatherings. Committees were appointed by both men's and women's meetings to address issues such as slavery, Indian rights, and education. In addition, questions raised at quarterly meetings had to be responded to, new business had to be undertaken, and time had to be set aside for representatives of the women's meeting to seek the concurrence of the men's meeting for their decisions. To ease the crush of business at the first GYM, participants had adopted the Discipline of New York Yearly Meeting as their own, but in 1835, some Friends sought changes. Notably, on Sixth Day, two women Friends informed the men's meeting for business that Lydia Mott and Lucretia Mott wished to raise a concern with them. While some men considered it inappropriate to address any significant issue so late in the proceedings, the men agreed to admit them. Entering the room, the two Motts took seats "on One of the low benches on the floor," even though "friends had left seats in the upper gallery," where the recognized ministers and elders sat. After being pressed to occupy this select seat, Lydia did so but claimed "that since she had had the liberty to occupy those high seats she had been uneasy in occupying them." She then returned to her seat on the floor, declaring that in her estimation "the high seats [were] no more Holy than others & that some people were desirous of promotion & being placed above their brethren &c, &c." Charles Townsend found her remarks "hackney'd" and claimed that "the meeting was not edified" by her "severe attack on Select Meetings."[38] Yet a significant contingent of Friends, including the Posts, shared her concerns about hierarchical authority—of ministers and elders over regular members, of select meetings (restricted to ministers and elders) over ordinary meetings, and of men over women.

In 1836 and 1837, GYM committees discussed these issues and other changes to the Discipline. Members of Scipio Quarterly Meeting—the spiritual home of the Posts—and Farmington Quarterly Meeting initiated these inquiries. In considering those "under dealing" for alleged disciplinary violations, for instance, Farmington Friends proposed "that the discipline be so alter'd that men & women shall stand on the same footing in all matters in which they are equally interested, such as deliberations respecting alterations of discipline; & that in receiving and disowning members, and in granting and receiving certificates of removal, the two branches of a monthly meeting shall each obtain the concurrence of the other before the subject matter be concluded."[39] Amy and Isaac no doubt supported these proposals, having been the object of disciplinary actions at the time of their marriage. Indeed, they advocated eliminating any vestiges of inequality between men's and women's meetings, a position they shared with many of their Scipio F/friends. While no action was taken on these proposals or on the role of ministers and elders, supporters continued to raise them until resolution was achieved. In 1840, GYM finally dropped separate instructions for women's meetings, after which men's and women's meetings abided by the same rules.[40]

Surrounded by family and F/friends, Amy, Isaac, and many other GYM members envisioned the new yearly meeting as an opportunity to dismantle traditional hierarchies. GYM seemed ripe for change as women and men converged on the frontier from diverse Quaker communities and forged bonds of fellowship. While not all yearly meeting participants agreed with critics of the existing Discipline, those who sought change developed increasingly close relationships with like-minded Friends. In Scipio Quarterly Meeting, the Posts worshiped with and worked alongside Susan and Elias Doty, Rhoda and Elias DeGarmo, Benjamin and Sarah Fish, Sarah Thayer, Lydia Mott, and other progressive Hicksites. Their common perspectives on the authority of inner light, the equality of women's and men's meetings, slavery, and Indian rights strengthened ties rooted in their shared experience as migrants and farmers. These friendships did not replace ties to family and F/friends on Long Island but became intertwined with older bonds of affection and obligation.

Of all the issues raised at GYM, that of Indian rights achieved the greatest consensus. The rights of the Haudenosaunee (Iroquois) who lived in central and western New York State had been of concern to Friends in New York and Philadelphia Yearly Meetings for decades. When Haudenosaunee leaders invited those meetings to send witnesses to the signing of the 1794 treaty with the U.S. government at Canandaigua, New York, Quakers in Farmington (then called New Salem) attended. In addition to befriending Red Jacket and other Haudenosaunee leaders in the early 1790s, they met some of the Quaker teachers sent in the following decades to the Cayuga and Seneca living on reservations in the region. In turn, Red Jacket and other leaders regularly visited Quaker settlements, including a visit to Friends in New York City in 1829. Adin T. Corey, an outspoken advocate of Indian rights and a resident of Scipio, offered passionate testimonies on the issue at monthly and quarterly meetings. GYM established a committee on

Indians at its inaugural meeting and, in 1838, sent Isaac Post and other representatives to a Joint Committee on Indian Affairs meeting that included Friends from Philadelphia and New York Yearly Meetings.[41]

Slavery was on the minds of many Friends as well, and in 1835, GYM appointed a committee to deliberate on the subject. Of course, weighty Friends such as Elias Hicks had been outspoken in their critiques of human bondage in the late eighteenth century, and British Quakers were among the leading proponents of ending the slave trade and abolishing slavery in the nation's West Indies colonies. In the 1810s, Benjamin Lundy, a New Jersey–born Friend, began publishing antislavery circulars in the Midwest. In 1821, he launched the *Genius of Universal Emancipation*, which he continued to publish as he moved from city to city. Lundy hired William Lloyd Garrison to assist him in editing the *Genius* in 1829–30 in Baltimore, which inspired the Bostonian to start a similar paper, the *Liberator*, in his hometown in 1831. Garrison then helped establish a national organization, the American Anti-Slavery Society. The founding convention, held in Philadelphia in December 1833, attracted black and white abolitionists, including Lucretia and James Mott and several other local Friends. The society's declaration demanded "immediate emancipation" with no compensation to slaveholders, embraced the nonviolent principles of the Friends, and supported the free produce movement, which was already thriving among Quakers and African Americans in Philadelphia.[42]

The desire of Friends to discuss their role in the movement at the 1835 GYM was reinforced by stirring antislavery appeals from Cadwalader, Mott, and Corey. Although some in attendance considered these abolitionist Friends too zealous, harming the cause by their use of "immoderate language," both men's and women's committees chose to act.[43] They jointly produced a "minute of advice" to subordinate meetings, asking "individuals to be attentive to the scruples in their own minds of partaking of articles which are the products of Slave Labour," and a memorial to Congress, seeking "an act to abolish Slavery in the District of Columbia."[44] Three of Amy's close friends served on that committee, and the Posts, like many GYM participants, were already boycotting slave-produced goods. They no doubt dismissed critics like Townsend, who claimed that central New York Quakers only supported the boycott because they made their own maple sugar and spun their own articles of clothing.[45]

Like Amy and Isaac, many central and western New York Quakers had learned the evils of slavery as children and embraced the need to fight racial prejudice and assist freed as well as enslaved blacks. The Posts had grown up near free black settlements and were introduced to the work of the New York Manumission Society by relatives and neighbors. Once in central New York, Isaac, Hannah, and Amy may have met relatives of Paul Cuffee as several of them had migrated to the region from western Massachusetts. They most certainly had heard the story of Austin Steward, who escaped slavery in New York State around 1814 and lived in Farmington with the Quaker Otis Comstock until 1817 or 1818. Otis had moved to the area in the 1790s with his parents and brother Darius. The two brothers helped found the Ontario Manumission Society in 1812 and assisted Steward in gaining his freedom. While working on the Comstock farm, Steward attended the local Friends school and likely helped build the Farmington Meetinghouse in 1816, where the quarterly meeting of Hicksites and later GYM met. Soon after, Steward moved west to Rochester.[46]

As importantly for the Posts, despite the traumas of the 1828 separation, efforts to assist fugitives crossed the Orthodox–Hicksite divide in central New York. Even on Long Island, Thomas Willis—an Orthodox Friend and the Kirbys' Jericho neighbor—joined the New York Manumission Society in 1829. Willis also hid the young fugitive Henry Highland Garnet on his farm. Garnet had been spirited out of New York City after he sought revenge for his sister's capture by slave catchers. Despite their doctrinal differences, Willis allowed Elias Hicks to visit the fugitive at his farm.[47] In the 1830s, Garnet became a noted abolitionist preacher. Within Farmington Quarterly Meeting, several Orthodox families embraced abolition. The leaders included John and Esther Hathaway, John's sister Phebe Hathaway, Maria Wilbur, and the families of William Smith and Asa B. Smith, who were related to the Comstock brothers. Their efforts were reinforced in the late 1830s when John Gurney, a wealthy Orthodox Friend from England, visited central New York. A learned minister and author, he envisioned reform as part of the religious work of Friends. Slocum Howland of Sherwood, a village near Ledyard, joined this group of Orthodox abolitionists, and his home became an important stop on the Underground Railroad.[48]

Among Hicksites, Pliny Sexton and Griffith M. Cooper, both members of Farmington Quarterly Meeting, led the cause early on, with support from the Dotys, Pounds, Priors, Searings, Fishes, DeGarmos, and Posts.[49] By the early 1840s, when Amy and Isaac played increasingly prominent roles in the movement, Orthodox and Hicksite Friends worked together in the mixed-sex, interdenominational, and interracial Western New York Anti-Slavery Society.[50]

The Posts' commitment to a broad and radical vision of social justice was reinforced by their friendship with James and Lucretia Mott. Following the 1835 GYM, the Motts traveled throughout central New York, visiting wealthy philanthropist and antislavery supporter Gerrit Smith in Peterboro; Lucretia's sister Martha and her husband, David Wright, in Aurora; and their daughter Anna Hopper, who was staying with her aunt and uncle on Lake Cayuga. At some point, the Posts drove the Motts from Aurora to Auburn and then to an antislavery meeting in a nearby town. In September, when the Posts were visiting Isaac's sister Phebe Post Willis in Westbury, Phebe received a letter from Lucretia that described her and James's time with the Posts the previous summer. "We hope you are planning a visit to this City with Isaac and Amy," she concluded. "We shall not soon forget their many kindnesses to us."[51] Over the next two decades, Amy and Lucretia often found themselves at the same meetings and conventions, where they shared a deep commitment to a universal vision of social change and social justice.

As central New York Friends migrated further west in the 1830s, bonds of friendship were constantly refreshed at quarterly and yearly meetings. Just as importantly, Quaker migrants carried challenges to hierarchical structures and concerns about Indian rights and abolition into the meetings they founded or joined in western New York, the Midwest, and Upper Canada. Indeed, Farmington became known as the "mother of meetings," spawning at least twenty other monthly and quarterly meetings and serving as the home of GYM.[52] Although the yearly meeting did not reach consensus on many of these issues, those members—including the Posts—who embraced progressive views forged bonds that eventually broke the constraints of religious meetings. At the same time, "worldly" associations were multiplying as the American Anti-Slavery Society spawned local and regional organizations.

Meanwhile, Hicksite migrants also continued to share religious and abolitionist commitments with family and F/friends back home. Indeed, such commitments strengthened the connection between Isaac and Amy in Ledyard and Long Island relatives such as Joseph and Mary Robbins Post and John and Rebecca Ketcham. The Posts, Ketchams, Kirbys, Willetses, and other like-minded family members read the same stories in the *Genius* and the *Liberator*, copies of which were circulated among relatives and F/friends. They corresponded regularly about their efforts to establish antislavery societies and the difficulties this posed for them as Quakers.

Although Friends had been involved in organizations like the New York Manumission Society alongside non-Quakers since 1785, meetings grew more anxious about such efforts as the antislavery movement grew. The Discipline of New York Yearly Meeting had no specific prohibition on participating in "worldly" or "popular" associations with non-Quakers, but Friends were advised "to avoid political controversies." In addition, the section on "Plainness" implied that Friends should remain separate from the world. In 1838–39, the *Friends' Intelligencer,* a New York City paper edited by Isaac T. Hopper, published a lively debate on popular associations. By that time, many weighty Friends insisted that "Friends should not be mingling with the world's people."[53]

Such prohibitions proved increasingly difficult to accept for Quakers convinced that the only way to rid the nation of the stain of slavery was to work alongside those who supported abolition and assisted free and fugitive blacks. Indeed, those who harbored fugitives in the early decades of the nineteenth century, before the Underground Railroad gained a label and a more systematic set of routes and conductors, found it inconsistent not to participate in secular antislavery meetings and conventions.[54] By the mid-1830s, Quakers in central New York had spun an activist web that reached to New York City and Long Island; Rochester, Lockport, and Buffalo, New York; Adrian and Battle Creek, Michigan; Salem, Ohio; and Upper Canada. At quarterly and yearly meetings, Friends urged like-minded souls to extend the network.

For many Quakers living in the Finger Lakes, Rochester was the next stop on their westward migration. Rhoda Rogers, born in Massachusetts, met Elias DeGarmo, from Dutchess County, New York, at Nine Partners Meeting. Once married, they moved their growing family to Oswego, then to Farmington, and finally to Rochester in 1834. Sarah Bills and Benjamin Fish had preceded them. Their families had migrated to Farmington from New Jersey and Rhode Island, respectively, where Sarah and Benjamin met and married in 1822. Seven years later, they resettled their family on the outskirts of Rochester.[55] When Charles Townsend visited the Fishes after the 1835 GYM, he claimed that Rochester "seems by nature to offer to man [perhaps] the greatest accommodation for mill seats, manufactories etc . . . in the united states by an unfailing supply of water from the Genesee River." Townsend lauded as well the magnificence of the "great falls," the beauty of the lower falls, and the convenience of the railroad cars.[56]

The reports of early Quaker migrants and of visitors sparked the Posts' interest in urban life. A little investigation reassured Isaac, always on the lookout for the next opportunity, of Rochester's potential. The Erie Canal had fueled an economic and demographic boom in the city. Indeed, Rochester was the fastest-growing city in the United States between 1825 and 1835. In 1836, an English-born engraver, Thomas Woodcock, was among thousands of tourists, journalists, laborers, and merchants who traveled from New York City to Buffalo via the Erie Canal. In Rochester, he marveled at the ten stone arches forming an aqueduct to carry the canal over the Genesee River. "Everything here is *new* but the Forests, log houses of all grades from the Whitewashed, neatly fenced in, to the black looking, mud-surrounding hovel." The corduroy roads, made of logs rolled together, were filled with traffic, while in the "thinly wooded country," where forests had been cleared, cattle grazed and the soil "yields enormous crops."[57]

Initially gristmills, grinding wheat from rural hinterlands, served as the engine for Rochester's expansion. But the barrels of flour flowing down the canal soon attracted steamboat and carriage companies, liveries and blacksmiths, taverns and bakeries, dry good stores, and apothecary shops. With workers and entrepreneurs pouring in, residents established schools, churches, fraternal orders, and voluntary societies. Amid this cacophony of activity, the Posts could depend on the presence of F/friends and an active Hicksite meeting to welcome them. And Rochester's three antislavery societies reassured them that the city attracted its share of progressive residents.

Isaac and Amy could continue to meet central New York F/friends at quarterly and yearly meetings, the distance from Rochester to Farmington being half that from Ledyard. Still, the city was nearly eighty miles farther from Jericho and Westbury. Increasing the distance from parents and siblings could not have been easy for the Posts or their relatives back home. Still, their Long Island kin were not necessarily surprised when Amy and Isaac announced their move. In 1835, a year before Isaac relocated to Rochester, Henry Post declared his nephew the most "independent" member of the family, a man willing, as Uncle Henry was not, to venture to new locales and explore new enterprises. That same spring, Isaac had floated the idea of moving farther west to Joseph and Mary Robbins Post. Mary replied that "the distance is trifling in comparison to Michigan which appears now to attract very many."[58] Perhaps the fact that several Scipio, Farmington, and Long Island families had already decamped to Michigan made the thought of Rochester—with its easy access to New York City via the Erie Canal and the Hudson River—less distressing for her and other relatives on Long Island.

Sometime in 1836—probably late summer—Amy and Isaac packed their worldly goods into boxes, sold off many of their farm implements, and moved with their four children and sister Sarah Kirby into a large house at 36 Sophia Street. The gable-roofed front was set back only a few feet from the street, while a mansard-roofed extension ensured room for a large family and lots of company.[59] A block from the local Hicksite meetinghouse, three blocks from the African Methodist Episcopal Zion Church, and four blocks from the junction of the Genesee River and the Erie Canal, the Posts' Sophia Street home was perfectly situated for them to extend their spiritual and political commitments and gain an economic foothold. Relationships forged in Farmington Quarterly Meeting and GYM would be enhanced by a larger community of Quaker activists and by ties with white and black Rochesterians of other faiths committed to a radical vision of social justice.

· ·

The rural town of Ledyard and the booming city of Rochester were separated by only sixty miles of rolling hills and farmland, yet in many ways,
they were worlds apart. While Ledyard remained a small farming village
of a few dozen households, the Flour City—so named for the numerous gristmills that lined the Genesee River—was one of the fastest-growing cities in
the United States.[1] Driving to Rochester over roads pounded firm by a steady
stream of wagons and carriages, the Posts entered a place brimming with
water-powered mills, canal barges, churches, and newly built homes and
shops.

In their early years in Rochester, Amy and Isaac engaged activist worlds
that did not exist in the farming communities of Long Island and central
New York. They had certainly met people of other faiths and been acquainted
with small numbers of African Americans. Not until moving to Rochester,
however, did the Posts fully realize the special character of their Quaker
faith as they labored for social change alongside large numbers of white
evangelical Protestants. Nor had Amy and Isaac worked so closely with
black activists—both freeborn and fugitive—who had established a vibrant
community of churches, schools, businesses, and civic organizations. The
importance to the Posts of these two largely distinct circles of activists—
white evangelical Protestants and African Americans—loomed large as the
antislavery movement rapidly expanded. While the Posts remained active
in Hicksite meetings, their vision of social justice and social change was increasingly shaped by interdenominational and interracial efforts.

As the Posts explored Rochester, they may have imagined some of the
changes to come. They passed by the neat log homes and muddy hovels,
flour mills, and stone aqueduct described by Woodcock, but they also
gazed on fine two-story brick-and-clapboard houses, a few elegant churches,
and the substantial but plain Hicksite Meetinghouse. The two-story
mansard-roofed home they purchased on Sophia Street was large enough
for a still-growing family as well as visiting relatives and friends. It sat near
the Hicksite Meetinghouse and just a few blocks west and north of where
the Genesee River and Erie Canal intersected in downtown Rochester. It

was also only a block north of the main east-west thoroughfare, Buffalo Street, that led to a bridge over the Genesee River connecting the well-developed west side of the city to the east, where farmland was slowly being turned into neighborhoods. Along that route, the Posts passed the impressive Reynolds Arcade, a four-and-a-half-story building containing the post office, stores, offices, and a hotel. Buggies, wagons, and pedestrians filled the streets heading to the river, which were lined with banks, factories, mills, and warehouses. Just across Buffalo Street, on the southern end of Sophia Street, a small but vibrant African American community thrived in a neighborhood of homes, shops, and churches.[2]

Before the Posts moved to the city, Benjamin and Sarah Fish likely showed them the area, pointing out fertile farms on the outskirts of Rochester as well as the dramatic upper falls and the steep bank that led down to the lower falls and a wide bow in the river. The falls and rapids along the Genesee River initially limited settlement in the region, but by the mid-1820s, it became the driving force for flour mills and saw mills that transformed the small village into a boomtown. Perhaps the Fishes drove their friends out to Charlotte (pronounced Sha-lott), a village seven miles north of Rochester's center, where the Genesee emptied into Lake Ontario. Lake steamers arrived daily in the spring, summer, and fall, providing opportunities not only for local residents but also for men and women fleeing bondage.[3]

Rochester had experienced a decade of impressive growth in the decade before the Posts arrived, and there were more transformations to come. The roads and canals that carried Isaac and Amy to the city had conveyed thousands of other people there for years. Even though a significant percentage continued farther west, Rochester's population nearly tripled from around five thousand in 1825 to over fourteen thousand a decade later.[4] The 1834 city directory tracked the expansion by the number of churches, businesses, public officials, and publications as well. It claimed fourteen houses of worship; nine "publick houses" offering rooms, food, and drink; two banks; and one each of a court house, jail, post office, market, museum, and seminary. An athenaeum provided residents access to four hundred books and twenty-eight newspapers and magazines. Fire inspectors, street inspectors, school inspectors, and overseers of the poor worked to maintain order in the bustling city, while ten newspapers—two dailies and weeklies such as the *Genesee Farmer*, the *Rochester Gem*, the *Rochester Observer*, and the *Liberal Advocate*—kept the populace informed of commercial dealings, boat and coach schedules, mercantile goods, municipal regulations, agricultural advances, political developments, and social events. Four years later, the 1838 city directory, the first to note the Posts' arrival, alerted residents to the latest developments. It noted sixteen insurance companies with agents in the city, where none had existed four years earlier; four times as many canal boat lines (expanding from 4 to 21), five new churches, a raft of new businesses, and an addition of nearly 7,000 residents (19,061 total).[5]

While city directories touted Rochester's advances and advantages, the city's boom also inspired changes that were less welcome, at least to white Protestant pioneers. Construction of the Erie Canal brought hundreds of Irish immigrants and other working-class men, many of them Catholic, to the region in the 1820s. Their demands for food, drink, and entertainment fueled the city's economy, but they also brought about the establishment of taverns, gambling dens, and brothels. Once the canal was operational, boats, barges, and their crews stopped regularly in Rochester, where they picked up flour and other commodities and refreshed themselves with whatever pleasures they could find along the docks. Hundreds of rural families poured into the city each year as well, with labor demands in construction, milling, manufacturing, and the trades promising exciting opportunities. While some rose up the economic ladder, others failed to find a toehold, creating a growing class of poor and needy souls.

At the same time, the financial opportunities offered by the flourishing canal trade attracted newcomers with substantial resources as well as aspiring men and women who hoped to secure a middle-class lifestyle. It was these affluent and rising residents who voiced the greatest concern about the potential crises fostered by growth. In 1820–21, even before the canal reached Rochester, middling and elite women who worried about the fate of poor and orphan children in the village opened a charity school. Aroused to greater concern by the condition of those who attended classes, these women recruited others to discuss more systematic ways of addressing the problems of poverty and disease. In 1822, they established the Rochester Female Charitable Society with representatives of all the mainline Protestant churches. Members visited impoverished neighborhoods, loaned needy families bedding and clothing, and offered them medicine and food. A temporary "Pest House," open only during outbreaks of cholera or smallpox, provided the only other medical care for poor people in the city. These charitable women regularly visited canal-side communities overflowing with single male workers, young couples, and barely clad children crowded into residences lacking sewers, wells, or cisterns. Recognizing that more help was needed, members supported the construction of a county almshouse in 1826, yet demand for assistance continued to multiply each year.[6]

In 1830, these benevolent efforts received a boost from the Reverend Charles Grandison Finney, a young evangelical minister who experienced his own conversion in Jefferson County, New York, where he was raised. He was invited to Rochester by affluent flour miller and Third Presbyterian Church leader Josiah Bissell, who promoted the Sabbatarian cause and sought help in combating the "large budget of evils rolling through our land & among us."[7] Bissell believed that keeping Sundays holy by closing down canal traffic along with saloons and other haunts would restrain the lower classes and remind more affluent Rochesterians of their Christian duty. From September 1830 through the following spring, Finney's revivals rocked the city. Hundreds of converts embraced the "new measures" of daily sermons, prayer circles, and protracted meetings as Baptist, Methodist, Episcopal, and other Presbyterian ministers followed Finney's lead.[8]

Although the widespread revivals brought business to a near standstill, they lessened economic and political conflict dramatically and gave "a new impulse . . . to every philanthropic enterprise."[9] The many shopkeepers, businessmen, and professionals who rededicated themselves to their faith advocated reform and supported the efforts of their female kin. Throughout the 1830s, associations to aid orphans and advance temperance, antislavery, and moral reform joined Bible, missionary, and benevolent societies in recruiting members, raising funds, and advancing the city's spiritual and moral climate.[10]

While a dense network of Anglo-American pioneers, upwardly mobile newcomers, and evangelical reformers dominated Rochester society and politics in the 1830s, the city was also home to African Americans, Catholic immigrants, and agrarian Quakers, who provided much-needed labor, skills, and entrepreneurial zeal.[11] None of these groups participated in Finney's revivals. African Americans embraced evangelicalism but established their own houses and styles of worship, and Catholics and most Quakers rejected revivalism. Blacks were among the region's earliest settlers. At least nine arrived as slaves with Colonel Nathaniel Rochester, who moved his family from Maryland to the western New York village that took his name in 1818. Two years later, twenty-seven African Americans lived in the area, and by the mid-1830s, the city welcomed several hundred more.[12]

The rapid increase of African Americans in the city was aided by New York State's final abolition of slavery on 5 July 1827. Black Rochesterians celebrated the event by parading through the streets alongside white supporters. Austin Steward, the fugitive slave who had lived in Farmington before moving to Rochester, gave the Emancipation Day address. He learned to read and write among central New York Friends and, after settling in Rochester, opened a meat market on Main Street that attracted customers of all races. Steward also helped establish a Sabbath school for local colored children in 1827.[13]

During the 1820s, African Americans met in local homes, forming distinct circles under the umbrella of Methodism. The Reverend Thomas James led one group of about twenty families and raised funds to build a sanctuary. James, like Steward, had fled enslavement in New York, escaping from Canajoharie as a teenager in the 1820s. He lived briefly in Canada and later worked along the canal in Lockport, New York, where he learned to read and write in a Sabbath school. In 1831, James preached for the first time in the new one-story wooden church, known initially as the African Methodist Church, on Spring and Favor Streets. In 1834, parishioners opened a school for black children at 34 Sophia Street, next door to the home that the Posts would purchase two years later. The church was incorporated in 1839, with Austin Steward and Zebulon Hebard overseeing the formalities. While men held the formal positions of authority, Caroline Hawkins was among the many women who contributed substantially to the church's growth. Finally, even though the incorporation papers carry the name "the first African Methodist Episcopal Church," the congregation was soon sanctioned by the African Methodist Episcopal Zion (AME Zion) family.[14]

Over the years the Posts, who lived a few blocks from the church, watched the congregation grow. Between 1831 and 1840, Reverend James increased church membership fourfold, from twenty to eighty families. The Jeffrey and Gibbs families, whose activist interests intersected with those of the Posts, were among the most active Methodists. The Jeffrey family settled on the east side of the city in the late 1820s, where Roswell Jeffrey, in his late teens, worked as a waiter at the Eagle Tavern and later owned the Massasoit House hotel. The Jeffreys joined the AME Zion Church, and Roswell agitated against the brutalities of slavery alongside Steward and James.[15] Isaac and Mary Gibbs also enlisted in the cause. Isaac, a grocer, porter, and carman, delivered goods all over the city, which gave him an excellent sense of the local geography and access to numerous sites where fugitives might hide. He and his wife remained committed to the AME Zion Church and the antislavery cause for decades.[16]

Black churches were the first institutions in the city to harbor fugitives, and they also hosted antislavery meetings and lectures. In 1834, a group of black women, possibly led by Caroline Hawkins, founded Rochester's first female abolition society, the Union Anti-Slavery Sewing Society. The year before, white men had established the Rochester Anti-Slavery Society; and a year later, white women organized the Rochester Female Anti-Slavery Society. Most participants in the Union Anti-Slavery Sewing Society were Methodists, like Hawkins and Mary Gibbs, and joined brothers, fathers, husbands, and ministers in support of abolition.[17]

While blacks slowly increased their numbers and visibility, Irish immigrants poured into the city, forming a canal-side community known as Dublin in the 1820s and 1830s. Despite some Rochesterians' concern about the growing influence of Catholicism and popular stereotypes of Irish drinking and poverty, most local residents recognized the value of Irish labor. Moreover, some affluent residents also hailed from the Emerald Isle. These included newspaper editor Henry O'Reilly, who migrated to Rochester from New York City in 1826; several Catholic priests; and members of the Hibernian Society, who urged their compatriots to become naturalized citizens.[18] Smaller communities of immigrants from other parts of the British Isles, Scandinavia, and Germany also emerged in the city, though only the last added significantly to the local population.

In 1836, the Posts joined this amalgam of ethnic, economic, and racial groups. Their Sophia Street home sat amid a mix of long-term and recent residents and a bevy of white Presbyterian, Baptist, and Methodist churches.[19] Friends had formed the city's first Quaker meeting in 1817 and, five years later, built the first meetinghouse on North Fitzhugh and Ann Streets, a block east of Sophia Street. At the time of the 1828 schism, Hicksites retained control of that meetinghouse, and by the mid-1830s, both Hicksite and Orthodox meetings attracted growing numbers of members. Like the Posts, most Rochester Friends migrated to the city in stages, moving from New England, New Jersey, Long Island, and Pennsylvania to eastern or central New York, then to outlying towns or into the city proper. As a result, most Hicksites sustained ties of kinship and faith with Quakers in Rochester's hinterlands and their more distant hometowns, creating a web of connections that stretched across the Northeast. And as some Friends migrated farther west, these networks extended into Ohio, Michigan, Indiana, and Upper Canada.

Once the Posts settled into their new home, Isaac established himself as a butcher, a skill he may have honed on family farms in Westbury and Ledyard.[20] Amy set up housekeeping with the help of thirteen-year-old Mary, whose main task was probably to look after her younger half-brothers: Jacob (age 6), Joseph (3), and Henry (1). The family gathered for First and Fifth Day services with thirty or forty families at the Hicksite Meetinghouse and served on committees for preparative and monthly meetings. For quarterly meetings, they traveled to Farmington, where they refreshed ties with F/friends in central and western New York. In addition to Quaker publications, Isaac and Amy likely read *Friend of Man*, a Rochester weekly that advocated abolition and labor reform; local dailies; and the *Liberator* and other reform journals. They also attended lectures, regularly presented on a variety of topics, and may have first met their African American neighbors when abolitionist speakers appeared.

Although the black community was small compared to the city's population, it was far larger than that in Jericho, Westbury, Scipio, or Ledyard. In those communities, the Posts had been aware of efforts to assist fugitives, though it is not clear whether they participated in them. In Rochester, far larger numbers sought safe haven. While it is not clear how many passed through Rochester in the 1830s, by the 1850s, local abolitionists claimed to aid 150 annually. Within a few years of settling in the city, the Posts joined black activists and other white allies in hiding fugitives and providing resources for their journey to freedom.[21]

Close proximity to African American activists was one of several novel experiences Amy and Isaac encountered in Rochester. Fortunately, both found the economic, cultural, and political ferment stimulating. Indeed, such ferment inspired them to think anew about their spiritual and social commitments even as news from Long Island intensified their anxiety about living so far from family and F/friends.

In April 1837, Amy opened a letter from her mother announcing the death of her grandmother a month earlier. Perhaps to ease the shock, Mary Kirby noted that a friend had told her that her mother "was the handsomest Corps[e] she ever saw, and I think she was for her age." She had delayed writing because her sister Hannah Seaman, Amy's aunt, fell ill shortly after the funeral. Hannah died just ten days later and was laid in the grave next to her mother.[22] It must have been startling to realize that for several weeks, as daily chores and new acquaintances occupied Amy's attention, family members back home had been mourning her grandmother and aunt.

Long Island relatives also wrote begging the Posts for reports on Hicksite meetings, antislavery activities, and other developments. Mary Robbins Post complained to her sister-in-law Amy that she expected more letters, since her "retirement from farm life must give [her] more leisure time."[23] Isaac's sister Phebe Post Willis sent a similar plea to her "Dear Brother and Sister" in April 1837: "How is it that you tell us nothing about Abolition movements in Rochester. I should scarcely suppose you were members of that

Society by your silence on that subject."[24] She, too, assumed that Amy in particular had time to spare, especially since seven-year-old Jacob was now staying with his maternal grandparents in Jericho and attending the local Friends school there.

It may have been his aunt Sarah who delivered Jacob to Jericho when she returned to her parents' home that spring for an extended visit. It was not unusual for Quaker parents to send their children away to Friends schools and to depend on extended family or close friends to serve in loco parentis. Indeed, the Posts would send each of their children to school in Jericho or central New York at some point, hoping they would forge closer bonds with family and F/friends in the process. Periodic family visits also enriched the epistolary conversations among adult siblings, cousins, and in-laws.

Mother Mary Kirby; siblings Sarah Kirby, Phebe Post Willis, and Joseph Post, along with his wife (and Kirby cousin) Mary Robbins Post; and cousins John and Rebecca Ketcham regularly exchanged news and views with Amy and Isaac. In March 1838, for instance, Phebe Post Willis reported on the success of Jericho Women's Monthly Meeting in gaining greater independence. They had "dispensed with asking the men to pleas[e] let them pass an offence or a transgression," and "the men re[a]dily acceded"; though, she admitted, "some if not many of the women are quite alarmed by the suppos'd in[n]ovation." John Ketcham, meanwhile, described the "spirit-stirring time" among abolitionists on Long Island and detailed the rousing Free Produce Convention in Philadelphia as well as the "labours of love and discord" between Hicksite Lucretia Mott, who participated in the event, and George F. White, who denounced such worldly labors as unQuakerly.[25]

Widespread bank failures in spring 1837 led to falling prices, tight credit, and the loss of homes and businesses for many Americans and left far-flung families anxious to hear news. Initially, Rochester weathered the recession better than most cities did, as local banks remained solvent and rising flour prices gave hope to farmers, millers, and shippers.[26] Still, in early July 1837, Mary and Sarah Kirby wrote Amy a joint letter, concerned that they had not heard from her in weeks. Nineteen-year-old Sarah wondered whether "hard times have at last affected you," while Mary worried that she had mistaken her daughter's plans to visit. Noting that Amy's son Jacob was eager to see her and that her sister-in-law Mary W. Kirby was ill, her mother demanded a reply.[27] Within a week, a letter reached them with the tragic news that the Posts' youngest son, Henry, had died on July 2 after a brief illness. A cousin who had visited Rochester earlier that year voiced the sentiments of many Long Island relatives: "The news gave me quite a shock, not knowing but that he had been a healthy child . . . [and] a lively interesting little creature."[28]

In mid-October, Isaac's nephew Edmund Willis traveled from Rochester to Westbury and immediately wrote Amy to tell her that people were asking him "over and over" why she "did not come down here with me." She and Isaac finally arrived a week or two later. However, their visit was brief, and they took Jacob home with them, leaving Amy's mother sad and agitated.[29] A few months later, Mary Kirby had even more reason to feel bereft. In February 1838, Sarah Kirby, who had been back in Jericho less than a year, announced her decision to marry Jeffries Hallowell and move to central New York. Jeffries, eight years Sarah's senior, had settled near Ledyard in the 1820s and likely met Sarah when she visited Amy and Isaac there. He worked as a pharmaceutical agent in the region, and Amy and Isaac hoped he might find work in Rochester. So did Mary Kirby, who noted that "the Sisters being settled near together" would somewhat "blunt the keenness of our sepperation [sic]." Still, as the time grew near for Sarah's departure, her mother could not reconcile herself. "It almost makes me tremble to think of parting with my last . . . darling daughter," she wrote Amy. "But yet if it is their choice, why should I cling to her so closely, knowing [my] time is almost run."[30] And she did have two married daughters—Mary Willis and Elizabeth Mott—and their families nearby, as well as her sons Edmund and Willets and their families.

Yet Mary Kirby felt keenly her distance from Sarah and Amy and her grandchildren, regularly including notes to and about them in her letters. "Jacob I think of thee often," she wrote in a February 1838 letter to Amy, and worried "how hard" it must be for fifteen-year-old Mary Post, who was then attending a Quaker boarding school, "to be separated from you."[31] Isaac was sensitive to his mother-in-law's disappointment, inviting her and Jacob to come live with them on Sophia Street or offering to find them a home of their own nearby. Indeed, the Posts had been renovating their home over the previous year to make it "much more convenient."[32] Mary thanked Isaac for "thy kindness" and said she had hoped to spend that summer in Rochester, "but my Jacob felt like being settled at home."[33]

Knowing his sister Phebe Post Willis was also eager to be in closer touch, Isaac sent her a detailed report on a grand antislavery convention that he, Amy, and their nephew Edmund Willis had attended on 10 to 12 January 1838. The lively lectures and debates attracted seven hundred to nine hundred men and women each day.[34] In response, Phebe wrote her nineteen-year-old nephew, "We think Rochester is indeed a privileged place [and] has many advantages that we country folk are deprived of; the Anti-Slavery meeting must have been peculiar and interesting." She was happy to hear that Thomas and Mary Ann M'Clintock were in attendance. Close friends of James and Lucretia Mott while living in Philadelphia, the M'Clintocks had moved to Waterloo, New York, in 1836. Once there, they quickly made friends—including the Posts—through Farmington Quarterly and Genesee Yearly Meetings. Quakers, however, formed only a minority of the hundreds of 1838 convention participants, and Phebe feared the influence of evangelical ministers. In her letter to Edmund, Phebe confided that she hoped such gatherings "would have a tend[e]ncy to overthrow Priestly influence."[35] While Friends like George White denounced ministers, including Mott, who participated in worldly associations, Phebe Post Willis expressed an explicitly anticlerical stance. She believed that ministers generally, Quaker as well as evangelical, wielded too much authority in religious and reform societies.

Amid family upheavals, antislavery conventions, and the ongoing economic panic, Isaac launched a new business venture, which might seem odd if not for his many earlier efforts to improve his family's economic position.[36] In November 1838, Jeffries Hallowell scolded his new brother-in-law for not letting him know he was going into the "oil business."[37] The oils Isaac was interested in were medicinal, as he planned to open an apothecary shop. Most apothecaries handled a range of items, including oils, paints, and dyes; sold popular medicines, such as Peleg White's All Healing Ointment; and produced medical compounds prescribed by doctors.

With neither a formal educational regimen nor an apprenticeship system in place for apothecaries in the early 1800s, most individuals who opened shops learned the trade from more practiced relatives or friends. In Isaac's case, the Whites may have been an important influence, but he must have also read the latest literature on herbs, packaged medicines, and prescriptions. Shop owners generally prepared and compounded medicines in storefronts, where the light was best, and stored a variety of items—salves, paints, instruments, and sundries—on shelves along the walls. Isaac Post, like many apothecaries, may have purchased a copy of *The Pharmacopoeia of the United States of America*, published in 1820 by two physician-chemists, which provided a list of 217 primary drugs and recipes for compounding many more.[38] Still, having only informal training, Isaac opened his apothecary shop in early 1839, with his neighbor and Friend Elihu Coleman and his nephew Edmund Willis as partners.[39]

As he launched his new enterprise, Isaac certainly called on his wife's medical knowledge and skills. Although a F/friend from Geneseo, New York, made fun of Amy's innovative efforts to care for Edmund Willis's "rheumatism" with "steam treatments," the patient reported that "Aunt Amy's doctoring" helped significantly.[40] Amy regularly excused interruptions in her letters by noting demands to nurse neighbors, relatives, elderly Friends, young mothers, or newborn babes, and correspondents often sent her news of ailments and therapies.[41] Her wealth of knowledge was a boon to Isaac.

The economic hard times also proved beneficial for those with resources to invest. As interest rates, land prices, and other costs fell, Post, Coleman, and Willis opened their apothecary shop in a double storefront in a new commercial building constructed by Silas O. Smith. The pioneer shopkeeper and flour miller expanded his holdings during the Panic of 1837, building the Smith Arcade at the corner of Buffalo and Exchange Streets, just blocks from the Post home. Shops on the ground floor provided goods for both local residents and visitors to the Irving Hotel above. Isaac walked to work past the county clerk's office and the post office or via the well-apportioned court house, a stone building with Greek revival facades.[42] The entire block was lit by whale oil lamps and was home to a jewelry store, a coal company, and a bank, as well as Post's apothecary shop and the street railway waiting room. Anyone passing by would have thought the city was thriving.

Isaac and his partners prepared "physicians' prescriptions and family remedies" and sold salves, balms, patent medicines, oils, paints, and a variety of other items.[43] The business flourished, providing sufficient funds for Amy and Isaac to maintain their house, visit Farmington and Long Island F/friends and family, become more involved in local reform activities, and loan money to relatives in need. Indeed, despite the unsettled economic times, the enterprise lifted the Post family out of the class of small farmers and skilled laborers and into the strata of shopkeepers. Thus, while some of Rochester's pioneer merchants suffered huge losses, others—like Silas Smith—bought up lots at bargain prices, and a few—like Post—launched new careers.[44]

In May 1840, amid changes in Isaac's and the city's fortunes, Amy gave birth to a daughter, Mathilda. Seventeen years younger than her half-sister, Mary, and eight years younger than her closest sibling, Joseph, Mathilda garnered copious attention and affection. At age thirty-eight, Amy may have thought that this would be her last child and that, freed from the labors of a farmwife, she could devote considerably more time to Mathilda's care.

Moreover, she and Isaac had recently hired Mary Dale, a seventeen-year-old English immigrant, to assist with housework and childcare. With the help of Dale and her older children, Amy soon returned to preparative and monthly meetings and kept up with her many correspondents as well as the latest news from the *Liberator*, the *Friend of Man*, and the newly launched *National Anti-Slavery Standard*.

Between their move to Rochester in 1836 and the birth of Mathilda, Amy and Isaac had become immersed in local religious and reform activities, cementing their marital partnership through their joint public labors.[45] While they joined Friends who were satisfied testifying against social evils within Quaker meetings, they also embraced worldly reform efforts that attracted Rochesterians from many faiths. Amy had taken the first small step in this direction by donating to the newly established Rochester Orphan Asylum in 1837. The group that opened the asylum recruited members from the Female Charitable Society and Finney's revivals along with two Orthodox Quakers and one Hicksite—Amy's F/friend Sarah Fish. Mrs. Susan D. Porter, an evangelical Presbyterian and a leader in the Rochester Female Anti-Slavery Society, was also a key figure in the Orphan Asylum Association. Although the Female Anti-Slavery Society was all-white, she persuaded the asylum's board to serve "colored" as well as white orphans.[46] Sarah Fish's work with Porter in the Female Anti-Slavery Society along with the asylum's biracial policy likely persuaded Post to donate.

Still, Amy and Isaac devoted most of their energy to the Hicksites in the late 1830s. Since Rochester preparative and monthly meetings were part of Farmington Quarterly and Genesee Yearly Meetings (GYM), the Posts knew many local Friends and felt at home in their meetings. In fact, just as the Posts prepared to move to Rochester in summer 1836, Amy served on a GYM committee studying manual-labor schools alongside Rhoda DeGarmo, who had already settled near Rochester with her husband, Elias. The next year, the two families traveled to Farmington, where Amy and Rhoda served with Mary Ann M'Clintock of Waterloo on the Committee on Epistles, writing minutes to other meetings on the issues of the day.[47] Isaac, too, served on a variety of committees, including those related to Indian affairs, alongside neighbors from both central New York and Rochester.

At the same time, the Posts and their closest F/friends were committed to altering the Hicksite Discipline. Circles of more progressive Quakers in Rochester, Scipio, Junius (the name of the meeting in Waterloo), and Farmington sought to limit the authority of ministers and elders and to change the Discipline so that "men & women shall stand on equal footing in all matters in which they are equally interested."[48] Despite relative equality compared to other religious denominations, most women's meetings still required the approval of the men's meeting to receive or disown female members and to approve marriages.[49] While progressive Friends called for change, GYM found "the way not open" in 1836 and 1837. Mary Kirby and Phebe Post Willis noted that New York Yearly Meeting was similarly unwilling to alter its Discipline, although in 1838, Jericho's Hicksite Monthly Meeting accepted the right of women to make decisions on their own.[50]

Rochester's Hicksites had embraced this progressive approach two years earlier. By 1836, men and women sometimes conducted business jointly, women disowned female Friends without needing the concurrence of men, and marriage proposals were approved by both the men's and women's meetings on the date of receipt—"a radical departure from all previous Quaker custom."[51] These changes certainly pleased the Posts. They were happier still when in 1838 GYM finally adopted similar rules, which were published in its 1842 printed Discipline. In the section explaining the functions of men's and women's meetings, the revised Discipline stated, "Agreeably to the conclusion of our Yearly meeting, men's and women's meetings stand on the equal footing of common interest and common right."[52]

Yet reaching consensus on this issue only raised expectations for further action, especially related to the authority of ministers and elders. The debate was fueled in part by the continuing controversy over Priscilla Cadwalader's marriage and ministry. Throughout 1837, news about the Cadwalader divorce proceedings, Joseph's behavior, Priscilla's health, and Orthodox and Hicksite attacks on Priscilla circulated among F/friends throughout New York State. The problem continued even after a divorce was granted in October 1837. Nearly two years later, Phebe Post Willis voiced her frustration over the continuing campaign to undermine Cadwalader's ministry. A Hicksite leader claimed that Priscilla's husband had not abused her and that she took "stimulants" to sustain herself.[53] These attacks reinforced the desire of her supporters to limit the power of ministers and elders, and GYM's willingness to grant men's and women's meetings equal standing gave them some hope of success.[54]

The Posts and their allies also challenged existing constraints on working with "popular associations."[55] They increasingly questioned whether testifying in Friends meetings and working alongside other Quakers was sufficient. Supporting the rights of Indians had long been accepted as part of the Friends mission, and in these efforts, Quakers generally worked separately from more evangelically oriented missions organized by Baptists,

Methodists, and Congregationalists. When the Joint Committee on Indian Affairs met with Seneca leaders at the Farmington Friends Meetinghouse in June 1838, they did not invite other Protestant groups to join them. Instead, Senecas worked with Hicksites to develop strategies for securing native ownership of those lands in western New York that the Ogden Land Company had acquired fraudulently under the Treaty of Buffalo Creek. Isaac Post, probably present at the meeting, was soon appointed to the committee. However, similar efforts on behalf of slaves were not confined to Friends and thus raised deeper concerns within Quaker meetings.

The Society of Friends had been well ahead of most denominations in denouncing slavery, and GYM continued the tradition with its 1835 minute of advice to subordinate meetings and a memorial to Congress. In June 1838, the GYM of Women also drafted a memorial to Congress, declaring that they were "under a deep feeling, over the wrongs practiced upon our coloured brethren and sisters in wresting from them the greatest of all external blessings, that of Liberty."[56]

Over the following decade, a significant cohort of GYM members pursued abolition, Indian rights, and women's rights, but many questioned whether epistles and memorials were adequate to address the various evils, especially the plague of slavery. Traveling Friends crisscrossed New York, Pennsylvania, and the Midwest in the 1830s, fueling lively discussions on the issue. Rachel Hicks and George White believed that Quakers should "keep in the quiet" and rely on God to make things right. Priscilla Cadwalader, Lucretia Mott, and Oliver Johnson claimed instead that their inner light led them to work for emancipation by whatever moral means existed. These debates continued in local meetings which the Posts and their many correspondents attended.[57]

While the issue was especially compelling for Friends living in urban settings, even those in farming communities engaged the issue. In spring 1837, while visiting Long Island, a surprised Amy reported to her family in Rochester that father Jacob Kirby had signed a popular petition "to the effect of buying the slaves freedom." When Amy noted that this was "contrary to Dissapline [sic]," he responded, "[I] think it is better to do so than that they should always be kept slaves." He also sought to rally like-minded Jericho Friends in hopes of disrupting "the lukewarm state that has so long pervaded this branch of the sect."[58] A few months later, Amy was asked to sign a petition from Rochester women opposing, among other issues, "the annexation of TEXAS to this Union." The eight hundred female petitioners, most of whom belonged to evangelical churches, argued that annexing Texas might provoke war with Mexico and that the incorpora-tion of a huge state that "expressly sanctions slavery" would "give predom-inant power, in our national councils, to the slave-holding interest."[59]

Petitions had emerged as a crucial means of female political expression in the early 1800s. Usually directed at local or state authorities, early peti-tioners employed deferential language and acknowledged their own subor-dinate status. The first female petitioners to address national policy opposed federal efforts to remove Cherokee Indians from their homelands in the Southeast. This effort, led by white Protestant women in 1829–30, served as a model for antislavery women, who sent eighty-four separate petitions to the U.S. Congress in 1834 alone.[60] The 1837 petition, which was larger and even more expressly political, responded in part to the decision of the U.S. House of Representatives the previous May to table all petitions related to slavery or its abolition.

Immediately after passage of this gag rule, the American Anti-Slavery Society (AASS) called for a campaign to flood Congress with petitions. That summer, Maria Sturges of Ohio initiated a campaign among women in her state to petition Congress for the abolition of slavery in the District of Columbia. The response was enormous, and Ohio women sent copies of their petition to allies in Boston, who circulated them more widely.[61] In May 1837, female abolitionists gathered in New York City at the first Anti-Slavery Convention of American Women built on the Ohio model by devel-oping a plan to circulate petitions by state, county, city, and district. Amy Post and other Quakers were well aware of these developments, since the meeting was both announced by and reported on in the *Liberator*. The elec-tion of Mott and four other Friends as officers of the convention along with African American activist Grace Douglass heightened their interest.[62] The petition devised at the convention included resolutions to rescind the gag rule, abolish slavery in the nation's capital, eliminate the slave trade, and oppose the annexation of Florida and Texas. Mrs. Susan Porter coordinated the Rochester campaign.[63]

It is not clear how many Rochester Friends were asked to join the effort, but Amy Post was ahead of most in her willingness to sign on. She may, again, have been persuaded by Sarah Fish, who had helped organize a petition campaign in spring 1835 "for the immediate Abolition of slavery in the District of Columbia." That campaign aroused opposition among local charitable women like Mrs. Jonathan Childs, the mayor's wife, who consid-ered abolition "more properly the business of those [men] who by the con-stitution of our government are entrusted with the management and direction of its political affairs."[64] Yet in Rochester, few male leaders were interested in addressing the issue. In September 1835, following an antislavery lecture by Theodore Weld, 250 prominent Rochesterians denounced abolitionists and insisted that the issue be left to each state.[65]

Despite such criticisms, the Rochester Female Anti-Slavery Society continued its work with the assistance of Hicksite Sarah Fish and Orthodox Friends (and sisters) Sarah Cornell and Abigail Moore. Their husbands— Benjamin Fish, Silas Cornell, and Lindley Murray Moore—joined them in worldly antislavery activities. A February 1836 petition signed by hundreds of Monroe County men included only a couple dozen Friends, among them Fish and Moore. Even in 1837, when Post signed the women's petition and the Rochester Female Anti-Slavery Society had ballooned to some four hundred members, only a handful of Quakers participated.[66] Among the eight hundred names on that petition, those of Sarah Fish, Amy Post, her stepdaughter Mary, and about three dozen other Hicksite and Orthodox Friends were nearly lost among the hundreds of Presbyterians, Baptists, Methodists, and Unitarians.[67]

Quaker testimonies against slavery and the Society's opposition to participation in popular associations likely account for the small number of Friends involved in interdenominational antislavery campaigns. Yet some prominent Quaker women were already playing outsized roles in the movement, most notably Lucretia Mott. In 1833, she and Mary Ann M'Clintock helped found the Philadelphia Female Anti-Slavery Society, which included black and white members with diverse religious affiliations. Mott was a leader as well in promoting the "free produce" movement, urging blacks and whites, Quaker and non-Quaker, to reject the use of slave-produced goods.[68] Angelina and Sarah Grimké gained even greater notoriety. The sisters had been born and raised on a South Carolina plantation, so when they moved to Philadelphia, rejected slavery, and joined the Orthodox Friends, they became instant celebrities among abolitionists. Their 1837 speaking tour, organized by the AASS, attracted large audiences of men as well as women and sharp denunciations by Congregational and other Protestant clergy.[69] While the work of Mott, M'Clintock and the Grimkés offered models for female Friends, criticisms of their efforts within and beyond Quaker meetings aroused concern among most.

The Posts were well aware of the Philadelphia women's activities and the protests they aroused. They had spent time with the Motts shortly after their marriage and again during the couple's visit to central New York in 1835, and both the Post and Kirby families were proud of their kinship ties to

James Mott. Mary Robbins Post and Phebe Post Willis maintained especially close friendships with Lucretia. In fact, Mary visited the Motts in Philadelphia in April 1837, just one month before the Anti-Slavery Convention of American Women. She wrote Isaac and Amy about the challenges the Grimké sisters raised for local Orthodox Friends by flouting their Discipline. Although Phebe Post Willis believed that the Orthodox "would hurt their cause very much if they did disown them," the meeting repudiated the sisters within the year. Once the M'Clintocks moved to Waterloo, the Posts saw them regularly at quarterly and yearly meetings of GYM, where they no doubt shared news of the Motts and Grimkés.[70]

Philadelphia Hicksites proved more lenient. Mott's Cherry Street Meeting continued to approve her traveling ministry despite her significant involvement in "popular" associations.[71] Still, it took effort on both sides to sustain her membership, and most Hicksite meetings refused to reconsider their stance on worldly activism even when anti-abolitionist violence escalated. Mary Robbins Post noted with distress that even after a series of anti-abolitionist mobs attacked antislavery meetings and presses, culminating in the death of Elijah Lovejoy in 1837, "indifference prevails in very many [Hicksites] to that degree that they can coolly say this is no time for us to do or act on this agitating subject."[72]

Like her cousin and sister-in-law Mary Robbins Post, Amy was far from indifferent. She signed the 1837 petition and may have persuaded Isaac to become more involved in worldly antislavery efforts as well. In January 1838, he served as a local delegate to the first convention of the New York State Anti-Slavery Society to be held in the western part of the state. Despite treacherous roads that had not yet fully frozen, hundreds of delegates from sixteen central and western counties convened in Rochester. The three-day meeting was hosted by the Bethel Free Church, a reform-minded Presbyterian congregation to which Samuel and Susan Porter belonged.[73] The vast majority of the delegates and attendees were white evangelical Protestant men, including a number of reform-minded ministers. However, Orthodox and Hicksite Friends participated, including a large contingent from central New York. Eight men and eight women constituted the Farmington and Waterloo delegations, the former entirely Orthodox and the latter Hicksite. Orthodox Friends Joseph Hathaway and his sister Phebe Hathaway represented Farmington along with Maria Wilbur and her Hicksite husband, Esek Wilbur. Hicksites Richard and Sarah Hunt and Thomas and Mary Ann M'Clintock served as delegates from Waterloo. However, the convention refused to recognize the female delegates.

Nonetheless, their participation demonstrates not only the central role of women in the Society but also the willingness of Orthodox and Hicksite, men and women, to work together for emancipation. In spring 1837, Orthodox women and men in Farmington had formed two separate antislavery societies, with the Hathaway siblings serving as president of their respective organizations. The two groups then worked to foster ties with other antislavery Friends as well as non-Quakers across central and western New York.[74]

The Rochester delegation to the January 1838 convention did not include any women, but a few Orthodox and Hicksite men joined—Lindley Moore, Benjamin Fish, and Isaac Post—as well as African American activist Austin Steward. They were far outnumbered, though, by Protestant evangelicals, including ministers from Bethel, Third, and Brick Presbyterian churches.[75] However, local women attended many convention sessions, particularly in the evening after domestic chores were done. Amy Post's participation was eased by her stepdaughter being away at boarding school and the presence of Mary Dale, who kept watch on the younger children. It was in the evening that delegates debated the only resolution related to women's efforts: "that female abolitionists ought to promote the abolition cause by their prayers, by signing and securing signatories to petitions . . . ; by early instilling into the minds of children the principles of anti-slavery; by the employment of their pens and voices, publicly and privately; by their own donations and the securing of donations by others." Although some ministers opposed the inclusion of the phrase "publicly and privately," the resolution passed as presented. A delegate from Seneca County, which included Waterloo, introduced the resolution after noting that "many ladies" traveled long distances to attend the convention, "who, but for the corrupt state of public sentiment, would have presented to us their certificates as delegates." Perhaps, he argued, male delegates were afraid that women would do more for the slave or show better judgment and warmer eloquence. "Let us give them their rights, sir."[76] The Posts and their F/friends certainly agreed.

In December 1838, Isaac signed his first antislavery petition, an all-male and largely non-Quaker effort to persuade Congress to abolish the gag rule. Still, he and Amy drew more sustenance from gathering with radical F/friends at their home or that of the Fishes for "numerous little abolition meetings." There was clearly work to be done, but also pleasure in sharing antislavery labors that were frowned on by more conservative Quakers.[77] Joseph and Mary Robbins Post were envious. They had been unable to organize a Friends antislavery society on Long Island, "where our dear relative E[lias] Hicks laboured so long." Joseph at least was not yet prepared to work with non-Quakers, being particularly opposed to the idea of paying lecturers. Like most Friends, he rejected the practice of most churches in providing ministers with salaries and considered paid antislavery lecturers as equivalent to a "hireling ministry."[78] Still, in May 1839, Joseph and Mary joined Isaac at the Chatham Street Chapel in New York City for the annual AASS Convention, where they mingled with a diverse array of evangelicals, Unitarians, and Quakers.[79]

Soon after, traveling Friends ignited passionate discussions over Hicksite participation in worldly associations throughout Genesee and New York Yearly Meetings. Speaking to monthly and quarterly meetings on Long Island in fall 1840, Rachel Hicks and George White decried such participation. Mary Robbins Post criticized their views, while John Willis, Amy's brother-in-law, "wish[ed] some of your warm Abolitionists and Teetotalers could have heard him [George White]. I think he would have removed some of the scales from [your] eyes."[80] Tensions increased as more moderate Hicksites began denying the use of their meetinghouses to antislavery lecturers and then to gatherings of their own members to discuss abolition. In March 1841, John Ketcham detailed the challenges of "get[ting] up a friends Antislavery association" in Jericho and finding a place to meet. Resistance to his efforts forced Ketcham to agree with the Posts: "Why should we exclude all who do not happen to be included within the pale of our religious faith. . . . I am therefore not far from thy sentiment, that our light (if we have any) would be more likely to shine where it would do good by uniting with all without distinction of Sect or creed."[81]

Amy and Isaac had far more opportunities to engage in worldly activism than did their family and F/friends on Long Island.[82] Consequently, they also had more chances to alienate Hicksites who opposed such efforts. Still, they were far from alone among antislavery activists in facing religious persecution. The famed orator and reformer Theodore Weld, who had lectured on temperance before a packed house at Rochester's Third Presbyterian Church in 1831, was received less enthusiastically five years later. Returning to Rochester, Weld, now married to Angelina Grimké, ignited "a small riot in the old Third Church" by trying to preach on abolition.[83] Over the next several years, while some local evangelicals continued to support abolition and attend lectures and conventions, a number spoke out against the use of their churches for antislavery meetings. A growing number of ministers also insisted that abolitionist work was inappropriate for female parishioners and sought to redirect women's zeal to more "respectable" paths.[84] In response, some evangelicals established new congregations. Thus, antislavery members of Third Presbyterian Church, including Samuel and Susan Porter, founded Bethel Free Church in 1836, which, as previously noted, hosted a convention of the New York State Anti-Slavery Society two years later.

At the same time, the main body of Hicksites in Rochester, like those in New York City and Long Island, began pushing back against members who engaged in popular antislavery efforts. The Posts were among those disciplined, as John Ketcham noted in spring 1841: "It appears that you do not meet with much encouragement to circulate the reformatory periodicals of the day; seeing you have been strictly forbidden to do so, in one instance at least," by local Friends.[85] That same year, New York Yearly Meeting investigated Charles Marriott, James Gibbons, and Isaac Hopper, who, as editors of the *Friends' Intelligencer*, had encouraged debate on the subject of participation in popular associations. The three men were disowned "for involvement 'in a publication of a paper calculated to excite discord and disunity among Friends.'" The article in question, which criticized George White for denouncing popular reform societies, was written by Oliver Johnson and published in the *National Anti-Slavery Standard* on 25 March 1841. At the time, Johnson was living with Hopper, who, along with Marriott and Gibbons, was thought by some Friends to have encouraged his critique. The men's disownment and Hopper's refusal to accept it aroused strong feelings among Friends throughout the North.[86] The Posts followed developments closely; and Joseph and Mary Robbins Post, John Ketcham, and Henry Willis—Phebe Post Willis's husband—signed a testimonial on Johnson's behalf.[87] In addition, despite a lengthy history of Long Island Quakers assisting fugitives, some Friends now argued that it was wrong to encourage slaves to flee their masters, stating that one could only help them once they had escaped. Mary Robbins Post worried that the escalating controversies might lead to a division much like that of 1828 and feared that Amy and Isaac's enthusiasm for worldly activities put them in danger of disownment.[88]

Nevertheless, the Posts did not retreat. Indeed, antislavery work took up more and more of their time. They were now joined by Jeffries and Sarah Kirby Hallowell, who had moved to Rochester in June 1840. Six months earlier, the pleas of abolitionists from central and western New York to create a regional organization separate from the New York State Anti-Slavery Society had been answered, and area activists called a convention for

January 1841 to create the Western New York Anti-Slavery Society (WNYASS). At the first meeting in LeRoy, members instituted several progressive measures. Most importantly for Amy and her sister activists, women were not only "entitled to all the privileges of membership" but also allowed to serve "*on the committee to nominate officers of the Society.*" Still, a report in the *National Anti-Slavery Standard* indicated that nearly all the positions at that meeting were filled by men.[89]

The Posts and other Rochester F/friends traveled the twenty-seven miles southwest to LeRoy, joining more than four hundred participants, at least a quarter of them women. Representatives from dozens of local societies elected Orthodox Friend Joseph Hathaway to preside over the convention. Many Hicksites attended as well, along with other Orthodox Quakers, evangelicals, Unitarians, and free and fugitive blacks of various faiths. Participants appointed a WNYASS board composed of eleven men from eight counties, including Isaac Post, to coordinate abolitionist efforts throughout the region. Another committee was established to further the "Canada mission" of Hiram Wilson, who assisted fugitives living north of the border.[90]

Men and women debated the best means of advancing the antislavery cause, a question that stirred growing dissension among abolitionists. The greatest disagreement arose over whether abolitionists should engage in partisan politics. Most abolitionists followed Garrison's lead in arguing that moral suasion—the effort to use moral arguments to persuade owners and their supporters to free the enslaved—was their most powerful weapon. However, in 1839, Myron Holley of Rochester had initiated a movement among New York abolitionists to run candidates for office as a way of forcing the major parties to address the issue of slavery. In a series of meetings and conventions held that year and the next, Holley's supporters founded the Liberty League and then the Liberty Party, believing that electoral politics offered more opportunities for advancement than did moral suasion. In Rochester, a significant number of evangelical and Orthodox men, including Samuel Porter and Lindley Moore, embraced political abolition. While most had been early followers of Garrison, they feared that moral suasion alone could never upend slavery. Some also worried that the AASS had become too entangled in extraneous issues, from nonresistance and women's rights to attacks on religion.[91] As political abolitionists gained ground, advocates of moral suasion, most of whom condemned the U.S. government as being proslavery, vigorously defended their views.

The majority of Hicksite and African American abolitionists remained staunch Garrisonians, at least for the moment, decrying both electoral politics and mainstream churches for perpetuating slavery. Female Garrisonians were especially incensed with the supporters of the Liberty Party because an electoral strategy would once again marginalize women. Yet Liberty Party leaders considered women critical to raising funds and ensuring spirited rallies. Still, the rise of political abolitionism in tandem with ministerial condemnation of women's antislavery efforts led many evangelical and some Orthodox Quaker women to retreat from public agitation on behalf of the cause.[92]

These debates arose as well at the AASS in May 1840, when the election of Quaker Abby Kelley to the business committee induced a couple hundred members of that organization to walk out. They formed a new society, the American and Foreign Anti-Slavery Society, which was dominated by white evangelical Protestants, although it attracted some black abolitionists as well. Its members, including many ministers and political abolitionists, denied women the right to speak, vote, or hold office in its organization even as it appealed to churches—in which women played crucial roles—to take an antislavery stance.[93]

In the newly formed WNYASS, the majority of members, including the Posts, rejected political abolitionism, which they claimed promoted "sectarian" and "party" loyalties over individual moral responsibility. Indeed, the WNYASS board was asked to organize a meeting that spring of abolitionists "who consider the organization of the '*third party*' unwise."[94] Still, Liberty Party men did not automatically break with the WNYASS. Many, including Porter and Moore, viewed electoral politics as an addition to, rather than a replacement for, moral suasion. Myron Holley died just two months after the 1841 LeRoy convention, but he inspired many of his Rochester neighbors to join the Liberty Party, ensuring a vibrant debate and a growing split in the movement there.

Samuel Porter, the Moores, and the Posts hoped that the two factions could work together, and area activists attempted to bridge their differences in January 1842 during a three-day WNYASS convention. While members sought to make the convention inclusive, speakers such as William Lloyd Garrison and Abby Kelley were the very activists who had alienated many evangelicals from the AASS. Still, hundreds of local residents attended the event, and Samuel Porter, Lindley Moore, Silas Cornell, and many of their allies participated. It was, however, the Posts, the Fishes, the DeGarmos, and their F/friends whose beliefs and priorities were generally advocated by the stellar cast of speakers. Time was set aside on the third day for an open discussion of antislavery methods, and advocates of third-party politics stated their case forcefully. Nonetheless, Garrisonians overwhelmed Liberty Party supporters in both number and fervor.

The convention intensified the Posts' activist commitment. A week later, Amy penned an exultant letter to her brother-in-law Joseph Post: "I can hardly find words to express our exceeding great enjoyment, we had [the] supreme pleasure of *having W L Garrison our guest*, and a more interesting one we have never had. . . . He was ever ready to converse on all subjects that came up, and such excellent Christian sentiments." In addition, "the excellent and powerful woman A Kelley, and powerful John Collins," spoke on several occasions and "were worthy of our esteem and admiration." Thomas and Mary Ann M'Clintock and their daughter Mary joined Garrison as guests at Sophia Street, and Amy reported that the company was so occupied with the meetings, we "could not get to our *sleeping* places until after twelve." It was not work, she assured Joseph, but the "conversation that kept us up."[95]

There were two discordant notes in Amy's otherwise glowing report. The first involved the conflict over party politics. Amy believed that the Garrisonians had bested their opponents, noting that Anna Mott, the daughter of Lindley and Abigail Moore, "attended all the sittings of the convention except the last which was a discussion between her particular friends the third party folks and they appeared so insignificant that I expect [she] could not be willing to witness any more of it."[96] Despite Post's dismissal, the Liberty Party attracted a growing number of members in the region, most importantly, perhaps, the wealthy abolitionist Gerrit Smith, who lived with his wife, Ann, in Peterboro, New York. He, like Porter and Moore, hoped to establish not just a third party but a third way that combined electoral politics and moral suasion.[97] Despite her interest in bringing diverse activists together, Amy Post had no apparent interest in bridging those worlds.

The second sign of discord—this time with family and Friends—involved Amy's decision to sign an announcement for an upcoming antislavery fair. She noted that it would appear in the February 1842 *National Anti-Slavery Standard*. "I expect some of my friends will grieve at it but I think that I shall do what little I can to raise a little money if it is only for the sake of having some *on hand to assist the poor helpless fugitives across the lake* as it is very often we are called upon for that purpose." Perhaps Amy revealed her participation in the Underground Railroad for fear family members would complain if the funds she raised supported "hireling" lecturers. However, she refused to worry about whether her public participation in the fair might lead to an investigation by local Hicksites. Instead, Amy leapt into the fray, regretting only that Rochester abolitionists were not yet "as spirited and noble" as their counterparts in Boston.[98]

Post's January 1842 letter is the first to acknowledge that she and Isaac worked with the loose aggregation of abolitionists who assisted fugitives in what would soon be known as the Underground Railroad. Certainly they were close to families in Jericho, Westbury, and Ledyard who served as conductors, and the coach line that Post helped found in central New York stopped at many towns along one of the main underground routes. Soon after moving to Rochester, the Posts befriended Austin Steward, whom they likely met in Farmington, and became acquainted with the Jeffreys, the Gibbses, and other blacks who aided their self-emancipated brethren. In addition, several WNYASS members, including the Hathaways and the Porters, joined in this work. Now the Posts announced that they did as well.

The Posts' involvement with the Underground Railroad heightened Amy's interest in fund-raising fairs. Female F/friends in the region began organizing fairs at least as early as January 1838, when women from Farmington, Palmyra, and Macedon joined with their Rochester sisters to hold a fair in conjunction with the New York State Anti-Slavery Society convention. Modeled perhaps on a Boston "Ladies Fair" held a year earlier or on local black women's fund-raising efforts, the western New York women contributed their profits to the *National Anti-Slavery Standard*. While no individual names are listed on the reports of these fairs, members of the Farmington Union Female Anti-Slavery Society, founded in April 1838, were certainly involved. This society was led by Phebe Hathaway; other Orthodox and Hicksite women were among the ardent abolitionists in Palmyra and Macedon. At about this time, white evangelical women retreated from public antislavery efforts in Rochester, and the city's Female Anti-Slavery Society dissolved, leaving Amy Post, Sarah Fish, and their F/friends to take over fair activities.[99]

Isaac clearly supported Amy's efforts as he expanded his own, attending a New York State Anti-Slavery Society convention in July 1838 at Lockport and an AASS convention the following May in New York City. At the latter, Oliver Johnson proposed an amendment substituting the word *person* for *men* in the call of the roll so that women delegates might be included in the discussions and voting. Anticipating the clash over Abby Kelley's election at the 1840 AASS convention, Johnson's amendment sparked a lengthy debate. Post voted yes along with forty-four other New York delegates, including F/friends Thomas M'Clintock, Richard Hunt, and Benjamin Fish; philanthropist Gerrit Smith; and African Americans Charles B. Ray, Henry Garnet, and

David Ruggles.[100] It ultimately passed 178 to 129. Commenting on a similar debate at a New Hampshire antislavery convention in June 1840, the Rochester *Daily Advertiser* noted "that the *women* are determined not to be *abolished* whatever may be the fate of slavery."[101]

Clearly, despite concerns about the reaction of family and F/friends, neither Isaac nor Amy curtailed their worldly activities. In March 1842, Amy not only signed but circulated an antislavery petition from men and women in Monroe County, New York, the signers of which signaled a significant shift in women's public advocacy of the cause. Although the petition focused on the "Children Born of Slave Mothers," not a single one of the evangelical founders of Rochester's white female antislavery society signed. Some of their husbands, including Samuel Porter, did, but the only charter members of the female society who affixed their signatures were Orthodox Friend Sarah Cornell and Hicksite Sarah Fish. Having lost female evangelicals to the admonitions of preachers and the turn toward third-party politics, only sixty-three female names appeared on the 1842 petition. Many of these women were signing a petition for the first time, and more than half of them were Quakers.[102]

For Amy Post, her first five years in Rochester transformed her activism in crucial ways. Within a year, she was contributing to and signing petitions circulated by organizations dominated by non-Quakers. Moreover, despite the fact that she was still bearing and raising children, Amy devoted more time to the abolitionist cause than ever before. She and Isaac became well known among the local antislavery movement and began assisting fugitives headed to Canada. Amy's letters to family and F/friends made clear the passion with which she regarded the antislavery movement as well as her growing concern over the limits prescribed by Hicksites. By 1841, as evangelical women retreated from abolitionist work and evangelical men turned to the Liberty Party, the Posts and many of their F/friends eagerly took the lead in the more radical wing of the western New York movement. This was no easy decision, as they knew it would certainly alter their relationship to the Society of Friends and to F/friends and family on Long Island.

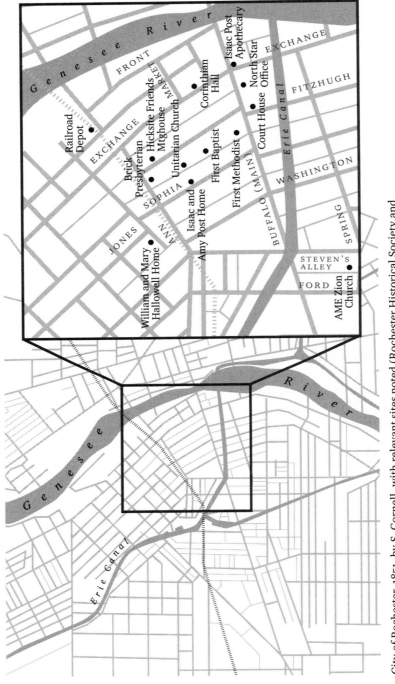

City of Rochester, 1851, by S. Cornell, with relevant sites noted (Rochester Historical Society and University of Rochester Digital Humanities Center).

4 Abolitionist Bonds, 1842–1847

By August 1842, when Abby Kelley returned to Rochester, the Posts and other radical F/friends had become central to the local movement. Kelley was now lecturing in the company of a relative newcomer to the platform, Frederick Douglass, as well as the antislavery physician Erasmus Hudson. The trio, lambasted as a "traveling seraglio," were joined by Hicksites from Junius Monthly Meeting as they made their way through central and western New York. When local abolitionists tried to claim the Third Presbyterian Church for their meeting, the minister objected. He was appalled by a woman speaking from the pulpit and no doubt by her African American companion as well.[1] The small gathering—Hudson claimed listeners nearly outnumbered speakers—was ejected from the building but soon reassembled at the African Bethel Church. Amy and Isaac were in the audience that 26th of August, excited to see Kelley and meet Douglass, whom they had agreed to host.[2] Weary from traveling and a long day of speaking, Douglass gladly headed to 36 Sophia Street. That brief visit initiated deep friendships that would shape the antislavery efforts of all three for years to come. For Amy in particular, it animated her vision of an interracial movement for social justice.

Over the next five years, as the Posts pursued abolition, women's rights, and Indian rights, they focused increasingly on the intertwined character of democratic struggles. Yet their growing involvement in these movements, especially abolition, put them at odds with many Hicksites. By 1845, this conflict led Amy and Isaac to withdraw from Rochester Monthly Meeting even as their progressive labors were inspired by an inner light. Their holistic vision fueled their work alongside African American activists as well as Friends, former Friends, and even some white evangelicals. Isaac took the lead as a member of the WNYASS board and an officer at numerous conventions, while Amy joined with other female activists—F/friends and neighbors as well as traveling lecturers—to expand women's efforts.[3] While she explored the ways that deeply entangled hierarchies of race, gender, and religion shaped interpersonal relations and social institutions, Amy's main contribution was performing the behind-the-scenes work crucial to any movement's success. Thus, she corresponded with a wide range of family, friends, and activists; befriended reformers from diverse backgrounds; hosted traveling lecturers in her home; wrote announcements and reports; circulated petitions; and organized fairs.

The Posts had developed ties to local black activists, including the Reverend Thomas James, which now strengthened their bonds with emerging race leaders. James had moved from Rochester to New Bedford, Massachusetts, in 1840 to become pastor of that city's AME Zion Church. While there, he met Frederick Douglass and his wife, Anna, who had moved to New Bedford in 1838 after their escape from Maryland. Douglass was licensed as a lay preacher, and James encouraged him to talk more openly about his experiences as a slave. He also invited Douglass to tell his story at a predominantly white antislavery meeting in New Bedford.[4] Then in summer 1841, Frederick spoke at a Friends meetinghouse on Nantucket; and that fall, he was invited to work as a paid lecturer by the Massachusetts Anti-Slavery Society. Soon after, Douglass moved his family to Lynn, Massachusetts, and a year later, he was on the road promoting the AASS with Kelley and Hudson. Douglass had befriended many white abolitionists—including Garrison, Kelley, and Wendell Phillips—and James had likely told him about the Posts.[5]

That Douglass was traveling with Kelley no doubt elevated him in Amy's view. For many antislavery women, Kelley was a compelling role model. A birthright Quaker, she had been educated and taught at Friends schools in New England. Converted to abolitionism through reading the *Liberator*, Kelley served as an officer in the Lynn Female Anti-Slavery Society as well as the local peace society, and in 1838 she joined Garrison in founding the New England Non-Resistance Society. Attending the first Anti-Slavery Convention of American Women in 1837 and lecturing alongside the Grimké sisters the next year, she proclaimed her deep moral commitments in a powerful voice. It was her election to office at the annual AASS convention in May 1840 that spurred hundreds of those opposed to women's equal role in the movement to form a rival organization, the American and Foreign Anti-Slavery Society.[6]

A year later, Kelley "disowned" the Society of Friends before it could disown her. Facing her Hicksite co-worshippers in Uxbridge (Massachusetts) Monthly Meeting, she assured them that the "fundamental principles of the Society . . . have taken deep root in my heart." But "bowed down with grief" that New England Yearly Meeting "took ground in direct opposition to its own professed principles on the question of slavery," she proclaimed it her duty to "come out and be separate, and have no communion with the un-fruitful works of darkness."[7] Publishing her "come-outer" logic to fellow abolitionists in a letter to the *Liberator* in September 1841, she encouraged other Friends to consider their own spiritual and moral path.[8] Come-outerism inspired abolitionists in a range of Protestant denominations to leave their churches and form explicitly antislavery congregations. Some established Wesleyan Methodist and Free Will Baptist churches; others, like Kelley, made the abolition movement itself their spiritual home.

Although Kelley continued to be reviled by anti-abolitionists and even moderate antislavery advocates, her fierce determination in the face of at-tack endeared her to radical activists like Post. During Kelley's 1842 tour, she was denounced from pulpits and papers, pelted with rotten fruits and vegetables, and refused the use of churches and town halls well before she reached Rochester.[9] Still, she continued to speak across the North and Mid-west, often in the company of black male abolitionists, ensuring further cal-umny. For Post and other female Friends, she made clear the importance of following one's inner light and forging interracial bonds. The contentious issue of faith and politics had generated heated debate for several years among Friends throughout the North. By summer 1842, Oliver Johnson que-ried the Posts about the ongoing disputes: "What will be the course of *your* Yearly Meeting?"[10]

When Kelley returned to Rochester in November 1842 for a three-day an-tislavery convention, many abolitionist Friends were prepared to embrace worldly activism more fully. Samuel Porter had written Kelley two months earlier, insisting that local abolitionists had been unjustly "styled agrarians, disorganizers, infidels & fanatics."[11] His Quaker coworkers—both Orthodox and Hicksite—probably found such descriptions less problematic. Most were farmers, and many were considered disorganizers and fanatics, if not quite infidels, by more conservative members of their meeting. Indeed, Samuel and Susan Porter were considered fanatics by some of their Presbyterian co-worshippers after abandoning Third Presbyterian to found Bethel Free Church, an antislavery congregation.[12]

The November 1842 convention, held at Bethel Free Church and hosted by the WNYASS, produced lively discussions on a wide range of issues. Ben-jamin Fish presided, and Isaac Post served on the executive board. Before the convention, Amy Post had worked with Mary Ann M'Clintock, Joseph Hathaway, Lewis Burtis, and five others to draw up a new constitution. That constitution, which the committee presented to the convention on the first day, established the WNYASS as an auxiliary of the AASS. Kelley, who was eight years younger than Amy Post, was staying at 36 Sophia Street. They likely discussed the best way to advocate the WNYASS's proposed affiliation with the AASS, which Liberty Party leaders Samuel Porter and William Chaplin would certainly challenge. The Garrisonians may have felt a greater need to proclaim their AASS affiliation, since the headquarters of the WNAYSS were to be moved from Farmington, a progressive Quaker stronghold, to Rochester, an anchor for the Liberty Party. After a lengthy debate, the constitution and the AASS affiliation were approved.[13]

While the WNYASS continued to welcome African Americans and women, none of the city's black activists were elected to office in November 1842. White women, however, filled more than a quarter of the positions. Sarah Hallowell and two other women served as vice presidents alongside six men, while Sarah Burtis, Sarah Fish, and Phebe Hathaway sat with two more women and thirteen men—including Isaac Post, Lewis Burtis, and Thomas M'Clintock—on the executive committee. Despite the dominance of Garrisonian moral suasionists among these officers, Samuel Porter was elected president, offering some hope that bonds with Liberty Party men could be maintained.[14]

Although WNYASS members "disclaim[ed] any intention of impeaching the anti-slavery fidelity of those abolitionists who deem it better to organize a distinct political party . . . and regard them as sincere co-workers in the same great cause," only a handful of third-party men joined Porter at the convention.[15] Evangelical Protestants proved scarce as well. John Kedzie had embraced that affiliation until two weeks before the convention, when he was excommunicated by Brick Presbyterian Church for his antislavery and anticlerical pronouncements.[16] Henry Bush, another Brick Church excommunicant, joined him among the newly elected WNYASS officers. However, it was Friends—mostly Hicksite—who took over positions earlier occupied by Presbyterians and Baptists, filling at least twenty of the twenty-five offices held by men.

The same pattern held true for women. Few of those active in the Rochester Female Anti-Slavery Society joined the WNYASS, and none of the evangelical women did so. Susan Porter, who helped found the earlier organization, paid membership dues to the WNYASS in 1842 but never participated in the society in any public way. As Sarah Burtis wrote Abby Kelley, with the exception of Susan Porter, "not one person belonging to a professed Church has given her name as [a] member."[17] Abigail Bush, Henry's wife, was the only female evangelical to participate in the 1842 convention, and she had resigned from Brick Presbyterian months earlier, before she could be excommunicated.[18] She soon befriended Amy Post, passing by her former spiritual home whenever she visited Sophia Street. Indeed, the Post home was surrounded by evangelical churches, including Brick Presbyterian Church, United Presbyterian Church, German Evangelical United Church, First Methodist Episcopal Church, First Baptist Church (directly behind 36 Sophia Street), and Central Presbyterian Church, built just south of the Post home in 1841. However, it was mainly ex-communicants from Brick Presbyterian who joined the Posts' circle.

In the aftermath of the November convention, there was much work to do. Amy had been appointed, along with Abby Kelley and Elizabeth M'Clintock, "to draft and present an address to the abolitionists of Western New York, setting forth the benefits of fairs."[19] As antislavery fairs spread from Boston to Philadelphia, Farmington, Rochester, and other cities, they became a critical vehicle for promoting a vision of the North as a free and democratic society, in contrast to the despotism tied to southern slavery. As the WNYASS women proclaimed in the *Liberator* on January 6, 1843, "Our only hope is in the regeneration of the public sentiment of the free States." Antislavery fairs would provide funds to ignite that sentiment via lecturers, periodicals, pamphlets, and petitions. Items purchased would also remind participants to embrace antislavery principles in all their "social, political and religious relations."[20]

Fairs were a common form of fund-raising among charitable societies, churches, and reform organizations, but the antislavery version had a more political edge. The initial event in Rochester, for instance, was scheduled for 22 February 1843, "a day easily remembered by the people. The birth day of the great, good, pious, immortal slaveholding Washington!"[21] Announcements in the *National Anti-Slavery Standard* and local papers were signed by Post, Kelley, M'Clintock, Sarah Anthony Burtis, Phebe Hathaway, and their coworkers. Arguing that the familiarity of the form was crucial to its success, they claimed that a fair "takes captive the strong-holds of prejudice unawares, . . . a kindly feeling is kindled up in the community, and many, before indifferent or cold-hearted, . . . become softened in their prejudices." The organizers recruited women throughout central and western New York to produce goods for sale, such as "caps, bags, [and] aprons," and children's clothing and toys. In return, they would offer fairgoers cider, pies, and jams to sweeten their antislavery message.[22]

The organizers' enthusiasm, however, could not overcome all the obstacles they faced. Certainly, the slow recovery from the Panic of 1837 affected fund-raising efforts generally. In addition, there was considerable competition from other fairs being held that winter by churches, the Orphan Asylum Association, and other groups, leading to both "indifference and opposition" regarding WNYASS claims on the community. More personal crises also challenged organizers. The Burtises' young daughter died in December 1842, after which Sarah lay ill with a severe cold and fatigue. Amy Post nursed her friend, stealing time away from her labors on behalf of the fair.[23] In mid-January, when Burtis had recovered sufficiently to write Kelley requesting assistance, she noted that the necessary work had barely begun. Twenty women had enrolled in the local antislavery sewing society, and others were willing to help, but several then "left us on account of our admitting colored persons to our society." At least a few African American women must have participated in this early WNYASS effort, though none of their names were listed on the fair announcements; ironically, the very idea that blacks might participate could frighten away some whites. Burtis assured Kelley that "we do not sacrifice principles to numbers, neither will colored people be rejected, yet it is very proving to some of our long professed abolitionists."[24]

At the same time, Rochester's black female abolitionists were committed to retaining their own society, which had been organizing events in the community since 1834. No black women served as officers in the interracial and mixed-sex WNYASS, nor were they reported as participating in discussions at its conventions. While contributing to the 1843 fund-raising fair, black women activists preferred to maintain their institutional autonomy even from white women like Post, who regularly attended events at black churches.[25]

While hoping antislavery fairs would gain a wider audience for their arguments, WNYASS fair organizers did not sacrifice their principles or mute their tone. They did, however, focus on the special concerns of female slaves. This emphasis on the specific brutalities faced by enslaved women gained heightened attention across the North with the spread of women's antislavery fairs. Black and white abolitionists had previously noted the horrors of female enslavement, but the publicity for and reports on fund-raising fairs provided a platform through which to restate such claims more adamantly. In a letter to Kelley, Burtis presaged the kind of language that would soon appear in public documents: "While the wings of every moment bear the wailings of kidnapped infants, the shriek of the agonized mother, the dumb anguish, and black despair of outraged daughters, and the deep groans of spirit-broken and imbruted mothers, . . . shall we sit listlessly by, without one effort to kindle the truth-fires, whereby the chain shall be melted?"[26]

Despite the forceful language, Burtis, Post, and their coworkers organized the fair "with an eye to the advancement of the *cause*" so that "instead of turning the public from *it*, there may be light spread more universally that the apathy and indifference may be thrown aside."[27] According to Joseph Hathaway, the February fair achieved its aims: "Considering the shortness of the time to prepare in, and the dreadful dull and 'hard times' it was quite a magnificent af*fair*."[28] The WNYASS women reported that they had raised "over three hundred dollars, a sum by no means contemptible in . . . hard times, and in a city so small as Rochester." They noted especially a "display of rich and elegant articles" from Boston that not only enhanced the profits but also "strengthens our hands" and "prepares us for persevering in every work of reform."[29] Part of those profits may have been used to support activities that summer. In late July 1843, Douglass headed to 36 Sophia Street, where he was joined in early August by Abby Kelley and Charles Remond. The three well-known lecturers participated in a stirring three-day convention organized by Isaac Post, Lewis Burtis, and Samuel Porter. From there, the two black orators headed to the National Convention of Colored Citizens in Buffalo. It was Douglass's first time attending a gathering organized and run by African American men, and it made a powerful impression on him.[30]

Meanwhile, the Posts continued to combine their abolitionist work with efforts on behalf of Indians. Isaac had been especially active in supporting the Seneca people as they fought to retain their remaining lands in western New York. The battle over the Treaty of Buffalo Creek, which would have removed Seneca peoples to lands in Kansas, had begun immediately after President Martin Van Buren approved it in January 1838. Controversy over the treaty led the U.S. Senate to seek assurances that each tribe or band, "separately assembled in council, . . . have given their free and voluntary assent" before ratifying the agreement.[31] The Joint Committee on Indian Affairs, on which Isaac Post served, assisted the Seneca in defending their rights, and in June 1838, GYM sent a petition to Congress opposing the treaty. At the same time, groups of Seneca petitioned the president and the U.S. Congress. Moreover, despite bribes offered to various chiefs, to be paid by the Ogden Land Company, only sixteen of eighty-one approved the Buffalo Creek treaty. Lawyers hired by the Seneca collected depositions documenting the bribes, forgeries, and fraud employed by government and land company agents seeking to coerce the Seneca. Nonetheless, in March 1840, the Senate approved the Buffalo Creek treaty by a single vote. Still, the Seneca refused to comply.[32]

The Joint Committee, working with the Seneca Nation, continued to gather letters, depositions, and petitions and published them in 1840 as *Case of the Seneca Indians*.[33] Then, in April 1841, newly inaugurated president and famed Indian fighter William Henry Harrison died, and Vice President John Tyler became president. Although an advocate of western expansion, Tyler was open to renegotiating the Buffalo Creek treaty. The following January, members of the Joint Committee on Indian Affairs worked out a compromise with Secretary of War John Spencer and the Ogden Land Company by which the Seneca retained Cattaraugus and Allegany lands, lost the Buffalo Creek and Tonawanda reservations, and agreed to grant any railroad company chartered by the state of New York right-of-way across Seneca lands.[34]

However, some Seneca and GYM delegates to the Joint Committee had not been informed of the agreement and were outraged. Claiming that "the Seneca Nation . . . are in great danger of being dispossessed of their most valuable possessions," they called a meeting at the Farmington Hicksite Meetinghouse.[35] Amy and Isaac likely attended the March gathering, since the day after the meeting, a group of Seneca women from Tonawanda either gave or sent the Posts a copy of their petition to President Tyler. It began, "We, the women of our race, feel troubled with deep anxiety, for our children, who are in our hands. . . . We pray you, our Great Father, the President, to unlo[o]se our bondage, which gives us much pain." Amy may have encouraged the Seneca women to draft the petition, since Minerva Blacksmith and her six cosigners stated that they had never before devised such a document.[36] Two months later, Isaac attended a council at Buffalo Creek as one of several representatives from the Joint Committee to discuss a resolution with Seneca chiefs and commissioners from the federal government, Massachusetts, and New York State. Seventy-nine of the eighty-one Seneca chiefs were ultimately convinced to accept the supplemental treaty. Still, many Hicksite Quakers from GYM, including the Posts, continued to address Seneca concerns and assist families at Cattaraugus and Allegany.[37]

The 1842 petition of Seneca women echoes the efforts of antislavery women to make their voices heard on crucial issues of national policy. It may also have reinforced a growing sense of women's centrality to movements for social change. As early as February 1838, Sarah Kirby had written Amy about a family visit to Manhasset, where she saw many interesting books, "among which were Sarah Grimké's letters on woman's rights. Probably you have seen them."[38] This was likely true, since Grimké's letters were originally published in the *Liberator* over several months in 1837 and addressed the controversy that swirled around female petitioners and lecturers.

Abby Kelley, Lucretia Mott, and other female abolitionists considered these letters a call to arms.³⁹

Sarah's sister Angelina Grimké was equally outspoken. At the first Anti-Slavery Convention of American Women in May 1837, she offered the following resolution: that "the time has come for woman to move in that sphere which Providence has assigned her, and no longer remain satisfied in the circumscribed limits with which corrupt custom and a perverted application of the Scripture have encircled her."⁴⁰ During the ensuing debate, several evangelical women protested both the notion that the Scriptures were perverted and that women had a right to speak publicly on political issues. However, after Mott and other Friends spoke in favor of the resolution, it passed.

The 1837 dispute resonated in Rochester, as growing numbers of evangelical women retreated from public antislavery efforts in the early 1840s. Debates within GYM and other Hicksite meetings raised similar concerns over the roles of women, while battles in the AASS and other antislavery organizations centered on women's right to petition, speak, vote, and hold office. By this time, the term "woman's rights" was being used with greater frequency to capture an array of issues and claims. In May 1845, Jeremiah Burke Sanderson attended the anniversary meetings of the AASS and other reform associations in New York City and reported to Post that "Woman is rising, becoming free. The progress manifest at the present of the idea of Woman's Rights in the public mind" demonstrates "what a few years comparatively may effect." Although Sanderson was black, he did not mention a speech made by Sojourner Truth, a relative newcomer to the antislavery circuit who from the beginning linked women's rights and racial justice.⁴¹

Some of Post's closest F/friends, including Benjamin and Sarah Fish and Asa and Huldah Anthony, embraced an even broader vision, believing that achieving women's rights and ending slavery were best gained through the development of "cooperative communities." In such communities, reformers could live according to the model of social interaction outlined by French sociologist Charles Fourier. Fourierist phalanxes, planted across the northern United States, attracted a wide range of activists. Two established in 1843–44—at Skaneateles and Sodus Bay, the latter some thirty miles east of Rochester—attracted more than a dozen WNYASS members and their families, including the Fishes, the Anthonys, Eliab Capron, John and Sarah Hurn, and the Reverend Roswell Murray and his wife, Laura Murray. All but the Murrays were also members of GYM. Embracing Fourier's regimen of physical and intellectual labor, a simple lifestyle, and egalitarian decision making, residents believed, as Benjamin Fish wrote to the Posts, that they were "engaged in a reform which if properly carried out will strike at the root of all *Slavery*."[42]

Still, most Quaker activists, including the Posts, continued to live within the larger society and viewed utopian communities as more of a distraction from than a vehicle for abolition and women's rights. Both Amy and Isaac served as officers in the WNYASS throughout the 1840s, and Amy helped organize antislavery fairs along with her stepdaughter, Mary Post; her sister Sarah; and her closest F/friends in western New York. The Posts were thrilled when William Hallowell, an active F/friend and WNYASS stalwart, announced his intention to wed Mary Post in January 1843. The couple exchanged vows at the Post home on Sophia Street, just three blocks south of Hallowell's home on Jones Street. Soon, the young couple was hosting traveling lecturers as well as fugitive slaves.

Their son-in-law was as deeply engaged in the WNYASS as the Posts and, like them, embraced Garrisonian moral suasion rather than third-party politics. Samuel Porter repeatedly tried to bridge the growing chasm, claiming that it was not electoral victory that Liberty Party men sought with their "appeal to the Ballot Box" but the *moral effect of numbers*."[43] He argued as well that remaining in established churches provided opportunities to move mainstream denominations toward antislavery views. While many black attendees likely agreed with Porter concerning the importance of churches to the abolitionist cause, they joined the vast majority of WNYASS members who condemned congregations that failed to oppose slavery. Moreover, given the restrictions on black men's voting rights in New York State, most did not view partisan politics as a significant vehicle for change.[44]

Still, some WNYASS leaders, including Isaac Post and William Hallowell, worried that Garrisonians lost the moral high ground when they criticized Liberty Party men too severely. As Isaac wrote Amy in May 1844, while she was attending the AASS meeting in New York City, "I do not like our friends battling with those that think they are called to work at the Ballot Box." After all, Liberty Party meetings in Rochester attracted people who "would not go any where else to hear the subject of liberty conversed." Once there, he continued, they have a chance to hear men like William C. "Bloss tell how powerful mor[al] suasion is and that political action only is calculated to hold what suasion gains." For Isaac, seeing the *Liberator* "continually saying so many hard things against the liberty party as though there was no honesty amongst them" only hurt the Garrisonian case. He hoped that

"zeal will be tempered with judgment" at the AASS convention, thereby encouraging Amy to play her usual role in fostering coalitions.[45]

Isaac was to be disappointed, as advocates of party politics came under
severe attack at the convention. As a WNYASS delegate, Amy participated
in debates not only over the utility of political means but also over whether
abolitionists should advocate the "dissolution of the American Union." Those
who supported the resolution claimed that the U.S. government was proslavery at its foundation, and thus true abolitionists should reject any involvement with government by way of the ballot box or otherwise. After
heated discussions, the resolution for disunion passed 29 to 21. Despite the
opposition of many F/friends and Isaac's cautionary note, Amy voted in
favor, alongside Lucretia Mott, Wendell Phillips, Abby Kelley, Charles Lenox
Remond, and Mary Robbins Post. Douglass supported the disunion camp a
month later at a convention in New England. The following February, the
WNYASS embraced disunion as well, although participants noted that in
western New York "there is among the Liberty Party less exclusiveness of
feelings than in the East." Samuel Porter and other Liberty Party members
were nonetheless affronted by the resolution and opposed it. Once again,
Amy joined the majority of the society in supporting it.[46]

The heightened activity on behalf of abolition intensified conflicts in
Farmington Quarterly Meeting and GYM. In 1843, Thomas M'Clintock, who
was active in the AASS, gave up his position as clerk of GYM, which he had
held since 1838. Even in Rochester Monthly Meeting, some Hicksites now
adamantly opposed participation in worldly associations. The overseers of
local preparative meetings apparently raised concerns about such behavior in the Post household. According to friend and fellow activist Lucy
Colman, Amy Post was singled out for investigation. Because she "left her
home for the purpose of holding bazars [sic] and fairs to raise funds" for
the abolitionist cause, a "committee was appointed to reason with [her]."
One of its objectives "was to advise her in regard to her duty towards her
family," but they could find no sign of domestic neglect. In fact, several
family members joined Amy in her questionable activities, including Isaac,
stepdaughter Mary Hallowell, and sister Sarah Hallowell.[47] The overseers
did not call for a formal inquiry, but their concerns were clear.

In December 1843, following the overseers' visit, Amy wrote Abby Kelley
and noted almost with regret that they have "taken no further notice of my
case." But, she continued, "I suspect they will have a fresh charge against me
soon, as I yesterday transcribed Epistles for the Preparative meetings on
such paper as this"—stationery embossed with the antislavery logo of a

slave in chains—"and have but little doubt but that imploring image will disturb their quiet."[48] Her willingness to challenge Hicksite overseers was reinforced by the support she received from ex-Quaker Abby Kelley, non-Quaker Frederick Douglass, and Hicksite minister Lucretia Mott.

In July 1844, Mott visited Rochester and spoke at the local meetinghouse. Julia Wilbur, an Orthodox Friend who had recently accepted a teaching post in the city, captured the event in her diary. Mott, she wrote, began by criticizing individual conformity to the "doctrines and creeds" of churches—all churches—as a sign "of servile fears or a lack of independence on the part of the conformist." After insisting on *morality as the great thing to be attained,*" Mott discussed the great movements of the day—"*the mental and spiritual degradation of women,' Peace, Temperance & Anti Slavery. . . .* She cannot conceive," Wilbur noted, "how any benevolent persons can fail to *act* in these causes, but . . . she well knows" they do, "and that her *own society* are as deficient as any in this respect." Indeed, Mott accused those Friends opposed to Quaker participation in worldly associations "as being guilty of joining in the hue & cry of 'going forward without being sent,' of 'disturbing the quiet,' etc." Wilbur concluded, "The effect of this preaching was very apparent, some being very much disturbed, others were evidently highly delighted at the approbation of their own proceedings, for the society has some members who are *very* active in these reforms."[49]

The Posts certainly counted in that "*very*" active" circle. After being investigated for her antislavery labors, Amy corresponded with Abby Kelley, fugitive slave and antislavery agent Williams Wells Brown, abolitionist Paulina Wright of Utica, and other Garrisonians about conventions, agents, and periodicals, as well as fund-raising fairs. Indeed, Kelley and Brown were depending on Amy and the women of the WNYASS to arrange a fair in fall 1844, since the central New York group, based in Utica, was ravaged by ill health.[50]

While applauded for their antislavery work by AASS leaders and like-minded radicals, the Posts' efforts caused grave concern among family members on Long Island. In January 1845, seventy-year-old Mary Kirby sent an anguished letter to her "dear children," pleading with them to "stand and wait patiently," believing that local Hicksite leaders "will be overcome by your good and consistant [*sic*] lives."[51] But the Posts found little reason for patience. Certainly they were convinced by 1845 that slavery could only be eradicated by working outside the confines of the Society of Friends. GYM still refused to alter its Discipline by eliminating the meeting of ministers and elders or allowing women and men to meet jointly for business. And if the 1841 disownment of Isaac Hopper had worried many abolitionist Friends, WNYASS member Eliab Capron's withdrawal in February 1844 caused an even greater stir in western and central New York. Capron was incited to give up his membership when Friends in the region refused Douglass, Remond, and other abolitionists use of their meetinghouses.[52]

The Posts shared Capron's dismay and were distressed as well about Rochester Monthly Meeting's ongoing investigation of Benjamin Fish. Fish had resorted to bankruptcy in the midst of the Panic of 1837, a decision that created problems for his creditors, many of them Friends. Amy and Isaac believed the meeting should embrace a "forgiving disposition," but other members argued that Fish had not taken enough care to protect the interests of his creditors.[53] Although Fish was not disowned, the inquiry may have encouraged him to move his family to the Sodus Bay Phalanx, where notions of communal property negated the focus on individual failure.

By 1844, Fish's case resonated more deeply for the Posts, who suddenly faced financial difficulties of their own. Isaac had weathered the Panic of 1837 well and had sufficient funds to help relatives in need, including his brother-in-law Jeffries Hallowell.[54] The Posts loaned money to Jeffries and likely to Amy's sister Elizabeth Kirby Mott when she and her two young sons were abandoned by her husband. In September 1843, a report for the credit agency R. G. Dun and Co., founded by Lewis Tappan to provide reliable financial information, noted that Post and Willis seemed to be doing well. Still, the agent noted, "we think P too ready to endorse for his friends."[55] That concern proved true in the case of Hallowell, who failed at a number of ventures. In 1843, he and Sarah were living with William and Mary Hallowell. The two men were at best distant cousins, but Sarah was very close to her niece Mary. William could likely have found Jeffries a position in his woolen factory, but apparently he did not. By winter 1844, Sarah and her husband had moved to a farm on the outskirts of Rochester, aided by Isaac, who cosigned a loan. Then, in July, Jeffries fell ill and died, leaving behind debts far greater than anyone had imagined.[56]

The economic burden fell mainly to Isaac, who felt obligated to set things right. The timing could not have been worse. He had recently suffered a $2,000 loss, when a building he owned with Edmund Willis burned. While insurance would cover the loss, it meant he was short on funds just when he needed them most. Moreover, Isaac discovered that his younger brother, Joseph, had also loaned money to Jeffries "with not the most distant idea of his not having enough property to pay his debts."[57] Of course, the situation left Sarah in difficult straits as well. Adding to the dismal situation,

Isaac and Joseph's mother, Catherine Willets Post, died in August 1844 in Westbury; with all the problems he was facing, Isaac could not attend the funeral. That summer, the Posts had moved in with Sarah on the farm, apparently renting out their Sophia Street home to save money. In October, unaware of the family crisis, an R. G. Dun agent wrote that Isaac was "reputed a man of considerable prop[erty], has just bo't a farm & we understand paid for it." An act that was apparently necessary to keep creditors at bay was viewed as a sign of Isaac's prosperity. The agent did, however, reiterate the concern that "Post is said to endorse pretty freely for his friends."[58] As Isaac worked to keep his family and business afloat, his fourteen-year-old son, Jacob, began helping out at the apothecary shop, while twelve-year-old Joseph was sent to live with Amy's parents in Jericho. Only three-year-old Mathilda seemed oblivious to the troubles surrounding her.

Then, in fall 1844, Amy and Mathilda took ill. While Amy soon recovered, her daughter continued to suffer severe pain and was ultimately diagnosed with scarlet fever. In that grim summer and fall, Amy stopped attending meeting, which led a women's committee to question her spiritual commitment. As F/friend and coworker Nathaniel Potter wrote Amy in November, "Thy trials are greater than I had supposed—and I am not sure but the spirit of opposition in the minds of those who control your meeting matters—[they] may excuse thee from what would be required if prejudice [against you] did not exist."[59] In January 1845, Mathilda died, making all other problems seem trivial.[60]

Isaac was grief stricken, and Amy inconsolable. Mary Hallowell and her aunt Sarah sent word to relatives on Long Island, and Amy's mother wrote immediately: "I due [sic] mingle with you in sympathy in these deep tryals [sic]. . . . I hope thou will endeavour to seek resignation, in thy keen tryal of thy darling and only *little* daughter, now in her lovely and innocent state, nothing to *mourn* for but our loss, hers is a sure and *Eternal Rest*."[61] In April, Amy sent twelve-year-old Joseph a long letter, lamenting "the loss of thy little interesting sister." "We must submit," she wrote, but admitted "the repressed tears often become too potent to obey the check, when reflecting on her loveliness, and our disappointed hopes." Still, she included pages of motherly counsel along with medical advice for family members, a temperance pledge, and a packet of antislavery songs, perhaps the *The Anti-Slavery Picknick*, a book the WNYASS hoped would encourage children to embrace the cause.[62]

Amy's mother, who had anticipated her daughter Sarah's return to Jericho following Jeffries's death, agreed that she must stay up north to watch over her devastated sister. Amy's F/friend Sarah Thayer sent comforting thoughts from Ledyard in three cramped pages, recalling a happy visit to Rochester a year earlier, commiserating on the declining spirit of Friends' meetings, describing the woes of a Catholic servant girl working in a nearby household, and praising the latest phrenological journal. She closed with thoughts of Amy's many losses: "How are the dear departed spirits of our loved ones called around us at times and is it wrong to indulge the pleasing thought that they are hovering above us—as it were—to strengthen us to submit to his ways." Certainly, she wrote, "we can be permitted to call the dear loved ones to mind to cheer us on to virtuous deeds."[63]

Amy remained physically and emotionally exhausted for months and found little solace in her faith. Indeed, she complained to family and friends of a "party spirit" among local Hicksites. While Isaac continued to be appointed to Friends committees, he, too, seemed less engaged. In March 1845, Phebe Post Willis combined condolences to Isaac on the loss of "your precious little darling" with concerns that their monthly meeting "must be exceedingly trying according to thy account." She urged her brother and sister-in-law to live down the spirit of opposition and not "gratify them by resigning . . . and if the worst must come, have no agency in it."[64] But it was too late. In May, Isaac and Amy asked to be released from Rochester Monthly Meeting, and the request was quickly granted. Some co-worshippers were no doubt relieved, whereas others were deeply concerned.[65]

Relatives on Long Island feared that economic stress and Mathilda's death had contributed to a hasty decision on Amy and Isaac's part. Mary Kirby Willis seemed especially unhappy with her sister's decision. Having read a letter that the Posts sent to Joseph and Mary Post, she felt her "dear sister went a little to[o] far in some expressions relative to the society of friends. Now thee is released from membership I hope thee may be preserved from censuring . . . lest *we* may conclude that thee is not right and censure thee."[66] Fortunately, most family members evidenced more sympathy, even those who disagreed with the decision.

Quaker coworkers in the WNYASS held more complicated views. The shifting stances of Nathaniel Potter of Buffalo capture the ambivalence of many. Writing as soon as the news reached him, Potter challenged the Posts' claim that "everyone who remains in society [the Society of Friends] share in the responsibility of the acts of the society although contrary to a decided and expressed opinion against the measure." But a few months later, he asserted, "I have no intention of letting the circumstances of your withdrawal from the monthly meeting make any differ[ence] in my feelings and trust you will not in yours." And by September, he admitted that he had "yet to suffer in society" for his antislavery activities. "If you have suffered your share—then of course it is time for you to journey forward. I confess you have been more faithful in the cause of the downtrodden slave than I have. . . . Blessed are they that are persecuted for righteousness sake for theirs is the kingdom of heaven."[67]

Certainly, those who had already been released or disowned were pleased to include the Posts in their ranks. In Rochester, women and men who had stopped attending monthly meeting or had been expelled from evangelical churches began holding "free meetings" in their homes, including 36 Sophia Street, where they could worship in their own way.[68] That August, the Posts joined a large group of antislavery Quakers from GYM and a few from New York Yearly Meeting in publishing a letter to Green Plain (Ohio) Quarterly Meeting in the *National Anti-Slavery Standard*. Aware of the conflicts in that meeting through their work with abolitionists Joseph and Ruth Dugdale, the signers sympathized with its trials, mourning "the progress of a spirit in our religious society calculated to sever the bonds of unity and brotherly affection. . . . [Still] there is so much cause for joy . . . joy, that pure principles of truth, love and mercy are breaking forth . . . and illuminating as it were the whole earth. And it is the faithful in heart, those who are willing to bear the scoffs and scorn of the world, . . . that are the fitted instruments to advance this glorious reform in the earth."[69] While many Friends continued to press their case in GYM, the Posts' gloried in their freedom to pursue reforms beyond its strictures.

The Posts' decision to leave the Hicksite meeting, entangled with their shared grief, drew Amy and Isaac even closer together. In 1846, Sarah Hurn, who resided with her husband, John, at the Wisconsin Fourierist Phalanx, noted the strength both of her marriage and that of the Posts. She concluded, "If the relation which *should* exist between husband and wife were better understood and appreciated, it appears to me that much domestic unhappiness . . . might be avoided." A few years later, Sarah Owen, a self-employed widow and WNYASS coworker, sent greetings to Amy and her "good Isaac. . . . I was quite inspired with the wish that I had an *Abram, Isaac*, or a *Jacob* if they should happen not to be a 'tyrant instead of a husband,'" and who, like Isaac, "heartily adopted the principles of equal rights."[70]

As Amy basked in her freedom from Friends constraints and the mutuality of her marriage, she threw herself into antislavery work. Indeed, it seemed the only activity that lifted her spirits. Just a month after Mathilda died, and in the midst of a fierce snowstorm, Amy and Isaac traveled into Rochester to attend the February 1845 WNYASS convention. Amy served on the resolutions committee with her sister Sarah Hallowell, William Wells Brown, and the indefatigable Samuel Porter. Isaac was elected president of the meeting, while his daughter, Mary, collected dues, and her husband, William, served on the executive board, to which Amy was also appointed.[71]

The meeting was at least as contentious as any Friends meeting, with a small circle of Liberty Party advocates fighting the Garrisonian majority on nearly every resolution. The battles over how best to achieve abolition led Rhoda DeGarmo to lament "the deviations and betrayals of those that once stood faithful," which from her perspective meant supporters of party politics.[72] The Posts, however, surrounded by family and friends, felt loved and supported. Their friends, all self-described radicals, now included not only the Fishes, DeGarmos, and Burtises but also ex-evangelicals such as Abigail Bush, John and Lemira Kedzie, and Sarah Owen (excommunicated from Brick Presbyterian Church in 1845), as well as local and national African American leaders. The presence of self-emancipated blacks infused Rochesterians—black and white, Garrisonians and political abolitionists—with pride. William Wells Brown was among the newest recruits to the WNYASS. While working on Mississippi steamers, he had fled his Missouri master in 1834 and found sanctuary in the home of Ohio Quakers. He was soon assisting other fugitives while learning to read and write and starting a family. Brown moved his wife and child to Buffalo in 1836 and joined abolitionist efforts there. In 1844, he was hired as a paid lecturer by the WNYASS; that June, he wrote to Amy, assuring her that people in rural areas and small towns were "wide awake." Eight months later, he attended his first WNYASS convention, where he won praise for his singing as well as his speaking and no doubt shared stories about his work with the Underground Railroad.[73]

As self-emancipated blacks, Brown and Douglass were considered heroes by many abolitionists and helped cement interracial bonds in many towns and cities. Rochester's black community had harbored escaped slaves since the 1810s, and the AME Zion Church remained a mainstay of that effort. By the 1830s, local blacks were aided by Orthodox Friends such as Lindley and Abigail Moore and Hicksites such as Benjamin and Sarah Fish, who lived on the outskirts of the city. As more Hicksites, including the Posts and Asa and Huldah Anthony, migrated to Rochester, they joined the ranks of Underground Railroad conductors. They shared this sacred labor not only with black neighbors but also with white evangelicals, including Samuel and Susan Porter; William Bloss, a reformed tavern keeper; Edward C. Williams, whose sail loft provided an excellent hiding place; and George Avery, who founded the Monroe County Bible Society.[74]

Rochester's proximity to Lake Ontario, the Genesee River, the Erie Canal, and regular stagecoach service to Buffalo and Niagara Falls had attracted fleeing slaves since the early 1800s. The central and western New York region was crisscrossed by lakes, canals, rivers, and roads and dotted with Quaker, Methodist, and Baptist meetinghouses, making it a hub of activity as the Underground Railroad developed more systematic routes in the 1830s. By the 1840s, commercial railroads—completed from Boston to Rochester in 1841—offered another, faster means of travel, while steamboats shuttled passengers from Charlotte, Lewiston, Pultneyville, and Oswego to Canada several times a day, adding to the area's importance for fleeing fugitives. Horatio Throop of Pultneyville and other reform-minded captains extended the Underground Railroad across Lake Ontario. In Rochester, the steep banks down to the Genesee River near Kelsey's Landing, where fugitives boarded Canadian-bound vessels, shielded them from prying eyes as they scrambled to safety.[75]

Perhaps the city's location at the nexus of major escape routes created the seemingly aboveground character of the Underground Railroad in Rochester. Many of the local conductors were well-known residents who were vocal about their opposition to slavery and, at least until mid-century, did little to hide their involvement. Self-emancipated blacks such as Austin Steward and Thomas James lived openly in Rochester in the 1810s and 1820s, as did Harriet Jacobs and John S. Jacobs in the late 1840s, at a time when Frederick Douglass publicized the plight of runaways in the region on a regular basis.[76]

Douglass had continued his periodic visits to the region throughout the 1840s. In June 1845, Douglass became the nation's most renowned fugitive with publication of his *Narrative of the Life of Frederick Douglass*. The famed orator was scheduled to lecture in Rochester in late July, and the Posts eagerly awaited his arrival. The visit offered Julia Wilbur the chance to hear "the eloquent" former slave lecture. She had never "heard a person of this description speak in public, & it was most deeply interesting." Responding as Amy Post might have following her first experience hearing Douglass, Wilbur concluded: "To see a person of his noble mien & commanding figure drawn to his full height pouring forth eloquence powerful enough to unchain a *Rochester* audience after 9 o'clock P.M. was a most impressive sight." While Wilbur considered his claim that slavery was "a covenant with death & an argument with hell" too strong for "all but the most ultra," Post had already embraced these views.[77] It was perhaps during this visit that Isaac and Mary Gibbs invited the Posts to join a circle of friends at their home, a center of antislavery activity in the black community.[78] A few months later, with Douglass's fugitive status fully revealed, he left the United States to tour Ireland, Scotland, and England, bringing the power of his experience and his voice to the British antislavery movement.

By fall 1845, Amy found renewed purpose in the beloved community of social and religious activists in western New York. Edmund Willis and his new wife, Julia, joined other family members in the antislavery circle as Post continued to work alongside dear friends Sarah Fish, Sarah Burtis, Rhoda DeGarmo, Huldah Anthony, Abigail Bush, and Sarah Owen. These women shared social as well as spiritual comradeship and deepened ties between faith and political action even as many left formal religious institutions behind. Several of these women had also survived the loss of children, a special if too frequent source of female bonding in the mid-nineteenth century. The Posts had returned to 36 Sophia Street, which held warmer memories of Mathilda than did the farm. Back home, Amy shared domestic labors with English servant Mary Dale and her widowed sister Sarah, who also took comfort in being back in the city.

In late November, the Posts and Sarah made a much-delayed visit to Long Island. Amy had still not fully recovered her physical or emotional strength, but at least the Posts' economic problems were largely behind them and their family had mostly accepted their religious choices. They visited widely in Jericho and Westbury, spending time with Amy's parents and with siblings and cousins in Jericho, Westbury, and nearby towns. The three Rochesterians spent a good deal of time with John and Rebecca Ketcham, who had had a year almost as difficult as that of Isaac and Amy. Rebecca was sick with fever when the Posts arrived and only improved "after Isaac's more throu [*sic*] doctoring." John Ketcham's cousin had died earlier in the year, two daughters had recently married and moved away, and a daughter-in-law living nearby had died in September. John seemed to take it all "with much evenness & composure."[79]

Despite the Ketchams' problems, the joy of seeing family and friends lifted the Posts' spirits. On the way back to Rochester, the trio stopped in New York City to see more relatives, including some cousins active in the

Colored Orphan Asylum. Recalling that just ten years before two women had started the asylum with "4 or 5 little orphans," Isaac noted that they now had "a very large house where comfort & learning are communicated to 130 poor children." He and Amy also attended the Rose Street Meeting with their cousins and listened to George White condemn "Transcendentalists & abolitionists" while "prais[ing] slaveholders." Isaac reported to his sister, we "did not see much good in what he said."[80] They also visited the local antislavery office, and Isaac conducted some business downtown before the family headed up the Hudson River.

Amy, Isaac, and Sarah stopped next at the home of cousins Lydia and Abigail Mott in Albany. There they found a letter from Douglass describing his adventures in Ireland and Scotland. His missive surely sparked tales of his visits to Rochester and his spellbinding lectures. Their last night on the road, the trio splurged on "fine accommodations" at the Auburn House, paying two dollars for a parlor, two bedrooms, and breakfast. Emotionally refreshed, they reached home in late December and soon after received a long letter from Amy's mother extolling her great joy at their visit and her deep love for them all.[81]

While warm memories lingered, Amy leapt into preparations for the WNYASS convention in January 1846. At the opening session, Isaac was elected vice president, while the Posts' old friend William Wells Brown served as corresponding secretary. When the executive committee met, Amy was among the ladies who "resolved to hold a fair . . . a year from this time." The *National Anti-Slavery Standard* reported that there "appeared to be more of a determination on the part of the Executive Committee to do something, than at any previous meeting, especially by the females . . . [who] are determined that their Fair shall be second to none, save the great Boston Fair."[82]

Eager to begin the work, Amy could not avoid painful reminders of all that was out of her control. Early in the new year, her mother reported that Jane Ketcham, Rebecca's daughter, had died of a fever on 5 January. She described the heartrending scene when Rebecca "could not consent to have her grave clothes put on, felt as though she could not give her up."[83] Then, in early February, even more devastating news reached the Posts. Isaac's older sister, Phebe Post Willis, who had spent precious time with the Posts' in Ledyard and Rochester, had died after catching cold at Jane Ketcham's funeral.[84] Although they were glad they had visited her so recently, her vitality just weeks before made the news all the more shocking.

Isaac and Amy seemed to believe that focusing on those who suffered more than they did could put their own pain in perspective. The Post home once again became a center of spiritual and reform activity, with free religious meetings vying with gatherings of the antislavery sewing circle and visits from itinerant lecturers, relatives, and friends. By spring 1846, Amy was actively soliciting goods for the antislavery fair to be held months later. She wrote to Douglass, in care of English abolitionist Elizabeth Pease, asking if he could solicit goods from his British friends. Although he replied that all the ladies' societies there were "Pledged to the Bazaar at Boston," he added, "I can not but admire the perseverance and determination you indicate in the course you have marked out." And he was sure that "Mrs. Chapman [of Boston] will aid you to whatever foreign articles the society has on hand." Douglass then described the efforts that he and George Thompson, a leading British abolitionist, were making to expose the proslavery conduct of the Church of Scotland and the freedom he felt being in a place "where I am treated as a man and an equal brother." I am "sometimes fearful," he admitted, "it will unfit me for the proslavery kicks and cuffs at home."[85]

Douglass sent greetings to the extended Post family and added, "I hope to embrace you all in the course of a few fleeting months." He then added a deeply personal message: "Amy your family was always Dear—very dear to me, you loved me and treated me as a brother before the world knew me as it does—& when my friends were fewer than they now are, and let me tell you that I never loved and admired you more, than since I last met you in Rochester."[86] Free from the responsibilities and aggravations attendant on participation in Hicksite meetings and encouraged by Douglass's praise, Amy both built on and sustained the extensive network of local, regional, and national activists formed since the advent of the WNYASS. She worked to maintain its interracial and mixed-sex character and began to engage the transatlantic circle that Douglass and others opened to her.

The international perspective that infused Douglass's letters was fully on display at the AASS Annual Meeting in May 1846. Isaac attended alongside Joseph and Mary Post and F/friends Lydia and Abigail Mott, Paulina Wright, and Thomas M'Clintock. The efforts of President James Polk to launch a war with Mexico in order to gain control of Texas riled abolitionists of every stripe.[87] The war connected issues long of interest to the Posts, who, with other Garrisonians, linked the "degradation of the country in relation to slavery, [and] the extirpation of the aborigines [Indians]" to the policies that fueled conflict with Mexico.[88] The war also reinforced abolitionists' understanding of the deeply intertwined character of local, national, and global politics. For the Posts and many others, Mexico, having outlawed slavery, sat next to St. Domingue and England on the roster of civilized nations. A war against that nation could be intended only to expand slavery and impose Anglo-Saxon domination over Mexican and indigenous populations.[89]

That June, at the behest of their British sisters, female activists in Philadelphia organized a public meeting to protest the war. Lucretia Mott and Sarah Pugh, longtime members of the Philadelphia Female Anti-Slavery Society, led the meeting. The women drafted a memorial in which they lamented "the false love of glory, the cruel spirit of revenge, the blood-thirsty ambition, the swelling breast of the soldier in the field," and the danger of extending slave territory. Concerned with the mistreatment of Mexican women by U.S. soldiers during the war and the consequences for slave families if the conquest was successful, some called for "women *en masse*" to petition Congress to withdraw American troops. Abolitionists organized protest meetings in a number of other communities in the Northeast and Midwest. In Syracuse, New York, Unitarian minister Samuel J. May was among those who called on laboring men to refuse to serve in Mexico. Progressive antislavery Friends gathered at Kennett Square, Pennsylvania, to condemn the "blind obedience" required by patriotism.[90] Amy followed these meetings and protests through reports in the antislavery press and Rochester's daily papers. Correspondence with Joseph and Mary Post and with other antislavery F/friends also linked the war against Mexico to U.S. politicians' imperial interest in Cuba.[91]

Many abolitionists and Friends had long embraced an internationalist perspective, tracking antislavery efforts in the British Isles, celebrating 1 August as Emancipation Day in the British Caribbean, and supporting communities established by fugitive and free blacks in Canada. They had also followed developments at the World Anti-Slavery Convention in London in 1840 and the dispute over seating Lucretia Mott and other female delegates. While lauding British Friends for their early agitation against slavery and the slave trade, radical Quakers nonetheless critiqued their transatlantic counterparts for their conservative views on women's activism.

Quakers were especially attuned to international concerns because of the exchange of epistles and testimonies among Friends' meetings in the United States and other nations, especially Britain. Printed testimonies and traveling ministers further expanded their horizons. In 1842, for example, Lucretia Mott corresponded with British reformer Richard Allen about a recent convention in Paris, William Knibb's London speech on "the privations & sufferings of the poor Irish emigrants to Jamaica," and George Thompson's speeches in Glasgow on the "Affganistan war." These exchanges circulated among abolitionists, and portions were published in the *National Anti-Slavery Standard* and the *Liberator*.[92] By 1846, even abolitionists who were relatively isolated commented on international developments. John Hurn, who had moved from Rochester to the Sodus Bay Phalanx and then to a Fourierist settlement in rural Wisconsin, wrote to Amy that October: "I should like to see the example of the [British] Anti-Corn Law League followed in all other reforms, which would hasten the 'good times coming' considerably."[93]

In July 1846, western New York abolitionists addressed local, national, and international developments at a convention held "to awaken, to inform, and to inspire the American people with a true sense of the iniquities of slavery."[94] They had seen the larger effects of such iniquities close to home when two "little colored girls," the daughters of the Reverend David Ray, were not allowed to attend the school where Julia Wilbur taught.[95] Some Rochesterians were offended by such displays of prejudice, but city officials insisted that black children attend only the "colored school" provided for them. Aware that segregation and discrimination were occurring across the North, the WNYASS hired William Wells Brown, "who has felt in his own person the evils of slavery," as its first full-time agent and lecturer. He would carry the resolutions of the WNYASS—in support of interracial education, black communities in Canada, disunion with slaveholders, and opposition to the war with Mexico—to audiences throughout the Northeast and Midwest. To support this effort, WNYASS women announced their plans for a grand antislavery fair, to be held from Christmas through New Year's Day. Hoping to raise interest among Canadian F/friends, Sarah Hallowell traveled to Ontario, Canada, that fall where cousins Thomas and Phebe Willis accompanied her on visits to black communities in the region.[96] Some of the residents had reached Ontario via western New York, and a few had no doubt been hidden in the Post home or store.

The December 1846 antislavery festival attracted widespread attention from the local press and enthusiastic reports in the *Liberator* and the *National Anti-Slavery Standard*. Of particular note to those, like Post, who viewed abolition, women's rights, and peace as deeply intertwined, the women sold copies of a sermon by Rev. Samuel J. May titled "The Rights and Condition of Women." May denounced the fact that "the *men* of our nation presumed to plunge us into the multiform calamities, crimes, and expenditures of a war, without so much as consulting the women, who will have to share equally, if not to endure the larger part of the losses and sufferings, that are inevitable upon such a measure of folly and wickedness." Noting these abuses of power, May called for women's enfranchisement.[97]

Amy Post reported that the earnings from the fair were "cheering," although the $100 profit paled relative to the exhaustive preparations. She also noted that some Rochesterians could not "leave off entirely the use of eggs as argument against A[bby] K[elley] Foster," who spoke at the event.[98] The WNYASS held its annual convention while the fair continued, having secured the court house for its proceedings. Giles Stebbins, an antislavery lecturer who had toured with Kelley, had married Benjamin and Sarah Fish's daughter Catherine earlier in 1846 and moved to Rochester. Stebbins sent an account of the convention to the *National Anti-Slavery Standard* and claimed it attracted "the attention of those who have seldom before visited the Anti-Slavery gatherings." Their interest was piqued by "the iniquity of the Mexican war" as well as by "the truthfulness and importance of our views."[99]

Amy had worked the fair while six months pregnant and spent the next two months nursing her niece Julia Willis, Edmund's wife, who had contracted measles. Anxious relatives on Long Island filled crosshatched pages with additional worries: the ongoing upheavals in Hicksite Quaker meetings, the machinations of "Liberty Party folks," the ongoing war with Mexico, and the Irish famine.[100] Meanwhile, Waterloo activist Mary Ann M'Clintock was depending on Amy to send her leftover items from Rochester so she might offer them at Waterloo's antislavery fair.[101] Julia Willis died on 11 February, but somehow Amy managed to box up and ship the goods soon after. She then retreated from the world, giving birth to Willet Edmund Post on 16 March. Anxious about going into labor at age forty-four, Amy had not told her Long Island family that she was pregnant, so they were shocked, but happy, when she announced Willet's arrival.[102]

Long Island F/friends did not hold back, however, on their litany of complaints while Amy recuperated. Relatives in Jericho expressed their "disquiet" over Edmund Willis's decision to bury his wife at the new Mount Hope Cemetery in Rochester rather than in the Rochester or Jericho Friends' graveyard.[103] At the same time, Isaac's family complained that Westbury Monthly Meeting had disowned a member for purchasing a piano and considered disowning another for joining the Odd Fellows. These seemingly petty concerns were entangled with more serious disputes. In 1846, New York Yearly Meeting had "laid down" (eliminated) Cornwall Quarterly Meeting because of its efforts to curb the authority of "select committees" of ministers and elders who judged the behavior of other members, including Friends involved in popular abolitionist movements. Cornwall and Marlborough Monthly Meetings were then attached to Westbury Quarterly Meeting. Two years later, Westbury would suffer its own insurgency led by Marlborough Friends who continued their antislavery activities.[104]

While these disputes certainly interested Amy and Isaac, they were no longer absorbed in the particulars of Friends debates. Indeed, since moving to Rochester, much about their lives had changed. Willet Post would grow up in worlds dramatically transformed from those familiar to his older siblings. The younger Posts had all been raised in farming communities, with conflicts among Quakers a central issue, including Friends' growing involvement in worldly associations. Willet was raised in a thriving urban center, where his father had become a solid middle-class business owner and his parents well-known activists in a variety of causes. Largely removed from conflicts within the Society of Friends—though still influenced by its emphasis on plainness, simplicity, and fairness—Willet was immersed from childhood in debates over abolition, interracial relations, women's rights, and spirituality. A hint of one of the most significant transformations to come arrived shortly after his birth, when Amy heard the joyous news that Frederick Douglass was a free man, his liberty having been purchased by friends in England.[105]

Meanwhile, Isaac, his eighteen-year-old son Jacob, and his nephew Edmund Willis oversaw a thriving apothecary shop. With the Panic of 1837 behind them and Jeffries Hallowell's debts mostly settled, the shop did a "fair bus[iness] and doubtless [a] safe profit[abl]e one" in 1847.[106] Those profits allowed Amy, Sarah, and Mary Dale to keep the domestic sphere in order while ensuring that no slave-produced goods were used in the home and no alcohol served. They regularly prepared the front rooms for WNYASS meetings and the bedrooms for the constant stream of itinerant lecturers, traveling F/friends, and family members visiting the city. And they always made sure that extra bedding, clothes, and food were at hand in case fugitive slaves arrived at their door.

The Posts were happy to hear from sister-in-law Mary Robbins Post in early May, who reported seeing Frederick Douglass, only recently returned from Great Britain, at the annual AASS convention. She noted that he "looked well and was greater than ever" and urged Amy and Isaac to look for his speech in the *National Anti-Slavery Standard*.[107] Yet not everyone was pleased with the enhanced stature Douglass gained through his autobiography and his British tour. Maria Weston Chapman, a powerful force in the Boston circle, was concerned. She had received letter after letter from British women extolling the virtues of "our beloved friend Frederick Douglass."[108] One of them mentioned they were providing financial support for Douglass to launch his own newspaper, news that Chapman passed on to Garrison and Edmund Quincy, who edited the *Liberator* in Garrison's absence. The trio tried to persuade the increasingly famous activist that such a venture would only create greater competition, possibly even diminishing support for the *Liberator* and the *National Anti-Slavery Standard*. They assured Douglass that he was far more valuable as a lecturer than an editor.[109]

Garrison, assuming he had convinced Douglass to remain part of the Boston group, applauded his protégé's rising fortunes as they lectured through Pennsylvania and Ohio that summer. In August 1847, Mary and Joseph Post reported on a rousing antislavery convention in Norristown, Pennsylvania, where the two men spoke to cheering crowds. They noted that Douglass and Garrison would be in western New York by fall.[110]

Douglass enjoyed the tour and made new friends along the way, including Martin Delany, the black editor of the *Mystery*, a Pittsburgh newspaper. When Garrison fell ill in Cleveland, Douglass continued on to western New York, where he joined forces with Charles Lenox Remond for lectures in Buffalo, Rochester, and other towns. Left behind in Ohio, Garrison wondered why Douglass did not write to inquire about his health or confide more about his future plans. Douglass, apparently oblivious to his old friend's concerns, was full of energy when he and Remond arrived in Rochester in mid-September for a two-day WNYASS convention and fair that attracted large mixed-race audiences.[111]

Encouraged by his enthusiastic reception throughout the tour, Douglass was determined to establish his own newspaper and finally revealed his decision to Garrison and other Boston colleagues on his return to that city. When the *Liberator* announced his intentions in its 1 October issue, his local supporters were deeply unhappy. They removed Douglass from his position as an AASS lecturer, leaving him without a salary; and Garrison privately informed friends that Frederick had been "impulsive, inconsiderate," and ungrateful for his early assistance.[112] Clearly Douglass could not remain in Massachusetts if he was going to make a success of his enterprise.

Rochester abolitionists soon heard rumors that the famed orator might relocate to western New York, their joy offsetting the anger of Boston's antislavery elite. While traveling with Remond, Douglass had written Sydney

Gay, editor of the *National Anti-Slavery Standard*, that "the meetings at Rochester were all that we could desire. They continued two days, and were interesting and spirit-stirring to the last."[113] In the fall, Douglass had talked to the Posts about the difficulties of sustaining his current relationship with Garrison; and back on the road, he wrote Amy, detailing his anxieties over his prospects for taking an independent course.[114] On 28 October, with all support from Garrison, the *Liberator*, and the AASS denied him, Frederick confided, "I have finally decided on publishing the *North Star* in Rochester, and to make that city my future home." Hoping to "issue my first number as early as the Middle of November," he mailed out the paper's prospectus from Lynn before traveling to Rochester to set up shop.[115]

By fall, Douglass did, indeed, make Rochester his new home, launching the *North Star* there in December. His presence in the city transformed the lives of local black and white activists, none more so than Amy Post, whose emerging role as a conductor across radical movements would be significantly enhanced. Over the next year, revolutionary events unfolded across Europe and within New York State that would extend her political ties and ensure that the Posts' activist circles became more interracial, their radical vision more international, and their commitment to abolition and racial justice more deeply entwined with women's rights and religious liberty.

5   Orchestrating Change, 1847–1848

· ·

On 3 December 1847, Frederick Douglass celebrated the publication of the
first issue of the *North Star* alongside coeditor William C. Nell and printer
John Dick. Mary and Isaac Gibbs, James P. Morris, and other representatives of the black community were jubilant, as were white allies like the
Posts. The *North Star* brought new energy to Rochester abolitionists, giving
them a powerful voice and a stronger connection to activists in Boston, New
York, Philadelphia, Pittsburgh, the Midwest, and Canada.[1] In the inaugural
issue, Amy Post inserted a call for an upcoming fair "to aid the great work of
emancipation." With twenty-two WNYASS coworkers, she sought donations from "mothers who can feel for the mothers of our own land that are
daily and hourly experiencing the torture of having their children torn
from the sight of their eyes, and the embrace of their love." These items
would be sold on "behalf of more than a million of our sisters, crushed,
abused and bleeding under the lash."[2] In the fair's aftermath, Nell applauded
the effort in the *North Star*. Despite heavy snow, the women made "every
effort" to aid "the cause of bleeding humanity," knowing that "their sisters
at the South are the greatest sufferers by the infernal system of slavery."
Recognizing women's potential, Nell proclaimed, "Impose upon her no
restrictions—clip not the wings of her lofty aspirations for liberty."[3]

Bolstered by the zeal of Douglass and Nell and committed to interracial
organizing, Amy Post emerged as a key player in efforts to transform society
in the late 1840s. Building on her base in the WNYASS and among radical
Quakers, she embraced burgeoning movements for women's rights, workers' rights, and spiritualism without diminishing her commitment to racial
justice. Indeed, by 1848, she viewed demands for racial and gender equality and religious liberty in the United States as part of a global democratic
surge with international critics of American slavery, European revolutionaries, and newly emancipated Caribbean blacks voicing their own demands.
Orchestrating events and transmitting ideas across diverse groups and
organizations, Post expanded her activist worlds, extending her alliances
and friendships with blacks and whites, men and women, Quakers and
non-Quakers, in rural communities, small towns, and cities across the

North. She took on more public roles as well, organizing and speaking at conventions and penning announcements and short articles for the *North Star*.

This burst of activity converged with improved prospects for Amy and Isaac. In spring 1848, business was thriving, and R. G. Dun and Co. reported that Post and Willis's apothecary "sup[lie]d the best in their line." Isaac, his son Jacob, and partner Edmund Willis filled physicians' prescriptions and offered family remedies, while expanding their stock to include more patent medicines as well as daguerreotype supplies.[4] Meanwhile, Amy felt as healthy as she had in years and, with the assistance of Mary Dale and the young Irish servants Sarah Birney and Bridget Head, was able to juggle domestic chores, childcare, and public activities.[5] In the latter, she was often joined by her widowed sister Sarah Hallowell and stepdaughter Mary Hallowell, whose husband's woolen manufactory was flourishing. William Hallowell and Edmund Willis were active in antislavery meetings and conventions as well. The extended Post clan was joined by George and Ann Willets and their daughter Georgianna, Isaac's cousins who had recently settled in Rochester. Isaac's brother Joseph had become more closely tied to Rochester, too, serving as the *North Star* agent for Westbury and the surrounding area.

At the same time, Douglass's arrival enhanced interactions between black and white activists. The WNYASS continued to invite members of both races to attend their lectures and conventions, and more blacks—both locals and visitors—participated in 1848 and after. Similarly, when Douglass spoke at black churches in the city, more whites attended. August 1 celebrations of Emancipation Day attracted large interracial audiences as well. Both white and black women continued to labor at raising funds and consciousness, and WNYASS fair organizers worked especially hard to appeal to both races. Finally, dozens of black and white Underground Railroad conductors established a well-organized network, secreting fugitives in basements, attics, barns, sail lofts, storerooms, and other safe havens, with the *North Star* alerting readers to Rochester's hospitable environs.

Moreover, like Post, Douglass fused campaigns for abolition and racial equality with demands for women's rights and religious liberty. The *North Star* masthead proclaimed these views: "Right Is of No Sex—Truth Is of No Color—God Is the Father of Us All, and All We Are Brethren."[6] Insistence on these intertwined efforts deepened his friendship with the Posts, while the *North Star*'s location a block from the Post and Willis pharmacy and six blocks from 36 Sophia Street nurtured frequent interactions. During

Douglass's first months in the city, before his wife and children arrived from Lynn, the trio spent considerable time together.

The interracial friendships furthered by the presence of Douglass and Nell transformed Amy's activist worlds. In fall 1847, Douglass had persuaded Martin Delany, a medical practitioner and abolitionist publisher in Pittsburgh, and William C. Nell, a free black writer, historian, and antislavery activist in Boston, to join his publishing venture. While Delany remained in Pittsburgh, Nell moved to Rochester along with John Dick, a white English-born printer who provided critical technical skills.[7] Dick boarded with the Douglasses, but Nell moved in with the Posts. Nell almost immediately felt at home at 36 Sophia Street and became a valued member of their extended family. He quickly endeared himself to one-year-old Willet, and thus to Amy, by "playing blindman's bluff in the Post's parlor."[8]

Nell and Post shared a 20 December birthday—he turned thirty-one and she forty-five in 1847—and became fast friends, sharing their political visions as well as their personal hopes and struggles. He undoubtedly told Amy about his father, William Guion Nell, the son of a free black mother and an enslaved father in Charleston, South Carolina. Taken captive on a British ship during the War of 1812, William was released as a free man in Massachusetts four years later.[9] He then married Louisa Marshall and opened a tailor shop in Boston. William Cooper Nell was born in 1816, and a half dozen siblings followed. When William was ten, his father helped found the Massachusetts General Colored Association alongside David Walker and James Barbadoes. Mainly educated at home, Nell attended classes at the African Meeting House from age eleven to thirteen and qualified for a citywide scholastic award. However, it was denied him because of his race.

Amy was impressed by Nell's accomplishments. Despite his limited formal education, he had been steeped in abolition and public service through his father's activist circles. When Garrison launched the *Liberator* in January 1831, William Cooper—then fourteen—worked for him as an errand boy. Before long, the young man was setting type and then writing articles. Nell always carried a small notebook in his pocket to capture scenes, conversations, and events. Increasingly part of the inner circle of Boston abolitionists, he befriended black activists such as Douglass and worked hard to integrate Boston schools and highlight black contributions to the nation. His ideals and talents endeared him to the Posts, as they had to Garrison and Douglass.[10]

Amy Post also hoped to befriend Anna Douglass, Frederick's wife. Anna and the youngest Douglass children arrived in Rochester in March 1848, but the move wrenched Anna away from the close friends she had made in Lynn's black community. The adjustment was made more difficult by the absence of her oldest daughter, Rosetta, who was being educated by Lydia and Abigail Mott in Albany. Her husband's frequent travels added to her burdens as did his decision to reside on the east side of the Genesee River rather than in the west side's black community. Amy invited Anna into the WNYASS circle, but she was not interested in joining a white-dominated society, however progressive its views.[11] Moreover, just as Anna Douglass settled in Rochester, some community leaders voiced concern about one of her husband's *North Star* editorials. In February 1848, Douglass claimed that black churches hurt the cause of racial advancement.[12] Forced to defend his claim a month later at the African Bethel and AME Zion churches, he insisted that while black churches had once been necessary, there were now white-dominated congregations willing to admit African Americans. Continuing to highlight "complexional distinctions" through segregated institutions, he argued, was thus detrimental.[13]

Most local blacks were happy to have Douglass in their midst, but his presence did publicize disagreements that were normally kept within their community. The fact that such disclosures revealed internal conflicts to white audiences concerned some blacks. Yet they also allowed, or forced, white allies to recognize African Americans' complicated understandings of race and racism. Perhaps of special interest to Amy Post was the fact that Douglass and Nell advocated integration, whereas the city's black female abolitionists preferred autonomy.[14] Some African Americans worked with Post and other WNYASS women on fund-raising fairs, and several attended an interracial dinner at the 1848 WNYASS convention, but the women always maintained their own Union Anti-Slavery Society.[15] Given black women's relationships with white women—for whom they often worked as servants, laundresses, or seamstresses—and their well-earned distrust of white men, it is not surprising that they chose to labor in a separate society. Anna Douglass might have helped bridge the gap, as her husband did within the wider antislavery movement, but she, too, seemed more comfortable among women of her own race. Even as the involvement of black men increased in the WNYASS—including barbers James P. Morris and James and Benjamin Cleggett, and hotel owner Roswell Jeffrey—their wives, daughters, or sisters offered only limited support to that society.[16]

Whatever the limits of interracial organizing, Post gained a critical understanding of debates in the black community through her friendships with Douglass and Nell. Nell, especially, confided in Amy about a range of personal and political matters, though the specific content of their discussions was rarely recorded for posterity. We know that Nell largely agreed with Douglass on racial integration; felt strongly about the importance of black history to current campaigns; and developed a deep connection to Amy, her family, and her activist circle.[17] The two surely mulled over ideas about black self-organization, the integration of churches and schools, and the ideological fault lines in black and white communities.

These discussions were eased by Post's astute sensibility to racial dynamics. Douglass had confided in her well before he moved to Rochester. Early on, Amy seemed to consider him a member of her extended family, and he was the same age as her sister Sarah. Nell, too, immediately felt at home in Amy's company and, for years after his return to Boston, he wrote her lengthy and detailed letters about politics, friends, even his love life. William Wells Brown appreciated Amy's empathy, revealing to her painful scenes related to his estranged wife; and Harriet Jacobs, another self-emancipated slave, developed an intimate friendship with Amy when she lived with the Posts in 1849. Indeed, it was to her that Jacobs first confided the bitter truths of her sexual exploitation by an abusive master. Sojourner Truth also befriended Amy and appreciated the material and personal support she and Isaac provided through the 1850s and 1860s.[18] Clearly Post was unusual, even among white abolitionists, in the deep connections she forged with black activists.

Amy Post had more difficulties building connections with local African American women, although she welcomed Douglass's efforts to foster such interactions.[19] Before his arrival, interracial ties among Rochester activists rarely stretched beyond formal settings, such as antislavery conventions, or secret communications related to harboring fugitives. This began to change when the Douglasses hosted interracial gatherings in their home. With Nell as a boarder, the Posts, too, invited black and white activists to Sophia Street. When William's younger sister Frances Nell moved to Rochester in 1848, she was warmly welcomed by Amy and Isaac. A year later, they hosted a party upon her engagement to local barber and abolitionist Benjamin Cleggett.[20]

In addition, black activists from other cities were eager to visit Rochester once Douglass settled there. Such visits became easier as more and more passenger boats plied the Erie Canal and railroad service slowly expanded.[21] On Sunday, 26 March 1848, for example, white abolitionist Jonathan Walker and fugitive slave John S. Jacobs stopped in the city as part of an extended lecture tour. They attracted "a large audience, which spoke well for the course of Anti Slavery in Rochester." According to teacher and abolitionist Julia Wilbur, "One year ago such a meeting could not be seen in R."[22]

For white residents of central and western New York, it was Rochester's shops, mills, and waterfalls that attracted them to the city more than its lectures and conventions. Nonetheless, the WNYASS opened an antislavery office and reading room in February 1848, "where our friends from the surrounding country can gain information in regard to the progress of our cause, and supply themselves with books and pamphlets." Located above the *North Star* office on Buffalo Street, the reading room was also a fundraising venture, with Amy Post and her WNYASS sisters providing "a rich array of Fancy and useful articles" for sale.[23] The space was first managed by Catherine Fish Stebbins, then by Amy's dear friend Sarah Owen, and later by John and then Harriet Jacobs.[24]

The reading room did not fill WNYASS coffers, however, and like most local or regional antislavery societies, the organization depended largely on female fund-raisers. In 1848, Post led these efforts, laboring alongside a bevy of family and neighbors, including stepdaughter Mary and sister Sarah as well as the old F/friends and ex-evangelicals who had come together in the WNYASS. Many of the Quaker women involved in the WNYASS lived or had lived in central New York, where they attended Farmington or Junius Monthly Meetings. Huldah Anthony was one of the most recent migrants, having moved with her husband, Asa, from Farmington to Gates, on Rochester's outskirts. Having met Amy years earlier at quarterly meetings, she quickly joined her activist circle. The ties among urban, small town, and rural activists were dense and continually reinforced. In addition, nearly all of Post's female coworkers were married to men who advocated abolition, religious liberty, and women's rights. Thus, even as women performed gender-specific tasks, they claimed an equal role as decision makers and officeholders in antislavery societies. While women had not yet achieved full equality in the WNYASS, they advanced their position considerably in the late 1840s.

Women in the Union Anti-Slavery Society, including barber Eliza Johnson and Mary Gibbs, shared the burden of fund-raising. They were joined by dozens of women from African Bethel and AME Zion churches, the latter located just blocks from the Post home. Post met these women at antislavery events and, after November 1847, from time to time at Douglass's home. On at least one occasion, Mary Gibbs and her husband invited the Posts to their home, and the Posts would certainly have reciprocated.[25] Like their white counterparts, many members of the Union Anti-Slavery Society were married to male abolitionists. Still, of the six black men who served as officers of the WNYASS in 1848, none were joined by wives, sisters, or daughters.

The WNYASS did not publish a membership roster and listed its many officers without racial or marital descriptors. Thus, in 1848, the thirty-eight individuals on the executive committee were listed in the *North Star* in seemingly random order. Husbands and wives, parents and children, and siblings were separated, each individual—black or white, male or female— appearing as an autonomous person. Nonetheless, the list contains several activist couples, with Amy and seven other white women serving alongside their husbands that year. Similarly, sons and daughters served alongside parents, and sets of siblings also appeared. The half-dozen black members of the committee, all men, included local activists as well as national figures like Charles Lenox Remond.[26]

The *North Star* covered the WNYASS as well as developments in Rochester's black community in rich detail, adding depth to the announcements and reports published in the *Liberator* and the *National Anti-Slavery Standard*. Coverage in those and other reform papers also expanded as the *North Star* provided reports on developments in western New York and as more national figures attended conventions in the region. Such coverage integrated the Posts and their coworkers more fully into activist networks from New England and the Mid-Atlantic states through the Midwest. Nell and Douglass also spread the word about their Rochester allies at the National Convention of Colored People and similar gatherings.

The *North Star* also broadened readers' understanding of their activist labors by highlighting national and international developments. In 1848, WNYASS members eagerly followed reports of protests against the U.S. war with Mexico at home and abroad and read speeches that denounced the proslavery intent of warmongers. Douglass provided riveting accounts of dramatic events in the West Indies, Ireland, the British Isles, and across Europe as well, providing even those who never traveled far from home with a transatlantic perspective. In April 1848, Post and her coworkers certainly agreed with Douglass's reaction to revolutionary developments in France. He declared the uprisings "a bolt of living thunder": "Thanks to steam navigation and electric wires, we can almost hear the words uttered, and see the deeds done as they transpire. A revolution now cannot be confined to the place or the people where it may commence, but flashes with lightning speed from heart to heart, from land to land, until it has traversed the globe." Celebrating the efforts of "the humble poor, the toil-worn laborer, the oppressed and the plundered" to overthrow "the despots of Europe, the

Tories of England, and the slaveholders of America [who] are astonished, confused, and terrified," he insisted that in the United States "only Negroes and Abolitionists" can truly rejoice over developments in Europe.[27]

For the Posts and their allies, whose only international travel might be to Canada, the *North Star* ensured that international events became integral to antislavery discourse and debate. Thus, when a local committee of arrangements began planning a "Sympathy with France" meeting for 9 May, abolitionists worried that many of the politicians and merchants involved were dedicated only to liberty for whites. The new French government had abolished slavery in its West Indies colonies, but the committee debated whether Douglass should even be invited to speak.[28] Once it added the famed abolitionist to the schedule, area activists eagerly joined some six thousand men, women, and children to cheer the revolution abroad. Claiming that the hearts of "working-men and mechanics . . . vibrate in sympathy with the grand movement of France," Douglass rejoiced that "the Provisional Government [has also] . . . set in operation measures which must bring about the entire overthrow of Slavery in all her dominions."[29] Like Douglass, the Posts viewed this emancipation, combined with the recent U.S. victory over Mexico, as damning evidence of their own nation's reactionary stance on race.

The Foreign News section of the *North Star* rapidly expanded as Douglass and Nell applauded rebels in Ireland, Chartists in England, abolitionists in Denmark, and revolutionaries across Europe. With local abolitionists imbibing vivid reports from Europe, they imagined changes there converging with their own desire for racial, gender, and economic justice. For WNYASS women especially, the accounts of French and German women demanding rights set their own work in a more global context. In June 1848, the *North Star* announced that "the 'Address of the Anti-Slavery Women of Western New York,' has been separately printed and circulated in England, with the view of helping the cause along."[30] To expand their transatlantic ties, Post and her coworkers also called on their sisters in New York State to send "contributions of every description" to the "noble-hearted women" of England, including the Misses Griffiths of Kent, who would soon make their way to Rochester. In letters to family and friends, the Posts and other WNYASS members eagerly discussed international developments and sought updates from antislavery lecturers and convention speakers as well as the press.[31]

Revolutions and emancipations abroad thus strengthened the convictions of radicals at home, whether among Quakers, abolitionists, or advocates of women's rights. In June 1848, long-simmering tensions among Hicksites erupted. The Hicksite Meetinghouse in Farmington had been closed to antislavery speakers for several years. It did open its doors for Douglass in fall 1847 but continued to lock out other abolitionists.[32] The following June, the GYM decided to disband Michigan Quarterly Meeting for eliminating its select committee of elders and ministers despite opposition from many members. In response, some two hundred Friends, about half of those in attendance, walked out and gathered to form a more progressive meeting. The dissidents included Rhoda DeGarmo, who had been serving as clerk of the meeting.[33] Lucretia and James Mott, who were attending GYM, joined the dissidents' gathering and then traveled to "all radical quarters" in the ensuing weeks.[34] They stopped first in Rochester, where they surely told the Posts about the latest insurgency among Friends. Lucretia later wrote friends in Scotland, "Agitation is in all the Churches—ours seems rocked to its centre."[35]

After leaving Rochester, the Motts visited Seneca Indians on the Cattaraugus Reservation near Buffalo, where the Posts were well known. The Seneca were in the midst of a major political transformation in 1848, as some leaders sought to replace the traditional clan-based system of government with an elective form based on a written constitution. In Mott's view, this effort suggested that Indians were "imitating the movements of France and all Europe, in seeking larger liberty—more independence."[36] Yet the Seneca did not need inspiration from Europe, having fought for decades to keep their land and sustain their independent existence.[37] Indeed, by adopting a new electoral process, the Seneca eroded the traditional authority of clan mothers to select chiefs for life and depose them when necessary. While women still had to approve land sales, other matters were to be determined by male voters alone. Mott did not immediately appear to recognize the ways that the proposed changes would undermine Seneca women's power, but the women themselves realized the risk and sought to protect their traditional authority.[38] Just a few weeks later, Lucretia might have thought differently about the situation.

In July, the Motts returned to the home of her sister Martha Wright in Auburn. Soon after, Lucretia and Martha went for tea at the Waterloo home of F/friend Jane Hunt, along with Mary Ann M'Clintock and Elizabeth Cady Stanton, who had moved to the neighboring town of Seneca Falls the previous May. Stanton and Mott were happy to reconnect after meeting in London and Boston in 1840–41. While the four Quaker women likely planned on discussing Mott's recent travels and developments among the Hicksites,

Stanton had her own agenda. As she later wrote, "I poured out the torrent of my long accumulating discontent, with such vehemence and indignation that I stirred myself, as well as the rest of the party, to do and dare anything."[39]

Responding to Stanton's grievances, the group organized a convention, an obvious step for Mott and M'Clintock, who had substantial experience with antislavery meetings. Proceeding quickly to ensure Mott's presence, the group sent an announcement to the *Seneca County Courier* of a "Woman's Rights Convention . . . to discuss the social, civil, and religious condition and rights of women," to be held 19 and 20 July.[40] Over the next two weeks, this circle, aided by M'Clintock's daughters Elizabeth and Mary Ann, organized the convention and drafted a Declaration of Sentiments.[41]

News of the convention soon reached Rochester. Mott sent an announcement to Frederick Douglass, who had applauded the New York legislature's passage of the Married Women's Property Act three months earlier.[42] Douglass was invited to participate and reported to Elizabeth M'Clintock that he would be bringing "one or two more of the Post family" with him.[43] Early on 19 July, a clear and sunny morning, Frederick Douglass, Amy Post, Sarah Hallowell, Mary Hallowell, and their friend Catherine Fish Stebbins headed to Seneca Falls, no doubt speculating along the fifty-mile route about the issues to be raised there.[44]

The Rochester circle joined the proceedings alongside large contingents from Waterloo and Seneca Falls. They met many F/friends—mostly Hicksite but also a few Orthodox—who constituted at least a quarter of the participants. These Quakers had already demanded greater rights for women in Friends meetings and had spoken, voted, and held office in the WNYASS. Nearly all the Hicksites had joined the dissidents during the recent upheaval in GYM. Many were also well aware of Priscilla Cadwalader's painful experience at the hands of an abusive husband, Quaker critics, and the Indiana courts. In addition, one of Amy's sisters had recently been abandoned by her husband, making issues of marital rights and custody especially compelling for the Post family.[45]

For radical Quakers as for Douglass, the Seneca Falls convention served not as an introduction to women's rights but as another step in the long fight for sex equality. Others in attendance were addressing these issues for the first time, at least in public. To ensure that these women were heard, the discussion on the first day was reserved for women. Even Stanton was nervous, having far less experience with public meetings than did her co-organizers. Nonetheless, she read out the Declaration of Sentiments to the assembled participants. It opened with the now famous proclamation: "We declare these truths to be self-evident, that all men and women are created equal." The list of grievances and resolutions that followed framed the two-day meeting.[46]

While the Declaration did not refer to international issues, Post, Douglass, Mott, and other activists at Seneca Falls likely envisioned the convention as an extension of revolutionary movements elsewhere in the world. Similarly, although neither race nor slavery was noted in the Declaration, the abolitionist labors of many participants formed the canvas on which women's rights came to life. Indeed, one of the resolutions was taken nearly verbatim from the 1837 Anti-Slavery Convention of American Women; and Elizabeth M'Clintock and Mott, both key players there, contributed to the Declaration of Sentiments in other ways as well.[47] Stanton brought a commitment to legal equality to the document, inspired by learning about law in the office of her father, a lawyer and judge in Johnstown, New York. A fierce advocate of married women's property rights, she also included a demand for women's enfranchisement among the resolutions. The idea was not entirely new; the Reverend Samuel J. May had called for women's enfranchisement in his 1845 sermon and pamphlet, *Rights and Condition of Women*, sold at WNYASS fairs. And many female abolitionists had fought for the right to speak, vote, and hold office in antislavery societies. In addition, three petitions to the New York State Constitutional Convention of 1846 called for female suffrage, though it is unclear whether the women at Seneca Falls were aware of them. They certainly knew, however, about the claims for black male suffrage made to the constitutional convention and the frustration of African Americans and abolitionists when delegates refused to remove the discriminatory property qualification.[48]

Although calls for women's rights had been made in other forums, this was the first convention focused solely on the issue, and many in the audience seemed hesitant to voice their views publicly. Still, lively debates ensued, with Mott, Stanton, Post, Stebbins, and Douglass eagerly joining the discussion.[49] The speakers agreed on many issues, but there was contention over Stanton's insistence that women seek equality at the ballot box. The disagreement was rooted not in critics' concern that the claim was too radical but rather in antislavery politics.[50]

Garrisonians, such as Mott and Post, argued that since the U.S. government was proslavery, abolitionists should refuse to participate in electoral politics. Quakers also opposed participation in a government that condoned war, which kept most male Friends from the ballot box in the 1840s. Stanton, on the other hand, embraced the political process that led to the recent Married Women's Property Law in New York State and was influenced by her husband Henry Stanton's ardent support for the Liberty Party. By the time of the Seneca Falls convention, the Liberty Party had largely merged into the Free Soil Party; and Free Soilers and their relatives constituted a significant contingent at the convention. Indeed, the Free Soilers formed the largest group from Seneca Falls itself. Moreover, even abolitionists and Quakers who opposed participation in partisan politics supported women's right to vote and hold office in antislavery societies and believed in principle that women should have the same rights as men. Thus, their critiques of voting were born not of a hesitant conservatism but rather from a deep and abiding suspicion of state power. Ultimately, the women's suffrage resolution was approved, and twenty-five Quakers—including Mott and Post—were among the one hundred signers of the final Declaration of Sentiments.[51]

At the end of the convention, participants appointed a committee of five women, including Amy Post, Elizabeth M'Clintock, and Stanton, to prepare the proceedings for publication in the *North Star*.[52] They also agreed to meet again in Rochester in two weeks.[53] An organizing committee was quickly assembled, headed by Post and her stepdaughter, Mary Hallowell, who invited three Rochester friends—Sarah Fish, Sarah Owen, and Rhoda DeGarmo—to join them. Like the Seneca Falls organizing committee, this one included four progressive Quakers and one non-Quaker, the ex-evangelical Sarah Owen. In this case, however, all five had worked together in the WNYASS.[54]

Not surprisingly given their abolitionist commitments, the women planned the Rochester Woman's Rights Convention for 2 August, the day after Emancipation Day. Douglass and Nell were among those organizing events to celebrate "the day which gave freedom to 800,000 human beings in the West Indian Isles" and to offer "a tribute of gratitude for the recent French demonstration of 'Liberty, Equality, Fraternity.'"[55] On 1 August, a "fine" morning, the Posts likely joined the hundreds of neighbors and visiting dignitaries who gathered at Ford Street Baptist Church for opening exercises.[56] Black Baptist James Sharpe convened the celebration, while twenty vice presidents represented a range of occupations, churches, towns, and cities. The Reverend Thomas James returned for the occasion, and other vice presidents traveled from Ohio, Illinois, and Philadelphia. James P. Morris and William Nell served as secretaries, recording the day's events.[57]

At noon, a procession of some five hundred men, women, and children paraded from Ford Street to Washington Square, led by three honorary marshals: Eliza Johnson, Henry Scott, and John Douglass. Scott, a barber, and Douglass, a fireman, were black homeowners and activists, while Johnson, also a barber, boarded with David Ray, a barber and lay minister, and his wife, Phebe, a cook.[58] Festooned with banners and bright ribbons, the marchers included musicians, clergymen, and representatives from the area's black benevolent societies and the local "colored school."[59] At Washington Square, Adams' Brass Band played "La Marseillaise," and the audience swelled to over two thousand people. A prayer was offered, a local choir sang "Ode to Freedom," and the English and French Emancipation Acts were read.[60]

Then Frederick Douglass rose to speak. The event, organized to celebrate the tenth anniversary of the "peaceful emancipation" of "eight hundred thousand slaves" in the West Indies, "is not one of color," he proclaimed, "but of universal man—from the purest black to the clearest white, welcome, welcome! . . . I extend to each and to all, of every complexion . . . a heartfelt welcome." After describing the horrors of slavery, Douglass insisted, "The long pent up energies of human rights and sympathies, are at last let loose upon the world. The grand conflict of the angel Liberty with the monster Slavery, has at last come. The globe shakes with the contest."[61]

As the speeches and entertainment continued through the afternoon, Eliza Johnson, Mary Gibbs, and other members of the Union Anti-Slavery Society hosted a fund-raising fair, while others prepared for an evening ball.[62] Meanwhile, Amy Post and her co-organizers headed to Protection Hall, where the Mechanics Mutual Protection Association provided space for them to meet. The reform-oriented Unitarian church, just a block east of Post's home, offered to host the Rochester Woman's Rights Convention; and Mott, Stanton, and the M'Clintocks all agreed to attend.[63] Seeking to broaden the woman's rights agenda approved at Seneca Falls to reflect their vision of holistic change, the organizers sent a committee to investigate the wrongs of the laboring classes and "to invite the oppressed portion of the community" to attend the convention "and take part in its deliberations."[64] The organizers appeared to focus specifically on working-class women, rather than African Americans, though the two groups overlapped considerably. Their official invitations to blacks went to Nell, Douglass, and Charles Lenox Remond although they certainly hoped other participants in the rousing Emancipation Day celebration would join them.

The claims of European revolutionaries may have stirred organizers' interest in working women's rights, but Post and her coworkers were well aware of the economic liabilities and challenges of being female. Two of

Post's sisters (and Mary Hallowell's aunts) had faced financial ruin because of the actions of their husbands. Sarah Fish's husband, Benjamin, had gone through bankruptcy and been publicly shamed by Rochester Monthly Meeting's investigation. The widow Sarah Owen supported herself through needlework and nursing, while Rhoda DeGarmo worked alongside her husband, Elias, running their farm. To highlight such economic issues, the Rochester women expanded the Seneca Falls call from discussing "the social, civil, and religious conditions and rights of women" to demanding "the Rights of women, Politically, Socially, Religiously, and Industrially."[65]

In another innovation, Post and her co-organizers nominated an all-female slate of officers. The committee chose three radical Quakers as secretaries—Catherine Fish Stebbins, Sarah Hallowell, and Elizabeth M'Clintock. They reached beyond that tight circle, however, to nominate two former evangelicals—Abigail Bush and Laura Murray—as president and vice president. Still, these two women, both white, were part of the same activist network. Bush had withdrawn from Brick Presbyterian Church and joined the WNYASS in 1842. Murray had worked with her husband in moral reform societies before joining the WNYASS in the mid-1840s and then the Sodus Bay Phalanx.

Not yet certain what the convention would bring, "an attentive audience" crowded the First Unitarian Church on the morning of 2 August, many exhilarated by the previous day's events. Post called the meeting to order, and the Reverend William Wicher, minister of the antislavery Free Will Baptist Church, offered a prayer.[66] Amy then read the nominations for convention officers. She was likely surprised when Elizabeth M'Clintock "declined accepting the office" of secretary "on the ground of being unprepared to have a woman the presiding officer." At Seneca Falls, her father and James Mott had presided, even though women had dominated the discussions. Mary Ann M'Clintock, Elizabeth's mother, was also opposed to the idea, as were Mott and Stanton, who declared it "a most hazardous experiment to have a woman President and stoutly opposed it." Post "assured them that by the same power by which they had resolved, declared, discussed, and debated, they could also preside at a public meeting."[67] The audience, including many relatives and F/friends, agreed, so Abigail Bush accepted the position, and her outspoken opponents stayed to observe.

Sarah Hallowell began reading the minutes of the preliminary meeting but could not be clearly heard in the overflowing church, so Sarah Anthony Burtis, an experienced Quaker teacher with a powerful voice, stepped forward and finished the job. When Abigail Bush took the chair, she acknowledged the challenges before them: "Friends, we present ourselves here before you, as an oppressed class, with trembling frames and faltering tongues, and we do not expect to be able to speak so as to be heard by all at first, but we trust we shall have the sympathy of the audience, and that you will bear with our weakness, now in the infancy of the movement. Our trust in the omnipotency of Right is our only faith that we shall succeed."[68] There was little need for concern, however, as the audience, including Mott, Stanton, and the M'Clintocks, joined the lively debates.

While this was a woman's rights convention, the organizers' commitment to abolition was clearly evident, from the selection of officers to the minister who offered a prayer and the opening speaker, William C. Nell. He stepped forward to commend "the energies and rare devotion of Woman in every good cause," adding "that he should never cease to award the grateful homage of his heart for their zeal in behalf of the oppressed class with which he stood identified"—enslaved and free blacks. Despite his good intentions, Nell was chided by Mott for employing "the language of flattering compliments," though she assumed he indulged in it "unaware." She assured him that it was often wielded to demean and trivialize the female sex. She also challenged his description of man as "a tyrant," claiming "it is power that makes him tyrannical, and woman is equally so when she has irresponsible power."[69] Stanton rose next and read the Declaration of Sentiments. Noting that critics at Seneca Falls had kept quiet during the convention only to denounce the proceedings afterward, she asked that those "who did not agree with [us] in [our] notions of the Rights of Woman" would "make their objections" known then and there.[70]

Several gentlemen obliged. Mr. Colton of New Haven, Connecticut, claimed that "he loved the ladies as well as they love themselves" but insisted that a woman's "proper sphere" was "at home, *it* was her empire and her throne." He was particularly opposed to her "occupying the pulpit." Mott advised Colton "to read his bible again," insisting he would find nothing there "to prohibit her being a religious teacher." Next, Rochester temperance and antislavery advocate William C. Bloss claimed that "good results would attend the exercise of the elective franchise by woman" but nonetheless "enquired if there was not a natural disqualification," since "boys and girls exhibit dissimilarity of taste in the choice of play things," distinctions that seemingly only increased with age.[71]

Bloss's comments inspired Rebecca M. Sanford, a young Quaker bride on her way to Michigan, to take the floor. For twenty minutes she "eloquently advocated the just claim of woman to an equality with man."[72] "From Semiramis [legendary Queen of Assyria] to [Queen] Victoria," she declared, "we have found the Women of History equal to the emergency before them!" Sanford was hopeful that "through these all-stirring inspirations of rights," women might "finish the work so nobly commenced by man—to wipe from our national escutcheon that spot—*slavery*." In addition, she argued, with women's rights in hand, the "honest earnings of dependents will be paid; popular demagogues crushed; impostures unpatronized; true genius seriously encouraged; and, above all, pawned integrity redeemed."[73]

Despite enthusiastic applause, abolitionist Milo D. Codding was not convinced. Although aware of women's many contributions to the cause as a member of the WNYASS, he objected to women's enfranchisement. He claimed it was "sufficient for women to vote through their fathers, husbands, and brothers." This time Douglass responded, noting "that the only true basis of rights was the capacity of individuals, and as for himself, he dared not claim a right which he would not concede to Woman."[74]

The afternoon session began with Amy Post reading "a long and interesting letter" from abolitionist and physician James Caleb Jackson, who, like Amy, emphasized the connections between women's work, women's health, and women's rights. Sarah Owen then read an address on female wage earners in which she "portray[ed] the evils to which women are subject." Arguing that the problem of women's economic hardship is rooted in "immemorial" notions of her physical and intellectual weakness and man-made laws that strip her of the rewards of "her own hard-earned toil," Owen called for better education, more equitable laws, and the right to labor in occupations currently "monopolized" by men, including bookkeepers and store clerks.[75] Two other working-class women also spoke. Mrs. Roberts, the wife of machinist and prison reformer George H. Roberts and a WNYASS supporter, reported on the average wage for seamstresses and the deductions for food and board that often left workers penniless. These conditions made it nearly impossible for a woman to maintain her health, much less a family, in the few occupations reserved for her sex. Widow Ann Galloy "corroborated the statement, having herself experienced some of the oppressions of this portion of our citizens."[76]

Post then presented a series of resolutions that expanded on the issues raised at Seneca Falls. The first suggested practical means to achieve women's right to vote—petitioning the state legislature for that right, "every year, until our prayer be granted." The second claimed that "woman, being taxed equally with man, ought not to be deprived of an equal representation in government." Clearly, radical Friends had gotten over any concerns about granting women suffrage. Other resolutions spoke to women's legal status. One labeled the husband's "legal right to hire out his wife for service, collect her wages, and appropriate it to his own exclusive and independent benefit" a "hideous custom" that reduced women "almost to the condition of a slave." Another resolved "to overthrow this barbarous and unrighteous law; and conjure women no longer to promise obedience in the marriage covenant," a practice already embraced by Quakers.[77]

Perhaps it was at this point that Post read a comment she had written out on the back of a prospectus for the *North Star.* Claiming "that there are men in our own city who have become so imbued with the [idea] of man's superiority . . . that he does assume the prerogative of judging for his wife in everything[,] almost even she needs some addition to her wardrobe—he must be the judge [before] he will allow her the means to make the purchase." But, she argued, in "reality it as rightfully belongs to her as to him— she either received it from her inheritance or contributed her ful[l] share of labour to produce it." She also denounced men who spent their wives' earnings on drink and then turned on them with "kicks and unkind words." Perhaps thinking of her sister Elizabeth Mott, whose husband abandoned her, Post concluded, "I have been supprized [*sic*] some times to see how supercilious some men do grow after marriage. . . . This is all calculated to bring about a very unharmonious state of society."[78]

Still, as deeply as Amy cared about the plight of abused wives, she was far more concerned about the brutalities faced by slaves. The abolitionist convictions of Post and her co-organizers inspired a resolution that incorporated all women, regardless of race, into the movement. It is "the duty of woman," they proclaimed, "whatever her complexion, to assume, as soon as possible, her true position of equality in the social circle, the Church, and the State."[79] While the term *complexion* had multiple meanings, skin color was its primary definition, and Douglass regularly used the word as a synonym for race. Just the previous day, he had welcomed women and men "of every complexion" to the Emancipation Day celebration. Mott reinforced the point, "compar[ing] the condition of woman with that of the free colored population," emphasizing "the progress they had made within the past few years, [and] urging imitation of their perseverance through opposition and prejudice."[80]

While race was rarely mentioned—or its discussion was not reported— at Seneca Falls, speakers at Rochester regularly referred to free blacks, slavery, and abolition. Nell, Mott, Sanford, and Douglass all compared the plight of women to that of people of color, and Post insisted that the movement must embrace women of all complexions. At least half the women who signed the WNYASS "Address of Anti-Slavery Women" in winter 1848 attended the Rochester convention, and many participants followed black women's activism in the antislavery press, especially via the *North Star*. Women of the AME Zion Church had been especially active in asserting their rights. In 1844 and 1848, at the AME's Quadrennial Conference, women recruited male delegates to raise the issue of licensing female preachers and to recognize women's critical role in the church. Although their calls for rights were defeated, they caused "quite a sensation" and set the foundation for future changes.[81]

Still, despite the attention to race at the Rochester convention, it does not appear that any black women spoke at the 2 August meeting.[82] Certainly the secretaries would have noted if Eliza Johnson, Mary Gibbs, or another woman of color offered remarks. Perhaps when organizers invited black men and white working-class women to speak, they also reached out to women from the Union Anti-Slavery Society or local black churches. If so, none apparently chose to participate.

At the final evening session, audience members voted to approve the new resolutions with only "two or three dissenting voices." Then participants were given the opportunity to add their signatures to the Declaration of Sentiments; 107 did so. The convention then adjourned.[83] While the list of Rochester signatories was never published and ultimately disappeared, it purportedly included "large numbers of influential men and women" from the city and surrounding towns. Organizers and officers who had not attended the Seneca Falls convention eagerly signed, and their husbands—including Isaac Post and William Hallowell—likely did so as well. Buffalo abolitionist Nathaniel Potter; fifteen-year-old Ellen Sully; and Daniel, Lucy, and Mary Anthony added their signatures as well.[84] Many Rochester speakers, including Nell, Sanford, Roberts, and Galloy, probably followed suit. And perhaps Mary Dale or Sarah Birney, Amy's employees and friends, added their signatures, or William Nell's sister Frances.[85]

We can never identify all of those who attended these two 1848 conventions, but within three short weeks that summer, the participants crafted an agenda that would shape the woman's rights movement for the next decade and a half. Many of the central issues were laid out at Seneca Falls, with Rochester activists heightening attention to both working-class women and women of color. The Rochester organizers also ensured that women would preside over the movement, continuing to chair conventions from Ohio to Massachusetts.

Moreover, despite the acerbic reports and ridicule that appeared in some newspapers, several local editors voiced at least mild support for the women's efforts.[86] Mixing satire and praise, Rochester's *Daily Democrat* claimed that convention participants considered "some new, impractical, absurd, and ridiculous proposition[s]" but applauded their introduction of one "practical good—the adoption of measures for the relief and amelioration of the condition of indigent, industrious, laboring females." The *Daily Advertiser* claimed, tongue in cheek, that this was "an age of 'democratic progression,' of *equality* and *fraternization*—the age when all colors and sexes, bond and free, black and white, male and female, are, as they of right ought to be, tending downward and upward toward the level of equality." While the reporter suggested that men and women exchange breeches and petticoats, he concluded that "the proceedings throughout were of a highly interesting character, and the discussions of the convention evinced a talent for forensic efforts seldom surpassed."[87]

Fellow activists and reform-minded editors offered more fully laudatory comments. Nathaniel Potter, who attended numerous conventions in 1848, wrote Isaac Post that "with the exception of the Buffalo free soil convention, I have not since at Rochester, seen a greater manifestation of talent than I did at the Woman's Rights convention in the Unitarian Church. Indeed, being in company with so much talent in female frame was calculated (as it did) to make me feel my own inferiority in the scale of intellect."[88] The *National Reformer*, published in Auburn, praised the Declaration of Sentiments as a document that "would do honor to any deliberative body ever assembled in this country" and claimed that the Rochester convention was "characterized by a zeal, spirit, talent, and enthusiasm rarely excelled in conventions of any character among us."[89] The *North Star* applauded the organizers and speakers and printed the official proceedings, while the *Liberator* offered detailed reports and enthusiastic praise.[90]

In the following months, white and black women sustained their campaigns for rights. Although their efforts were generally undertaken separately, they were not unconnected. For instance, when African American women insisted on their right to speak and vote in abolition meetings and colored conventions, they now received enthusiastic support from Douglass, Nell, and Remond, all of whom participated in woman's rights conventions and were friends and confidantes of Post.

Black and white women's campaigns overlapped in other important ways. On 20 July 1848, as Douglass defended women's enfranchisement at Seneca Falls, black women in Cincinnati spoke for the first time at a meeting of the United Colored Americans Association, which sponsored cemeteries and civic events in the city. Although the women in Cincinnati did not demand rights or challenge the gender order, Douglass praised their enterprise in the *North Star*.[91] A month after the Rochester convention, Douglass and Martin Delany called for the rights of women to speak and vote at the National Convention of Colored Freemen in Cleveland, Ohio. A heated debate erupted, and in its midst, Douglass—chair of the convention—called on Rebecca Sanford to present the case for women's rights. Sanford reiterated the claims she had made at Rochester, but cognizant of her sex and her whiteness, she ended on a deferential note. The delegates ultimately proclaimed, "We fully believe in the equality of the sexes."[92]

Reports of these events excited activists like Post, despite the racial divide. Several of the national woman's rights conventions held in the 1850s included resolutions on race, though only a handful of black women participated. Perhaps more confounding to Post and her allies, in 1849, when African American women demanded the right to speak and vote at the State Convention of Colored Citizens, they compared themselves to "the ladies of England, Scotland, Ireland and France," who "made strenuous efforts in behalf of right, liberty and equality." But they did not note the similar efforts of women at Seneca Falls and Rochester.[93]

In fall 1848, Post looked forward to Douglass's return from the National Convention of Colored Freemen in Cleveland, eager to discuss developments there. However, he was immediately caught up in a conflict over his daughter Rosetta's schooling. The nine-year-old had easily passed the entrance exam for Miss Seward's Seminary and begun the term while Douglass was away. Upon his return, he learned that Rosetta was hidden away in an alcove rather than sitting in the room with other students.[94] When an outraged Douglass confronted Lucilia Tracy, she polled the opinions of her students and their parents. Only one—Horatio Warner, editor of the conservative *Rochester Courier*—publicly objected, but that was sufficient for Tracy to remove Douglass's daughter from school.[95] The incident angered abolitionists both white and black and outraged Douglass as well as Nell, who had battled segregation in Boston schools.

Addressing inequalities of class proved more successful, as local women formed a branch of the Working Women's Protective Union (WWPU) in September 1848. The organizers, including Post, declared that "the laws of nature and of nature's God, entitle women equally with men to the products of their labor or its equivalent." Signers of the union's constitution agreed to "associate ourselves together for the purpose of our individual and collective benefit and protection." Mrs. George Roberts was chosen president, Mrs. Charlotte Cavan vice president, Sarah Owen secretary, and Post treasurer. The Union met semimonthly, and men were invited to attend the meetings for double the fee for women—two cents each—the "inequality of assessment" to cease only when "women receive an equal remuneration for the same labor performed as men."[96] It is not clear whether Charlotte Cavan had joined Mrs. Roberts at the August woman's rights convention, but the thirty-three-year-old mother of three had worshipped alongside Sarah Owen and Abigail Bush at Brick Presbyterian Church in the early 1840s. She likely worked alongside her husband, James, a tailor; and the two would join the Unitarian Church in the 1850s, home to many abolitionists and women's rights advocates.[97]

Throughout the fall, the WWPU met biweekly on Friday afternoons or evenings at Protection Hall. Announcements appeared in the *North Star* and the *Daily Advertiser*, urging "all interested in raising woman from her present state of degradation" to attend.[98] News of the union appeared erratically after that fall, but members continued to produce resolutions for woman's rights conventions and send letters to reform papers. They later petitioned the state legislature, demanding that married women be granted full rights to control their property and wages. In addition, women in the region wrote Sarah Owen for advice on organizing similar societies.[99]

Post, too, was called on to advance the women's rights agenda. In September 1848, Stanton wrote Amy, noting how well "our conventions both went off." Asking "What are we to do next?" she proposed "a simultaneous petitioning for this right [suffrage] among women of the several states" and wondered whether it might be wise "to have an agent to travel all over the country & lecture on the subject." Stanton suggested Lucy Stone and thought Amy, who knew Stone personally, could broach the idea with her. Stanton also apologized for "my foolish conduct in regard to the President of the convention at R. The result proved that your judgment was good, & Mrs. Bush discharged her duties so well that I was really quite delighted."[100]

In early October, Mott asked Stanton if she had written to "Rochester [to] stir up those women to their duties?"[101] However, Amy did not need outside encouragement to "stir up" local women. Considering, like Mott, that women's rights and abolition were intertwined, she had published a letter in the *North Star* on 1 September 1848, urging the women of western New York to continue their work "for the cause of the oppressed." She lauded "the pleasure of meeting once a week" at the antislavery reading room "with the free and cheerful spirits of such men and women as are engaged in this holy and unselfish cause. . . . Oh, the blessedness of Anti-Slavery!" she proclaimed. "Even the broad Atlantic forms no barrier to this expansive work of reciprocal righteousness, for we see a noble band of trans-Atlantic women . . . not only sympathizing, but co-operating with us."[102]

Sarah Thayer, an old F/friend from Ledyard, was inspired by Post's efforts, praising the reading room in particular. She considered "giv[ing] our attention to the constant supply of articles of usefulness, Books of information etc, keeping on hand goods that we might sell on commission or make up for a yearly exhibition" even more fruitful than "a thing so novel and *lottery like* as a fair." She was, however, too burdened at the moment with Friends' investigations of her daughters Abby and Phebe Thayer to take part in the work. Here, too, Sarah planned to follow Amy's path. "I have no unity with the friends who sit as judges," she insisted; the only question is whether we should "ask for a release" or "wait for them to sit in judgment."[103]

Plenty of other antislavery women in western and central New York took up the mantle and organized fourteen antislavery fairs and eleven stores for the sale of antislavery items over the next six months. To stock them, WNYASS women produced endless streams of hats, scarves, handkerchiefs, embroidery, infant wear, and other goods. They arranged for space at civic halls and churches; printed notices and posted fliers; gathered baskets of fruits and vegetables; baked cakes and pies; sorted items sent from nearby towns and from England, Scotland, and Ireland; and decorated halls and tables. On the day of each fair, local women rose early; arranged the goods and set out plates of cheese, pickles, dried beef, ham, and turkey; then spent hours cajoling customers, refreshing food items, and counting change.[104]

Amy's commitment to the reading room on Thursdays, the WWPU on alternate Fridays, numerous antislavery fairs over the course of the year, a house filled with family and friends, and a year-old son and two teenage boys was only possible with help on the home front. Nell attested to the devoted labors of Birney and Dale, who cooked, cleaned, and laundered for the Post family. Nell himself was happy to care for Willie, now eighteen months old, as was Sarah Hallowell, who continued to live with her sister, and stepdaughter Mary Hallowell, who lived nearby.[105] Of course, Nell, Sarah, and Mary were also deeply engaged with antislavery efforts. Still, they juggled attendance at meetings and fairs and depended on Birney and Dale when all of them were busy at once.

The Posts' oldest son, Jacob, turned nineteen in 1848 and continued to work in the store with Isaac and Edmund. He rarely required Amy's attention, but fifteen-year-old Joseph did. In fall 1847, the Posts had sent Joseph to Macedon Academy. The private coeducational manual-labor school was founded by Orthodox Friends but also attracted the children of reform-minded Hicksites. Amy and Isaac hoped that the curriculum, which combined "classical and scientific study" with physical labor, might instill some discipline in their son.[106] But Joseph soon got in trouble. In February 1848, he and a friend were disciplined for breaking regulations while other boys were expelled. Joseph then begged his parents to let him come home, arguing that he would "get expelled eventually." Still, he assured them he "was just fooling Jacob" about smoking tobacco. Indeed, he thought the school was perfect for his older brother, noting that there were "some fine girls here just about his age and size."[107] Joseph apparently stayed the term, but that was the end of his formal education.

Joseph was back home that summer when another cause captured his parents' attention. In June 1848, just as dissident Hicksites walked out of GYM, the Posts were invited to meet Kate and Margaretta Fox. The two girls, fourteen and twelve, were staying with their older sister, Leah Fox Fish, a friend of the Posts, and had agreed to demonstrate their ability to communicate with the spirit world to a select few. The Posts immediately embraced spirit communication as a new means of addressing both personal and social issues. They regularly held séances at their home that summer, inviting local residents and recent converts, which included dissident Quakers as well as a large number of Methodists and ex-evangelicals. The Fishes, Willetses, and Burtises, along with Asa Anthony, often joined the Posts in their spiritualist gatherings, although most of their antislavery circle did not. William Nell and a few other African American activists—though not Douglass—were also drawn to spiritualism, ensuring that this circle, too, was interracial.[108]

For Amy, embracing the spirit world lent new power to her faith. She may have been drawn to spiritualism in part by the death of her daughter, Mathilda, and the sense of the fragility of life that it engendered. She and Isaac also knew the Fox sisters personally and could not imagine that they would be involved in fraud. The broad appeal of the movement also attracted them, bringing together diverse women and men who viewed spirituality—rather than institutionalized religion—as central to their lives. Moreover, spiritualism served as both a sign of and a vehicle for progressive reform. Spirit communication was often linked to telegraphy, another symbol of a progressive age introduced in the late 1840s. Both offered invisible means of communication over long distances, one carried through the atmosphere by wires, the other by mental telepathy. Spiritualism allowed deceased family members, friends, and leading religious and political figures, far removed from the controversies of the day, to offer insights on current debates and developments. Moreover, by eliminating the need for male authorities and intermediaries, spirit communication also widened the reach of female faith.[109]

Spiritualism converged as well with Amy's long-standing interest in alternative healing. In the 1840s, she became friends with James Caleb Jackson, an abolitionist and editor who turned to the water cure to improve his fragile health. He then trained in hydropathy, an alternative medical regimen that relied on cold and warm baths and wet body wraps. It was especially attractive to female patients, who found the treatments relaxing and at least as effective as mainstream medicine for a variety of female complaints. Amy incorporated some hydropathic methods into the healing techniques she employed to assist friends and relatives. She also corresponded with Jackson and other "irregular" healers and joined Isaac in learning about treatments involving diet and magnetism as well as hydropathy.[110] Amy shared new techniques with family members, writing her mother about possible therapies to cure sister Sarah's "disordered" stomach, sending "remedies" for a niece in Jericho, and exchanging medical information with Mary Robbins Post.[111] Isaac no doubt provided crucial ingredients from the pharmacy for Amy's treatments, but she probably also grew herbs in her backyard and gathered ingredients from the farms of the DeGarmos and Anthonys.

When family members took ill, the Posts asked for advice from other lay healers. In 1847, abolitionist Milo Codding agreed to help their son Jacob. Codding suggested that Jacob's problem was caused by the "unclean and impure" state of his "arterial system" and recommended a mixture of roots and herbs. William Nell would have been surprised that Amy needed any such advice. He regularly benefited from her medical treatments, especially her wild cherry cough syrup, cod-liver oil with phosphate of lime, and "use [of] the wet bandage" as well as Sarah Birney's "Dyspepsia Bread."[112]

The Posts' use of alternative medical treatments and their embrace of spiritualism baffled some of their Long Island F/friends, but in 1848 many were more worried about Amy and Isaac's participation in the Congregational Friends, also known as the Progressive Friends. Mother Mary Kirby voiced concern about the very idea of creating a new Friends meeting. She had been reading "old writings of friends, in George Fox's time," who "set up meetings by themselves, but they seemed not to continue long but died away."[113] Even Mary Robbins Post warned that the new venture would not last because "it has not sectarian feelings enough to bind together" the members.[114]

Others, however, were more sympathetic. John Ketcham claimed, "The Farmington Revolution has had a good share of my more thoughtful moments. I hope the revolutionists will soon show themselves prepared for a more liberal government than the old dynasty [the Hicksites]." While believing that some structure was needed, he hoped that "every man and every woman too has rights which cannot be rightfully compromised by any compact with their fellows."[115]

Ketcham would have felt right at home among the Progressive Friends who gathered at Waterloo in October 1848 to finalize the plans laid at Farmington in June. Thomas M'Clintock and Rhoda DeGarmo were selected as clerks of the new meeting, and M'Clintock drafted a document to frame the discussion. His "Basis of Religious Association" formed the foundation of a democratic structure.[116] Women and men were to meet and share jointly in the governance of the society. The organization would be strictly egalitarian, with no special authority given to ministers, elders, or other groups. Indeed, other than clerks to record the proceedings, no members would be granted positions of authority. Moreover, like other congregational religious societies, each meeting would be autonomous, eliminating the powers of yearly or quarterly meetings to discipline smaller or more local gatherings. All meetings were expected to undertake "the promotion of righteousness— of practical goodness—love to God and to man—on the part of every member composing the association and in the world at large."[117]

For these Friends, faith and practice were inseparable, and members pledged to promote "the exemplification of these [Divine] principles in the actions of moral agents." Rather than isolating spiritual testimony from worldly efforts, the Progressive Friends agreed with the Posts that "no laws nor institutions of men should restrict th[e] individual exercise of conscience of responsibility."[118] Indeed, they were committed to "the removal of the existing evils of the day, War, Slavery, Intemperance, Licentiousness, or in whatever form cruelty, injustice, and other perverted principles may operate."[119] They invited both ex-Quakers and non-Quakers to join them in these efforts, and Amy and Isaac Post, Elizabeth Cady Stanton, Frederick Douglass, and Charles Lenox Remond did so on many occasions. In the early 1850s, Stanton considered herself a Progressive Friend, having left the Episcopal Church in which she was raised. By then, dissident Quakers had organized meetings in Indiana, Pennsylvania, Ohio, and Michigan.[120]

While Progressive Friends seemed optimistic about achieving spiritual and social transformation, the November 1848 election suggested that difficulties lay ahead. The Free Soil Party had been founded in Buffalo that August, bringing together members of the Liberty Party, "conscience" Whigs who deplored slavery, and even some northern Democrats. The new party sought to expand the appeal of political abolitionism by emphasizing restrictions on the spread of slavery rather than its elimination where it already existed. Indeed, some Free Soilers focused more on keeping western lands open for white settlement than on abolishing slavery. Many Liberty Party advocates were disappointed with this more moderate antislavery stance and with the party's nomination of former Democratic president Martin Van Buren for U.S. president. Douglass was disappointed as well. Nonetheless, he—like many black abolitionists—was increasingly drawn to political action and grudgingly endorsed Van Buren in the *North Star*.[121]

In that fall's election, the Whig Party candidate Zachary Taylor, a Mexican War hero and Louisiana slaveholder, won the presidency. Taylor had no declared position on slavery in the territories and ran with vice presidential candidate Millard Fillmore from Buffalo, New York, who had opposed the annexation of Texas. Most abolitionists watched Taylor's inauguration with horror and some worried that Free Soiler Van Buren had captured just enough support in New York State to ensure the Whig's victory. Still, Douglass argued for the value of political abolitionism. The "free soil movement," he claimed, had "rallied a large number of the people of the North in apparent hostility to the whole system of American slavery"; "rebuked and humbled" a good number of "corrupt and cringing politicians"; and perhaps "checked the proud and arrogant pretensions of the slaveholder with respect to the extension of slavery." He concluded, "There is no question . . . that the anti-slavery movement will always be followed to a greater or lesser distance by a political party of some sort. It is inevitable."[122]

Most WNYASS members were less sanguine about electoral politics than Douglass. At their December 1848 annual meeting, they reminded New Yorkers of the great work to be done. Some two dozen Progressive Friends—including the Posts, Fishes, Hallowells, M'Clintocks, Stebbinses, and Anthonys—played prominent roles in the event, which began with a fair at Rochester's Minerva Hall on 20 and 21 December. A group "small in numbers, yet large in principles and spirit," then walked to the newly opened concert hall on State Street for its convention. Amy Post and Sarah Owen moved from selling fair goods to serving on the nominating committee, drawing up a slate of officers while the executive committee, on which Amy and Isaac had served, presented its report.[123]

The executive committee applauded the establishment of the antislavery reading room and blamed any shortcomings on the "fierce excitement of a Presidential election—one of those periodical contests in which conscience is disregarded, right trampled under foot, and profligate mendacity, cunning trickery, and bold, bad acts . . . stifle for the time the better nature of the people, and close every ear to appeals for the slave." WNYASS members voiced outrage with both major party candidates and disgust with Free Soilers' failure to condemn "the existence or even the Constitutional support of slavery." Still, perhaps at Douglass's urging, they proclaimed their hope that for some party members "the same spirit which leads them to be opposed to slavery in Mexico may lead them to oppose slavery in Virginia" next. In a rousing conclusion, the committee demanded, " 'No Union with Slaveholders,' either in the glittering goldmines of California or the wasting plantations of the Old Dominion—'No Compromise with Slaveholders,' either in the beautiful valleys of Mexico or on the banks of the majestic Mississippi."[124]

The slate of officers elected that December completed the shift from white evangelical to radical Quaker and black leadership of the WNYASS. Progressive Friends Benjamin Fish, Susan Doty, and Giles Stebbins, along with William Nell and Edmund Willis, won the major offices; only Roswell G. Murray represented the evangelicals, and he had largely given up his ministry. Amy and Isaac Post were reelected to the executive committee, along with three other family members, twenty other Progressive Quakers, and a handful of African Americans, including Douglass. Four ex-evangelicals also served on the committee, including Sarah Owen.[125]

A series of resolutions captured the radical vision of the WNYASS. Participants resolved that "slaveholding is a sin against God" and that "God is a God of justice . . . and his justice will be meted out upon this guilty nation for her sins of commission and omission" with respect to her three million enslaved subjects. Living in "an age of progressive reform," they added, those who oppose such progress are "traitors to the race of man." The white members of the WNYASS then turned a critical eye on themselves, acknowledging that "too little attention has been given to our identity with our colored citizens" and noting "that upon it and their exertions depend the success of emancipation." Yet emancipation was not sufficient; racial justice must prevail. It is "the duty of the friends of humanity to labor with untiring zeal for the overthrow of every law which deprives the colored American of one right enjoyed by those of a paler complexion."[126]

WNYASS members reserved their greatest disgust for slaveholders and those who refused to condemn them, arguing that churches and clergy who held "fellowship with those who make merchandize of the bodies and souls of men . . . deserve the scathing rebuke of all lovers of humanity." They also denounced those who admitted slaveholders to the bastions of political power: "The election of a warrior, slaveholder, and bloodhound importer, to the highest office of our country, proves that the vast majority of the American people are at heart slaveholders, slave traders, and bloodhound importers." Even Douglass could not keep the society from denouncing the Free Soil Party platform "as an unwarrantable compromise of the principles of human liberty." Fearing further expansion of U.S. territory, they opposed "the annexation of Cuba, unless it shall be free territory, and pledged to remain so." Finally, expanding the Garrisonian view of the federal Constitution as a proslavery document, the WNYASS proclaimed it "the duty of every colored man of the State of New York to spurn with indignation the offer of voting under its Constitution for the price of two hundred and fifty dollars."[127]

Still, WNYASS members believed there were reasons for hope "in view of the obstacles removed—the rapid spread of Anti-slavery sentiment among the people . . . the extensive discussion of the subject—the freedom of speech tolerated in Congress, and the growing respect with which antislavery petitions are treated," the gag rule having been eliminated. Members praised the "eloquent appeals of a galaxy of lecturers—the potent influence of a free press; and the example of true words and deeds in the intercourse of everyday life." The WNYASS then "tender[ed] our sincere thanks to the untiring and devoted anti-slavery women . . . whose contributions of genius and industry . . . are indeed noble offerings on freedom's altar."[128]

As Amy Post and her coworkers left the concert hall on 23 December 1848, they felt exhilarated by the revolutionary developments that had unfolded over the previous year. Revolutions in Europe and emancipation in the French West Indies had spurred American activists to recognize the connections between their vision and that of other radicals around the world. Over the past year, the WNYASS had engaged more fully in interracial labors aimed not only at abolition but at racial justice more broadly. At the same time, the woman's rights conventions at Seneca Falls and Rochester heightened awareness of the ways that gender inequities were intertwined with economic and racial discrimination. For the Posts and many of their radical friends, the emergence of spiritualism and the founding of the Progressive

Friends also ensured that secular transformations would remain rooted in faith, but a faith that recognized inner light, purity of conscience, and a higher plane of belief and action.

Nonetheless, radical activists faced a troubling future. Zachary Taylor was headed to the White House, the Free Soil Party had gained more votes than earlier antislavery parties by diluting its abolitionist stance, and plans were being hatched for extending U.S. territory into the Caribbean. Even worse, perhaps, the revolutions in Europe, once a beacon of hope, were being turned back. Most had been led by ad hoc coalitions of middle-class reformers, working-class radicals, and others with grievances against their government. These coalitions proved a shaky basis for creating stable democratic institutions. By June 1848, tensions between liberal and radical forces in France led to renewed uprisings among workers. In December, presidential elections led to the inauguration of Louis-Napoléon Bonaparte, who would slowly turn the nation in a more conservative direction and eventually suspend the elected assembly. In the German states, too, conflicts between reformers and radicals, workers and the middle class, allowed the conservative aristocracy to reclaim power.

That fall, Lucretia Mott had voiced grave concern about these developments: "Even the non-resistant indulges the secret wish that, if they [the revolutionaries] will fight, the right may prevail, and larger liberty diffuse itself over the world." Instead, "There seems . . . a temporary settling down, with far less change than anticipated—especially in revolutionary France."[129] By the end of the year, hopes that radicals might prevail had been crushed in Germany and Italy as well as France, and the possibilities for a transatlantic transformation had dimmed considerably. While slavery had been abolished in the French West Indies, serfdom eliminated in Austria and Hungary, and a more democratic government established in the Netherlands, hopes for sweeping political change were dashed.

Perhaps this meant only that the United States would now have to take the lead in revolutionary activities, demanding the eradication of slavery and corrupt political systems and battling for racial and gender equality, economic justice, and religious liberty. Amy Post believed these struggles could be won, but only by working in interracial coalitions; building regional, national, and international networks of visionary agents; and combining radical faith with moral action. In the coming years, she would continue to orchestrate such changes by working across a broad network of radical friends and widely scattered activists, always pushing to merge distinct campaigns into an integrated movement for social justice.

Shifting Alliances, 1849–1853

Whereas 1848 offered revolutionary hopes in both Europe and western New York, 1849 required reckonings, with European counterrevolutions, deepening dissension among abolitionists, and multiplying movements for change. Yet Amy Post believed that the enthusiasm inspired by the emergence of woman's rights, Progressive Friends, and spiritualism could offset the dispiriting news from abroad and strengthen ties between faith and activism at home. At the same time, she insisted that new movements not dilute campaigns for abolition and racial equality. Even with the joy that two-year-old Willie provided at home, Post engaged in a hectic schedule of meetings, conventions, fairs, and lectures. Those public labors proved unexpectedly challenging as the WNYASS waned and Douglass turned increasingly to political abolitionism and to Julia Griffiths as his main confidante and supporter. In response, Post reconfigured her activist worlds. She intensified her bonds with other black activists, pursued women's rights and religious liberty in diverse arenas, expanded her efforts to assist fugitives, and continued to transmit ideas and carry tactics and strategies from one movement to the next.

As 1849 dawned, Post could not imagine the changes ahead. That winter, the Posts helped lead the WNYASS, retained their close friendships with Douglass and Nell, and nurtured racially integrated networks. Their home life was happy as well. Amy's sister Sarah was being courted by Isaac's nephew and business partner, Edmund Willis; but she continued to live at Sophia Street, where she helped care for Willie and shared domestic and activist labors.[1] Meanwhile, old F/friends John and Sarah Hurn had moved to the outskirts of Rochester, settling near Sarah's sister Huldah Anthony and her husband, Asa. On many Sundays, the Posts, the Hurns, and other antislavery friends gathered at the Anthony farm. In 1845, Asa's cousin Daniel and his wife, Lucy, had purchased a farm near Asa and Huldah's and next to that of Elias and Rhoda DeGarmo. Daniel and Lucy attended the Rochester Woman's Rights Convention in August 1848 with their daughter Mary and wrote their daughter Susan about signing the Declaration of Sentiments. The next spring, when Susan Anthony, a teacher and temperance advocate in central New York, moved to Rochester, she joined these activist circles.[2]

Spring 1849 was propitious on the economic front as well. Amy and Isaac had once again gained financial security, with a local representative for the R. G. Dun credit agency describing the Post and Willis apothecary as an "old establish[ment] doing good bus[iness]" and the proprietors "of good char[acter] and in good cr[edit]." The next year, another agent noted, "I'd trust for any sum they want."[3] Twenty-year-old Jacob, a clerk in his father's store since the financial crisis of the mid-1840s, could finally return to school. In fall 1850, he moved in with Joseph and Mary Robbins Post in Westbury to attend the Buckram Institute.[4] Meanwhile, fifteen-year-old Joseph had completed his last term at Macedon Academy in spring 1848, but remained restless after returning to Rochester. Amy and Isaac were relieved when Douglass hired Joseph, and by spring 1850, their son claimed to "feel quite like a journeyman-Printer." He had also started courting a local woman, Mary Jane Ashley, who might dissuade him of "going west."[5]

The Posts still enjoyed the company of William Nell in winter 1849, though his professional relationship with Douglass had cooled. Within six months of joining the *North Star* staff, William realized that Frederick did not plan to fully use his reportorial and writing skills, nor could he guarantee a steady income. Nell's name was removed from the newspaper's masthead in June 1848, and he considered returning to Boston.[6] Still a staunch Garrisonian, Nell worried about Douglass's growing interest in political abolitionism. However, Douglass published more of Nell's dispatches and reports after their formal partnership ended, so Nell stayed on at 36 Sophia Street.

Moreover, by remaining with the Posts, Nell stayed close to his sister Frances, who was working as a domestic in the city. Frances Nell was being courted by Benjamin Cleggett, a local barber whose family were devoted abolitionists. In February 1849, the Posts hosted a party to celebrate their engagement, with William welcoming the Cleggetts, the DeGarmos, the Fishes, and other black and white guests.[7] That same month, in reviewing a series of local lectures delivered by Douglass, Nell applauded the presence of a "large delegation of colored citizens," which "produced a beneficial effect on the large mass of their white fellow attendants."[8]

However triumphant Post and her circle felt about these interracial events, the occasions sparked serious complaints from local residents and Long Island relatives. A cousin reported to Mary Robbins Post that the engagement party "had caused great dissatisfaction in the Rochester community" and that she "regretted [the Posts'] social mingling very much." She claimed that "the people are not ready for it yet . . . for they [African Americans] are an inferior class." Mary assured Amy and Isaac that she and the cousin "had a pretty warm talk."[9] Still, to relatives who dismissed spiritualism as folly and viewed the establishment of the Progressive Friends as a betrayal to Hicksites, the Posts' insistence on socializing across the color line confirmed their belief that Isaac and Amy had been swept away by ultraism. Even Amy's mother voiced concern that the couple's radicalism was pulling them away from Quaker values and Long Island kin.[10]

Amy regretted her parents' uneasiness but was more immediately distressed by Nell's decision, finally, to return to Boston. Before he headed east in April 1849, Amy gave William an inkstand in hopes he would think of her whenever he put pen to paper.[11] Fortunately, shortly after Nell departed, Harriet Jacobs arrived. After fleeing an abusive master in North Carolina in 1835, she hid for seven years in an attic crawl space in the home of her grandmother, a free black. In 1842, Harriet fled north by steamship with her son, Joseph. Landing in Philadelphia, she traveled to New York City to find her daughter, Louisa, and brother, John S. Jacobs, who were also fugitives. After a joyous reunion, John, a popular antislavery lecturer, headed to Boston, while his sister and niece remained in New York. Harriet found work as a nursemaid for the daughter of author and publisher Nathaniel Parker and his wife, Mary Willis. However, when Harriet heard in 1843 that her owner had sent slave catchers to the city, she, too, headed to Boston. While there she met Nell, who befriended her and sent her on to the Posts.[12]

In spring 1849, Jacobs moved to 36 Sophia Street, eager to reunite with her brother, John, who was then managing Rochester's Anti-Slavery Reading Room. Like Nell, Harriet quickly felt at home with the Posts, joining in meals, visits from friends and relatives, and spiritual séances around the dining room table. Also like Nell, she doted on two-year-old Willie and found in Amy a trusted confidante. Harriet was a decade younger than her hostess, but they had sons the same age, both named Joseph, who caused them similar anxieties. Just as importantly, they shared commitments to abolition and spiritualism. When her brother left on a lecture tour, Harriet took over management of the reading room and joined fund-raising efforts for the *North Star.*[13]

Douglass, who had been lecturing on Long Island when Jacobs arrived in Rochester, met her on his return to the city. Their introduction was brief, as he was heading back to New York City for the May AASS convention, accompanied by Amy Post and Sarah Hallowell. Amy was eager to reconnect with Nell at the annual meeting and to visit family and friends on Long Island. The traveling trio spent the night in Albany with cousins Lydia and Abigail Mott and then boarded a steamer down the Hudson. Although it was blustery and cool, Sarah wrote her niece Mary Hallowell that "we had a fine view of the everlasting rocks and mountains and the numerous princely mansions that adorn their rugged peaks . . . and we wished for all we love to sit beside us on the stern of the *Confidence* with our noble Frederick and enjoy all that we enjoyed." Frederick had sat with them in the dining room that morning, where "we were observed by all . . . with a scrutinizing eye. Frederick thought the people could understand him but we [Amy and I] were a sort of riddle to them. . . . So long as they treated us with respect and pleasant faces, we did not mind the observation."[14]

When they reached New York harbor, Douglass remained in the city while Sarah and Amy traveled to Jericho. The sisters enjoyed visits with family and friends, even those who questioned the religious, political, and personal choices the Posts had made. They soon returned to New York City with Joseph and Mary Robbins Post for the AASS convention, where Amy took an active part in the debates. Mary described Amy's remarks as "acceptable and edifying, tending to stir up" participants "to more zeal and faithfulness." Amy's own zeal was fortified by visits with William Wells Brown and William Nell and by a meeting she attended at which Douglass spoke with local African Americans. She was deeply impressed, but she worried that his rising fame stirred up "Jealousy, Sectarianism and Envy" among some black leaders.[15]

It was precisely Douglass's fame that brought Julia and Eliza Griffiths to New York City. Family friends of the great British abolitionist William Wilberforce, the sisters had been captivated by Douglass during his tour of Britain and Scotland. They arrived in the United States in hopes of using their connections to wealthy abolitionists back home to raise funds for Douglass's work. Douglass introduced the Griffiths sisters to Amy and Sarah in New York City and a week later to Isaac in Rochester, where the sisters assured him they were "very much in love" with his wife and sister-in-law.[16]

Isaac sent Amy news of the introduction in a letter to Westbury, assuming she had returned there after the convention. Instead, his wife had traveled to Boston with Nell, apparently planning to stay for the New England Anti-Slavery Convention in late May. Thus began a period of great excitement for Amy and great anxiety for Isaac. His 12 May letter to Westbury urged Amy to bring Joseph and Mary Robbins Post back to Rochester with her. A few days later, when he realized that she had not yet returned to Long

Island, he wondered if "Father and Mother think it hard of you to stay in New York so long." Douglass, he noted, was back in Rochester, and "you *will be very welcome home*" as well.[17] However, his wife was already in Boston.

Amy may have felt freer to take the long way home because her stepdaughter, Mary Hallowell, who had no children of her own, had agreed to care for two-year-old Willie in her absence. Isaac often dined with the Hallowells and Willie after long days at the store. In addition, Harriet Jacobs, Mary Dale, and Sarah Birney were all living at 36 Sophia Street, and Isaac had many other commitments to keep him busy: attending spiritualist séances, delivering medicines to and enjoying visits with old F/friends, and participating in antislavery meetings. Nonetheless, he was relieved when he finally received a letter from Amy on 19 May. Still, when she urged him to join her for the New England Anti-Slavery Convention, Isaac replied that he felt "very little draft toward Boston" and instead tried to draw her home with tales of friends and spirits.[18]

Amy's absence sharpened Isaac's anxiety that the old circle was breaking apart. Nell was gone, and other friends were departing to assist family or advance their economic interests. Sarah Owen left for Michigan in early May to join her sister and brother-in-law and their two young children. Soon after, Giles and Catherine Fish Stebbins headed to Michigan as well, with thoughts of frontier opportunities.[19] At age fifty-one, Isaac had no desire to move again and little interest in traveling to conventions, whereas forty-seven-year-old Amy seemed eager to be out working for abolition and extending her networks.

Isaac often calmed his apprehensions through conversations with spirits, sending detailed reports to Amy about séances with Leah Fox Fish and others. In a letter marked "Private," Isaac described a visit from Hannah, Amy's sister and Isaac's first wife. She told Leah that Edmund, Henry, and Mathilda, his departed children, could visit Isaac when he was "*asleep*"— that is, in a trancelike state. When Leah asked the spirits about Isaac and Amy's relationship, they claimed "it was not true that first love was best for after the object [of affection] was removed we are left free to have the same feeling center on another." Isaac suggested that the message was "alluding to Charles Willets," Amy's fiancé who had died unexpectedly.[20] A week later, Isaac wrote that another spirit sent a message to Amy: "You should not let your friends convince you to stay away longer."[21]

Meanwhile, Amy was enjoying visits with William and Louisa Nell and Louisa's daughter Harriet and grandson Ira. She was also spending time with Charles Remond and his family in Salem. Despite some "unpleasant weather," Amy did not rush home, even after Isaac passed on the news that Harriet Jacobs was "in an exticy [sic]" after hearing that her son, Joseph, who had been at sea, would soon travel to Rochester.[22] When Amy did finally return home in early June, she journeyed from Boston to Rochester with a black friend—perhaps William Wells Brown, who was promoting his recently published autobiography. Isaac was simply happy she was back, but a cousin on Long Island had complained that it "was a bad thing to be seen traveling with a colored person."[23] John Willis, Amy's brother-in-law, agreed and also criticized the Posts' friendship with Douglass, who, he claimed, "wanted to promote insurrection." Willis warned Amy that she "might as well make up thy mind that abolition does as much harm as good."[24]

The Posts were well aware that their friendships with African Americans dismayed some of their kin, but they took pride in challenging segregation. Writing to Amy in Jericho that spring, Isaac asked, "Did you frighten" Aunt Phebe "with your talk about eating with coloured persons so that she will not like to come[?]" Still, he predicted, "I think she would not be troubled for long for I wish our family all behaved as well as Harriet [Jacobs]." Indeed, he added, "I don't believe she would object [to] sleeping with her after three days acquaintance."[25] When Phebe Post Willis finally did arrive, she enjoyed herself. Clearly, whatever her or other relatives' reactions, Amy and Isaac had taken their stand on the high ground of interracialism and would not be moved.

While the Posts were being denounced for reaching across the color line and supporting Douglass, they worried that their dear friend was about to renounce his Garrisonian roots. Frederick had drawn closer to Gerrit Smith, one of New York's leading political abolitionists, and had endorsed the Free Soil Party in fall 1848, even if hesitantly. As Douglass wrote to Smith in March 1849, he now looked "with grateful friendship upon all classes of abolitionists."[26] He was not, however, entirely free to assert his ideological independence, as the *North Star* was in serious financial trouble. Hoping to persuade Frederick of the severity of the problem, Amy and Isaac urged him to allow the WNYASS Executive Committee, on which they served, to audit the books. Despite approaching their friend with gentle concern, Douglass took offense.[27]

When Amy met the Griffiths sisters in New York City in May 1849, she hoped they might help restore the *North Star* to a sound footing. Isaac, however, voiced concerns about Julia from the start. He acknowledged that she was "very talented," but noted her elaborate dress and abundant jewelry, a quite un-Quakerly style.[28] He had also witnessed an argument between Julia and Frederick, right after her arrival in Rochester, over Gerrit Smith's embrace of Adventism. Isaac had been impressed with the way she stood up to Frederick and with how seriously Frederick took her critiques, but concluded, "I wish F.D. would treat all that differ with him in [p]ublic as kindly as he did her."[29]

Initially, Amy played her usual role, working with Julia and Eliza to bring them into her activist worlds. In fall 1849, she organized a dozen WYNASS fairs throughout the region to raise funds for the *North Star* and invited Douglass and the Griffiths sisters to join her at each. On 11 September, despite a bad cold, Amy traveled to East Bloomfield to help set up the fair there. When Douglass arrived, the two talked about the paper's financial difficulties before Amy headed home to bed. Later that day, she received a letter from Douglass and was shocked to read the opening lines: "The conversation I had with you this morning . . . has left a very uncomfortable impression on my mind—and especially do I feel grieved at your declaration of intention not to vote in favor of any further [WNYASS] donations to the Star until I put the economical concerns of the paper under the charge of a committee." Douglass insisted that he had "*no* possible objection" to having the accounts examined by any member of the WNYASS Board, yet "the paper is my *own*" and "I am personally responsible for its character—and for its debts." Giving up "entire control" to others "would be degrading to me as a man—making me a mere Cypher—in my own affairs." Nonetheless, Douglass said he would ask William Hallowell and Edmund Willis "to perform the duty I have already indicated" and closed "with sincere Love to Dear Isaac and the same to yourself."[30]

The accusatory tone of Frederick's letter stunned Amy. A month earlier, she had written Nell about "controversies with the 'Lords of Creation'" on the WNYASS Executive Committee over business operations.[31] While it is not clear whether that controversy involved funding for the *North Star*, Post was devoting enormous time and effort to the paper's success and felt battered from all sides. Drafting a reply, she sought Frederick's sympathy while defending her intentions. "I just received thy letter," she began, "and have crept up from my sick cough to answer it, desiring as speedily as possible to remove if I can all that is uncomfortable between us." Saying she was "sorry and ashamed" of having even joked about her "influence," she was surprised that he would think she would ever try "influencing thee . . . by the *threat* as thee calls it." How could he "believe me willing to treat this in so disrespectful a manner[?]" After all, she reminded Frederick, you made "the proposition for the Com[mittee]" to help with the finances, and I "advocate[d] it for thou advantage and thine alone."[32]

Post denied any desire to remove control of the paper from Douglass. If she had ever appeared "deficient in interest" for the welfare of the *North Star*, or Frederick personally, she had "acted as wide as the poles from my true judgement and feelings." Perhaps hoping to gain allies as well as mend fences, Amy applauded the "glorious example" set by the Griffiths sisters in promoting abolition.[33] The letter apparently had a beneficial effect. In mid-September, Frederick invited William Hallowell, Edmund Willis, Isaac Post, and Asa Anthony to serve as a committee, "which should take the financial management of the North Star into their own hands" and "advise with me" on relevant matters. In early October, the WNYASS donated $100 to the *North Star*, suggesting the society's renewed confidence in Douglass and the continuing importance of Amy Post in his life.[34]

Just as this crisis passed, another emerged. Ever since the Fox sisters had gained fame as spirit "rappers," Rochesterians had debated whether they had opened a new spiritual path or executed a fraud. In fall 1849, Leah Fox Fish sought to both settle and benefit from the rising controversy. At a séance at the Post home, she reported that spirits demanded a public demonstration at Corinthian Hall. That large and beautiful lecture hall had opened in the summer and hosted lyceum lectures and touring shows, as well as antislavery, reform, and political conventions. The nation's first public spiritualist demonstration took place there on 14 November, attracting four hundred women and men, including reporters from local papers and the *New York Tribune*.[35] The audience heard rappings, which Kate and Margaretta Fox translated into spirit messages, but skeptical audience members demanded further investigation.

During two successive exhibitions, committees examined the stage and the girls and found no alternative explanation for the rappings. Indeed, one of the judges, John Worth Edmonds, was converted to spiritualism by the experience. Finally, a fourth exhibition was arranged at Corinthian Hall, with tickets sold at half price so that more people could attend. That night, Amy Post and three other women went backstage and undertook intimate examinations of the sisters. They had the girls disrobe in a private room and looked through their gowns, petticoats, and underwear. The girls then got dressed and stood barefoot on feather pillows with their skirts tied around their ankles, and even then the spirits made themselves known via distinct rappings.

The committee reported its findings, and the girls returned to the stage accompanied by Amy and Isaac Post, Isaac's cousin George Willets, and a Methodist minister. Given the half-price tickets, the hall was filled with a rowdier and more hostile crowd, and a bucket of tar had been discovered behind a curtain. The final report could barely be heard as rowdies showered huzzahs and boos at the Foxes and their supporters. When the audience realized the report was favorable to the girls, several groups tried to storm the stage. The Posts and their friends surrounded the girls, and the whole circle was then rescued by local police, who had been hiding backstage in case of a mob scene. Despite the positive reports, many local papers ridiculed the idea of spirit communication, including the *North Star*. Others, however, such as the *New York Tribune* and Rochester's *Daily Democrat*, suggested that spirit communication might, indeed, be another sign of the era's progressive discoveries.[36]

As critics became more vocal, the Posts described their experiences with spirits in long letters to friends and family members, who were alternately dismissive, skeptical, and intrigued. Stephen and Matilda Rushmore of Westbury wrote a letter to their uncle Isaac that was typical of many. Although they could not quite convince themselves "how a spiritual sound affects a corporeal ear," they nonetheless granted it might be true. Meanwhile, Amy sent Nell, a devoted spiritualist, a detailed account of the November exhibitions. In reply, Nell noted Garrison's interest in "spiritual matters" and suggested that he might reprint the *Tribune* account of the "mysterious knockings" in the *Liberator*. Three years later, Nell wrote Amy that labor reformer Eliza Kenny, who had joined the Boston antislavery circle, was also a believer and sent her "best love" to the Posts. Harriet Jacobs and Sojourner Truth, too, became ardent spiritualists, deepening their bond with Amy.[37]

In contrast, Douglass considered spiritualism a distraction and focused his energies on nurturing ties between the WNYASS network and the Griffiths sisters' affluent British supporters.[38] Although the two groups shared a common goal, they did not share a common vision. Eliza and Julia Griffiths were not interested in universal transformation. They were focused instead on abolition and advocated on behalf of Douglass, whatever brand of abolitionism he embraced. Still, Post and the Griffiths sisters encouraged their coworkers to join forces during the spate of WNYASS fairs in fall 1849. After the East Bloomfield event in September, fairs were held in Williamson, Henrietta, Palmyra, Macedon, and other nearby towns. Nell applauded Post's devotion to the cause and her "General-ship of the series of antislavery Fairs."[39] That generalship involved coordinating schedules and publicity with local allies, writing a steady stream of letters and articles, and aiding in the preparation and collection of sale items. Many goods were hand-made by WNYASS women; others were donated by farmers and shopkeepers or sent by supporters in the Midwest, Philadelphia, and, most recently, Britain. Leftover items from one fair were passed on to the next or sold in small antislavery shops set up in church basements or at the Anti-Slavery Reading Room in Rochester.

Post began publishing appeals in the *North Star* in June 1849 that high-lighted both the economic importance of the upcoming fairs and "the general enlightenment of the public mind" they fostered. Acknowledging the small number of truly dedicated activists, she claimed, "[We are] doubling our diligence . . . [as] the means of advancing this holy cause." She reminded readers that while "[we labor within] our domestic circle, with none to mo-lest us," "three millions of men and women . . . are doomed to abject slavery and chains, robbed of every right—civil, social, personal, political." Still, she wrote, abolitionists must consider themselves "bound with" the enslaved: "we desire to plead their cause as though the galling chain were on our own limbs and the knotted lash were applied to our own backs." In an editorial, Douglass applauded the "earnest desire" of the women who "labor zealously and industriously" for emancipation and the *North Star*.[40]

Many WNYASS members believed that the moral power of their efforts was at least as important as any pecuniary profits. Sewing circles crafted pillow cases, towels, quilts, baby clothes, scarves, and handkerchiefs; baked pies; and collected produce and other goods in hopes of raising funds. Amy sustained enthusiasm for these efforts by encouraging her antislavery sisters across western and central New York. In August 1849, old F/friend Susan Doty wrote Amy about the upcoming fair in Macedon, a canal town east of Rochester that was home to the Quaker academy Joseph had attended. Her neighbor Maria Wilbur, an Orthodox Friend, was helping arrange coffee, cake, lemonade, and ice cream for the event. Susan sought advice on man-aging a sewing circle in hopes of producing "cradle quilts" for the Macedon and Rochester fairs.[41]

Organizers also hoped the numerous festivals and the calls for aid might induce new women to join the antislavery fold. One prime candidate in Rochester was Julia Wilbur, the niece of Maria and Esek Wilbur, who had moved to the city to work as a teacher. Maria and Esek worked with Amy in the WNYASS and had joined her at the Seneca Falls Woman's Rights Con-vention. On 6 January 1849, although it was "quite cold," Julia attended her first WNYASS meeting at the Posts' home. The next month, she helped boost the fair in East Avon by obtaining "the Baptist House" there for lectures by Frederick Douglass and John S. Jacobs. A few weeks later, Wilbur chatted with John's sister, Harriet Jacobs, at the Anti-Slavery Reading Room and described her as "intelligent & agreeable." In mid-June, Wilbur called on Douglass, whose daughter was to enroll in her class that summer, and met the Griffiths' sisters. She described them as "like 2 fearless spirits regardless of the prejudice against color which exists here." By then, Wilbur considered herself an abolitionist, though she worried that some WNYASS members were "infidels."[42]

Fortunately, Wilbur was comfortable working in interracial arenas, a fundamental principle of the WNYASS. The women often met to sew, talk, and plan at the Anti-Slavery Reading Room, a space accessible to both black and white women. Meeting there also allowed manager Harriet Jacobs to participate while being available to other visitors. WNYASS women also gathered at 36 Sophia Street, again a comfortable place for Jacobs and Frances Nell Cleggett to join in, or at the Douglass home, which accommodated not only Anna Douglass and her newborn daughter, Annie, but also female leaders from the black community as well as the Griffiths sisters.[43]

Nonetheless, the radical reputation of the WNYASS meant that recruiting visitors to fairs could be as difficult as recruiting members. At a small-town fair in January 1849, weeks of preparation produced only an eighty-dollar profit. A report in the *North Star* highlighted problems other than race: short notice, "bitter cold," and the fact that "the goods were altogether too ornamental to meet the ideas of hard-handed, industrious farmers."[44] By fall, however, WNYASS organizers felt confident that better weather and a wider selection of goods would result in greater success. In October, Douglass expressed his "deep and warm gratitude" for the women's work, "especially to Mrs. Amy Post, and to Misses Julia and Eliza Griffith[s]." Having helped organize and attended half a dozen fairs in just the last six weeks, the women "have stemmed the current of opposition, met coldness and indifference, overcome prejudice, and the various obstacles thrown in their way." Still, the money raised was far less than what was needed.[45]

A month later, Amy published a detailed report in the *North Star*, thanking supporters in eleven villages that had hosted fund-raising fairs. Hoping to cement an alliance with the British newcomers, she noted that the WNYASS was "especially grateful to our English friends Julia and Eliza Griffiths, for their persevering and strenuous efforts," and to Douglass, "whose indomitable energy saw no obstacle, and whose soul stirring eloquence dissipated doubts wherever they existed." Fairs, Post maintained, provide "a medium through which a knowledge of our principles, our measures, our faith and our works have been spread more extensively and usefully among the people than they otherwise would have been in any other way."[46]

Amy and her coworkers hoped the Rochester Bazaar, scheduled for December 1849, would attract Christmas shoppers and whet the appetite for the annual WNYASS convention. Both events, however, were postponed until mid-January and then pushed back another week.[47] The WNYASS invited "all classes and colours" to attend the fair when it finally opened on 23 January, but it did not attract the anticipated crowd, the hoped-for funds, or the usual plaudits from the *North Star*. The fair generated $215, about half of what it had generated the previous year. In addition to holding it after the holiday season, the fair may have drawn smaller crowds and a few rowdy anti-abolitionists because of a racially integrated dinner held the first night. Still, Amy considered the dinner "a glorious achievement," demonstrating as it did the possibility of racial harmony.[48]

Douglass, however, offered a harsh critique. In a one-paragraph report on 1 February, he claimed that from "a financial point of view the Fair must be considered a failure" and that "morally, it has been far from successful."[49] The next day, a "soarly agrieved" [*sic*] Amy wrote Frederick a pointed letter: "Will my dear friend . . . explain what necessity there was of giving so discouraging an account of the Rochester Fair[?] . . . That we came very far short of realizing in a pecuniary point of view what we wished is true, yet we would not despise even the sum of one hundred dollars, but rejoice to have it to add to other hundreds that have been raised and used in the cause, during the past year." "Was it nothing," she asked, "that one hundred people, of all classes and colours, sat down to one table, and the most perfect decorum and order prevailed[?] . . . Dost thou really wish to bring thy Western New York friends into disgrace, and turn all donations in another direction[?] [I]f so, thou has done the deed."[50]

Douglass responded in a businesslike tone: "I had two duties to perform in that notice—to give credit to our few Dear friends who have labored faithfully to make the fair successful—and at the same time to do justice to the absent by making them know the truth with respect to the results." He insisted, "*I do not despise the sum realized.* . . . Nor have I said that the tendency of the fair was wholly immoral. These are your remarks dear friend, not mine certainly." With that he closed, "Faithfully and affectionately."[51]

The contentious character of this exchange reflected much deeper tensions between Douglass and the WNYASS circle. Although he may not have intended for the Griffiths sisters to take over fund-raising efforts for the *North Star*, Julia planned to do just that. Her decision dramatically transformed the dynamics of Rochester women's antislavery activism. Initially eager to befriend Post, Griffiths soon realized that there were significant differences between her and WNYASS stalwarts. For instance, in encouraging "ladies" from Canandaigua to start a sewing circle, she made it clear, "I am not 'woman's rights' or a public speaker."[52] This alone made any partnership with Post and her coworkers unlikely. In addition, Griffiths forged close friendships with Gerrit Smith and other political abolitionists as she built an independent circle of supporters.

The national debates that erupted in winter 1850 forestalled any immediate change, as abolitionists made common cause in the face of proslavery forces. Congress debated a series of measures, together known as the Compromise of 1850, in hopes of settling disputes over California's admission as a free state, lingering conflicts over territories acquired in the war with Mexico, and white southern outrage over northern aid to fugitives. The Compromise was finally passed that fall, including a Fugitive Slave Act that required individuals, not just state authorities, to assist in returning runaways or risk being fined or imprisoned. The law also eliminated jury trials for alleged fugitives and paid judges more for returning fugitives to owners than for sending free blacks back to their communities. For Douglass, the Posts, and hundreds of other Underground Railroad conductors, the Fugitive Slave Act raised the stakes of their work while fueling new passion for the cause.

Douglass's freedom had been purchased by British supporters three years earlier, but for those who remained fugitives—including Harriet Jacobs—the danger of remaining in the United States increased dramatically. And the people who harbored these fugitives faced greater risks as well. To address these challenges, Rochester abolitionists tried to set aside their differences. At the WNYASS convention in January 1850, as Congress debated the Compromise, Douglass and Remond condemned the once-lauded Senator Daniel Webster and other politicians willing to betray "the cause of Freedom" by supporting the bill. That winter, the society's executive committee met monthly at 36 Sophia Street to plan events that would alert the public. At the same time, black community leaders and white radicals joined demonstrations against segregation in the city's schools, and Isaac Post served on an interracial committee "to draft 'a remonstrance' to the Board of Education." In April, political abolitionists organized a mass meeting at Corinthian Hall on the hated Compromise and invited Douglass and Isaac Post to speak. Participants resolved that nothing "but a bill of sale from God

Almighty can establish the title of the master to his slave, or induce us to lift a finger to aid in his return to the house of bondage."[53]

In May, AASS members crowded the Broadway Tabernacle in New York City, eager to denounce the proposed Fugitive Slave Act. Douglass attended with the Griffiths sisters, and Rochester friends were shocked to learn that a gang of white thugs accosted the three while walking along the Battery. Douglass was savagely beaten before police intervened.[54] Violence never deterred Douglass, however, and he lectured against the draconian measure throughout the summer. In June 1850, he joined Progressive Quakers at the second Yearly Meeting of Congregational Friends in Waterloo. Participants there sent a memorial to Congress that began: "Open then your ears to the wailing of millions in our own land whose only crime is the color of their skin. . . . We entreat you in the name of humanity, to set your faces against this horrible homicide—American Slavery."[55]

In August, Gerrit Smith and the New York State Vigilance Committee convened a meeting at Cazenovia, New York, where free blacks, fugitives, and their white allies considered how best to protect African Americans from the clutches of slave catchers. Smith encouraged "old guard" Garrisonians to join the effort, and a few did. The Posts, who were on Long Island at the time, followed reports of Douglass's speech as well as those of fugitives, such as the Edmondson sisters, whose harrowing tale of escape from Washington, D.C., reminded abolitionists that challenging the law was a matter of life and death.[56]

All the efforts to derail the Fugitive Slave Act failed, however, and President Millard Fillmore signed it into law on 18 September 1850. While abolitionists were horrified, many northerners were angered by the federal government's intrusion into their communities. Betsy Mix Cowles, an Ohio abolitionist and spiritualist, queried Amy Post, "That accursed 'Fugitive Bill,' is it not enough to make the vilest spirits blush?" Mary Robbins Post, however, hoped it might expand abolitionist support. The recent arrest and attempted arrest of African Americans in New York City, she reported, "has caused a great sensation and among a class . . . who before have been quite indifferent to the subject. . . . I have a strong hope that this infamous act will act as an engine against the evil it is designed to perpetuate and secure."[57] Nell, too, hoped the law would fuel wider protests. Active in the Boston Vigilance Committee, he pledged to intercede if slave catchers or government officials sought to send any black person into slavery. He hoped that those who had been silent before would now join forces against such efforts.[58]

Post's most immediate fear was likely for Harriet Jacobs's safety. In fall 1850, she had moved back to New York City, where her brother, John, was organizing demonstrations on behalf of fugitives. However, he soon headed for California to seek his fortune and avoid the slave catchers swarming New York and New England. Harriet remained in the city, as she was once again working for the Willis family as nursemaid to the children of Cornelia Grinnell Willis, Nathaniel's second wife. Although she was convinced that Cornelia Willis did not have "any prejudice against color," her husband was well known for promoting proslavery views.[59]

While Jacobs only discussed the dangers she faced with close friends like Post, other black activists openly debated how best to respond to slave-catchers. At the Cazenovia convention in August 1850, Douglass proclaimed that fugitives should meet slave catchers with bloodhounds. Writing Douglass afterward, Amy confessed to anxiety about "express[ing] any dissent from thy judgement." Still, "allow me in the fre[e]dom of an own sister to say to thee that I cannot feel happy . . . since thy conclusion to give slave catchers a blood-hound reception." Thinking only of his safety and the good of the cause, she insisted that he must see the problem of meeting force with force.[60]

Nell tried to reassure Amy. He, too, had helped organize a vigilance committee, considering, as Douglass did, that armed self-defense was significantly different from the proactive use of force. In numerous letters in 1850 and 1851, he reiterated his devotion to Garrisonian principles and to what he called the "Sophia Street Circle." Indeed, in summer 1850, he yearned "to be once more sitting down conversing with [you] and Sarah L. Hallowell and the *relatives, friends* and visitors who together have so oft times rendered 36 Sophia St such a charmed spot to me . . . an Oasis in the Desert."[61]

Amy could have used an oasis herself that summer. In June, Wendell Phillips wrote the Posts from Boston asking for insights on William Wells Brown's marriage after his wife accused him of desertion. Isaac let Amy respond, noting that both William and his wife, Betsey, confided more freely "with my wife than with me." Reluctant to reveal confidences to Phillips, Amy did so only to reinforce the truth of William's version of events. Early on, Brown had spoken lovingly of his wife and child, so when problems first arose, Post urged him to mend relations for his family's benefit and that of the cause. However, after William accused Betsey of having an affair with a neighbor in Buffalo and she refused to deny the allegations or move with William to Farmington, Amy "much lament[ed] the trouble she is giving

William and his friends." She and Isaac both hoped that his friends "will stand by him and give him all the support in their Power."[62]

In this same period, relations between Isaac and his son Joseph caused anguish for the entire Post family. Although Isaac's relationships with Mary, Jacob, and Willet were close, he was often frustrated by Joseph's inability to forge a career. He had hoped that his son would learn the printing trade at the *North Star*, but despite early enthusiasm, he headed to Chicago in May 1850, seeking a better position. He left while Isaac was in New York City at the AASS convention, but he wrote his father to request money for the trip. Although Isaac disapproved of the venture, he told Jacob to give his brother one hundred dollars from the pharmacy account. After that, he insisted, "he must depend upon his own exertions for success."[63] Joseph wrote from Chicago two months later, thanking his father for the "favor," which he admitted was "more than I deserve."[64] He wrote more frequently to his mother, however, begging her not to tell others of his failure to find work. In August, just before Amy and Isaac traveled to Jericho to celebrate her father's eighty-fifth birthday, Joseph asked his parents to help his fiancée, Mary Jane Ashley (whom he called Mate), who was "out of Flour and everything else."[65]

That fall, Joseph journeyed to New York City, keeping his decision secret for fear of his father's objections. After finding work on the railroad, he asked his mother to send him some clothes and to "tell Mate I want her to answer my letters if she is a going to or if she is not to let me know and then I shall know what to depend upon." He also complained that his father took "more interest in the Burtis Family than in me."[66] While Joseph assured Amy that he was not running wild in New York, his constant movement, lack of employment, and grievances against his father, as well as Mate's impatience with his unsettled state, must have provoked anxiety.

The Posts could no longer turn to Rochester's Hicksite Monthly Meeting for comfort, as they and many of their F/friends had withdrawn or been released after the meetinghouse closed its doors to antislavery and other reform meetings. Some turned to the Progressive Friends, while others, including William and Mary Hallowell, joined the Unitarian Church. William Henry Channing, its reform-minded minister, attracted many to the fold in the early 1850s.[67] Amy Post likely joined family members on occasion for weekly services at the Unitarian church and attended annual meetings of the Progressive Friends. Both maintained the democratic structure and universalist vision of social change that she and Isaac embraced, but they did not provide the community bonds that Friends meetings had offered in Jericho, Westbury, Ledyard, and Farmington.

When Amy missed the Progressive Friends' 1850 yearly meeting, she gathered reports from Douglass, other F/friends, and reform papers. She applauded the participants, who resolved that "the Creator has established an equality in the human family, perfect and beautiful as it is beneficent, without limitation to sex, or complexion, or national peculiarities." She also approved their invitation to "the Christian, the Jew, the Mohammaden, or the Hindoo" to share what light they had, and supported their memorial to Congress opposing the Fugitive Slave Law.[68] In addition, a committee that included Elizabeth Cady Stanton drafted "An Address to the Women of the State of New York" that defined women's rights in the broadest possible terms. It drew examples of degradation and achievement from around the world and insisted that women's rights apply to all races and classes. Indeed, the Progressive Friends declared "the Rights of Woman are Human Rights."[69]

The inclusive stance of Progressive Friends cheered Amy considerably. That fall, her spirits were also lifted by letters from Douglass, who was touring Massachusetts. Delighted to see mutual friends in New Bedford, Frederick discussed future antislavery events in Rochester, clearly assuming Post would be involved.[70] Perhaps Amy had retreated from her criticism of Douglass's advocacy of force against slave catchers after realizing that Nell, too, supported the need to protect fugitive and free blacks by any means necessary. And Douglass needed the Posts' support since his relationship with Julia Griffiths continued to arouse criticism from allies.

The Griffiths sisters lived in the Douglass home and accompanied him on lecture tours and at conventions while Julia worked beside Frederick at the *North Star* office. Abolitionist coworkers worried—and some gleefully gossiped—about the nature of their relationship. Even many of those impressed with Julia's financial and intellectual skills voiced concern about an unmarried white woman spending so much time with a married black man. The situation became more problematic when *North Star* printer John Dick married Eliza Griffiths in summer 1850. The couple soon moved to Toronto, leaving Frederick and Julia without their constant chaperone.[71] For activists unhappy with Douglass's drift toward political abolitionism or his advocacy of black self-defense, the situation provided another weapon against him. Julia, aware of the gossip, moved out of the Douglass home in July 1850, but she still spent a great deal of time with Frederick.

Eighteen months later, Samuel Porter warned Douglass about the negative effects of his relationship with Griffiths, but to no avail.[72]

By 1853, even the Posts, who rarely commented on Douglass's friendship with Griffiths, became embroiled in the scandal, at least indirectly. In early December, a letter purportedly written by Anna Douglass was sent to Garrison to be published in the *Liberator*. Garrison printed the letter but voiced his doubts about its authenticity. Amy Post called at the Douglass home while the letter was being written and sometime afterward talked with Susan B. Anthony. While Anthony was not one of Amy's closest friends, she was equally concerned about Griffiths's influence on Douglass. Shortly after their conversation, Anthony wrote Garrison that Post told her Anna Douglass's letter was "concocted by Frederic & Julia." In the letter, Mrs. Douglass claimed that Griffiths's presence in Frederick's office did not cause "unhappiness in the family," but, Post reported, Anna insisted she "would *never* sign a paper that said, *Julia has not made her trouble*." Apparently Anna was not concerned with Griffiths's work in the *North Star* office, but she told Amy, "I won't have her in my house."[73] Whether Post knew that Anthony revealed these confidences to Garrison is unclear, but she was certainly upset over Anna Douglass's plight as well as Frederick's willingness to appropriate his wife's words to his—and Griffiths's—benefit.

Harriet Jacobs also sympathized with Anna Douglass, and her presence at 36 Sophia Street may have strengthened Amy's relationship with Frederick's wife. Yet Jacobs, too, refused to criticize Griffiths, at least in public. Perhaps her own fears of being condemned for submitting to a relationship with a white man when enslaved as protection against her master's brutality made her unwilling to criticize others. Whatever the reasons, she and Amy had collaborated with Griffiths and Douglass in a variety of ways during Jacobs's year in Rochester.[74] Post continued to do so in the following years, most importantly in bringing a "beloved transatlantic Brother," George Thompson, to the city during his 1850–51 tour of the United States.[75]

Thompson's visit energized abolitionists throughout the Northeast, as he lectured alongside Sojourner Truth and Douglass; but his presence infuriated anti-abolitionists, who viewed him as an outside agitator intent on challenging American racial traditions. News of a mob attack on Truth and Thompson in Springfield, Massachusetts, reached Rochester before the trio did, strengthening abolitionists' resolve. Truth was certainly undaunted. She had been enslaved, under the name Isabelle Van Wagenen, on an Ulster County farm and fled to New York City in 1826, before the New York State emancipation law took full effect. After struggling to find economic security and spiritual comfort in New York City, she took the name Sojourner Truth and moved in 1843 to a utopian community in western Massachusetts that included many abolitionists. Seven years later, she happily joined Thompson's tour.

In Rochester, numerous abolitionists, including Post and Griffiths, organized events for Thompson, Truth, and Douglass. The Athenaeum Association, a group of Rochester businessmen, invited Thompson to speak at Corinthian Hall on 11 March 1851, after which a two-day meeting open to abolitionists of every stripe would convene there. In response, the *Daily Advertiser* raged against the British orator, condemning him as a "pestilent presence" who seeks to "desecrate our State." The editor urged residents to shun him as they would "a man polluted with the plague, and the exhalation of whose breath was a foetid poison, contaminating all within its reach."[76] Nonetheless, some twelve hundred women and men paid a small fee to attend Thompson's lecture. He was ushered to the stage that evening by a group of five local men, including Isaac Post, and received a warm reception.[77] Having arrived in Rochester "with the most serious apprehensions of disturbance," the British orator instead found as "respectable and intelligent" an audience "as I ever addressed in my life."[78]

Area abolitionists continued to impress Thompson. The presence of Truth and Abby Kelley, now Abby Kelley Foster, certainly heightened interest in the convention and ensured the Posts' intimate involvement. This time it was Truth who stayed at 36 Sophia Street. As the *Liberator* noted, the Posts were "untiring in their services to the cause, and most generous in their hospitality to the strangers who have visited Rochester."[79] However, the Posts and their WNYASS coworkers had only a limited role in organizing the convention. Evangelical abolitionists and Free Soil Party members, like Samuel Porter, were the major players. The difference was immediately visible. Men alone presided over Thompson's lecture and the convention. Among WNYASS participants, only Daniel Anthony served as an officer. The other officers were all political abolitionists, and the only woman among them was Griffiths.[80] Foster and Truth spoke at the convention, but few other women gained the platform. Still, if the goal was to attract a large audience, it was certainly met, as more than one thousand people attended the convention's sessions.

Thompson spoke to a rapt audience as he decried slavery, lambasted civil and church authorities for cooperating in its continuation, and highlighted the guilt of ordinary women and men in failing to challenge the institution. After noting that the Fugitive Slave Law was bringing the crisis to a head nationally, he proclaimed, "[We must] rejoice that the battle is at hand, for . . . [the] God of the oppressed is with us," and "certain victory awaits us."[81] While talk of "battle" always worried the Posts, they were nonetheless thrilled with Thompson's oratory and Truth's decision to remain with them following the convention.

The excitement generated by the convention convinced Griffiths that the moment was ripe for expanding the local movement. Thompson had agreed to return to Rochester in late April, and Julia was determined to organize a Grand Anti-Slavery Festival for the occasion. If the hundreds thrilled by the British orator could be persuaded to purchase goods there, antislavery coffers would be filled to overflowing. Griffiths formed a festival committee that included but reached well beyond the usual WNYASS circle. In addition to Amy Post and her longtime coworkers, Griffiths invited white evangelical women, who had not identified with public antislavery efforts since the 1830s, to join. Four black women from the Union Anti-Slavery Society added their names to the call as well. Sojourner Truth did not, but she was likely still involved, as she used 36 Sophia Street as her home base in spring 1851, lecturing at Corinthian Hall and the AME Zion Church and in surrounding towns. Representatives from area towns were not part of the festival committee, however. This was a strictly urban affair.[82]

Like the composition of the committee, the tone of the announcement was refined rather than indignant. The appeal for "a grand ANTI-SLAVERY FESTIVAL," to be held on 29 April, appeared in the *North Star*. Attendees would find "generous contributions from Anti-Slavery Ladies in Bristol, Bridgewater, Manchester, and Cork," including "a fine assortment of Useful and Fancy Articles," such as "a beautiful Swan's Down Muff and Tippet" and "a rare and choice collection of Irish Sea Weed, tastefully arranged." Not wishing to diminish the luster of these foreign items with the usual contributions from small towns, area women were asked only to provide food for "the Refreshment Tables." Moreover, unlike WNYASS announcements, readers heard no pleas from brutalized workers or wails of devastated black mothers. Finally, the announcement listed committee members by their respective marital titles—Mrs. Post, Miss Porter, Mrs. Weddle—a form never used by WNYASS women. At least the policy also applied to black women, such as Mrs. Hawkins and Mrs. Paul.[83]

Whether inspired by the desire to disentangle abolition from women's rights or simply to recruit new blood to the cause, Griffiths launched a reconfiguration of women's antislavery activism through the Thompson festival. In doing so, she replaced Post as the conductor of this collaborative venture. Griffiths was savvy enough to invite Amy Post, Mary Hallowell, Sarah Burtis, Huldah Anthony, and a few other WNYASS stalwarts to join the festival committee and sufficiently dedicated to interracialism to include Mrs. Caroline Hawkins and three other black activists. More importantly, however, a new circle of white women was recruited for the festival. Two— Susan Porter and her sister Maria G. Porter—were founding members of the 1834 Rochester Female Anti-Slavery Society. They returned to the abolitionist fold along with nine women new to the cause. Five were, like Griffiths, British born, including Mrs. Theodore Weddle, who served as president of the committee. All were from evangelical churches or the Unitarian church, many were involved in benevolent efforts, and several came from families of Liberty Party and Free Soil men.[84]

In April 1851, this collective effort achieved great success. Despite unusually cold temperatures and the threat of snow, crowds filled Corinthian Hall, where "Useful and Fancy" goods were displayed for sale and an array of refreshments provided. Despite being excluded from the organizing committee, "Country friends" donated "poultry, eggs, cream, butter, fruit, &c." to feed the visitors, while "rich, elegant and beautiful articles" from England and Ireland ensured they spent their money. For the evening, the hall was "finely lighted up," and Thompson spoke passionately of "those who suffer and are dumb, who are oppressed and reviled, and cannot plead for themselves." Esther Lukens, an abolitionist visiting from Ohio, "saw the secret of his power, and ceased to marvel that the world bowed down and listened."[85] Indeed, everyone seemed impressed by Thompson and by the city's antislavery women.

Still, the 1851 festival proved the culmination rather than the initiation of local women's united efforts in the cause. In the months that followed, white women abolitionists broke into opposing camps. Their black coworkers, momentarily visible as their efforts converged with those of whites, once again faded from the public record. On 23 May 1851, Douglass deepened these divisions by finally announcing his conversion to political abolitionism.[86] In response, the Posts and other WNYASS members redirected their fund-raising efforts to Boston and the *Liberator*. That decision allowed Griffiths to take full charge of efforts on behalf of the *North Star*.

By August 1851, Griffiths had organized a new association, the Rochester Ladies' Anti-Slavery Sewing Society (RLASS), dropping "Sewing" from the name soon after. Douglass quickly anointed the group. In the 4 September issue of the newly titled *Frederick Douglass' Paper*, he lamented that "during the last two years, this city has been without a Female Anti-Slavery

Society; and the want of such an auxiliary has been deeply felt by us." He applauded the new society as the "firm and faithful friends of freedom, . . . the same who gave the memorable Anti-Slavery Festival in honor of George Thompson."[87]

Douglass's editorial stunned Post and her coworkers, who had labored tirelessly on his behalf from December 1847 through the Thompson festival. It must have angered members of the Union Anti-Slavery Sewing Society as well. It was the WNYASS women, however, who had dedicated the bulk of their efforts to the *North Star*. Douglass both erased their efforts of recent years and anointed the newly formed RLASS as Rochester's *only* female antislavery organization. That society's officers—the Porters, Mrs. Weddle, and six others—were all recruited by Griffiths. A longer list of RLASS members appeared in a January 1852 announcement for another antislavery festival. No WNYASS members signed this call, replaced by evangelical and Unitarian women. Many had ties to political abolitionists, led by the wife, sister, and daughters of Samuel Porter. Although the RLASS insisted that "this association *did not deem it duty* to make an election be-tween *old* and *new* organization . . . but preferred to assume an independent position," its membership roster made its affiliations clear.[88]

Griffiths did urge Amy Post to join the new association, which would en-sure its primacy in the city. Although Post usually embraced opportunities to bring activists together and bridge religious and institutional differences, she refused to do so this time. While Post's alienation could be explained by her dismay over Douglass's embrace of political abolition, it was also fu-eled by her knowledge that Griffiths had wrested control of Thompson's visit from her. In 1850, Post had sent Thompson an invitation to speak in Rochester but learned from William Nell that her invitation had been re-sponded to in a letter to Julia Griffiths. Garrison, who had relayed the news to Nell, was "surprised that you [Post] were yet ignorant of it."[89] Whatever suspicions this raised in Post's mind were heightened by Griffiths's insis-tence on sole direction of the April 1851 festival. The establishment of a ri-val organization was the last step. While Griffiths complained to Gerrit Smith that "bigotry precluded many of the old friends from joining" the RLASS, she had steadily undermined any possibility of allying with Post.[90]

No members of the Union Anti-Slavery Sewing Society appeared on the roster of RLASS members either. Sojourner Truth attended a few RLASS meetings, but only those held at Douglass's home, where she often visited Anna Douglass. Her commitments—Garrisonian abolition, women's rights, and spiritualism—ensured her loyalty to Post. Thus, within months of the

Thompson festival, the RLASS stood alone as an all-white, all-female organization dedicated to supporting Douglass. Although women in the WNYASS and the Union Anti-Slavery Society remained active, they received little coverage in *Frederick Douglass' Paper*. The rift was not without its costs. In August 1851, Griffiths noted that Douglass's "change on the Constitution has thinned our Subscription list considerably." She used this claim to justify her formation of a new "Anti-Slavery sewing circle" that will be "influential, permanent, & efficient."[91] Yet not all of his former friends abandoned him. The Posts were among those who continued their subscriptions, though not their avid support, of Douglass's paper.

Throughout this ordeal, newsy letters from Nell, who critiqued Douglass's turn to political abolitionism and Griffiths's influence on him, raised Amy's spirits. He detailed developments in Boston, including the activities of the vigilance committee and fears for fugitives William and Ellen Craft. In turn, Nell depended on Amy for news of Rochester friends and his sister Frances. In December 1850, amid the machinations over Thompson's visit, he wrote Post about his fears of Frances dying in childbirth. However, he soon received a telegram announcing the birth of William Albert Cleggett and the survival of Frances, and Amy visited them to reassure Nell that all was well.[92]

In September 1851, much to the Posts' delight, Nell returned to 36 Sophia Street and stayed for a year. Drawn in part by the arrival of his nephew and namesake, he also came to promote his newly published *Services of Colored Americans, in the Wars of 1776 and 1812*, which highlighted the crucial role of black soldiers and civilians in the founding of the American Republic. Nell sought Amy's ministrations for unspecified but painful ailments as well. And he was eager to rejoin local spiritualist circles and soon sent messages to Garrison from deceased abolitionists and repentant slave owners, including John C. Calhoun, for whom Isaac served as medium.[93]

Despite the conflicts in local antislavery circles, Nell worked intermittently with Douglass in resisting the Fugitive Slave Law and contributed articles to his paper. The two activists agreed on the right of blacks to use force to protect their community, and William attended an October meeting of the Colored Citizens of Rochester, where participants resolved that they would follow the Boston model. They agreed to "constitute ourselves a vigilance committee" to notify citizens immediately of any arrests and do all in their power to secure the liberty of the city's free black population as well as any "who, guided by the *North Star*, have declared their independence of slavery."[94] Nell certainly discussed these developments with the

Posts as he worked with the local vigilance committee, and Amy at least seemed to take his appeals for armed self-defense to heart.

In March 1852, the Posts, Nell, and other friends and family members attended a "Grand Anti-Slavery Convention" and fair at Corinthian Hall. Although the organizers of the convention were mainly political abolitionists, and the RLASS managed the fair, some WNYASS members participated. They may have ridiculed the RLASS's claim that only now "the evils of slavery have reached our own fire-sides," but they must also have hoped that differences between Garrisonians and political abolitionists could still be bridged, as had been done in many parts of the Midwest.[95] Or perhaps WNYASS members were there simply to defend their turf. For many, the purpose of the March convention—to form a new statewide antislavery society—demanded that they challenge the rising tide of political abolitionism. While most speakers were committed to partisan efforts, Stephen S. Foster, Abby Kelley Foster, and Benjamin Fish spoke for the Garrisonians. Similarly, Amy Post, Abigail Bush, and Benjamin Fish joined a committee to craft the society's constitution, although they were outnumbered two to one by political abolitionists. In fact, William Goodell, a Liberty Party and Free Soil leader from Utica, played the primary role in drafting the document. Perhaps most surprisingly for a western New York convention, Abby Kelley Foster was the only woman listed among the speakers, and Amy Post and Abigail Bush the only women listed as committee members.[96]

When the constitution of the new New York State Anti-Slavery Society was presented, Stephen Foster "labored earnestly, and against much opposition," to make the new organization auxiliary to the AASS. While "able speeches were made on both sides," Nell noted that "as usual, in the best of debate, expressions were used that tended to widen the breach rather than harmonize differences." It was "evident," he concluded, "that no union would be made with the American Anti-Slavery Society, and the result so proved."[97] Once the constitution was ratified, a fourteen-member executive committee was elected. Of the twelve men chosen, all but Daniel Anthony were active in the Liberty League or the Free Soil Party. Only two women served on the committee, both members of the RLASS. Gerrit Smith was elected president of the society, and the seventeen vice presidents also heavily favored political abolitionism.[98] While Douglass applauded the outcome, many WNYASS members were no doubt offended by his claim that "some who had stood foremost in our ranks" have now been "led to think that anti-slavery effort was useless." Post and her coworkers took issue as well when Douglass proclaimed that that spring's festival "made an impression upon our community *far* more favorable . . . to the cause of freedom than any previous one."[99]

Critics of the convention made their feelings known. Sarah Hallowell immediately wrote Douglass challenging his claims. "For years," she noted icily, WNYASS women "labored earnestly and trustingly to get up Annual Fairs, as a means for aiding our great cause." Noting the burdens that "fell on a few," Hallowell reminded him that they were often forced to purchase their own goods in order to raise the necessary funds. She also insisted that the WNYASS circle was "never thinking of a final cessation of our associated efforts for the *slave*." Indeed, the group had "labored steadily for months" to send contributions to the Boston bazaar. She was publicizing these facts "because from your letter in last week's paper to the Ladies of the 'Rochester A.S. Society,' and from their report, it might be supposed that *we* had no existence, were dead, disheartened, disbanded. Justice to our friends, and a due self-respect, alike prompt us to make our existence known."[100]

Douglass published Hallowell's letter and simultaneously dismissed it. In an editorial comment, he wrote that he "fail[ed] to perceive either utility or pertinency" in the letter and claimed "it would be easy to point out many defects and inaccuracies." Douglass then critiqued specific points while pretending that the society on whose behalf Hallowell had written was some unknown entity, rather than the same WNYASS circle that had helped sustain the *North Star* in its infancy.[101]

Perhaps hoping to provide some redress for WNYASS grievances, Nell wrote Garrison that "a vast deal of good would be accomplished by holding the [May AASS] anniversary meeting in Rochester."[102] After a proslavery mob disrupted its convention in New York City in May 1850, the AASS held its next annual meeting in Syracuse. Nell was convinced it was time to bring Garrison back to Rochester. The AASS board accepted Nell's suggestion and reserved Corinthian Hall for 11–13 May 1852.

A host of famous activists attended the AASS convention, including Parker Pillsbury, Wendell Phillips, Robert Purvis, and Eliza J. Kenny. They joined activists long familiar to Rochesterians, such as Garrison, Remond, Kelley Foster, and Nell. An array of local abolitionists participated as well, including the Posts and the Hallowells as well as Douglass, Porter, and Griffiths. Surprisingly, however, the organizing committee was composed solely of men, including Isaac Post; and men dominated the speakers' platform. Nonetheless, the women who spoke, especially Abby Kelley Foster, enjoyed enthusiastic responses, and a few women were represented on AASS committees. Amy was elected to the fifteen-member business committee with Mary Hallowell, Abigail Bush, and Lydia Mott. While the four women brought extensive experience to the committee, they were no doubt glad of one another's company as they debated issues with prominent male activists from New York, Boston, and Philadelphia. Sallie Holley served on the finance committee with Abby Kelley Foster, and Eliza Kenny was the lone woman elected among the four secretaries.

Despite the excitement among western New York abolitionists, the death of Isaac Hopper just four days before the opening session lent a somber atmosphere to the convention. The first morning was dedicated to tributes to the beloved Quaker. Perhaps his spirit led Garrison and Gerrit Smith, the latter via a lengthy letter, to bridge tensions between supporters of the AASS and Free Soilers. Garrison offered a resolution that the AASS "gladly welcome all (however they may differ in other respects) who will aid faithfully in our great work." Even Douglass "was pleased with his exposition" of the society's principles.[103]

Yet the common ground laid on the first day was quickly trampled. Douglass wrote a lengthy epistle to Smith, complaining "that the practice of the [AASS] Society had not been according to its theory" and listing numerous examples. His frustration flared during debates over the proslavery character of the U.S. Constitution, the refusal to make the New York State Anti-Slavery Society auxiliary to the AASS, and the recent visit of Hungarian revolutionary Louis Kossuth. During a tour of the United States, Kossuth had refused to denounce slavery, and most Garrisonians indicted him on that ground. Douglass was convinced that the various critiques were aimed at him, and some certainly were. Black activists Charles Lenox Remond and Samuel Ringwold were particularly harsh, claiming that an article by Douglass praising Kossuth was unworthy of a true abolitionist. Garrison, Phillips, and a few others tried to calm the waters by distinguishing between personal disagreements and the policies of the AASS.[104]

The convention might have dissolved in rancor but for the announcement by Douglass that slave catchers had arrived in Rochester to capture three fugitives.[105] Two self-emancipated brothers and a cousin had reached the Posts' house a week earlier. From there, one was taken to Douglass's home, another to Asa Anthony's farm, and the third to a family in nearby Irondequoit. It was Jacob Post who first alerted Douglass of the danger and then immediately set out in his carriage to take the fugitive from Douglass's home to Anthony's farm. The two hid out in the nearby woods, armed with knives and guns, until dark. Another abolitionist then took the two brothers to Irondequoit, picked up their cousin, and spirited them to Williamson, where they were smuggled across the lake to Canada.[106] When news reached the convention on its last day that the three fugitives were safe, participants joined hands in joy and relief.

Hoping to suture some of the wounds inflicted at the convention, Douglass was elected one of thirty-six AASS managers for the following year, alongside Isaac's brother Joseph Post. Still, Garrison was chosen president, and he and nearly all the twenty-eight vice presidents, including Isaac Post, were ardent disunionists.[107] Nell, who took copious notes during the convention, recognized the near impossibility of bridging the growing differences in antislavery ranks. His rift with Douglass made a longer stay in Rochester difficult. Nell spent much of the summer traveling in central New York, and in August 1852, he returned to Boston.

That same summer, Douglass moved his family from their home on Alexander Street to a farm, two miles south of the city center. Convenient for fugitives heading north to Rochester because of its proximity to the road but distance from other houses, the South Avenue location also provided some relief from the constant prying of local residents—friends and foes alike. Anna Douglass may have been particularly happy to be farther away from the intrusions of Frederick's coworkers. Even Griffiths had to make special arrangements to reach the new house.

The physical distance between Douglass and the city paralleled the emotional distance between him and the Posts, although all three remained deeply committed to abolitionism. Amy took no part in RLASS activities and chose not to salve wounds or orchestrate ties between the new organization and WNYASS women. On this occasion, she removed her conductor's hat as frustration, anger, and disappointment led to fatigue. At the same time, she was concerned that the new emphasis on vigilance committees as central to aiding fugitives might curtail women's roles even in the most progressive antislavery organizations. At the May 1852 AASS convention, only nine women were chosen as officers out of the eighty-one positions filled. Conventions of black activists, too, became more male centered and less open to women's participation and influence.[108] While Post remained committed to addressing issues of race and gender simultaneously, the challenges to such a universalist vision seemed more daunting than ever.

In this context, Amy Post's activist worlds both narrowed and expanded. Nearly all her radical friends provided safe havens for fugitives or supported such work by others. In fact, the one aspect of the RLASS that Amy and her coworkers fully approved was its commitment to fugitives. After 1852, the

WNYASS circle left local fairs to their rival organization, albeit with some reluctance. Instead, Amy and her coworkers prepared goods for the Boston fair and stockpiled food, clothing, and medicine to assist fugitives. They still attended antislavery lectures and conventions; and the Posts hosted Truth, Nell, William Wells Brown, Lucy Stone, Garrison, and other itinerant lecturers to reinforce the bonds among radical friends.

As the WNYASS faded away, local "free meetings" provided arenas in which the advocacy of abolition remained intertwined with women's rights, peace, and other progressive causes. Local radicals also gathered on Sundays at Asa Anthony's or Daniel Anthony's farm, and at the Anti-Slavery Reading Room or the Post home during the week, discussing and debating the latest events, developments, and challenges. In addition, after missing the first three annual meetings of Progressive Friends, Amy attended four of the next eight.[109] These meetings became the site where Amy's activist worlds most fully converged, as participants continued to insist on nothing less than a "thorough re-organization of Society."[110] Addressing "social evils" from slavery and intemperance to capital punishment and the wrongs of women, Progressive Friends believed it "necessary to strike deep at the root . . . though it should expose us to the violence of sectarian bigotry, anathema and reproach."[111]

In June 1852, less than a month after the tumultuous AASS convention, the Posts eagerly joined the Progressive Friends in Waterloo.[112] As epistles and letters were read from like-minded meetings in Ohio, Michigan, Indiana, Pennsylvania, and eastern New York, Amy saw her activist world expanding outward to incorporate new allies and new issues. She and Isaac served on committees to respond to epistles, distribute the proceedings, and publicize the next year's meeting. Stanton was in attendance as were Amy's cousins Sarah Thayer and Lydia Mott, who traveled from central New York, and F/friend Catherine Fish Stebbins from Ann Arbor. As they grieved for dear Susan Doty, who had died that spring, "the conviction pervaded the assembly that LOVE, as it resides in Divinity . . . and is recognized in the human soul,—is at once the mightiest and most reliable Principle of Reform— the realization and actualization of it in the human character individually, the only hope of the world."[113] For Amy, the bruising conflicts of the previous year may have momentarily faded from view.

For Post as for Progressive Friends generally, "progression, or the tendency of all nature to higher degrees of refinement and development," is one of God's laws. For Amy and Isaac, spiritual communication was one manifestation of progression. And they did not have to choose between religious affiliations, since Progressive Friends formed "a Universal Church; emphatically, the Church of Humanity; the portals of which may be open to Christian, Jew, Mohammedan, . . . Pagan," or spiritualist.[114]

In epistles to other meetings of Progressive Friends, which the Posts helped draft, members addressed the critical issues of the day. They characterized slavery as "a crime most revolting and sacrilegious," and noted "its hideous cruelties" and "the heart-crushing despair of its victims." Once again employing the potent language of the WNYASS, they called upon Progressive Friends to " 'scatter the living coals of truth / Upon the nation's naked heart' to awaken the conscience of the people." They resolved as well that "the Fugitive Slave Bill is the legitimate offspring of the *American Slave Power*, and that we are bound not to respect its demands, but to trample it under feet, by rendering to the fugitive slave all the assistance in our power." At the same time, they urged Friends to take up "the great work of woman's elevation and regeneration," for "on her elevation depends that of the race."[115]

Amy returned home with a more open heart, eager to return to the struggle. Nell was still with the family that June, and though both were disappointed with Douglass's actions, they likely attended his 5 July lecture. The RLASS had invited Douglass to speak on 4 July, but he refused to celebrate the day that honored the independence of a nation committed to slavery. He spoke instead the following day, when five to six hundred abolitionists, paying admission of twelve and a half cents each, crowded the main floor of Corinthian Hall. Given the size of the crowd and the significance of the day, the audience surely included a wide range of antislavery activists, black and white, women and men, Garrisonians and Free Soilers.[116]

In his opening, Douglass pointed to the distance between the slave plantation where he was raised and the magnificent Corinthian Hall. He then noted the relative youth of the United States, only seventy-six years old that 4th of July, which gave hope to those who sought to change the nation's course. As he warmed to his subject, his voice rose. "The signers of the Declaration of Independence were brave men" who placed public good above private gain, Douglass declared. But, he asked, "What have I, or those I represent, have to do with your national independence?" Addressing the white members of the audience, he admonished them: "This Fourth [of] July is *yours*, not *mine*. *You* may rejoice, *I* must mourn." For nearly an hour, he offered an impassioned condemnation of the conditions of the slave, the silence of the church, the limits and possibilities of the Constitution, and the horrors of the Fugitive Slave Law. Douglass then prophesied the war to come and the intractability of racism even after slavery was eradicated. Still, after this long journey through the darkest aspects of the nation's existence, he concluded: "I do not despair of this country. . . . 'The arm of the Lord is not shortened,' and the doom of slavery is certain."[117]

As Douglass fell silent, the audience rose and cheered. Many realized immediately they had heard one of the greatest antislavery orations ever given and insisted on its immediate publication. Relieved and excited by the response of such a large and diverse group, Douglass printed the speech in his paper the next week and published seven hundred copies in pamphlet form.[118] His 5 July oration quickly became a touchstone for other antislavery lecturers. It also helped ease some of the strain that had developed between Douglass and Post in the preceding months. In early August, Douglass responded to a letter from Amy, thanking her for her "kind wishes" and hoping that he would see her before leaving for Pittsburgh the next afternoon. He also urged her to "stay calm" in the face of a cholera epidemic in the city. "We are all subjects—part of a great *whole*—in the hands of a Supreme power—and you and I have decided that power is *good*." Closing with love to Isaac, Douglass added, "Julia desires her warm regards to yourself and friends."[119] Apparently, some hope of reconciliation existed on both sides.

Yet the breach in women's antislavery ranks remained wide. For the next several years, RLASS and WNYASS women met regularly, but separately. Only the rare individual bridged the two societies. Two who did carry news of the RLASS to Post were Lucy Colman, a longtime friend, and teacher Julia Wilbur, whose sister-in-law Charlotte Wilbur was active in the RLASS. Both Wilbur and Colman gained Douglass's approbation for their efforts to integrate Rochester's schools, and Colman hosted RLASS meetings on occasion.[120] At the same time, the two women met periodically with members of the "old organization," the WNYASS.

Wilbur, who had unsuccessfully tried to enroll Rosetta Douglass in her class at the lily-white public school in 1849, chronicled the differences between Griffiths's organization and the WNYASS circle in her diary. On 4 June 1852, she noted that the RLASS was "favorable to views entertained by Douglass. They have little sympathy with the old Society, but *I* can sympathize with both." Acknowledging that there "is more influence & 'respectability' belonging, perhaps, to this new Society," she nonetheless "doubt[ed] whether there is that self-sacrificing, martyr-like spirit among its members wh[ich] is necessary to make an organization useful & efficient." She did, however, recognize that the RLASS might "have a good influence upon a class who has hitherto been indifferent" to the cause, and on that basis concluded to "help them when I can."[121] By November, she was moving back and forth between old society and new, attending meetings at Amy Post's and Mary Hallowell's on the 11th and 18th and at Mrs. Weddle's on the 12th. She found the RLASS more "lively" as women prepared for "the approaching festival." Similar work was being done by the old society, but it was being sent off to Boston; and Julia admitted, "I do not enjoy the meetings of this society as much as I do those of the new society."[122] The Quakerly quiet embraced by the WNYASS circle may have influenced Wilbur's views, or the fact that the RLASS attracted more young and fashionable members.

Griffiths and Post maintained a distant but cordial relationship, and Julia still tried to recruit Amy for the RLASS. In October 1852, she wrote "My dear friend" Amy, who she hoped was "enjoy[ing] a thorough holiday." She regretted hearing "of your son Joseph's illness" and "fear he is worse by your sister being sent for." She added, "I miss you very much . . . for although we do differ on 'the Constitution,' we *agree* to differ & that's a good thing!" Still, Julia pressed Amy to "read *our Rochester* Society Constitution" and assured her the members "would _all_ like to have Mrs. Post with them—*can you say no?*"[123]

The Posts' refusal to engage in the kind of gossip that enveloped Griffiths may have endeared them to her. She certainly believed that if she could recruit Amy to the new society, other "old friends" would follow. Yet however cordial Amy appeared and however much she valued collaboration across activist networks, she refused to join the RLASS or reorient WNYASS fund-raising efforts back to Douglass. Still, she corresponded with Douglass; subscribed to his paper; and joined him and Julia in assisting fugitives, advocating mixed-race social and political efforts, and hosting antislavery lecturers.

Amy never did join the RLASS. For all her skills as a conductor, this was one bridge she would not cross. Post's dedication to Garrisonianism, women's rights, and a holistic approach to activism certainly stood in the way. So, too, did Griffiths's need for control and Douglass's dismissal of the work of the WNYASS. In addition, Amy's sister Sarah and stepdaughter Mary had little patience for Griffiths. Sarah wrote Mary, "rejoic[ing] at Julia's removal" from the Douglass household and wishing Anna Douglass would "express some wholesome truths" that "could send J[ulia] to Australia after her brother, or some other desirable retreat."[124] If Amy's nearest and dearest kin and coworkers held such views, she was not going to seek a public rapprochement.

Instead, Amy devoted more energy to her friendships with Nell, Jacobs, and Truth. Their correspondence was reinforced by intermittent visits, and their discussions ranged over topics political, personal, and spiritual. Truth, who never learned to write, had friends send missives to Amy, and all three stayed with the Posts when they visited Rochester. Bound by their advocacy of abolition, women's rights, and spiritualism, they remained devoted to each other's well-being and supported each other's work.[125]

During the early 1850s, popular interest in spiritualism grew across the country, though not all believers embraced the Posts' support for abolition and racial equality. Eager to publicize the intelligence gained from spiritual communications, Isaac Post published *Voices from the Spirit World*, a series of articles *"written under the control of spirits,"* in 1852. It contained transcripts of sixty-two brief remarks and forty-two longer messages *"by the hand of Isaac Post, Medium."* The book was advertised in reform as well as mainstream papers and sold at some antislavery conventions. Nell, who lectured across central New York in spring and summer 1852, wrote from Waterloo that he had sold three or four copies of *Services of Colored Americans* and five "Voices from the Spirit World."[126]

For the Posts, Nell, and like-minded activists, spiritualism did not detract from their worldly endeavors but helped sustain their commitment to social justice. Isaac's book contained multiple messages from Elias Hicks, George Fox, William Penn, John Woolman, and other Friends, as well as activists Nathaniel P. Rogers, Margaret Fuller, and Abby Fowler. Although not all spirits are clearly identified, none appear to be African American. Several messages are aimed at abolition, however, including denunciations of slavery from John C. Calhoun, Thomas Jefferson, and other slaveholders. Taken together, the spirits in *Voices* promise enlightenment in both this life and the world beyond. The large crowd that attended Andrew Jackson Davis's appearance at a spiritualist convention in Rochester in January 1853 added to the audience for Isaac's book.[127]

Sarah Thayer, a cousin and dear F/friend in central New York, insisted on the feminist potential of spiritualism. In March 1853, she wrote to Amy that a "fond mother ought to be better qualified to direct the spiritual life of her own sex than any belov'd disciple or even Jesus himself as a man or a brother."[128] Thayer's letter resonated with debates among women's rights advocates over the role of religion in furthering or constraining the cause. Women in more progressive religious circles, including Progressive Friends and Unitarians as well as spiritualists, often viewed religious leaders as important allies in social justice campaigns. After all, Lucretia Mott was a Quaker minister; Samuel J. May, William Henry Channing, and Theodore Parker advocated abolition and women's rights from Unitarian pulpits; and some spiritualist mediums assured the living that sex equality was well supported in the next world.[129] Recognizing that most churches did not embrace women's rights, these activists supported resolutions demanding spiritual as well as social, economic, educational, and political equality, yet they did not denounce religion itself as a barrier to women's advancement. Leaders who had grown up in more traditional churches—for example, Elizabeth Cady Stanton, raised as an Episcopalian, and Ernestine Rose, raised as an Orthodox Jew—considered religion itself as central to women's oppression.[130]

This controversy emerged at nearly every woman's rights convention from 1848 through the 1850s, with participants often spending hours on the issue. Lucretia Mott and other movement leaders challenged ministers who claimed women's subordination was divinely ordained, but woman's rights advocates also argued among themselves over religion's potential to serve as a progressive force.[131] Post stood clearly on the side of Mott and the possibilities of progressive religions to foster gender equality. Reading reports on the 1850 woman's rights conventions in Worcester, Massachusetts, and Salem, Ohio, Amy likely paid particular attention to the comments of friends Betsy Mix Cowles and Esther Lukens in Salem and of Mott, Douglass, Kelley Foster, Stone, and Rose in Worcester.[132] Ernestine Rose, a self-proclaimed atheist, was unique in insisting on the oppressive character of *all* religion, a position that Post opposed even as her admiration for Rose grew.[133] Other issues debated at these two meetings echoed fundamental questions that Post and other radical activists had discussed for years. Were women and men essentially the same, necessitating equal rights in every sphere, or were they essentially different, which required redrawing the spheres to ensure equality despite those differences? Were custom and tradition to blame for the current injustices, requiring women and men to work together to achieve change, or must women demand their rights, recognizing that—despite male allies—it was men who wielded the power that constrained them?[134]

Post certainly discussed reports of the first National Woman's Rights Convention at Worcester with friends who were there, including Douglass, Colman, and Abby Kelley Foster. Amy was pleased with the participation of labor activists such as Eliza Kenny and radicals such as Ernestine Rose, who ensured attention to the economic aspects of female subordination. She must have been equally excited by a resolution that explicitly linked woman's rights to enslaved women's emancipation: "That the cause we are met to advocate,—the claim for woman of all her natural and civil rights,—bids us remember the million and a half of slave women at the South, the most grossly wronged and foully outraged of all women." The resolution had incited a furious debate. Some participants opposed efforts to link woman's rights and abolition, while others insisted that race and sex oppression were deeply intertwined.[135] Like Post, a majority of convention participants supported the latter position.

By 1851, Post viewed woman's rights conventions as a crucial arena in which to promote her universalist vision of social justice and was eager to organize another meeting in Rochester. With Willie in school and family members happy to share childcare, Amy wrote Lucretia Mott, suggesting that a National Woman's Rights Convention be scheduled for Rochester in 1853. Mott passed the suggestion on to Stanton, along with a similar plea from friends in Syracuse.[136] Post was inspired no doubt by news of conventions elsewhere, including one in Akron, Ohio, in May 1851. Sojourner Truth had been staying with the Posts since March, using it as her home base as she traveled for lectures and conventions. During a tour of the Midwest in May, Truth stopped in Akron and offered extemporaneous remarks to the woman's rights convention there. The transcript that Marius Robinson published in the *Anti-Slavery Bugle* must have riveted Amy: "I am a woman's rights. I have as much muscle as any man, and can do as much work as any man. I have plowed and reaped and husked and chopped and mowed, and can any man do more than that? I have heard much about the sexes being equal; I can carry as much as any man, and can eat as much too, if I can get it. I am strong as any man that is now."[137]

Inspired by reports from Akron and other conventions, Post and her coworkers invited Ernestine Rose to speak at Corinthian Hall on 19 June 1851. Julia Wilbur described Rose as "a sensible lady" and an independent thinker. Although she was slightly bored by her speech, she refused to align herself with her "very sensitive" neighbors who "thought she was an infidel."[138] Post, on the other hand, was delighted with Rose and thrilled that she added Rochester to her lecture circuit for the next two years.

When Rose arrived in the United States in 1836 with her English husband William, she carried with her European and British radical traditions that combined women's rights, workers' rights, and abolition. She had earlier rejected a marriage arranged by her Jewish father and become an atheist. Many Americans, including some reformers, criticized her as a heathen, socialist, and free lover. Ernestine and William Rose's participation in celebrations of Thomas Paine's birthday, which memorialized the transatlantic revolutionary, added to her suspect reputation. Although Ernestine Rose's campaign for married women's property rights in New York State in the 1840s garnered support from Stanton and a few other female activists, others feared being linked with infidels and fanatics.

Post, however, agreed with Rose's claims for the deep connections among sexual, racial, economic, and religious oppressions and liberations. Rose reinforced the Progressive Friends' 1850 proclamation that women's rights were human rights and insisted that the universalist approach to social change was the only path to meaningful transformation. Moreover, Post's conception of religious liberty allowed her to see atheism as a choice, and Rose's admiration of Paine strengthened Amy's esteem for the revolutionary ex-Quaker. Indeed, Post admired Rose so much that she ordered a copy of her portrait from William Nell.[139]

Throughout the early 1850s, the woman's rights agenda was expanded and debated as lecturers, petition campaigns, and local, state, and national conventions received growing coverage in the reform and mainstream press, and as advocates testified before state legislative committees and constitutional conventions across the North. Some women, including Susan B. Anthony, worked to link woman's rights with temperance. A temperance advocate since the 1840s, Anthony had become increasingly frustrated by male temperance leaders' refusal to grant women a voice in the movement. After hearing about early woman's rights conventions and befriending Stanton, she took a stand at a statewide convention in Albany in winter 1852 organized by the Sons of Temperance. Anthony rose to speak as a delegate from Rochester and was told that "the sisters were not invited there to speak but to listen and learn." She then walked out with four other women, and they quickly organized a women's meeting with the assistance of Lydia Mott and newspaper editor Thurlow Weed. At the end of that meeting, Anthony agreed to chair a committee to call a Woman's State Temperance Convention.[140]

Anthony returned to Rochester and rented Corinthian Hall for the 20 April event. Some five hundred women, including Post, listened as Anthony read the widely circulated call, which had been signed by well-known activists from central and western New York. Here, as at the Thompson antislavery festival, women crossed existing boundaries of ideology and faith to show their solidarity for the cause. Anthony, Stanton, Post, and other woman's rights advocates lent their names, as did several evangelical women active in the local Daughters of Temperance. Men signed the call as well, including Daniel Anthony and William Hallowell. Woman's rights advocates dominated the organizing committee and prepared the slate of officers. Amy Post, Rhoda DeGarmo, Sarah Fish, and Mary Hallowell were elected alongside the Reverend Antoinette Brown, Amelia Bloomer, and Susan B. Anthony. The participants then elected Elizabeth Cady Stanton to preside over the meeting.[141]

Although woman's rights advocates had organized the temperance meeting, the speeches and discussions that followed revealed deep tensions within the convention. Stanton outraged many moderate participants by calling for states to legalize divorce for women married to "drunkards" and grant them custody of their children. She also proposed withdrawing women's funds from foreign mission work in order to "devote ourselves to the poor and suffering around us."[142] The many temperance advocates who held traditional views on marriage and supported foreign missions were horrified. Stanton tried to calm the waters by declaring that she did not consider "divorce as a *remedy* for the evil" of drunkenness. Rather, it was simply "a moral duty on the part of the wife" to leave an intemperate husband. While several women immediately spoke out in agreement, others challenged the very idea of divorce. Some participants also claimed that woman's rights advocates were "unjust towards temperance men of the Empire State" and preferred to remain auxiliary to their society.[143] While progressive participants prevailed, forming the Woman's New York State Temperance Society, they left many participants disgruntled. Still, the majority elected Stanton as president and Anthony as one of two women to organize auxiliaries, collect funds, certify memberships, and circulate petitions.

Three months later, the Men's State Temperance Convention in Syracuse refused to seat Anthony and instead attacked her. Anthony's courage in the face of these venomous assaults came in part from the vibrant activist community in Rochester. Susan did not move to Rochester with her family until 1849, but then she immediately became enmeshed in the city's multiple reform circles. She eagerly attended temperance and antislavery conventions and, at the May 1852 AASS convention, was stirred by the oratory of Garrison, Phillips, Douglass, and other luminaries. She was also inspired by the dedication of the Rochester activists among whom she sat—the Posts, the Fishes, the Hallowells, and her cousin Sarah Anthony Burtis.[144] She was likely impressed as well with Julia Griffiths, another single woman dedicated to social change.

In September 1852, Anthony attended her first woman's rights convention when the national meeting was held in Syracuse. Although Post and her coworkers were disappointed that Rochester was not selected to host the event, they traveled the sixty miles east for the grand affair. A central committee now helped organize and publicize the national conventions and invited well-known orators—men and women—to speak. The meeting "was densely packed at every session," despite a small fee charged at the door.[145] Delegates attended from eight states and Canada, and some prominent reformers, like Garrison and Angelina Grimké Weld, sent letters. The pioneers of 1848 were well represented by Lucretia Mott, who presided, and her sister Martha Wright, who served as one of three secretaries, as well as by James Mott, Amy Post, Mary Hallowell, Sarah Hallowell, Catherine Fish Stebbins, and Thomas and Mary Ann M'Clintock. Anthony was appointed to the nominating committee and selected as one of the secretaries, while a pregnant Stanton stirred the masses from afar by urging property-owning women, via letter, to refuse to pay their taxes until they gained political rights.[146] Several women donned the new bloomer costume, a short skirt worn over trousers. Mingling with women in fashionable dress and others in simple Quaker garb, those in bloomers attracted the most attention. They included Elizabeth Smith Miller, who had designed the outfit, and Amelia Bloomer, who popularized it in the *Lily*, as well as Anthony and Post, who praised the benefits of such practical and comfortable attire.

The Syracuse convention was notable for energetic disagreements among participants. The long-simmering debate over whether women deserved rights because of their difference from or equality with men erupted in full force. Lucretia Mott declared that woman's "moral feelings" were not "more elevated than man's; but that with the same opportunities for development, with the same restrictions and penalties, there would probably be about an equal manifestation of virtue."[147] While applauded by Post and other radical F/friends, plenty of participants insisted that it was women's moral superiority that necessitated her entrance into the professions, politics, the church, and other institutions. Most of the discussion focused on practical strategies to advance the cause, and here, too, differences abounded. Some wanted to establish a newspaper and a national organization; others demanded state legislative action and pushed for suffrage; still others focused on local efforts, including raising wages, expanding employment opportunities, and empowering property-owning women.

If Post voiced her views, they were not recorded. Still, she must have been pleased when Dr. Harriot K. Hunt, one of the pioneer women physicians in the nation, declared, "Unseen spirits have been with us in this Convention; the spirits of our Shaker sisters whom untold sorrows have driven into those communal societies, the convents of our civilization."[148] Other advocates of spiritualism and health reform also took part in the debates, including Lydia Fowler, whose lectures on women's health, water cures, and nutritious diets had attracted large audiences across the North, including Rochester. She and Post joined Rose, Mott, and others in opposing a resolution by the Reverend Antoinette Brown, who now served a church in South Butler, New York, that sought to make the Bible central to woman's rights demands. While Brown offered a liberal reading of its texts, Post and her radical coworkers refused to take any written text as truth and rejected any attempt to present a specific interpretation of the Bible as "the doctrine of the Convention."[149]

The following year, 1853, Post focused increased attention on women's rights, incorporating her commitment to spiritualism, health reform, temperance, religious liberty, and abolition into her efforts. Perhaps Post's new focus was inevitable. Not only had she fought over women's roles in Friends meetings and antislavery societies for decades, but Rochester now hosted both county and state woman's rights conventions as well as the Woman's New York State Temperance Society meeting. Susan B. Anthony's residence in Rochester also ensured increased activity around women's rights.

At the Monroe County woman's rights convention in mid-January, Post, Anthony, Mary Hallowell, Rhoda DeGarmo, and Sarah Anthony Burtis shared the stage with delegates from nearby towns and national leaders such as Stanton, Rose, and Reverend Brown. Representatives from throughout the county "nearly filled" Corinthian Hall to discuss "the disabilities which the customs and laws impose on the industrial rights and powers of Woman." Rose offered a powerful address on the "Legal Wrongs of Women." Cheers and applause greeted her claim that the movement formed "one link in the chain of progressive reform" and her insistence that women not only gain the right to vote but also "the privilege of being voted for."[150] The delegates also discussed civil, religious, and political rights, and debated the best means for improving the lives of working as well as middle-class and affluent women.

Although the convention aroused great enthusiasm, Post must have missed her pioneering coworker Abigail Bush, who had just given birth to a baby girl. Weeks later, Bush headed to New York City with her five children to board the *Star of the West* steamer, carrying them through the Panama Canal to California. Her husband, Henry, had already traveled to California twice, spending two years there before returning to Rochester to move his family west. However, before final arrangements could be made, Abigail discovered she was pregnant. She insisted on waiting until after the birth to join her husband and oldest son on the Pacific Coast. Harriet Jacobs and

Sarah Hallowell, who were both in New York City when Bush arrived there, noted her sorrow at leaving. On board the ship, she poured out her despair to Amy, lamenting those who were "leaving Home, its Comforts and Endearments," only to be "Doomed to Disappointment, Sorrow & a Grave." She concluded that she never again expected "to find *another* to stand side by side with me, Heart to Heart, in our Labours of Love . . . to our Afflicted and Downtrodden Fellow Ones."[151]

Amid a hectic schedule, Post could not grieve Bush's absence for long. With Sarah on Long Island and Mary Dale, now Mrs. George Johnson, having moved to Buffalo, Amy took on more domestic chores without diminishing her activist efforts. In addition to ongoing campaigns for abolition, temperance, and women's rights, Post was involved in efforts to launch the People's College in New York State. The college would offer classes for women and men more cheaply than all-male institutions, meet "the wants of the practical community," provide training for "useful female employment," and promote "bodily health." Asked to circulate a petition to the state legislature supporting these plans, Post enthusiastically agreed.[152]

At the same time, the problems of working women once again gained attention. In April 1853, the Reverend William H. Channing of Rochester's Unitarian Church lectured on "Woman's Wages." Two weeks later, a group of local women founded a Sempstresses Protective Union, in which, much like the WWPU, members encouraged middle-class reformers to support their demands for economic security.[153] That spring, Amy's friend and coworker Sarah Anthony Burtis, a forty-year-old activist and mother of three, became the first local woman to secure a position as clerk at a clothing store, opening the door for other women to do the same.[154]

Amid these developments, on 20 May, Amy and Isaac invited family and friends to their home to celebrate the long-anticipated marriage of Sarah Hallowell and Edmund Willis. Edmund had ended his partnership with Isaac Post the previous year to join forces with William Hallowell in the woolen business. Although Edmund and Sarah made an extended visit to Westbury and Jericho, they settled in Rochester.[155] While they were on Long Island, Isaac headed to Hartford, Connecticut, for a progressive Bible convention that attracted Unitarians, radical Friends, spiritualists, women's rights advocates, and abolitionists. By the 1850s, he rarely traveled far for any convention but was eager to join in the discussions at Hartford. A euphoric Isaac wrote Amy that on the very first morning he had met Andrew Jackson Davis, Lucy Stone, Parker Pillsbury, Henry C. Wright, and Lewis and Sarah

Burtis. The next day the rooms were so crowded that many audience members had to stand, "even women." Post found the speakers alternately "delightful" and "grand" and praised Garrison in particular for a "worthy" speech. However, some Hartford residents considered the event anti-christian, and a group disrupted the proceedings when Ernestine Rose took the platform. Isaac knew Amy admired Rose and he certainly supported her right to speak. Still, he believed "she would do much more good if she had the knowledge of Spiritual life as some of us have."[156]

While Isaac pondered matters of faith, Amy attended to more practical matters at the first annual meeting of the Woman's New York State Temperance Society in Rochester. Although feeling ill for days beforehand, Post joined Anthony, Stone, and Stanton at the convention, all attired in bloomer costumes to signify their woman's rights politics. She also proudly watched as her stepdaughter, Mary Hallowell, was recognized as chair of the executive committee. Some four hundred women and men attended the opening session, during which Stone, Bloomer, and Reverend Brown lectured on the poisonous effects of alcohol on women, families, and the larger society. But it was Stanton, as usual, who raised the hackles of moderate reformers, this time by claiming that all persons were welcome to join in the society's activities "without regard to sect, sex, color, or caste." While some members were likely concerned about creating an interracial organization, it was the introduction of men that inspired heated debates. Having fought hard the first year to exclude men from membership, Stanton now argued that women, having demonstrated their "self-reliance, dignity, and force," should open the society to everyone. Inspired, perhaps, by the People's College and the Progressive Friends, Stanton and her supporters wanted to transform the "Woman's Society" into the "People's New York State Temperance League."[157]

Protests erupted immediately, and a heated debate ensued. A few men, including Douglass, favored Stanton's proposal on the principle of absolute equality. Others, including several ministers, wished to maintain single-sex societies, eager no doubt to keep women's rights issues out of their temperance gatherings. Several women also argued eloquently for sex segregation. Emily Clark, one of the society's first two agents, stated that her experience the past year "had taught her that the power of the Society lay in the fact of its being a Woman's Society." Amelia Bloomer seconded her view, pointing to "the conduct of men in this Convention," who occupied the floor at length with little concern for women's opinions. "The time has not come," she concluded, "when *men* are prepared to come on a platform with us and acknowledge our equality."[158]

Post, Hallowell, and their radical friends, who had long worked along-side men in antislavery societies, supported Stanton's proposal, but they could not convince large numbers of their view. Instead, the majority of women rejected the change and elected Mary C. Vaughn, an advocate of separate societies, as president over Stanton. Anthony, who was elected secretary, declined to serve because "the Society had taken a position in opposition to Woman's Rights." Post also refused to accept election to office and was replaced by Maria G. Porter, a coworker of Julia Griffiths.[159] After reading about the proceedings in the *New York Tribune*, Isaac wrote Amy from Hartford: "I hope the prospect of a rupture nor the realization of it will injure thy health nor retard its spe[e]dy recovery. I rejoice that the result has been reached for it is better to live in peace though alone than to [contend?]."[160]

More contention lay ahead, although in this case, the Posts were observers rather than participants. A month after the temperance convention, Douglass invited black communities to send delegates to the meeting of a new organization, the National Council of Colored People, at Corinthian Hall. In the late 1840s, Post and her F/friends had been impressed with black organizations' embrace of women's rights. Following passage of the Fugitive Slave Law, however, these organizations shifted their focus to vigilance committees, legal redress, and political organizing, marginalizing women in the process. At the same time, many colored conventions opened their doors more readily to white supporters.[161] Julia Wilbur, for instance, attended the Rochester meeting and noted, "There is a large audience assembled & perhaps some 200 colored persons among them. The [140] Delegates occupied the body of the Hall & the Platform & I never saw an equal number of white men with so many fine looking persons among them." After a full day of speeches, she admitted, "I never felt so intensely the fearful wickedness of slavery as now."[162] Despite opposition from some black leaders, Douglass succeeded in creating a national organization with a federal structure to tighten the bonds among African Americans and promote their advancement.[163]

Although many local abolitionists—old organization and new, black and white, women and men—attended the convention, it failed to heal divisions within their ranks. Most importantly, Nell opposed the formation of a national council and its plans for a blacks-only school. Although in the minority, he was adamant that integration was far more beneficial to the race than segregation. Douglass and Nell had maintained cordial relations amid conflicts over the *North Star* and differences over political abolitionism, but this latest disagreement led to a rupture that would not be easily healed.[164] It also turned some of Nell's Boston friends against him, but he was always assured of Amy's loyalty.

Amid these upheavals, Post received an urgent letter from Harriet Jacobs, who was still working for the Willis family. "I stop in the midst of all kinds of cares and perplexities to scratch you a line and commit to you a breach of trust which I have never breath[ed] to anyone." She had found a newspaper story by Mrs. John Tyler, the former First Lady, about buying and selling slaves, and "felt indignant." Staying up after the family was asleep, Harriet wrote a reply and sent it to the *New York Daily Tribune*, which to her shock published it under a pseudonym. Only able to glance at it before Mr. Willis took the paper to his study, Harriet was afraid to let anyone know that she had written the piece. She asked Amy to send her a copy, assuming it might have been reprinted in *Frederick Douglass' Paper*. When Amy did not find it there, she contacted Nell, who sent a copy from the *National Anti-Slavery Standard*.[165]

While reluctant to reveal her authorship to anyone but Post, Harriet did write a second letter to the *Tribune* in July. And when Jacobs's grandmother, Molly Horniblow, died in September 1853, Harriet confided to Amy that she was ready to reveal her life story. "I must write just what I have lived and witnessed myself," she proclaimed, though she worried that God had not given her the gift of literary talent. However, he "gave me a soul that burned for freedom and a heart nerved with determination to suffer even unto death in pursuit of that liberty which without makes life an intolerable burden."[166] It would be eight years before her narrative appeared in print, and she continued to depend on Amy's support throughout that long process.

That summer and fall, the Posts assisted numerous fugitives from bondage. With self-emancipated women and men flooding Rochester, fugitives were hidden in every available space. In this work, old and new abolitionist groups, women and men, black and white, joined forces while antislavery editors kept readers aware of the dangers they confronted, even on the verge of freedom.[167] In September 1853, Post wrote Nell that a free black woman and her husband, whom the wife had purchased from his owner, and their ten children had arrived at the Post home on a Saturday. They had fled north after neighbors "set about trying to steal" the children. Amy knew how anxious they were to get to Canada, but a boat would not be available to take them cross Lake Ontario until Monday. After a good meal and a full night's sleep, some of the family became so excited "that they were forgetful of any danger either to us, or to themselves," popping their heads out of windows and otherwise making themselves visible. During the long wait, the mother told Amy her story, including that she had had to give up the farm she and her sons had worked so hard to gain. "I don't care now," she concluded, as long as "I have got all my children, and my husband, too, thank the Lord." On Monday, she and her family left the house, "with all the stillness and quietness possible." Taken along the river to Kelsey's Landing, they soon boarded a Canada steamer, which hoisted the British flag as it moved out into the lake. Nell printed Amy's letter in the *Liberator* and urged friends to supply her and other Rochester conductors with goods and funds to assist the many fugitives passing through the city.[168]

Although local abolitionists agreed on the need to assist self-emancipated fugitives, female abolitionists continued to work through separate associations. Julia Wilbur moved back and forth between them. On 29 September, "Quite a large company" met at Mary Hallowell's to prepare "a box of goods" for the Boston bazaar. The next day, Wilbur joined RLASS women creating items for their own fair. She then traveled with Julia Griffiths to Syracuse to celebrate the two-year anniversary of the rescue of a fugitive named William "Jerry" McHenry from the clutches of slave catchers. There, Julia reported to her diary, Griffiths claimed that she "*despises* the Garrisonians," while "I have a *very profound respect* for them, being myself *one of 'em*."[169]

In October, RLASS members were "all in a ferment," this time over bloomers. Lucy Colman "wore a *dress shorter* than any other members of the Society & some individuals, not very weighty ones . . . have taken it in high dudgeon," reported Wilbur. Colman, who generally favored the Garrisonians and women's rights, left the meeting after several women voiced their outrage. Wilbur was "indignant that they c[oul]d Object to a useful member on account of her dress" and noted that those same women never criticized young ladies in dresses with "*short sleeves* & *low necks*."[170] Although Wilbur's disdain for many of her RLASS coworkers and her criticisms of Griffiths intensified, she apparently voiced them only in her diary while continuing to attend meetings with her sister-in-law Charlotte Wilbur.[171] Still, her descriptions of both the substance and the style of the RLASS make it clear why Amy Post never joined.

For once, in fall 1853, Amy remained isolated from conflicts at home. She had persuaded Lucy Colman, who was trying to launch a lecturing career, to travel with her to the Western Anti-Slavery Society convention outside Detroit, Michigan. The night before the convention, Post arranged for them to lodge with a black family, the Wallaces, whom she "had entertained at her house." The Wallaces had fled slavery via Rochester a decade earlier and shared their home with a more recent fugitive, Henry Bibb. After a lovely reunion, Post and Colman journeyed on to the convention, meeting up with Henry DeGarmo, the son of Rhoda and Elias DeGarmo, and "an Infidel in the Thomas Paine stamp." They also visited with Marius Robinson, the black journalist who had reported Sojourner Truth's 1851 Akron speech.[172]

Just weeks after returning from Michigan, Amy and Isaac headed to Cleveland for the fourth National Woman's Rights Convention. They were especially eager to attend after a September woman's rights convention in New York City had been disrupted by a crowd that hissed, booed, stamped, and jeered the speakers. Despite the presence of seasoned veterans on the platform—Mott, Anthony, Garrison, Rose, Truth, and others—the women faced repeated disturbances that made it impossible to hear their remarks or conduct the convention's business.[173] Several participants in that "mob convention" were scheduled to appear in October in Cleveland, which offered a much warmer welcome.[174]

Amy Post was elected one of the vice presidents of the Cleveland convention along with Mott, Reverend Brown, and several Midwestern activists. Early on, a letter from Rochester's Reverend Channing was read, which suggested the adoption of a "Declaration of Woman's Rights" and listed nine resolutions, several of which echoed those approved in 1848. The Posts may have wondered whether Channing was aware of the documents signed at Seneca Falls and Rochester. Still, they were likely surprised when, after that earlier Declaration of Sentiments was read aloud, Garrison admitted that he "had forgotten it till this morning." Fortunately, he was still "deeply impressed with its pertinacity and power." Yet several participants argued that a new document was needed that provided a clear and concise statement of the movement's goals. Once drafted, it should be circulated widely, along with petitions to implement those items that required legislative action. However, the lengthy debates that erupted over its content made clear that fundamental disagreements remained over the source of women's oppression and strategies for advancement. The new declaration was never written.[175]

Nor was the debate over religion resolved. Indeed, woman's rights advocates who viewed faith as an instrument for oppression or for liberation seemed more entrenched than ever. There was far broader agreement over the necessity of female enfranchisement, but substantial disagreements remained about how to obtain that right and to what extent suffrage would alleviate other forms of gender discrimination.

Nonetheless, the Cleveland convention left the Posts energized. Just seeing Truth, Garrison, Mott, Rose, and a host of midwestern friends was refreshing. Upon her return, Amy leapt into planning the New York State Woman's Rights Convention scheduled for 30 November and 1 December. The call, signed by thirty-six women and men, went out to black and white activists across the state. Many in Post's circle signed the call, including Isaac Post, Mary and William Hallowell, Lemira Kedzie, Sarah Anthony Burtis, Mary Fenn Love, and Lydia Mott, as did Douglass, Stanton, Anthony, and Rose. Some two hundred women and men were inspired to attend. Once again, Post was elected a vice president alongside Ernestine Rose, Sarah Burtis, spiritualist Mary Love, five other white women, and three men, including black activist Jermain Loguen. Amy also worked with Douglass, Rose, and Channing on the business committee, while her sister Sarah Hallowell Willis served as secretary with two other white women and William J. Watkins, a free black activist who had recently moved to Rochester to join *Frederick Douglass' Paper* as an associate editor. As in 1848, radical Quakers and free and freed blacks played a significant role in the convention, though they were now joined by more Unitarians and a scattering of evangelicals.[176]

One significant change, particularly noted by Post no doubt, was the selection of the Reverend Samuel J. May to preside. Stanton was expected to chair the convention, but illness kept her at home. At least May had supported women's rights, including suffrage, since 1846, and he repeatedly linked issues of women's legal disabilities to that of enslaved southerners. He also led with a light hand, encouraging women to take the stage. When Ernestine Rose did so, she insisted that "this movement ought . . . to be called a human rights movement," a position Post embraced.[177]

The state convention was primarily focused, however, on practical efforts to address women's legal and civil disabilities, which too often meant leaving aside issues of race to address economic and political discrimination based on sex. The resulting laws might affect black as well as white women, but there was little effort to engage the distinctive challenges confronting black women, nor were any black women elected to committees or quoted in the published proceedings.

A great deal of discussion focused on ways to expand existing laws, such as married women's property rights, and petitions and legislative hearings remained the primary weapons of choice. Promoting the achievements of individual women who broke occupational barriers was also considered an important means of transforming public opinion. Dr. Sarah R. Adamson, who had opened an office in Rochester, was recognized as the nation's second female medical school graduate; and the Reverend Antoinette Brown was praised as a pioneering Congregational minister. Douglass noted as well the presence of two young women assistants in the county clerk's office and the entrance of women into typesetting at a number of papers. In demanding better working conditions for women, Rose surprised the audience by including prostitutes among those whose situation must be improved. Ultimately, the convention resolved "to prepare an address to the capitalists and industrialists of New York on the best modes of employing and remunerating women" and, in a separate resolution, noted "the inseparable connection between dependence and degradation" that could be seen through the impoverishment of women.[178]

For the final session, the hall was "packed to its utmost." It was there that the Reverend Channing circulated copies of petitions for women's property rights and suffrage and asked editors to publish the forms in their papers. While tremendous work lay ahead of them, the convention organizers succeeded in attracting enthusiastic crowds; highlighting critical issues; and developing practical plans for advancing women's economic, legal, and political rights. In the following months, Post was among the sixty women who carried petitions door-to-door across New York State.[179]

On 20 December, as Amy Post turned fifty-one, she could look back on the previous decade with a sense of accomplishment. Between 1843 and 1853, she had been a central figure in some of the most important and innovative movements of the era: abolition, women's rights, temperance, health reform, spiritualism, and the Progressive Friends. A confidante of numerous activists, both black and white, she continued to campaign for social justice and a universalist agenda even as she embraced practical means to achieve specific gains. She was fortunate in her ability to integrate her radical vision into her domestic life, due largely to the loving partnership she had forged with Isaac and the political engagement of many family members. Similarly, her friendships with Nell, Jacobs, Truth, and Colman and her working relationships with Douglass, Kelley Foster, Stanton, Rose, and Anthony bolstered her participation in a wide range of movements. While many of these coworkers were national leaders, Post was dedicated instead to carrying ideas and arguments from one organization or convention to another and linking activists from Long Island and central and western New York to those in Boston, New York, Philadelphia, and the Midwest. Although there were moments—as with the Rochester Ladies' Anti-Slavery Society—when Post refused to play the conductor, she spent much of her time orchestrating alliances across race, class, faith, and region. In this way, she served as a lynchpin of radical activism across the Northeast.

(92)

Whereas Joseph Post of Westbury Town of North Hempstead, County of Queens and State of New York, Son of Edmund Post and Catharine his wife, and Mary Robbins daughter of Willet and Esther Robbins of Jericho Town of Oysterbay, County and State aforesaid, having laid their intentions of Marriage with each other before two monthly meeting of the religious Society of Friends at Jericho aforesaid they having consent of Parents and nothing appearing to obstruct their Marriage was allowed by the meeting —

These are to Certify that for the accomplishment of their intentions this twenty fifth day of the ninth month in the year of our Lord one thousand eight hundred and twenty eight, they the said Joseph Post and Mary Robbins appeared in a public meeting of the said Society held at Jericho and the said Joseph Post taking the said Mary Robbins by the hand, did on this Solemn occasion declare that he took her to be his wife promising thro divine assistance to be unto her a kind and affectionate husband until separated by death, or words to that

(93)

effect, and then the said Mary Robbins did in like manner declare that she took the said Joseph Post to be her husband promising thro divine assistance to be unto him a kind and affectionate wife until separated by death or words to that import. And they the said Joseph Post and Mary Robbins (she according to the custom of marriage assuming the name of her husband) as a further confirmation thereof, did then and there to these presents set their hands.

Joseph Post
Mary W. Post

And we being present have subscribed our names as witnesses thereof —

Mary Hurley Jr.	Edmund Post
Edmund Post Jr.	Catharine Post
Henry Willis	Willet Robbins
Samuel Willis	Esther Robbins
Rachel Willis	Mary Hurley
David Seaman	Lydia Rushmore
Sarah R. Seaman	Phebe P. Willis
Joseph Hicks	Isaac Post
Lydia Seaman	Amy Post
Esther Seaman	Wm. S Robbins
Esther Willits	Mathew F. Robbins
Jane Willits	Willet S Robbins
Elizabeth Rushmore	Samuel Willis
Obadiah Willits	Jacob Hurley

and a number of others

1828 marriage certificate of Mary Robbins and Joseph Post (Friends Historical Library, Swarthmore College, Swarthmore, Pennsylvania).

1816 Farmington Hicksite Friends Meetinghouse (Photo by Edwin Gardner, 1890s; Margaret Hartsough and Ontario County Historical Society).

AFRICAN CHURCH,
ROCHESTER, NY.

African Methodist
Episcopal Zion Church,
Rochester, New York,
c. 1830 (Central
Library of Rochester
and Monroe County,
Rochester, New York).

THE OLD POST RESIDENCE ON SOPHIA STREET.—The Headquarters of the Underground Railway.

36 Sophia Street, home of Amy and Isaac Post, c. 1895 (Central Library of Rochester and Monroe County, Rochester, New York).

Frederick Douglass, *My Bondage and My Freedom*, 1856 (Rare Books and Special Collections, University of Rochester, Rochester, New York).

William C. Nell, c. 1850 (Collection of the Massachusetts Historical Society).

My Dear Mrs Post:

Please shelter this sister from the house of bondage till five O'Clock this afternoon — We will then be sent on to the land of freedom.

Yours truly —
FredK

Underground Railroad pass, Frederick Douglass to Amy Post, c. 1850 (Isaac and Amy Post Family Papers, Rare Books and Special Collections, University of Rochester, Rochester, New York).

Corinthian Hall, Rochester, New York, 1851 (Central Library of Rochester and Monroe County, Rochester, New York).

Hallowell

173136

INCIDENTS

IN THE

LIFE OF A SLAVE GIRL.

WRITTEN BY HERSELF.

"Northerners know nothing at all about Slavery. They think it is perpetual bondage only. They have no conception of the depth of *degradation* involved in that word, SLAVERY; if they had, they would never cease their efforts until so horrible a system was overthrown."
A WOMAN OF NORTH CAROLINA.

"Rise up, ye women that are at ease! Hear my voice, ye careless daughters! Give ear unto my speech."
ISAIAH xxxii. 9.

EDITED BY L. MARIA CHILD.

BOSTON:
PUBLISHED FOR THE AUTHOR.
1861.

Harriet Jacobs, *Incidents in the Life of a Slave Girl*, title page, 1861 (Rare Books and Special Collections, University of Rochester, Rochester, New York).

Amy Kirby Post, c. 1870 (Rare Books and Special Collections, University of Rochester, Rochester, New York).

Isaac Post, c. 1870
(Rare Books and
Special Collections,
University of
Rochester, Rochester,
New York).

7 Practical Righteousness, 1854–1861

· ·

Progressive Friends dedicated themselves not only to a universalist vision of social change but also to the "promotion of practical righteousness."[1] In 1853, a relative newcomer to reform exclaimed, "Where else but in Rochester c[oul]d I attend so many *conventions* in one year. *Temperance, Anti-Slavery, Colored National, Teachers, Woman's Rights!!*"[2] For many Rochesterians, grand public events defined social activism in the city. For the Posts and their radical F/friends, however, social transformation was rooted at least as much in behind-the-scene efforts. As Lucretia Mott insisted, "We need to understand the worship that is more in our everyday life, that is manifested more by efforts of love and devotion to truth and righteousness."[3] For Amy and Isaac Post, social activism had become a form of worship, and they displayed their devotion in their home and store and in intimate gatherings as much as in public arenas. The Posts had long rejected the use of slave-produced goods; opened their home to fugitives and itinerant lecturers; socialized across racial lines; assisted Seneca Indians; challenged barriers to women's equality; refused to participate in a government built on slavery and war; and provided alternative medical treatments to friends, neighbors, and fellow activists. As political conflicts intensified, the Posts sustained these efforts and added to them.

From 1854 to 1859, Amy Post organized no major conventions or fundraising fairs, a change shaped by both familial and political factors. The WNYASS faded from view as the Rochester Ladies' Anti-Slavery Society, the New York State Anti-Slavery Society, the Athenaeum Society, and the Free Soil Party managed most reform-oriented public events in Rochester. Just as importantly, 1854 was marked by illness and death in the Post family and a short-lived financial panic that endangered their economic security. Still, the Posts would face prodigious demands on their time and resources over the next several years: friends, fellow activists, and fugitives would call on them for assistance; lecturers, spiritualists, healers, and family members would make 36 Sophia Street their home for days, weeks, or months at a time; and a new movement against capital punishment would demand their attention.

At the same time, antislavery battles increasingly played out at the highest levels of government, demanding different kinds of responses from abolitionists both locally and regionally. Between 1854 and 1861, Congress passed the Kansas-Nebraska Act, the Republican Party emerged as a counterweight to the Democratic Party, the Supreme Court ruled against African American rights in the *Dred Scott* case, federal troops captured John Brown following his raid on Harpers Ferry, Abraham Lincoln was elected U.S. president, and eleven southern states seceded. Women's rights advocates, too, focused increasingly on legislation over agitation, though mainly at the state level. Such efforts often marginalized radicals who did not participate in electoral politics or partisan rituals. In 1860–61, however, the stark choices demanded by a nation in crisis pulled Post back onto the public stage as she organized and chaired conventions, served as clerk of the Progressive Friends, and brought abolitionists of all stripes together once war erupted.

Throughout the 1850s, Amy remained an active conductor in social movements from Boston and New York to Ohio and Michigan. Indeed, she reached out often to activists in the Midwest in the 1850s as well as to small-town advocates of spiritualism, health reform, and women's rights. She sent letters and copies of newspapers to friends near and far; accompanied Lucy Stone on two New York State lecture tours; and offered solace, practical assistance, and medical advice to family, friends, and near strangers. Though often working behind the scenes, she helped women activists, mediums, and healers reach wider audiences and played a crucial role in Harriet Jacobs's effort to write and publish her life story.

Isaac's support was essential to Amy's efforts. Indeed, her ability to advocate social change and orchestrate connections across regions and campaigns was grounded in her husband's financial and emotional support. He only rarely joined her at yearly meetings of Progressive Friends—which took the name Friends of Human Progress in 1854 to avoid any "sectarian feeling"—or at AASS conventions. However, they attended local lectures and séances together as well as protests against capital punishment and continued to share an overall vision of social justice even as they embraced different priorities. Isaac became more involved in free religious societies and spiritualist gatherings, while Amy continued to focus on abolition and a broad understanding of women's rights. John Brown's raid in 1859 and the eruption of civil war in 1861 would highlight another difference: Isaac spoke out against any use of force to solve the nation's crisis, whereas Amy now agreed with Nell that a resort to arms might be justified if it led to the eradication of slavery. The shock of these events refocused Isaac's attention on abolition and fueled Amy's return to leadership in that movement and in the Friends of Human Progress. Whatever their differences, the Posts continued to move seamlessly across gendered spheres and racial boundaries in their promotion of practical righteousness.

In winter 1854, the Post household was smaller than usual. William Nell, Harriet Jacobs, and Sojourner Truth had all left Rochester; Amy and Isaac's son Joseph was seeking his fortune in New York City, while Jacob was in Westbury, continuing his studies. Seven-year-old Willie was at home, but his parents planned to send him, as they had their other children, for a summer in Jericho and then to a Friends school in Union Springs, New York. Sister Sarah had taken up housekeeping with her husband, Edmund Willis, though she visited Amy regularly, as did Amy's stepdaughter, Mary. Sarah Birney was enjoying a family reunion in Ireland, but she planned to return that summer; and Mary Dale Johnson was settled in Buffalo with her husband, George. In addition, Isaac's cousins George and Ann Willets, who had joined the Posts in antislavery and spiritualist circles for a few years, had moved to Jersey City, while Sarah Owen remained in Michigan and Abigail Bush had joined Henry in California. Amy also saw far less of Frederick Douglass, now that he lived south of the city. Isaac, whose pharmacy was close by the *North Star* office, still spoke with Frederick regularly, but Amy was more likely to cross paths with Julia Griffiths, who boarded in the city, or with Susan B. Anthony, who spent the winter circulating petitions on behalf of women's property rights and suffrage.[4]

Other friends tried to fill the gap. Sarah Burtis spent more time with Amy, while her husband and two older sons traveled the Midwest seeking new economic opportunities. Rhoda DeGarmo also had more time to visit now that her oldest daughter was married, and Asa and Huldah Anthony and Daniel and Lucy Anthony continued to hold Sunday gatherings at their farms. Amy and Isaac also enjoyed the company of fellow activists at the Hallowells', without the burdens of hosting. With William's wool business thriving, he and Mary often hosted the antislavery meetings, visiting lecturers, and dinners once held at Sophia Street. And Amy still met regularly with the remaining members of the WNYASS antislavery circle, producing goods for the Boston fair and exchanging news of conventions, lecture tours, and political debates.

The Posts attended numerous lectures in the 1850s, as renowned orators appeared regularly under the auspices of the Athenaeum Society, the RLASS, local Garrisonians, or women's rights advocates. In January 1854 alone,

Wendell Phillips, Theodore Parker, Solomon Northup, and Horace Greeley all attracted large audiences to Corinthian Hall. Amy was surely excited to hear Phillips, with whom she had served on AASS committees, and Solomon Northup, the free black man from Saratoga, New York, who was sold into slavery and freed after twelve years.[5] She and Isaac also organized a few lectures, particularly by spiritualists and health reformers. For instance, that March they arranged a talk for Andrew Jackson Davis, a noted spiritualist and clairvoyant healer, and invited him to stay at 36 Sophia Street. Unfortunately, he arrived in the city the day after Lucy Colman's husband, Luther, was killed in a railroad accident along with a Seneca Indian, John Spencer. Isaac and Amy, who were friends with both men, mourned their loss. On 23 March, a coroner's jury placed the blame on an inexperienced switchman. Three days later, Davis followed Colman's funeral with a lecture on "harmonial philosophy," which he believed would infuse the bereaved with hope of future communion with the dead.[6]

The Posts' enjoyed one harmonial event that year. Their son Joseph returned to Rochester in spring 1854 to work alongside his father and Jacob in the drugstore and marry Mate Ashley. He still hoped for a position with more independence and opportunity, and that summer he was offered one by Thomas Hallowell, a relative of the deceased Jeffries Hallowell. Joseph took the job in Hallowell's shoe store in Brockville, Ontario, on the north shore of the St. Lawrence River. The couple boarded with Thomas and his wife, Phebe—the daughter of cousins John and Rebecca Ketcham—which eased their transition. Even Isaac expressed optimism about his son's prospects. He and Amy sent clothes, fresh peaches, and other items to the newlyweds, while Joseph and Mate begged family members to visit.[7]

Within months, however, Joseph was complaining that Thomas was often away, visiting boot and shoe factories in other Canadian towns, and that business was "very dull."[8] He likely knew that business was even worse in Rochester. A panic, fueled by speculation on railroad securities, had swept private banks in Ohio that summer and led to dozens of closures throughout the Midwest, as well as among corresponding banks in New York City. While the 1854 panic was limited in scope, it created problems for many merchants, including Isaac Post. In late July, he was in such difficult straits that he and Jacob were on the verge of selling a second store they had just recently opened.[9] Surprisingly, R. G. Dun and Co. agents offered no indication of their financial problems. In September 1853, they noted that despite Post's belief "in spiritual rappings," he, Jacob, and their new partner,

William Bruff, displayed "good char[acter] & hab[i]ts" and were "careful, prudent, & hon[est]." Five months later, an agent reported the opening of the second store; and in July, another claimed "bus[iness] increasing." In the following years, credit reports were equally positive based on the good character and credit of its owners.[10] The expansion noted in February 1854 may have caused problems that were exacerbated by the panic, and Post may have sold the new store soon after it was purchased. By year's end, Isaac Post & Co. had recovered, with many suppliers and consumers none the wiser.

In the midst of this crisis, during the third week of July, the Posts hosted William Nell along with old F/friends Henry and Dorcas Collins. The year before, Frederick Douglass had attacked Nell in his hometown of Boston, after Douglass himself was publicly disparaged by Wendell Phillips. William's friend Robert Morris, a black lawyer, joined in the "ungenerous and ungentlemanly attack" on Nell. Soon after, another close friend, William Watkins, seemed to choose sides when he agreed to help edit *Frederick Douglass' Paper*.[11] So perhaps it is not surprising that William did not stay long in Rochester. Instead, Amy traveled with him and the Collinses to Cleveland, where they attended a contentious meeting of the National Council of Colored People. There, too, Nell clashed with Douglass over antislavery tactics and political priorities. Nell, Post, and the Collinses then returned to Rochester, where they enjoyed the company of the Sophia Street circle. The Posts and their friends eagerly listened to Nell's account of the capture of fugitive slave Anthony Burns in Boston that May, and they certainly discussed passage of the Kansas-Nebraska Act by the House of Representatives, which would repeal the Missouri Compromise and open territory north of the 36°30′ line to slavery. As soon as Nell returned to Boston, he wrote Amy, already reminiscing about his recent visit but also noting of Douglass, "I cannot easily imagine the circumstances that would result in my speaking to him."[12]

Amy's ongoing friendship with Nell reinforced her connections to activists in Boston and beyond. Their correspondence always included greetings to a variety of abolitionists, women's rights advocates, and spiritualists, allowing each to sustain ties to those they rarely saw. Amy visited Frances Nell Cleggett, then reassured William that she and her growing family were well. In return, Nell, who saw Harriet and Louisa Jacobs far more than Amy did, sent detailed accounts of their visits. William also reported on the comings and goings of mutual friends. In September 1854, he alerted Amy to William Wells Brown's return to the States from an extended stay in England and arranged for him to lecture in Rochester alongside Charles Lenox Remond.[13]

On the evening of 4 October, Brown, Remond, and the Posts joined AME Zion congregants and the Sophia Street circle at Corinthian Hall. Stormy weather, a series of church services, and a newspaper announcement that the meeting was intended for political abolitionists limited the crowd. Still, the audience was attentive as Brown recounted his experiences abroad and contrasted "the liberal sentiment which the colored man meets in Europe, with the prejudices which degrade him in his own country." Remond then offered a compelling critique of northern whites, demonstrating "that the evil of slavery was not confined to the States and the people of the South where it exists" but had "a reflex influence upon the free States and the people of the North."[14] While the visit was short, it refreshed Amy's bonds with Brown and Remond.

The visit of the two orators also relieved the Posts' grief. Just two weeks before their arrival, on 21 September, Amy's mother, Mary Seaman Kirby, died. She and her husband Jacob and the Post's son Willie had all been sick with ague for a few weeks, but Mary Kirby had asked family members not to alarm Amy and Sarah. Finally, on 14 September, a friend alerted the sisters to their mother's illness. It was too late, however, for them to reach Jericho before Mary passed away.[15] The sisters decided to wait until after Brown's and Remond's visit to travel south, but then Amy fell ill. In late October, Mary Willis wrote her younger sister Sarah, describing their father's loneliness and the family's need to discuss his care. Mary Robbins Post wrote as well, mourning the death of "my dear and honored aunt, *your* beloved and venerated mother." Finally, on 1 November, Amy and Sarah boarded a train for New York City.[16]

The sisters spent more than a week on Long Island, reminiscing about their mother with friends and relatives. Recognizing her father's loneliness and his need for more care, Amy took Willie back to Rochester, believing that the seven-year-old was more a burden than a comfort. By the time she and Sarah returned, Sarah Birney was back in Rochester as well, though very ill. She had sailed out of New York City the previous summer and written Amy from Belfast that she had been extremely sick on the voyage. Birney improved in her family's care and remained with her parents and siblings until November 1854.[17] On the return, however, she again fell dangerously ill. Hearing the news, Nell was certain that "she cannot be in better quarters than 36 Sophia St. with Amy Post for Nurse." Isaac wrote family on Long

Island that Sarah, "who has been a most worthy friend to us," was in pain, but assured them "we will not let her suffer." As Amy watched over Sarah, she was "knitting as fast as possible for the Boston Fair," completing five pairs of mittens in her friend's sickroom.[18]

The constant care that Amy provided Sarah Birney illustrates the unusual role this Irish servant played in the family circle. As Birney wrote earlier that year from Ireland, "I suppose you never thought your name ever would be as much spread through [our] land as it is Misses Post for your kindness to myself. . . . Father, mother and sister join me in love to you in the Kindest manner."[19] Of course, the Posts had extended housing, medical care, friendship, and financial aid to wide-ranging circles of friends. Indeed, Lucy Colman claimed that Amy Post welcomed anyone who knocked on her door.[20] Many friends, relatives, and fellow activists not only called on the Posts but also asked them to assist their friends, which the couple regularly did. All of this was in addition to their work with fugitives—perhaps 150 a year in the 1840s and 1850s—who passed through Rochester. Douglass's relocation south of the city made it even easier for self-emancipated women and men to reach his home without detection, and Frederick continued to rely on the Posts and other experienced conductors to get them safely to Canada.[21]

While testimony from freedom seekers is necessarily limited, it is clear that the Posts were well known to them and to many other conductors. In 1853, Amy had visited black communities in the Midwest and Canada with Lucy Colman, and residents greeted her warmly, having partaken of the Posts' hospitality or having heard about it from others. After Amy returned home, James S. Gibbons, who provided refuge for freedom seekers in New York City, contacted Isaac for help. A free black woman's husband and two sons had reached Rochester, but once there, they had faced some disaster. At least one son had survived, and his mother wanted to learn more about what occurred. Gibbons asked Isaac to serve as the mother's "guide to the scene of her sorrow" and raise funds to allow "the poor boy" to return to New York with her.[22] Indeed, the Posts were so well known on the underground circuit that they were defrauded at least once. Reuben Nixon, a free black man serving time at Dannemora State Prison, asked the chaplain to write to Isaac, pleading his "forgiveness for imposing on you when I first arrived in R[ochester]." Having heard of your generosity, "I posed as an escaped slave from the South to excite your commiseration & obtain assistance." Now he felt guilty for duping him.[23]

Seneca Indians, too, trusted that the Posts would aid them in times of need. John Joe Mack, who lived on the Cattaraugus Reservation, visited the

Posts regularly in the 1840s and 1850s. In January 1853, his health was poor, and he wrote Amy: "I am hard up for Provisions now days. . . . I write to you because [we] love you Just the same as our own Brother and Sister and wish you to write me." Mack planned a visit for mid-summer, but by that time he had gone blind, so in June he asked Asher Wright, a teacher on the reservation, to contact Amy for him. Wright noted the death of Mack's friend John Peter, hoping that Amy might assist Peter's widow, who was left with "the care of a large number of orphans." Peter's wife wanted her oldest daughter to attend school and "wishes to know if you cannot take her into your family."[24]

Many white women also requested aid, several seeking Post's help in escaping bad marriages or surviving widowhood. Amy served as a conductor to them as well, offering shelter, solace, and funds. In letters and notes, often hastily and poorly written, friends and friends of friends poured out their woes. Elizabeth Bowen and her husband Ansel, a schoolteacher, had boarded with the Posts in 1850. By 1857, however, Mrs. Bowen's situation had become desperate: "Suffize [sic] it to say that I am worse than a *widow* for the one that should be my *Protector* is changed to a cruel *Enamy* [sic], and that is harder to be reconciled to than my extreme destitution." Nancy Hassey, who was living with her mother and child in rented rooms in Buffalo, reached out to Amy when her husband left her bereft. Afterward, she thanked Amy for "your kindness to me and in taking an interest for my child." She added, "I will exert myself for a living as long as I have strength to do so." Libbie Rees, who worked on a farm south of Rochester, thanked Amy for being her "counselor and adviser. . . . You have given me the strength to maintain myself and had it not been for your kindness, where should I have been now but a poor miserable broken hearted one." Amy later agreed to take in Libbie's daughter Amelia, so she could get an education and a better job. Bowen had boarded with the Posts, and Hassey may have once lived in Ledyard, but myriad women contacted Amy to seek help in times of crisis.[25]

Radical activists and former employees also reached out to Amy for support. Longtime F/friend Susan Doty apologized to Amy for intruding, since "thee devotes so much of thy time to services for others." Still, she, like many others, wondered if the Posts could board her daughter so that she could attend school in Rochester.[26] Mary Ann Pitkin, a fourteen-year-old African American girl who lived with and worked for the Posts in the mid-1850s, wrote Amy on an even more personal matter. She found out that her sister Sarah had died in Albion, New York, and hoped Amy could get her body shipped to Rochester and buried in Mount Hope Cemetery. At the time, Mount Hope only accepted burials of people who lived in or died in Rochester. Having "tried every way to plan and arrange to have dear Sarah's remains brought here for internment," Amy concluded it was impossible. She suggested, however, that if the poor master of Albion could furnish a coffin, hearse, and carriage "and charge the expence to our county," Monroe County would take care of the burial, which Amy hoped Mary Ann would not see as "any disgrace."[27]

Correspondents, including relatives, close friends, and acquaintances, also regularly received financial help from the Posts. Cousin George Willets, boarder Ansel Bowen, Canadian abolitionist Hiram Wilson, spiritualist Elizabeth Hamilton, and many others depended on Isaac and Amy's largesse to get them through difficult times, support their activist efforts, or cover small debts left behind. Willets had borrowed money from the Posts for his move to Jersey City, and a year later, in the midst of the 1854 panic, blamed the delay in repayment on the Erie Railroad, which was two months behind on wages. Bowen, who had moved with his wife to Ohio and opened a medical practice, owed the Posts a large sum but enclosed three dollars to show his good faith. His wife Elizabeth's plea to Amy for protection a few years later suggests the Bowens' situation continued to deteriorate[28] Hamilton, a spiritualist with little schooling but a profound belief in "god and holy angles [sic]," realized that she "forgot to pay my 50 sents a month before i left Rochester i hope you will forgiv me. . . . My Lov to you all."[29]

The Posts took on a variety of other economic tasks for friends and family. A cousin, Esther Titus, who shunted between central New York and central Michigan in the 1850s, asked Amy to get twenty dollars from the bank and send it to her. She also wrote Amy from Battle Creek on behalf of Sojourner Truth, who hoped to get to New York City to lecture but needed funds for the trip: "She is very desirous to ask thee whether collection[s] could not be taken up for her in Rochester." A spiritualist in the tiny town of Johnson's Creek, New York, asked Isaac if he could find employment for healing medium Cora Hatch for a few days and, if so, how much it would pay. Henry C. Wright sent the Posts a gift of his latest book, *Marriage and Parentage*, along with a batch for sale, presumably for Isaac's pharmacy. And Mary Dale Johnson sent two dollars to the Posts, asking Isaac if he could arrange subscriptions for her to *Frederick Douglass' Paper* and the *Liberator*.[30] Requests like these poured into the Posts, as they became widely known for their activism, their kindness to strangers, and their largesse.

Amy and Isaac offered material support even when their own financial situation was fragile, but for most of the 1850s, their economic fortunes were secure. Isaac had invested in real estate and railroad stocks, and by 1852, he owned a second house on Sophia Street. Two years later, during the panic, Post could save his apothecary business because he had other investments to draw on, such as shares of New York Central Railroad Company stock, which paid dividends in 1854. Isaac also offered loans on fair terms to neighbors, friends, and family members. Even after Jeffries Hallowell's death led to financial difficulties, Isaac continued to extend credit to in-laws, siblings, and cousins.[31] Post's business acumen and reputation for integrity also led businessmen to seek his advice for their own economic ventures. Progressive Friend Thomas M'Clintock, who owned a pharmacy in Waterloo, considered opening a second in Rochester with his son and asked Isaac if there were any druggists willing to sell.[32]

Friends also continued to seek out the Posts for medical advice and treatment. Harriet Jacobs included regular medical updates in her letters to Amy and often asked advice about particular doctors and diagnoses, including a possible tumor on her womb.[33] Priscilla Cadwalader required Amy's nursing skills a second time while touring Hicksite meetings in western New York in fall 1855. Some local Hicksites looked askance at Cadwalader's staying with the Posts, since they had left the meeting, but Amy saw Priscilla's decision as evidence that she "was no sectarian in spirit." Indeed, Amy was happy to care for her old F/friend even though Isaac had only recently recovered from a fever that languished for two months. Priscilla later took ill in Albany, but returned to the Posts healthy when she headed back to Ohio the next spring.[34] In the interim, the Posts had become grandparents. Joseph's wife, Mate, gave birth to a daughter, Alice, in 1855, and soon after the couple moved back to Rochester. They lived at 36 Sophia Street while Joseph searched for a job, allowing Amy and Isaac to spend precious time with Alice and Mate.

Whether the Posts were grieving or joyous, friends and strangers called on them for spiritual as well as medical interventions, the former often related to sick and deceased relatives. Increasing numbers of these requests came from midwestern activists, who met or knew of the Posts through radical Quaker, antislavery, and women's rights networks. Betsey Mix Cowles wrote Amy in 1850, after visiting Rochester on a lecture tour the previous year. She begged her to seek a message from her niece's husband, who had died on his way to California. Cowles hoped that contact with his spirit would keep her niece from utter despair.[35] Valentine Nicholson, of Warren

County, Ohio, was moved to write the Posts by F/friend Joseph Dugdale, who touted Isaac as a medium. Nicholson hoped that Isaac could offer some "spiritual advice" about his future, following his and his wife's loss of a good deal of property while attempting to establish a utopian community. He also provided the names of departed family members, including a "sweet spirited daughter," in case Isaac was able to reach them. Even other mediums, such as Kate Fox, sought support. Touring the Midwest, Kate wrote "my *dearest* friend" Amy about her homesickness, her woes regarding men and courtship, her strange dreams, and a variety of other cares. She thanked her repeatedly for the "beautiful" and comforting letters she sent.[36]

Another group of correspondents focused on the interplay of spiritual and physical health. Just as communication with the deceased offered solace to the spirit, water cures offered relief to the body. The treatment, hydropathy, was imported from Europe in the early 1840s and consisted of "the internal consumption and external application of cold water for the prevention and cure of all diseases."[37] Mrs. G. B. Bushnell Marks, who visited Rochester in 1849, worked as a medium and spiritualist lecturer in Cincinnati. She corresponded regularly with Amy, detailing her personal and professional transformations. In fall 1854, after leaving her husband, Mrs. Marks moved to New York and secured a job as a clairvoyant at a water cure establishment. By the late 1850s, female mediums and clairvoyants like Marks easily outnumbered abolitionist and women's rights speakers on the lecture circuit, and many of them found ready audiences at hydropathic institutes.[38] Mary Ann Johnson and her husband, Oliver, were dedicated abolitionists and Progressive Friends, who were sympathetic to spiritualism. Mrs. Johnson also lectured to women "on Anatomy and Physiology" and hoped Amy might help arrange a class in Rochester. She inquired as well about the Halsted Medical Institute in the city, wondering if Dr. Halsted's water cure treatments could help a friend desperate for relief from a prolapsed uterus.[39] These efforts to improve women's health and minds through alternative medical treatments and spiritualism expanded and strengthened Post's network of radical friends.

Given her broad connections and multifaceted activism, Post became a crucial contact for women who sought to build careers as healers and mediums. She forged friendships with Kate and Margaretta Fox, Betsey Mix Cowles, Mary Ann Johnson, and Mary Fenn Love, who had attended the state woman's rights convention in 1853 and two years later married Andrew Jackson Davis. In expanding her abolitionist, spiritualist, and women's rights networks, Post came to the attention of a wide range of editors as well as lecturers. Anna E. W. Dowell wrote to Post from Philadelphia in January 1855, announcing the launch of a newspaper, the *Woman's Advocate*, "to be executed exclusively by Women, and devoted to their interests. . . . If you feel an interest in the ultimate success of this enterprise," perhaps "you will favour me with an Article from your pen." Just a month later, the Boston publisher of the *Una*, a women's rights paper founded by Paulina Wright Davis, wrote Amy, thanking her for the five dollars she sent for subscriptions and appointing her an agent for one year. John Dick, Douglass's former partner, had reached out to Amy a year earlier, sending her a copy of the *Provincial Freeman*. The Toronto-based paper was run by several "respectable colored men," and Dick asked Post to encourage friends to subscribe.[40]

Other activists sought Post's support for their vocation. Cora Hatch launched her career as a medium in 1851, at age eleven, and three years later was a regular speaker for a spiritualist society in Buffalo. In 1856, she moved to New York City but continued touring across the North. In the late 1850s, her second husband, N. W. Daniels, contacted Post, asking her to write the *National Anti-Slavery Standard* about Cora's "*Political*" lectures, hoping she would be "more identified with Anti-Slavery and Woman's Rights work." Many involved in these movements worried that spiritualists would distract attention from the most important issues of the day; a recommendation from Amy Post eased such concerns. Elizabeth Lowe Watson, another spiritualist, peppered Post with requests for information on both speaking engagements and medical treatments.[41]

While Post's circle now extended to a diverse array of lecturers and editors, she did not neglect her dearest friends and longtime coworkers. Amy was particularly solicitous of Harriet Jacobs's desire to publish her life story. After Jacobs's employer, Cornelia Grinnell Willis, paid $150 to purchase her freedom, Harriet was ready to begin serious work on her narrative. In February 1853, she asked Post to write a letter of introduction to Harriet Beecher Stowe, thinking the famed author of *Uncle Tom's Cabin* might be willing to tell her story. Stowe invited Jacobs to visit for a month, but Jacobs soon realized that her host had her own agenda. Stowe encouraged her guest to reveal agonizing episodes of abuse and brutality with the idea of fictionalizing the horrors she had endured. An outraged Jacobs confided to Amy that Stowe planned to exploit her and decided right then that she must write the book herself, even if she had little time to spare for such work.[42]

Garrison and the Motts still called on the Posts as well. Garrison stayed at 36 Sophia Street in November 1854 while lecturing in the area. "We had a delightful visit," Isaac wrote family on Long Island. "The more we see him, the more we love him." Hopefully Amy felt the same, even though she was nursing Sarah Birney and knitting socks for the Boston bazaar during his stay.[43] The next fall, the Motts asked Amy to plan appearances for Lucretia in Rochester for early January 1856. Although James and Lucretia were staying with Orthodox abolitionists Silas and Sarah Cornell, they asked Amy, who was no longer bound by Friends constraints on worldly activism, to organize and publicize Mott's lectures.[44] A less well-known women's rights lecturer, Elizabeth Kingsbury, spoke in Rochester in winter 1857 and stayed at Sophia Street for a couple of weeks. She left a trunk there and in April had Amy ship it to Columbus, Ohio, where she was then lecturing. That summer, Post wrote Abby Kelley Foster to recommend Aurelia Raymond, Lucy Colman's sister, as a lecturer for the AASS. The executive committee agreed to have her accompany Colman if Post would "undertake the task of raising" funds to cover the costs.[45]

Post had always been generous with her time and resources, but it was especially difficult to refuse requests in the mid-1850s as the women's rights movement flourished and the antislavery movement faced severe crises. Congress passed the Kansas-Nebraska Act in 1854, which opened up those territories to slavery. Ferocious battles erupted in the Kansas Territory between proslavery southerners and northern abolitionists, and the conflict escalated as the flood of migrants put statehood within reach. By 1856, the political upheavals wrought by the Kansas-Nebraska Act ensured the decline of the Whigs and the rise of the Republican Party, where former Whigs, Free Soilers, and some northern Democrats sought a new political home. By then, southern migrants had installed a proslavery government at Shawnee Mission, Kansas, and northern migrants an antislavery government at Lawrence. The ensuing violence left some two hundred residents dead in the next six months. The 1856 presidential election was poisoned by vitriol and recriminations. When Democrat James Buchanan, a proslavery man from Pennsylvania, won, northern fears were exacerbated. Two days after his inauguration, the Supreme Court handed down its decision in the case of *Dred Scott v. Sandford*, in which Chief Justice Roger Taney wrote the majority opinion, declaring that a slave was not a citizen and therefore could not sue in court. In addition, the court ruled that Congress had no constitutional authority to exclude slavery from any territory, thereby nullifying past compromises as well as future efforts to restrict the institution. At every turn, it seemed, slavery was becoming further entrenched, shocking many northerners and fueling further expansion in antislavery ranks.

Amid these upheavals, in winter 1855, Amy agreed to accompany Lucy Stone as she lectured through central and western New York. The two women had met on several occasions, including at woman's rights conventions in Rochester and Cleveland. Post admired Stone's willingness to stand up to Douglass over his embrace of political abolitionism, to Anthony over donning bloomers, and to various radical activists over questions of marriage and sexuality. She also shared Stone's insistence on the intertwined character of abolition and women's rights.[46] In spring 1854, Lucy had married Henry Blackwell after struggling over whether such an act would mean giving up her independence. The marriage contract they signed allowed Lucy to keep her birth name, and they jointly protested legal inequalities between husband and wife.[47] Amy no doubt reassured Lucy that marriage did not mean an end to activism, and Post's friends in the region helped arrange Stone's lectures.

The two women spent long hours together on lightly traveled roads and chilly nights in whatever accommodations they could find. While only Stone lectured, Post provided companionship and introductions to friends along the way. Having tramped through snow and rain as they moved from town to town, Amy was thrilled when she and Lucy reached Macedon the first week of March. It was a relief, she wrote Isaac, to be "back so near our dear home." Having heard that her sister Sarah was ill, Amy thought of heading directly home, but she decided to stay after news arrived that Sarah was improving. That evening, her old F/friend Elias Doty accompanied her and Lucy to a local school hall when church trustees refused to open their buildings. A small but enthusiastic group raised their spirits as Stone's tour neared its end.[48]

Post may have looked forward to settling back into her domestic routine, but she was faced instead with a cholera epidemic that claimed lives on Long Island as well as Rochester and numerous cities and towns in between. Cholera epidemics had hit the United States in the 1830s, the 1840s, and the early 1850s. To curtail its severity in the 1850s, officials in Rochester and elsewhere cleaned up sewers and pools of contaminated water and removed refuse from city streets. Nonetheless, in spring 1855, Isaac reported to his brother Joseph that many were still afflicted with the disease, helping to explain why antislavery lectures were so lightly attended. He also mentioned an unexpected confrontation between Amy and Frederick Douglass. That March, probably while on the road with Stone, Amy had written a note to Rosetta Douglass, who was away at school. This "so disturbed her father" that he visited Isaac and asked him to tell Amy "that he would not wish her to write his daughter." Isaac was stunned. He could not believe that Douglass "suppose[d] that [Amy] would say to her [Rosetta] what she would not be willing her parents to see."[49] Distressed, Amy wrote her old friend Sarah Owen, whose move to Michigan made her a safe confidante. Owen, too, was shocked: *Never* was I so much astonished at such a return for such unbounded exertions for his interest and happiness." "Oh, Frederick," Sarah concluded, "from what heights hast thou fallen!"[50]

Post had little time to worry about Douglass, however. She had been anxious about her father for months, especially after his house was burglarized in January 1855. Two months later, she traveled to Jericho to help care for her father, who was suffering from a debilitating fever. The visit gave her a chance to catch up with son Jacob, who was back at the Buckram Institute, and to tell Mary Robbins Post about her adventures with Lucy Stone.[51] For Mary, the stories likely brought back memories of the 1853 National Woman's Rights Convention in New York City, where mobs disrupted the scheduled speakers, including Stone. The opportunity, so rare by the 1850s, for the sisters-in-law to share confidences must have been a balm to both.

Still, Amy was well aware that her sojourn at Jericho created problems for those left behind, as a stream of letters testified. Her sister Sarah, deeply concerned for her father's health, was one of the few who wrote reassuringly. Still, even she noted the ailments of close friends, Isaac's continued cough, and the abrupt departure of Mary Dale Johnson, who was helping out at Sophia Street in Amy's absence. Sarah's main reason for writing, however, was to provide news from Julia Wilbur. Wilbur had confided to Mary and William Hallowell that Julia Griffiths was headed to England in early June. Some members of the RLASS apparently feared she might act in the name of the society; but, Sarah noted, "they have not quite the strength to oppose her or expose her if she does."[52] Certainly, for Sarah and Amy, Griffiths's departure was a relief, whatever her intentions back home.

Other family members called Amy home as well. Jenny Curtis, Jacob Post's fiancée, wrote in mid-May to say she was leaving Rochester temporarily to assist a sick sister. Isaac added a postscript, urging Amy not to postpone her return to Rochester, and son Joseph pleaded with his mother to "come Home soon," so he could tell her about his plans to open his own business.[53] In early June, Isaac complained, "No letter nor wife either comes [but I] will try to bear my loneliness as philosophically as possible" though I pass "night after night" with no person "in the house connected to me" by blood. More than a week later, Amy wrote that she needed to stay a few more days as her father had again taken "a chill," but commiserated about Isaac's "comfortable though lonely sojourn."[54] By late June, she was home along with Jacob, whose school term had ended.

Although Isaac complained about being lonely, he had many visitors while Amy was away. In early June, following the Friends of Human Progress meeting in Waterloo, radical Quakers from New Jersey and eastern New York visited Isaac, and soon after, two or three spiritualists stayed at Sophia Street and attended a séance there.[55] Mary Dale Johnson also returned to Sophia Street and helped tend to domestic chores, though she periodically returned to Buffalo, as her husband complained about her absence. Mary Ann Pitkin, the young African American woman living with the Posts, sometimes assisted Johnson and helped entertain guests as well. The previous summer, she had enchanted Nell by singing "Wait for the Waggon," and she likely offered up songs to other visitors, too.[56]

Still, Amy's absence took a toll on Isaac. In late June, soon after her return, he fell ill with ague and a fever. Jacob took over duties at the store while his mother nursed Isaac back to health.[57] In mid-October 1855, with the family back at full strength, the Posts once again welcomed William Nell along with his sister Louisa Gray to 36 Sophia Street. They discussed the latest developments in the antislavery movement, including Douglass's increasingly pointed attacks on Garrisonians. Still, Amy and Nell were relieved that Griffiths had returned to England. William spent time with his sister Frances Cleggett and her three children, as well as with other friends in the black community, attending gatherings at their homes and at the Posts'. When Nell returned to Boston, Louisa Gray stayed on for several more weeks, enjoying "the many attentions you and your Husband and relatives bestowed upon me."[58]

Early the next year, Amy and Sarah's father, Jacob Kirby, was again in failing health. Sister-in-law Mathilda Kirby updated Sarah on his care, as she did not want to trouble Amy, "fear[ing] she has too many cares. . . . We doctored him in our fashion with bitter teas and a dose of salts." He improved enough that he enjoyed reading and reminiscing again, though Mathilda noted that "the print is so small" in the book "dear sister Amy sent him that I have to read that and the newspapers to him." Amy also sent a "memorandum book" of her mother's, which sparked happy memories for Jacob about early events in his married life.[59]

As news of Jacob Kirby arrived in Rochester by post, William Lloyd Garrison arrived by train. Although the Posts were thrilled to see him, his

February 1856 visit did not begin auspiciously. Isaac was annoyed that Susan B. Anthony insisted Garrison go to her house for at least one night even though she was out of town. Isaac assured friends that Garrison "wished himself at our house." Then, suffering from a cold, the eminent abolitionist tried to cancel his speaking appointment, but the manager of the venue insisted he go on. Isaac thought the crowd of two hundred "very good" given the severe weather and competition from a Finney revival and a "Citizens' Meeting" about events in Kansas. Once Garrison was happily ensconced at Sophia Street, he accompanied the Posts to the wedding of Lewis and Sarah Burtis's daughter to the son of George Avery, a local abolitionist and Underground Railroad conductor. The wedding supper was crowded, but the "old folks"—the Burtises, the Posts, Garrison, and the Baptist minister— were given seats at one of the few tables. Garrison talked of his experiences with spiritualism, which the minister found fascinating. At midnight, the honored guests rode home through the icy cold in two sleds, and Garrison stayed on through the next day's snowstorm.[60]

Soon after these pleasurable days, Isaac received news that his cousin Isaac Willets had died. He left behind a bond and mortgage that Post had cosigned and on which $6,000 was shortly due. While it is not clear how the matter was handled, the Posts retained their financial standing, and the store's credit did not suffer.[61] Still, Willets's sudden death, like that of Jeffries Hallowell a decade earlier, reminded Isaac of the dangers of overextending himself, especially as he approached his sixties. The concern was especially clear in 1856, as another panic swept the nation, curtailing commerce and forcing more vulnerable enterprises out of business. Fortunately, Isaac Post and Co. survived these crises without a significant loss.

The circumstances certainly did not limit Amy's activities. She and her circle continued to provide goods for the Boston bazaar, and Amy helped organize several lectures in winter 1856. One by Theodore Parker sparked controversy, as he spoke one evening on behalf of the "old society" and a few days later on behalf of the RLASS. William Hallowell wrote a "sharp letter" to that society's secretary, Julia Wilbur, accusing her "of trying to keep people away from *their* lecture." The accusation outraged Wilbur, whose election as secretary had been contested because several members considered her too much "a Garrisonian." Hallowell's criticism was likely more surprising, since Julia had boarded with him and Mary for six months just the year before. Whereas Amy seemed to accept Julia's divided loyalties, neither Hallowell nor Nell did. After applauding Post on the winter lecture series, Nell noted, "My own sentiment toward Miss Wilbur has been one of distrust—the position she occupies of close fellowship with your enemies materially unfits her for confidence of your circle."[62]

Perhaps Wilbur's relationship with Lucy Colman and their efforts to integrate the city's classrooms lessened Amy's concerns about Julia. For years, local blacks had protested the separate school the board of education set aside for their children. Colman had agreed to serve as principal of the "colored school" in Rochester in winter 1856, with the intention of working with parents to force the board's hand. If black families refused to send their children to segregated and underfunded classrooms, then the school would have to close. Wilbur and Post supported Colman's efforts, as did Douglass. By fall, both the school and Colman's position were eliminated, and the board of education was forced to integrate the city's public schools.[63]

The preceding spring, Post had agreed to accompany Lucy Stone on another lecture tour, although she had not attended the woman's rights conventions held in Albany, Saratoga, or New York City the previous two years. Those meetings had focused mainly on persuading the New York State legislature to expand women's economic and political rights, and Susan B. Anthony served as the chief organizer. Post could have easily stayed with her old F/friend Lydia Mott in Albany or with Mary Robbins Post on Long Island, but not even the chance to hear Ernestine Rose, Samuel J. May, or Elizabeth Cady Stanton inspired her to go. In April 1856, however, she eagerly joined Stone on visits to Saratoga and other eastern New York towns. Stone's reasons for the tour were largely economic. That winter, Henry Blackwell had sold his hardware store in Ohio so that he and his wife could move east. However, the expenses involved required Stone to return to the lecture circuit before joining Henry in New York City in May for the annual AASS convention.

Post was no doubt eager to discuss the turmoil that Lucy's refusal to take her husband's name had caused as well as the criticism she received for marrying at all.[64] Stone was also thinking about having children, and once again, Amy could reassure her that this did not mean giving up her political commitments. Traveling by coach, rowboat, and train, the pair tried to pack in as many speeches in as many towns as possible. Like Stone, Post planned to have her husband join her at the AASS convention and sent Isaac directions for meeting at Troy, New York. With only a few days left of Stone's tour, Amy took time off to visit an old friend and fix a broken tooth. Not willing to go "out toothless among the strangers here," she journeyed to Poughkeepsie to pick up a new plate.[65]

When the Posts arrived in New York City for the May anniversary meetings, they luxuriated in visits with their families while everyone, including Jacob Kirby, was healthy and happy. Still, Isaac and Amy were eager to get to the AASS meetings and spend time with Nell, William Wells Brown, Harriet and Louisa Jacobs, and the Motts. That spring, the discussions and speeches were largely focused on the bloody clashes in Kansas. Mott noted that the radical demands of younger abolitionists made stalwarts like Samuel J. May, who called for "gradual steps" in Kansas, appear "quite in the conservative ranks."[66] Among black abolitionists, however, both young and old insisted on the immediacy of emancipation, and not only in Kansas. As William Wells Brown reminded his audience, "Those of us who have lived in slavery could tell you privately of the degradation of the domestic circle of the master." Jacobs knew full well the meaning of his claim, though a bad cold meant she saw Amy "for only a few fleeting moments."[67] Nell, on the other hand, enjoyed a welcome respite with his old friend.

On returning home, Amy wrote a long letter to Sarah Owen, taking her old friend's mind off the hours spent caring for her sister, nieces, and nephews by vicariously sharing Post's travels and conversations. Owen did attend lectures when possible, but Grand Blanc, Michigan, where she now lived, attracted more missionaries and moderate reformers than Garrisonians and women's rights advocates. Having been widowed as a young woman, she valued not only the advantages Amy gained by living in a vortex of activism but also her marriage to Isaac. Sarah had written Amy earlier, asking her to send some muslin and dress patterns. She closed, "Now dear sister Amy, the Lord bless you abundantly and brother Isaac *full as much* if not more, for all your kindness to the children of men and *me* in particular."[68] Amy was, indeed, fortunate to have a husband who not only adopted the principles of equal rights but also practiced them on a daily basis. In the 1850s, when Isaac was less eager to leave home, he supported Amy's right to travel in the interest of social justice or family even as he lamented her absence. Still, he was happiest when they could share their interests with close circles of friends and family.

One of Isaac's favorite gatherings was the local "free meetings," often held at 36 Sophia Street. Based on the same principles as the Friends of Human Progress, free meetings combined faith and activism and admitted people regardless of religious affiliation, race, or sex. Isaac claimed he almost forgot that Samuel J. May and Theodore Parker were ministers "when they are on the free platform pleading for humanity, for justice." Still, he felt that "priests stand in the way of progress . . . and I think Amy felt [*sic*] the same." Although Isaac admitted that some free meetings were poorly attended, others attracted a larger group, including Benjamin Fish, Lucy Colman, and Huldah and Asa Anthony. Frederick Douglass even appeared now and then, as did itinerant activists and spiritualists. "Nothing," Isaac concluded, "can be higher [than] each one feeling free to give their highest ideas."[69] Mary Robbins Post wished such gatherings occurred in Westbury. She and Joseph still attended the local Hicksite meeting but suggested to some dissatisfied members that they "meet as you do for mutual improvement and the free interchange of thought on any of the great subjects of the day."[70]

By the mid-1850s, outside the relatively limited circles of the Friends of Human Progress, spiritualists, and Garrisonians, interest in universalist visions of social justice had waned. This was particularly true in election years, when partisan struggles for political power loomed large amid ongoing battles over slavery. In 1856, Democratic standard bearer James Buchanan ran against Republican John C. Frémont and former President Millard Fillmore, who headed the nativist American Party ticket. The election proceeded in an atmosphere poisoned by violence. Bloody clashes had spread from Kansas to the floor of the U.S. Senate. In May, Charles Sumner, the Massachusetts senator, railed against what he termed the "Slave Power" and planter politicians like South Carolina Senator Andrew Brooks. Brooks's nephew, who served in the House of Representatives, chose to protect his family's honor by assaulting Sumner in the Senate chambers, beating him senseless with a cane. News of the attack headlined papers across the country, and the incident met with shock and anger in the North. Frederick Douglass declared the act "an outrage" at a May meeting in Rochester, and many believed that the "Union will be saved or lost" by the fall election.[71]

That June, delegates at the first national Republican Party convention in Philadelphia "demonstrated a fervor and moral zeal never before seen at a political convention." They stomped, yelled, applauded, and cheered as Frémont was nominated, even though the candidate and his wife, Jessie, remained at home in California, as was customary at the time. Former Free Soilers and Whigs were enthralled with the frontier soldier and politician, and his wife, who was a power in her own right.[72] Ratifying meetings were held in cities across the North to arouse enthusiasm. The Rochester meeting attracted three thousand people, with William Hallowell serving as one of its vice presidents. Unlike Amy and Isaac, Hallowell had shed any constraints about political action. Douglass, too, supported the Republican candidate, insisting to Gerrit Smith, who was running for president on the

Liberty League ticket, that it is "the best thing I can do *now*." He did recognize the limits of a Republican platform, which rejected calls for abolishing slavery in the South in favor of ending its further expansion. A mass meeting and procession for Frémont on 5 September attracted large crowds in Rochester as local papers celebrated their favored candidate and excoriated his opponents.[73] The Posts, like most Garrisonians, did not join the partisan fray, but Amy must have admired Jessie Frémont's skills as an orator and a campaigner.

For radical circles in Rochester and elsewhere, presidential elections meant smaller crowds and diminished funds. Religious revivals throughout 1856 further diminished participation in secular campaigns. In Rochester, the Reverend Finney's return was especially disruptive. J. Elizabeth Jones, an Ohio abolitionist and spiritualist, commiserated with Amy: "I am sorry to hear that your lectures have not been well attended this winter. That is, however, the general complaint everywhere." Jones had been scheduled to speak in Rochester, but a snowstorm kept her from reaching the city. Shortly afterward, she sent Amy a newspaper clipping that listed important American books, complaining that it included no African American authors.[74] Lucy Colman also wrote Amy from the Midwest, where she sought to spread Garrisonian principles. She longed for Amy's company as she battled political abolitionists along with radicals focused on spiritualism and free love, which she considered pure "nonsense."[75]

The election of Buchanan on 4 November 1856 aroused dismay among abolitionists. Although the new president was from Pennsylvania, he was a proslavery advocate and a Democratic Party stalwart. He captured majority votes across the South and in Indiana, Illinois, New Jersey, and his home state. Still, his election encouraged Garrisonians and political abolitionists to work more closely, especially in assisting freedom seekers. In western New York, the appearance of Harriet Tubman, who escaped Maryland in 1849, nurtured those bonds. She returned to the South several times in the 1850s to guide enslaved family members and others to safety. Tubman likely made her first connections in Rochester in 1851 through Frederick Douglass and the AME Zion Church, which had long provided sanctuary for fugitives. She later worked with leaders of the RLASS, bringing a party "out of the land of servitude" to the home of Maria G. Porter just weeks after Buchanan's election.[76]

Although the Posts met Tubman, Amy did not develop the kind of close relationship with her that she had with Nell, Jacobs, and Truth. In part, Tubman's ties to Douglass and the RLASS explain the distance. Certainly Amy admired the famed conductor's courage, and William and Mary Hallowell hosted Tubman on at least two occasions. Still, Amy's universalist vision bound her more closely to Nell, Jacobs, and Truth, all of whom used 36 Sophia Street as a home base for extended periods and happily joined the radical circle of family and friends gathered there. Tubman, on the other hand, slipped quietly into the city and left as soon as it was safe to continue her mission.[77]

Another woman who entered the local antislavery scene in the late 1850s was Ottilie Assing, a German journalist whose political vision was forged in the European revolutions of 1848. She arrived at Douglass's South Avenue home in summer 1856 and made numerous extended visits there over the following summers. Much as was the case with Griffiths, neither Anna Douglass nor the WNYASS circle was pleased with the situation. Indeed, Assing's intrusions seemed more problematic, since unlike Griffiths, she did not contribute financial or strategic assistance to Douglass or the movement. Post, despite her interest in European perspectives on social justice, had little contact with Assing, but then she had little contact with Douglass in this period.[78]

Instead, Post forged a closer relationship with Charles Lenox Remond and his sister Sarah Remond, compatriots of Nell in Massachusetts. Given the upheavals of fall 1856, Amy and Isaac were happy to welcome the Remonds to Rochester that December. They had been lecturing across the state and enjoyed a respite at 36 Sophia Street. Charles returned in February 1857, when the AASS held a convention in the city, with Garrison and May among the speakers. While the Posts and several close friends participated, the turnout was smaller than in earlier years and the fractiousness more evident. Indeed, Douglass berated Remond in his report on the event.[79] Meanwhile, Nell worried that Amy was ill, as no Rochester box had been received for the Boston bazaar that winter. She replied in April, reporting that she had been busy organizing an antislavery lecture series and hosting visitors at Sophia Street. She also mentioned that Douglass had informed her that Julia Griffiths, now back in England, was seriously ill. In addition, Amy was preparing for her son Jacob's marriage to Jenny Curtis on 2 May. The Hallowells and Willises joined Amy, Isaac and Willie at Sophia Street for the occasion, along with Joseph and Mate and their daughters, two-year-old Alice and two-month-old Hattie. Several friends also shared in the festivities, including visitor Sarah Remond, who offered "an interesting account of the pleasant scenes" to Nell on her return to Boston.[80]

Still, it was difficult to forget for long the grave issues that loomed that spring, especially after the *Dred Scott* decision on 6 March. Following the ruling, protest meetings were held across the North, including one at Rochester's city hall in April that attracted both Garrisonians and political abolitionists. Then, following the May AASS convention in New York City, Sojourner Truth organized a lecture tour through western New York, staying with the Posts and offering her unique perspective on the latest developments.[81]

In June, Amy Post returned to the yearly meeting of the Friends of Human Progress. By then, the group had added health reform, land reform, and prison reform to its ongoing commitments to peace, abolition, racial equality, women's rights, and religious liberty. Even the positive value of spiritualism was accepted by many. Progressive Friends in Michigan "urged all the friends of Progression to investigate the facts, the philosophy and claims of Spiritualism" as an antidote to popular ideas about "the authority of the Bible," ideas of total depravity, and "a fixed and eternal hell."[82] Those in western New York were pleased that Andrew Jackson Davis joined their colloquy in 1857, at which participants advocated a range of issues and, for the first time, called for "disunion." The idea had caused heated debates within abolitionist ranks since the 1840s, when some Garrisonians argued that those who truly opposed slavery must cut all ties with a proslavery government. This meant refusing to participate in electoral politics, a position that political abolitionists denigrated as wholly ineffective in eradicating slavery. After the *Dred Scott* decision, more Garrisonians argued that only dissolving the union could save the North and West from proslavery control of federal authority. Over two nights in May 1857, Douglass and Remond debated the issue at New York City's Shiloh Presbyterian Church, gaining widespread news coverage. Although some Progressive Friends believed that disunion would only lead to war, the Posts joined Mott, Nell, and other radical F/friends in supporting the strategy.[83]

Earlier that spring, Harriet Jacobs had written Post from Idlewild, the home the Willises, her employer, had built at Cornwall on the Hudson. She and Amy had not seen each other since the 1856 AASS in New York City, and then only briefly. Jacobs had continued to work on her book, despite the difficulties of juggling the demands of the Willis family and the need to hide her literary efforts from the proslavery patriarch, Nathaniel Willis. However, the *Dred Scott* case convinced her that she must finish her book as soon as possible. "When I see the evil that is spreading throughout the land my whole soul sickens," she wrote Amy. "Oh my dear friend this poor heart that has bled in Slavery—is often wrung most bitterly to behold the injustice the wrongs—the oppression—the cruel outrages inflicted on my race." Her anguish was clear. Has "not the decision of the last few days . . . decided this for us," she lamented. "I see nothing for the Black Man—to look forward to—but to forge his old Motto—and learn a new [one. H]is long patient hope—must be might—and Strength—Liberty—or Death." In a postscript, penned upside down along the top of the opening page, she added that she would not show Amy "the Book until I see you."[84]

Over the next year, Jacobs and Post corresponded regularly. Unfortunately, Post did not make it to the 1857 AASS convention in New York City, but Jacobs spent time there with Lucy Colman and William Nell. On 18 May, Harriet put in writing what she had hoped to ask Amy in person: "I have thought I wanted some female Friend of mine—to write a Preface or some introductory remarks for my Book—and there is no one whose name I would prefer to Yours. . . . I know my dear friend it is a great deal to ask of one whose time is so [illegible] invaluable," but "you know me better than most of my friends." Well aware that "there are many painful things" in the book, including descriptions of enslaved women's sexual exploitation, which might shock readers, Jacobs shrank "from asking the sacrifice from one so good and pure as yourself."[85] Nonetheless, she believed Post's endorsement would curtail criticism of the book and its author. Although Jacobs planned to publish under a pseudonym, she wanted to convince readers that the story she told was true. Given Post's reputation for integrity and her devoted friendships with black activists, a few lines from her could lend authenticity to Jacobs's tale.

Taken ill with congestion of the lungs, Jacobs did not send the letter until early June and assured Amy she did not need a preface until late August. Post wrote back within the week assuring her support. Although she had written epistles, fair reports, petitions, and hundreds of letters, she had not authored anything like the preface Jacobs proposed. Nonetheless, Harriet responded with "a heart full of thanks" and some ideas for Post's remarks. She added, "My kind friend, I do not restrict you in anything for you know far better than I do what to say." While Jacobs knew several activists more famous than Post, she trusted no one to better understand and endorse her life story. She also hoped Amy could advise her on a plan to sell the book in England, perhaps by lecturing there: "By identifying myself with it I might do something for the Antislav[e]ry Cause." But this would require letters of introduction, which she hoped Post could help her obtain.[86] Although the process of reading Jacobs's book and offering suggestions would have been eased by meeting in person, the best they could do was communicate through Nell. Harriet visited him while in Boston, securing Maria Weston Chapman's "interest in her forthcoming book" as well as letters of introduction to British abolitionists. Nell then wrote Post, offering to read her introduction and assuring her, "All you have said about the Book and its Author as also cherished by yourself is understood, accepted and will be considered and adopted by me in the manner suitable to the wishes of all."[87] Jacobs had hoped to have books to sell that fall, but obstacles repeatedly delayed publication.

Amid anxiety over the *Dred Scott* case and Amy's intense efforts on behalf of Jacobs's book, the Posts continued to embrace other causes. The most important of these was prison reform and capital punishment. These issues had long interested Friends, who had written testimonies seeking to improve penal regimes they considered brutal to mind and body. Philadelphia Friends had been especially active in prison reform; and in the days before the Seneca Falls Woman's Rights Convention, Lucretia Mott had visited Auburn State Prison and applauded its efforts to educate and convert its inmates. A decade later, Joseph Post wrote his brother Isaac about a recent visit he had made to Sing Sing, where he preached to one thousand male prisoners. He and his wife Mary had visited the sick and met with a group of about eighty-five women prisoners, "some of them looking very intelligent." He noted that there were no distinctions of color, but all the prisoners, black and white, mixed together.[88] While Isaac and Amy supported Quaker testimonies, they had not been deeply involved in the movement until a sensational murder case in Rochester inspired them to act.

On 20 December 1857, Rochester police found the body of Charles W. Littles, a local lawyer, and in January arrested his wife, Sarah, and her brother, Ira Stout. The investigation dragged on through the winter, with trials finally set for mid-April 1858.[89] Among the 150 men questioned for the Stout jury, a few—all F/friends of the Posts—announced their "conscientious scruples against bringing a man in guilty of murder" if execution was to be his end. When the Stout trial finally took place, Amy was in Jericho, helping care for her father and visiting friends and family. Jacob, now father to an infant daughter, kept his mother apprised of developments. It took the judge "three days or more," he wrote, to impanel a jury "that had no minds of their own." The court house was crowded every day, and on the day of the verdict, it was packed, and "the stairs wer[e] crowded (so full that the plastering on the underside cracked)." Crowds of people also surrounded the court house, and "the street from Fitzhugh Street Bridge was full around the Court House, all trying to get a sight of Ira Stout."[90]

After a brief trial, Stout was declared guilty and was sentenced to hang on 18 June. Jacob reported that "Mrs. Littles, who I think is much more to blame than Ira was," refused to plead guilty to manslaughter in the first degree so will stand trial, "which will certainly be no worse for her, and she may be acquit[t]ed." Like others who opposed capital punishment, Jacob "hope[d] that the governor will interfere and commute the sentence to imprisonment for life."[91] After the trial, many Rochesterians, both women and men, visited the convicted murderer in prison. To those who opposed capital punishment, Stout appeared intelligent and capable of rehabilitation.

Several radical F/friends were bent on saving Stout from hanging. Isaac, though busy with the store and the return of Joseph, Mate, and their children to 36 Sophia Street, sent updates to Amy. He reported that Sarah Burtis "has been to see the Prisoner. She is very much interested in the condemned man Ira Stout [and] had a free conversation with him. . . . The Jail has been crowded with visitors and one [group] has to wait until another goes." Burtis, wanting to "commune with him in a more private way," asked Stout to take off his cap so she could feel his head, after which she concluded that "his combativeness is small but firmness large." Amy's cousin Esther Titus went with Amy's daughter-in-law Jenny Curtis Post to visit Stout the next day. Although Jenny sympathized with "poor Ira" and held his "*cold* hands," she worried that "it was too much like going to a show." Indeed, the jail charged admission.[92] Sarah Willis, too, conversed with Stout, telling Amy that each time someone visited, "sympathies were so aroused" that the whole circle "felt it the more." Some considered "the jury and Judge . . . equally guilty with Ira Stout," while others felt "as guilty as they," having not earlier "bestirred [them]selves for the abolition of so horrible a law." Most made it clear that their concern was not "for this man above others" but for the "barbarous" practice itself.[93]

Challenges to Stout's sentence postponed his execution, allowing protesters time to organize a mass meeting for those who believed "Capital Punishment to be unfriendly to the progress of civilization[,] hostile to a true religion, [and] repulsive to the best instincts of humanity." The call was signed by more than thirty local activists, including the Posts, the Anthonys, the Hallowells, Frederick Douglass and his daughter Rosetta, and Lucy Colman. On 9 October, activists gathered to denounce capital punishment "with special reference to the case of Ira Stout." Many Garrisonians and political abolitionists agreed on the issue, and the hall was crowded, though "every effort [was] made by a group of rowdies to break up the meeting." The officers—president Frederick Douglass, vice president Isaac Post, and secretary Susan B. Anthony—managed to proceed with their efforts, but they failed to change the outcome. Stout was hanged two weeks later. Participants sent resolutions to be printed in the *Liberator* and other reform papers, as well as to New York governor John King.[94] However, with Stout's case out of the news, the campaign to abolish the death penalty subsided.

Of course, abolition remained a major concern among capital punishment opponents even in the midst of the Stout campaign. John Brown arrived in Rochester in late January 1858 and stayed with Douglass for the next month, laying out his plans for emancipating slaves by force of arms and creating an independent state in the Virginia mountains. It is likely that Isaac met Brown because Douglass's office was so close to his store, but neither he nor Amy mentioned the fiery abolitionist until months later. That May, "4 strongminded women" represented Rochester at the AASS anniversary meetings in New York City: Lucy Colman, Sarah Anthony Burtis, Sarah Willis, and Amy Post.[95] Unfortunately, Harriet Jacobs was unable to attend because her employer fell ill just days before the meeting, but Nell promised to carry news from Amy to her on his way back to Boston.[96] In late August, Nell headed west to lecture in Ohio and Michigan with Frances Ellen Watkins, a freeborn black poet and the cousin of his friend William Watkins. She had been inspired to join the abolitionist lecture circuit by the Fugitive Slave Law. Nell stopped to visit the Posts on his return to Boston in late September and joined in the passionate discussions over capital punishment, abolition, and spiritualism. The Posts also dined with Harriet Tubman that fall, invited by William and Mary Hallowell, who were honored to entertain the famed conductor.[97]

While the Hallowells took over some of the responsibility as hosts, 36 Sophia Street remained a center of activism, and Amy continued to orchestrate ties among movements and friends. Indeed, the effort was easier now, with Willie away at school in Union Springs for much of the year and her other children establishing homes of their own. The Posts maintained a free produce household and used alcohol only for medicinal purposes, but they offered hospitality to all who called. In 1857, Andrew Jackson Davis and Mary Fenn Davis lectured across central and western New York and stayed with the Posts during their time in Rochester. Davis had just published his autobiography, *Magic Staff*, which gained a wide readership among spiritualists and alternative medical practitioners. While some activists shied away from the couple because charges of adultery had been leveled at Mary Fenn

Davis by her first husband, Amy and Isaac believed in their spiritual powers, welcomed them into their home, and promoted their efforts among friends and family.[98]

Over the next year, Amy Post's relationship with Frederick Douglass slowly improved, and in June 1859, she traveled with him, Lucy Colman and Lewis Burtis to the Friends of Human Progress meeting in Waterloo. Old F/friends Oliver Johnson, Ruth and Joseph Dugdale, and Giles Stebbins attended, along with the Reverend Samuel J. May and Aaron Powell.[99] The meeting, while still infused with a Quakerly spirit, was increasingly organized like a reform society, with a chairperson and nominating and business committees as well as a committee to respond to epistles from other Friends of Human Progress meetings. Post served as one of two secretaries, while Colman joined Douglass on the business committee. Like the AASS, participants attacked northern churches that failed to speak out against proslavery forces. Passionate in their critiques, they characterized mainstream churches as "superstitious, idolatrous, and [full of] atrocious absurdities, . . . a wild hallucination and an utter futility." They linked the proslavery stance of mainstream religion to its opposition to women's rights. Churches, they claimed, branded blacks with the "awful curse of slavery" and women with "false and depressing notions of dependence and inferiority." Progressive Friends also condemned "what is popularly called prejudice against color" and insisted that women's "rights are co-extensive with her being, and are bounded only by her capacity." A debate then erupted over whether the enslavement of blacks or the oppression of women "was the greatest atrocity in the land." Colman and Douglass argued the former, and Lewis Burtis the latter by insisting that marriage was the most stultifying of all institutions.[100]

Given the incendiary claims made by Progressive Friends and the ongoing debates among them, Charles D. B. Mills, who was in charge of publishing the *Proceedings*, asked Post for help. She readily agreed despite being ill much of the summer. Working with progressive editor and printer Charles Hebard, she and Mills had fifteen hundred copies of the *Proceedings* published in September.[101] By that time, Amy was once again focused on the publication of Jacobs's book. Jacobs had traveled to England, with introductory letters from Maria Weston Chapman in hand, hoping to gain a sponsor for the publication of her book there. She met many prominent Garrisonians, including George Thompson and Irish abolitionists Richard and Hannah Webb, who had stayed with the Hallowells' during their U.S.

tour a year earlier. Jacobs was excited to meet black expatriates in London but, failing to find a publisher, she returned exhausted and depressed.

John Brown's raid on Harpers Ferry on 16 October 1859 snapped Jacobs out of her melancholic state and many Americans out of their complacency over slavery.[102] Although Douglass, like other prominent black activists, refused to get entangled in Brown's revolutionary plan, six white abolitionists, including Gerrit Smith, provided funds for his venture. With twenty-two followers—including three of his sons—Brown captured the federal arsenal at Harpers Ferry, Virginia, planning to arm slaves in the immediate area and ignite a wider rebellion against slaveholders. However, local authorities were quickly alerted, and federal troops under the command of Colonel Robert E. Lee cornered the rebels, killing fourteen. Two days later, Brown and his three remaining compatriots were captured. As news spread, some devoted abolitionists hailed Brown as a hero even though they disapproved of his use of arms. Still, his friends, blacks in particular, were in immediate danger of arrest and of being charged as co-conspirators. Federal authorities lost little time in seeking out Douglass, who was lecturing in Philadelphia.[103]

Fortunately, the Posts' old F/friend John Hurn, an abolitionist and utopian communalist, was then working as a telegrapher in Philadelphia. When Hurn received a telegram instructing the local sheriff to arrest Douglass, he immediately headed to the home where Frederick was staying and rushed him to a ferry that carried him to Camden, New Jersey. From there he took a steamer to New York City, fearing that at any moment he might be taken into custody. Hurn, however, had delayed delivery of the telegram for three hours, giving Frederick time to escape. Douglass found his way to Hoboken, New Jersey, and spent "an *anxious* night" in the house where Ottilie Assing boarded. Assing sent a message to a telegrapher in Rochester who was a friend of Douglass, asking Frederick's son Lewis to "secure all important papers in my high desk." Douglass then took a circuitous route home, arriving at South Avenue on 21 October. That night, the Posts received a message from William Still, an underground conductor in Philadelphia, and early the next morning, Amy hurried to the Douglass home. A local paper published an incriminating letter from Douglass to Brown that very day, convincing the famed orator he must flee to Canada. When night fell, Amy and Isaac secreted Frederick to the wharf below the Genesee Falls, where many a fugitive had boarded boats to freedom. Now it was Douglass's turn to escape his pursuers, who arrived in Rochester the very next day. By then,

Frederick had reached Canada, where William Hallowell, on business north of the border, escorted him to a safe haven.[104]

The Posts' role in ensuring Douglass's safety finally broke through the lingering tensions between them. Frederick wrote "My dear Friend" Amy from Canada, thanking her for her "kind notes. They seemed like good news from a far country. Your face here w[oul]d be quite a benediction." He was staying at "a low Dutch tavern," where authorities were unlikely to find him. She had urged him "to remain on this side of the water," but he only felt safe across the Atlantic.[105] In November, he left for England.

Amid the excitement surrounding Brown's raid and Douglass's flight, Amy drafted the preface for Harriet Jacobs's book, which she hoped would be published by the end of the year. On 30 October 1859, she sent it to Jacobs, who found it deeply moving. Amy identified the author as "my highly-esteemed friend. . . . She was a beloved inmate of our family nearly the whole of the year 1849. . . . Her appearance was prepossessing, and her deportment indicated remarkable delicacy of feeling and purity of thought." Post then recounted how Jacobs gradually confided her story, relating her "baptism of suffering." Despite the "mental agony" this caused, Amy "urged upon her the duty of publishing her experience, for the sake of the good it might do." She catalogued the obstacles Jacobs faced, including the lack of formal education and the need to support herself and her daughter while constantly on the alert for southern "man-hunters and woman-hunters." Still, Post was certain that Jacobs's "story, as written by herself, cannot fail to interest the reader. It is a sad illustration of the condition of this country, which boasts of its civilization, while it sanctions laws and customs which make the experiences of the present more strange than any fictions of the past."[106] Despite Post's endorsement and the intensifying crisis over slavery, publication was once more delayed.

Meanwhile, abolitionists gathered around the country to mourn Brown's execution on 2 December 1859. Although they disagreed over his use of force and his dream of an armed uprising among slaves, many abolitionists, both black and white, viewed Brown as a martyr. Isaac and Amy sympathized with Brown's outrage even as they opposed his use of violence. Nonetheless, Isaac joined other Rochester abolitionists to honor Brown's memory on the day of his execution.[107] Amy did not, but only because that very day she had been called to Jericho, where her father lay dying. She and twelve-year-old Willie rushed off as soon as the news reached them, but they did not arrive in time—Jacob Kirby was already gone. Isaac soon joined them, and the three stayed for two weeks, helping with arrangements to transfer the Kirby homestead to one of his grandchildren and visiting family and friends across Long Island.

Before returning home, Amy received medical treatments in New York City for an unnamed illness, giving her and Isaac the chance to see Leah Fox, now Leah Fox Underhill, who resided there. Amy found a letter from Douglass awaiting her return and replied immediately. She thanked him for his kind words and admitted, "I do not know what to say myself. . . . I am so sorry that we have lost five years of *beautiful friendship*." Still, she loved to think back on the many pleasures of their earlier times together and the "last few holy hours" we spent together. "Dear Frederick," she continued, "be no more sad about all those scenes of the past, so unspeakably painful, we will all resolve to be unspeakably good." She then described a trip she, Isaac, and Leah Fox Underhill made to New Jersey: "When we arrived at the grave of Thomas Paine we all alighted, so as to *press our feet* upon the soil this gifted man so oft had trod." She related the story of the various religious sects that refused him burial and the property owners who denied the right of his friends to erect a monument in his memory. Thus, they built it next to the highway, "a monument, not only to the genius of one man, but of the ignorance and superstition of many."[108]

The letters between Amy and Frederick reveal a fault line in the Posts' reaction to recent events. Isaac stood "his ground well on the peace question—amid all the warlike utterances of his Garrison friends," while Amy prayed for "the 'restoration to freedom of speech' " within radical convocations. In part, she sought to ensure that both pacifists like her husband and advocates of armed vigilance like Douglass and Nell would be heard. Douglass, meanwhile, was surprised that abolitionists in Britain objected to his "war views" while even Garrisonians in the United States were "deeply interested in the whole Brown invasion."[109] Amy tried to explain her husband's rationale to Douglass. Isaac, she wrote, sees "John Brown [as] a great man, viewing him from *Moses* and his own standpoint," but finds "the life of Jesus," who refused to raise a hand against anyone, the better model for mankind. While Amy did not openly endorse the use of violence, she understood why some might see force as the only response to human bondage. And she did not want divisions over its use to create discord among abolitionists just when unity was needed most. Moreover, while maintaining her universalist vision of change, Post clearly viewed abolition as the critical issue of the day. Thus, she lamented to Frederick that Lucy Colman has been busy, "I am sorry to say, not as thee supposes in the Anti-Slavery ranks, but under the less desirable auspices [of] *Wendell, Lucy, & Susan*," campaigning for women's rights.[110]

Wendell Phillips, Lucy Stone, Susan B. Anthony, and Lucy Colman tried to draw Post into their efforts to expand women's property rights and gain woman suffrage via state legislative action. In January 1860, Anthony wrote Amy from Albany: I left "my petition with the few signatures with you" and hope you will collect "as many more names as you can." Anthony urged her to "get the names of a few business men, lawyers, judges, etc," preferably at the head of the list. "The Legislature will be more strongly impressed than merely our *'fanatic'* names." Anthony then asked that Amy "forward to me all that you have by Monday night."[111] Whether Amy fulfilled her mission is unclear. Perhaps she passed it on to her stepdaughter, Mary, who more fully embraced Anthony's agenda. The Hallowells were both more inclined than Amy to partisan politics, with William having joined the Republican Party in 1856. He was also now counted among the city's prosperous businessmen, so Mary had access to that circle, while Amy remained intimately tied to the "fanatics."[112]

As abolitionists lectured and debated across the North, it was increasingly difficult to find venues willing to rent them space; and even when the staunchest opponents of slavery spoke out publicly, few turned out to hear them. The Posts insisted that this "lack of interest" was "the very reason" to call a convention. A core of powerful speakers was touring the state, providing the chance to host an event despite limited funds. Thus, on 21 and 22 March 1860, a stellar group of speakers convened in Rochester. Amy Post presided over the meeting, and Mary and William Hallowell, Sarah Willis, and Susan and Mary Anthony were among the officers. During the proceedings, Parker Pillsbury, Aaron Powell, Giles B. Stebbins, Susan B. Anthony, and Lucy Colman offered speeches and resolutions to an enthusiastic, if small, audience.[113]

Just two weeks earlier, Amy Post had attended the AASS annual meeting in New York City, where she was elected one of thirty-two vice presidents alongside old F/friends Lydia and Lucretia Mott.[114] While she was speaking at the AASS, a letter from Abigail Bush was wending its way cross-country. Perhaps Bush was inspired to write after reading of the Rochester convention in the *Herald of Progress* or the *National Anti-Slavery Standard*. Abigail described Henry's efforts to extend antislavery and spiritualist beliefs in northern California along with news of children and grandchildren, but reminders of earlier days overwhelmed her. "Memory with her never

Dying Loves & remembrances, brings *you* before my Heart, as I speak *now* . . . after a Silence of *years*." But if "spiritual Intercourse" is only measured "by verbal or written expression," she concluded, "*how* sadly would Our Heart's Love be mismeasured in *Length, Breadth & depth*."[115]

Douglass had returned from England that spring, driven home by the death of his dearly beloved youngest daughter, Annie. Although he mourned her loss deeply, he was quickly swept up in abolitionist labors, none more compelling than assisting fugitives to freedom. As he wrote William Still in July, since reaching home, "I had the satisfaction of passing nearly a score on to Canada, only two women among them all." Speaking for Post and other conductors, he declared, "The constant meeting with these whip-scarred brothers will not allow me to become forgetful of the four million still in bonds."[116]

Amid the growing political turmoil, Amy Post traveled to Waterloo for the yearly meeting of the Friends of Human Progress. Chosen to serve as clerk, she summarized the remarks of Douglass, Colman, and Lewis Burtis while scribbling a letter to Isaac from her desk. She described visits with old F/friends from Ledyard, Skaneateles, and other central New York towns, including Elias Doty, and her dinner plans with Asa and Huldah Anthony, stopping periodically to copy down resolutions. Soon after returning home, she wrote a long letter to Nell, detailing events in New York and Waterloo but regretting the discontinuation of Rochester's free meetings. Nell reciprocated with news of Boston's abolitionist circle and a recent woman's rights convention he attended, as well as updates on William Wells Brown and Louisa Jacobs. In October, he wrote again, describing a gathering of abolitionists at the Boston Music Hall, which led him to recall conversations he had had with Amy and her sister Sarah during an 1852 visit to Rochester. Nell also proudly noted his first public discussion of spiritualism and provided an update on Harriet Jacobs's book. "I wish it was my good fortune to spend a few days with you and the Circle in Rochester this fall," he concluded.[117] Amy surely wished for that, too, particularly with the political upheavals fueled by the presidential election.

By August it was clear that no political party could bridge the growing abyss between northern and southern positions. Within the Democratic Party, northern and southern branches could not even agree on a candidate. The northern faction chose Senator Stephen A. Douglas of Illinois, and the southern faction, John Breckinridge, a Kentucky slaveholder. A group of southern Whigs, unhappy with both choices, formed the Constitutional Union Party and nominated Tennessee senator John Bell. The Republicans, however, remained united despite taking three ballots to select their nominee, former Illinois congressman Abraham Lincoln. A small group of former Liberty League members created the Radical Abolitionist Party, which nominated Gerrit Smith, but even Frederick Douglass had no hesitancy in supporting Lincoln over his dear friend Smith. Douglass reminded voters that political purity had failed in recent presidential contests, with votes for third-party candidates ensuring the election of Democrats James K. Polk and James Buchanan. While recognizing that the Republican Party is far from "an abolition party," he nonetheless gave Lincoln the best chance of beating "the wickedly aggressive pro-slavery sentiment of the country."[118]

Lincoln was elected president on 6 November 1860, gaining a minority of the popular vote nationwide but a clear majority of Rochester's vote and, more importantly, the electoral vote. Although Isaac Post and other radical F/friends of his generation did not cast ballots, their younger allies, including William Hallowell and Edmund Willis, did. For them, only a Republican in the White House, even one who had not fully embraced abolition, could keep proslavery forces from taking control of the nation. By January 1861, many northern businessmen were frightened of the economic impact that Lincoln's election might have on trade, as southern politicians threatened secession. In the midst of these anxious times, in the early hours of 18 February, fifteen thousand women and men gathered at the Rochester train station to salute Lincoln on his way to Washington, D.C. Local families walked to the station, while those from outlying areas arrived in buggies and carriages. The president-elect's train arrived at 7:35 A.M., in the pitch dark of a winter morning. Lincoln stepped to the rear platform, and as the cheering crowd grew silent, he thanked them for coming out and claimed it was "the largest assemblage" he had met since leaving Illinois the week before. He spoke for just five minutes, then turned and was gone.[119] It is likely that the Hallowells and Willises were among the crowd that day, and Douglass and other members of the black community probably attended as well. If Amy and Isaac Post saw Lincoln speak, they did not describe it to friends or family.

Even before Lincoln's 4 March 1861 inauguration, the nation was in chaos. Southern sympathizers in the North increased their attacks on abolitionists, while proslavery advocates in the South demanded secession. In December 1860, Douglass and Nell had attended an anniversary meeting of Brown's martyrdom at Boston's Tremont Temple, where antislavery speakers were attacked by supporters of the Constitutional Union Party. When Douglass tried to speak, white men rushed the stage, throwing chairs in anticipation of fists. The battle raged for hours, and five black men were seriously injured.[120]

Worse was to come. By the time Lincoln took the oath of office in March, seven southern states had seceded from the union and formed the Confederate States of America. A week later, the Posts and other abolitionists rallied in Rochester. The AME Zion Church was one of the few venues that still welcomed antislavery meetings. Douglass again joined Parker Pillsbury, Aaron Powell, Giles Stebbins, Susan B. Anthony, and Lucy Colman on the podium. Douglass applauded Lincoln's rise to national leadership, but hoped the president could be induced to take on the southern states and eradicate slavery, by force if necessary.[121] On 8 April, Lincoln ordered ships to carry supplies to Fort Sumter off the South Carolina coast. The Confederate president, Jefferson Davis, then demanded that officers at Fort Sumter surrender. They refused, and four days later, Confederate guns opened fire. The Civil War had begun.

It was in this volatile context that Harriet Jacobs's book, *Incidents in the Life of a Slave Girl*, was finally published. Two final hurdles had delayed the book's appearance. Most importantly, in fall 1860, Jacobs's Boston publisher insisted on a preface by Harriet Beecher Stowe, which Jacobs refused even to request. Then Thayer and Eldridge agreed to publish the book if Lydia Maria Child wrote a preface, clearly considering Amy Post not sufficiently prominent to promote Jacobs's work. Jacobs wrote Amy that she "tremble[d] at the thought of approaching another Sattellite [*sic*] of so great magnitude." However, Nell arranged an introduction, and Child agreed not only to write a preface but also to edit the manuscript. With Child's assistance, Jacobs reorganized and polished the manuscript in fall 1860. That October, Jacobs wrote Post, noting that her original preface would now appear at the end of the book. She assured Amy that she had told Child "of the feeling that has existed between us—that your advice and word of encouragement had been my strongest prom[p]ter in writing the Book."[122] Finally, in January 1861, Harriet Jacobs held a copy of *Incidents in the Life of a Slave Girl* in her hands, even if the title page listed Linda Brent, her pseudonym, as author.

As Jacobs launched a tour to promote her book, the nation was coming apart at the seams. Nell wrote an admiring letter about the book to Garrison, which he printed in the *Liberator*. Antislavery Friends in Philadelphia also applauded the book and its author, with pioneering abolitionist Sarah Pugh calling Jacobs "a faithful and true witness, a worthy and noble representative of her race." However, in traveling through much of Pennsylvania and New York, Jacobs feared being assaulted and found few people eager to read her searing condemnation of slavery's brutal effects on women.[123]

That June, as northern men rallied to Lincoln's call for troops, the Friends of Human Progress gathered in Waterloo. Once again, Amy Post and Frederick Douglass attended, perhaps traveling together as they had journeyed to neighboring Seneca Falls in 1848. Catherine Fish Stebbins and her husband, Giles, came from Michigan, and Samuel J. May and Gerrit Smith came from Syracuse. Susan B. Anthony joined the discussions, as did Lucy Colman, Lewis Burtis, and Benjamin Fish. After the first day, Amy urged Isaac to come. Douglass "speaks grandly," she reported, while once again "I have the honourable seat at the Clerk's table."[124] There was considerable tension, however, over participants' reaction to the war. Catherine Stebbins confronted her brother's decision to join the Union army. Torn by "great and conflicting emotions," she argued in opposition to her brother's choice and her husband Giles's prowar pronouncements. The oppressive institution of slavery, she contended, could not be ended by the enslavement of thousands to the oppressive institution of war. Anthony also voiced skepticism about Union war aims, while Douglass insisted that the war was against slavery and must end with emancipation. One of the only points of consensus was the need to aid the enslaved and those who escaped to free territory.[125]

At the Friends meeting and after, Douglass tried to persuade northerners to support the war and President Lincoln to support emancipation. In Rochester on 16 June, old friends heard his demand that Union leaders confront the divisive issue of slavery. Titling his talk "The American Apocalypse," Douglass declared, "Not a slave should be left a slave in the returning footprints of the American army. . . . Sound policy, not less than humanity, demands the instant liberation of every slave in the rebel states."[126] That very week, Amy received a letter from Harriet Jacobs in which she enclosed a missive to Isaac from her brother John. He was touring England to buttress antislavery and anti-Confederate views there. John Jacobs hoped that we "are beginning to see the moving of His hand to execute judgement and bestow mercy," but he worried that too many Englishmen and Americans were not ready to break their ties with the South. "If the American flag is to be planted on the altar of freedom, then I am ready to be offered on that altar, if I am wanted; if it must wave over the slave, with his chains and fetters clanking, let me breathe the free air of another land, and die a man and not a chattel."[127]

The letters arrived while Amy Post was sending invitations to women across central and western New York to attend a Fourth of July "Anti-Slavery

Pic Nic" near Frederick Douglass's home. Douglass, Parker Pillsbury, Elizabeth Cady Stanton, Giles Stebbins, and others would address the crowd, and Post urged women to bring their husbands and "as many of those noble women of *Colloquy* reputation as you can." She even reached out to members of the RLASS. Many of Post's allies responded. So, too, did Maria G., Susan, and Samuel Porter and their coworkers. Finally bridging the gap that had divided local antislavery advocates for nearly a decade, Post declared, "We abolitionists surely have work to do now in influencing and directing this bloody struggle, that it may end in Emancipation, as the only basis of a true and permanent peace."[128]

8 Coming Together, 1862–1872

On 25 March 1862, a year after Lincoln took office, Frederick Douglass gave a rousing oration on "The War and How to End It" at Rochester's Corinthian Hall. Believing that black soldiers were the key to victory, he was increasingly frustrated by Lincoln's refusal to allow African Americans to serve in the Union army. After a series of military defeats, Union forces had finally gained footholds in Confederate territory that spring. Still, Douglass's tone was bellicose and bitter—toward southern officials and soldiers who turned traitor by joining the Confederacy and toward northern officers who seemed to admire the enemy. General George B. McClellan, he intoned, "is careful to tell us that the Southern army is composed of foemen worthy of our steel." To Douglass, "They are traitors worthy of our hemp." Although the Posts and other radical F/friends took a less vitriolic tone, they too worried that Lincoln either could not lead the Union to victory or would do so without abolishing slavery.[1]

While Douglass and the Posts insisted that blacks should be enrolled in the army and abolition must be the war's primary goal, plenty of northerners, including activists, disagreed. Moderate abolitionists were concerned that black soldiers and emancipated slaves would only heighten tensions among northern whites at a moment when unity was critical. As thousands of the enslaved escaped behind Union lines, conflicts emerged over how the government should treat them, who should care for them, and even what to call them. At first many Union commanders sent fleeing slaves back to their owners, but eventually the federal government recognized them as "contrabands" and claimed them as prizes of war—like captured weapons. Abolitionists considered such language dehumanizing and preferred "refugees" or "freed people."

Although these conflicts fueled divisions among government officials, army officers, and abolitionists, many female activists mended fences to aid men, women, and children who had emancipated themselves. Vastly more northern women organized on behalf of soldiers' aid, but female abolitionists—both Post's circle and the RLASS—focused their efforts on black refugees. Still, the bonds forged during the war between black and white, political and Garrisonian, and female and male abolitionists would not be strong enough to hold once peace was achieved. In the late 1860s, struggles over black citizenship and suffrage divided former allies and fueled new organizations and agendas.

From the outbreak of war in April 1861, northern newspapers flooded readers with optimistic claims for a quick victory followed by shocking reports of death and defeat. The Posts were committed to a Union victory only if it ensured emancipation. But at least they had time to work toward that goal. In the late 1850s, Isaac had officially passed his pharmacy business on to his son. Married and, by 1861, father to a baby girl, Jacob Post had invited another clerk, William Bruff, to become his partner. R. G. Dun and Co. assured its clients that Post and Bruff pharmacy remained a "well establ[ishe]d firm, in the oldest location in town," and that the two partners are "careful, indus[trious] and experienced." As war erupted, the Posts' younger son Joseph, now the father of three children, was hired by Flour City Oil Works, which offered steady employment. Meanwhile, son-in-law William Hallowell and brother-in-law Edmund Willis continued to thrive in the woolen trade while their wives, Mary and Sarah, labored beside Amy to achieve abolition, expand women's rights, and assist black refugees. Although Isaac helped out in the store part time, he could participate more fully in activist endeavors and, for the first time in many years, seemed as drawn to abolition and peace work as spiritualism.[2]

Domestic obligations were reduced as well. Willie, now in his teens, lived at home only a couple of months a year, spending much of the war at Union Springs Friends Academy or in Jericho and Westbury with family. The Posts were happy to have the company of Mary Ann Pitkin, the black boarder who had entertained Nell with her beautiful singing. In addition, widowed dressmaker Margaret King and single friend Susan Humphrey, both committed spiritualists, boarded with Amy and Isaac as the war began. Before Humphrey left to get married, the Posts took in the daughter of a friend living in the country. They also enjoyed visits from an array of family members and fellow activists. Mary W. Willis, Amy's older sister, and her husband, John, visited in October 1862. Whatever tensions the Willises' criticisms of abolition and spiritualism fueled were soon offset by a cherished visit from Mary Robbins and Joseph Post. An old friend from Ledyard then stayed for at least a week in December, and other friends and relatives stopped at Sophia Street in the following months.[3]

These visitors no doubt exchanged views on the war and its meaning. The Posts and their allies agreed on promoting emancipation as the ultimate goal of a Union victory though they sometimes disagreed on priorities and tactics. Amy and Isaac, for instance, "disapproved of the [*National Anti-Slavery*] *Standard's* publishing [of] the speeches and doings of prominent antislavery [R]epublicans," but their sister-in-law Mary Robbins Post tried to persuade them that these activities served as "a moral thermometer." Such speeches provide "strong incentives to abolitionists to labor more earnestly to arouse & quicken this sentiment which is being expressed by politicians." Perhaps to placate her dear relatives, Mary concluded, "It is a cheering sign that the most radical speakers on this issue [of war and emancipation] are the most loudly applauded and draw the largest audiences."[4]

While the Posts viewed emancipation as the central issue, many of their Rochester neighbors focused far more attention on military matters. Even some abolitionists embraced a martial spirit. In December 1861, the Reverend Henry Ward Beecher lectured in Rochester on "The Cause and the Country." He said "there was no use mi[ncin]g the matter, everybody knows that slavery is the cause of the war." Yet he highlighted the military, rather than the moral, prowess of abolitionists. He even gave credit to Quakers, who he claimed "are now the most belligerent class in the community." Although radical F/friends rejected this assessment, many former pacifists did support the war effort. Beecher noted in particular a company of Quaker soldiers in Pennsylvania.[5] And despite Lucretia and James Mott's protests, their son-in-law Edward Davis signed on as quartermaster for General John C. Frémont's Department of the West.

At least abolitionists could laud Frémont for declaring martial law in Missouri and freeing slaves there. However, this act only heightened concerns about Lincoln, who rejected Frémont's plan for fear of alienating white Missourians and residents of other border states in the Union. When Lincoln removed the general from his command, Lucretia Mott labeled the president a "miserable compromiser." Still, she was no doubt pleased that the president's action convinced Davis to resign from the army.[6] Mary Robbins Post was equally disappointed in Lincoln, berating him for undercutting Frémont's authority at a time "when the most heroic acts are liable to misconstruction, suspicion and the ingratitude of the people."[7] The administration's policies also ensured that Mott, the Posts, and their allies would have much work to do in addressing the needs of fugitive families.

Frustration gripped many abolitionists as 1862 dawned. Mary Robbins Post again captured their feelings: "Is there not great danger that slavery will survive this do nothing policy[?]"[8] That May, Lincoln was denounced at the AASS convention for his failure to make emancipation a wartime goal and to grant freedom to slaves who fled to Union lines. Amy Post, who served as a vice president for the convention, was joined in the deliberations by Mary Robbins and Joseph Post as well as Lucretia and Lydia Mott, Williams Wells Brown, and Lucy Stone. Garrison spoke eloquently on the important work being done to aid freed people but reminded participants that the great work of "Emancipation" must be the organization's main focus. Brown, Stone, and Ernestine Rose echoed the claim that abolition was the only outcome that could render this bloody conflict meaningful. Yet on a practical level, the needs of refugees were immediate, as was the demand for resources to continue supporting lecturers and the antislavery press. Questions of principle also arose. Some wondered how, given their disunionist principles, Garrisonians could demand that the "pro-slavery" federal government use its wartime powers to abolish slavery. Despite these contentious issues, the *Liberator* reported that different points of view were offered in a "thoroughly cooperative" spirit.[9]

At the end of May, Progressive Friends meeting at Waterloo embraced Garrisonian critiques of Lincoln and demands for emancipation as they debated the role of Quakers in wartime. It proved far easier to denounce Lincoln and support the right of blacks to serve than to reach consensus on whether Friends should take up arms.[10] The Posts were fortunate that none of their sons sought to enlist, but some of their F/friends wrestled with family members' choices. Catherine Fish Stebbins's brother, John Hurn's sons, the Motts' son-in-law, and Jane Hunt's brother-in-law all enlisted. Of course, some radical F/friends considered volunteering for service honorable. In 1862, Esther Titus, a Kirby cousin in central New York, supported her sons' enthusiasm for the war. Even though Edward Titus "*fell from sunstroke with the wounded,*" she wrote Amy, he "*is now able to go back into the army again.*" Her son James, she claimed, would also "go willingly to the war, was it not for his little family." She seemed more worried that he "will have to give a thousand for a substitute" should the conscription law go into effect. Still, she thought it worthwhile that abolitionists, even Quakers, serve. Jane Hunt's brother-in-law, she noted, "brought a bright, intelligent contraband with him" to Waterloo on his first visit home.[11]

The Sophia Street circle, too, divided over the benefits of military service. Lucy Colman and Giles Stebbins supported Quakers signing up for Union service, and Douglass and Nell fought for African American enlistment, believing it was a powerful means of proving blacks' right to full citizenship. However, Catherine Fish Stebbins, Benjamin Fish, Isaac Post, and Asa Anthony stoutly maintained their pacifist principles. Amy wavered, believing that the war could be considered righteous if it led to emancipation, though she would not encourage her sons or others to enlist.[12]

By fall 1862, the landscape had shifted, as Union forces finally achieved some notable victories and war fever once again gripped the North. Julia Wilbur reported that Rochester was "full of soldiers, excitement and bustle." That spring, the United States had signed a treaty with Great Britain that would more effectively suppress the African slave trade, and Congress finally abolished slavery in the District of Columbia. Just as importantly, Union troops captured the Sea Islands in South Carolina, while the army and navy combined to take control of key forts along the western front. On 19 September, just two days after the Union army declared victory at Antietam, the 140th Regiment departed Rochester, and local residents crowded the train station and nearby streets to cheer them on their way.[13] In the following months, speakers on the war attracted enthusiastic crowds to Corinthian Hall, and even pacifists were buoyed when Lincoln announced a preliminary Emancipation Proclamation in September and agreed to accept blacks into the Union army. Former slaves from South Carolina composed the first black unit while Douglass and his allies rushed to enlist northern blacks in the Massachusetts 54th Regiment.

Still, abolitionists were not entirely persuaded that emancipation would follow or that it would be universal. Moreover, for many whites, the proposed conscription law was of more immediate concern. Long Island relatives reported that it was causing "great excitement around us, particularly among the Irish." At the same time, Union generals continued to return runaways to their plantations. Mary Robbins Post found the military's decision to send some one thousand enslaved blacks, "poor defenseless people who had faithfully dug the canal at Vicksburg," back to their masters "shocking" and "disgusting."[14] Another friend, however, who had been with the "Western Army" in Alabama, assured Post that there was much good to tell about "the Slave and the war," claiming "we Free them as we go."[15]

With the Union army gaining ground, Post and her circle doubled their efforts on behalf of the burgeoning communities of black refugees. Amy fell ill for a time that fall as she tried to juggle far-flung correspondents, activist endeavors, and domestic responsibilities. Among her many tasks was managing the financial affairs of several female friends, including her cousin Sarah Thayer, who depended on her to handle banking, a mortgage, and the repayment of debts.[16] Still, neither age nor illness could keep Post down for long. She wrote William Nell that she was determined "never to grow old" despite her fifty-nine years. Nell agreed, claiming he was too busy planning exhibitions and tableaux, fighting against the color bar for employment in the U.S. Post Office, writing for the *Liberator*, and participating in debates over the Emancipation Proclamation.[17]

Like Nell, Post focused on the good to be accomplished. Her Sophia Street home remained "a Refuge" for widows, activists, spiritualists, and the children of friends and acquaintances even as Amy focused increasing amounts of energy on aiding refugees. Freedmen's Aid societies sprang up across central and western New York as well as in Boston; Philadelphia and West Chester, Pennsylvania; and throughout the Midwest. Orthodox and Hicksite yearly meetings in several regions, including New York, also labored on behalf of freed people.[18] Post's efforts were reinforced by her participation in the 1862 AASS annual meeting in New York City alongside Joseph Post, Williams Wells Brown, Ernestine Rose, Aaron Powell, Susan B. Anthony, and other longtime allies. She was again honored to be elected a vice president with Lydia and Lucretia Mott, Samuel J. May, Robert Purvis, and other old friends.

Post's enthusiasm intensified when Harriet Jacobs started working among self-emancipated refugees in Washington, D.C., and Alexandria, Virginia. In late May 1862, Jacobs attended the Pennsylvania Yearly Meeting of Progressive Friends at Longwood, outside Philadelphia. The former fugitive had become acquainted with the Progressive Friends through the Posts. Encouraged by Longwood attendees Lucretia Mott and Garrison, Jacobs began working among the contraband. Initially, Jacobs relied on assistance from black abolitionists and Quaker groups to collect blankets, clothing, and other items in New York City and deliver them to refugees in the District of Columbia and Alexandria.[19] She continued to promote her book but spent more time raising awareness of the plight of freed people and calling on old friends like Post to provide much needed resources. In September, Jacobs wrote a long article for the *Liberator* on "Life among the Contrabands," describing in stark detail the chaos, disease, poor housing, and "pitiable condition" of men, women, and children. "Each day," she reported, "brings its fresh additions of the hungry, naked and sick," dozens of whom would not survive their first weeks in freedom.[20] Yet Jacobs also noted the courage of these self-emancipated blacks and their efforts to forge families and communities in freedom.

Jacobs's reports inspired many abolitionists, including the Sophia Street circle and the RLASS, to expand their efforts. The RLASS asked Julia Wilbur to serve as its agent in Washington, D.C., and she readily agreed. Friends meetings and newly established Freedmen's Aid societies, which had begun organizing shipments of bedding, clothing, and other goods to Jacobs, now extended the same resources to Wilbur. The urgency provoked by the war ensured that, after years of keeping their distance, women from the "old organization" increasingly cooperated with members of the "new." Providing necessities for the thousands and then tens of thousands of southern blacks who found their way to Union outposts demanded new coalitions that crossed old divisions. Although it was the RLASS that sent Wilbur to Washington, Amy Post, Mary Hallowell, Sarah Willis, and other radical friends leapt into action, supplying funds and goods to her as well as to Jacobs.[21]

In November, Wilbur reached out to Post to spread the word about her need for funds and goods. Julia noted the severe overcrowding in the nation's capital and described the especially dreadful conditions for refugees and contrabands. She reported on her visit to "an old slave pen" in Alexandria, where "20 women & children, many of them sick," were huddling around a little fire. They "were wrapped in their old rags, the weather has changed & they feel the cold very much now." In other places, several orphans were fending for themselves, one of whom was badly burned. Other children had mothers, but all adults were required to work for their rations and paltry accommodations, which rarely included sufficient food, beds, or bedding. In addition, many "secesh" women—that is, Confederates living in Alexandria—refused to pay the refugees after making them work for hours or days. Wilbur was outraged as well by the treatment of many soldiers. Sometimes loads of "sick soldiers" arrived, with no idea where to go for treatment, food, or housing. She described officers who "care no more for the comforts of the soldiers than they can for the beasts" they ride. After describing these various horrors, she concluded, "It makes me sick of my country, sick of mankind. . . . I wish thee w[oul]d come & see for thyself." If that was impossible, she hoped Amy could persuade Emily Howland, Lucy Colman, or another activist to join her in Washington. Finally, she asked Post to show her letter to Anna M. C. Barnes, the president of the RLASS, ensuring that the two women would discuss their overlapping efforts.[22]

Wilbur understood the importance of having both networks labor on her behalf, and she knew that the Sophia Street circle, which was already assisting Jacobs, was well prepared for the work. Post dutifully circulated copies of Wilbur's letter to Barnes as well as to Howland and the Searing sisters in central New York, who had been shipping goods to the Sea Islands for the past year.[23] This flurry of correspondence along with ongoing reports from Wilbur published by the RLASS, *Frederick Douglass' Paper*, and *Douglass' Monthly*—the British version of Douglass's weekly paper—inspired many abolitionist women to assist in whatever ways they could.[24]

Then, on 1 January 1863, the Emancipation Proclamation took effect. The document did have its limits—it did not abolish slavery in the border states, over which the federal government held control, but only in Confederate states, where such control was tentative or nonexistent. Nevertheless, blacks across the nation celebrated, including Post's closest friends. In Boston, Douglas, Nell, and Jacobs waited for a telegram confirming that the proclamation had indeed been signed.[25] Nell presided over an all-day vigil at the Tremont Temple, which attracted some three thousand people. Speakers moved to the Boston Music Hall for the evening, where Anna Dickinson, John Greenleaf Whittier, Ralph Waldo Emerson, and Harriet Beecher Stowe spoke and the Boston Philharmonic played Beethoven's "Ode to Joy." It was nearly midnight before an official raced into the hall, telegram in hand, and read Lincoln's words: "I do order and declare that all persons held as slaves within said designated States and parts of States are, and henceforward shall be, free."[26]

Amy eagerly read reports of Boston along with the responses of close F/friends like Mary Robbins Post, who captured the thoughts of many radical abolitionists: "The proclamation is a great act of justice, more than I feared but much less than I hoped[;] . . . whether it will be carried out fully remains to be proved. The sufferings of the escaped slaves in many places is enough to deter many from the attempt to leave. Their present is filled with uncertainty and peril." In early February, she wrote Amy and Isaac again, noting that Frederick Douglass, Charles Lenox Remond, and Robert Purvis were "all energetically urging" black men to enroll in regiments "as a means of success." Waxing philosophical, she claimed that despite discouraging incidents, "it [is] well to review the past and the triumphs achieved lest in view of the difficulties and dissentions here at the North we took a wrong estimate of things and faint by the way."[27] For Sojourner Truth, who lay seriously ill throughout late 1862, the proclamation renewed her vigor, and she sent word to her friends that she longed "to speak to the people a few more times in this glorious day of emancipation."[28]

Personal crises, however, did not disappear in the wake of Lincoln's long-awaited promulgation. Isaac's brother Joseph seemed especially worried about rising costs fueled by the wartime economy. He and Mary were also anxious that Edmund Willis continued to suffer from "chronic disease" despite the attentions of Sarah and the best doctors in Rochester and on

Long Island. At the same time, the Posts' old Jericho friends John and Rebecca Ketcham were assailed by financial, medical, and parental troubles. Harriet Jacobs's daughter, Louisa, was also taken ill that winter. Willie Post, however, seemed far removed from personal or political crises. Now fifteen and boarding at Union Springs Friends Academy, the complaints in his letters home focused only on cold rooms and homesickness. While other young men imagined or feared heroics on the battlefield, Willie daydreamed about "hear[ing] the birds sing their sweetest melody while the dew is on the ground" and having "a garden" in which I could "exercise and experiment."[29] His letters were welcome relief from most his parents received.

Letters from Alexandria were especially heartrending. In early 1863, the Alexandria slave pen that had first housed contrabands had been turned over to the army to hold disorderly soldiers. In response, the U.S. government, which had never set up designated contraband camps in Alexandria as it had in Washington, D.C., sent these and other refugees to government-built barracks. Others fended for themselves, but the city was bursting at the seams. Moreover, federal assistance to refugees was largely confined to food and a room—any room—with no funds for furniture, coats, bedding, shoes, or other necessities. Since families fleeing plantations rarely arrived with more than the clothes they wore and the children they carried, their situation was dire. Even in the District of Columbia, Wilbur claimed that there were four times more blacks than whites by February 1863, and the small number who had money for rent found most boardinghouses closed to them.[30]

Despite the success of Post, Howland, and the RLASS in collecting large quantities of goods for refugees, serious challenges remained. As Wilbur wrote Post, not only did "boxes and bales" go astray, but she had few resources for moving items from Washington, D.C., to Alexandria, where the need was even greater. Wilbur had also discovered that some boxes were opened before they arrived and suspected that items were missing. In response to these problems, she asked that goods be shipped in her name to a specific express company that would deliver them where needed. In addition, supporters should "send a list of the goods & their value, and a duplicate receipt" in a separate letter to ensure that all the items were intact.[31]

Wilbur did have some good news: Harriet Jacobs had just returned to Alexandria with support from New York Yearly Meeting of Friends. Harriet had written Amy in December that she was eager to return to Virginia, noting, "The good God has spared me for this work." Still, she believed that "a just God is settling the account [and] it is fearful to think what Man will suffer before he is willing to do justice to his fellow man." Jacobs "craved more than one pair of hands & money," so was thrilled to find Wilbur in Alexandria when she arrived. Although Julia was not immediately taken with her coworker, she acknowledged to Amy that Jacobs "can do many things better than I can do," particularly when it came to gaining the trust of refugee families. Smallpox had broken out among them, but many were unwilling to admit that family members were sick for fear of being separated. Jacobs, who befriended local black families, was more successful than Wilbur in gathering information as she distributed clothing and bedding among them. The two women came to depend on each other and believed they could manage the workload, at least once the smallpox outbreak ended and their need for additional bedding, pails, towels, and basins subsided.[32]

While female abolitionists engaged in the practical work of assisting self-emancipated blacks, they remained committed to expanding the reach of the Emancipation Proclamation. More needed to be done to ensure slavery's eradication, and some, particularly Elizabeth Cady Stanton and Susan B. Anthony, hoped that liberating the enslaved might lead to greater freedom for women. Concerned about Lincoln's commitment to abolition, much less women's rights, the pair organized the Women's Loyal National League to give voice to their hopes about the war and its outcome. Their specific aim was to gather one million names on petitions for a constitutional amendment ensuring the abolition of slavery throughout the nation. Stanton, then living in New York City, helped create the Woman's Central Committee as an umbrella group for women's rights and antislavery organizations. That committee then called a meeting to organize the Women's Loyal National League. Anthony contacted dozens of women leaders across the North, including Post, to meet in New York on 14 May 1863, establish the league, and organize the massive petition campaign.[33]

The call for the meeting recognized the thousands of mothers who laid "their sons on the altar of [their] country," as well as the thousands of women laboring on behalf of soldiers and freed people. "It is high time the daughters of the revolution, in solemn council[,] . . . lay hold of their birthright of freedom, and keep it a sacred text for all coming generations." Anthony enclosed the call with invitations to Amy Post, Jane Elizabeth Jones, Betsy Mix Cowles, Josephine Griffing, and other local and regional leaders. She sent letters not only to women committed to racial equality but also to those dedicated to soldiers' aid. Anthony sweetened the appeal, at least for more radical activists, by announcing that Lucy Stone, Antoinette Brown Blackwell, Ernestine Rose, and Anna Dickinson had agreed to speak. She also stated that she and Stanton were preparing an address to the president of the United States "to be adopted by the meeting." Working out of New York City's busy antislavery office, Anthony took a moment to pen a personal message on Amy's letter—"your brother Joseph Post just comes in" and "looks as fresh and joyous as ever."[34]

The women who convened that May at the Church of the Puritans held a wide range of views, but the leaders were staunch women's rights advocates. Lucy Stone presided, Stanton served as one of three vice presidents, Lucy Colman and Martha Wright served as secretaries, and Amy Post sat on the business committee alongside Anthony and Rose. Anthony offered a resolution that "there never can be a true peace in this Republic until the civil and political rights of all citizens of African descent and all women are practically established." Some moderates objected, but Post and Rose joined Stone and Angelina Grimké Weld in insisting that the cause of women and slaves were intertwined.[35] After a lengthy debate, Anthony's resolution was adopted. Still, the petition that the organization circulated focused solely on abolition, recognizing that in the moment, emancipation for slaves was the primary aim. Signatories thus "earnestly pray that your Honorable Body [U.S. Congress] will pass . . . an Act emancipating all persons of African descent held to involuntary service or labor in the United States." Post was among two thousand women who agreed to circulate petitions in local areas. Within fifteen months, these agents collected some 400,000 signatures, helping to gain approval for a Thirteenth Amendment, ending slavery in the United States.[36]

As usual, while Post gathered signatures for the league, she continued to labor on other fronts as well. In early June, she attended the Friends of Human Progress meeting at Waterloo, enjoying time with Lucy Colman and cousins Esther Titus and Sarah Thayer, all of whom were circulating the league petition. Aaron M. Powell, a Garrisonian whom Post admired, attended the meeting for the first time in several years. He was soon to take over editorship of the *National Anti-Slavery Standard*, an especially critical position during the war. Despite participants' respect for each other, tense times ensured that disputes erupted. Colman disagreed passionately with Giles Stebbins's prowar stance, and although Thayer probably agreed with Colman in principle, she considered Lucy "very disagreeable and annoying."[37] Still, Post found the Progressive Friends inspiring, an oasis in the midst of the militaristic passions voiced by so many Union supporters.

Soon after Amy returned home, antidraft riots erupted in New York City. The mid-July uprising shocked many Americans, and abolitionists were appalled by the savage attacks white mobs launched against African American residents, including the Colored Orphan Asylum. Although blacks were taking up arms against the Confederacy and facing some of the most brutal fighting of the war, many working-class whites were angered by a draft that allowed wealthier men to buy their way out of service as Union casualties rose. In the midst of the riots, an anxious Esther Titus wrote Amy from Canandaigua, New York, "What is going to become of us all—will right eventually prevail [in] *miserable New York*. I am glad that I am not there. I feel safe—away off here—but perhaps we shall have trouble among ourselves. *There was great excitement until the drafts were stop[p]ed.*"[38] The hiatus was short, however. The federal government ensured conscription's peaceful resumption in New York City in mid-August by stationing 20,000 troops there.[39] While riots erupted in other cities, none occurred in Rochester. Still, as the war dragged on, deaths and injuries mounted, and refugees continued to pour north; residents there, too, wondered how the conflagration would ever end and how many lives would be sacrificed along the way.

Throughout fall 1863, Post gathered signatures on petitions and collected goods to send to Washington, D.C., and Alexandria. As she poured more of her energy into ensuring the war would end with emancipation, she may have become less critical of the conflict and more dissatisfied with receiving her news secondhand. After reading dozens of agonizing letters and reports about conditions in the nation's capital, Amy felt as if her "soul went there, with its heavy load."[40] Finally, she decided to visit Wilbur and Jacobs. Isaac, who had no desire to go, was relieved when his cousin Ann Willets, whose daughter Georgianna was working in a D.C. contraband camp, joined his wife. Amy traveled to the Willets home in Jersey City around 1 December. The two women then headed to Philadelphia, where they met up with Benjamin Fish, visited the Motts, and dined with Frederick Douglass, in town for an AASS convention celebrating the founding of the society in Philadelphia thirty years earlier. Fish, Post, and Douglass also lunched with Dr. Aurelia Raymond, Lucy Colman's sister, at the Female Medical College, which Amy was eager to see.[41]

Amy had been gone a week when she stopped by the photography studio owned by old F/friends John and Sarah Hurn and found a quiet moment to write Isaac. There, "surrounded by the comers and goers, and bargain makers for pictures," she apologized for the delay caused by constant traveling and visiting. That day alone, she and Ann had already dined with the Motts, visited Camp William Penn with James Mott, and met two soldiers from

Rochester, whose "countenances shone very bright when they grasped my hand." Despite concerns among some Friends when the camp was being built, the first for black recruits, Amy reported that "James and Lucretia now seem delighted to have them so near." Then, after visiting the Hurns, Post and Willets met up with the Motts at an antislavery convention, which a number of the soldiers also attended, "giving our meeting a martial appearance."[42] Despite her pacifist beliefs, Amy recognized that at least black men in arms shared their dream of emancipation.

While Amy tried to assuage any grievance caused by her tardy correspondence, she also noted that Isaac could have traveled with her. "I have wished continually that thee was with me. . . . It makes me almost give out going any further, but I am afraid if I wait to go with thee, I shall never go."[43] Clearly, by 1863, the Posts embraced different notions of an activist life. Sixty-one-year-old Amy was still eager to attend meetings of the AASS and the Friends of Human Progress and to journey south to see conditions for herself. At sixty-five, Isaac preferred to stay at home. The two also differed on their feelings about the war. While Isaac maintained his pacifist views, pure and simple, Amy embraced the possibility that military victory might be justified by gaining emancipation.

Finally, on 9 December, Post and Willets, excited and curious, arrived in Washington, D.C. They had traveled at night by train with Benjamin Fish, arriving the next morning at Camp Barker, where Georgianna Willets and her roommate, Carrie Nichols, worked with black refugees. They invited Amy and Ann to stay in their "rough boarded room," which contained "a good fire, good bed, three chairs, a table—washstand, [and] two or three shelves with books, plants etc." Despite their overnight journey, Amy and Ann were eager to tour the camp and found the place "kindly and pleasantly managed." Yet even there, Amy noted, "much destitution [was] apparent among so many poor creatures just [out] from under the hand of oppressors, their tales of cruelty [are] heartrending."[44]

The next morning, the two women met Benjamin Fish and headed to the provost marshal's office "to get permits to go over [to] Dixey"—that is, Alexandria—after "affirm[ing] our loyalty." Amy described crossing "the *famed Potomac*," where they saw, for the first time, the preparations "for defence [sic] or attack. Oh! The innumerable multitudes of horses we saw on the Eastern bank, . . . the great Arsenal, and cannon on each side was a great sight," with flags "flying from almost every hill top." Her enthusiastic response to the battlements testified to the change in her view of the war, while her stunned reaction to conditions in Alexandria mirrored her deep concern for the treatment of blacks, enslaved, fugitive, and free. "I can't [describe] how shocking bad every thing almost looked," she wrote Isaac, claiming it was too horrid to put down on paper. The trio then visited the "old slave pen," which now held "disorderly soldiers." Their guide "did not point out the dismal dark cells around the sides, but pompously showed us the shower bath where they punish [men], sometimes ten minutes at a time," in the December cold. Amy noted that the pen held "twenty or twenty-five prisoners today, our Union soldiers, how my heart ached for them."[45]

Post and Willets were soon confronted by the Reverend Albert Gladwin, a Baptist missionary who had been appointed superintendent of contra-bands. Although initially hopeful of Gladwin's support, Wilbur was soon complaining to Anna Barnes, and no doubt to Post, that the superintendent abused the refugees, "threatening to flog them & scolding them as if they were animals." Jacobs also criticized Gladwin as well as the doctor in charge of the nearest smallpox hospital, who proposed to gather together all the orphans and send them to the pox house.[46] Gladwin was no doubt incensed that Post, Willets, and Fish arrived in Alexandria on the same day that a committee of New York Friends, who helped fund Jacobs's work, appeared to examine the conditions she had detailed.

Earlier in the day, Wilbur had taken the Friends committee to the hospi-tal, which had "*been scrubbed for them to see*," and hoped the visitors would not be fooled. They were not. Even with efforts to conceal the worst condi-tions, committee members were "indignant at what they saw" and de-manded that stoves be put into the hospital rooms before nightfall. Already angry at what he considered an intrusion, Gladwin tried to put off Post and her friends. He "kept us as long as he could from finding Julia and com-panions, showing [us] all the best, and keeping us out of all the worst abodes." When they finally met up with Wilbur and Jacobs, Amy and com-pany received the grand tour "to the Long House & to the school, & to the old mill. They all climbed up the old ladder & the stairs, & were indignant that rent sh[ould] be paid for these places to the U.S. government." Glad-win was angry that the visitors had been shown the sites he sought to hide, and Amy was haunted by the scenes. Later that night, she wrote Isaac, "I can't get Alexandria out of my mind, the poor contrabands, it seems to me the conditions can't be much worse than slavery, such wretched smoky hovels—not a bit of light."[47]

Post carried these horrific images with her for years, but she visited more uplifting sites as well. She sat with Fish and Willets in the gallery of the House of Representatives and listened to a debate, then toured "the Capitol, very grand," and "searched out the Senate chamber." Despite Amy's earlier embrace of disunion, she wrote enthusiastically of being "invited in" to the Senate's "sacred floor" and seeing Charles Sumner conversing with Horace Greeley. She was equally interested in the Union soldiers. She, Ann, and Benjamin saw soldiers' camps "all astir . . . their four-horse covered wagons in numbers surpassing anything we had ever conceived of. . . . Soldiers all over everywhere." Amy and Ann then returned to Camp Barker and "attended [a] meeting in the old schoolhouse with the ex-slaves [t]here— we were astonished to hear what good language they used, though some misplaced words—their voices seemed very melodious both in preaching, praying & singing."[48]

The next day, Post and Willets visited hospitals throughout the city and met some wounded men from Rochester. One, John Jessup, "appealed so earnestly to us to go to the United Stat[es] Agent to interced[e] for him in get[t]ing a discharge, that we went." The two women did persuade the agent to work on Jessup's behalf but did not know how it would end, as discharges were one of the most "difficult things to accomplish." They then toured the White House, where the president lay ill. Afterward, Amy and Ann traveled by a mule-driven contraband ambulance to Arlington Heights, where a plantation with a splendid view of the Potomac had been confiscated and the mansion house turned into a school for black children. Janet Jackson, a Philadelphia woman who served as caretaker, "sprang to her feet, and grasped my hand . . . when she heard my name, said she had known me ever since she could remember anything about Antislavery." Post believed that the "little bright" children were "impressed with the idea, that they were the hope of our country's salvation."[49]

From there, the pair traveled to a contraband camp set up on General Robert E. Lee's plantation, where Amy picked some ivy to bring home to her stepdaughter, Mary. They then "called to see Aunt Sally, her husband & one son, who were his [Lee's] slaves, [and] she could hardly find language adequate to express her sense of horror & scorn of the man, who had deliberately sold her nineteen children away from her." Four of Aunt Sally's children had returned since the war began, but even their presence could not dislodge the terrifying memories in her mind. In the last camp Post and Willets visited, the women noted Douglass's autograph in the school room, "the first intimation that he had visited any camps of the kind." Harriet and Julia, she told Isaac, were still awaiting Frederick's appearance in Alexandria. That night, a young black woman with measles shared the room with Amy, Ann, Ann's daughter Georgianna, and her coworker Carrie. She was suffering from nightmares of being pursued by slave catchers, or "murderers" as Amy called them, and needed the security of a crowded room.[50]

On Sunday, Post met Jane Grey Swisshelm, a moderate abolitionist, woman's rights advocate, and journalist, who with her daughter now visited "the poor wounded and sick men" in Washington, D.C., hospitals. Swisshelm related numerous stories of hospital life and accompanied Amy to the Soldiers' Home, a stately retreat "where 130 of the old Mexican soldiers remain." That evening, Post and Willets enjoyed services at the church of the Reverend William H. Channing, who had previously presided over Rochester's Unitarian church. Amy "spoke to him [and] he remembered us, and desired love to his Rochester friends," who included William and Mary Hallowell. Anxious not to miss anything on what "will be *my* only visit here," Amy persuaded Ann to stay two more days so that they could visit the patent office and the Smithsonian.[51]

While Amy spent hectic days touring Washington, D.C., and Alexandria, Isaac worried back home. Immediately after her first letter arrived, he wrote her at Jersey City, the only address he had, to assure her all was well. He scoured the *Liberator* and the *Standard* for any mention of the meetings she attended in Philadelphia and for developments in Washington, D.C. Despite wanting Amy to return as soon as possible, Isaac urged her to visit family on Long Island on her way home. He also reported news of family and friends, as he oversaw a full house. Mrs. King was still living at Sophia Street, and George W. Clark, the famed abolitionist singer, stopped there for a few nights. Esther Titus also arrived soon after Amy left and stayed for at least a week, and a Mrs. Abbott was resting in one of the rooms, awaiting a doctor's call. Although Mary Ann Pitkin provided much needed help, she was not fond of Mrs. King; thus, Sarah Willis spent a good deal of time at Sophia Street.[52]

By mid-December, on her way back to Jersey City, Amy did stop on Long Island, though not for long. Indeed, her sister Mary Willis complained, "How short your visit was here—can't reconcile myself to it." Willis also chided her niece Mary Hallowell and sister Sarah Willis for always disappointing her by writing so rarely.[53] Amy had stayed long enough to see Joseph and Mary Robbins Post, John and Rebecca Ketcham, Leah Fox Underhill, and her former boarder Susan Humphrey, who had moved to New York City. She then spent a day or two in Jersey City with the Willetses before heading back to Rochester.[54]

Post's return was timely for many reasons. In mid-January, Willie fell ill and had to be brought home from Union Springs. Schoolmates hoping to hear of his quick return were disappointed, and he remained home for at least three months.[55] At the end of February, the Posts awaited the arrival of Sallie Holley, who also labored on behalf of "slaves who escaped from the rebel to the Union Army." She was touring the North with a "beautiful child she has saved from a life of shame [who] will tell her own story."[56] Soon after Holley's visit, she wrote Amy and enclosed a letter to Mr. Bishop at "the colored church in Rochester," as she hoped to lecture there on 8 April if Bishop "succeeds in getting me three subscribers to the Anti-Slavery Standard."[57] Clearly Amy was still the one to contact to organize events in Rochester.

Sarah Thayer, Amy's cousin and sister activist, wrote as well that winter, having turned seventy-five in early March. She owned property in Rochester, which Amy and Jacob Post managed and which Thayer hoped would provide an inheritance for her daughters. She now lived quietly in King's Ferry on the Hudson with one of those daughters, as too much activity led to debilitating headaches. Despite the recurring illness, Thayer enjoyed reading the *Herald of Progress* and rereading Andrew Jackson Davis's *Magic Staff*. She also took comfort in Amy and Jacob overseeing her finances. She viewed it "as a case of 'woman's rights'" to rely on the Posts, rather than her own family, for such decisions. The choice also allowed her "to keep up an interchange with 'the Friends' *there*," where "I have enjoyed the most elevated intellectual and soul satisfying hours of my life history." An avowed spiritualist, Thayer was certain "that Time will bring us into the same *life* some day."[58]

Letters like Thayer's sustained Post in her personal and activist labors. So, too, did communion with Mary Robbins Post, who shared Amy's political sympathies as well as her familial joys and challenges. In spring 1864, Mary asked for updates on Isaac's "frequent turns of pain" and reported on the health of family and F/friends on Long Island, as well as Joseph's efforts to keep the Post family farm thriving. She sent news, too, of her antislavery sewing circle, which now produced clothes for black fugitives, and described recent lectures, including Anna Dickinson on women's economic independence and Wendell Phillips on the need for racial equality. In words that touched a chord with Amy, Mary acknowledged "a great advancement in liberality." She was "sometimes amused," and clearly at other times vexed, "in hearing" that "we all are abolitionists now . . . when in fact [many] have scarcely learned the A B C of real antislavery. . . . We see prejudice and intolerance are not entirely removed in respect to the negro [and] they feel the old prejudice and weary in hearing equality spoken of."[59] Still, she, like Amy, continued her labors to achieve both emancipation and racial justice.

While the Posts in Rochester and Westbury felt compelled to support the work of Jacobs, Wilbur, Georgianna Willets, and others working with black refugees, more moderate activists in Soldiers' Aid societies devoted themselves to military men. Women carried on these complementary labors as the political environment heated up in anticipation of the fall 1864 election. Debates between Republican supporters of Lincoln and Democratic backers of his likely opponent, General George McClellan, intensified even as many Garrisonians remained on the sidelines. Lucretia Mott did not think this was a bad thing, warning abolitionists at the May AASS meeting, "Let us be careful how we commit ourselves, as a body, as a Society, to one candidate or another. We are in danger of becoming partisans in our feelings, by holding up one man or crying down another. . . . I am glad to hear Abraham Lincoln held up as we have just now, for the many things that he has done; and where he has fallen short, it is our duty to rebuke him." As the Posts read her speech in the *Liberator*, they applauded her claim that "it is our duty to ourselves to keep the standard high, and to bring the acts of all classes, even Kings and Governors, to the test of that standard."[60]

That summer, Amy collected goods to send to Wilbur and Jacobs and arranged a visit for Sojourner Truth. Having recovered from a near fatal illness the year before, Truth now threw herself into the work of Freedmen's Aid societies in the Midwest. By July 1864, she was eager to head south. With the help of her grandson Sammy, she slowly traveled through Ohio and western New York, making speeches and selling her *Narrative* and *cartes de visite* to raise funds. Truth aroused great interest, and the overflowing churches and lecture halls infused her with a new vigor. In Rochester, Truth stayed at 36 Sophia Street, eager to hear from Amy about conditions in Alexandria and Washington, D.C., as she prepared to address local residents. Sallie Holley and Frederick Douglass were also in the city, the former reporting on her speeches and the latter joining Sojourner on the platform.[61]

Now sixty-seven and gray haired, Truth was happy to have Douglass, twenty years her junior, by her side at Corinthian Hall. Both former slaves had seen part of their dreams come true and described the war as "a howling jeremiad—a bloodletting fulfillment of divine justice." Truth testified about the brutalities her people had suffered, brutalities so foul "that she 'hated to put them into her mouth.'" Douglass offered powerful denunciations of the Confederacy: I would rather be "the most whip-scarred slave in all the South," he proclaimed, "than the haughtiest slave-master." Still, capturing the hopes of Douglass, Post, and other abolitionists, Truth proclaimed, "After the blood and smoke and storm of battle are gone, this country will be beautiful [in] justice and freedom."[62]

Truth remained with the Posts a few more weeks, but not long enough to see Julia Wilbur and Harriet Tubman. An exhausted Wilbur had returned to her family in Avon, New York, to regain her health and accepted only the occasional visitor. In early August, Lucy Colman traveled the twenty-five miles south to tell Julia that she, too, was headed to Washington, as matron of the Colored Home in Georgetown. Several weeks later, Wilbur traveled to Rochester, reporting on her work to a meeting of the RLASS one day and calling on Amy Post and Mary Hallowell the next. A month later, still in the city, she spent an evening at the Hallowells' with Anna Barnes and Maria G. Porter of the RLASS and Harriet Tubman, a combination of guests unlikely before the war. Wilbur was especially excited to see Tubman, who had been working as a scout for the Union army. Finally, in early November, Julia headed back to Alexandria, reinvigorated for the labors ahead.[63]

The work for refugees only increased over the next year. By late 1864, following Lincoln's reelection, the Union army and navy had gained control of vast expanses of the Confederacy. Although battles continued into the new year, the battering of southern strongholds in Atlanta and the Carolinas signaled that the end was near. But this also meant more blacks fleeing northward, increasing the pressure on those working with refugees in Washington, Alexandria, and elsewhere. By January 1865, Sojourner Truth had joined Wilbur, Jacobs, Willets, and Colman in laboring for the tens of thousands of blacks pouring into northern Virginia and the capital city. Back home, Post and her allies worked harder than ever to meet the needs their friends described in agonizing detail. While anticipating a Union victory, they knew it would only create greater demands for clothes, bedding, medicine, schooling, and jobs.

At least one item on the women's agenda was achieved, however. On 31 January 1865, Congress met the demands of black activists, the Women's Loyal National League, Ohio congressman James Ashley, and President Lincoln by approving the Thirteenth Amendment to the Constitution, abolishing slavery in the United States. The amendment was quickly ratified. Several weeks later, at the urging of Lincoln and advocates for refugees like Josephine Griffing, Congress established the Bureau of Refugees, Freedmen, and Abandoned Lands (known as the Freedmen's Bureau). While the bureau provided federal assistance for millions of newly freed African Americans in the South, voluntary associations, missionary societies, and educational organizations continued to dispense critical aid to blacks in Washington, D.C.; Alexandria; and many other communities. All these efforts were complicated by the racial prejudice that existed not only throughout the country but in the nation's capital and the Freedmen's Bureau itself.[64] Sojourner Truth confronted discrimination on a regular basis, including on D.C. streetcars and among government officials who supposedly supported her work among black refugees.

Colman, Wilbur, and Truth all sent Amy stories of blacks' experiences in Washington, which Post shared with Louisa Nell Gray when she visited 36 Sophia Street in February 1865. Louisa brought news of her brother William, who had finally gained a position with the post office. She then headed on to nearby Geneva, where she spent two months with her younger sister Frances and helped care for her six children while their father, Benjamin Cleggett, served on a U.S. naval vessel patrolling the James River. Despite ongoing racial discrimination, activists displayed some optimism. That winter, Joseph Post wrote his brother Isaac that public opinion was evolving. If people "change as much in the next year as they have the last four years I think they will be ready to give blacks the right to vote [on] equal terms with whites."[65]

In March, Lucy Colman returned to Rochester to raise funds and consciousness about conditions among refugees and blacks more generally. She stayed with the Posts for a night, and Amy accompanied her on calls around the city, where Colman expounded on her experiences in Washington. "The things she has accomplished in that city and Alexandria, for the freed people, is truly wonderful," Amy wrote her cousin Esther Titus, whose daughter Frances had for several years assisted Truth by writing letters, responding to invitations, and carrying out other small chores. Post admitted that she was surprised to hear that Lucy had hired Truth, who "scarcely knows a letter," as a teacher. She was teaching housekeeping, which paid $10 a month plus room and board. Amy wished that she and Esther "could be down there with Sojourner a while. There is a great deal being done for those people," she noted, "but not near enough as necessary." Instead, Amy gave Lucy money to buy Truth "a rocking chair. She is too good and to[o] old to be neglected by her friends who are sitting on cushioned seats at home."[66]

The rush of news from Washington temporarily halted as the Posts and their Rochester neighbors dealt with a more immediate crisis. After a winter of heavy snow and extreme temperatures, a major flood hit the city in mid-March. Aqueducts overflowed, railroad bridges crashed into the river below, water rushed through homes and businesses, and telegraph wires snapped. Isaac, who had been lying sick in bed, headed to the store, where the water was eighteen inches deep. At home, where the cellar was flooded, Amy was left to pull things "up out of the mud." The Willises' house, where Edmund was confined to bed with "Cholera morbus," was in even worse shape; but the roads were impassable, so it was days before the family could gather at 36 Sophia Street and exchange stories. Fortunately, Edmund and Isaac recovered their health, their homes, and their businesses, though it took weeks to clean up the damage, which cost city residents a million dollars.[67]

Amid the cleanup, Rochesterians, like northerners generally, began to imagine that the long and brutal war might soon be over. As Joseph wrote Isaac after the fall of Charleston, "I am in hopes that they [the Confederates] will keep evacuating and deserting until they are satisfied their cause is a bad one."[68] On 9 April 1865, General Robert E. Lee surrendered to General Ulysses S. Grant at Appomattox Court House, Virginia. Despite scattered battles in a few locations, the war was over; the Confederacy had been defeated; slavery was abolished. Then, just five days after the celebrations in Boston, New York, Philadelphia, Rochester, and other northern cities ended, the shocking news arrived that Lincoln had been assassinated. Soon after, Vice President Andrew Johnson took the oath of office as president, putting a southern unionist and Democrat in the White House. The uncertainties that already engulfed the nation were multiplied a hundredfold. Rather than diminishing the labors of Post and her radical friends, the "peace" promised only more battles.

Many of those battles occurred in the Deep South, where Harriet and Louisa Jacobs traveled after the war to assist freed people. The plight of blacks in Washington and Alexandria remained dire as well, and Truth continued to work there. The Posts offered support to both Jacobs and Truth, but they could provide the most immediate help to refugees in D.C. and Alexandria. Fortunately, Amy and Isaac, sixty-two and sixty-six when the war ended, were comfortable financially as well as domestically. Mary Ann Pitkin, now twenty, continued to provide company and assistance, now with the aid of twenty-four-year-old Julie Pitkin, her sister. In 1865, the Posts' only boarder was seventeen-year-old William Maher, although other young men—some former soldiers—moved in and out of their home over the next few years. Willie was happily back home as well, working as a clerk at Post and Bruff while attending classes in writing and bookkeeping.

Jacob remained head of the family business, which provided a middle-class lifestyle for Jenny and their two daughters. Joseph was still working for Flour City Oil, which allowed Mate to stay home and care for their three children. They had taken in Margaret King, a widowed dressmaker who now listed herself as a "Picture dealer," and her board likely helped the family finances.[69]

Amy and Isaac focused their efforts on freed people, well aware of the challenges. Many recently emancipated blacks preferred to remain in the South to reunite their families, locate friends, establish churches, and find work. The women who had worked with refugees during the war could understand that desire and also worried that freed people heading north would face patronizing attitudes at best and full out discrimination at worst. Even in the nation's capital, as Post learned from friends there, most whites rejected racial integration at every turn. In October 1865, Truth wrote Amy of her persistent struggle to ride the city's streetcars. When conductors did not throw her off bodily, white passengers made racist remarks, which Truth responded to with her characteristic wit.[70] But freed people needed more than wit to survive in this environment. A government that did not enforce its own laws concerning integration on streetcars was not likely to meet the tremendous needs of blacks, either in Washington, D.C., or in the former Confederacy.

In winter 1866, Josephine Griffing wrote Post of the horrifying conditions refugees faced—"We are needing help for our freedpeople here in the District"—and asked Amy to send food, wood, clothes, beds, and bedding. While Congress debated whether to extend the Freedmen's Bureau's tenure beyond the one year initially planned, families were perishing. Even black soldiers, alone or with wives and children, found it impossible to find work, shelter, or food in the capital, while single mothers were paid a pittance for a few days' labor. Laura Haviland, another white woman working among refugees in Washington, pleaded with Amy for assistance: "You cannot imagine the destitution in this very severe weather." Cora Hatch Daniels, the spiritualist friend of Truth and the Posts, had written to Amy that January, insisting that it was critical to be in Washington: "There are important events transpiring here now."[71]

Not everyone agreed on which events were most important, however. Truth berated Douglass for spending more time seeking ballots for black men than necessities for refugee families. He did, however, join in the push to get the tenure of the Freedmen's Bureau extended. As Congress debated a bill to achieve that end, Douglass sat in the black section of the gallery alongside Garrison, Haviland, Truth, Purvis, and Giles and Catherine Stebbins. The bill was finally approved, but by the time Haviland wrote to Amy in February, President Johnson had vetoed it. His veto caused a "great sensation" in Washington, Haviland reported, "as it must [have] everywhere among the lovers of *freedom* and *eternal* rights."[72]

In April 1866, Republicans in Congress overrode President Johnson's veto, allowing the Freedmen's Bureau to continue its work. By then, Truth had concluded that the best hope for freed people was to relocate them in northern towns and cities where they could be ensured of jobs and housing. She fought for resources from the bureau, but relied heavily on her extensive network of abolitionist friends. The work began with the assistance of Griffing and northern supporters, most importantly the Posts. During 1866 and 1867, Truth transported refugees to western New York and Michigan, where she used her personal contacts to supply them with food, shelter, and jobs. When ferrying men, women, and children north by train, she took along bundles of clothing, bedding, and food that had been sent to Washington to help them survive the journey. During her travels across New York State and the Midwest, she sought employment for her charges and contributions to further the work. Rochester proved a crucial site in Truth's scheme for freed people. Two of her grandsons, Sammy and James Caldwell—the latter released from a Confederate prison at the end of the war—now lived there, though Truth continued to use 36 Sophia Street as her local headquarters. Coworkers in Washington and friends and family in Michigan sent letters to Truth in care of Amy Post.[73]

Truth organized a committee in Rochester, on which Isaac Post served, to assist her in raising funds and soliciting applications from prospective employers in central and western New York. The area included prosperous farms, small towns, and thriving cities, thus providing a diverse array of job opportunities. Rochester newspapers advertised the project, Julia Wilbur sent a letter of support, and applications poured in.[74] Many were sent directly to the Posts, who compiled a long list of potential employers, including shopkeepers, farmers, homeowners, and merchants. Those who sought workers reached west from Rochester to the tiny village of Jeddo; south to Canandaigua; and east to Geneva, Macedon, and Union Springs. A Civil War veteran from Spencerport, eleven miles west of the city, sought "two freedmen for farm work and driving Hors[e] team." An applicant from Macedon, seeking a housekeeper, offered the Posts' old F/friend Elias Doty as a reference. Mr. A. C. Van Epps of Geneva assured Truth he could place workers with several families in the area. Mrs. James Cavan, who had labored alongside Amy in the Working Women's Protective Union, requested a girl "*very dark*." Mary H. Thomas was eager to hire freed people, but worried when one man left for Rochester after not immediately finding work in Union Springs. Thomas, the daughter of Isaac's old Ledyard business partner Humphrey Howland, realized the challenge freed people and their employers faced in small farm towns but continued to request workers.[75] Other applications came from members of the Thayer, Beebe, Curtis, Willis, and Kingsbury families, all linked to the Posts as relatives, former neighbors, or activist coworkers.

Despite the enormous numbers of refugees and newly emancipated blacks, Truth considered each individual or family placed in a home and a job an accomplishment. She wrote Amy periodically, requesting information: "How are the women I brought you getting along? I do want very much to know."[76] She also repeatedly traveled back and forth from Washington, D.C., with new groups of workers, supplying them with items from the Freedmen's Bureau for the trip and asking her committee in Rochester to construct temporary housing for the new arrivals. On 26 March 1866, Griffing wrote Post on Truth's behalf: "I shall reach Rochester Wednesday or Thursday night next week with ten or twenty freed people." She asked the Posts to please have everything in order for their arrival. A year later, the *Rochester Evening Express* announced the arrival of "fourteen able-bodied young unmarried colored men," who arrived "in charge of a sojourner South." Further information could be obtained "at Post & Bruff's drug store."[77]

Truth often held meetings and lectures in Rochester to raise awareness and collect contributions. She likely spoke in the lyceum series that Amy organized at the time, where Truth would have fit easily among the spiritualists, reformers, and other notable individuals who offered programs.[78] In 1866 alone, Truth transported at least 140 freed people to western New York, seeking places for entire families, for women and children, and for single women and men. Although the numbers were infinitesimal compared to the need, each one was considered a small victory against racial injustice.

Despite these achievements, Truth had to deal with criticisms even from her supposed allies. Wilbur was particularly harsh, claiming that Truth was making a profit off her speeches and the sales of photographs and books while purportedly raising money for freed people. Such criticism shocked Truth, who had volunteered so much of her time and resources to blacks North and South.[79] One wonders what conversations took place between Julia and Amy when Wilbur visited the Posts in August 1866. She arrived at 36 Sophia Street with Sarah Willis after dinner at the Hallowells and discovered that spiritualist medium Cora Hatch Daniels and her husband, Colonel Daniels, were staying there. Colonel Daniels had lobbied for the Freedmen's Bureau and had supported the organization of black regiments during the war, though he often exaggerated his role in both. He also shared Griffing's and Truth's criticism of General Oliver Howard, the first head of the bureau, which he expressed to Wilbur. She, in turn, vehemently defended Howard, noting in her diary, "There was quite a war of words between us. I dislike the man very much." And despite all the efforts Amy had made on behalf of Wilbur's work, Julia added, "I[saac] Post's home is a rendezvous for many very dubious people."[80]

Perhaps not surprisingly, Post worked more closely with Truth and Griffing after the war and let the RLASS fund Wilbur's efforts. Amy still sent contributions now and then to Harriet Jacobs, but she, too, had gained new organizational support. In November 1865, Harriet and her daughter, Louisa, headed to Savannah, Georgia, to work with newly emancipated blacks under the auspices of the New England Freedmen's Aid Society. Despite a strong and organized black community in the city, the situation deteriorated after military rule ended in Savannah in fall 1865. While white urban leaders used every means at their disposal to limit black autonomy, disappointed Confederates wreaked havoc on the countryside. Hearing such reports from multiple sources, Mary Robbins Post wrote Isaac and Amy that "injustice now reigns" in "the South land. . . . It will be sad indeed if all the suffering and sorrow of the past years are of no avail and if so heavier calamities must come to teach justice to the people."[81]

Still, with the war ended and emancipation achieved, the Posts combined their work for freed people with other causes and turned more attention to familial and domestic obligations. Isaac spent a few hours each week at Post and Bruff pharmacy, while Amy handled most of the domestic duties, at least in fall 1866 when Mary Ann Pitkin took ill and was cared for at the Post home by her sister. Amy reported to Mary Robbins Post, "I am getting along with my household work pretty well yet[;] though sometimes rather wearied, I am not yet ready to give it up." She added, "Where one pair of hands does all, they must be busy and functional." At the same time, Post happily attended to her "Lyceum duties," which involved organizing lectures as well as housing for visiting speakers, such as Cora Hatch Daniels and Truth. Speakers often stayed with the Posts or at the Hallowells', and Amy was pleased that "spectators come in more and more so that we are under the necessity of looking out for a larger Hall."[82] The Posts also hosted séances at 36 Sophia Street, but their spirits were raised mainly by the arrival in December 1866 of Jacob and Jenny's third child, whom they named Isaac.

That fall, the elder Isaac reported that both "Spiritualists and Progressives"—that is, Friends of Human Progress—had "passed resolutions" on another hotly debated issue: suffrage. The Posts embraced universal suffrage—the simultaneous enfranchisement of blacks and women. Still, they did not often partake in the debates that erupted in the late 1860s between those who prioritized black male suffrage, such as Wendell Phillips, and those who insisted woman suffrage was at least as important, led by Stanton and Anthony.[83]

Amy did join in discussions at the 1866 yearly meeting of the Friends of Human Progress in Waterloo, along with Lucy Colman, Frederick Douglass, and the Reverend Samuel J. May. Amy was likely most involved in the lengthy discussions on spiritualism and its relation to other religious and reform movements, but reports in the National Anti-Slavery Standard focused more on debates over race and suffrage. The article applauded Colman's "pointed and excellent remarks" on racial prejudice, which included stories about Sojourner Truth being thrown off streetcars in Washington and turned away from one of Lincoln's presidential receptions. Yet it was Douglass's "unrivalled eloquence" in appealing for black men's enfranchisement that garnered the greatest attention. Douglass supported two resolutions, one calling for black male suffrage and a second proclaiming that the "grand and fundamental idea" of equality and justice "will not have been practically carried out till woman, equally with man, shall have secured to her the power to cast her ballot and to choose those who are to make the laws under which she lives."[84] Douglass, like Post and most Progressive Friends, supported the enfranchisement of both blacks and women, but he preferred to express that support through two distinct resolutions, suggesting they might be dealt with separately, and at different times.[85]

Similar debates had erupted a year earlier at the May 1865 anniversary meetings of reformers in New York City. While there, Garrison had declared the work of the American Anti-Slavery Society finished. Many of his followers, however, argued that the society's work must continue until, as the AASS founding declaration declared, "the colored population of the United States" has gained "all the rights and privileges which belong to them as men [sic] and Americans."[86] Despite powerful protests, Garrison and several of his Boston associates refused to change course, closing down the Liberator and resigning from the AASS. When the National Anti-Slavery

Standard cut back from a weekly to a monthly publication, Amy was distraught. As she wrote editor Aaron Powell, "The thought of not . . . see[ing] the Standard entering our door, but once a month, fell upon my living, earnest soul like the death-knell of a dear, and ever welcome friend who had . . . ever kept the chane [*sic*] bright, that has bound the co-workers so pleasantly together." In hopes of reviving the *Standard*, she and Mary Hallowell agreed to serve as agents for the paper. Indeed, the only reason Post could bear to part with the AASS itself was her concern that so many speakers "should touch the *Woman question* so gingerly, when *so many* of the speakers, *so well understand* the fearful danger of procrastination of that theme."[87]

Other AASS members shared Post's concern and considered creating a new organization to fight for racial and gender justice simultaneously. Stanton and Anthony launched the effort in early 1866, and Douglass and Aaron Powell agreed to support it. However, Wendell Phillips, who in 1865 had declared it "the Negro's hour," challenged the plan. So, too, did some women's rights stalwarts, including Lucy Stone and Lucretia Mott, who wondered whether this was the moment to emphasize issues of sex equality. Still, believing in the principle of universal suffrage, the two attended the May 1866 AASS meeting, and Mott suggested that "the negro's hour was decidedly the time for woman to slip in."[88] Phillips, however, had no intention of giving ground and foiled every effort to transform the AASS into an equal rights association.

Stanton and Anthony quickly regrouped and decided to use the Eleventh National Woman's Rights Convention, scheduled for the day after the AASS convention closed, to launch the American Equal Rights Association (AERA). Anthony had sent Post an invitation to the event, but her work with freed people and the lyceum kept her at home. While this was the first national woman's rights convention since the outbreak of the Civil War, Stanton, Anthony, and their allies were willing to forgo the single focus on sex equality to make what they considered the more important claim of joining woman suffrage and black suffrage.[89] Still, ideological differences among old allies as well as political realities in Congress made any attempt to bridge the two movements difficult. Initially, however, Stanton, Anthony, Douglass, Stone, and Mott, as well as black activists Robert Purvis and Frances Ellen Watkins Harper, sought common ground. Even Phillips had softened his position by late 1866.[90]

That December, AERA members held equal rights conventions in several New York cities. A curious reporter from Canandaigua, who considered

Rochester home to "leading fanatics," reported on the convention there. Some three hundred people—men and women, black and white—waited impatiently at Corinthian Hall the first evening until the entire group of speakers trouped on stage at 9:00 P.M. Anthony led off the speeches, followed by Stanton, "a venerable old lady . . . quite fleshy and unusually short." However, Stanton read "a very polished lecture" on Reconstruction, the main point of which was that the nation would never attain permanent prosperity and peace until "universal suffrage" was granted. The evening closed with lengthy speeches by Charles Lenox Remond and Parker Pillsbury. The next day's gathering focused on practical means for gaining "suffrage for all," until Dr. James C. Jackson, head of a Danville, New York, water cure establishment, took the stage in the afternoon to lay out "long-winded" claims about the similar natures of man and woman, leading to a hasty adjournment.[91]

Despite the reporter's critiques, six to seven hundred people attended the second evening session, where Pillsbury read the list of resolutions, including a memorial to the New York State legislature to make the state constitution "blind to the distinctions of color and sex." Sojourner Truth was among the final speakers. Though in "her dotage," the reporter claimed, Truth manifested considerable "mental and bodily vigor." Still, he noted that some in the crowd laughed and hooted during her speech. Most audience members took matters more seriously, however, including Abigail Bush, who was making a rare visit from California. Thrilled to be reunited with the Posts and other dear friends, she was excited to meet Truth for the first, and only, time.[92]

By 1867, the battle over woman suffrage and black suffrage moved to Kansas, where separate referenda both lost after a bruising battle. Stanton, Anthony, and their new supporter, the wealthy Democrat George Francis Train—well known for his racist beliefs—were blamed for the result, although it is unlikely that either black or woman suffrage would have passed on its own. Still, the rhetoric wielded by Stanton and the reputation of Train tainted the woman suffrage cause even for many longtime allies. Stanton combined elitist and racist rhetoric by insisting that it was an insult to give the ballot to blacks and immigrants before women, and contrasted freedmen's "incoming pauperism, ignorance, and degradation with the wealth, education, and refinement of the women of the republic," ignoring freedwomen altogether.[93] Train advocated suffrage for white women only and was opposed to enfranchising black men or women.

Following the defeat in Kansas, congressional efforts to pass a Fifteenth Amendment, guaranteeing black male suffrage, revived. Clashes over that amendment fractured the AERA along complicated and shifting fault lines. At its May 1867 meeting, Sojourner Truth was one of the most prominent participants, demanding rights for freedwomen along with freedmen, and cutting across the arguments of those pitting black male suffrage against white woman suffrage. Stanton, however, fueled antagonism by continuing to degrade African American along with Chinese, Irish, and other immigrant men in order to uplift women, making it difficult for Abby Kelley Foster, Charles Lenox Remond, and others to maintain their universalist stance. The fact that neither Phillips nor Douglass attended the meeting also raised concerns.[94]

Truth must have discussed these contentious debates with Post as she ferried freedmen and freedwomen to Rochester. Nell participated in the conversations as well, having finally managed a brief visit to 36 Sophia Street in May 1867 before heading to nearby Geneva to see his sister Frances and her family. Nell likely met the Posts' seventh grandchild, a son named Jacob, the fourth of Joseph and Mate's children. He wrote Amy from Boston in June that his visits with "Yourself and Isaac, the trio of Post boys," and other Rochester friends provided "much solace . . . to cheer my otherwise lonely seasons." Yet Nell seemed hardly ever alone, reporting in the same letter on numerous outings with the abolitionist fraternity, spiritualists, and the Walden Pond circle, as well as conversations with Sallie Holley, Wendell Phillips, and William Wells Brown. He had also recently seen William Hallowell, who was in Boston on business.[95]

Amy, meanwhile, was busy organizing the yearly meeting of the Friends of Human Progress at Waterloo, where she served as one of two clerks, now called secretaries. Despite dissension at the AERA, discussions over suffrage among Progressive Friends—including Charles Lenox Remond, the Reverend Samuel J. May, Lucy Colman, Giles Stebbins, Aaron Powell, and Post—remained cordial. The group agreed to a trio of resolutions that both incorporated and moved beyond universal enfranchisement. Most importantly, the resolution on black suffrage demanded that newly emancipated men *and* women receive not only the vote but also land. A separate resolution advocated congressional passage of a universal suffrage amendment that enfranchised both women and blacks. Finally, the Friends approved a memorial to the New York State Constitutional Convention advocating woman suffrage and the elimination of property qualifications for black men. They delegated Amy Post, Reverend May, and Remond to present this resolution in person.[96]

If Post and Remond did travel to Albany for the opening of the state's constitutional convention on 10 June, they were not allowed to submit their resolution to the participants in person. Instead, the Progressives' memorial, the first submitted to the convention, was read by delegate George William Curtis, a reform-minded Rochester journalist and influential Republican who supported both woman suffrage and black equality. A few days later, a petition from Rochester women, sent by Emily Collins, was presented with a stack of others from counties and cities throughout New York. The delegates, however, seemed deaf to the outpouring of petitions and the arguments of Elizabeth Cady Stanton on woman suffrage. They voted 125 to 19 against enfranchising women but did eliminate property qualifications for black male citizens.[97]

Congress, too, was committed solely to black male suffrage, approving the Fifteenth Amendment, which prohibited discrimination against voters on the basis of race. The choice to oppose or support the amendment split the AERA's fragile coalition. Indeed, by its May 1868 meeting, participants had become more entrenched in their opposition. Douglass joined the contentious debates and, upon his return to Rochester, complained to Truth, who was staying at Sophia Street, about Stanton's and Anthony's racist appeals and their alliance with Train. The Posts avoided the AERA convention, luxuriating instead in the happiness of a Long Island wedding as Mary and Joseph Post's younger daughter Elizabeth married Edward Post. Amy and Isaac signed the marriage certificate surrounded by siblings, cousins and dear F/friends. Within three weeks, however, Mary and Joseph's other son-in-law, Sam Willis was dead, and grieving replaced joy.[98]

The presidential election campaign in summer and fall 1868 added another layer of stress to relations among friends and former allies. Douglass and Truth campaigned for the Republican candidate Ulysses S. Grant, while Stanton and Anthony supported the Democratic nominee, Horatio Seymour of New York City.[99] Isaac Post likely found it hard to choose between a Democrat and a military hero known for his bloody battlefield tactics. However, Amy supported Grant, even if ambivalently, because of her close relationship with Truth. Shared efforts to provide freed people homes and jobs anchored their relationship, while their shared views on suffrage and spiritualism strengthened their bonds.

In August 1868, Truth joined the Posts at the American Association of Spiritualists convention in Rochester, where the equality of women and men was hailed as a sign of enlightened progress.[100] Celebrating the twentieth anniversary of the first "rappings," the meeting attracted some three hundred women and men. Charles W. Hebard, editor of the *Rochester Evening Express* and husband of local suffragist Mary Hebard, presided, and Isaac Post opened the meeting by recalling "the wonderful things he had seen in a spiritual way." Although Amy rarely appeared as a main speaker at conventions, she now offered a vivid account of the first public investigations of the Fox sisters at Corinthian Hall in 1849. Recounting the threatening atmosphere, vulgar taunts, and "explosions of torpedoes in every part of the audience," Post reminded listeners of the obstacles that stood in the movement's path. Despite this, she concluded, the Fox sisters "led us to a higher and diviner conception of spirit consciousness and spirit light within ourselves, which, if listened to, will lead and guide us in paths of wisdom and goodness."[101] Raised in the belief that one's inner light was the ultimate source of knowledge and action, Amy considered spiritualism an advanced form of this concept.

Post began writing as well as speaking on behalf of those she had long worked beside. In 1868, Sojourner Truth campaigned across New York State for Ulysses S. Grant, including an "Emancipation Jubilee" in Geneva in late August, where she shared the platform with Benjamin Cleggett, the Reverend Roswell Jeffrey, Douglass, and Remond. In early November, she headed to the Posts to celebrate Grant's victory, and Amy wrote to the *National Anti-Slavery Standard* describing Truth's long months of campaigning for Grant "(of whom we hope the best things)." She noted the aged activist's many "long cold rides" in trains and carriages across New York State, which aggravated the lameness in her legs and convinced her "to rest a little" in Rochester before returning to Battle Creek.[102] Old friends sent letters to Truth at 36 Sophia Street, including Jonathan "Branded Hand" Walker, who had met the Posts while speaking in Rochester in the 1840s. He marveled at Truth's energy given her "advanced age" and invited her to stay with him in Muskegon.[103]

When Sojourner returned to Michigan in early 1869, she did not leave activism behind. As her Battle Creek host, Eliza Leggett, wrote Post, Truth spoke at a Unitarian church, which was "so crowded that we had to go up into the Church" rather than use the smaller lecture room. She enthralled the crowd with tales of her experiences in Washington, both "her labors with Freedmen" and "her troubles with the Cars," describing the rude behavior of conductors and passengers. "She spoke with power," Eliza assured Amy, "and gave her testimony with a Spirit of wonderful clearness."[104]

Post had long recognized the local Unitarian church as a home for advocates of social justice. It had hosted the Rochester Woman's Rights Convention in 1848; and the Hallowells, Susan B. Anthony, and other reformers were drawn to the congregation in the following years by William Henry Channing, who served as minister in the early 1850s. In 1859, the church, which stood just two blocks east of the Post home, burned to the ground. It was rebuilt through the leadership of Reverend Frederick W. Holland, who took over the pulpit in 1865. He, too, attracted a wide array of reformers, including Emily Collins, who had promoted women's rights since 1848, and a younger cohort of women suffragists, such as Mary Hebard. The Unitarian church thus offered a comfortable respite for Post, and she was welcomed at services despite her ongoing ties to Progressive Friends and spiritualists. Her son Willie, though also a spiritualist, eventually joined the church.[105] Her eighth grandchild—little Amy Post, born to Joseph and Mate—may have been christened there as well.

In the winter of 1869, Post, along with Truth and Mott, avoided a New England suffrage convention that attracted black and white supporters of the Fifteenth Amendment. Their decision not to participate was tied in part to the burdens of such a long journey, plus Amy was enjoying her latest grandchild. But the three women were also disturbed by the organizers' refusal to invite Anthony and their withdrawal of an invitation to Stanton. Such actions were an affront to the free speech principles that drove Post and many radical F/friends. Nor did any of the three attend the AERA anniversary meeting that May, at which Stanton's elitist and racist sentiments made even old friends like Douglass wonder whether they could ever find common ground.[106]

Immediately after the AERA's conclusion, Stanton and Anthony founded the National Woman Suffrage Association (NWSA), which attracted significant numbers of women from the Midwest and West, who were less embroiled in eastern debates over the Fifteenth Amendment. By fall, a group of New Englanders led by Lucy Stone and Henry Blackwell established the rival American Woman Suffrage Association (AWSA) and endorsed the Fifteenth Amendment.[107] Amy had worked with Stanton and Anthony since the 1840s and traveled with Stone in the 1850s. Her old spiritualist friend Mary Fenn Davis sided with the AWSA, as did many black activists because of its stance on the Fifteenth Amendment. Post, however, turned down Stone's request that she serve as a delegate to the first meeting because organizers had decided that only elected delegates would be allowed to speak. Writing to Stone, Post lamented, "Oh! I do not want to be an outsider in this glorious cause, I want to be folded and sheltered in your beneficent arms and hearts, but how can I go back into the bondage of exclusiveness?"[108]

While Post did not feel completely comfortable in either organization, she was pulled toward the NWSA, which Sarah Willis, Mary Hallowell, Catherine Fish Stebbins, and Rhoda DeGarmo all joined. Willis and Hallowell developed close friendships with Anthony and joined Susan and her family for annual dinners celebrating matriarch Lucy Anthony's 2 December birthday. Certainly, Susan assumed Amy's involvement with the NWSA. In December 1866, while in New York City, she asked Post to secure speakers and a place "where the *working women* may call for their *free* tickets" for a Monroe County Woman's Rights Convention later that month. She also directed Post to place announcements in local papers and arrange for posters if she thought they were needed.[109] However, Post maintained her independence, helping to found a local Equal Suffrage Association in 1869 and serving as its president. She opened a 5 July "celebration of Independence" at the farm of Asa and Huldah Anthony, declaring, "It was a great day, but not so grandly great as it would have been had our Government fully carried out its fundamental principles." Noting that "it was a fitting time" to protest "against the wrongs and disabilities still imposed upon certain classes by our Government," Amy invited men and women to speak, as the "platform was free, [and] the day was propitious." Some women then read the Declaration of Independence, "either that of the Fathers or of their own." Two weeks later, Post did agree to serve as a vice president for the newly organized New York State Suffrage Association, which Anthony had helped organize and on which Martha C. Wright, Lucretia Mott's sister, served as president.[110]

Whatever the battles among suffragists, Post continued to view women's rights as broader than enfranchisement. To that end, she attended a meeting of the local Magdalen Society, part of a nationwide movement to rescue women from prostitution. In 1867, Amy corresponded with spiritualist and women's rights advocate Lois Waisbrooker about the new movement. Waisbrooker insisted that "just as long as *woman* is a subject, a servant, a defendant, just so long will she be . . . a *slave* to" man's "passions."[111] She suggested that fallen women must be taken out of their situation and offered the chance to improve their lives. Two years later, a Rochester Magdalen Society was formed. Amy Post, Emily Collins, and Lucy Colman attended an evening meeting at which two "fallen women" appeared seeking asylum. Unsure how to respond, the society's members debated erecting a house of refuge. Collins argued that such efforts would be "futile" and "that only by enfranchising woman and permitting her a more free and lucrative range of employments could they hope to suppress the 'social evil.'" Post agreed with Collins, but neither a house of refuge nor lucrative employment was available to the two women who needed help. Thus, Post announced, "'I will take one, and if there is no second place for the other, I will take her, too.'"[112] Post likely took the two women home, but the Magdalen Society faltered, and no house of refuge was built.

The suffrage movement, on the other hand, flourished in Rochester and beyond, and Post followed developments closely. She surely read about the seven women—five white and two black—who tried to register to vote in a local election in Washington, D.C., on 22 April 1869. Julia Wilbur was part of the group and reported that although the women were not allowed to register, "they did not experience any remarkable inconvenience, and were not subjected to any disagreeable remarks."[113] Women's excursions to the polls would become a regular feature of elections as suffragists Virginia and Francis Minor devised a legal argument for women's right to vote under the Fourteenth and Fifteenth Amendments.

The Minors argued that women were "persons" and thus included among the national citizens guaranteed rights by the Fourteenth Amendment. The Fifteenth Amendment then recognized that the right to vote was central to and inherent in national citizenship. If women attempted to register and vote and were denied, they could initiate test cases that would force the Supreme Court to recognize women's enfranchisement without further congressional action. Even before this "New Departure" was officially launched, black and white women attempted to register and vote in Washington, D.C.; Vineland, New Jersey; Topeka, Kansas; Schenectady, New York; and Columbia, South Carolina. In some cases, women were allowed to vote; in others, they cast ballots in a separate box; and in most, they were rejected by registrars and election officials but were not charged with any crime. By 1871 and 1872, growing numbers of women—some white, some black, and a few in interracial groups—made concerted efforts to vote across the North and West as well as in Washington, D.C.; Baltimore, Maryland; Memphis, Tennessee; and Johnson County, North Carolina.[114]

Several of Amy's radical friends joined the New Departure in its early days, including Lucy Stone, Catherine Fish Stebbins, Julia Wilbur, and Sojourner Truth. Sarah Grimké and Angelina Weld Grimké also joined the effort, and in 1871, Frederick Douglass accompanied a group of black women to the polls in Washington, D.C.[115] The excitement surrounding these efforts may have inspired Post to accept an invitation to revise and republish the proceedings of the 1848 Rochester Woman's Rights Convention.

By the late 1860s, the printed proceedings of the first woman's rights conventions had become a rare commodity. Fearing that suffragists would forget their origins, Stanton and Anthony proposed publishing new and revised proceedings. In April 1867, they planned a meeting at Hallowell's home and directed Mary to have Amy bring the 1848 Seneca Falls and Rochester reports there.[116] When Stanton and Anthony launched a woman's rights newspaper, the *Revolution*, in January 1868, they asked its printer, Robert J. Johnston, to publish the revised 1848 proceedings as well. Stanton and Anthony hoped by this means to turn the Seneca Falls Declaration of Sentiments into "a sacred text" for the woman suffrage movement. Thus, they decided to create separate pamphlets on Seneca Falls and Rochester and recruited Post to revise the Rochester proceedings. She happily agreed, eager to emphasize that meeting's emphasis on economic rights. Post added a fuller version of Sarah Owen's address on women and work than had appeared in the original report. She also included several commentaries comparing racial and gender advancement, among them a longer version of Rebecca Sanford's speech, as well as the full list of resolutions approved at Rochester. While highlighting the election of Abigail Bush to preside, Post did not out Stanton or Mott as among those who opposed the selection of a woman to preside, as both, she claimed, had quickly regretted their objections.[117] Certainly, working on the pamphlet brought back fond memories of those heady days of radical action.

By the time the pamphlet was published, however, Post was overwhelmed with problems at home. In July 1870, Mary Dale Johnson, widowed at age fifty, moved back to 36 Sophia Street with her twenty-four-year-old daughter Betsy and Betsy's son, four-year-old Henry. Willie was still living at home at age twenty-three, and two boarders—a white laborer and an Irish dressmaker—rounded out the household. According to the census, seventy-year-old Isaac was no longer employed and sixty-seven-year-old Amy was "Keeping House." She likely shouldered numerous domestic chores. Although the Johnsons offered some assistance, Mary Dale was not well. Fortunately, the Posts were financially secure and could afford extra help when needed. Isaac claimed real estate valued at $4,000, Amy owned real estate valued at $2,500, and their personal estate had reached $12,000. However, they were far from wealthy. Others in their neighborhood claimed two to four times as much real estate, and two neighbors nearly tripled the Posts' personal estate.[118] Nonetheless, they lived comfortably and, having always lived plainly, had plenty to assist friends and family in need.

Joseph and Mate likely needed some help, as their seventh child—and the Posts' ninth grandchild—Wallace, arrived in 1871. He competed for attention not only with his siblings and cousins but with the demands of elderly relatives and friends. Edmund Willis continued to battle maladies of various sorts, and Isaac was increasingly frail. There was, in addition, always some in-law, cousin, or childhood friend taking sick or passing away on Long Island. Yet it was harder than ever to visit those far away, as the Posts were aging right along with their circle of F/friends and family in central New York, Jericho, and Westbury. Some of their closest friendships from the previous decades also waned. Amy heard less and less frequently from Harriet Jacobs, Sojourner Truth, and William Nell. For Nell, at least, inattentiveness resulted from newfound happiness. He had finally married in 1869 and fathered sons in 1870 and 1872. Charles Lenox Remond wrote in February 1872, but only to lament the recent death of his wife and his fears for his ailing daughter.[119]

When Remond's letter arrived, Isaac was also ill. He and Amy traveled to Westbury, hoping doctors there might offer help. Amy also wanted to visit her sister Mary W. Willis, who was losing her memory and hardly recognized family members. In late March, Amy wrote family in Rochester that she found "some encouragement in the most important object of our visit," for "Isaac certainly seems stronger and better."[120] But Isaac's strength did not last long. On 9 May, just five weeks after returning home, he died. He and Amy had been married forty-four years, sharing domestic happiness, activist labors, and the progressive unfolding of the spirit. The latter Isaac also shared with his dear friend Asa Anthony, who passed away on 10 May. Whether Amy's and Huldah's belief in an existence beyond the grave diminished their grief is unclear, but at least they had faith that their husbands were together in another realm.

Children, grandchildren, in-laws, cousins, and old F/friends came together to celebrate Isaac's life. Douglass, who was in Washington, D.C., sent a telegram: "Would gladly be with you at this sad supreme moment . . . but it is impossible. I am with you in sympathy."[121] Following the funeral, Amy seems to have spent a quiet summer in Rochester, visiting Isaac's simple gravestone at Mount Hope Cemetery and carrying out Isaac's will, for which she served as co-executor with Edmund Willis. Perhaps she shared with friends and family a letter Isaac had written her in April 1858, in which he meditated on "the great business of life": "If we progress ourselves[,] if we improve by every opportunity[,] the Great Spirit will be gratified [and] the lesser ones[,] our attendant Spirit companions[,] will rejoice and we will be as happy as can be under the circumstances in which we are placed."[122] Isaac had certainly fulfilled that vision.

Less than a month after Isaac's death, on 4 June 1872, Frederick Douglass's South Avenue home went up in flames. All his original runs of the *North Star, Frederick Douglass' Paper,* and *Douglass' Monthly* were lost, along with many of his books, files, and letters. Fortunately, neither Anna nor the children living at home were injured. Douglass rushed back from Washington to comfort his family and see the devastation for himself. Angered by the horrific loss and the failure of the police to find the "incendiary" who set the blaze, Douglass spilled his outrage onto the pages of the *New National Era,* for which he now served as editor.[123] He thanked the neighbors who pulled furniture and books out of the flames, but made no reference to the close friends, including the Posts and the Porters, who had supported him and his work for decades. Instead, Douglass spurned Rochester and moved his family to Washington, D.C.

Despite these tragic events, by fall, Amy was ready to reenter her activist worlds, drawn by the efforts of women in cities and towns across the North and West to register for that year's presidential election. In October, Susan B. Anthony conferred with local activists, including Post, about a plan to register and vote. On 1 November, Anthony—joined by her three sisters, Rhoda DeGarmo, Mary L. Hebard, and ten other women from the city's Eighth Ward—walked to a local barber shop, where after much debate, two officials allowed them to register. The evening and morning papers carried the story, and other women soon followed suit. But a threat in the Democratic *Union and Advertiser* to prosecute election officials who enrolled women made it much harder to register thereafter. Nonetheless, on 3 November, twenty or thirty more women tried to register. In the First Ward, Amy Post led a contingent that included Mary Fish Curtis (the sister of Catherine Fish Stebbins), Mrs. L. C. Smith, and Dr. Sarah Adamson Dolley, but they were turned away. So, too, were Mary Hallowell, Sarah Willis, Eliza Mann, the wife of the new Unitarian minister, and two hydropathic women physicians, Drs. Dutton and Wheeler.[124]

On 5 November, the Eighth Ward women were allowed to vote, with longtime reformer Edwin T. Marsh and his coworker, W. Baugh Jones, accepting the votes against the instructions of federal authorities. Mary Hallowell and Sarah Willis visited the Anthony sisters in the afternoon, eager to hear in person their triumphant tale of casting ballots. That evening, Anthony wrote an exultant letter to Stanton: "Well, I have been and gone and done it!!—positively voted the Republican ticket—strait this a.m. at 7 Oclock." She noted that fifteen other women had registered in the Eighth Ward and that others had tried elsewhere in the city but were denied. "Amy Post was rejected & she will immediately bring action for that," and "Hon. Henry R. Selden will be our Counsel." Franklin K. Orvis, a thirty-year-old Civil War veteran and entrepreneur, who had been staying with Post during the election, wrote from his home in Illinois: "I hope you women of Rochester mean to carry your cases to the courts of last resort, and if beaten in the courts, appeal to Congress."[125]

By the time Orvis's letter reached Rochester, Anthony had been arrested along with Marsh and Jones, though not Post or others who only attempted to register and vote. The trio were sent home to await a hearing with U.S. Commissioner William C. Storrs. He finally heard legal arguments on 23 December and remanded all three into the custody of a deputy marshal until each paid the bail set. Jones paid quickly and was released. Marsh refused to pay and was "deluged with bouquets and a vast variety of elegant foods and drink." He was finally released without paying. Anthony, hoping to take her case to the U.S. Supreme Court, had Selden ask a U.S. district judge in Albany to issue a writ of habeas corpus releasing her. The judge denied Selden's request and raised Anthony's bail from $500 to $1,000, but his refusal provided grounds to take her case to the higher court. That hope was dashed, however, when Selden, claiming he could not abide having a respectable lady imprisoned, paid her bail. Having lost her chance to take her case to the Supreme Court, Anthony remained under threat of a federal indictment.[126]

The excitement of the election, Anthony's arrest, the court challenges, and her possible indictment aroused intense interest among local activists. Mary Hallowell and Sarah Willis, who were near in age to the fifty-two-year-old Anthony, were fully engaged with her case. So, too, was seventy-three-year-old Rhoda DeGarmo, who registered and voted alongside Anthony in the Eighth Ward. Amy Post, however, apparently did not join in the many meetings and discussions that followed the election. Instead, she helped care for her grandson Isaac, her husband's namesake, who had taken ill. Amy felt all her seventy years that December when six-year-old Isaac died. Perhaps it was time to retire from the world and enjoy the comforts of home, family, and friends.

· ·

In January 1873, Susan B. Anthony's case was brought before a grand jury. The twenty men assembled to hear evidence indicted her for "knowingly, wrongfully, willfully," voting for a member of Congress "without having the right to vote . . . the said Susan B. Anthony being then and there a person of the female sex."[1] While awaiting trial, the strong-willed suffragist lectured widely and sent letters and pamphlets to activists and political leaders across the North. Area suffragists rallied to her cause, including Amy Post, Mary Hallowell, and Sarah Willis. Concerned that the defendant was receiving too much positive publicity, the prosecutor moved the trial, which began in June, to the U.S. circuit court at Canandaigua in neighboring Ontario County. In May, as Anthony awaited trial, local allies founded the Women's Taxpayers Association of Monroe County, which supported Anthony in her battle with the federal government and campaigned for women's suffrage. Their first meeting was held at the Rochester mayor's office, and Anthony and the association's vice president, Mary L. Hebard, spoke.[2]

Anthony was hoping to create a test case to take to the U.S. Supreme Court, but Judge Ward Hunt, who presided over the June trial, short-circuited that effort. He refused to let Anthony testify on her own behalf and, over Selden's protest, directed the jury to bring in a guilty verdict. Anthony's only triumph was the passionate plea she made for women's political equality before the sentence was handed down. Judge Hunt fined her $100 but did not jail her before the fine was paid, depriving Anthony of the one remaining means of appealing his decision.[3]

Following Anthony's conviction, the Women's Taxpayers Association condemned Hunt's ruling, made plans to petition the U.S. Congress to reverse his judgment, and threatened to have him impeached. About the same time, Hebard published a pamphlet on "Female Suffrage," based on speeches she had given, that combined older claims for sex equality with a renewed emphasis on women's moral superiority.[4] This merging of radical and moderate justifications for suffrage attracted diverse members to the Women's Taxpayers Association; its name may have helped as well, suggesting a focus on the rights of property-holding women. Although Post did not find the combination appealing, her younger relatives and coworkers—including Mary Hallowell, Sarah Willis, and sisters Catherine Fish Stebbins and Mary Fish Curtis—embraced the venture. The four longtime activists joined two of Anthony's sisters as officers, along with Hebard and Mrs. L. C. Smith, the former leader of the Magdalen Society, who served as president. Unitarians were well represented in the group, including Smith, Hebard, the Anthonys, Hallowell, and Willis, along with Laura Ramsdell, an early abolitionist and recent widow, and Sarah Blackall, a social worker.[5] While the organization did not fulfill Post's radical vision of social justice, she likely applauded its practical efforts to raise consciousness and create change.

Although Anthony's case did not reach the U.S. Supreme Court, Frances Minor's case did. In March 1875, that court dealt suffragists a severe blow when it ruled in *Minor v. Happersett* that citizenship did not automatically provide access to the ballot. Instead suffrage was a privilege to be granted by states or territories. Achieving women's political equality would be a long struggle, one complicated by divisions within the movement itself. The Women's Taxpayers Association was affiliated with the NWSA, led by Stanton and Anthony, but its chief rival, the AWSA, attracted large numbers of supporters as well. Moreover, many regional associations in the West considered themselves independent of either group. They largely focused on state and territorial efforts, having achieved success in Wyoming and Utah territories in 1869 and 1870, respectively.[6]

Suffragists also battled over symbolic issues, including the birth of the movement. In 1870, Paulina Wright Davis, a member of the NWSA, organized a "Twentieth Anniversary" celebration of "the Inauguration of the Woman Suffrage Movement" and sought to bring the divided movement together for the occasion. While the date was chosen to honor the 1850 National Woman's Rights Convention in Worcester, Davis's allies in the NWSA led the effort. Stanton, in particular, helped organize the event, called the meeting to order, and declared that the "movement in England, as in America, could be dated from the first National Convention."[7] However, any unified vision of the origin of women's rights was soon engulfed by the same conflicts that led to the split between AWSA and NWSA. Anthony, especially, challenged the narrative that set the birthplace of woman suffrage at the Worcester convention.

In winter 1873, while lecturing across western New York, Anthony planned, rather hastily, a commemoration of the twenty-fifth anniversary of the Seneca Falls convention for NWSA's annual May meeting in New York

City. With Anthony presiding, a trio of 1848 organizers—Stanton, Mott, and Martha Coffin Wright—sat on the dais next to a silver wreath. However, when Mott spoke, she gave more credit for the emergence of women's rights to Quakers and abolitionists in the 1830s and 1840s than to the Seneca Falls convention. Few other 1848 participants attended the May meeting, and none of the Rochester contingent did. Still, it planted the seed for later anniversary celebrations that would be more successful in creating a singular origin story.[8]

While the struggle over origins and agendas raged among women's rights advocates, Amy Post focused on practical ways to enact suffrage. In October 1873, after Anthony's conviction, she once again marched to the registration office, this time with her old friend Sarah Owen, who had returned from Michigan. While recalling their days as organizers of the Rochester Woman's Rights Convention and the Working Women's Protective Union, the two attempted, unsuccessfully, to register for state elections that fall.[9] Still, this act did not signal Post's embrace of a singular, or even primary, focus on suffrage. Instead, over the next sixteen years she combined efforts to advance political and economic equality, freedom of expression, religious liberty, spiritualism, and racial justice with celebrations of past achievements and the mourning of lost comrades.

As in earlier decades, Post never settled for a single cause when many demanded attention. In spring 1874, she hosted the founding meeting of the Rochester branch of the Sovereigns of Industry. The organization, an offshoot of the Patrons of Husbandry (the Grange), was founded in 1868 in Fredonia, New York. It sought to counteract monopolies and promote "the moral and social elevation of working men and women." The twenty-five members of the "Pioneer" Council of Rochester met at 36 Sophia Street.[10] In addition, although Amy did not attend the National Anti-Slavery Reunion held in Chicago that summer, she followed its proceedings. Reports of the speeches by abolitionist allies, who recalled key incidents from the 1830s and 1840s, must have sparked memories of past struggles and lasting friendships. And on 31 August, she held a reception at her home to honor Parker Pillsbury that attracted local abolitionists and women's rights advocates.[11]

Post had certainly been thinking of the old days since hearing of William Nell's sudden death in Boston on 25 May 1874. Although deeply saddened, Amy was happy that his final years had been blessed. Having long decried his bachelorhood, Nell wrote Amy in spring 1868 of meeting Frances Ames, a delightful young woman from New Hampshire. He hoped that "at this eleventh hour," she will be the one. A year later, Ames, twenty-seven, and Nell, fifty-two, married; and by 1872, they had two sons, William and Frank. Gleeful over the "Double Blessedness" of marriage and fatherhood, Nell was proud that he could provide for his family, having broken through the racial barrier at the U.S. Post Office. Following his death, Nell's Boston friends and coworkers came out in droves to memorialize his lifelong dedication to racial equality. Garrison, Phillips, and William Wells Brown spoke at his funeral, and the "colored citizens" of Boston held their own service a week later to commemorate Nell's contributions to school desegregation, abolition, and black history.[12] Undoubtedly, Post hoped Nell's spirit would come calling, or perhaps imagined him chatting with Isaac on the other side.

When old friends died, Amy drew comfort from the intimate circle of family members who, in the 1860s, had moved within a few blocks of 36 Sophia Street. Jacob and his family had purchased a home at 97 Plymouth Avenue, the new name for Sophia Street south of Main Street. In 1865, William and Mary Hallowell also moved to Plymouth Avenue, buying a home next door to Edmund and Sarah Willis, who had settled there four years earlier. Mary and Sarah shared reform labors in the Women's Taxpayers Association and regularly visited Amy and Willie, who still lived at home. After his father's death, Joseph Post moved his family into a second house that Isaac had purchased on Sophia Street, on the same block as his mother. Economic bonds reinforced geographical proximity. William and Edmund continued as partners in the woolen trade, while Joseph and Willie clerked at their brother Jacob's drugstore on Exchange Street, of which Amy was now part owner.[13] Thus, even as Rochester's population ballooned to more than sixty thousand, the Posts forged a tight-knit family enclave.

The proximity of her sons also allowed Amy to enjoy her grandchildren as the oldest began forming households of their own. Hattie Post, Joseph and Mate's eighteen-year-old daughter, married Thomas Pollay at her parents' home in April 1875; and the next year, Hattie's twenty-one-year-old sister, Alice, married Frank Tabor. For both ceremonies, the Unitarian minister, Reverend Newton M. Mann, presided. His wife, Eliza, who had tried to register and vote in 1872, joined Hallowell and Willis in the Women's Taypayers Association.[14] For many in the younger generations, Unitarians provided the religious and reformist bonds that Hicksite Friends had once offered Isaac and Amy. Only Willie seems to have followed his parents' lead in embracing spiritualism.

Amy was surrounded as well by longtime neighbors and a variety of religious institutions. The five houses between Amy's and that of her son Joseph were all owned by widows, as were at least three other houses on that single block of Sophia Street. These female neighbors could exchange family news, suggestions for medical treatments, and memories of Rochester's early days. Most of them likely worshipped at one of the six churches that backed onto Montgomery Alley, which ran between Sophia and Fitzhugh Streets. The Central Presbyterian Church, just seven doors down from Amy's house, loomed over the block, as First Baptist Church dominated Fitzhugh Street. The smaller First Methodist Episcopal and German Evangelical United churches occupied lots in the middle of Fitzhugh Street, and the spacious Brick Presbyterian Church sat just across the alley from its small United Presbyterian counterpart at the northern corner, where Fitzhugh and Sophia Streets intersected Allen.[15]

In the years following Isaac's death, having family and neighbors close by was particularly important for Amy. She suffered from "General Debility of the Nervous System" and sometimes found it difficult to walk. Convinced of the value of alternative medical regimens, she received "magnetic treatments" from Dr. E. B. Fish, which provided significant relief. They could not, however, relieve her sense of loss as she mourned her dear friend William Nell and other of her early coworkers. Sarah Fish and Lewis Burtis had both died in 1868, though they left behind spouses who remained active into the 1870s. Rhoda DeGarmo died in 1873, not long after she registered and voted alongside Anthony. Her husband, Elias, followed in 1876.[16] Around that time, Lucy Colman moved to Syracuse, piercing one more hole in Amy's circle.

Although Amy's health remained fragile, she continued meeting with the Sovereigns of Industry, convened gatherings of spiritualists at her home, and attended lyceum lectures and other reform-oriented events in the city. In October 1877, Corinthian Hall hosted the first annual meeting of the National Liberal League. The league, founded in 1876, sought to stop states and municipalities from passing Sunday laws and requiring Bible reading in public schools. It promoted religious liberty and campaigned against government efforts to legislate morality and limit free speech. Many members also advocated women's rights. So when it was pointed out that the 1877 nominating committee had chosen no women among the twenty-eight vice presidents, Amy Post, Elizabeth Cady Stanton, Elizabeth Thompson, and Sallie Holley were added to that list of progressive ministers and politicians, rabbis, spiritualists, lawyers, and free speech advocates. Women and men joined in lively debates over public education, moral versus political action, women's rights, and other liberal causes.[17] A month later, Amy hosted the wedding of her youngest son, Willet, now thirty, and welcomed his bride, Josephine Wheeler, into their Sophia Street home. By then, Hattie Post Pollay had given birth to Amy's first great-grandchild, while Hattie's mother (and Joseph's wife), Mate, had borne another son.[18] By December, Amy and Willet Post had organized a Liberal League auxiliary in Rochester, which included spiritualists, health reformers, and other activists.[19]

In spring 1878, Post was excited to hear that the NWSA annual meeting would be held in Rochester on 19 July to celebrate the "Three Decades" anniversary of the nation's first woman's rights convention. Although Stanton and Anthony increasingly focused on Seneca Falls as *the* birthplace of woman's rights, Rochester was more suitable for housing the large number of delegates expected. Anthony asked Post to serve as co-organizer, and Amy was pleased that the Unitarian church, now in a new and larger building, agreed to host the event, as it had the city's 1848 convention. In an effort to attract a significant number of women from around the country, Anthony assured "friends from abroad" that they would be "entertained free of expense." It was Post, however, who handled most of the arrangements, and visitors were told to "report to . . . 36 Sophia Street" upon their arrival. The day before the convention, as delegates flocked to the city, Amy attended the NWSA business meeting and was appointed to the resolutions committee.[20]

An exhausted Post also served as one of forty-two honorary vice presidents for the convention, sharing the honor with Lucretia Mott, Sarah Pugh, Mathilda Anneke, Ernestine Rose, and Sarah Owen, as well as delegates from London, England, to Olympia, Washington, and Little Rock, Arkansas. Not all were in attendance, however. Rose, Owen, and Bloomer sent letters to be read to the gathering, as did Catherine Fish Stebbins and eighty-eight-year-old Abigail Bush. So, too, did Robert Purvis and Aaron Powell, who had been invited to participate. Of the original 1848 participants, Post appeared in person along with Mott; Stanton, who was the NWSA president; Mary Hallowell, of the NWSA executive committee; and featured speaker Frederick Douglass. Sarah Willis likely attended as well, perhaps sitting with Lucy Colman, her sister Dr. Aurelia Raymond of Philadelphia, and Mathilda Joslyn Gage, or with Sojourner Truth, whom cousin Frances Titus had brought to Rochester a few days earlier.[21]

Truth had published an expanded version of her *Narrative* and brought copies to sell as she and Titus toured the Midwest and western and central New York. At the NWSA convention, Sojourner closed the morning session by urging women to demand their rights rather than plead for them.[22] She and Douglass were the most prominent African Americans to speak at the meeting, and newspapers reported extensively on their speeches. Mott and Post had long stood with Truth and Douglass on a broad platform of women's rights defined by racial and economic justice as well as sex equality and religious liberty. Mott reiterated many of these issues in her remarks, the last she would make at a woman's rights convention. Her reminiscences, though reported only in snippets, recalled women's efforts to emancipate the slaves and promote civil rights.[23] Post's speech, on the other hand, sounded oddly out of character. Douglass introduced his old friend as "Rochester's warmest exponent of anti-slavery and liberty, religious and civil," over the past forty years. Amy, however, was too frail to speak, so Lucy Colman read her speech, which sounded as though Post had succumbed to the promptings of Anthony and Stanton. She claimed Seneca Falls as home to "the first Woman's Rights Convention known in history," but did not link it to the Rochester convention as she usually did. Post then portrayed women as "the slave and man the master," the kind of explicit equation of gender and racial oppression she generally rejected. She also mentioned only one resolution, the first passed at Rochester, calling on women to petition the state legislature for the elective franchise. From there, the speech leapt forward to Anthony's voting rights trial in 1872, following the trajectory that Anthony had laid out of a broad movement for women's rights narrowing to the contemporary demand for female enfranchisement. Post had certainly become more committed to woman suffrage after the ratification of the post–Civil War amendments, the last ratified in 1870. Still, she continued to promote a broad platform that included economic and racial justice, religious liberty, and free thought, topics ignored in her 1878 speech.[24]

The gap between Post's universalist vision and the more limited claims she made at the three decades celebration may have been influenced by ongoing battles over women's enfranchisement in New York State. Or she may have known that she was appearing after Mott, who would lay out the larger context for the events of 1848. Or her speech may have been a collaborative effort. Amy had taken ill just before the convention, and perhaps Colman or Anthony, or both, helped craft her remarks, highlighting certain of her memories over others. One anecdote in the talk is particularly peculiar. According to Colman's presentation, Post recalled a morning in 1843 when "that far seeing prophet, William Lloyd Garrison," was breakfasting at 36 Sophia Street and remarked, "Well, when the slavery question is decided the next question is the Woman question." Post/Colman continued, "I hardly understood what he meant by the 'woman question.' I was a happy wife rejoicing in the strength and uprightness of my husband."[25] Yet

Post knew from childhood that Friends were unusual in recognizing women as ministers and had clearly sided with the more progressive Hicksites in the 1820s. By the 1830s, Post was among those supporting full equality between women's and men's meetings in Genesee Yearly Meeting and urging Hicksites to recognize men's and women's right to participate in worldly movements for reform. She had signed her first antislavery petition in 1837, six years before Garrison stayed at the Post home, and by 1843 labored within the interracial and mixed-sex WNYASS. She may have been a happy housewife, but she was also well aware of the "woman question."

At other points in the speech, Post's voice came through clearly. She, like Abigail Bush and Sarah Owen, noted that the organizers of the Rochester convention had overcome serious challenges to ensure a woman presided. And even as Amy highlighted a resolution on suffrage, she chose one passed at Rochester, not Seneca Falls. Finally, she closed on a spiritualist note, recognizing the passing of coworkers Sarah Fish and Rhoda DeGarmo, who, "no doubt, from their spirit home to-day join hands and hearts with us."[26]

Following the three decades convention, Post continued to work on multiple fronts and with diverse activists. Truth and Titus remained with Amy for the next six to seven weeks, using her home as the launch pad for Sojourner's lectures across western and central New York. The next year, 1879, Post again served as a vice president of the NWSA but also devoted considerable time to the National Liberal League. Truth's companion, Frances Titus, represented Battle Creek at that year's Liberal League convention in Cincinnati, where former abolitionists, ardent spiritualists, and free thinkers, along with Unitarians, agnostics, and atheists, met to advance liberal ideals and policies.[27]

"Only feeble health" kept Post from "the cherished hope" of attending the Cincinnati convention, but she wrote the league's secretary, A. L. Rawson, praising the young organization's work in promoting an anti-sectarian spirit. She lauded its campaigns against the Victorian sexual mores embodied in the 1873 Comstock Law, by which Congress sought to ban obscene publications and contraceptive items. She also circulated league pamphlets "amongst our hopeful freethinkers" in western New York. Still, Post criticized the organization for continuing to marginalize women. She had discovered in the proposed "Liberal compact for government" an "omission which seemed to me to be unworthy [of] the thoughtful and conscientious men by whom it was signed—that omission was the word *woman*." Just as Post insisted that women's rights involved more than suffrage, she cautioned the league not to "forget that we—Women—are the long downtrod[d]en class of National Citizens." She noted that the phrase "*All* who believe etc" does not automatically include women, "as the exponents of our statutes still persist in denying our right to Citizenship—and the Ballot Box." To erect a new structure on this same old ground, she insisted, "is to ignore and trample upon the rights of one half of the human inhabitants."[28]

Post also acknowledged that her absence would make little difference, as "more useful delegates" from Rochester would attend, including her son Willet. Along with her personal letter to Rawson, Amy enclosed a letter to be read at the convention and was no doubt pleased that it was published with the proceedings in the *Boston Investigator*, one of the leading free thought journals. There, she combined calls for gender inclusivity in any compact for a new government with support for the league's principles. Post applauded D. M. Bennett, a publisher of marriage-reform pamphlets that included birth control information, as "our champion of [free] thought, free speech, free press and free mails." She then noted that he "is at this moment incar[c]erated in a loathsome prison, deprived of almost every comfort that life, health and happiness demand." Post insisted that such dangers faced all who supported "the sweeping current of Freedom that is fast breaking away from bonds [of] long imprisonment, shewing manly and womanly [strength?] no longer enslaved to Church or State." Although recognizing that "some of us are growing old in the cause of fre[e]dom," she declared it inconsequential, since "there are the young, and the mature minds of both sexes, already in the work, who keep their standard high and erect as long as health and strength lasts." Finally, she linked her support for female enfranchisement to the need for a government built on "equal justice to all citizens" as "the only foundation . . . that will stand the test of this living-searching-scientific and philosophical age of reason."[29]

If Post's health remained fragile, her mind and spirit were strong. Fortunately, she was surrounded by caretakers. Willet and Josephine continued to live at 36 Sophia Street with their infant son Ruden, born in January 1879. Willet clerked at the family drugstore, while his wife helped Amy with domestic chores. Mary Dale Johnson resided at 36 Sophia Street as well, but at sixty years old and with a dislocated hip, she now required the assistance of others. Perhaps that is why Ellen Romayne, a servant from Canada, joined the household, along with a fourteen-year-old hired boy, Henry Van Auken. Joseph and Mate, with five children at home and a nanny, continued to live close by, although Joseph had recently given up his position at the oil company to open up his own drugstore in Charlotte (pronounced Sha-lott), just north of Rochester on Lake Ontario.[30]

By the next year, Jay Chaapel, whose family lived in Oneida, New York, but ran a funeral home in Rochester, was boarding with Amy. In his mid-forties, he may have exchanged housing and meals for assistance with heavier chores after Joseph and Mate moved to Charlotte. Just as importantly, Chaapel and Post shared an interest in Thomas Paine. In early February 1880, the two attended a celebration organized by the "Liberals of Rochester" to commemorate the 143rd anniversary of his birth. Dorus M. Fox, a midwestern spiritualist, opened the meeting, after which his wife, medium Nettie Pease Fox, Chaapel, and Post offered comments, upholding "the memory of the departed Deist."[31]

The Foxes had published a spiritualist newspaper in Springfield, Missouri, in the late 1870s but by 1880 were in Rochester, where they soon befriended Post. Nettie Fox accompanied Amy to a meeting on 22 February to discuss a new state law granting women the right to vote for school officials. They may have been surprised when the presiding officer, Mrs. Lysander Farrar—a leader of the city's Soldiers' Aid Society in the 1860s—immediately questioned the constitutionality of the new law. She then read a letter from a schoolteacher, who stated she was "averse" to having "lady commissioners to preside over the cause of education." She believed that "gentlemen" were "much better adapted to look after the business affairs of the schools and direct the discipline and intellectual development of the pupils." Farrar noted that if there was any question about the law's constitutionality, she thought it would show "a lack of dignity in the women of Rochester registering when they could not vote." A committee then introduced resolutions, the first of which declared it "not expedient" for women "to favor the nomination of women for the position of School Commissioners."[32]

Post, who had joined the Women's Political Equality Club (heir to the Women's Taxpayers Association), immediately moved that the "not" be removed from the resolution. Her amendment inspired a lively debate, in which several participants raised questions about the new law's constitutionality. An astonished Post asked whether "legislators in Albany would pass a law without knowing whether it was constitutional or not" and urged women to nominate commissioners as well as vote for them. Fox agreed, insisting that "the ladies could not make a greater mistake than the legislators did, and was in favor of women asserting their rights." Mary Anthony and other members of the Women's Political Equality Club joined Post and Fox in urging that women take the law at face value.[33] However, the suffragists' pleas were ignored. The majority at the meeting adopted one resolution opposing women's registration and another declaring it inexpedient to nominate commissioners. A few days later, Amy Post, the "well-known freethinker," tried to register to vote in the First Ward but was again refused.[34] Clearly, suffragists faced challenges not only from male naysayers but also from large numbers of more moderate women reformers. Perhaps it was this fact that had led Post to join the Women's Political Equality Club.

Having suffered these defeats, Post hoped for a better outcome at a local trial that received substantial publicity. In early March 1880, she appeared at the trial of Martha Van Auken, who was related to Amy's hired boy, Henry. Mrs. Van Auken, a spiritualist medium and magnetic healer, had supposedly stolen a cloak from a tailor, whom she had asked to repair the garment. She claimed that she paid him two and a half dollars for the repair since it was not worth the five dollars he demanded. Post and Chaapel were called in as character witnesses, and both attested to her good name. When the young prosecuting attorney raised questions about Van Auken's role as a medium, Chaapel insisted that the lawyer knew nothing about spiritualism and should not suggest that believers were somehow tainted. The jury acquitted Van Auken, who joined her supporters to celebrate.[35]

When the NWSA met in Chicago that June, several spiritualists were in attendance, and Post was once again selected as an honorary vice president. Her name was listed right below those of Lucretia Mott, Ernestine Rose, and Clarina Howard Nichols. Post was certainly honored to be in their company, although, like them, she did not attend the convention that year. Stanton's and Anthony's laser focus on the fall presidential election and the decision to hold the annual meeting in Chicago, alongside the Republican National Convention, held little appeal for Amy. Still, she may have been among the seventeen hundred women who sent letters and telegrams advocating a Sixteenth Amendment to the U.S. Constitution granting woman suffrage.[36]

Instead, Post gathered her strength and joined Chaapel, Martha Van Auken, and others at a New York Freethinkers Association convention held over four days in Hornellsville, some seventy miles southwest of Rochester. The convention attracted delegates from New England to the Midwest. Post, Giles B. Stebbins, Lucy Colman, Frederick Douglass, and Horace Seaver, editor of the *Boston Investigator*, were among the scheduled speakers; and the presence of D. M. Bennett, just out of prison, added excitement to the occasion. Among these freethinkers, Post found the sustenance that Lucretia Mott gained in her final years at peace conventions and free religious meetings.[37] While there, she supported Dr. A. E. Tilden, a Rochester physician, in promoting efforts to send funds, food, and clothing to Kansas. Black and white settlers had streamed into the territory in the late 1870s but now faced desperate times. Drought and an overcrowded labor market left families bereft and children near starvation. Sojourner Truth had gone to Kansas with Frances Titus the previous year, visiting southern blacks who had fled the South's escalating violence. She wrote friends back East, "I have not the language to tell you what rags and wretchedness and hunger and poverty I saw among them." Truth's concerns were circulated via Quaker and abolitionist networks even before Kansas activists reached out to Tilden, and Post had begun gathering contributions at her home.[38]

In September, Post did travel to Chicago for the Fourth Annual Congress of the National Liberal League, where she served on the finance committee. Her old friend Lucy Colman served as assistant secretary. Although men still dominated the major offices, more women were selected as vice presidents—including Lucy Colman, Dr. Aurelia Raymond, Frances Titus, and Amy Post—and women's rights were incorporated into the league's platform. Former abolitionists, such as Parker Pillsbury, had joined the league, as did freethinker A. L. Rawson and members of suffrage and labor associations. By fall 1880, while participants debated the wisdom of organizing a political party, members organized a committee "to defend through the courts . . . any American citizen whose equal religious or moral rights are denied."[39] Post was no doubt more committed to defending the rights of Americans who held distinctive moral views than to running Liberal League candidates for political office.

Two months after returning home, news of Lucretia Mott's death must have caused Post to ruminate over the shared principles that drove their activism. Mott had offered a model not only for Post's activism but also for her marriage to Isaac and her friendships with black and white coworkers. The elderly Hicksite had not traveled much in recent years, and Post was glad to have seen her at the 1878 anniversary in Rochester. There, Mott spoke in favor of resolutions on "the right of 'individual conscience' and the insidious influence of 'priestcraft and superstition,'" issues that were equally important to Post. Perhaps Amy recalled Lucretia leaving Corinthian Hall that day and the entire convention rising to its feet as Douglass bade her good-bye.[40]

As Post contemplated the deaths of early coworkers, from Sarah Fish, Lewis Burtis, and Rhoda DeGarmo, to her dear Isaac and beloved Nell, to Garrison (who passed away in May 1879) and Mott, she must have wondered how much time she had left and whether her younger coworkers would carry on her work. Perhaps it was in this spirit that Amy presented Jay Chaapel with a copy of Harriet Jacobs's *Incidents in the Life of a Slave Girl* in

January 1881. Post had apparently told him much of her life story during the four years he spent at Sophia Street, as he made clear when he gave the book to the Pennsylvania State University Library in 1884. On the inside cover, he described Mrs. Amy Post as "a most amiable noble woman; an early Hicksite Quaker, a Garrisonian Abolitionist, a prominent advocate of Women's Rights, Freethought, etc. Defending D. M. Bennett, E. H. Heywood and others in their persecutions by the church bigots." Knowing that the author listed on the book's title page was Linda Brent, Chaapel noted that the "correct name of the author of this valuable book is Harriet Jacobs" and claimed that he had once met her at 36 Sophia Street.[41]

Throughout the early 1880s, nostalgia regularly mingled with grief in Post's world. Despite her steadfast embrace of spiritualism, Post was stricken in 1882 when both her sister Sarah and her stepdaughter, Mary, buried their husbands. The death of Amy's brother-in-law Edmund Willis in March "was the occasion of deep and sincere regret among his many friends." Although Edmund had been plagued by illness much of his adult life, he had been an active abolitionist and Republican Party member and worked for decades in the woolen trade with William Hallowell. Success in that business allowed Edmund to buy stock in the Commercial Bank of Rochester, where he served on the board of directors from its establishment in 1875. As a result, he left Sarah a well-to-do widow. Just three months later, William Hallowell died after a brief illness. He, too, had been active in antislavery ranks, the Republican Party, the woolen trade, and the Commercial Bank of Rochester. He also served as a school commissioner in the 1850s and was a faithful member of the local Unitarian church, whose pastor conducted his funeral at his home on Plymouth Avenue. A large group of "sorrowing friends" and family gathered there to remember this "most kind-hearted, generous and genial" man.[42] Though Sarah and Mary inherited fine homes and substantial wealth, neither had expected to be widowed so soon. Still, their close bond and the proximity of Amy and other family members eased their grief, as did their continued work in the service of suffrage and social justice.

These were not, however, the only distressing events. In July 1882, just a month after William Hallowell's death, Frederick Douglass Jr. reported to Amy, "Mother had a paraletic stroke yesterday" and is "dangerously ill." A week later, his father assured Amy that while Anna was not out of danger, "her mind is clearer and her speech and appearance is better." Despite his hopes and the efforts of Washington doctors, Anna died on 4 August. Her grieving husband wrote, "My dear friend Amy, You kindly said come to me in your trouble"—and come he did, with daughter Rosetta and his oldest granddaughter, Annie Sprague. They brought Anna's body to Rochester, where, surrounded by friends, they buried her at Mount Hope Cemetery. Frederick and his family stayed one last time at 36 Sophia Street before returning to Washington, D.C., where Douglass battled sorrow and depression for many months.[43]

That December, Amy Post turned eighty, but any celebration was delayed when she was called to Long Island upon the death of her younger brother, Willett Kirby. Amy and Sarah made the trip to mourn with his widow Mathilda and their only other surviving sibling, Elizabeth Kirby Mott. Family and friends gathered at Sophia Street in March 1883 to honor Post's lifelong dedication to social change. Dr. Fred C. Farlin, a leading spiritualist, served as master of ceremonies. Stories of Amy's role in advancing abolition, women's rights, and spiritualism were offered by Lucy Colman; Mrs. Cornelia Gardner, who, after the war, had joined Post in efforts to uplift "the weak, the oppressed and the forsaken"; and Reuben D. Jones, a newspaper editor who had long covered Post and her activist circles. Family members and friends shared memories; and Amy was presented with a framed testimonial, an easy chair, a gold pen, and a sandalwood photograph album filled with pictures of family and friends.[44]

In the coming years, Post continued to attend a few conventions and meetings, including the September 1883 National Freethinkers Convention, which was held in Rochester. When she was announced as a member of the executive committee, the audience responded with enthusiastic applause. Participants then reaffirmed "the principles of the national liberal league in its advocacy of a total separation of church and state"; demanded that woman be granted equal rights and privileges with man, "be they industrial, marital, educational, or religious"; and "sympathize[d] with the cause of struggling labor throughout the world."[45] These themes, so resonant of the call for the Rochester Woman's Rights Convention thirty-five years earlier, must have pleased Post even as it worried her that the issues remained so relevant.

Unfortunately, Post could no longer care for Mary Dale Johnson, who had resided at 36 Sophia Street for the previous decade. By 1880, Johnson's two children had apparently died, and in October 1883, she moved to the county poorhouse. Though only sixty-one, the widowed Johnson was described as "old, feeble and destitute," with no living relatives and no capacity to perform labor.[46] The parting must have been painful, as Post rarely turned anyone away from her door, and this aged widow had become a dear friend. Less than a year later, Johnson died and was buried in the Post family plot at Mount Hope Cemetery.

Sojourner Truth, too, had a "hard summer" in 1883, and after months of pain and suffering, she died peacefully in Battle Creek on 26 November. Another of her old and dear friends and coworkers was gone, but at least her life had been captured in print when she told her story to Olive Gilbert, who edited the narrative and helped get it published in 1850. A new edition of *A Narrative of Sojourner Truth* appeared in 1884 with a thirty-two page "memorial chapter." In honor of her old friend and coworker, Amy bought a copy and presented it to her son Willet.[47]

The losses Post suffered may have inspired her to reach out to Frederick Douglass when he came under attack for marrying Helen Pitts, his former secretary and a white woman. After their wedding in January 1884, he was criticized widely by black and white coworkers and old friends, but Post sent "congratulations and good wishes." The couple kept a low profile for several months and then took a wedding trip from their Anacostia, D.C., home to Chicago, Battle Creek, western New York, and New England. He wrote Amy on his return, regretting that they had missed her in Rochester and reporting "that the momentary freeze of popular disfavor caused by my marriage has passed away. . . . You would laugh to see the letters I have received and the newspaper talk on such matters . . . but there is one [point] on which I wish you as an old and dear friend to be entirely satisfied and that is: that Helen and I are making life go very happily and that neither of us has yet repented our marriage."[48]

When she read Douglass's letter, Post had just completed an article on the Underground Railroad for William F. Peck's *Semi-Centennial History of the City of Rochester.* After the 1870 publication of the revised proceedings of the Rochester Woman's Rights Convention, Amy had sent a few letters to the *National Anti-Slavery Standard* but otherwise had not written for the world at large. Nor had she initially intended to write about her experiences as a conductor for fugitive slaves. Instead, her chronicle of antislavery days in Rochester had begun as a talk to the Women's Political Equality Club, where stepdaughter Mary, sister Sarah, and many friends, young and old, provided a companionable audience. Amy presented two other papers there—"on the political interests of women" and on the "condition of Indians on state reservations"—that illustrated the continued breadth of her activist vision.[49] As she revised her latest talk for publication, Post relived the anxious and exciting moments that she and Isaac shared as they worked alongside black and white neighbors to shepherd fugitives to freedom.

Peck's book appeared to great fanfare during the city's sesquicentennial celebration, and the residents who contributed to it were fêted along with the author and editor. That same year, Jane Marsh Parker published *Rochester: A Story Historical*, which offered a breezier account of the city's history. In it, she quoted the *New York World* in proclaiming her hometown a "hot-bed of isms," and added that Amy Post's home "had ever been the hottest place in our 'hot-house of isms.' "[50]

While Peck and Parker documented earlier decades of activism, Post looked forward as well. As she wrote Joseph and Mary Robbins Post in March 1884, "I am mostly the first up in the morning . . . as in former days. And still feel that it is good to live, strange, strange, when I know the dear loved ones on the other side stand ready to receive me. . . . I should be ready for when I am no longer needed here on this side." She accepted that her domestic life had become one mainly of "forebearance and economy," but she was glad to have family members still busy with worldly affairs. Still, she had not fully retreated from such affairs. That spring, Sarah, Mary, and Jacob's daughter Jessie visited New York City, where they toured the sights and attended the NWSA convention. Amy enclosed a letter Sarah had written about the meeting in her missive to Joseph and Mary Robbins Post, but noted her differences with her sister over Belva Lockwood and the controversial issue of Mormon women's enfranchisement and polygamy.[51]

In 1884, NWSA delegates divided over the 1882 Edmunds Law, which disenfranchised polygamists in Utah. Although worried about collateral damage—that efforts to disenfranchise polygamists might end up disenfranchising all women who had gained the vote in the Utah Territory in 1870—most suffragists refused to condemn the Edmunds Law. The AWSA embraced it, believing disenfranchisement was a reasonable response to plural marriage. Many NWSA members shared in the national outrage over polygamy in the Church of Jesus Christ of Latter-day Saints, but initially they fought to maintain woman suffrage in Utah. By 1884, however, many leaders, including Anthony, worried that standing with Mormons would limit the NWSA's appeal. Belva Lockwood, a lawyer who testified before Congress on suffrage issues, did not agree, viewing the Edmunds Law as "punishing innocent women for the crimes of men."[52] Having met with various Mormon groups, she assured the 1884 convention, they were "a gentle, harmless people," with the right to practice their religion "without Washington's 'unwarranted usurpation of power.' " In defending Mormons as a means of criticizing Congress, Lockwood lost more supporters than she gained.[53]

Mary Hallowell and Sarah Willis sided with Anthony, but Amy Post heard Lockwood's defense in person and was persuaded by it.

In the midst of the NWSA convention, Lockwood was called away for a family emergency and spent a day in Rochester waiting for a train. Having spent much of her adult life in western New York, she knew Post and had worked alongside her at the 1878 third decade anniversary convention in Rochester. Instead of wasting time at the station, Lockwood headed to 36 Sophia Street, where she explained her side of the debate to Post and a local reporter, who came to interview her. Lockwood told them that "her speech could not be turned into a plea for polygamy, but for women's equality everywhere, and nothing else." Accused of profiting from her efforts to overturn the Edmunds Law, she insisted that "she had *never been employed by the Mormons* and had never received any money from them." Most importantly, she feared that if the Edmunds Law was allowed to stand, Congress "could disfranchise all women of the Territories where they now have the right of suffrage."[54]

When the reporter suggested that the matter had caused a rift between her and Anthony, Lockwood objected: "I have no controversy with her. . . . I am astonished at Susan's misunderstanding" of my remarks. Nonetheless, she added, "I had rather stand in my shoes today than in hers." Post clearly agreed, rejecting any efforts to curtail religious liberty. She admitted to Joseph and Mary that she might "excuse Susan somewhat as being President, her attention might have been frequently withdrawn to other cares required of such officers." She was clearly perturbed, however, that "Sarah and Mary saw" the matter "as Susan [did]." Amy was even more upset that Anthony had slighted Frederick Douglass, "who was in almost constant attendance—and has always before been invited to speak, *how cowardly, just because he has married a white intelligent wife*" he should be ignored. After all, she concluded, "He is two-thirds white" himself.[55]

If Amy was unhappy with certain aspects of the woman suffrage movement, she remained devoted to free thought. In August 1884, she traveled to a spiritualist camp meeting at Onset Bay in Wareham, Massachusetts, and on the way visited the Thomas Paine Memorial in Boston as well as the office of the *Boston Investigator*. Noting her labors on behalf of abolition, free thought, female suffrage, temperance and other moral and social reform, *Investigator* editor Horace Seaver applauded "her good works," which he claimed, "are the crowning glory of old age in woman as in man."[56]

Post shared her enthusiasm for spiritualism with her son Willet, who also advocated woman suffrage. Indeed, he served as secretary of a Rochester meeting of the state woman suffrage society in October 1884. There, Hamilton Wilcox, a pro-suffrage legislator, spoke on behalf of a bill eliminating penalties for election officials who accepted women's ballots. This bill, Wilcox claimed, would make it possible for women who desired to vote to do so, while women who were opposed to suffrage could simply stay home. A similar bill had failed by only four votes the previous winter, and Wilcox was surprised that three of the nay votes came from Monroe County, "which has been looked upon as in advance of most sections of the state on this question." He urged supporters, especially male voters, to recognize the importance of suffrage for working women, farmwives, and other less privileged groups who needed political rights to ensure their economic security. A few days later, Amy accompanied Willet to a suffrage meeting in Buffalo at which participants decided whom to support in the upcoming elections. Although the gathering was devoted to partisan politics, Amy Post, the "Veteran Abolitionist," made a speech, though her remarks were not recorded.[57]

Post regularly held spiritualist meetings at her home in the mid-1880s and saw no conflict between her religious beliefs and women's enfranchisement. Thus in December 1885, she helped organize a new woman suffrage society at the home of Mary Anthony. Leaders of the Women's Political Equality Club were among those present, but so were a few women who, a generation earlier, would not have allied themselves with a radical like Amy Post.[58] While some suffragists questioned Post's advocacy of spiritualism and her affiliation with the National Liberal League, both the league and spiritualists happily embraced woman suffrage and other aspects of Post's holistic vision of change. In summer 1886, Amy Post was honored as "the Mother of Modern Spiritualism" by the *Carrier Dove*, a monthly spiritualist-suffragist magazine published in San Francisco. The article was written by Dr. A. E. Tilden, with whom Post had shared freethinking platforms on several occasions. It covered more than six columns, accompanied by a full page etching of the elderly honoree. Noting her stature in activist ranks, Tilden claimed that Post "has attracted attention among reformers, more perhaps than any other female reformer, not a public speaker" due to "her firmness in the defense and advocacy of truth, and the wisdom of her counsels." Describing her labors among radical Friends and on behalf of abolition and women's rights, he proclaimed her "a sure and guiding star." Tilden then detailed her crucial role in promoting modern spiritualism. She and "her noble loved companion Isaac Post" had supported the Fox sisters from the earliest day and harbored them in their home when a mob threatened violence. He quoted the well-known trance medium Mrs. F. O. Hyzer, who wrote to Amy in 1877 on behalf of herself and her sister: "You, dear Amy, have been mother, sister, friend, and comforter in a time and a place that no one but yourself could have filled for us. . . . Surely your house is the Temple of Truth!" Noting that foreign as well as American reformers sought out 36 Sophia Street as a beacon for progressive change, the author recalled that Post was cheered by audiences in Chicago and New York for "her great works for mankind." Having access to the spirit world, Tilden included a message from Isaac, who claimed "he was guided by the superior wisdom of his wife in nearly all things."[59]

That September, Post sat next to Lucy Colman on the platform of the state Freethinkers convention in Albany. A *New York Herald* reporter suggested that with her "long, white curls falling from beneath her bonnet," she "might be called the grandmother of liberalism." Colleagues from the National Liberal League were in attendance as well as fellow spiritualists, former abolitionists, and pioneering women's rights activists, who chose the eighty-three-year-old Post to serve on the society's executive committee.[60] Such tributes became more common as the pioneer activist aged, though they must have been slightly embarrassing for a woman who had rarely sought the spotlight.

Post had served neither as presiding officer or public speaker in her younger days, instead laboring among the organizers, committee members, and correspondents who created the infrastructure of movements for change. This was clearly her choice. Even when she organized events, such as the Rochester Woman's Rights Convention, she lobbied others to fill leadership roles and offer keynote speeches. The passage of time did not change her preference for mobilizing and orchestrating behind the scenes, although she was no doubt pleased to be recognized as an honorary vice president of the NWSA and the National Liberal League.

Still, despite her age, Post was not content to rest on her laurels. In May 1887, she drove herself and a friend to the Friends of Human Progress meeting in Waterloo in her carriage and enjoyed the three days of speeches and conversation. The next year, in November 1888, Amy hosted a meeting of spiritualists at her home to form a joint stock company that would advance "spiritualistic philosophy and the cultivation of spiritual phenomena and measures of reform," a project that would carry on Isaac's and her work long after she was gone.[61]

Her last appearance at a major gathering of reformers had been in Washington, D.C., in March 1888, where forty delegates from ten nations and two dozen U.S. organizations met for five days to consider forming a permanent International Council of Women. Participants devoted long sessions to religion, social purity, labor, legal disabilities, and political conditions and women's right to the ballot. On the final morning, delegates honored "the pioneers" of the U.S. women's rights movement. Post joined Stanton, Anthony, Stone, Gage, and Douglass on the stage, alongside Robert Purvis, Mary Hallowell, Sarah Willis, Sarah Anthony Burtis, Catherine Fish Stebbins, Mary Anthony, Julia Wilbur, and Virginia Minor. Following speeches and reminiscences, female descendants of the pioneers hosted a reception for their famous mothers, aunts, and grandmothers. Since Amy's stepdaughter and younger sister were also pioneers, granddaughter Jessie Post filled the role of hostess for her trio of family members.[62]

Amy Post must have been delighted to be among the honorees, surrounded by family and those few dear friends who remained from her early activist days. And here, at least, postwar rivals Stone and Stanton stood together, while Douglass and Purvis reminded the room of predominantly white women that black activists had expounded women's rights from the beginning. Moreover, the trip gave Post the chance to recall her 1863 visit to the city and her work with Wilbur, Jacobs, Truth, and hundreds of freed people.

Over the next several months, Post continued to visit family and welcome friends to her home. Her grandchildren and great-grandchildren played in the basement where fugitives once hid, while her sons became successful businessmen and her stepdaughter and sister leaders in local reform circles. None of her descendants fully embraced the universalist vision that had inspired Amy and Isaac, although Sarah Willis and Mary Hallowell dedicated themselves to educational reform and liberal religion as well as suffrage. Still, many in the following generations took pride in the Posts' involvement in abolition and especially the Underground Railroad. Most worshipped at the Unitarian church, a font of progressive ideas; and some descendants believed it had been the original religious home of the Post family, a view easier to embrace as the Friends of Human Progress faded from view.[63]

In late January, a month after her eighty-sixth birthday, Amy too began to fade. Taken ill on a Thursday, she passed away five days later, on Thomas Paine's birthday, 29 January 1889. In the following days, numerous papers carried obituaries, including Rochester's *Democrat and Chronicle* and the *Union and Advertiser*, both of which covered her death and her funeral in long and detailed articles. Lengthy accounts also appeared in the *Union*

Springs Advertiser, read by many of her old F/friends in central New York, and the *Buffalo Courier*, where fellow Underground Railroad conductors and spiritualists resided. Readers of the *New York Herald*, the *Troy Daily Times*, and the *Daily Register* in Medina, New York, viewed shorter notices. The *Democrat and Chronicle* described her "political agitation" against slavery "at a time when it was not only unpopular, but sometimes unsafe" and as "a champion of woman suffrage." It also noted that "she was especially interested in the condition of Indians on the state reservations," hosted annual visits from "Blind John," who lived on the Cattaraugus Reservation," and "never turned an applicant, white or black, from her door." The *Union and Advertiser* headed its obituary with an image of Post, under which it noted her "Identification With the Abolition Cause, the Woman Suffrage Movement, and With Spiritualism." The article described Amy and Isaac's friendships with Douglass and Garrison, assistance to fugitive slaves as well as American Indians, belief in spiritualism, and work with Susan B. Anthony. The *Buffalo Express* repeated much the same story, concluding that "her chosen work was long of an unpopular and even unsafe nature, but she stood up to it bravely and acquitted herself with honors."[64]

Shorter obituaries focused on Post's abolitionist efforts, particularly her involvement with the Underground Railroad. While the *Troy Daily Times* described her as "one of the most famous of her sex in three fields of endeavor, as a spiritualist, abolitionist, and suffragist," it emphasized her involvement "in several conflicts with the authorities through her endeavor to free the slaves chance threw in her way." The *New York Herald* similarly remarked on her three main causes but expanded on her contributions to "the famous underground railway," which she supported financially, and "by running many a hazard in the work of aiding slaves to reach Canada." The *Union Springs Advertiser* highlighted her abolitionist work as well, proudly noting that she was "a former resident of Sherwood, this county," though in fact she had lived in Ledyard.[65]

On 1 February, Post's friends and family packed Sarah Willis's home on Plymouth Avenue for the funeral. Frederick Douglass, unable to leave Washington, sent his condolences: "Few better than I know the excellence of her character, the kindness of her heart, the strength and firmness of her convictions, the serenity of her spirit, the breadth and fullness of her benevolence." He, along with William Nell, William Wells Brown, Charles Lenox Remond, and Harriet Jacobs, were noted as among her longtime friends and coworkers, as were Mott, Stanton, Anthony, and Garrison. The local Douglass League, a black mutual aid society, honored her advocacy of abolition and racial justice and recalled her labors "for the good of their race." Members passed a series of resolutions to be published in the press, "lament[ing] the loss of one whose untiring devotion to the cause of the oppressed, whose Christian courage in sharing the hospitalities of her home; and whose love for humanity . . . have endeared her name to the homes of the grateful and to the hearts of the good." League President J. V. Thompson and eight other members served as honorary pallbearers.[66]

By the time of her death, spiritualism had become "the anchor of Amy Post's soul," and spiritualists were well represented in the circle of friends offering remarks at the Willis home. Dr. Frederick Willis, Sarah and Edmund's nephew, conducted the proceedings. Although he praised Post's work for fugitives and the enslaved, Dr. Willis noted that she "was an advocate of liberty not only for the African race but of all mankind" and that her death "was but a transition to an existence beyond." He was followed by spiritualists George Clark and Mrs. Lucy Carpenter, and then by Lucy Colman. Although Colman was a critic of spiritualism, she remained fast friends with Amy and best captured the breadth and depth of her universalist worldview, recognizing the links she made between gender equality, racial justice, and religious liberty. The Women's Political Equality Club, which attended the funeral as a group, "accompanied the remains to the cemetery at Mt. Hope" along with the Post family and a number of local black activists who watched Amy's casket being lowered next to her beloved Isaac.[67]

Obituaries, memorial resolutions, and funeral orations enumerated Post's many contributions to progressive causes and to the oppressed of all backgrounds. Yet despite such recognition, the narrative of Post's activist career was refashioned almost from the moment of her passing. Perhaps most tellingly, all the obituaries conflated women's rights with woman suffrage, obscuring Post's universalist vision of gender equality with a narrower and specifically political understanding of rights. The *Democrat and Chronicle* also confused Post's roles in the abolition and women's rights movements, claiming that Post was "present at" the "first antislavery convention held in the North" rather than the first woman's rights convention. Meanwhile, the *Union and Advertiser* identified that pioneering venture as the first meeting of the "National Association" for "woman suffrage" and located it in Rochester, not Seneca Falls.[68]

Through the 1890s, area papers referenced Isaac and Amy Post as they celebrated the region's ties to the Underground Railroad and the career of Frederick Douglass. In 1894, the *Rome Daily Sentinel* reported on Douglass's recent visit to Rochester, where he was fêted as a hero. His early appearances in the city had garnered far more hostility, particularly from white residents; but, the reporter noted, Amy Post was among his avid supporters from the beginning, attending the young orator's first speech at the Bethel AME Church. When Jacob Post was interviewed in February 1895 by the *Elmira Telegraph* following Douglass's death, he related colorful tales of Frederick's early visits to his parents' home and their joint involvement in rescuing fugitives. A *Democrat and Chronicle* article the next year included the story of the three fugitives who had to be ferried to Canada during the 1853 antislavery convention in Rochester, and noted the role of Jacob Post in hiding the fugitives until they could escape northward.[69]

Lucy Colman, who published her *Reminiscences* in 1891, offered some of the most detailed recollections of Post's activist career, covering the full range of her work with abolition, women's rights, freed people, and spiritualism, and touting her courage and generosity to all who sought her aid. She had offered similar comments at Amy's funeral, where, despite her criticism of spiritualism, she concluded in a way that Post would have appreciated: "My friends, you have just laid this noble woman into the silent grave, but do you not remember of who it was said, 'being dead, yet speaketh!' Let us listen, my sisters, possibly we may find echo in our own hearts."[70]

Unfortunately, by the time Jacob and his siblings died in the 1910s, that echo was growing faint. The Posts' four surviving children and Amy's sister Sarah all died between 1913 and 1917. Mary Hallowell and her aunt Sarah Willis, who died in March 1913 and April 1914, respectively, likely drafted their own obituaries. They were both childless widows, and each had a clear sense of how she wanted to be remembered. Both noted, for instance, that they had taken up the work of "woman's rights even before the day of the late Susan B. Anthony," who had died in 1906. Hallowell also tried to clarify the difference between women's rights and suffrage, explaining that in the early days, "the right to vote was not the definite object" of the movement. Instead, her obituary claimed, it highlighted the legal disabilities of married women and employed suffrage as a means of addressing other issues rather than as a goal in its own right. Hallowell was equally committed to the abolitionist work she shared with her husband, noting that their home, like that of her parents, served as a stop on the Underground Railroad. Still, Hallowell and Willis were proud of their suffrage work and their close friendships with Anthony. And as they aged, they embraced causes that Amy might have seen as tame. Hallowell was prominent in the United Charities, the First Unitarian Church, and the Women's Political Equality

Club. Willis shared all these interests and also left significant bequests to the Rochester Female Charitable Society, the Rochester Orphan Asylum, the Industrial School, and the Athenaeum and Mechanics Institute. Willis had already endowed a scholarship for women at the University of Rochester, and her obituary noted that it "was largely through" her "influence and endeavor" that the institution opened its doors to women, another achievement usually credited to Anthony.[71] The two obituaries only mentioned Amy and Isaac Post briefly and only Hallowell's in relation to any form of activism.

The Posts' three sons were less involved in reform efforts, but their obituaries all referred to their parents' activism. In December 1915, eighty-three-year-old Joseph Post passed away at his home in Charlotte, where he spent the last decades of his life. His early job at the *North Star* office was noted in his obituary, and his youthful ties to the Underground Railroad activity of his parents. His own civic interests involved support for the Rochester Industrial School and his successful efforts to have Rochester annex Charlotte and build a bridge to that community across the Genesee River. He was also an active Mason and a member of the Chamber of Commerce, having finally established a successful pharmacy business in Charlotte.[72] His brother Jacob was ill for several years before his death at eighty-seven on Thanksgiving Day in 1916. He was praised for his long career as a druggist, his integrity, and his staunch Republican politics. While his parents' activism was mentioned, Isaac was identified solely with abolition and the Underground Railroad, while Amy was noted simply "as a coworker with Susan B. Anthony in the cause of equal suffrage."[73] By the time Willet Post died a year later, at the relatively young age of seventy, his mother was misidentified as "Mrs. Kate Post," "an early worker in the woman-suffrage movement and an associate of Susan B. and Mary S. Anthony." Isaac was not mentioned at all. Willet himself was described as a loyal Republican and "an active worker in the earliest days of the Spiritualist Church of Rochester," though the paper did not link his interest in that faith to his parents' early advocacy.[74] As these obituaries suggest, the lives of Amy and Isaac's sons had taken them on different paths, contributing to the waning knowledge of their parents' multifaceted activism.

The Posts rarely found their way into local newspapers or histories again until 1948, when the Rochester *Democrat and Chronicle* ran a story on the centenary of the first woman's rights conventions written by Mrs. George Howard, president of the Susan B. Anthony Memorial. The article began with four local women and one man attending the convention in Seneca Falls and noting it was adjourned until 2 August, when participants met at

Rochester's First Unitarian Church. Frederick Douglass, Amy Post, Mary Hallowell, Sarah Hallowell Willis, and Catherine Stebbins were rightly named as the local representatives at Seneca Falls, and the women were identified as Quakers who attended the First Unitarian Church. While the broad outline of the Post family history was accurate, Howard was far more interested in describing the homes of Mary Hallowell and Sarah Willis and the various items each had donated to the Anthony house, which was then being preserved as a historic site. Douglass's role in the two conventions and the Posts' commitment to abolitionism and spiritualism were never mentioned.[75]

Not until 1979, when the *Democrat and Chronicle* ran an article on the Post Family Papers being deposited at the University of Rochester, were the activist worlds of Amy and Isaac revived. The papers, donated by the widow of Willet Post's son Ruden, revealed a story that even their descendants barely knew. Great-great-granddaughter Amy Post Foster and her daughter and grandchildren were thrilled to learn that Amy and Isaac Post were not only prominent activists but close friends with Frederick Douglass, Sojourner Truth, the Fox sisters, Susan B. Anthony, Elizabeth Cady Stanton, Harriet Jacobs, and William Nell, as well as Progressive Friends, abolitionists, conductors on the Underground Railroad, women's rights and Indian rights advocates, and, perhaps most surprisingly to them, spiritualists.[76] The letters also illuminated the complex and overlapping activist networks that Amy Post helped create and sustain from her young adulthood in Jericho, New York, through her years in Ledyard and her decades in Rochester. Serving as a conductor not only on the Underground Railroad but also among abolitionists and between them and radical Quakers, women's rights advocates, spiritualists, and freethinkers, Post built close friendships with regional and national leaders and demonstrated her commitment to racial and gender equality personally, spiritually, and politically. She and Isaac lived out their politics in their everyday lives, refusing to serve alcohol and slave-produced goods in their home, and taking in fugitives, Indians, activists, itinerant lecturers, and women in need. Some stayed for a day or two, some for weeks or months at a time, and a few for a year or more, turning 36 Sophia Street into a center for progressive activism, interracial gatherings, and spiritualist séances. And at a time when most women, especially mothers, remained close to home, Amy traveled widely, attending AASS, woman's rights, and other conventions from New York City and Washington, D.C., to Cincinnati, Cleveland, and Chicago; visiting freed blacks in Canada and freed people in Alexandria, Virginia; and sustaining friendships and family connections from Long Island to Philadelphia and throughout central and western New York.

When Amy Post was not traveling, she was writing. While only several dozen of her outgoing letters survive, hundreds of incoming letters chart the reach and strength of her bonds to activists far and wide. Those from Douglass, Nell, Jacobs, and Truth trace not only major developments in the movement for emancipation and racial equality but also a unique set of links between a white woman and some of the most prominent black activists and writers of the nineteenth century. Others track key moments in the women's rights and suffrage movements and in the development of radical Quakerism; spiritualism; and a liberalism focused on religious liberty, the separation of church and state, and moral freedom. Many illuminate intimate details of women's lives, from marriage and childbirth to abuse and penury to mourning and faith.

In these letters, friends from diverse walks of life testify to Post's remarkable influence on them. Abigail Bush, the first woman to chair a woman's rights convention, wrote Amy as she headed to New York City on her way to California. After recalling their shared labors and asking Amy for a daguerreotype to set on her table, Bush proclaimed, "You live unfading and undying in my Heart of Hearts, yeh I would love thy Shadow." Spiritualist Susan Lee Humphrey, who lived with the Posts during a difficult period of her life, wrote of Amy from Michigan, "She is like the Saviour, every sufferer, all Humanity, to her are worthy. . . . I was thinking of your letter," she continued, "and your remarks on Liberty. . . . Truly Liberty is Thy watch word—Glorious Woman."[77] In 1877, Amy herself had noted, in her daughter-in-law's "Mental Photograph Album," that the character trait she most admired in men and women was "Truthfulness" and claimed as her motto, "Think for thyself."[78]

The life of Amy Kirby Post illuminates the remarkable effects that one ordinary woman—a wife and mother, a sister and F/friend, an activist and a conductor—had on transforming the world through the steady application of radical principles and practical righteousness. She embraced a series of ideas and movements—Progressive Quakerism, abolition, racial equality, interracial friendships, women's rights, religious liberty, spiritualism, free speech, and universal suffrage—each of which challenged conventional wisdom and inspired society's condemnation. Yet Post did not retreat but instead piled cause on cause, orchestrating bonds between activists and organizations as well as among local allies and national leaders spread across the Northeast and Midwest. Without the support of her family, especially of

Isaac, her ability to sustain such activism over so many decades would have been sorely diminished. Instead, engaged with global as well as local concerns, she remained engaged in myriad movements as well as attentive to the lone fugitive, abandoned wife, sick neighbor, and needy child. She strove as well to forge bonds across generations, welcoming younger activists within her family and the wider society, and rarely suggesting that old age made one a more astute observer or actor. While the memory of Amy Kirby Post was lost to us for generations, her spirit lives on in all those who speak against systemic racism and gender inequality and demand democratic structures and personal and religious liberty. Post's dedication to understanding the interwoven character of these issues and to forging bonds across movements is as critical today as it was in her own time.

Acknowledgments

Mary M. Huth, then an assistant librarian at the University of Rochester, introduced me to Amy Kirby Post forty years ago. I was starting dissertation research on women reformers in nineteenth-century Rochester, and the Isaac and Amy Post Family Papers revealed a landscape of radical activism I had only hoped existed. I never met Charles Ray, the undergraduate student who processed the papers, but I am deeply grateful for his exceptional work. I spent months in the University of Rochester Rare Books and Manuscripts Room with Mary Huth and Karl Kabelac, who expanded my intellectual worlds and have remained staunch and patient advocates of my work. Karl answered every query and gave me a rare first edition of Isaac Post's *Voices from the Spirit World*, while Mary Huth and Barbara Billingsley offered lively conversation over decades of lunches, dinners, and drinks.

My experiences at the University of Rochester ensured my deep appreciation of librarians and archivists. Time and again they have led me to new sources, other collections, and revelatory scholarship. Since the late 1970s, Christopher Densmore, now curator of Friends Historical Library at Swarthmore College, has shared his deep knowledge of the Society of Friends and has guided me to endless diaries, meeting minutes, and other sources. He also introduced me to the late Elizabeth H. Moger, keeper of the New York, Genesee, and Congregational Yearly Meeting Records at the Haviland Record Room in New York City. Her generosity in answering endless questions eased my way as a young scholar.

In studying the Posts for so long, I met whole new generations of librarians and archivists. Lori Birrell, Melissa Mead, and Melinda Wallington have carried on the exceptional work and collegial spirit of Mary and Karl at the University of Rochester. They welcomed me back to the Special Collections Department on many occasions, invited me to present my work, and, even as the Post Family Papers were being digitized, scanned letters I needed to recheck. Christine Ridarsky and Elizabeth Spring at Rochester Public Library, Ann Upton at Special Collections at Haverford College, Janet Bloom at the William L. Clements Library at the University of Michigan, Victoria Aspinwall at the Long Island Studies Institute at Hofstra University, and Sean P. Casey at the Anti-Slavery Collection at Boston Public Library were also generous with their knowledge and time.

The librarians, historians, and volunteers who run local archives and historic sites have also been critical to my research. Thomas Abbe of Jericho, New York, showed me the Hicksite Friends Meetinghouse where Amy Kirby worshipped for a quarter century; Kathleen Velsor gave me a tour of the Kirby and Post homesteads and Underground Railroad sites in Jericho and neighboring Westbury; and Betsey

Murphy showed me early books, drawings, and photographs at the Jericho Public Library. The opening chapter of Amy Kirby's life could not have been written without their help and the books they published. The second chapter, which follows Amy Kirby and Isaac Post to central New York, owes much to the local knowledge of Judy Furness of Sherwood and Pat White of Ledyard, as well as to Aurora historian Reginald W. Neale, Carol Darling of the Cayuga-Owasco Lakes Historical Society, and Ed Varno of the Ontario County Historical Society. In Rochester, New York, William Keeler of the Rochester Historical Society, city historian Christine Ridarsky, and Cynthia Howk of the Landmark Society of Western New York added to my treasure trove of information on the nineteenth-century Flour City. And when a last-minute glitch sent me into a state of pure panic, they, along with Nora Dimmock and Blair Tinker of the Digital Humanities Center at the University of Rochester, helped me locate, revise, and produce the 1851 map that appears in this book.

Dr. Judith Wellman introduced me to many of the central New Yorkers noted above who keep the region's vital history alive. Judy and I worked together at the Seneca Falls Woman's Rights National Park in summer 1982, where we first shared ideas about women's activism, interracial organizing, and progressive Friends. Over many years, I have benefited from Judy's friendship, conversation and insights and, more recently, from the remarkable collaborative research that she inspires and undertakes as head of Historical New York Research Associates. In illuminating the rich history of the Underground Railroad across central and western New York, she and her coworkers have reclaimed the central role of the 1816 Farmington Quaker Meetinghouse in campaigns for abolition, Indian rights, and women's rights.

Charles Lenhart, who works with Historical New York Research Associates, has made major contributions to this book. We both grew up in Spencerport, New York, but only in the past decade have we become friends and colleagues. Charles has amassed a remarkable archive of newspaper articles, genealogies, advertisements, photographs, and other sources documenting antislavery, women's rights, Indian rights, temperance, and other local and regional movements. A descendant of Esek and Maria Wilbur, signers of the Seneca Falls Declaration of Sentiments, Lenhart has discovered and recovered materials that trained historians have missed. His research has allowed me to trace family and friendship networks and incorporate key events in the lives of Amy and Isaac Post that would have otherwise been impossible. The numerous footnotes to his collection cannot capture the insights he has provided or the enthusiasm he brings to this work.

I have also benefited from joining the luminous and lively circle of Quaker scholars. Dr. Susan Mosher Stuard, my undergraduate adviser at the College at Brockport, SUNY, in 1973–74, first alerted me to the importance of women Friends to social movements. In 1987, she invited me to participate in the conference Witnesses for Change: Quaker Women over Three Centuries at Haverford College. Over the next thirty years, my work was significantly reshaped by my participation in Friends conferences; and in 2013, Stuard, then professor emerita, welcomed me back to Haverford, where I read Julia Wilbur's extraordinary diaries. By then, I had met Beverly Palmer and Carol Faulkner, whose work on Lucretia Mott allowed me to place Post in a wider world of activist and abolitionist Friends. With them and Christopher Densmore, I coedited *Lucretia Mott Speaks* while finishing the final draft of this manuscript. That work and our many conversations and email exchanges deepened my understanding of Friends faith, their attitudes toward race and gender, and their contentious relations to "worldly" activism.

Faulkner is one of several historians whose recent studies of nineteenth-century activists inspired me as I completed this book. Thanks to Bonnie Anderson, Leigh Fought, Ezra Greenspan, Wanda Hendricks, Stephen Kantrowitz, Paula Tarnapol Whitacre, and Dorothy Wickenden for sharing ideas, questions, and chapters. John Kaufman-McKivigan, a dear friend and editor of the Frederick Douglass Papers, has offered sage advice for decades. Numerous other scholar-friends who study nineteenth-century life—Anne Boylan, Ann Braude, John L. Brooke, Bruce Dorsey, Faye Dudden, Paula Giddings, Lori Ginzberg, Julie Roy Jeffrey, Martha Jones, Sydney Nathans, Stacey Robertson, Nikki Taylor, Margaret Washington, Judith Wellman, and Jean Fagan Yellin—have created models of engaged scholarship that raise issues central to this book. And just as I thought I was done, Manisha Sinha's *The Slave's Cause* appeared, reminding me, once again, that the best books help us reimagine the past as a way of re-envisioning the present.

Several of these scholars generously offered to read all or parts of my manuscript. Bonnie Anderson, Stephen Kantrowitz, Judith Wellman, and Paula Whitacre provided important insights on key chapters. Christopher Densmore, John Brooke, and Carol Faulkner read the whole manuscript, helping me hone major arguments and saving me from minor errors. Brooke and Faulkner evaluated the manuscript twice. Their perceptive critiques framed in enthusiastic prose improved the book and my spirits as I made final revisions. Steven Lawson, my wise in-house critic, read more versions of this manuscript than I can count, in many iterations and over many years. His edits and insights appear on every page.

I have been fortunate over my career to work with outstanding editors. The insights I gained working with Marlie Wasserman, Leslie Mitchener and the Rutgers University Press Board deepened my respect for those who, by laboring in academic publishing, sustain intellectual collaborations and exchanges within and beyond the academy. It also made me appreciate even more the patient support of Charles Grench, my editor at the University of North Carolina Press, who waited fifteen years before seeing the first draft of this book. When I finally started spewing out polished chapters, he offered sage advice and the right balance of encouragement and critique. He then arranged for the wonderful Jad Michael Adkins to shepherd the manuscript through the next stages of production. My thanks as well to Dino Battista and Iris Oakes at UNC Press and Annette Calzone and the production team of Westchester Publishing Services for easing the final steps to publication. And special thanks to Susannah Link for her keen eye and insights.

In the midst of final edits, it is often hard to remember the intellectual exchanges that shaped this book through years of conferences, panels and workshops. I cannot begin to acknowledge all the people whose questions, comments and critiques found their way into this study, but I do want to recognize several institutions whose invitations to speak significantly enriched my work. First, the University of Rochester, thanks to Mary Huth and Lori Birrell, hosted me several times, and audiences there offered numerous ideas and constant encouragement. The College at Brockport, my alma mater, has been equally generous in bringing me back to speak. Dr. Alison Parker has arranged three such events over the last decade, each one shaping my thinking and this book. In the early 2000s, Sharon Harley asked me to join a four-year project on Women of Color and Work, and although I was working on another study at the time, those discussions and presentations substantially shaped this book. In 2007 and 2008, Schlesinger Library Summer Institutes, organized by Nancy Cott, provided exciting opportunities for extended conversations on biography and activism, respectively. Soon after, the University of Cambridge invited me to become the Pitt Professor for 2009–2010. My conversations with Tony Badger, Andrew Preston, Deborah Thom, Lucy Delap, and the late Michael O'Brien and my presentations to the Cambridge American History Seminar in 2010 and 2014 spurred me to think anew about Amy Post. Then, as I was finishing my first draft of the full manuscript, John Brooke asked me to workshop chapter 5 at the Early American Seminar at Ohio State University. The questions, critiques, and insights I received there from faculty and graduate students reconfigured that central chapter and thus the book as a whole.

Colleagues and former graduate students, now friends, have helped mold this book as well. Although I cannot mention them all, those listed here have been particularly important during my long communion with Amy Kirby Post: Judith Bennett, Jacqueline Castledine, Dorothy Sue Cobble, Belinda Davis, Kirsten Delegard, Kayo Denda, Ann Fabian, Jacquelyn Dowd Hall, Sharon Harley, Judy Gerson, Temma Kaplan, William Link, Susannah Link, Jen Manion, Joanne Meyerowitz, Margaret Sumner, Anne Valk, Deborah Gray White, and the late Leslie Brown. Two PhD students took time from their own work to offer crucial help at critical moments: Andrew Pope, of Harvard University, and Julia Bowes, of Rutgers University. Many thanks.

Friends outside the academy have nurtured this book as well. High school classmates Karen Irwin Teske, Mary Dollinger, Holly Bauer, and Kathy Casey proved enthusiastic audience members when I spoke near our hometown of Spencerport. Ann Repplier, who has known me since my shaky undergraduate days, has never wavered in her enthusiasm for my work. More recent friends—Allen and Harriette Weingast and Paula and Mark Goldberg—have asked about Amy for years and surely must wonder how long a book can take. The camaraderie of these and many other friends, and their faith that I would finish one day, sustained me over this long journey.

I also gained inspiration from a source that few nineteenth-century scholars enjoy. In the late 1980s, I met Amy Post's great-granddaughter, Amy Post Foster, and great-great-granddaughter, Nancy (Foster) Owen. Early on, I spent a wonderful afternoon at Nancy's home, around the dining room table where Amy and Isaac once gathered their family and friends. Before she passed away in 2006, Amy Post Foster was always eager to hear about new aspects of her namesake's life. Nancy Owen has shared paintings, photographs, and stories as well as her detailed research on the Post and Kirby families. These personal connections have enriched my work and my life.

My own family has heard about Amy Kirby Post and her activist worlds for decades. My cousin Patty Carley and I have spent hours discussing our lives and our writing over prolonged breakfasts at the Neptune Diner in Newburgh, New York. My mother, Irene Hewitt; brother Will Hewitt; and sister-in-law Neerja Bhatnager live just outside Rochester, where I've given more than a dozen talks on Amy Post in the last thirty years. They have attended so many that they are now well known in local women's history circles, have become friends with Mary Huth and Barbara Billingsley, and have visited the Post family gravesite at Mount Hope Cemetery. This book is a small token of my love and appreciation for a family that appreciates the past but lives in the present. No one has spent more time with the Post family than my husband, Steven Lawson. In the early 1980s, when we were colleagues at the University of South Florida, he met Amy and Isaac in the pages of my first book. Since then, he has attended endless lectures and panels, edited a dozen articles, read several drafts of this book manuscript, and engaged in innumerable conversations on nineteenth-century activism and women's history. As a pioneering civil rights historian, he has offered ideas central to this book, including the concept of Amy Post as a conductor across multiple forms and circles of activism. He once suggested that Isaac Post was the first feminist husband. If so, Steven has followed in his footsteps. Along with his intellectual contributions to my life, he has taught me to love the Yankees, Sanibel, and Australian television, and has persuaded me to slow down, enjoy time with our "boy" Scooter, and savor sending my *last* monograph out into the world.

Note on Sources

I began research on Amy Post in 1978 for my dissertation and continued over the following four decades. Many sources that I consulted at the time have now been digitized, but I cite the original manuscript sources from which the vast majority of the citations come. Most importantly for this book, the Isaac and Amy Post Family Papers at the University of Rochester Rare Books, Special Collections and Preservation Department have been digitized and are available online at rbsc.library .rochester.edu. The Post Family Papers Digitization Project has been invaluable for rechecking material and adding additional context and quotes. Similarly, when I first researched the records of Genesee Yearly Meeting and its constituent meetings as well as the Yearly Meeting of Congregational Friends and the Yearly Meeting of the Friends of Human Progress, I viewed the manuscript sources at the Haviland Records Room, New York City. These materials, now microfilmed, have been moved to the Friends Historical Library at Swarthmore College. I cite both the original manuscript sources as well as additional materials that I used at Friends Historical Library on microfilm.

In addition, I have had access to a treasure trove of materials collected by Charles Lenhart of Hilton, New York, for the 1816 Farmington Quaker Meetinghouse preservation project as well as other scholarly research projects. He has discovered abundant reportage of people and events related to the lives of Amy and Isaac Post as well as other abolitionists and advocates of women's rights, Indian rights, and religious liberty in western and central New York State using a wide range of sources, including Fultonhistory.com, Ancestry.com, Accessible Archive, the James E. Hazard Index to New York Yearly Meeting, digitized newspaper collections, and cemetery records. For these sources, I follow the name of the newspaper or other source with Charles Lenhart Collection (CLC).

Many of the historic structure reports cited in the notes can be found on "Following the Freedom Trail" or "Uncovering the Freedom Trail" websites for specific cities or counties across the North. These are periodically updated with links to new or revised reports.

Notes

Introduction

1. Of many examples of this argument by pioneering women's historians, see Hersh, *Slavery of Sex*; Smith-Rosenberg, "Cross and the Pedestal"; and DuBois, *Feminism and Suffrage*. For more recent studies, see Ginzberg, *Women in Antebel-*

lum *Reform*, esp. 5–8. For a focus on western New York, see Cross, *Burned-Over District*. On the importance of evangelical religion for men's reform activities in Rochester, New York, see Johnson, *Shopkeeper's Millennium*.

2. Kaplan, *Taking Back the Streets*, 5.

3. Lucretia Mott, letter, *Boston Liberator*, 6 October 1848. On Mott, see Faulkner, *Lucretia Mott's Heresy*; Palmer, *Selected Letters*; and Densmore et al., *Lucretia Mott Speaks*.

4. Faulkner, *Lucretia Mott's Heresy*, 10.

5. For early work on Quakers as social activists, see Bacon, *Mothers of Feminism*; Chmielewski, *Guide to Sources on Women* and "'Binding Themselves Closer to Their Own Peculiar Duties'"; and Brown and Stuard, *Witnesses for Change*. More recently, see Wellman, *Road to Seneca Falls*; Dorsey, *Reforming Men and Women*; Faulkner, *Lucretia Mott's Heresy*; and Carey and Plank, *Quakers and Abolition*. In Carey and Plank, see especially Nash, "Hidden History of Quakers and Slavery."

6. The Michigan activist Laura Haviland, who left the Society of Friends to join the Wesleyan Methodists as a means of furthering her antislavery work, was central to an equally important interracial network in the Midwest that reached across the U.S.-Canada border. Although her work focused more on education and less on women's rights, she, too, carved out a decades-long career focused on social justice. See Miles, "'Shall Woman's Voice Be Heard?'"

7. Robnett, "African-American Women in the Civil Rights Movement." Robnett describes these efforts as building bridges "between movement organizations and potential adherents, between prefigurative and strategic politics, between potential leaders and those already predisposed to movement activities," and considers them crucial to "the micromobilization of a social movement" (1661).

8. Steven Lawson first suggested the term "conductor" to describe Amy Post's role in social movements. Conductors both direct—choirs, orchestras, trains—and transmit—electricity, sound, heat—across groups and venues.

9. See Fought, *Women in the World of Frederick Douglass*, especially chap. 4, on the intertwined and conflicted relationships among Post, Griffiths, and Douglass.

10. Good, *Founding Friendships*, 5.

11. On the danger of gossip and scandal in interracial friendships, see Fought, *Women in the World of Frederick Douglass*, introduction and chap. 4.

12. Thanks to John Brooke for his insights on the confounding character of historical time. His view is demonstrated in the chapters that follow, which cover anywhere from thirty-eight years to one year in Post's life.

13. On friendships between black and white activists in the antebellum era, see Faulkner, *Lucretia Mott's Heresy*; Fought, *Women in the World of Frederick Douglass*; and Stauffer, *Black Hearts of Men*. The best twentieth-century counterpart to Amy Kirby Post is probably Anne Braden, who was active alongside her husband, Carl, during the civil rights era. See Fosl, *Subversive Southerner*.

14. I use the term F/friends to indicate Quakers who were also close friends of Amy Kirby and the Posts.

15. For two important studies of women's nineteenth-century activism that range well beyond the standard single-issue study, see Jeffrey, *Great Silent Army of Abolitionism*; and Wellman, *Road to Seneca Falls*. For an excellent synthetic work on women's activism in which chapters are focused on distinct movements, see Ginzberg, *Women in Antebellum Reform*.

16. Mary Robbins Post to Amy Post, n.d., IAPFP; this was likely sent c. 1848–50; A. E. Tilden, "Amy Post: The Mother of Modern Spiritualism," *Carrier Dove*, July 1886. Thanks to Ann Braud for sending me a copy of this article thirty years ago.

17. On letter writing in early America, see Decker, *Epistolary Practices*. The most important collection of Amy Kirby Post correspondence can be found in the Isaac and Amy Post Family Papers at the University of Rochester.

18. Of the more than 2,300 letters in the IAPFP, only forty-two are written by Amy Kirby Post. Another eight letters written by Amy Kirby in the late 1820s are held at the William Clements Library at the University of Michigan. Three Amy Kirby Post letters exist in the Post Family Papers at the Friends Historical Library, Swarthmore College, and perhaps half a dozen others can be found in scattered archives.

19. For examples of such mirroring, see letters from William C. Nell and Mary Robbins Post to Amy Post in the IAPFP.

20. On female friendships and family networks related to economic development in the Atlantic World, see Davidoff and Hall, *Family Fortunes*. On the crucial role of friendship and kinship among antebellum women activists in the United States, see Lasser and Merrill, *Friends and Sisters*. On friendships and networks among black male activists, see Kantrowitz, *More Than Freedom*.

21. Stauffer, *Black Hearts of Men*, 1. He claims: "These four men, two black and two white, forged interracial bonds of friendship and alliance that were unprecedented in their own time and were probably not duplicated until well into the twentieth century." The relations between Post, Douglass, Nell, and Jacobs belie this claim, as do the friendships between white and black women in the Philadelphia Female Anti-Slavery Society. On the latter, see Faulkner, *Lucretia Mott's Heresy*; and Yellin and Van Horne, *Abolitionist Sisterhood*.

22. On the role of couples in the abolition movement, see Sinha, *Slave's Cause*, 284–85.

23. Harriet Jacobs to Amy Post, 18 May–7 June [1857?], IAPFP; and Tilden, "Amy Post." On Post's importance to Douglass's decision to launch his newspaper in Rochester, see chap. 3; on the importance of her friendships with Nell, Jacobs, Remond, and Wells, see chaps. 4 and 5; on Anthony's reliance on Post, see chaps. 8 and 9.

24. Thanks to the December 2015 Seminar in Early American History at Ohio State University for an insightful discussion on the "second-hand" character of many "internationalist" or "transatlantic" activist contacts in the United States.

25. For examples of these connections, see especially chap. 4.

26. See Ginzberg, *Elizabeth Cady Stanton*, 108–10. The Women's Loyal National League ultimately collected 400,000 names on its petition.

Chapter One

1. The area that became Jericho was initially called Lusum or Lewisum, perhaps after an Algonquian word or after Lewisham, England, which may have been the home of Robert Williams, the first British landowner in the area. See Murphy, *Jericho*, 17, 19.

2. Murphy, *Jericho*, 9–13. On Dutch settlement of New Netherland and New Amsterdam more generally, see Taylor, *American Colonies*, 251–62; and Shorto, *Island at the Center of the World*.

3. On conflict with the Dutch, see Murphy, *Jericho*, 10.

4. *Jericho Friends Meeting House*; "History of Jericho," accessed 10 March 2015, http://ms.jerichoschools.org/about_us/jericho_s_history. Robert Williams has been linked to both Welsh immigrants and Roger Williams, who established religious tolerance in Rhode Island.

5. Levy, *Quakers and the American Family*, 5.

6. Barbour et al., *Quaker Crosscurrents*, 1–4, 3 (quotes).

7. On the success of Pennsylvania Quaker settlements, see Levy, *Quakers and the American Family*, 6.

8. Velsor, *Underground Railroad*, 13; and Murphy, *Jericho*, 15–19, 26–27.

9. On Mary Washburne Willets family history and conversion to Quakerism, see "Willets Family of Long Island," accessed 10 March 2015, http://longisland genealogy.com/Surname_Pages/willets.htm. (Mary's family name was also spelled Washbourne and Washbourn.) See also "History of Jericho," http://ms.jericho schools.org/about_us/jericho_s_history. On Robert Williams and Washbourne family settlements on Spring Pond, see Murphy, *Jericho*, 15–19. Quote from "Willets Family of Long Island," accessed 10 March 2015, http://longislandgenealogy.com /Surname_Pages/willets.htm.

10. Murphy, *Jericho*, 15–19.

11. On the early history of Africans and African Americans on Long Island, see Velsor, *Underground Railroad*, 21, 24–25, 32–33; Murphy, *Jericho*, 12.

12. Velsor, *Underground Railroad*, 24–25, 30–35.

13. Quoted in ibid., 32.

14. Velsor, *Underground Railroad*, 20–21, quote on 21 from Hicks Family Papers.

15. On Friends and early antislavery efforts, see Carey and Plank, *Quakers and Abolition*; and Rediker, *The Fearless Benjamin Lay*; on early developments in Brooklyn and Long Island, see Velsor, *Underground Railroad*, 21, 25; and Wellman, *Brooklyn's Promised Land*, chap. 1.

16. Velsor, *Underground Railroad*, 25. See also Barbour et al., *Quaker Crosscurrents*, 67, 73–75.

17. Forbush, *Elias Hicks*, 24 (quote); Barbour et al., *Quaker Crosscurrents*, 116–19.

18. Thanks to Christopher Densmore for explaining the various kinds and levels of meetings. See also Palmer, *Selected Letters*, liii–liv.

19. On New York City ties to southern slavery and commerce, see Foner, *Gateway to Freedom*, 8–9, 44–46, 78, 94, 129–30, 138, 172, 213–14, 219–20, 228.

20. Forbush, *Elias Hicks*; Henry Hicks, "Freeing of Slaves on Long Island by Members of the Religious Society of Friends or Quakers and Self-Help Organization among Colored People," Speech, 9 January 1941, Hicks Family Papers.

21. On the American Revolution loosening the bonds of slavery, see Quarles, *Negro in the American Revolution*; Berlin, "Revolution in Black Life"; and Nash, "Forging Freedom." Thomas Paine, the author of *Common Sense* as well as an early antislavery pamphlet, was a birthright Friend but did not participate in Quaker meetings in the American colonies.

22. Murphy, *Jericho*, 33–35.

23. Ibid., 35–36. Mary Seaman would have been a child during the war, and Jacob Kirby a young man by the time the war ended. An obituary of Amy Kirby Post notes that her grandparents' home in Jericho "was occupied by the Tories during the war of the revolution." See *Democrat and Chronicle*, 30 January 1889. However, the newspaper misstates the owners as Jacob and Mary Post rather than Willet and Hannah Kirby.

24. Onderdonk, *Documents and Letters Intended to Illustrate the Revolutionary Incidents*, 19.

25. See Barbour et al., *Quaker Crosscurrents*, 71, 75; and Mathilda [Kirby?] to Sarah Hallowell Willis, 3 February 185[6?], IAPFP, in which she notes Jacob Kirby reminiscing about these events.

26. Hicks, "Freeing of Slaves on Long Island," Hicks Family Papers. Members of New York Monthly and Yearly Meetings were also active in efforts to manumit slaves, dominating membership of the New York Manumission Society, founded in 1785, and the board of the New York African Free School, established in 1787. Friends constituted a majority of the members in both organizations. See also note 50.

27. Quoted in Velsor, *Underground Railroad*, 44. On the importance of free black communities in the region, see Wellman, *Brooklyn's Promised Land*.

28. The Jericho school for blacks opened in 1817. See "History of Jericho," http://ms.jerichoschools.org/about_us/jericho_s_history.

29. *Jericho Friends Meeting House.*

30. Lavoie, "Historic American Buildings Survey," 4–5, 25–26. For influence on meetinghouses in central New York State, see "North Street Meetinghouse (Brick Meetinghouse), 1834," 12.

31. Dunn, "Later Light on Women of Light," 73–74.

32. Lavoie, "Historic American Buildings Survey," 25–26. On concerns about marrying out of meeting, especially in the revolutionary era, see Miller, *Betsy Ross*, 98–105.

33. *Jericho Friends Meeting House.* This meetinghouse looks much as it did by the early nineteenth century. Larger meetinghouses had two full floors rather than a gallery.

34. *Jericho Friends Meeting House*; and Barbour et al., *Quaker Crosscurrents*, 45–47. No public school opened in Jericho until 1870.

35. Barbour et al., *Quaker Crosscurrents*, 100–103, 101 (quote).

36. Thanks to Christopher Densmore for a description of Quaker marriage practices.

37. Sarah Kirby Willis quoted in "Long Island Houses," Painting #57, Jericho Public Library.

38. The genealogies of the Seaman and Kirby families were especially complicated around the time that Amy Kirby's parents wed, but many Quaker families in Jericho and Westbury intermarried in multiple generations. Thanks to Nancy Foster Owen and Charles Lenhart for helping disentangle these family ties. See also James E. Hazard Index to the Records of New York Yearly Meeting of the Religious Society of Friends, accessed 20 February 2017, www.swarthmore.edu/Library /friends/hazard/.

39. On the interlacing of men's and women's chores on late eighteenth- and early nineteenth-century farms, see Ulrich, *A Midwife's Tale*, introduction; see also Jensen, *Loosening the Bonds*.

40. No family letters exist before c. 1817, but extensive correspondence between Mary Seaman Kirby and her children indicate a loving relationship between Mary and Jacob. Later in life, the Kirbys did differ over visiting their children in western New York, and here their nine-year age difference may have been a factor.

41. On fugitive slaves in Jericho, see Velsor, *Underground Railroad*, especially 45–48.

42. Mary Seaman Kirby was first cousin once removed of Jemima Hicks, a relation that was close enough to include Elias and Jemima Hicks in family gatherings. Elias had a close relationship with Amy Kirby, as noted later in this chapter. Mary Seaman Kirby was also a first cousin once removed from James Mott, the husband of Lucretia Mott. Amy Kirby and her cousin Mary Robbins visited the Motts in Philadelphia as young brides and as mature women. They also maintained close ties with Lydia and Abigail Mott, who were cousins of the Kirbys and of James and Lucretia Mott.

43. Barbour et al., *Quaker Crosscurrents*, 108–12.

44. Ibid.

45. Genealogical information on the Kirby and Post families are based on compilations of genealogies by Nancy Foster Owens, Douglass E. Post, and Charles Lenhart, all in the author's possession as well as in Abbott, *Post, Albertson, and Hicks Family Letters*.

46. Amy Kirby's brothers were four and six years younger than she; a brother born in 1795 died before she was born. Two of her sisters were eleven and three years older than Amy, and two were twelve and sixteen years younger. She was

closest throughout her life to Hannah, three years older, and Sarah, sixteen years younger. Amy and her cousin Mary Robbins, four years younger, were also close and married the Post brothers.

47. The free produce movement urged individuals to refuse to purchase slave-produced goods. After developing in Britain in the 1790s, the movement found ready adherents in Philadelphia in the 1820s. See Faulkner, "Root of the Evil." On the Hickses' refusal to consume slave-produced goods, see Barbour et al., *Quaker Crosscurrents*, 118.

48. On the New York Manumission Society, see Barbour et al., *Quaker Crosscurrents*, 69–71; Foner, *Gateway to Freedom*, 40–44. On Willet Robbins, see New York Manumission Society Membership Book, 1787–1818, accessed 9 December 2016, www.triptych.brynmawr.edu/cdm/ref/collection/HC-QuakSlav/id/4605; and American Abolitionists and Antislavery Activists: Conscience of the Nation, accessed 9 December 2016, www.americanaabolitionists.com/new-york-manumission-society .html#Officers.

49. Mathilda [Kirby?] to Sarah Hallowell Willis, 3 February 185[6?], IAPFP, describes Jacob Kirby's memories of these events.

50. Thanks to Thomas Abbe, email correspondence, 28 December 2014, for his description of plain speech based on Buckley, *Essential Elias Hicks*.

51. Barbour et al., *Quaker Crosscurrents*, 146–55.

52. Most preparative meetings held worship services twice a week, on First Day and one other day. In Jericho, preparative meetings met on First and Fourth Days.

53. Mary Seaman Kirby to Hannah Post, 30 May 1823, IAPFP. Mother Mary Kirby notes that she had to hire a black girl to take over some of the chores that Amy usually performed.

54. On black women's participation in church activities—including fund-raising, decision making, and preaching—in the eighteenth and nineteenth centuries, see Brekus, *Strangers and Pilgrims*, 132–37, 145–61, 227–31, 287–90; Pope-Levinson, *Turn the Pulpit Loose*, chaps. 1, 3, 6; and Jones, *All Bound Up Together*, 40–44, 66–67, 74–76, 88, 107, 155–57, 160–61, 185–86, 191–92, 195–99, 202.

55. See Women's Meeting Minutes, Jericho, New York, 1820s and 1830s, FHL, to find numerous examples of such activities in preparative and monthly meetings.

56. There is a vast literature on the divisions among Friends, especially their separation into Orthodox and Hicksite branches in 1828. Among the most helpful for this study are Barbour et al., *Quaker Crosscurrents*, chaps. 7 and 8; Ingle, *Quakers in Conflict*; and Dorsey, "Friends Becoming Enemies." My contribution to this literature appears in Hewitt, "Fragmentation of Friends."

57. Thanks to Christopher Densmore and Judith Wellman for insightful discussions on Friends debates in this period.

58. This appears in a letter from evangelical Quaker John Butler to his English mother describing Hicks's visit to the Rose Street Meetinghouse; quoted in Barbour et al., *Quaker Crosscurrents*, 122. This description fits with visual images of Hicks.

59. Elias Hicks, *Quaker*, 271, quoted in Barbour et al., *Quaker Crosscurrents*, 120.

60. Barbour et al., *Quaker Crosscurrents*, 121–24; Ingle, *Quakers in Conflict*, chaps. 6–9; and Hewitt, "Fragmentation of Friends."

61. Abbey Gifford to Amy Kirby, 16 May 1823, IAPFP. See also Ann P. Titus to Hannah Kirby, 12 April 1819; Amy [Willis?] to Amy Kirby, 8 December 1822; Phebe [Willis?] to Amy Kirby, 25 December 1822; and Lydia [Seaman?] to Amy Kirby, 26 August 182[3?], all in the IAPFP. All the letters discuss young men interested in Amy Kirby as well as other potential matches in Jericho, Westbury, and Scipio.

62. Information for this paragraph is based on genealogies of the Hicks, Post, and Kirby families, CLC; and Abbott, *Post, Albertson, and Hicks Family Letters*.

63. Amy [Willis?] to Amy Kirby, 8 December 1822, IAPFP.

64. Phebe [Willis?] to Amy Kirby, 25 December 1822, IAPFP. Details on Amy Kirby's appearance and character are from Amy Post, "Mental Photographs Album," 1877, compiled by Josephine Wheeler Post, Amy's daughter-in-law, in author's possession.

65. Levy, *Quakers and the American Family*, 132.

66. Mary W. Willis to Amy Kirby, 182[0?], IAPFP.

67. Ledyard was separated from Scipio in 1823 and established as an independent town. It lay on the east shore of Lake Cayuga.

68. Hannah Post to Amy Kirby, [1823?], IAPFP.

69. Maria Willets to Hannah Post, 18 April 1823, IAPFP.

70. Amory, "Expedition under General Sullivan"; Graymont, *Iroquois in the American Revolution*; Calloway, *American Revolution in Indian Country*, chap. 5; and Wellman, "1816 Farmington Quaker Meetinghouse," 14–16.

71. Hartsough, foreword to *Farmington*. On the founding of Farmington, see Neale, *Farmington*, 8–9, 23; and Wellman, "1816 Farmington Quaker Meetinghouse," 17–21, 37–43.

72. Isaac Post attended several quarterly meetings in Farmington in 1823 and 1824 as well as the rare quarterly meeting held at Scipio before it was granted its own quarterly meeting in 1825. Quarterly meetings generally lasted two or three days, and those from afar might spend a day traveling to and from such gatherings.

73. On development of Friends meetings in central New York, see "North Street Meetinghouse." On Hannah's involvement in these activities, see Minutes, Women's Monthly Meeting, Scipio, 11 March 1824 and following months, Microfilm, FHL.

74. On William Willets family, see http://longislandgenealogy.com/Surname _Pages/willets.htm; and Willets family genealogy, CLC.

75. Hannah Post to Amy Kirby, 14 May 1823, IAPFP.

76. On Isaac's absences for work, see Mary Seaman Kirby to Hannah Post, 2 June [1823?], IAPFP; and Phebe Kirby to Hannah Post, 27 June 1825, IAPFP.

77. On Isaac's absences for meetings, see Isaac Post to Hannah Post, 23 May 182[4?] (quote), IAPFP; and Amy Kirby to Mary Seaman Kirby, 24 July 1823, IAPFP.

78. Hannah Post to Amy Kirby, 1 February 1824, IAPFP.

79. Mary Seaman Kirby to Hannah Post, 30 May 1823, IAPFP. This letter was written diary style between 4 and 27 May and posted on 30 May, after Amy Kirby's arrival. It is not clear why Amy did not travel with Hannah and Isaac.

80. Mary Seaman Kirby to Hannah Post, 14 December 1823, IAPFP.

81. Amy Kirby to Mary Seaman Kirby, 24 July 1823, IAPFP.

82. On Amy's social network in the Ledyard area, see Hannah Post to Amy Kirby, 14 May 1823, IAPFP; Abbey Gifford to Amy Kirby, 16 May 1823, IAPFP; and Phebe Kirby to Amy Kirby, 26 May 1823, IAPFP. On the illness of Hannah and Mary Post, see Phebe Post Willis to Isaac Post, 2 June 1823, IAPFP.

83. Abbey Gifford to Amy Kirby, 16 May 1823, IAPFP. See also Wellman, "1816 Farmington Meetinghouse," 26–27.

84. Amy Kirby to Mary Seaman Kirby, 24 July 1823, IAPFP; and Lydia [Seaman?] to Amy Kirby, 26 August 182[3?], quoting Amy's previous letter, IAPFP.

85. Anna Greene to Amy Kirby, 12 May 1824, IAPFP. Underlining in the original suggests that the two had had a specific conversation about this issue.

86. Amy Willis to Amy Kirby, 30 August 1823, IAPFP.

87. Amy Kirby to Charles Willets, 9 March 1824, Amy Kirby Papers, William Clements Library, University of Michigan, Ann Arbor. In the letter, Amy refers to Charles's previous letter, which has not been found, and indicates that she did not anticipate "a declaration of this kind" and is not prepared to accept it.

88. Mary S[eaman?] to Amy Kirby, 4 September 1823, IAPFP; and Phebe Post Willis to Isaac and Hannah Post, 11 November 1823, IAPFP.

89. Mary Seaman Kirby to Hannah Post, 8 December 1823, IAPFP.

90. Mary W. Willis to Hannah Post, 5 January 182[4?], IAPFP. Although the Mary W. Willis letter is dated 5 January 1823, it was likely written in January 1824, at the time of Amy Willis and Townsend Rushmore's wedding.

91. Amy Willis to Amy Kirby, 26 December 1823, IAPFP.

92. Amy Kirby to Charles Willets, 9 March 1824, Amy Kirby Papers, William Clements Library, University of Michigan, Ann Arbor.

93. Hannah Post to Amy Kirby, [Jan/Feb 1824?], IAPFP. The letter was written the day that Isaac returned from taking Amy to Long Island.

94. Amy Kirby to Charles Willets, 9 March 1824, Amy Kirby Papers, William Clements Library, University of Michigan, Ann Arbor.

95. Ibid., 3 April 1824.

96. Joseph Post to Hannah Post, 15 September 1824, IAPFP.

97. On apologies for "expressions," see Amy Kirby to Charles Willets, 26 October 1824, Amy Kirby Papers, William Clements Library, University of Michigan, Ann Arbor. Hannah Post gave birth to Edmund on 14 March 1825, five months after her parents' visit.

98. See advertisements, for example, in *Ontario Repository*, 26 January and 16 February 1825, and *Geneva Gazette*, 6 April 1825, CLC. The quote appears in all three papers. The name Post Coaches referred not to Isaac Post but to the role of the coaches in carrying mail as well as passengers. Isaac's co-investors included I.

Roy in Jersey City, Isaac Mott in North Milford, N.Y., and S. Hemenway (hometown unknown).

99. Thanks to Judy Furness, Ledyard town historian, for information regarding Isaac Post's appointment as overseer of highways, District 22, in 1825, 1826–29, and 1834.

100. "The Full-Blooded English Horse Roc Planter" advertisement, *Auburn Cayuga Republican*, [182?], CLC.

101. Amy Kirby to Charles Willets, 26 October 1824, Amy Kirby Papers, William Clements Library, University of Michigan, Ann Arbor.

102. Ibid., 30 January 1825.

103. Ibid., 9 March 1824 and 26 October 1824.

104. Barbour et al., *Quaker Crosscurrents*, 124–25.

105. See, for example, Mary Seaman Kirby to Hannah Post, 30 May 1823; Mary Seaman Kirby to Hannah Post, 14 December 1823; Mary W. Willis to Amy Kirby, 182[4?]; Phebe Post Willis to Isaac and Hannah Post, 11 November 1823; Phebe Post Willis to Isaac Post, 28 April 1824; and Lydia Post Rushmore to Hannah and Isaac Post, 9 November 1826, all in the IAPFP.

106. Lydia Post Rushmore to Isaac Post, 9 November 1826, IAPFP.

107. Amy Post to Charles Willets, 15 May 1825, Amy Kirby Papers, William Clements Library, University of Michigan, Ann Arbor.

108. Ibid., 4 May 1825.

109. Ibid., 7 March 1825.

110. Ibid., 4 and 15 May 1825.

111. Mary Kirby to Hannah Post, 29 June [1825?], IAPFP.

112. Amy Kirby to Hannah Post, 28 July 1825, IAPFP.

113. Amy Kirby to William Willets and Family, 28 June 1825, Amy Kirby Papers, William Clements Library, University of Michigan, Ann Arbor.

114. Hannah Post to Mary Seaman and Jacob Kirby, 6 October 1825, IAPFP.

115. Hannah Willets to Amy Kirby, 15 January 1826, IAPFP; and Hannah and Isaac Post to Amy Kirby, 17 November 1825, IAPFP.

116. Hannah Post to Amy Kirby, 10 February 1826, IAPFP. Hannah began her letter on 29 January but did not complete it until 10 February. On rheumatic fever, see www.mayoclinic.org/diseases-conditions/rheumatic-fever/home/ovc-20261251.

117. Hannah Post to Amy Kirby, 25 December 1825, IAPFP.

118. A[nna] G[reene] to Amy Kirby, [March/April 1826?], IAPFP.

119. Caroline [?] to Amy Kirby, 15 April 1827, IAPFP; and M[ary?] Lefferts to Amy Kirby, 23 April 1827, IAPFP.

120. Joseph Post to Isaac Post, 29 November 1827, IAPFP. Amy Kirby spent extended periods in Ledyard, Jericho, and Westbury with Hannah's children.

121. Lucretia Mott to Anne Mott, 26 February 1827, in Palmer, *Selected Letters*, 16.

122. Barbour et al., *Quaker Crosscurrents*, chap. 6, especially 125–30.

123. On separation, see ibid., chap. 7; and Wellman, "Sherwood Equal Rights Historic District."

124. Cornell, *Adam and Anne Mott*, 146–49, 147 (quote). See also Barbour et al., *Quaker Crosscurrents*, 125–30, 130–34.

Chapter Two

1. No extant letters between Amy Kirby and Isaac Post exist for this period, and letters from Amy Kirby to friends and family contain no hint of their changing relationship.

2. New York Yearly Meeting Discipline, 1836. Although this wording comes from 1836, the statement reflected Friends practice in the 1820s as well. Thanks to Christopher Densmore for clarifying this issue.

3. On definitions of incest by Protestant churches, see Connolly, *Domestic Intimacies*, chap. 2.

4. On attendance by family and friends, see John Ketcham to Isaac Post, 20 January 1829, IAPFP. Scipio Monthly Meeting of Women was concerned about Quakers marrying out of the Society, so perhaps marrying a Quaker was more important to them than degrees of kinship. See Scipio Preparative Meeting, Women, 7 Third month 1828, FHL. All references to Friends meetings below refer to Hicksite meetings unless otherwise stated. On Isaac being disciplined, see Lydia Post Rushmore to Isaac Post, 30 May 1829, IAPFP. She claims Isaac lost his membership temporarily and the "right to sit in favored meetings"—that is, business or select meeting—for a longer period.

5. Scipio Monthly Meeting, 4 Ninth month 1828; Women's Meeting, Jericho Monthly Meeting, 16 Tenth month 1828 and 14 Third month 1829; and Men's Meeting, Jericho Monthly Meeting, 16 Fourth month 1829, FHL.

6. Lydia Post Rushmore to Isaac Post, 30 May 1829, IAPFP.

7. On the threat of dismissal, see Jericho Preparative Meeting, Women, 18 Twelfth month 1828 and 3 Third month 1829; on letting transgression pass, see Jericho Preparative Meeting, Men, 16 Fourth month 1829, FHL. Scipio Monthly Meeting acknowledged a certificate for Amy Kirby Post on 16 Sixth month 1829, while Isaac Post was still being investigated. See Scipio Monthly Meeting, 17 Sixth month 1829, FHL.

8. Quotes from John Ketcham to Isaac Post, 20 January 1829, IAPFP. Ketcham's mother, Jane Seaman, was first cousin to Amy Post's mother, Mary Seaman Kirby.

9. Quotes from John Ketcham to Isaac Post, 20 January 1829, IAPFP.

10. Scipio Preparative Meeting, Women, 5 Second month 1829, FHL.

11. Ibid., 12 Third month 1829, FHL. Anna Greene and Phebe Underhill submitted this report from Poplar Ridge Preparative Meeting.

12. On Ledyard farms, houses, and meetinghouses, see "North Street Friends Meetinghouse (Brick Meetinghouse)"; and "Cayuga County Homes of Susan White Doty and Elias Doty." By 1820, a second meetinghouse was built in Scipio at Barber's Corner and called the North Street meetinghouse. Its members and those at Poplar Ridge became Hicksite meetings in 1828.

13. On Susan White and Elias Doty, see "Cayuga County Homes of Elias and Susan Doty," 2–3.

14. Quote from Stroke, *History of Cayuga County*, 417. See also "North Street Friends Meetinghouse (Brick Meetinghouse)"; and "Cayuga County Homes of Susan White and Elias Doty."

15. Undated letters from this period suggest a variety of family visits to Ledyard. In summer 1830, the federal census taker noted 1 white male under 5 (Jacob Post), 1 white male 5–9 years (Edmund Post), 1 white male 30–39 (Isaac Post), 1 white female 5–9 (Mary Post), 1 white female 20–29 (Amy Post), and 1 white female 40–49 (probably Phebe Post Willis). Fifth U.S. Federal Census, 1830, Ledyard, Cayuga County, New York, Series Microfilm 19, Roll 88, 283.

16. Mary Seaman Kirby to Amy Post, [9 month 183?], IAPFP

17. Mary Seaman Kirby to Amy Post, 4–27 April 1831, IAPFP. On illnesses and deaths, see also Mary W. Willis to Isaac Post, 22 March 1832, IAPFP; Amos Willets to Isaac Post, 4 July 1832, IAPFP; and Anna Greene to Mary Robbins Post, 6 April 1833 and 1 March 1834, MJPFP.

18. Mary Seaman Kirby to Amy Post, 4–27 April 1831, IAPFP.

19. Ibid.

20. "REWARD," *Long Island Advertiser*, 23 January 1832, CLC; Mary W. Willis to Isaac Post, 22 March 1832, IAPFP; and Amos Willets to Isaac Post, 4 July 1832, IAPFP. Amos Willets was related to Catherine Willets, Isaac's mother. He visited Edmund and Mary Post on 4 July and sent news to Isaac.

21. Amos Willets to Isaac Post, 4 July 1832, IAPFP.

22. Anna Greene to Mary Robbins Post, 4 June 1833, MJPFP.

23. On the struggle between "heroic medicine" and alternative treatments offered by midwives, "irregular" physicians, and lay or folk healers, see Ulrich, *A Midwife's Tale*, 49–50, 61–64. Ulrich highlights the centrality of women to "social medicine," which she defines as being practiced by cooperative, informal, but complex circles of female healers in the late eighteenth and early nineteenth centuries. By the 1830s and 1840s, a popular health movement involving both women and men emerged that highlighted homeopathy, hydropathy, herbs, and diet. See also Rosenberg, *No Other Gods*; and Gordon, *Woman's Body, Woman's Right*, 159–65. While Amy Post read widely, we do not know which books related to health and medicine she owned or borrowed from friends.

24. On indigenous healing knowledge used by white Americans, see Ulrich, *A Midwife's Tale*, 52–53; and Butler, "Dark Ages of American Occultism," 59–61. On Peleg White's All Healing Ointment, see "Improvement on White's Salve," *Auburn Journal and Advertiser*, 4 September 1839, CLC. Eunice White continued its production and sale after her husband died in 1838. On sharing information among women, see Ulrich, *A Midwife's Tale*, 49, 61–66. See also Obituary for Eunice White, *Livonia Gazette*, 23 March 1877, CLC; and Postcard advertisement for Peleg White's All Healing Ointment, 1886, from Wauregan Pharmacy, Norwich, Connecticut, CLC.

25. Numerous letters to and from Amy and Isaac Post discuss medical issues and health matters, and many note Amy Post caring for family members and friends. The decision to place Cadwalader in the Post home for several months suggests that the couple were recognized for their medical knowledge and skills. Cadwallader, *Memoir*, 106–8, 106 (quote). Published after her death, the book is a compilation of testimonies from a variety of Quakers, including Amy Post (identified as A.P., of Western New York). Post describes her interactions with Cadwalader in 1833–34 in Scipio and in 1855 in Rochester. Priscilla Hunt Cadwalader's name is also spelled Cadwallader. I use the first spelling, which Quaker scholar Thomas D. Hamm considers correct, although her posthumous *Memoir* is published under Cadwallader.

26. Anna Greene to Mary W. Willis, 6 April 1833, MJPFP. Phebe Post Willis, born in 1790, had attended Nine Partners Friends School with Lucretia Coffin and was, like Isaac and their siblings, second cousin to Lucretia's future husband, James Mott. Phebe married Henry Willis in 1813, bore one son in 1815, and began traveling with Mott in 1830. The Seamans and Seaman Kirbys were also cousins of James Mott.

27. Cadwallader, *Memoir*, 106, 107.

28. These discussions of Joseph and Priscilla Cadwalader are deeply indebted to Hamm, "Quakerism, Ministry, Marriage, and Divorce."

29. Ibid., 415.

30. Ibid., 421, 423–27 (quote 421). The Posts' view was reinforced in 1837, when Joseph was disowned by his Indiana meeting for the "vending of spirituous liquors," 425. Amy Post heard directly about Cadwalader's disownment: Phebe K. Carpenter to Amy Post, 24 June 1837, IAPFP. After a civil (all-male, non-Quaker) jury granted Joseph a divorce, Priscilla Cadwalader returned home, where she was received warmly by Blue River (Indiana) Monthly Meeting.

31. Noah Haines to Isaac Post, 10 February 1834, IAPFP; and David Evans to Isaac Post, 22 July 1834, IAPFP. All three circulated testimonies to Priscilla Cadwalader's moral character.

32. It is possible that Isaac Post attended the inaugural meeting. See reference to his sending news about the June 1834 GYM in David Evans to Isaac Post, 22 July 1834, IAPFP. On Lydia Mott, see GYM, Minutes, 1834, HRR.

33. Mary W. Willis to Isaac and Amy Post, 22 March 1832, IAPFP; Amos Willets to Isaac Post, 4 July 1832, IAPFP; and Anna Greene to Mary W. Post, 6 April 1833 and 1 March 1834, MJPFP.

34. Information on size of yearly meetings and possibilities for accommodations and meals from Christopher Densmore, emails to author, 22 April 2011 and 18 December 2014. See also Mary Durfee Diary, 9–17 June 1838, Wayne County Historian's Office, Lyons, N.Y.; and Charles Townsend Diary, 1835, vol. 2, 92–97, FHL.

35. Charles Townsend Diary, 1835, vol. 2, 92–95, FHL. See Mary Durfee, Diary, 9–17 June 1838, Wayne County Historian's Office, Lyons, N.Y., for similar descriptions

of GYM from a resident of nearby Palmyra, New York. It is not clear where the Posts stayed during the 1835 GYM.

36. GYM, Minutes, 1835, HRR.

37. On the four separate gatherings on Fourth Day, see Charles Townsend Diary, 1835, vol. 2, 93, FHL. Quote is from A[my] P[ost] in Cadwallader, *Memoir*, 109.

38. Charles Townsend Diary, 1835, vol. 2, 95–96, FHL. The GYM published its first Discipline in 1842. Changes made before then were noted in meeting minutes.

39. GYM, Minutes, 1837, HRR.

40. This practice was included in the printed edition of the GYM's Discipline in 1842.

41. Taylor, *Life of William Savery*; and email to author from Douglas Fisher, 24 July 2014. On developments in the early 1800s to 1838, see Wellman and Lewandowski, "Farmington Quaker Meetinghouse." Further discussion of the 1838 meeting and its aftermath appear in chap. 3. See also Spence, "Women at the Crossroads," 7.

42. On Lundy and Garrison, see Dillon, *Benjamin Lundy*; and Mayer, *All on Fire*; on the founding of American Anti-Slavery Society and early Quaker influences, see Faulkner, *Lucretia Mott*, 64–66.

43. Charles Townsend Diary, 1835, vol. 2, 92, FHL. Townsend was particularly critical of Adin Corey.

44. Ibid., 94.

45. On deliberations over slavery, see GYM, Minutes, 1835, HRR; on critiques of boycott, see Charles Townsend Diary, 1835, vol. 2, 94, FHL. The 1842 GYM Discipline included "advice" that Friends should consider on whether dealing or consuming the products of slave labor was equivalent to supporting the system of slavery.

46. On Austin Steward's life, see Steward, *Twenty-Two Years a Slave*, 111–13; and "1816 Farmington Quaker Meetinghouse," 33–35, 42. On the 1823 case in Lockport, where Comstock was overseeing work on the Erie Canal, see Lockport, New York, Underground Railroad, accessed 26 September 2016, http://www.math.buffalo.edu /~sww/ohistory/hwny-ugrragents.html.

47. On Willis's part in Garnet's story, see Velsor, *Underground Railroad*, 114–16.

48. On Wilburites in central New York, see Barbour et al., *Quaker Crosscurrents*, 144–45. Thanks to Judith Wellman, Christopher Densmore, and Charles Lenhart for discussions about the importance of Orthodox and Hicksite partnerships among abolitionists in this region. See Wellman, "1816 Farmington Quaker Meetinghouse," 46–47.

49. "1816 Farmington Quaker Meetinghouse," 47–48; and Densmore, "Dilemma of Quaker Anti-Slavery," 81–82. Thanks to Charles Lenhart for tracing these Orthodox families over three generations.

50. See chaps. 3 and 4 for more on the WNYASS.

51. Lucretia Mott to Phebe Post Willis, 2 September 1835, in Palmer, *Selected Letters*, 34.

52. On Farmington as the "mother of meetings," see Spicer, "Farmington Centenary," 666–67.

53. New York Yearly Meeting first adopted the London Yearly Meeting Discipline in 1763. Christopher Densmore summarized Friends attitudes toward participation in worldly associations. Emails to author, 19 and 20 December 2016.

54. The activities of Post family members in Rochester and Long Island will be detailed in the following chapters. On the importance of New York City and Long Island Friends in early abolitionist activities, see Barbour et al., *Quaker Crosscurrents*, 67–75, 83–86, 172, 183–90. See also Foner, *Gateway to Freedom*, 40–41, 55–58, 93–94.

55. The movements of the Fish and DeGarmo families were tracked through monthly meeting minutes with the help of the late Elizabeth Moger of HRR. She mailed me pages of the relevant meeting minutes, which remain in my possession.

56. Charles Townsend Diary, 1835, vol. 2, 97–98, FHL.

57. Woodcock, "Some Account of a Trip to the 'Falls of Niagara,' " 166.

58. Joseph and Mary Robbins Post to Isaac Post, 19 April 1835, IAPFP. Their letters often contained separate sections written by each of them. Here Mary quotes Uncle Henry about Isaac's independence.

59. The Posts moved to 36 Sophia Street on arriving in Rochester, and it remained Amy's home until her death in 1889. The first indication of the move appears in a letter from Phebe K. Carpenter to Isaac and Amy Post, 17 September 1836, IAPFP.

Chapter Three

1. McKelvey, *Rochester*, 165, 229. Lowell, Massachusetts, is the only rival for fastest-growing city in the United States between 1825 and 1835.

2. On the development of Rochester in this paragraph and the next, see French, *Historical and Statistical Gazeteer*, 402–5; and McKelvey, *Rochester*, chaps. 3 and 4.

3. On the importance of Charlotte and lake steamers, see, for example, Calarco, *Underground Railroad in Upstate New York*, 16.

4. McKelvey, *Rochester*, 165, 229, on population growth and turnover from the 1820s to the 1840s.

5. See Rochester City Directories, 1834 and 1838.

6. On the Charity School and Rochester Female Charitable Society, see Hanmer-Croughton, "Rochester Female Charitable Society," 68–70; and Hewitt, *Women's Activism and Social Change*, 64, 70–71.

7. Josiah Bissell to Charles Grandison Finney, 15 September 1829, quoted in Johnson, *Shopkeeper's Millennium*, 94. The Society of Friends opposed the kind of state intervention in religious life that Sabbatarians proposed, such as stopping canal traffic on Sundays.

8. For detailed analyses of Rochester revivals, 1830–31, see Johnson, *Shopkeeper's Millennium*, chap. 5; McKelvey, *Rochester*, 190–94; and Cross, *Burned-Over District*, chap. 5.

9. Quote by Finney convert, the Reverend Charles Bush, in Ogden-Malouf, "American Revivalism and Temperance Drama," 146.

10. See Hewitt, *Women's Activism*, chaps. 3 and 4. On the spread of revivals and reform in western and central New York more generally, see Cross, *Burned-Over District*.

11. See Hewitt's *Women's Activism*, chaps. 1 and 2; Johnson, *Shopkeeper's Millennium*, chaps. 1 and 2; and McKelvey, *Rochester*, chaps. 4 and 10.

12. On the African American population, see McKelvey, *Rochester*, 69, 286. He claims that about 360 African Americans lived in the city by 1834, but if their migration rates—in and out—were anywhere near those of whites, then twice that many would have passed through Rochester between 1820 and 1834.

13. Steward, *Twenty-Two Years a Slave*, 292–98; and Frazier, *Old Ship of Zion*. Other self-emancipated slaves also lived openly in Rochester, including the Reverend Thomas James, see below, and John Reed, who escaped slavery in 1832, moved to Rochester, and became a barber and an abolitionist. See Oliver Johnson, "Letters," *NASS*, 31 March and 5 May 1842.

14. Information on the establishment of the AME Zion Church is scattered and often contradictory. The church is listed under multiple names before officially affiliating with the AME Zion Church, likely in 1839. There was at least one other African American church, African Bethel Church, in the city before 1850. See Frazier, *Old Ship of Zion*, 3, 6–8, for early history and documents with different names. See also James, *Life of Rev. Thomas James*; and "Memorial AME Zion Church: History," accessed 20 June 2015, https://sites.google.com/site/memorialamezionchurch/church-history.

15. See James, *Life of Rev. Thomas James*; Coles, *Cradle of Freedom*; and McFeely, *Frederick Douglass*, 82. On Roswell Jeffrey and family, see Rochester City Directories, 1834 and 1838; and Frazier, *Old Ship of Zion*, 10–12. On dates and locations of various black churches, see Halsey, "Religious Congregations in Rochester, NY, Formed before 1900," accessed 18 May 2014, http://mcnygenealogy.com/church1.htm#ame#ame. On possible merger of other black churches with AME Zion, see "Memorial AME Zion Church: History," https://sites.google.com/site/memorialamezionchurch/church-history.

16. On Isaac Gibbs, see Rochester City Directories, 1834, 1838, and 1841. Like most women and many African Americans, Mary Gibbs is not listed. See *Liberator*, 8 March 1834, on the founding of a black women's antislavery society in Rochester. Caroline Hawkins was likely one leader. She was a single woman or widow who was a mainstay of the society until at least 1851. See chap. 5.

17. No list of members of the black women's antislavery society has been located. The black women's organization appeared in antislavery papers with and without "Sewing" in the name. References to individual women, like Caroline Hawkins and Mary Gibbs, appear in reports on fairs and celebrations in the 1830s, 1840s, and 1850s. Most known leaders of the society came from families in which black men were also active in the abolitionist cause.

18. On Irish residents, see McKelvey, *Rochester*, 104, 229, 284, 300, 306, 334.

19. Johnson, *Shopkeeper's Millennium*, 53–55.

20. Isaac Post's services as a butcher and his home address are noted in Rochester City Directory, 1838. The address is variously listed as 36, 136, and 137 Sophia Street, but 36 Sophia Street is the correct address for the decades the Posts lived in the house. Houses were renumbered as the city expanded. The part of Sophia Street south of Buffalo Street (later Main Street East) was renamed Plymouth Avenue by the 1860s, and eventually all of Sophia Street became Plymouth Avenue. The Post home no longer stands, but a historic plaque has been placed at its site on Plymouth Avenue.

21. It is not clear when precisely the Posts first hid fugitives, but their proximity to the AME Zion school and church, their knowledge of fugitives hiding on Long Island and in Ledyard, and their attendance at antislavery lectures at AME Zion and African Bethel churches suggests they became part of the network of safe houses soon after reaching Rochester. See page 126 for evidence of their involvement by January 1842.

22. Mary Seaman Kirby to Amy Post, 2 April 1837, IAPFP.

23. Mary Robbins Post to Amy Post, [183?], IAPFP.

24. Phebe Post Willis to Isaac and Amy Post, 5 April 1837, IAPFP. This letter also details Willis's travels and connections with the antislavery movement and with Lucretia Mott.

25. Phebe Post Willis to Amy and Isaac Post and Edmund Willis, 14 March 1838, IAPFP; and John Ketcham to Isaac Post, _ September 1838, IAPFP. Many letters in this period discuss issues raised at Friends meetings and offer comments on traveling ministers and antislavery lecturers.

26. On the impact of the Panic of 1837 on Rochester, see McKelvey, *Rochester*, 213–15.

27. Mary Seaman Kirby and Sarah Kirby to Amy Post, 5 July 1837, IAPFP.

28. Phebe K. Carpenter to Amy Post, 24 June 1837, IAPFP. The date on this letter is in error, since Henry died on 2 July 1837, and the news likely reached Carpenter a week or so later. The most likely date is 24 July 1837.

29. Phebe Post Willis and Edmund Willis to Amy and Isaac Post, 20 October 1837, IAPFP; and Mary Seaman Kirby to Amy Post, 1 November 1837, IAPFP. See also Phebe Post Willis to Edmund Willis, 24 November 1837, IAPFP.

30. Mary Seaman Kirby to Amy Post, 12 July 1838, IAPFP.

31. Mary Seaman Kirby to Amy Post, 20 February 1838, IAPFP. Amy and Isaac's daughter Mary Post may have been attending school near the family's former home in Ledyard in anticipation of Aunt Sarah Kirby settling in nearby Aurora.

32. Mary Seaman Kirby and Sarah Kirby to Amy Post, 5 July 1837, IAPFP.

33. Mary Seaman Kirby to Amy Post, 20 February 1838, IAPFP.

34. Isaac Post's letter has not been found, but for coverage of the event, see "Proceedings of the Anti-Slavery Convention for Western New York," *FOM*, 31 January 1838.

35. Samuel Willis and Phebe Post Willis to Edmund Willis, 12 February 1838, IAPFP. Samuel Willis was Edmund's brother. Phebe tells Edmund to thank "uncle Isaac" for his detailed account of the convention.

36. Sarah and Jeffries Hallowell to Amy and Isaac Post, 5 November 183[8?], IAPFP.

37. Jeffries Hallowell to Isaac Post, 5 November 183[8?], IAPFP.

38. On the history of pharmacy, see Higby, "Chemistry and the 19th-Century American Pharmacist"; and Stieb, "A Professional Keeping Shop."

39. On Smith Arcade, see "To Build at the Four Corners," *Democrat and Chronicle*, 10 January 1903, which recounted its history.

40. Henry Clayton to Amy Post, 22 December 1838, IAPFP; and Phebe Post Willis to Isaac and Amy Post, 14 October 1838, IAPFP. See also Mary Robbins Post to Amy Post, 3 —— [184?], IAPFP.

41. On Amy's medical skills and treatments, see, for example, Anna Greene to Mary Robbins Post, 6 April 1833, MJPFP; Amy Post to Joseph Post, 13 January 1842, MJPFP; Amy Post to Joseph Post, [1842?], IAPFP; and Cadwallader, *Memoir*, 106–7.

42. See Rochester City Directory, 1827, Map; McKelvey, *Rochester*, 75. On Silas O. Smith's financial trajectory, including the Panic of 1837, see McKelvey, *Rochester*, 43, 44, 48, 127, 209, 296.

43. Quote from *History and Commerce of Rochester, Illustrated*, 77. On development of Irving Hotel and commercial block, see "To Build at the Four Corners," *Democrat and Chronicle*, 10 January 1903; and J.K. Post Drug Co., Advertisement, *Democrat and Chronicle*, 19 September 1938, CLC, which reproduced an old ad. On early plans for business, see Isaac Post to Amy Post, 1 May 1839, IAPFP. The business changed names several times. Coleman left the business shortly after it was established, and it became Post & Willis, then Isaac Post & Co., Post and Bruff, and finally J.K. Post and Co. when son Jacob K. Post took full control of the store in the 1860s.

44. On the effects of the Panic of 1837 on local businesses, see McKelvey, *Rochester*, 213–18.

45. On the importance of the shared labors of abolitionist couples, see Sinha, *Slave's Cause*, 284–85.

46. On the Orphan Asylum Association, see Hewitt, *Women's Activism*, 88–93; and "History of the Asylum," Ms., [186?], Hillside Children's Center Papers, SpecColUR. It is not clear if many African American children were admitted to the institution; few are mentioned in the Asylum records. After 1839, Amy Post and Sarah Fish stopped donating to the Orphan Asylum Association.

47. Minutes, GYMWF, June 1836 and June 1837, HRR.

48. Minutes, June 1837, GYMWF, HRR. The proposal was initially made by Junius Monthly Meeting in 1836 and quickly approved by Farmington Quarterly Meeting so that it could be presented to that year's GYM.

49. On the relation of women's meetings to men's meetings in the Society of Friends, see Soderlund, "Women's Authority in Pennsylvania and New Jersey Quaker Meetings"; and Barbour et al., *Quaker Crosscurrents*, 165–67.

50. On GYM's decision not to act, see GYMWF, Minutes, June 1835, 1836, 1837, and 1840, HRR. On New York Yearly Meeting's decision not to alter the Discipline, see Mary Seaman Kirby and Sarah Kirby to Amy Post, 5 July 1837, IAPFP; and Phebe Post Willis to Isaac and Amy Post and Edmund Willis, 14 March 1838, IAPFP.

51. Quote from Rochester Monthly Meeting, "Marriage Intents, 1825–1850," compiled by John Cox Jr., 1911, New York Public Library, New York, N.Y.

52. GYM, *Discipline*, 11.

53. See Phebe Post Willis to Isaac and Amy Post, 25 August 1839, IAPFP. For other letters related to Cadwalader or debates among Hicksites over ministers and elders, see Phebe K. Carpenter to Amy Post, 24 June 1837; Samuel Lundy to Amy Post, 16 August 1837; Hannah C. Greene to Amy Post, 12 December 1837; Joseph Post to Isaac Post, 13 December 1837; Phebe K. Carpenter to Isaac and Amy Post, 19 December 1837; and Mary Robbins Post to Isaac and Amy Post, 9 December 1838, all in the IAPFP.

54. See Hamm, "Quakerism, Ministry, Marriage, and Divorce," 430–31, on how Cadwalader's story illuminates challenges for Friends dealing with unsuccessful marriages and women's rights.

55. For discussion of the central issues, see Barbour et al., *Quaker Crosscurrents*, 183–88.

56. GYMWF, Minutes, June 1835 and June 1838 (quote), HRR. Orthodox Friends in Rochester also affirmed an antislavery minute, published in the *Liberator*, 27 January 1837. For the importance of GYM in forging an antislavery, women's rights, and Indian rights coalition, see Wellman, "1816 Farmington Meetinghouse," 51–52, 55–57.

57. On Hicksite debates over antislavery activism, see Barbour et al., *Quaker Crosscurrents*, 183–90; Densmore, "The Dilemma of Quaker Anti-Slavery"; Hamm, "George F. White and Hicksite Opposition to the Abolitionist Movement"; and Jordan, *Slavery and the Meetinghouse*, chap. 4. For a typical example of correspondence among the Post circle, see John Ketcham to M[ary] and J[oseph] Post, 27 December 1838, MJPFP.

58. Amy Post to [Family], [1837?], IAPFP. Amy sent this letter to Rochester while visiting Long Island between fall 1836, when she moved to Rochester, and summer 1837, when she signed her first antislavery petition.

59. Anti-Slavery Petition of the Women of Rochester, New York, 19 September 1837, House of Representatives, Document HR25-H1.7. Thanks to Paul Johnson for providing me copies of several Rochester and Monroe County petitions decades ago.

60. On women's early petition campaigns, see Zaeske, *Signatures of Citizenship*, 21–27; Hershberger, "Mobilizing Women, Anticipating Abolition"; and Theodore, "'A Right to Speak on the Subject.'"

61. On Ohio women's antislavery petitions, see Robertson, *Hearts Beating for Liberty*, 32–36; and Zaeske, *Signatures of Citizenship*, 74–75. On Midwestern networks more broadly, see Miles, "'Shall Women's Voices Be Heard?'"

62. On the Anti-Slavery Convention of American Women, see Zaeske, *Signatures of Citizenship*, 85–90. Coverage of the convention appeared in the *Liberator*, 4 March and 16 June 1837. On New York State antislavery petition campaigns, see Wellman, "Women and Radical Reform in Antebellum Upstate New York."

63. See Zaeske, *Signatures of Citizenship*, especially 69–72, 74–77, 83–90, 92–99. Zaeske argues that the Anti-Slavery Convention of American Women introduced the strategy of systematic petitioning embraced by the AASS later that spring. On Porter's leadership in Rochester, see Julianna Tappan to Mrs. Samuel D. Porter, 20 May 1837, Samuel D. and Susan F. Porter Family Papers, SpecColUR. (Hereafter Porter Family Papers.)

64. Sophia E Child to Sarah D. Fish, 14 May 1835, Benjamin Fish Family Papers, SpecColUR. Sophia E. Child was the daughter of city founder Nathaniel Rochester and the wife of political leader Jonathan Child. Jonathan Child submitted the 1837 women's petition to Congress.

65. *Daily Democrat*, 24 September 1835. The establishment of the RFASS was announced on the same page of the paper. See also *Daily Democrat*, 26 September 1835, for the resolutions of the anti–immediate emancipation meeting.

66. "Anti-Slavery Societies," *Liberator*, 23 June 1837. The Rochester [Men's] Anti-Slavery Society was listed as having seven hundred members, making it the second largest chapter in the country. In the 1810s, Silas Cornell and Lindley M. Moore had worked alongside Willet Robbins, Amy Post's uncle, in the New York Manumission Society.

67. The Anti-Slavery Petition of the Women of Rochester, New York, 19 September 1837, cited in note 59 includes signers from the Frost, Frink, and Underhill families, all common Hicksite names in western and central New York. Orthodox Friends Sarah Cornell and her daughter and Abigail Moore and her daughters also signed the September 1837 petition and were not disowned.

68. On Lucretia Mott's antislavery activism and its effect on her relations with the Society of Friends, see Faulkner, *Lucretia Mott's Heresy*, chaps. 4 and 5.

69. On the Grimké sisters' antislavery activities and relationships with the Philadelphia Orthodox Friends meeting, see Dorsey, *Reforming Men and Women*, 172–82.

70. Mary Robbins Post to Amy and Isaac Post, 13 December 1837, IAPFP, in which she quotes Phebe Post Willis. See also Lucretia Mott to Phebe Post Willis, 2 September 1835, Phebe Post Willis Papers, SpecColUR; and Mary Robbins Post to Isaac and Amy Post, 15 December 1837, IAPFP.

71. On the Cherry Street Meeting response to Mott's activism, see Faulkner, *Lucretia Mott's Heresy*, 120, 133.

72. Mary Robbins Post to Isaac and Amy Post, 13 December 1837, IAPFP.

73. "Proceedings of the Anti-Slavery Convention for Western New York," *FOM*, 31 January 1838, CLC, which met 10–12 January. Information in this paragraph and the next are from the *FOM* report.

74. Judith Wellman, "1816 Farmington Hicksite Meetinghouse," 53–54.

75. List of delegates, "Proceedings of the Anti-Slavery Convention for Western New York," *FOM*, 31 January 1838, CLC. The only other female delegate on the list was Martha Mann, from Lockport, who attended with her husband Joseph Mann.

76. Ibid.

77. On small abolition meetings, see Harper, *Life and Work of Susan B. Anthony*, 1:48. See also Isaac Post to Amy Post, 1 May 1839, IAPFP. Isaac attended the May 1839 AASS convention in New York City. See "Proceedings of the American Anti-Slavery Society Anniversary Meeting," *Liberator*, 24 May 1839. Isaac Post's signature appears on an anti–gag rule petition: Anti-Slavery Petition from Monroe County, New York, 22 December 1838, House of Representatives, Document HR25A-H1.7. This all-male petition was circulated at an antislavery meeting in Rochester that attracted a few Quakers and many evangelical Protestants if the signatories reflect the audience.

78. Mary Robbins Post to Isaac and Amy Post, 9 December 1838, IAPFP. Many Friends considered paid lecturers the equivalent of "hireling" ministers and thus opposed fund-raising for such a purpose. On the difficulties of organizing a Friends antislavery society on Long Island, see also [John Ketcham?] to [Joseph] and Mary Robbins Post, 27 December 1838, MJPFP.

79. "American Anti-Slavery Convention," *FOM*, 29 May 1839, CLC.

80. Mary Robbins Post to Isaac and Amy Post, 26 October 1839, IAPFP; and John Willis to Amy Post, 26 November 1839, IAPFP. See corroboration of Mary Robbins Post's view in Lucretia Mott to Phebe Post Willis, 25 April 1840, IAPFP, although Mott wrote in a gentler tone. Mott's letter is in the IAPFP, suggesting that Phebe Post Willis sent it to Rochester.

81. John Ketcham to Isaac and Amy Post, 11 March 1841, IAPFP.

82. Some Jericho and Westbury Friends did join the Long Island Anti-Slavery Society, though it was far smaller than Rochester societies. See Haynes, "Quaker Conflict over Abolition Activism." The society had about fifty members, including Isaac's siblings—Lydia Post Rushmore, Phebe Post Willis, and Joseph Post—and their spouses, as well as Amy's cousins John and Rebecca Ketcham.

83. On Weld's visits, see Johnson, *Shopkeepers' Millennium*, 113–14; McKelvey, *Rochester*, 285; and quote from Mary S. Mathews to Mrs. Charles Finney, 22 June 1836, Charles Grandison Finney Papers, Microfilm, Roll 3.

84. On the efforts of evangelical clergy to limit women's antislavery efforts, see Hewitt, *Women's Activism*, 85–88, 103–7.

85. John Ketcham to Isaac and Amy Post, 11 March 1841, IAPFP.

86. See Barbour et al., *Quaker Crosscurrents*, 186–87, on the Isaac Hopper case. See also "The Society of Friends—Developments," *NASS*, 26 August 1841.

87. Testimonial is reprinted in "The Society of Friends—Developments," *NASS*, 26 August 1841.

88. Traveling ministers and outspoken members of New York Yearly Meeting kept these disputes vibrant and public. See Mary Robbins Post to Isaac and Amy Post, 26 October 1840 and 23 November 1841; John Willis to Amy Post, 26 November 1840;

Sarah Hallowell to Amy Post, 24 January 1841; and John Ketcham to Isaac and Amy Post, 11 March 1841 and 17 [May?] 1841, all in the IAPFP.

89. H. C. Wright to "My Brother," [William Lloyd Garrison], *Liberator*, 10 April 1840, italics in original. On the state society's approval for WNYASS, see "Convention at Waterloo," *FOM*, 25 February 1840, CLC. On LeRoy Anti-Slavery Convention, see James C. Jackson, "Letter," *Liberator*, 29 January 1841; "Address of the Western New York Anti-Slavery Convention," *Liberator*, 5 February 1841; and "The LeRoy Convention," *NASS*, 21 January 1841. Charles Lenhart has traced the complex history of the WNYASS and compiled minutes for meetings through the 1840s, CLC. A Central New York Anti-Slavery Society was founded in November 1842, whose members had strong ties of kinship and friendships networks with the WNYASS.

90. James C. Jackson, "Letter," *Liberator*, 29 January 1841; and "Address of the Western New York Anti-Slavery Convention," *Liberator*, 5 February 1841. Isaac Post attended the convention and probably Amy as well. The official roll of the convention, published in *NASS*, 21 January 1841, was taken before most of the Rochester contingent arrived. During the convention, several Rochesterians not on that list, including Isaac Post, were appointed to major committees.

91. On the rise of the Liberty League and Liberty Party, see Johnson, *Liberty Party*; and Brooks, *Liberty Power*.

92. On debates over party politics versus moral suasion, see "The LeRoy Convention," *NASS*, 21 January 1841, especially resolution 14. See also McKivigan, *War Against Pro-Slavery Religion*, chaps. 3, 4, 8; Pierson, *Free Hearts and Free Homes*, chap. 2; Jordan, *Slavery and the Meetinghouse*, chap. 2; and Robertson, *Hearts Beating for Liberty*, chap. 3. On ministerial critiques of women's antislavery activism in Rochester, see Hewitt, *Women's Activism*, 85–88, 103–7.

93. On the 1840 AASS split, see McKivigan, *War Against Pro-Slavery Religion*, 61–64; Jeffrey, *Great Silent Army of Abolitionism*, 96–100; and Fought, *Women in the World of Frederick Douglass*, 71.

94. "The LeRoy Convention," *NASS*, 21 January 1841, resolution 14, CLC.

95. Amy Post to Joseph Post, 13 January 1842, MJPFP. All quotes in this paragraph are from this letter.

96. Ibid.

97. When Henry Brewster Stanton and his wife, Elizabeth Cady Stanton, moved to Seneca Falls, New York, in 1847, they also promoted the idea of a third way. Email from Judith Wellman, to author, 4 February 2017.

98. Amy Post to Joseph Post, 13 January 1842, MJPFP. Emphasis in original.

99. On early female antislavery fairs and societies, see "The Ladies' Fair," *FOM*, 19 January 1837; "Anti-Slavery Fair," *FOM*, 31 January 1838; "Ladies' Society in Palmyra," *FOM*, 28 February 1838; "Farmington Union Anti-Slavery Society," *FOM*, 23 April 1838, CLC; and "Announcements," *NASS*, 26 September and 14 November 1838, CLC. On dissolution of the Rochester Female Anti-Slavery Society, see Hewitt, *Women's Activism*, 104–5.

100. "American Anti-Slavery Society," *FOM*, 29 May 1839, CLC. A majority of New York State delegates opposed the measure, including James G. Birney, O. N. Bush, and Lewis Tappan. All three men left the AASS in 1840 when Abby Kelley was elected to the business committee.

101. Ibid.; and editorial, *Daily Advertiser*, 15 June 1840.

102. "Anti-Slavery Petition from the Men and Women of Monroe County, NY," 1 April 1842, House of Representatives Document HR27A-H1.7, National Archives, Washington, D.C. Thirty-five women signers have been identified as Quakers, but it is likely that some unidentified signers were also Quakers. Amy Post circulated a temperance petition in June 1842, but perhaps only among Friends. See "Petitions and Claims," *Daily Democrat*, 16 June 1842, CLC.

Chapter Four

1. Abby Kelley to Maria Weston Chapman, 13 August 1843, AKFP; and Trustees Book, 24 August 1842, Third Presbyterian Church, Rochester, N.Y., Presbyterian Historical Society, Philadelphia, Pa. See also Wellman, *Road to Seneca Falls*, 111–13.

2. Erasmus Darwin Hudson, Journal, 26 August 1842, cited in McFeeley, *Frederick Douglass*, 99. African Bethel Church was also involved in antislavery work but was smaller than the AME Zion Church. An elderly Maria G. Porter recalls Amy and Isaac Post attending the Bethel Church speech. See "Frederick Douglass in Rochester," *Rome Daily Sentinel*, 22 November 1894, CLC.

3. Although Amy Post did serve on WNYASS committees in the early 1840s, Isaac Post was chosen for more prestigious positions, such as the WNYASS Executive Board.

4. On Thomas James and Frederick Douglass, see McFeeley, *Frederick Douglass*, 82; on Douglass staying with the Posts, 99.

5. On James and Douglass in New Bedford and Douglass in Lynn, Nantucket, and on tour with Kelley, see McFeely, *Frederick Douglass*, 82–83, 86–88, 91–99; and Fought, *Women in the World of Frederick Douglass*, 76–79.

6. On the May 1840 antislavery division, see Kraditor, *Means and Ends in American Abolitionism*, chap, 3; Sterling, *Ahead of Her Time*, chap. 6; Jeffrey, *Great Silent Army of Abolitionism*, 96–98; and McKivigan, *The War Against Pro-Slavery Religion*, chap. 3.

7. Abby Kelley to Uxbridge Monthly Meeting of Friends, 22 March 1841, copy enclosed in Abby Kelley to William Lloyd Garrison, 30 September 1841, William Lloyd Garrison Papers, Boston Public Library, Boston, Mass. See also Melder, "Abby Kelley Foster."

8. See Abby Kelley, "Letter," *Liberator*, 20 September 1841.

9. On Abby Kelley as role model, see Elizabeth I. Neall to Abby Kelley, 12 March 1843, AKFP. On hostility, see Wellman, *Road to Seneca Falls*, 112–13; and Sterling, *Ahead of Her Time*, chap. 7 and 137, 141, 153, 155–57.

10. Oliver Johnson to Isaac Post, 7 June 1842, IAPFP.

11. Samuel D. Porter to Abby Kelley, 16 September 1842, AKFP.

12. On Bethel Free Church, renamed the Washington Street Presbyterian Church in 1845, see Samuel Porter to Pastor, Washington Street Presbyterian Church, 29 September 1845, Porter Family Papers, SpecColUR.

13. On the reorganization of the WNYASS, see "American Anti-Slavery Society," *Liberator*, 5 January 1843. This article suggests that the WNYASS was a newly formed society, but it was founded in LeRoy in 1841. On Kelley staying with the Posts, see Sterling, *Ahead of Her Time*, 164–65.

14. "American Anti-Slavery Society," *Liberator*, 5 January 1843. The list of officers was checked against the Rochester City Directory, 1843.

15. Ibid.

16. Second (Brick) Presbyterian Church, Session Minutes, 31 October 1842, Presbyterian Historical Society, Philadelphia, Pa. The women and men who were excommunicated from or left Brick Presbyterian Church and allied with the Posts did not join Bethel Free Church or another antislavery congregation.

17. Sarah Burtis to Abby Kelley, 17 January 1843, AKFP. Burtis claimed that Porter explained her lack of participation by noting her involvement in recruiting a minister for her church.

18. See William Channing Gannett, Speech for the Fiftieth Anniversary of the Rochester Woman's Rights Convention, 1898, Unitarian Society of Rochester Records, SpecColUR.

19. "American Anti-Slavery Society," *Liberator*, 5 January 1843.

20. Ibid. On the importance of antislavery fairs in forging what John Brooke calls "northern nationalism," see Brooke, "Cultures of Nationalism, Movements of Reform," 29–30.

21. Elizabeth M'Clintock to Abby Kelley, 10 January 1843, AKFP. The next year, the women held their fair on the same date. See "Anti-Slavery Fair," *Rochester Republican*, 19 February 1844, CLC.

22. "Western New York Anti-Slavery Fair," *NASS*, 2 February 1843; and "Western New York Anti-Slavery Fair," *Rochester Republican*, 13 February 1843, CLC. The latter article listed the names of the fair committee, which included Amy Post's stepdaughter Mary and sister Sarah, as well as central New York F/riends Ann and Mary Bunker and Ann Pound.

23. Sarah and Lewis Burtis to Abby Kelley, 17 January 1843, AKFP. On Post's nursing efforts, see Amy Post to Mary and Joseph Post, [December 1842?], IAPFP.

24. Sarah Burtis to Abby Kelley, 17 January 1843, AKFP.

25. For further discussion of black women's interactions with white abolitionists, see chap. 5.

26. "Western New York Anti-Slavery Fair," *NASS*, 2 February 1843; and *Rochester Republican*, 13 February 1843.

27. Sarah Burtis to Abby Kelley, 17 January 1843, AKFP. The only coworker Burtis names specifically, and more than once, is Amy Post.

28. Joseph C. Hathaway, quoted in Wellman, *Road to Seneca Falls*, 115.

29. E. I. Neall to Abby Kelley, 12 March 1843, AKFP; "Our Cause in Western New York," *Liberator*, 24 March 1843. See also "First Annual Report of the Executive Committee," *Daily Democrat*, 28 March 1843.

30. "Anti-Slavery Convention," *Daily Democrat*, 24 July 1843. On the 3–5 August meeting, see "Anti-Slavery Convention," *Daily Democrat*, 25 August 1843, CLC; and *Liberator*, 25 August 1843. On the Buffalo convention, see McFeely, *Frederick Douglass*, 105–6.

31. Wellman, "Land and Identity," 12.

32. See Spence, "Women at the Crossroads"; Hauptman, *Conspiracy of Interests*; and Resnick-Day, "Debating the 'Inevitable,'" chaps. 4 and 5; Spence is especially attentive to the ways religious affiliation and gender played out across these multi-decade negotiations.

33. See *Case of the Seneca Indians*. Sixty-two of the documents published were produced by the Seneca. See also Wellman, "1816 Farmington Meetinghouse," 58–62.

34. See Hauptman, *Conspiracy of Interests*; and Resnick-Day, "Debating the 'Inevitable,'" chaps. 4 and 5.

35. Statement of special meeting of GYM Friends, Farmington, N.Y., [13?] March 1842, quoted in Wellman, "Land and Identity," 22.

36. Minerva Blacksmith et al., Petition to President John Tyler, 14 March 1842, IAPFP.

37. On Isaac Post's role, see "Council with the Nations," *Troy Daily Whig*, 21 May 1842, CLC. On overall agreement, see Wellman, "Land and Identity," 23–24.

38. Sarah Kirby to Dear Sister inserted at end of letter from Mary Seaman Kirby to Amy Post, 20 February 1838, IAPFP. The fifteen letters that comprise Sarah Grimké's *Letters on the Equality of the Sexes* appeared in the *Liberator*, July to October 1837, and were published in book form in 1838.

39. See, for example, Lucretia Mott to Elizabeth Cady Stanton, 16 March 1855, in Palmer, *Selected Letters*, 234; and Bartlett, *Sarah Grimké, Letters*, 4.

40. Quoted in Faulkner, *Lucretia Mott's Heresy*, 72.

41. Jeremiah Burke Sanderson to Amy Post, 8 May 1845, IAPFP. Sanderson is described as "slightly colored" in Washington, *Sojourner Truth's America*, 173, where the author notes his failure to mention Truth's presence.

42. Members of Sodus Phalanx, 1844–1866, Benjamin Fish Family Papers, Spec-ColUR.; quote from Benjamin Fish to Isaac Post, [184?], IAPFP. See also Wellman and Perez et al., "Sodus Bay Phalanx"; Noyes, *History of American Socialism*, chap. 24, claims Sodus Bay Phalanx was plagued by problems and faltered in the late 1840s.

43. Samuel D. Porter to Gerrit Smith, 14 March 1845, Gerrit Smith Papers, Syracuse University Library, Syracuse, N.Y. The sentiments expressed here suggest why he remained active in the WNYASS through 1846, despite substantial opposition in the group to third-party politics.

44. On church-based efforts to expand abolitionist sentiment, see McKivigan, *The War Against Pro-Slavery Religion*. The New York State Constitutional Convention of 1821 granted suffrage to all white men without property qualifications but allowed black men to vote only if they owned $250 worth of property. Property restrictions remained in effect until ratification of the Fifteenth Amendment to the U.S. Constitution in 1870.

45. Isaac Post to Amy Post, 5 May 1844, IAPFP. See also Sarah D. Fish, "Party Spirit," *Liberator*, 9 February 1844. William Hallowell eventually embraced third-party politics as an alternative route to abolition.

46. Giles B. Stebbins to William Lloyd Garrison, *Liberator*, 7 March 1845.

47. Lucy N. Colman, *Reminiscences*, 84. Two overseers were appointed by monthly meetings for each preparative meeting. They could investigate behavior they considered suspect, but no report was made unless the preparative or monthly meetings pursued further investigations. Amy Post notes a visit from overseers in a letter to Abby Kelley, 4 December 1843, AKFP, but no further investigation occurred.

48. Amy Post to Abby Kelley, 4 December 1843, AKFP.

49. Diary, 21 July 1844, Box 3, JWP. Amy Post likely attended Mott's speech or certainly heard of its substance from F/friends and family members.

50. See, for example, William Wells Brown to Amy Post, 23 June 1844 and 3 September 1844, IAPFP; and Abby Kelley to Amy Post, 16 July 1844, IAPFP.

51. Mary Seaman Kirby to Isaac and Amy Post, 9 January 1845, IAPFP.

52. Eliab W. Capron (E.W.C.), "Letter," *Liberator*, 15 March 1844, criticized Farmington Monthly (Hicksite) Meeting's failure to support antislavery, temperance, and other reforms.

53. Amy Post to Joseph Post, 13 January 1842, MJPFP. Friends did not disown members for bankruptcy, but they expected business owners to deal with customers and creditors fairly and avoid injuring others as a result of their financial dealings.

54. On Isaac's business dealings, see Henry Clayton to Amy Post, 21 October 1838, IAPFP; and Sarah and Jeffries Hallowell to Amy and Isaac Post, 5 November [1838?], IAPFP.

55. New York/Rochester, vol. 162, p. 127, September 1843, R. G. Dun & Company Credit Report Volumes, Baker Library, Harvard Business School, Cambridge, Mass. R. G. Dun and Co. was founded in 1841 by Lewis Tappan as the Mercantile Agency in New York City. It used local correspondents to report on businesses and their owners in their area. The company later became Dun and Bradstreet.

56. An obituary of Hallowell appeared in *NASS*, 1 August 1844.

57. On fire, see *Rochester Republican*, 18 April 1843, CLC. On Jeffries Hallowell's debts, see Joseph Post to Isaac Post, 16 November 1844, IAPFP. Joseph was responding to a letter from Isaac requesting information. On Hallowell's death, see also Mary W. Willis to Amy Post and Sarah Hallowell, 14 November 1844, IAPFP.

58. New York/Rochester, vol. 162, p. 127, October 1844, R. G. Dun & Company Credit Report Volumes, Baker Library, Harvard Business School, Cambridge, Mass.

59. Nathaniel Potter to Amy Post, 19 November 1844, IAPFP.

60. "Died," *NASS*, 20 February 1845, CLC.

61. Mary Seaman Kirby to Amy Post, 9 January 1845, IAPFP.

62. Amy Post to Joseph Post, 11 April 1845, IAPFP. On *The Anti-Slavery Pick-nick* (or *Pic-Nic*), see Resolutions 10 and 11, "Monroe County Anti-Slavery Convention," *NASS*, 22 September 1842, CLC.

63. Mary W. Willis to Amy Post, 1 April 1845, IAPFP; and Sarah Thayer to Amy Post, 1 December 1844, IAPFP. Willis notes that mother Mary Kirby agreed to have daughter Sarah stay with the Posts.

64. Phebe Post Willis to Isaac Post, 7 March 1845, IAPFP. Willis mentions Amy's concerns about party spirit.

65. Minutes, May 1845, Rochester Monthly Meeting, HRR. The Posts asked to be released. Their request was granted, although Isaac was still being appointed to committees that spring.

66. Mary W. Willis to Amy Post, 1 April 1845 and 1 May [184?], IAPFP. The May letter was likely written in 1845.

67. Nathaniel Potter to Isaac Post, 9 May, 10 July, and 18 September 1845, IAPFP.

68. For a detailed description of free meetings, see the *Circumstance*, 20 December 1845, edited by Eliab W. Capron, CLC. See also Joseph Post to Edmund and Julia Willis, 17 September 1845, IAPFP. Edmund Willis had married Julia Lawton of Jericho earlier that year.

69. The letter was sent to Green Plain (Ohio) Quarterly Meeting and published in *NASS*, 21 August 1845. Most of the 107 signers were GYM members. The dozen or so non-GYM signers included Amy and Isaac Post, his brother Joseph Post, and Maria E. Wilbur, an Orthodox Friend active with her husband Esek, a Hicksite, in the WNYASS. On continuing conflict in GYM, see Wellman, "1816 Farmington Meetinghouse," 87–88.

70. Sarah Hurn to Amy Post, 11 October 1846, IAPFP; and Sarah C. Owen to Amy Post, 31 July [185?], IAPFP. By 1850, Sarah Owen had moved to central Michigan.

71. For proceedings, see "Annual Meeting of the Western New York Anti-Slavery Society," *NASS*, 6 March 1845; and "An Address," *Liberator*, 28 February 1845.

72. Rhoda De Garmo to Maria W. Chapman, 26 January 1845, quoted in Jeffrey, *Great Silent Army of Abolitionism*, 99.

73. William Wells Brown to Amy Post, 23 June and 3 September 1844, IAPFP. On Brown's early work as an antislavery lecturer, see Greenspan, *William Wells Brown*, 129–34.

74. On the Underground Railroad in Rochester and vicinity, see Coles, *Cradle of Freedom*, 97–98, 133–40, 151–61; Frazier, *Old Ship of Zion*, 376–83; Dorn, "A History of the Antislavery Movement in Rochester and Vicinity"; and Switala, *Underground Railroad in New York and New Jersey*, 115–16. George Avery was married to Henry B. Stanton's sister, providing familial and activist connections for Elizabeth Cady Stanton when she and Henry moved to Seneca Falls in 1847.

75. Ibid. See also Judith Wellman, Historical Context Statement for sites related to the Underground Railroad, Niagara County, N.Y., accessed 7 February 2017, http://niagarafallsundergroundrailroad.org/history-and-documents/historical -resources-survey/#; and Advertisements of Lake Ontario Steamboats, including the *Ontario* under Captain Throop, 1849, CLC. On extension of the railroad, see "Important Event," *Madison County Abolitionist*, 16 November 1841, and "Governor's Message," *Madison and Onondaga County Abolitionist*, 11 January 1842, CLC.

76. John S. Jacobs, a fugitive from North Carolina, lectured in Rochester and lived there in 1848–49, while his sister, Harriet Jacobs, who escaped separately, lived with the Posts in 1849–50. See chap. 6.

77. Diary, 23 and 24 July 1845, Box 3, JWP.

78. Isaac and Mary Gibbs invitation to the Posts, n.d., IAPFP.

79. Mary Seaman Kirby to Amy Post and Sarah Hallowell, 28 December 1845, IAPFP.

80. Isaac Post to Phebe Post Willis, 15 December 1845, IAPFP, describes their visit and journey home. George F. White considered himself "consistently antislavery" yet voiced animosity toward Quaker abolitionist and temperance advocates. It was criticisms of White in the *NASS* that led to Isaac Hopper's disownment in 1841.

81. Isaac Post to [Phebe Post Willis?], 15 [December?] 1845, IAPFP; and Mary Seaman Kirby to Amy Post and Sarah Hallowell, 28 December 1845, IAPFP.

82. "Second Annual Meeting of the Western New York Anti-Slavery Society," *NASS*, 22 January 1846, CLC.

83. Mary Seaman Kirby to Amy and Isaac Post, 5 January 1846, IAPFP. Like many of her letters, Kirby began this one on 28 December 1845, but completed it on 5 January 1846.

84. Mary W. Willis to Amy and Isaac Post, 3 February 1846, IAPFP.

85. Frederick Douglass to Amy Post, 28 April 1846, IAPFP.

86. Ibid.

87. "American Anti-Slavery Society Annual Meeting," *Liberator*, 22 May 1846.

88. Joseph and Mary Robbins Post to Isaac and Amy Post, 29 May 1846, IAPFP, describing discussions at the AASS convention.

89. For an insightful discussion of these concerns, see Isenberg, *Sex and Citizenship*, 135–47.

90. *Pennsylvania Freeman*, 25 June 1846 and 23 September 1847, and *Anti-Slavery Bugle*, 17 September 1847, quoted in Isenberg, *Sex and Citizenship in Antebellum America*, 139–40.

91. See, for instance, Joseph and Mary Robbins Post to Isaac and Amy Post, 29 May 1846, IAPFP; Mary Robbins Post to Post Family, [May?] 1847, IAPFP; and Nathaniel Potter to Isaac and Amy Post, 26 September 1847, IAPFP.

92. Lucretia Mott to Richard Allen, 25 June 1842, in Palmer, *Selected Letters*, 119–20.

93. John W. Hurn to Amy Post, 11 October 1846, IAPFP.

94. "Third Annual Western New York Anti-Slavery Society Meeting," *Liberator*, 24 July 1846.

95. Journal Briefs, 29 May 1846, Box 1, JWP.

96. Sarah Hallowell to Amy Post, 12 September 1846, IAPFP.

97. Samuel J. May to Isaac Post, 29 December 1846, IAPFP, notes donation of fifty copies of his sermon to that year's fair. See also "The Rochester Anti-Slavery Fair," *North Star*, 3 December 1847 and 29 January 1848. For pamphlet, see Samuel J. May, *The Rights and Condition of Women*, 1–2. The 1847 WNYASS fair sold the 1846 edition.

98. Joseph and Mary Robbins Post to Amy and Isaac Post, 9 February 1847, IAPFP. An earlier letter from Amy Post, which has not been located, is quoted in this letter. Kelley married abolitionist Stephen Foster in December 1845.

99. Giles Stebbins, "Report on Western New York Anti-Slavery Society," *NASS*, 28 January 1847.

100. Joseph and Mary Robbins Post to Amy and Isaac Post, 9 February 1847, IAPFP. Joseph and Mary Robbins Post also discussed the debate over purchasing Douglass's freedom.

101. Mary [Ann M'Clintock] to Amy Post, 9 February 1847, IAPFP. Julia Lawton Willis died on 11 February 1847.

102. See Mary Seaman Kirby to Amy and Isaac Post and Sarah Hallowell, 14 March 1847, IAPFP. Kirby notes that Amy "concealed her troubles to so late a period." Mary W. Willis to Amy Post, 21 March 1847, IAPFP, laments that she heard no news from Amy until Edmund Willis delivered a letter in mid-March.

103. Mary Seaman Kirby to Amy and Isaac Post and Sarah Hallowell, 14 March 1847, IAPFP; and Mary W. Willis to Amy Post, 21 March 1847, IAPFP. Mary W. Willis identifies Julia Willis's illness as measles. Kirby's letter, written on 14 March, would have arrived in Rochester after Willet's birth. Mount Hope was the nation's first municipal "rural" cemetery, laid out in 1838 on fifty acres along Rochester's southern boundary. See McKelvey, *Rochester*, 244, 249, 355. Mount Hope allowed large ornamental monuments, which were opposed by Friends.

104. On minor disputes, see [Joseph Post?] to Amy and Isaac Post, 9 February 1847, IAPFP; and Mary Robbins Post to Amy and Isaac Post, 1 May [1847?], IAPFP. On major disputes, see Barbour et al., *Quaker Crosscurrents*, 134–35.

105. There was disagreement among abolitionists over whether buying fugitive slaves from their former owners was tantamount to trafficking with slaveholders. Lucretia Mott was strongly opposed to the practice. See Faulkner, *Lucretia Mott's Heresy*, 115–16. However, Amy and Isaac Post were pleased that their friend was beyond his master's reach.

106. New York/Rochester, vol. 162, p. 127, 1 February and 12 August 1847, R. G. Dun & Company Credit Report Volumes, Baker Library, Harvard Business School, Cambridge, Mass.

107. Mary Robbins Post to Isaac and Amy Post, _ May 1847, IAPFP.

108. Eliza Whigham to Maria Weston Chapman, 2 April 1847, quoted in McFeely, *Frederick Douglass*, 148.

109. McFeeley, *Frederick Douglass*, details the struggle over Douglass's decision, 146–49.

110. Quotes from Joseph and Mary Robbins Post to Amy and Isaac Post, 5 August 1847, IAPFP. This letter was a continuation of a letter from Joseph Post to Amy and Isaac Post, 1 August 1847, IAPFP.

111. William Lloyd Garrison to Helen Benson Garrison, 20 October 1847, *The Letters of William Lloyd Garrison*, 3:532. On Douglass and Remond in Rochester, see Diaries, 18 and 19 September 1847, Box 3, JWP.

112. William Lloyd Garrison to Helen Benson Garrison, 20 October 1847, *Letters of William Lloyd Garrison*, 3:152. See McFeely, *Frederick Douglass*, 147–51, for a detailed discussion of this crisis.

113. Frederick Douglass to Sydney H. Gay, 26 September 1847, in McKivigan et al., *Frederick Douglass Papers*, 252–53.

114. Frederick Douglass to Amy Post, 29 September 1847, IAPFP.

115. Frederick Douglass to Amy Post, 28 October 1847, IAPFP; and Frederick Douglass to Isaac Post, 3 February 1848, on moving his family to Rochester, Phebe Post Willis Papers, SpecColUR.

Chapter Five

1. North Star Mail Book, 1849–1851, Frederick Douglass Papers, Beinecke Library, Yale University Manuscripts and Archives, New Haven, Conn.; and McFeely, *Frederick Douglass*, 151–53. On responses of black editors and activists, see McKivigan et al., *Frederick Douglass Papers*, 281–89, 295–96.

2. "The Rochester Anti-Slavery Fair," *North Star*, 3 December 1847. The fair committee included women from Rochester, Farmington, and Waterloo and was composed of Hicksite and Orthodox Friends, ex-Friends like Post, and a few ex-evangelicals.

3. "Anti-Slavery Fair," *North Star*, 7 January 1848. The article is signed W.C.N. (William Cooper Nell).

4. New York/Rochester, vol. 162, p. 127, 19 April 1848, R. G. Dun & Company Credit Report Volumes, Baker Library, Harvard Business School, Cambridge, Mass. See also advertisements for Post and Willis Drugs, Rochester *Daily Advertiser*, 14 October 1846, and Rochester City Directory, 1851, CLC.

5. Letters between Isaac and Amy Post and Amy Post and William Nell, cited below, demonstrate that Birney and Dale were more than servants.

6. This motto appears on the *North Star* masthead from the first issue in December 1847.

7. McFeeley, *Frederick Douglass*, 151–52.

8. Ibid., 152.

9. Biographical details of Nell's life are from Wesley and Uzelac, *William Cooper Nell*, 6–12.

10. Wesley and Uzelac, *William Cooper Nell*, 6–12. See also McFeeley, *Frederick Douglass*, 92, 150, 152. While Nell worked with Douglass, he remained close with Garrison and moved back to Boston in 1849.

11. See Fought, *Women in the World of Frederick Douglass*, chap. 2, on the effects on Anna Douglass of the family's moves and Douglass's rising career as an abolitionist.

12. "Colored Newspapers" appeared in *North Star*, 7 January 1848, and "Colored Churches," 25 February 1848. For reactions to these editorials, see William Whipper to Frederick Douglass and Martin R. Delany, 23 January 1848, and Leonard Collins to Frederick Douglass, 3 March 1848, in McKivigan et al., *Frederick Douglass Papers*, 283–85, 298–300. On lack of black support, see David Ruggles to Frederick Douglass and Martin R. Delaney, 1 January 1848, and Horatio W. Foster to Frederick Douglass and Martin R. Delaney, 18 February 1848, same volume, 281–82, 294.

13. "Colored Churches," *North Star*, 24 March 1848.

14. See "First of August," *North Star*, 21 July 1848 and "Announcement," 5 December 1850. The Union Anti-Slavery Society was likely a continuation of the black women's antislavery group noted in the *Liberator*, "Announcements," 30 December 1833 and 8 March 1834.

15. On interracial dinners and joint fund-raising efforts, see chap. 6.

16. Occupations of local African American abolitionists is based on Rochester City Directories, 1845, 1847, and 1849. The distinction between black men's and women's representation at WNYASS meetings and events is documented through names published in the *North Star* and other antislavery newspapers.

17. Nell wrote Amy Post regularly after returning to Boston, describing his bond with Post and her circle and recalling lengthy conversations at Sophia Street. See, for example, William Nell to Amy and Isaac Post, 30 June 1849, IAPFP; and William Nell to Amy Post, 11 August 1849, IAPFP. None of Post's letters to Nell have been found.

18. See, for example, Frederick Douglass to Amy Post, 28 April 1846, IAPFP; the Nell letters cited in note 17 and dozens of others in the IAPFP; William Wells Brown to Amy Post, 16 July 1848, IAPFP; Amy and Isaac Post to Wendell Phillips, 20 June 1850, Anti-Slavery Collection, Boston Public Library, Boston, Mass.; Harriet Jacobs to Amy Post, [7–21?] May 1849, 12 February 1852, 14 February 1853, and a dozen more in the IAPFP; and letters written for Sojourner Truth to Amy Post, especially 1865 to 1869. Biographers have noted these friendships with Post. See McFeeley, *Frederick Douglass*, 99; Fought, *Women in the World of Frederick Douglass*, chaps. 4 and 5; Wesley and Uzelac, *William Cooper Nell*, 22–23; Yellin, *Harriet Jacobs*, 101–2, 118–24; and Washington, *Sojourner Truth's America*, 214–17.

19. No correspondence exists between Amy Post and local black women. Their interactions would likely have occurred informally at lectures, fairs, and conventions. Post periodically worked alongside black women in Rochester, but there are no references to Mary Gibbs, Eliza Johnson, or other local black female activists in

her sixty extant letters, in WNYASS materials, or in the numerous fair reports other than 1851 (see chap. 6).

20. On Cleggetts and Posts, see Mary Robbins Post to Amy Post, [1849?], IAPFP; and William Nell to Amy Post, 5 December 1850, 15 January 1851, and 9 October 1852, IAPFP. Frances Nell worked as a domestic (Rochester City Directory, 1849) before marrying Cleggett.

21. Between 1840 and 1850, the miles of railroad track increased across New York State from 453 to 1,409. See Switala, *Underground Railroad in New York and New Jersey*, 85; and "Important Event," *Madison County Abolitionist*, 16 November 1841, CLC. On transportation improvements in the 1840s, see McKelvey, *Rochester*, 221–28.

22. Diary, 26 March 1848, Box 3, JWP. Jonathan Walker had been imprisoned in Florida for helping enslaved workers escape, and "SS" was branded on his hand for "slave stealer."

23. "Address of the Executive Committee of Western New York Anti-Slavery Society to the Abolitionists of Western New York," *North Star*, 25 February 1848. On the sale of goods, see advertisement for the reading room in *North Star*, 12 April 1848.

24. The *North Star* noted the various managers of the reading room in its announcements. On Harriet Jacobs, see *North Star*, 23 March 1849.

25. Isaac and Mary Gibbs, Invitation to their home, n.d., IAPFP. Douglass held numerous interracial events at his home, some of which likely included the Gibbs, J. P. Morris, and the Posts.

26. "Fourth Annual Meeting of the Western N.Y. Anti-Slavery Society," *North Star*, 7 January 1848. See also, "Fourth Annual Meeting of the Western New York Anti-Slavery Society," *NASS*, 27 January 1848.

The identities and marital status of WNYASS officers were determined by matching names through city directories, census data, and church membership lists for cities and towns represented in the society.

27. Editorial, *North Star*, 28 April 1848. See also *North Star*, Foreign News, 4 February 1848 and following weeks. Douglass published dozens of articles on developments in Europe during 1848–49.

28. "Sympathy Demonstration," *North Star*, 5 May 1848; on members of the Committee of Arrangements, see "French Sympathy Meeting," *North Star*, 12 May 1848.

29. "French Sympathy Meeting," *North Star*, 12 May 1848. The Treaty of Guadalupe-Hidalgo ending the war with Mexico was approved by the U.S. Senate in March 1848. It was assailed by abolitionists and Whigs as a land grab, while proslavery advocates and many Democrats criticized it for limiting the territory gained. See Foos, *A Short, Offhand Killing Affair*, 8, 151, 153–54.

30. "Aid from England," *North Star*, 9 June 1848.

31. Ibid.

32. On conflicts at Farmington Hicksite Meetinghouse over antislavery lectures, see Wellman, "1816 Farmington Meetinghouse," 84–85, 87–89. The local Orthodox meetinghouse remained open to antislavery speakers.

33. Minutes, GYM, June 1848; Minutes, GYMWF, June 1848; Minutes, GYM Men's Meeting, June 1848, HRR. Minutes recorded the consensus from a discussion but few details of debates. The conflict was more fully described in the records of the dissidents. See YMCF, *Proceedings, 1849*. For an eyewitness account, see Gue, *Diary of Benjamin F. Gue*, 40. See also Bradley, "Progressive Friends in Michigan and New York"; and Barbour et al., *Quaker Crosscurrents*, 134–35. The support for Michigan Friends was partly tied to the migration of progressive Hicksite families from central New York to Michigan in the 1840s. On migration, see Davidson, "Profile of Hicksite Quakerism in Michigan."

34. Lucretia Mott to Elizabeth Cady Stanton, 16 July 1848, quoted in Wellman, *Road to Seneca Falls*, 185; see also 99–101.

35. Lucretia Mott to George and Cecilia Combe, 10 October 1848, in Palmer, *Selected Letters*, 169.

36. Mott, letter, *Liberator*, 6 October 1848. See also Faulkner, *Lucretia Mott's Heresy*, 134–36.

37. See Wellman, *Road to Seneca Falls*, 66–68, 106–7, 185–86; and Spence, "Women at the Crossroads." See also chap. 4.

38. Wellman, *Road to Seneca Falls*, 185–86. See also Spence, "Women at the Crossroads." Sally Roesch Wagner claims direct links between Seneca and other Haudenosaunee (Iroquois) women and the development of the U.S. woman's rights movement; see Wagner, *Untold Story of the Iroquois Influence* and *Sisters in Spirit*.

39. For events leading up to and during the Seneca Falls Woman's Rights Convention, see Wellman, *Road to Seneca Falls*, chap. 8. Quote from Elizabeth Cady Stanton, *Eighty Years and More*, 147–48.

40. The announcement was published in the *Seneca County Courier* on 11 July 1848. The convention was held at the Wesleyan Methodist Chapel, the only place in the village willing to host antislavery meetings and therefore the logical venue for this convention.

41. See Wellman, *Road to Seneca Falls*, 186–92, 275n11, on organizing the Seneca Falls convention. Stanton likely produced the first draft of the Declaration of Sentiments, using ideas from the M'Clintocks and local lawyers.

42. Editorial, *North Star*, 21 April 1848, and an announcement, 14 July 1848. The announcement of the convention also appeared in the *Seneca County Courier* and the *Ovid Bee*, CLC.

43. Of the national figures invited to attend, only Douglass and Mott participated. No letters were read from Grimké, Chapman, or Childs, who did not respond in time.

44. Frederick Douglass to Elizabeth M'Clintock, 14 July 1848, quoted in Wellman, *Road to Seneca Falls*, 191. All five Rochesterians signed the Declaration of Sentiments.

45. On the Quaker contingent at Seneca Falls, see Wellman, *Road to Seneca Falls*, 207; Hewitt, "Feminist Friends"; and Densmore, "The Quaker Tradition" and "Quaker Comeouters." On links between the Cadwalader case and women's rights, see Hamm, "Quakerism, Ministry, Marriage, and Divorce," 430–31.

46. *Report of the Woman's Rights Convention, held at Seneca Falls*, 6. See also an announcement, *Seneca County Courier*, 21 July 1848.

47. For the resolution adopted at the 1837 convention, see Sterling, *Turning the World Upside Down*, 13. Mott offered a long extemporaneous speech at the convention, which was not transcribed. It was likely similar to her remarks on 9 May 1848 at the "Fourteenth Annual Meeting of the American Anti-Slavery Society," published in *NASS*, 18 May 1848, which linked U.S. developments to revolutionary events abroad.

48. "Declaration of Sentiments," *Report of the Woman's Rights Convention, held at Seneca Falls*, 7–11. On Elizabeth M'Clintock's crucial role in that convention, see Wellman, *Road to Seneca Falls*, 190; and Hawkes, "The Life of Elizabeth McClintock Phillips." On earlier claims for female enfranchisement, see Wellman, "Women's Rights, Republicanism, and Revolutionary Rhetoric"; Wellman, *Road to Seneca Falls*, 148–51; Ginzberg, *Untidy Origins*, especially chap. 6; and Jones, *All Bound Up Together*, chap. 2.

49. *Report of the Woman's Rights Convention, held at Seneca Falls*, 6–7. The manuscript minutes of the convention have not survived, so we have only the printed version as a record of debates. The only list of participants is the one hundred signers of the Declaration of Sentiments. Of those signers, twenty-five percent were Quakers, although Quakers constituted only about 2 percent of the U.S. population.

50. On Mott's views on suffrage, see her "Discourse on the Rights of Women, 1849," in Densmore et al., *Lucretia Mott Speaks*, 76–77. Tetrault, *The Myth of Seneca Falls*, examines Stanton's and Susan B. Anthony's efforts to entrench the Seneca Falls convention as *the* origin of the U.S. woman's rights and woman suffrage movements. On the role of radical Friends in debates over woman suffrage, see Wellman, *Road to Seneca Falls*, 197, 204, 206; and Hewitt, "Feminist Friends."

51. On radical Friends and Free Soilers at the 1848 Seneca Falls Convention, see Wellman, "The Seneca Falls Woman's Rights Convention"; and *Road to Seneca Falls*, chap. 8. One dissident Quaker claimed that "every member" of that group was at the Seneca Falls convention. Wellman, *Road to Seneca Falls*, 207. DuBois, *Feminism and Suffrage*, argues that the right to vote was the most radical demand at Seneca Falls.

52. Wellman, *Road to Seneca Falls*, 203–4, 223. The other members of the committee were Mary Ann M'Clintock and Eunice Newton Foote.

53. This decision was not mentioned in the *Report of the Woman's Rights Convention, held at Seneca Falls*, but it served as the opening line of the report of the "Rochester Convention, Rochester, New York, 2 August 1848," in Stanton, Anthony, and Gage, *HWS*, 1:75.

54. Owen was excommunicated in December 1845 for her continued work with the WNYASS. See Session Minutes, Second (Brick) Presbyterian Church, 8 December 1845, Presbyterian Historical Society, Philadelphia, Pa.

55. "Freedom's Jubilee," *North Star*, 14 July 1848. Charles Lenox Remond was expected to speak at the celebration but arrived too late to participate. However, he apparently remained in Rochester for the woman's rights convention. See "August 1st Celebration," *North Star*, 11 August 1848.

56. On the schedule of events for the August 1 celebration, see "Freedom's Jubilee," *North Star*, 14 July 1848. The Ford Street Baptist Church was established in 1845 and became another center for black activism.

57. For the list of officers, see "August 1st Celebration," *North Star*, 11 August 1848.

58. See Rochester City Directories, 1847 and 1849, for occupations and residences of parade leaders. The officers included three barbers, a carpenter, a white-washer, a boatman, and a cartman. See also *Daily Advertiser*, quoted in "August 1st Celebration," *North Star*, 11 August 1848, for numbers and groups in parade. On the importance of barbers among black activists, see Taylor, *Frontiers of Freedom*, 133–34.

59. "August 1st Celebration," *North Star*, 11 August 1848, included reprints of coverage from the local papers, including the *Daily Democrat*, *Daily Advertiser*, and *National Reformer*.

60. On arrival at Washington Square, see William C. Nell, "First of August in Rochester," in *Liberator*, 1 September 1848.

61. "Speech at West India Emancipation Celebration," *North Star*, 4 August 1848.

62. Ibid.; "August 1st Celebration, *North Star*, 11 August 1848. The 4 August 1848 *North Star* estimated the crowd at 2,000 to 3,000, while the *Daily Democrat* of 3 August 1848 claimed 1,500 to 2,000 participants.

63. Lucretia Mott to Thomas and Mary Ann M'Clintock, 29 July 1848, in Palmer, *Selected Letters*, 164. Mott notes that Post persuaded her to attend the Rochester meeting and Mott also hoped "that some of you and Elizabeth C. Stanton may conclude to go—to help make the Women's Convention interesting."

64. The preparatory efforts were described in *Daily Advertiser*, 3 August 1848, and in Manuscript Minutes, RWRC, 2 August 1848, Phebe Post Willis Papers.

65. Quotes from Manuscript Minutes, RWRC, and Gordon, *Selected Papers*, 1:94–95. There are at least four additional versions of the proceedings. A report on the Rochester "Woman's Rights Convention" appeared in the *North Star*, 11 August 1848, and in the *Liberator*, 15 September 1848. A revised version of the Manuscript Minutes was published in Stanton, Anthony, and Gage, *HWS*, 1:75–87, 808–9. A revised version of the report was published in 1870 as *Proceedings of the Woman's Rights Convention . . . Revised by Mrs. Amy Post*. All four sources will be referenced in stitching together this version of events.

66. Manuscript Minutes, RWRC. The First Unitarian Church was between ministers, so organizers asked Rev. William Wicher [or Whicher] of the Free-Will Baptist Church to open the convention. Quakers did not begin meetings with an opening prayer, but organizers included one to avoid offending non-Quakers.

67. Stanton, Anthony, and Gage, *HWS*, 1:75. Since this incident was included in a volume coedited by Stanton, it seems likely that the event occurred largely as described. The 1870 *Proceedings of the Woman's Rights Convention . . . Revised by Amy Post* notes Elizabeth M'Clintock's refusal to accept the office, but refers to the others only as "two or three other women—glorious reformers, well deserving the name."

68. Manuscript Minutes, RWRC, and *Proceedings of the Woman's Rights Convention . . . Revised by Amy Post*, 1. This quote was inserted into the Manuscript Minutes later and in the past tense. In the 1870 *Proceedings*, Post replaced it with the present tense version used here. Post also claims Sarah Hallowell was reading the minutes when shouts of "louder" rang out, but says it was the size of the space that created the problem rather than diffidence on the part of her sister.

69. Manuscript Minutes, RWRC, and "Woman's Rights Convention," *North Star*, 11 August 1848.

70. Manuscript Minutes, RWRC and *Proceedings of the Woman's Rights Convention . . . Revised by Amy Post*. Both documents describe this event, but the language in the 1870 version is fuller and better captures Stanton's voice. It is not clear if the phrase "cordially adopted" means that there was a formal vote at this point. Later in the day, following lengthy debates, there was a formal vote.

71. Manuscript Minutes, RWRC.

72. Ibid.

73. The report of the Rochester "Woman's Rights Convention" in the *Liberator*, 15 September 1848, provides an expanded version of Sanford's speech, as do the *Proceedings of the Woman's Rights Convention . . . Revised by Amy Post*. For background on Rebecca Sanford and her husband, see Gordon, *Selected Papers*, 1:129n4.

74. James C. Jackson to Amy Post, 1 August 1848, IAPFP. In it, he encloses a letter to be read at the RWRC. Jackson established the Glen Haven Water Cure on Skaneateles Lake in February 1848.

75. "Rochester Woman's Rights Convention," Stanton, Anthony, and Gage, *HWS*, 1:78, first quote. Other quotes in this paragraph are from *Proceedings of the Woman's Rights Convention . . . Revised by Amy Post*.

76. Manuscript Minutes, RWRC.

77. Only two resolutions approved at the RWRC are listed in the Manuscript Minutes. The full list, including those quoted here, are in Stanton, Anthony, Gage, *HWS*, 1:808.

78. Speech Notes, RWRC, 2 August 1848, IAPFP. The handwriting appears to be that of Post. As an organizer, she could have prepared her comments ahead of time. These comments do not appear in the various reports, but she likely read them.

79. Stanton, Anthony, Gage, *HWS*, 1, 808–9.

80. See *North Star*, 24 March 1848, and "West Indies Emancipation Day Speech," *North Star*, 4 August 1848. The term "complexion" appears numerous times in his speeches and writings in this period, and he nearly always uses it as a synonym for

"race." For alternative meanings, see Jones, "Overthrowing the 'Monopoly of the Pulpit,'" 127.

81. Both the facts and the interpretation regarding black women's activism are based on Jones, "Overthrowing the 'Monopoly of the Pulpit,'" 124–27, 124 (quotes). For signers of the WNYASS "Address of Anti-Slavery Women," see *North Star*, 31 March 1848. It was reprinted several more times, including 28 July 1848, right between the Seneca Falls and the Rochester woman's rights conventions.

82. Terborg-Penn first raised this question in *African American Women and the Struggle for the Vote*. See also Jones, *All Bound Up Together*, 70–82.

83. Manuscript Minutes, RWRC. The list of signers at the RWRC was not published with any of the reports, and no original copy has been found. Stanton, Anthony, and Gage, *HWS*, 1:808, notes, "Many persons signed the Declaration at Rochester, among them Daniel Anthony, Lucy Read Anthony, Mary S. Anthony, the officers of the convention, and others." See also Manuscript Minutes, RWRC, and *Proceedings . . . Revised by Amy Post*, 8–9.

84. On Rochester signers, see Stanton, Anthony, and Gage, *HWS*, 1:87 (quote), 810. See also Nathaniel Potter to Isaac Post, 29 October 1848, IAPFP; "Third Decade Anniversary," *National Citizen and Ballot Box*, August 1878, which mentions Ellen Sully Fray's attendance; and Ida Husted Harper, *Life and Work of Susan B. Anthony*, 1:59.

85. Mary Robbins Post notes that Amy Post sent her a detailed description of the convention and its participants, but the letter has not been found. See Mary Robbins Post to Amy and Isaac Post, 12 September 1848, IAPFP. Mary argues that Stanton and the M'Clintocks were largely responsible for Mott's opposition to a woman presiding at the RWRC. By 1870, Post had retreated from her earlier critiques of Mott, Stanton, and Mary Ann M'Clintock in her otherwise more detailed version of the Rochester proceedings. The list of signers at Rochester was likely sent with the handwritten minutes to the *North Star* office and destroyed when Douglass's home burned in 1872.

86. For coverage of the Seneca Falls Woman's Rights Conventions, see Stanton, Anthony, and Gage, *HWS*, 1:802–6. The *HWS* prints largely negative coverage of the convention in its appendix.

87. "Woman's Rights Convention," *Daily Democrat*, 3 August 1848; and "Woman's Rights Convention" and "Editorial," *Daily Advertiser*, 3 August 1848. Their coverage suggests that reporters from each attended the convention. The *Daily Advertiser* article was reprinted as "Woman's Rights Convention at Rochester," *Daily Gazette* (Utica, N.Y.), 5 August 1848, CLC. See also, "Woman's Rights Convention," *New York Evening Express*, 7 August 1848, CLC.

88. Nathaniel Potter to Isaac Post, 29 October 1848, IAPFP.

89. Clipping, *National Reformer*, 3 August and 17 August, 1848, in Susan B. Anthony Scrapbook, vol. 1, Susan B. Anthony Papers, Library of Congress, Washington, D.C.

90. See "Woman's Rights Convention," *North Star*, 11 August 1848; and "Proceedings of the Woman's Rights Convention," *Liberator*, 1 September and 15 September 1848, and "Rebecca Sanford Speech," *Liberator*, 22 September 1848.

91. See Jones, *All Bound Up Together*, 70–82. On p. 73 she quotes "U.C.A. Association," *North Star*, 25 August 1848, and on pp. 74–75 she provides details of events at that meeting.

92. "Proceedings of the Colored Convention Held at Cleveland, Ohio," *North Star*, 13 September 1848, quoted in Jones, *All Bound Up Together*, 59–60.

93. Quoted in Jones, *All Bound Up Together*, 81. See also Quarles, "Frederick Douglass and the Woman's Rights Movement."

94. Douglass described the scene in an open letter to H. G. Warner, *North Star*, 30 March 1849.

95. Ibid. For details of this incident and its aftermath, see Ruchkin, "The Abolition of 'Colored Schools' in Rochester"; and McFeeley, *Frederick Douglass*, 160–61.

96. Quotes from "Woman's Protective Union," *North Star*, 15 September 1848. See also "Woman's Protective Union," *Rochester Republican*, 7 September 1848, CLC; and "Women's Protective Union, *Daily Advertiser*, 3 August 1848; and "Woman's Protective Union," *Daily Democrat*, 18 August and 2 and 25 September 1848. The September articles reprint the Preamble and Constitution of the Rochester Working Women's Protective Union from the *National Reformer*.

97. On Charlotte and James Cavan, see Rochester City Directories, 1849 and 1854; and Membership lists, 1850s, Unitarian Society of Rochester Records, SpecColUR.

98. "Woman's Protective Union," *North Star*, 13 October 1848. For other announcements, see *North Star*, 15 September, 27 October, and 2 November 1848.

99. See Emily Collins's correspondence with Sarah Owen in Stanton, Anthony, and Gage, *HWS*, 1:91–92. Collins lived in Ontario County, N.Y., until 1858, when she moved to Rochester and engaged in women's rights activities there throughout the next decade. For examples of the Union's ongoing work, see Sarah D. Fish, "A Word for Domestics," *Liberator*, 22 August 1852; and "Letter," *Lily*, 2 January 1854.

100. Elizabeth Cady Stanton to Amy Post, 24 September [1848?], in Gordon, *Selected Papers*, 1:123–24. Lucretia Mott to Elizabeth Cady Stanton, 3 October 1848, in Palmer, *Selected Letters*, 172–73.

101. Lucretia Mott to Elizabeth Cady Stanton, 3 October 1848, in Palmer, *Selected Letters*, 172–73.

102. A[my] P[ost], "The Bazaar," *North Star*, 1 September 1848.

103. Sarah Thayer to Amy Post, [1848?], IAPFP. Given Thayer's references to the reading room and to a schism twenty years earlier among Friends, this letter was likely written in 1848.

104. For descriptions of antislavery fairs, see, for example, "Rochester Anti-Slavery Fair," *North Star*, 3 December 1847, and "Anti-Slavery Fair," *North Star*, 14 January 1848. For more upscale affairs after affluent women entered antislavery ranks, see "Circular, the First Report of the Rochester Ladies' Anti-Slavery Sewing Society," 1852, Porter Family Papers, SpecColUR, and *FDP*, 30 December 1853.

105. On Birney and Dale (who added Johnson to her name after marrying, c. 1850), see Nell's letters to Amy Post after his return to Boston. For example, Wesley and Uzelac, *William Cooper Nell*, 305, 307–8, 320, 324.

106. On Friends manual labor schools, see Barbour et al., *Quaker Crosscurrents*, 153–54.

107. Joseph Post to Amy and Isaac Post, 8 February 1848, IAPFP.

108. On the Fox sisters and early spiritualism, see Stuart, *Reluctant Spiritualist*, especially chaps. 1 and 2. On Rochester and the Posts' connections to spiritualism, see McKelvey, *Rochester*, 289–90; Hewitt, *Women's Activism and Social Change*, 142–43, 169; and Abbott, *Post, Albertson and Hicks Family Letters*, 1:164, 184–86, 188–90, 193, 198–200, 205, 214–18, 225, 234, 237–38. On Nell's belief in spiritualism, see Wesley and Uzelac, *William Cooper Nell*, 22. On Harriet Jacobs's embrace of spiritualism, see Yellin, *Harriet Jacobs*, 131–32. On Truth, see Washington, *Sojourner Truth's America*, 146–47, 278–80, 324, 379.

109. On spiritualism and women's rights, see Braude, *Radical Spirits*.

110. On James C. Jackson's medical career, see *Dictionary American Biography*, 9:547. Milo D. Codding to Amy and Isaac Post, 24 September 1847, IAPFP; and Mary Seaman Kirby to Sarah Hallowell, 11 February 1849, IAPFP.

111. Mary Seaman Kirby to Sarah Hallowell, 11 February 1849, IAPFP. Mary Robbins Post and Amy and Isaac Post regularly exchanged information on medical treatments.

112. Milo D. Codding to Amy and Isaac Post, 24 September 1847, IAPFP; William Nell to Amy Post, 11 August 1849, 2 June and 5 December 1850, 15 January 1851, and 11 September 1853, IAPFP. For quote on "wet bandages," see Wesley and Uzelac, *William Cooper Nell*, 22.

113. Mary Seaman Kirby to Amy Post Isaac Post and Sarah Hallowell, 8 September 1848, IAPFP.

114. Mary Robbins Post to Amy and Isaac Post, 12 September 1848, IAPFP.

115. John Ketcham to Isaac and Amy Post, 24 July 1848, IAPFP.

116. On the history of the Congregational Friends (also known as the Progressive Friends and the Friends of Human Progress), see note 33 above.

117. "Basis of Religious Association, adopted by the Conference Held at Farmington, in the State of New York, On, the Sixth and Seventh of Tenth month, 1848," published as appendix to *Proceedings of the Yearly Meeting of Congregational Friends, 1850*, 44–48 (hereafter cited as "Basis of Religious Association").

118. Ibid., 45.

119. Ibid., 48.

120. On Congregational/Progressive Friends spreading to other regions, see Bradley, "Progressive Friends in Michigan and New York"; and Davidson, "A Profile of Hicksite Quakerism in Michigan, 1830–1860."

121. Editorial, 22 September 1848, *North Star*. See Kantrowitz, *More Than Freedom*, 158–62.

122. "What Good Has the Free Soil Movement Done?," *North Star*, 25 March 1849. The Democrats nominated Senator Lewis Cass of Michigan in 1848. Though Cass was an ardent expansionist, he argued that residents in each territory should decide whether to make the region slaveholding or free.

123. Description of the group as small but spirited appears in *North Star*, 5 January 1849.

124. "Proceedings of the Western New York Anti-Slavery Society," *North Star*, 29 December 1848. The description of events described in this paragraph and the next are from these "Proceedings."

125. It was not possible to identify all the individuals on the list of officers and committee members, but none of the white evangelical men or women involved in the WNYASS in previous years were listed. At least three African Americans, including Frederick Douglass, were elected to the executive committee, but some of the individuals who have not been identified may have been black.

126. The resolutions from the December 1848 Annual Meeting of the WNYASS were published in the *North Star*, 7 January 1849. All quotes of resolutions are from this issue of the paper.

127. Ibid.

128. Ibid.

129. Lucretia Mott to George and Cecelia Combe, 10 September 1848, in Palmer, *Selected Letters*, 168–71.

Chapter Six

1. Mary Seaman Kirby to Sarah Hallowell, 11 February 1849, IAPFP.

2. The Hurns and both Anthony families lived on farms in Gates, New York, just west of Rochester. See Sixth U.S. Federal Census, 1850, Gates, New York, CLC, for listing of the neighboring farms of Asa Anthony, Gershon Griffin (brother of Huldah Anthony and Sarah Hurn), and John Hurn.

3. New York/Rochester, vol. 162, p. 127, March 1849 and March 1850, R. G. Dun & Company Credit Report Volumes, Baker Library, Harvard Business School, Cambridge, Mass.

4. On Jacob Post's enrollment at Buckram Institute, see Jacob Post to John Ransom, Isaac Post, Amy Post, and all the folks, 7 January 1851, IAPFP.

5. Sarah Fish to Amy Post, 19 September 1848, IAPFP; and Isaac Post to Amy Post, 22 May 1849, IAPFP.

6. See McFeeley, *Frederick Douglass*, 152.

7. This event was referred to as Frances Nell and Benjamin Cleggett's wedding in a Post family letter, but was instead an engagement party. William Nell wrote to Amy Post about Frances's upcoming wedding on 11 August 1849, IAPFP.

8. William C. Nell, "Anti-Slavery Lectures at Minerva Hall," *North Star*, 19 February 1849.

9. Mary Robbins Post to Isaac and Amy Post, 23 February [1849?], IAPFP.

10. Mary Seaman Kirby to Sarah Hallowell, 11 February 1849, IAPFP.

11. Nell moved back to Boston in mid-April. He visited Henry Garnet's school in Geneva on 3–4 April and wrote an article for the *North Star* on 27 April from Boston. See "Progress in Geneva" and "A Means of Elevation," in Wesley and Uzelac,

William Cooper Nell, 221–22, 224–25. On the gift of the inkstand, see William Nell to Amy Post, 12 December 1849, IAPFP.

12. For the story of Harriet Jacobs's life as a slave, a fugitive, and a freewoman, see Jacobs, *Incidents in the Life of a Slave Girl*; and Yellin, *Harriet Jacobs*.

13. Yellin, *Harriet Jacobs*, 103.

14. Sarah Hallowell to Family, 5 May 18[49?], IAPFP. The envelope was addressed to William, Mary, Harriet, Willie, Isaac, Jacob, Joseph, Bridget, and Joanna. The last two worked in the Post household.

15. Mary Robbins Post to Isaac and Amy Post, 10 June 1849, IAPFP; and Isaac Post to Amy Post, 19 May 1849, IAPFP. Isaac is quoting an earlier letter from Amy that has not been found.

16. Isaac Post to Amy Post, 15 May 1849, IAPFP. On the background of Julia Griffiths and her arrival in the States, see Fought, *Women in the World of Frederick Douglass*, 93–94, 96–97.

17. Isaac Post to Amy Post, 12 and 15 May 1849, IAPFP.

18. Isaac Post to Amy Post, 19 May 1849, IAPFP, notes a letter received from Amy that has not been found. On visits of friends and spirits, see Isaac Post to Amy Post, 7, 12, 15, 19, and 22 May 1849, IAPFP.

19. Isaac Post to Amy Post, 7 May and 12 May 1849, IAPFP.

20. Isaac Post to Amy Post, 15 May 1849, IAPFP.

21. Isaac Post to Amy Post, 22 May 1849, IAPFP. This letter appears to have been written over several days.

22. William Nell to Amy and Isaac Post, 30 June 1849, IAPFP; and Isaac Post to Amy Post, 7 May 1849, IAPFP. Nell described several events from Amy's visit as well as developments after she returned home.

23. Mary Robbins Post to Isaac and Amy Post, n.d. (probably 5 June 1849), IAPFP.

24. John Willis to Amy Post, 21 June 1849, IAPFP. Willis also calls spiritualism "absurd and ridiculous."

25. Isaac Post to Amy Post, 19 May 1849, IAPFP.

26. Frederick Douglass to Gerrit Smith, 30 March 1849, Gerrit Smith Papers, Syracuse University Library, Syracuse, N.Y. On Douglass's gradual shift toward party politics, see McFeeley, *Frederick Douglass*, 156–58, 168–69. On black men and Free Soil efforts of 1848–50, see Kantrowitz, *More Than Freedom*, 158–66. On concerns about Douglass's change of heart among radical friends, see Sarah [Owen?] to Amy Post, 15 April [185?], IAPFP; and Mary Robbins Post to Amy and Isaac Post, January 18[50?], IAPFP.

27. On initial conflict, see McFeeley, *Frederick Douglass*, 164–65.

28. Anne Warren Weston to Maria Weston Chapman, 5 June 1849, noted in McKivigan, *Frederick Douglass Papers*, 513–14.

29. Isaac Post to Amy Post, 19 May 1849, IAPFP.

30. Frederick Douglass to Amy Post, 11 September 1849, IAPFP.

31. William Nell to Amy Post, 11 August 1849, IAPFP. Nell quotes an earlier letter from Amy Post on "controversies with the 'Lords of Creation.'"

32. Draft of Amy Post to Frederick Douglass, 11 September 1849, IAPFP. In the draft, the word "implied" is inserted before "*threat*" but then crossed out.

33. Ibid.

34. Frederick Douglass to William Hallowell, 16 September 1849, IAPFP; and Frederick Douglass to Isaac Post, 16 September 1849, IAPFP. He apparently wrote the same day to Edmund Willis and Asa Anthony.

35. Stuart, *Reluctant Spiritualist*, 50–58; and McKelvey, *Rochester*, 290. This paragraph and the next are based on these accounts, especially Stuart. Leah Fox Fish began charging up to a dollar per person for séances in the early 1850s to support herself and her sisters, since spiritualism led to the loss of her piano students. Maggie Fox later charged that Leah "ruled over us with an iron rod." See Stuart, *Reluctant Spiritualist*, 48–49.

36. Stuart, *Reluctant Spiritualist*, 56–58; and McKelvey, *Rochester*, 290.

37. William Nell to Amy Post, 9 October 1852, IAPFP; Yellin, *Harriet Jacobs*, 103–4, 131–32; and Washington, *Sojourner Truth's America*, 217.

38. Douglass did attend a few séances at the Post home, but found little evidence to support the idea of spirit communication. See *North Star*, 21 December 1849 and 5 April 1850; and Frederick Douglass to Amy Post, [April?] 1850, IAPFP.

39. William Nell to Amy Post, 16 October 1849, IAPFP.

40. Amy Post, "An Appeal on Behalf of the Western New York Anti-Slavery Fair," and Frederick Douglass, editorial on "Anti-Slavery Bazaar," *North Star*, 29 June 1849.

41. Susan Doty to Amy Post, 8 August and 5 November 1849, IAPFP. See also Mary Chapin to Mrs. Post, 4 October 1849, IAPFP, on the West Mendon and West Bloomfield fairs. Numerous other letters to Post from Nell, Douglass, and Mary Robbins Post mention these antislavery fairs.

42. Amy Post was involved in antislavery activities every week, but many women attended less regularly, even as they contributed to the cause in a variety of ways. On Wilbur's involvement, see 21 January, 18 February, 19 April, 20 May, and 17 June 1849, Diaries, Box 3, JWP. Quotes are in chronological order.

43. Yellin, *Harriet Jacobs*, 106–7.

44. "Anti-Slavery Fair at Williamson," *North Star*, 26 January 1849. Antislavery fairs in farm towns were generally less profitable because the population was smaller and more scattered.

45. Frederick Douglass, "Acknowledgement," *North Star*, 5 October 1849.

46. Amy Post, "Report of the Fair Committee," *North Star*, 16 November 1849. On the importance of antislavery fairs, see Jeffrey, *Great Silent Army*, 108–26; Hewitt, "Social Origins of Women's Antislavery Politics," 205, 212–14, 222–25; and Brooke, "Cultures of Nationalism, Movements of Reform," 29–30.

47. Originally postponed until 16 January, the events had to be postponed another week when *NASS* announced an antislavery convention in Syracuse for 15 January 1850. See Amy Post, "To the Anti-Slavery Friends of Western New York," *North Star*, 14 December 1849; and Sarah D. Fish, "The Rochester Annual Meeting," *North Star*, 23 November 1849.

48. WNYASS, Anti-Slavery Fair Report [1850?], IAPFP; for "glorious achievement," see Amy Post to Frederick Douglass, 2 February 1850, IAPFP.

49. "Rochester Anti-Slavery Fair," *North Star*, 1 February 1850. The British goods were most likely sent at the request of the Griffiths sisters. Post reported the proceeds of the 1848 WNYASS fair as $435.15 in the *North Star*, 17 January 1849.

50. Amy Post to Frederick Douglass, 2 February 1850, IAPFP. This letter is a draft. Notes in pencil appear at the end, including: "The[e] knows that the Star has been my Idol, and I could not see its idolized Ed destroy its home without the most poignant grief."

51. Frederick Douglass to Amy Post, 4 February 1850, IAPFP.

52. Julia Griffiths to Gerrit Smith, 26 October [185?], Gerrit Smith Papers, Syracuse University Library, Syracuse, N.Y. The letter was likely written between October 1849, amid the fall fairs, and the April 1851 antislavery festival for George Thompson.

53. On the WNYASS convention and fair, see *North Star*, 15 March 1850. On the Corinthian Hall mass meeting, see "Fugitive Slave Law Meeting," *North Star*, 12 April 1850; and Yellin, *Harriet Jacobs*, 107. The officers of the mass meeting included political abolitionists James Fogg, William Goodell, and Samuel Porter, along with WNYASS members Frederick Douglass and George W. Clark. Isaac Post and Benjamin Fish were among the participants. No women were listed as officers or speakers, though some were certainly in attendance.

54. "American Anti-Slavery Society Anniversary Meeting," *Liberator*, 17 May 1850; McFeely, *Frederick Douglass*, 165.

55. YMCF, *Proceedings, 1850*, 10.

56. See "Announcement," Cazenovia Convention, in *NASS*, 1 August 1850, and "Anti-Slavery Convention," 29 August 1850, *NASS*. Siblings, Orthodox Friends, and Garrisonians Joseph and Phebe Hathaway were the only WNYASS leaders to serve as officers. On the Edmondson sisters' escape, see Ricks, *Escape on the Pearl*.

57. Betsy Mix Cowles to Amy Post, 1 December 1850, IAPFP; and Mary Robbins Post to Isaac and Amy Post, 1 October 1850, IAPFP.

58. On Nell's efforts with "colored citizens" and vigilance committees in Boston, see "Meeting of the Colored Citizens of Boston" and "Declaration of Sentiments of the Colored Citizens of Boston, on the Fugitive Slave Bill!!!" in Wesley and Uzelac, *William Cooper Nell*, 270–75.

59. Yellin, *Harriet Jacobs*, 109. Quote, Jacobs, *Incidents in the Life of a Slave Girl*, 190.

60. Amy Post to Frederick Douglass, [August 1850?], IAPFP.

61. William Nell to Amy Post, 15 July 1850, IAPFP. Nell often closed letters with greetings to the Sophia Street circle, naming some individuals and including the rest in the "Circle." See William Nell to Amy Post letters from the 1850s in IAPFP.

62. Amy and Isaac Post to Wendell Phillips, 20 June 1850, Anti-Slavery Collection, Boston Public Library, Boston, Mass. Phillips's letter to the Posts is missing, but

Amy repeats his queries as she addresses each one. William Wells Brown replied to the accusations in "To the Public," *Liberator*, 12 July 1850. See also Greenspan, *William Wells Brown*, 128–30, 135–38, 180–81, 235–36.

63. Isaac Post to Jacob Post, [May 1850?], IAPFP. Isaac was writing from Jericho, New York, where he and Amy were visiting family and attending the May AASS meetings.

64. Joseph Post to Isaac Post, 9 [July 1850?], IAPFP.

65. Joseph Post to Isaac Post, 17 August [185?], IAPFP.

66. Joseph Post to Amy Post, 8 and 15 August and 12 December [185?], IAPFP.

67. Members List, 1850s, Unitarian Society of Rochester Papers, SpecColUR. On Channing's ministry, see McKelvey, *Rochester*, 347–50.

68. YMCF, *Proceedings, 1850*, 3, 11, 23, 40.

69. Ibid., 13–18. The quote on women's rights as human rights is on 14. Lori Ginzberg notes that Stanton had given several lectures expressing ideas similar to those that appear in the YMCF address. Ginzberg, *Elizabeth Cady Stanton*, 69–71. Mott often critiqued women's rights advocates for assuming that men were the main source of women's oppression. See, for instance, her response to Nell at the Rochester Woman's Rights Convention in 1848, chap. 4.

70. Frederick Douglass to Amy Post, 20, 25, and 31 October 1850, IAPFP.

71. McFeeley, *Frederick Douglass*, 164–66; Fought, *Women in the World of Frederick Douglass*, 131; and William Nell to Amy Post, 15 July 1850, IAPFP.

72. On Julia Griffiths's new address, see "Announcement," *North Star*, 27 June 1850. Anna Douglass was likely glad to empty her home of *North Star* coworkers, though Griffiths's move did not silence the gossip. See Frederick Douglass to Samuel D. Porter, 12 January 1852, Porter Family Papers, SpecColUR. Douglass refers to an 8 January 1852 letter from Porter that has not been located. On gossip about Griffiths and Douglass, see McFeeley, 165, 170–71; and Fought, *Women in the World of Frederick Douglass*, 96–97, 109–11, 131, 134–35, 138. Fought argues against contemporaries' and historians' assumption that the gossip indicates an affair between Douglass and Griffiths, 6–8.

73. Quotes from Fought, *Women in the World of Frederick Douglass*, 124.

74. See numerous letters in which Amy Post applauds the Griffiths sisters' and especially Julia's commitment to the cause, interracialism, and Douglass. For example, Amy Post to Frederick Douglass, 11 September 1849, IAPFP. See also Fought, *Women in the World of Frederick Douglass*, 111–12; and McFeeley, *Frederick Douglass*, 163, 182. On Gerrit Smith, see McFeeley, *Frederick Douglass*, 165. On Jacobs, see Harriet Jacobs to Amy Post, [1850?], IAPFP. The letter was likely written in July 1850, when Douglass, the Griffiths sisters, and Jacobs were in the Boston area. See William Nell to Amy Post, 15 July 1850, IAPFP. See also Yellin, *Harriet Jacobs*, 108–10. Nell criticized Griffiths in letters to Post, but mainly in terms of her political influence on Douglass.

75. Frederick Douglass to Amy Post, 20 and 31 October 1850, IAPFP. Douglass acknowledges receiving important news from Amy in his 31 October letter, but her

letter has not been located. Thompson, born in Liverpool, was a prominent Garrisonian abolitionist in England and Scotland.

76. "From the *Daily Advertiser*" and "George Thompson in Rochester," *Liberator*, 28 March 1851. This was likely a Rochester article from 9 or 10 March that George Thompson sent to Garrison along with a letter to be printed in the *Liberator*. See "Letter from George Thompson," *Liberator*, 21 March 1851. Similar attacks had been published in the *Daily Advertiser* since January 1851.

77. "George Thompson at Rochester," *Liberator*, 28 March 1851. George W. Putnam regularly reported to the *Liberator* on George Thompson's tour.

78. "Letter from George Thompson," *Liberator*, 21 March 1851.

79. "Anti-Slavery Convention at Rochester, N.Y.," 4 April 1851, *Liberator*. Truth stayed with the Posts for two to three months following her appearance with Thompson. See Washington, *Sojourner Truth's America*, 215–17.

80. "Anti-Slavery Convention at Rochester, N.Y.," 4 April 1851, *Liberator*. Several officers were members of the Free Democracy Convention of Monroe County, N.Y., the name for the Free Soil Party in western New York. See "Free Democracy of Monroe County," *FDP*, 8 October 1852. Daniel Anthony settled his family in Rochester in 1845.

81. "Anti-Slavery Convention at Rochester, N.Y.," *Liberator*, 4 April 1851.

82. On the fair committee, see "Anti-Slavery Festival," *North Star*, 24 April 1851. Committee members were identified through church and organizational records and city directories.

83. Ibid. The women's names are listed as they appear in the announcement, with marital titles but generally without their husband's name or initial. The detailed description of fancy goods is longer than quoted here and especially noteworthy.

84. Ibid. A few of the newly recruited white women worshipped at the First Unitarian Church, where they would have met Mary Hallowell and perhaps Amy Post.

85. "George Thompson in Rochester," *Anti-Slavery Bugle*, 17 May 1851 (first and third quotes). The report was sent by E[sther] A[nn] Lukens, an abolitionist and women's rights advocate from Columbia County, Ohio (second quote), "Rochester Anti-Slavery Fair," *North Star*, 17 April 1851. In describing goods to be sold, there is no mention of the handcrafted items that made up the bulk of goods at earlier fairs.

86. "Editorial," *North Star*, 23 May 1851.

87. "Editorial," *FDP*, 4 September 1851.

88. "Circular, the First Report of the Rochester Ladies' Anti-Slavery Sewing Society, 1852," Porter Family Papers, SpecColUR. The report was professionally printed on three pages of good stock paper and included a letter of appreciation from Douglass. The involvement of Porter's wife, Susan, and sister Maria G. in the RLASS may have led Samuel Porter to write Douglass in January 1852 regarding rumors of an inappropriate relationship with Julia Griffiths. See note 72.

89. William Nell to Amy Post, 24 December 1850, IAPFP. On 5 December, Nell visited the Boston Anti-Slavery Office just as Thompson "received thy letter of invitation to Rochester." Nell to Post, 5 December 1851, IAPFP.

90. Julia Griffiths to Gerrit Smith, 26 August [1851?], Gerrit Smith Papers.

91. Ibid.

92. William Nell to Amy Post, 5 December 1850, IAPFP. See also Nell to Post, 2 June 1850, 3 and 15 July 1850, 5 and 29 August 1850, 5 and 24 December 1850, 15 and 29 January 1851, and 27 June 1851, all in the IAPFP. In September 1851, Nell returned to Rochester for an extended visit.

93. William Nell to William Lloyd Garrison, 15 and 17 September 1851, William Lloyd Garrison Papers, Boston Public Library, Boston, Mass. On Calhoun's changing views on slavery, see Isaac Post, *Voices of the Spirit World*, 87–91.

94. "Meeting of the Colored Citizens of Rochester," *FDP*, 23 October 1851, written by Nell. See also "Material Aid for American Fugitives," *NASS*, 17 June 1852, on a May meeting of the Rochester Vigilance Committee at the AME Zion Church.

95. Announcements of the festival, bazaar, and convention appeared in *FDP* on several occasions beginning with 29 January 1852. They also appeared in the *National Era*, 11 March 1852; and the *American Baptist*, 18 March 1852, CLC. Amy Post noted many early instances of efforts to hide and rescue fugitives in Rochester, including in 1823 and 1832. See Post, "The Underground Railroad in Rochester," 458–59.

96. "The Recent Anti-Slavery Festival and Convention in Rochester," *FDP*, 25 March 1852.

97. "Rochester Anti-Slavery Convention, Extract from a letter from William C. Nell," *Liberator*, 26 March 1852.

98. "New York State Anti-Slavery Society," *FDP*, 15 April 1852. See also, Douglass's response to Giles Stebbins report on the convention in *NASS*, *FDP*, 22 April 1852.

99. "The Recent Anti-Slavery Festival and Convention in Rochester," *FDP*, 25 March 1852. All quotes in this paragraph are from the same article. Emphasis in original.

100. Sarah Hallowell to Frederick Douglass, *FDP*, 22 April 1852.

101. Editor's reply to Sarah Hallowell, *FDP*, 22 April 1852.

102. "Rochester Anti-Slavery Convention, Extract of a letter from William C. Nell," *Liberator*, 26 March 1852.

103. Garrison's comments and resolutions and Gerrit Smith's letter appear in "Report on American Anti-Slavery Society Convention," *Liberator*, 21 May 1852. Douglass's comment appears in his letter to Gerrit Smith, 15 May 1852, in McKivigan, *Frederick Douglass Papers*, 1:536.

104. "Report on American Anti-Slavery Society Convention," *Liberator*, 21 May 1852; and Frederick Douglass to Gerrit Smith, 15 May 1852, in McKivigan, *Frederick Douglass Papers*, 1:536.

105. Journal Briefs, 13 May 1852, Box 1, JWP. Rest of paragraph from "Report on American Anti-Slavery Society Convention," *Liberator*, 21 May 1852.

106. On 1852 escape, see Post, "Underground Railroad in Rochester," 459–60. The story was retold in *Democrat and Chronicle*, 22 February 1896, following

Douglass's death. See also "Report on American Anti-Slavery Society Convention," *FDP*, 27 May 1852.

107. "Report on American Anti-Slavery Society Convention," *Liberator*, 21 May 1852.

108. See list of officers in *FDP*, 27 May 1852. On the declining concern for women's rights in black organizations, see Jones, *All Bound Together*, chap. 3.

109. Christopher Densmore compiled a list of participants at YMCF in Waterloo, New York, from extant proceedings. Amy Post did not attend the yearly meetings of 1849–51, although she followed developments through reports and F/friends. She then attended four YMCF between 1852 and 1859.

110. YMCF, *Proceedings, 1849*, 6.

111. Ibid., 6–7, for quotes in this paragraph. References to the purported heresy of members and the range of social evils addressed appear throughout the *Proceedings*.

112. The published proceedings, including those cited below, provide the most complete record of discussions, debates, epistles, and communications, but in many years the YMCF also received extensive coverage in reform papers, and even in mainstream papers. See, for example, a *New York Tribune* article reprinted in the *Liberator*, 6 July 1849.

113. YMCF, *Proceedings, 1852*, 3 (quote).

114. Ibid., 8.

115. Ibid., 6, 7, 8, 13.

116. On 5th of July Speech, see Colaiaco, *Frederick Douglass and the Fourth of July*, 7–8, 23–24; McFeeley, *Frederick Douglass*, 172–73; announcement of event in *FDP*, 2 July 1852; and "Oration," *FDP*, 9 July 1852. In the announcement, the RLASS claimed they scheduled the speech on Monday, 5 July, because 4 July was a Sunday. But Douglass told the audience he was unwilling to speak on 4th of July.

117. Douglass's *Oration* from 5 July 1852 was published in pamphlet as well as in book form. The quotes are from the pamphlet, Frederick Douglass, "Oration."

118. "Oration," *FDP*, 9 July 1852; and McKivigan, *Frederick Douglass Papers*, 546n1.

119. Frederick Douglass to Amy Post, 4 August 1852, IAPFP.

120. See examples of Wilbur's participation in RLASS below. On Colman, see Wilbur's descriptions and "The Rochester Ladies' Anti-Slavery Sewing Society will meet," *FDP*, 22 April 1853.

121. Diaries, 4 June 1852, Box 3, JWP.

122. Diaries, 11, 12 and 18 November 1852, Box 3, JWP. See also Sarah Hallowell to Mary Hallowell, 24 December 1852, IAPFP, for discussions of the competing societies and Sarah's disappointment in Colman joining the RLASS.

123. Julia Griffiths to Amy Post, 16 October 1852, IAPFP.

124. Sarah Hallowell to Mary Hallowell, 27 December 1852, IAPFP. Sarah refers to a letter from Mary that has not been located.

125. On the spiritualist beliefs of Nell, see Wesley and Uzelac, *William Cooper Nell*, 6, 22, 23, 308, 320–27, 375, 379, 402–3, 417, 430, 448–49, 494, 533, 594, 670–71. Many of his comments are contained in letters to Amy Post. On Truth, see Washington, *Sojourner Truth's America*, 55, 146–47, 160, 213, 216–18, 220, 274–75, 278–80, 324, 342–43, 350, 368, 378–79. On Jacobs, see Yellin, *Harriet Jacobs*, 103–4, 131–32.

126. Isaac Post, *Voices from the Spirit World*; William Nell to Isaac and Amy Post and Sarah Hallowell, 19 July 1852, IAPFP. On Jackson visit, see Journal Briefs, 23 January 1853, JWP.

127. Post, *Voices from the Spirit World*. Thanks to Karl Kabelac for a copy of this rare book.

128. Sarah Thayer to Amy Post, 9 March 1853, IAPFP.

129. Braude, *Radical Spirits*.

130. On Stanton, see Ginzberg, *Elizabeth Cady Stanton*; on Rose, see Anderson, *Rabbi's Atheist Daughter*.

131. See Faulkner, *Lucretia Mott's Heresy*.

132. On speakers at these conventions, see "Salem Convention," in Stanton, Anthony, and Gage, *HWS*, 1:103–11; "National Woman's Rights Convention," in *North Star*, 15 November 1850; and "The Woman's Rights Convention," *Liberator*, 1 November 1850. See also McClymer, *This High and Holy Moment*.

133. McClymer, *This High and Holy Moment*, 68 (quote), 88–89, 109, 122, 147.

134. Ibid., 72–74; and Davis, *Proceedings of the Worcester Woman's Rights Convention*. A speech by Abby Kelley Foster, in which she suggested that women take up arms like Revolutionary patriots, was not reported in newspapers or the official *Proceedings*. See McClymer, *This High and Holy Moment*, 87–88, 109–10.

135. McClymer, *This High and Holy Movement*, 168–74.

136. Lucretia Mott to Elizabeth Cady Stanton, 11 September 1851, in Gordon, *Selected Papers*, 1:186–87. Massachusetts women had already claimed the second, 1852, National Woman's Rights Convention for Worcester. Mott mentions the letter received from Amy Post, but it has not been found.

137. For Robinson's report on Truth's speech, see, "Women's Rights Convention: Sojourner Truth," *Anti-Slavery Bugle*, 21 June 1851. Other contemporary accounts appear in *Liberator*, 7 June 1851; *New York Tribune*, 6 June 1851; and *Ashtabula Sentinel*, 14 June 1851. A later version was published by Frances Gage, who was at the Akron convention but did not transcribe Truth's speech at the time. Although often quoted, Gage's version has been challenged for its use of southern dialect and its variation from contemporary reports. See Painter, *Sojourner Truth*, 124–25, 164–78; and Washington, *Sojourner Truth's America*, 226–29.

138. Diaries, 19 June 1851, Box 3, JWP.

139. On the life and vision of Ernestine Rose, see Anderson, *Rabbi's Atheist Daughter*. On Amy's order of Rose's portrait, see William Nell to Amy Post, 10 November 1857, IAPFP. Hers was part of a series of abolitionist and woman's rights portraits.

140. Harper, *Life and Work*, 1:65.

141. Ibid., 1:67.

142. Ibid., 1:68.

143. "New York State Women's Temperance Convention," *Lily*, 1 May 1852. This paragraph is based on this report as well as a review of the previous year's proceedings, published in "New York State Women's Temperance Meeting," *Lily*, 1 June 1853. See also, "Proceedings of the Women's New York State Temperance Society," *Daily Democrat*, 21 April 1852.

144. Harper, *Life and Work*, 1:69–71.

145. On the Syracuse Woman's Rights Convention of 1853, see Stanton, Anthony, and Gage, *HWS*, 1:517–46, 517 (quote).

146. Ibid., 1:519–20. Women had refused to pay taxes on several earlier occasions in order to voice their opposition to political decisions, the use of funds for wars, and their lack of representation, but this may have been the first time the strategy was suggested as a collective effort on behalf of women's political rights.

147. Ibid., 1:522.

148. Ibid., 1:535.

149. Ibid., 1:535–37 on resolution, and 1:539–40 on opposition.

150. "Monroe County Woman's Rights Convention," *Daily Democrat*, 15 and 17 January 1853, CLC, for the call and a list of local organizers and participants.

151. Abigail Bush to Amy Post, [185?], IAPFP. See also Harriet Jacobs to Amy Post, 20 December [1852?] and n.d., IAPFP; and Sarah Hallowell to Amy Post, 8 January 1853, IAPFP.

152. Amy Post to Harrison Howard, 2 November 1852, IAPFP; and Harrison Howard to Amy Post, 25 November 1852, IAPFP.

153. *Daily Democrat*, 7 and 23 April 1853, quoted in McKelvey, *Rochester*, 349.

154. William F. Peck's Scrapbook, 72, cited in McKelvey, *Rochester*, 349.

155. See "MARRIED," *FDP*, 27 May 1853.

156. Isaac Post to Amy Post, 3, 4, and 5 June 1853, IAPFP.

157. "Woman's N.Y. State Temperance Society," *Lily*, 15 June 1853. On Mary Hallowell's position, see "Woman's N.Y. State Temperance Society," *Lily*, 15 April 1853. See also Journal Briefs, 1 June 1853, Box 1, JWP.

158. "First Annual Woman's N.Y. State Temperance Society," *Lily*, 15 June 1853.

159. Ibid. Within two years, the Woman's New York State Temperance Society disbanded, and moderate women again organized auxiliaries to the men's society, while radicals folded their temperance concerns into woman's rights meetings.

160. Isaac Post to Amy Post, 4 June 1853, IAPFP.

161. On the marginalization of women and women's rights in the colored convention movement, see Jones, *All Bound Up Together*, chap. 3.

162. Diaries, 6 July 1853, Box 3, JWP.

163. Kantrowitz, *More Than Freedom*, 150–57, describes the convention and its aftermath.

164. Ibid., 153–54.

165. Harriet Jacobs to Amy Post, 25 June [1853?], IAPFP. For the full story of this incident, see Yellin, *Harriet Jacobs*, 122–24.

166. Harriet Jacobs to Amy Post, 9 October 1853, IAPFP. See also Yellin, *Harriet Jacobs*, 123–25.

167. A typical tale of disaster, focused on fugitives heading from Rochester to Canada, appeared in the *Liberator*, 1 November 1850, CLC.

168. On hiding twelve fugitives, see "Slavery and Colonization," *Liberator*, 23 September 1853, quoting a September 1853 letter from Amy Post to William Nell. See also Post, "Underground Railroad in Rochester," 461–62; and Jacob Post interview in "After Almost Half a Century," *Democrat and Chronicle*, 30 December 1900, which claims fifteen slaves were hidden. Nell urged support for Rochester conductors in "Help the American Kossuths," *FDP*, 25 December 1851.

169. Diaries, 1 and 2 October 1853, Box 3, JWP. On the Jerry rescue, see McKivigan, *Frederick Douglass Papers*, 514–20, 550–55.

170. Diaries, 4 November 1853, Box 3, JWP.

171. Journal Briefs, 11 November 1853, Box 1, and Diaries, 12 November 1853, Box 3, JWP.

172. Colman, *Reminiscences*, 22–24. Following this meeting, Colman became a lecturer for the Western Anti-Slavery Society and spent much of the next year traveling the Midwest.

173. The "Mob Convention" of 6–7 September 1853 is described in detail in Stanton, Anthony, and Gage, *HWS*, 1:546–77.

174. When Rochester's *Daily Democrat* reported that this meeting, too, broke up in disorder, Isaac Post wrote the editor describing the enthusiasm and decorum at the convention. "Letters to the Editor," *Daily Democrat*, 11 October 1853.

175. Stanton, Anthony, and Gage, *HWS*, 1:124–52, 1:136 (Garrison quote).

176. See call for convention, "The Just and Equal Rights of Women," *Warsaw Wyoming County Mirror*, 22 November 1853; and proceedings in "Woman's Rights Convention," *Carson League*, 29 December 1853, CLC.

177. Stanton, Anthony, and Gage, *HWS*, 1:577–91, 1:579 (quote). See also "Woman's Rights Convention," *Carson League*, 29 December 1853, CLC.

178. Stanton, Anthony, and Gage, *HWS*, 1:580–81. See also *FDP*, 23 December 1853. Despite their disagreements over antislavery issues, Douglass continued to participate in women's rights efforts with the Posts. On Rose's discussion of prostitution, see Diaries, 30 November 1853, Box 3, JWP.

179. Stanton, Anthony, and Gage, *HWS*, 1:588–89. The petitions themselves are included as a note on these two pages. The report claims that thirteen thousand signatures were collected in two months in just half of the state's sixty counties.

Chapter Seven

1. YMCF, *Proceedings, 1849*, 6–7.

2. Diaries, Box 3, 1 December 1853, JWP.

3. Lucretia Mott, Sermon at Cherry Street Meeting, Philadelphia, 4 November 1849, in Densmore et al., *Lucretia Mott Speaks*, 62. On "practical righteousness," see YMCF, *Proceedings, 1850*, 12.

4. On the various family members and fellow activists noted in this paragraph and the next, see Rochester City Directories, 1853 and 1855, as well as numerous letters for these years in the IAPFP regarding the current location of individuals and families. On Anthony's petition drives, see Stanton, Anthony, and Gage, *HWS*, 1:619. The Union Springs school was established by Orthodox Friends, but many Hicksites and non-Friends sent their children there.

5. Journal Briefs, 1854, Box 1, JWP. These events were covered in *FDP* and mainstream Rochester newspapers, with varying responses to the political positions taken. Many were also noted in the *Liberator*, *NASS*, or the *Anti-Slavery Bugle*.

6. Andrew Jackson Davis to Isaac Post, 4 March 1854, IAPFP. On Jackson's career as a clairvoyant and author, see Braude, *Radical Spirits*, 34–43, 34 (quotes). On Luther Coleman's and John Spencer's deaths, see "Things about Home," *Syracuse Evening Chronicle*, 23 March 1854, CLC; and "Obituaries," *FDP*, 31 March 1854. Lucy Coleman, who changed her last name to Colman, was close with Amy Post despite working with the RLASS; she initially embraced spiritualism but later rejected it. See Post, preface to Colman, *Reminiscences*.

7. Isaac Post to Mary Robbins and Joseph Post, 25 August 1854, MJPFP; Mary Jane Ashley to Isaac and Amy Post, 25 September 1854, IAPFP; and Joseph Post to Parents, 9 October 1854, IAPFP.

8. Joseph Post to Isaac and Amy Post, 9 October 1854, IAPFP.

9. Isaac Post to Amy Post, 29 July 1854, IAPFP. See also George Willets to Isaac Post, 13 September 1854, IAPFP. On the 1854 panic, see Van Horn, "The Ohio Banking Panic of 1854."

10. New York/Rochester, vol. 162, p. 127, 10 September 1853, and vol. 162, p. 240L, February 1854 and 22 July 1854, R. G. Dun & Company Credit Report Volumes, Baker Library, Harvard Business School, Cambridge, Mass. No second Post store appears in any Rochester City Directory.

11. William Watkins in *FDP*, 12 August 1853, quoted in Kantrowitz, *More Than Freedom*, p. 155.

12. William Nell to Amy Post, 20 January 1854 (quote) and 13 June and 21 and 31 July 1854, IAPFP. See also "The National Council Meeting at Cleveland," *FDP*, 28 July 1854; and "A Denial," *FDP*, 1 September 1854, in Wesley and Uzelac, *William Cooper Nell*, 385–86, 387–88.

13. William Nell to Amy Post, 15 September 1854, IAPFP.

14. "Anti-Slavery Meetings in Syracuse and Rochester," *Liberator*, 27 October 1854, reported by Nell; and Greenspan, *William Wells Brown*, 321.

15. John Ketcham to Amy Post, 14 September 1854, IAPFP. See also Isaac Hicks to Isaac and Amy Post and Edmund and Sarah Willis, 12 September 1854, IAPFP; and Rachel Hicks to Amy Post and Sarah Willis, 12 September 1854, IAPFP.

16. Mary Robbins Post to Amy and Isaac Post, 26 October 1854, IAPFP; Mary W. Willis to Sarah Willis, 29 October 1854, IAPFP; and Isaac Post to Amy Post, 1 November 1854, IAPFP.

17. On Sarah Birney's illness before leaving New York City, see George Willets to Amy and Isaac Post, 18 August 185[3?], IAPFP. See also Sarah Birney to Amy Post, 17 September 1853, IAPFP, sent from Belfast, Ireland.

18. William Nell to Amy Post, 21 November 1854, IAPFP; and Isaac Post to Mary Robbins and Joseph Post, [1854?], MJPFP.

19. Sarah Birney to Amy Post, n.d., IAPFP. This letter was likely sent in winter 1854, since it is after Sarah and Edmund were married and before fall 1854, when Birney became ill.

20. Colman, "Amy Post," in *Reminiscences*, 85.

21. For numbers and descriptions of freedom seekers in Rochester in the 1850s, see Annual Reports, RLASS, William Clements Library, University of Michigan, Ann Arbor, which offer stories of those who were assisted as they passed through the city.

22. Colman, "Amy Post," in *Reminiscences*, 84. J[ames] S[loan] Gibbons to Esteemed Friend (Isaac Post), n.d., IAPFP, likely sent in the early to mid-1850s. Gibbons begins, "Will thee excuse me for this still further trouble," suggesting he had called on the Posts for help earlier.

23. Reuben Nixon to Isaac Post, by the Chaplain, 16 November [1850?], IAPFP.

24. John Joe Mack to Amy Post, 30 January 1853, IAPFP; and Asher Wright to Amy Post, 5 June 1854, IAPFP. The letter from Mack was signed with an *X*, indicating that someone else wrote it for him. He referred to himself as "your brother" and said he would repay money the Posts had lent him. Wright was not a Quaker but worked with the so-called Pagan Party of the Seneca. John Peter may have been the "Indian John Spencer" who was killed in the railroad accident in March 1854. The names the Seneca used among themselves and among whites sometimes differed. It is not clear whether the Posts took in Peter's daughter.

25. E[lizabeth] Bowen to Amy Post, 19 November 1857, IAPFP; Nancy Hassey to [Amy Post], n.d., IAPFP; Libbie Rees to Amy Post, n.d., IAPFP; and Libbie Rees to Amy Post, 3 May [186?], IAPFP. While requests for help are often undated, their content suggests that many were sent in the 1850s to early 1860s. See also Jenny Dods to Mrs. Post, n.d., IAPFP.

26. Susan Doty to Amy Post, 14 August [185?], IAPFP. Doty's letter was likely written in 1851, as she died in May 1852. It is likely the Posts did board Doty's daughter since the two families had been close since their days in Ledyard. See also S[arah] H. Hallock to Amy Post, 1 December [185?], IAPFP.

27. M[ary Ann] Pitkin to My Dear Mrs. Post, n.d., IAPFP; and Amy Post to Mary Ann [Pitkin], n.d., IAPFP. These were likely written after Pitkin had lived with the Posts for at least a few years, so the mid-1850s.

28. George Willets to Isaac Post, 29 September 1854, IAPFP; and Ansel F. Bowen to Isaac Post, 28 June 1852, IAPFP. Bowen later abused his wife, Elizabeth, who called on Amy for assistance.

29. Hiram Wilson to Isaac Post, 23 November 1853, IAPFP; and Elizabeth Hamilton to Isaac and Amy Post, n.d., IAPFP. The Hamilton letter was probably written in the 1850s, when free meetings and séances were held regularly.

30. Esther Titus to Amy Post, n.d.; Esther Titus to Amy Post, n.d.; H. O. Loper to Isaac Post, 22 August [185?]; Henry C. Wright to Isaac and Amy Post, 7 June 1855; and Mary Dale Johnson to Amy Post, 20 March 1854, all from IAPFP. William Nell confirmed receipt of Isaac Post's letter regarding Johnson's subscription on 6 November 1855, IAPFP.

31. New York/Rochester, vol. 162, p. 127, 1 March 1852 and 10 September 1853, R. G. Dun & Company Credit Report Volumes, Baker Library, Harvard Business School, Cambridge, Mass. On loans, see John V. S. L. Pruyn to Isaac Post, 12 April 1854, IAPFP; Russell Dyer to Isaac Post, 27 September 1854, IAPFP; and William Titus to Isaac Post, 28 February 1856, IAPFP. The loan to Isaac Willets was made jointly by Post and Charles Frost.

32. Thomas M'Clintock to Isaac Post, 4 October 1855, IAPFP. Neither M'Clintock nor his son opened a pharmacy in Rochester.

33. Harriet Jacobs to Amy Post, 7 August [185?], IAPFP. Many of Jacobs's letters were sent to Post from New York City; Idlewild, New Jersey; and Cornwall, New York, and include updates on Jacobs's health as well as her book. See below for a discussion of her autobiography.

34. Quote from A[my] P[ost] in Cadwallader, *Memoir*, 137. See also Nathaniel Mead to Isaac and Amy Post, 26 December 1855, IAPFP. On Isaac's illness, see Henry C. Wright to Isaac and Amy Post, 7 June 1855, IAPFP; and Mary W. Willis to Amy Post, 5 August 1855, IAPFP. On Jacob Kirby and Edmund Willis's illnesses, see Mary W. Willis to Amy Post, 4 October 1855, IAPFP.

35. Betsey Mix Cowles to Amy Post, 18 November [185?], IAPFP. See also Elijah Pound to Isaac Post, 16 January 1854, IAPFP.

36. Valentine Nicholson to Isaac and Amy Post, 16 December 1849, IAPFP; and Kate Fox to Amy Post, n.d. IAPFP. At least three Fox letters exist from this Midwest tour, probably written in 1851–52.

37. Braude, *Radical Spirits*, 154.

38. Mrs. G. B. Bushnell Marks to Amy and Isaac Post, 30 April 1854, IAPFP; and George Willets to Amy Post, 13 September 1854, IAPFP. Willets notifies Post that Mrs. Bushnell Marks is working at a water cure establishment. On female mediums as lecturers, see Braude, *Radical Spirits*, 91–93, and on female mediums and water cures, 154–57.

39. Mary Ann W. Johnson to Amy Post, 10 April [185?], IAPFP. Johnson was already part of Amy's network and sent love to Isaac, Sarah Hallowell Willis, and Mary and William Hallowell. See also Benjamin Starbuck to Isaac Post, 14 November and 8 December 1856, IAPFP, on arranging events for spiritualist Charlotte Beebee.

40. A[nna] E. W. Dowell to Amy Post, 2 January 1855, IAPFP; S. C. Hewitt to Amy Post, 27 February 1855, IAPFP; and John Dick to Amy Post, 28 March 1854,

IAPFP. Dowell addresses Post as Dear Madam, Hewitt as My Friend, and Dick as Mrs. Post, suggesting that editors who were friends, acquaintances, and strangers all reached out to Post for assistance. Dowell and Hewitt may have sought reports on the 14 January 1855 Rochester woman's rights convention at which Ernestine Rose spoke. See Journal Briefs, 14 January 1855, Box 1, JWP.

41. N. W. Daniels to Amy Post, n.d., IAPFP. Cora Hatch was born Cora Scott, but she married four times, always taking her new husband's name. Her second marriage to N. W. Daniels places this letter in the late 1850s. Elizabeth Lowe Watson to Amy Post, n.d., IAPFP. There are four undated letters, all from Livingstone Place and all related to the same visit in the late 1850s. She signed her letters Libbie Watson or L. L. Watson.

42. Harriet Jacobs to Amy Post, 14 February and 4 April 1853, IAPFP. For a full discussion of Stowe's mistreatment of Jacobs, see Yellin, *Harriet Jacobs*, 119–21.

43. Isaac Post to Joseph and Mary Robbins Post, 19 November [1854?], IAPFP.

44. James Mott to Mary Anthony and Amy Post, 25 October 1855, IAPFP. The letter was written on one page and addressed to Mary Anthony, who then passed it on to Amy Post.

45. Elizabeth Ann Kingsbury to Amy Post, 18 April 1857, IAPFP; and Abby Kelley Foster to Amy Post, 12 September 1857, IAPFP. Kelley Foster was on the road in Salem, Ohio, at the time and notes an earlier exchange that led Post to apologize for suggesting an untested speaker. Kelley Foster assures her there is no need to apologize for one "who has done service" to the cause "for a quarter of a century." Post's letter has not been located.

46. Million, *Woman's Voice, Woman's Place*, chaps. 16, 17.

47. Ibid.,191–95.

48. Amy Post to Isaac Post, 6 March 1855, IAPFP.

49. Isaac Post to Mary Robbins and Joseph Post, 24 [April 1855?], IAPFP. Isaac's letter was likely written in April 1855, since it discusses the cholera epidemic, which hit Rochester that spring and meshes with Owen's response to the incident with Douglass.

50. Sarah C. Owen to Amy Post, 15 April 1855, IAPFP.

51. Sarah Willis to Amy Post, 11 May 1855, IAPFP.

52. Ibid.

53. Jenny Curtis and Isaac Post to Amy Post, 18 May 1855, IAPFP; and Joseph Post to Amy Post, 29 May 1855, IAPFP.

54. Isaac Post to Amy Post, 2 June 1855, IAPFP; and Amy Post to Isaac Post, 14 June 1855, IAPFP.

55. Isaac Post to Amy Post, 2 and 8 June 1855, IAPFP.

56. Sarah Willis to Amy Post, 11 May 1856, IAPFP, notes Mary Dale Johnson's movements. On Mary Ann Pitkin's singing, see William Nell to Amy Post, 31 July 1854, IAPFP.

57. Mary W. Willis to Amy Post, 8 July 1855, IAPFP.

58. William Nell to Amy Post, 28 October and 30 November 1855, IAPFP; and Louisa Nell Gray to Amy Post, n.d., IAPFP. Louisa Gray wrote sometime in the spring, probably April 1856.

59. Mathilda Post to Sarah Willis, 3 February [1856?], IAPFP.

60. Isaac Post to Mary Robbins and Joseph Post, 19 February 1856, MJPFP.

61. William Titus to Isaac Post, 28 February 1856, IAPFP. See also New York/ Rochester, vol. 162, p. 127, 30 January and 31 July 1856, R. G. Dun & Company Credit Report Volumes, Baker Library, Harvard Business School, Cambridge, Mass.

62. Journal Briefs, 24 and 28 February 1856, Box 1, JWP. Wilbur copied a portion of Hallowell's letter to her on the side of the page that listed Theodore Parker's two lectures on 24 and 28 February 1856. On Nell's suspicions, see William Nell to Amy Post, 12 April 1856, IAPFP.

63. Journal Briefs, 22 February 1856, Box 1, JWP; and Colman, *Reminiscences*, 16. Colman does not mention the organizing efforts of black parents. See also Nell, "Equal School Rights for Colored Children," *Liberator*, 20 February 1857.

64. Million, *Woman's Voice, Woman's Place*, 195–97, 198–202.

65. Amy Post to Isaac Post, 28 April 1856, IAPFP.

66. Lucretia Mott to Elizabeth Neall Gay, 27 May 1856, in Palmer, *Selected Letters*, 250; and *Liberator*, 16 May 1856, on May's comment.

67. William Wells Brown quote in Yellin, *Harriet Jacobs*, 131. Yellin notes that Jacobs had been ill on and off over the previous year yet was still managing to move forward, slowly, on her life story. On the 1856 AASS, see Harriet Jacobs to Amy Post, March [1857?], IAPFP.

68. Sarah C. Owen to Amy Post, 3 May [1853?], IAPFP.

69. Isaac Post to Mary Robbins Post, 30 August 1857, MJPFP.

70. Mary Robbins Post to Amy and Isaac Post, 16 January [1858?], IAPFP. This letter seems to have been written in 1858, after Jacob Post married Jenny Curtis in 1857.

71. Quotes from Journal Briefs, 22 May and 4 November 1856, Box 1, JWP.

72. Herr, *Jessie Benton Frémont*, 253 and generally 252–55.

73. "Republican Meeting," *FDP*, 11 July 1856, on Hallowell; Frederick Douglass to Gerrit Smith, 13 August 1856, Gerrit Smith Papers, Syracuse University Library, Syracuse, N.Y.; Journal Briefs, 5 September 1856, Box 1, JWP, on mass meeting and procession.

74. J. Elizabeth Hitchcock Jones to Amy Post, 4 February 1856, IAPFP.

75. Lucy Colman to Amy Post, 5 March 1857, IAPFP. On free love and appraisals by abolitionists, spiritualists, and women's rights advocates, see Braude, *Radical Spirits*, 127–36.

76. W. E. Abbott to Maria G. Porter, 29 November 1856, RLASS Papers, William Clements Library, University of Michigan, Ann Arbor. On Tubman's career, see Clinton, *Harriet Tubman*, especially 84–85 for her relationship with Douglass.

77. On Sojourner Truth's relationship with Tubman and with Nell, Jacobs, and the Posts, see Washington, *Sojourner Truth's America*, 198, 214–17.

78. Diedrich, *Love across the Color Line*, 208–9. On Assing, see Fought, *Women in the World of Frederick Douglass*, chaps. 5, 6.

79. William Nell to Jeremiah Burke Sanderson, 17 December 1856, in Wesley and Uzelac, *William Cooper Nell*, 461–62; and "American Anti-Slavery Society," *FDP*, 13 February 1857.

80. William Nell to Amy Post, 7 June 1857, IAPFP. Nell refers to a 28 April 1857 letter from Amy Post, and summarizes some of its content. Jacob's wedding date was set in February, according to Mary Dale Johnson to Amy Post, 4 February 1857, IAPFP.

81. "Dred Scott Meeting in Rochester," *FDP*, 24 April 1857; and Washington, *Sojourner Truth's America*, 272.

82. "The Union for Man, Not Man for the Union," *Liberator*, 17 October 1856.

83. YMCF, *Proceedings, 1857*, 21–24; and Densmore, "Friends of Human Progress (Waterloo, New York), Participants at Annual Meetings, 1849–1871," in author's possession. On the Douglass-Remond debates, see "American Anti-Slavery Society Anniversary Meeting," *New York Times*, 21 and 22 May 1857; and William Nell to Amy Post, 7 June 1857, IAPFP.

84. Harriet Jacobs to Amy Post, __ March [1857?], IAPFP.

85. Harriet Jacobs to Amy Post, 18 May and 8 June 1857, IAPFP. This was a single letter that Jacobs delayed sending due to illness and the arrival of a new Willis baby.

86. Harriet Jacobs to Amy Post, 21 June [1857?], IAPFP. Post's letter to Jacobs has not been located, but Jacobs indicates the basic content of that letter.

87. William Nell to Amy Post, 22 September 1857, IAPFP.

88. Faulkner, *Lucretia Mott's Heresy*, 138; Joseph Post to Isaac Post, [1857?], IAPFP.

89. "Charles Little Murdered," *Rochester Democrat and American*, 21 December 1857, CLC; "Marion Ira Stout: His Life, Crimes, Last Hours and Execution," *Union and Advertiser*, 22 October 1858; Dewey, *Rochester and the Post Express*, 33; and Malczewski, "Heinous High Falls Murder." Stout was buried in Mt. Hope Cemetery.

90. Jacob Post to Amy Post, 25 April 1858, IAPFP.

91. Ibid.

92. Isaac Post to Amy Post, 29 April 1858, IAPFP; and Jenny Curtis Post to Amy Post, 11 May 1858, IAPFP.

93. Sarah Willis to Amy Post, 9 May 1858, IAPFP.

94. Dewey, *Rochester and the Post Express*, 33; *Geneva Courier*, 13 October 1858, CLC; and "Disgraceful Riot," *Liberator*, 22 October 1858.

95. Isaac Post to Amy Post, 10 May 1858, IAPFP.

96. Harriet Jacobs to Amy Post, 3 May 1858, IAPFP.

97. William Nell to Amy Post, 25 October 1858, IAPFP.

98. Sarah Thayer to Amy and Isaac Post, _ August 1858, IAPFP; Charles Plumb to Amy Post, 1 October 1858, IAPFP; and William Nell to Amy Post, 25 October 1858, IAPFP.

99. Densmore, "Friends of Human Progress, Participants."

100. YMCF, *Proceedings, 1859*, 5–7, 18. See also "Waterloo Yearly Meeting," *Liberator*, 1 July 1859, based on a report sent by Rochester activist Zerviah T. Watkeys.

101. Charles D. B. Mills to Amy Post, 22 and 28 June and 5 August 1859, IAPFP. See the 5 August letter for references to Amy suffering ill health that summer. Mills was an abolitionist and a member of the Reverend Samuel J. May's Unitarian congregation in Syracuse, N.Y.

102. Yellin, *Harriet Jacobs*, 137–40.

103. McFeely, *Frederick Douglass*, 198–200, explains the specific circumstances that made Douglass's arrest likely.

104. Ibid., 199–200; Gregory, *Frederick Douglass: The Orator*, 46–48, which contains selections from an interview with John Hurn; William Still to Amy Post, 21 October 1859, IAPFP; and Frederick Douglass to Amy Post, 27 October 1859, IAPFP. Douglass's letter was sent from Clifton, Canada West. Thanks to Charles Lenhart for piecing together this story.

105. Frederick Douglass to Amy Post, 27 October 1859, IAPFP.

106. Amy Post to Harriet Jacobs, 30 October 1859, IAPFP; and Jacobs, *Incidents in the Life of a Slave Girl*, 203–4.

107. Amy Post to Frederick Douglass, 13 February 1860, IAPFP.

108. Ibid. Douglass's letter to Post has not been located.

109. William Nell to Amy Post, 8 July 1860, IAPFP; and Frederick Douglass to Amy Post, 25 [January 1860?], IAPFP. Nell quotes Post on "the restoration to freedom of speech" from a 23 June 1860 letter she sent him, which has not been located. Douglass's letter likely preceded Amy Post's letter to Douglass on 13 February 1860, IAPFP.

110. Amy Post to Frederick Douglass, 13 February 1860, IAPFP.

111. Susan B. Anthony to Amy Post, 28 January [1860?], IAPFP.

112. On William Hallowell at the 1856 Republican Party Convention and among prosperous businessmen of Rochester, see "Obituaries," *Union and Advertiser*, 14 and 17 June 1882; and "William Hallowell," McIntosh, *History of Monroe County*, 128.

113. On "Rochester Convention," see *Herald of Progress*, 7 April 1860; and "Anti-Slavery Convention at Rochester," *NASS*, 31 March 1860. Lucy Colman sent the latter report.

114. "American Anti-Slavery Society," *New York Morning Express*, 10 May 1860, CLC.

115. Abigail Bush to Amy Post, 3 May 1860, IAPFP.

116. Frederick Douglass to William Still, 2 July 1860, quoted in Still, *Underground Railroad*, 430.

117. Amy Post to Isaac Post, 3 June 1860, IAPFP; and William Nell to Amy Post, 8 July and 26 October 1860, IAPFP. Amy Post's letter of 23 June 1860 is quoted in Nell's 8 July 1860 letter.

118. McFeely, *Frederick Douglass*, 208.

119. Charles True, "Lincoln in Rochester, A Memorable Journey," *Rochester Post-Express*, 11 February 1909, CLC.

120. McFeely, *Frederick Douglass*, 209–11.

121. Diaries, 10 March 1861, Box 3, JWP; and McFeely, *Frederick Douglass*, 207–8.

122. Harriet Jacobs to Amy Post, 8 October [1860?], IAPFP. For the final ordeal in getting the book published, see Yellin, *Harriet Jacobs*, 140–43.

123. William Nell to William Lloyd Garrison, 21 January 1861, published in *Liberator*, 8 February 1861. Pugh, quoted in Yellin, *Harriet Jacobs*, 146. Yellin describes Jacobs's experiences on her tour and responses to her book, 144–48.

124. Amy Post to Isaac Post, [31 May?] 1860, IAPFP.

125. YMCF, *Proceedings, 1861*, 26–32.

126. Blassingame et al., *Frederick Douglass Papers*, 3:435.

127. Yellin et al., *The Harriet Jacobs Family Papers*, 1:353–56. Excerpts from John Jacobs's letter were published in the *National Anti-Slavery Standard*, 29 June 1861.

128. Amy Post to Dear Friend, 18 June 1861, IAPFP. Although this letter is sometimes listed as being sent to Sallie Holley, it was instead addressed to someone in Holley, New York. Copies were sent to many female friends in the area. Antislavery picnics were held in other parts of the North as well, with the goal of demanding that emancipation become a declared aim of the war.

Chapter Eight

1. Douglass, "The War and How to End It," 25 March 1862, in Blassingame et al., *Frederick Douglass Papers*, 3:512.

2. On Post and Bruff pharmacy, see New York/Rochester, vol. 162, p. 240L, 30 January 1862, R. G. Dun & Company Credit Report Volumes, Baker Library, Harvard Business School, Cambridge, Mass. On Isaac Post's reengagement with movements other than spiritualism, see Joseph Post to Isaac Post, 4 November 1862, IAPFP. Information on the Posts' circumstances in the early 1860s was taken from Rochester City Directories, 1859, 1861; Eighth U.S. Federal Census, Rochester, N.Y., 1860, CLC; Abbott, *Post, Albertson and Hicks Family Letters*; and genealogical information compiled by Nancy Foster Owen and given to the author.

3. Susan B. Anthony to Joseph Post, 28 October 1861, IAPFP. Anthony sent instructions to Amy Post via her son. For other residents and visitors at Sophia Street, see Libbie Rees to Amy Post, 3 May [186?]; Sallie Holly to Amy Post, 27 March [186?]; Joseph Post to Isaac Post, 24 December 1861; and Mary Robbins Post to Amy and Isaac Post, 25 December 1861, all in the IAPFP.

4. Joseph Post to Isaac Post, 2 December 1861, IAPFP; and Mary Robbins Post to Amy and Isaac Post, 25 December 1861, IAPFP.

5. Diaries, 3 December 1861, Box 3, JWP.

6. Faulkner, *Lucretia Mott's Heresy*, 178.

7. Joseph and Mary Robbins Post to Isaac Post, 9 February 1863, IAPFP. The Frémont incident had been revived by Mrs. Jessie Benton Frémont's article about her husband's efforts to emancipate Missouri's slaves.

8. Mary Robbins Post to Isaac and Amy Post, 6 January 1862, IAPFP.

9. "American Anti-Slavery Society, Business Meeting," *Liberator*, 16 May 1862.

10. "Notice for Friends of Human Progress Meeting, Waterloo," *Herald of Progress*, 24 May 1862, CLC; and YMCF, *Proceedings*, 1862.

11. Esther Titus to Amy Post, [186?], 28 May [186?], and [May 186?], IAPFP, emphasis in original. These letters were likely written in spring and summer 1862. Some Friends refused to serve or pay for a substitute, since doing so would support the war effort. While Orthodox and Hicksite meetings often disowned men who supported the war, Progressive Friends allowed members freedom of conscience. Neither Post son, Jacob or Joseph, who were thirty and twenty-seven when the war began, served in the Union Army.

12. On debates among Friends, see YMCF, *Proceedings, 1861*, 26–32. These debates continued throughout the war.

13. Diaries, 19 September 1862, Box 3, JWP.

14. Mary Robbins Post to Amy and Isaac Post, 16 August 1862, IAPFP. Union forces used enslaved labor to help build the canal, which saw white soldiers and laborers dying at a frightening rate, but then the slaves were returned to their owners when the job was completed.

15. Henrietta Platt to Amy Post, 10 September 1862, IAPFP. Platt suggests that she is serving in or with the army. She was sending money to Post, perhaps to save until her service ended. The spelling and grammar in the letter make it difficult to understand.

16. For examples, see Henrietta Platt to Amy Post, 10 September 1862; Sarah Thayer to Amy Post, 26 October 1862; Esther Titus to Amy Post, [186?]; and William Nell to Amy Post, 10 June 1862, all in the IAPFP. Thayer's letter also refers to Post's ill health.

17. William Nell to Amy Post, 10 June 1862, IAPFP. Nell quotes an earlier letter from Post that has not been found.

18. For quote on the Post home as "a Refuge," see Sarah Thayer to Amy Post, 26 October 1862, IAPFP. On Waterloo work for contrabands/freed people, see Esther Titus, [May 186?], IAPFP. On central New York, see Breault, *World of Emily Howland*; on Philadelphia, West Chester, and elsewhere, see Faulkner, *Women's Radical Reconstruction*, 14, 26, 33, 49–53, 85, 110.

19. On attendance at the May 1862 Yearly Meeting of Friends of Human Progress in Pennsylvania, see Yellin, *Harriet Jacobs*, 158–59.

20. "Life among the Contrabands," *Liberator*, 5 September 1862, quoted in Yellin, *Harriet Jacobs*, 158–60. See also Harriet Jacobs to Amy Post, 8 December [1862?], IAPFP.

21. Whitacre, *A Civil Life*. On RLASS wartime work, see Hewitt, *Women's Activism*, 193–94; and Faulkner, *Women's Radical Reconstruction*, 15–26, 27, 32, 50, 85, 87, 91, 92, 96, 122.

22. Julia Wilbur to Amy Post, 1 November 1862, IAPFP. Since the original letter is in the IAPFP, it is likely that Post kept it and sent copies to coworkers.

23. Emily Howland to Amy Post, 23 November 1862, IAPFP; and Mary Searing and Anna Searing to Amy Post, 7 December 1862, IAPFP.

24. See published reports of the RLASS for 1862 to 1866, RLASS Papers, William Clements Library, University of Michigan, Ann Arbor. See also Anna M. C. Barnes, "An Appeal," *Douglass' Monthly*, January 1863. Barnes, secretary of RLASS, based "An Appeal" on Wilbur's reports.

25. "Emancipation Day" and "Emancipation Day in Boston," *Liberator*, 24 December 1862 and 16 January 1863, in Wesley and Uzelac, *William Cooper Nell*, 632–33.

26. McFeely, *Frederick Douglass*, 215.

27. Mary Robbins Post to Amy and Isaac Post, 13 January and 6 February 1863, IAPFP; and Joseph and Mary Robbins Post to Amy and Isaac Post, 9 February 1863, IAPFP.

28. Sojourner Truth, quoted in Washington, *Sojourner Truth's America*, 299.

29. Joseph Post and Mary Robbins Post to Amy and Isaac Post, 9 February 1863, IAPFP; and Willet Post to Amy Post, 31 January 1863, IAPFP. Edmund Willis's illness was first mentioned in Sarah Willis to Amy Post, 2 August 1861, IAPFP.

30. Julia Wilbur to Esther Titus, 20 February 1863, IAPFP. Wilbur's letter was likely sent to Esther Titus's daughter Frances—who worked with Truth in Battle Creek, Michigan—and then forwarded to her mother, who was visiting the Posts.

31. Julia Wilbur to Amy Post, 23 January 1863, IAPFP. On Douglass's efforts to promote Wilbur's cause, see Julia Wilbur to Esther [Titus?], 3 February 1863, IAPFP.

32. Harriet Jacobs to Amy Post, 8 December [1862?], IAPFP; and Julia Wilbur to Amy Post, 23 January 1863, IAPFP. The first set of quotes in this paragraph are from Jacobs, the second from Wilbur. Although Wilbur suggests that Jacobs had just arrived in the area, she had in fact been working there before Wilbur appeared. Jacobs left to visit her daughter and collect more goods before returning in mid-January 1863.

33. Ginzberg, *Elizabeth Cady Stanton*, 108.

34. "Call for a Meeting of the Loyal Women of the Nation"; and Susan B. Anthony to Amy Post, 13 April 1863, IAPFP. The call was included with Anthony's letter to Post and other women and printed in the *New York Tribune*.

35. Ginzberg, *Elizabeth Cady Stanton*, 108–10; and Faulkner, *Women's Radical Reconstruction*, 84.

36. "War and Women's Rights," *New York Herald*, 15 May 1863, CLC; Ginzberg, *Elizabeth Cady Stanton*, 110; and Stanton, Anthony, and Gage, *HWS*, 2:58–61, 893. The Women's Loyal National League disbanded once Congress approved the Thirteenth Amendment.

37. Sarah Thayer to Amy Post, 10 September 1863, IAPFP, in which she discusses the 1863 Friends of Human Progress meeting.

38. Esther Titus to Amy Post, [186?], IAPFP. Emphasis in original. While the letter has no date, it was no doubt written following the New York City Draft Riots of early July 1863.

39. On draft riots and the resumption of conscription, see McPherson, *Battle Cry of Freedom*, 610–11; and Gutknecht, "Urban Legend."

40. Esther Titus to Amy Post, [December 1863?], IAPFP. Titus notes "how many times thy soul went there, with its heavy load." The rest of this paragraph is based on Amy Post to Isaac Post, 8 December 1863, IAPFP.

41. Amy Post to Isaac Post, 8 December 1863, IAPFP. The Female Medical College of Pennsylvania was founded in 1850 with support from Philadelphia Friends. Aurelia Raymond, a widow with two children, received her degree there. In 1867, the school was renamed the Woman's Medical College.

42. Amy Post to Isaac Post, 8 December 1863, IAPFP.

43. Ibid.

44. Amy Post to Isaac Post, 10 December 1863, IAPFP.

45. Ibid.

46. Julia Wilbur to Mrs. A. M. C. Barnes, 27 February 1863, RLASS Papers, William Clements Library, University of Michigan, Ann Arbor. On Jacobs's and Wilbur's opposition to Gladwin, see Yellin, *Harriet Jacobs*, 165–66; and Whitaker, *A Civil Life*, 89–90, 110, 112–14, 119–21, 128–32, 146–47.

47. Journal Briefs, 10 December 1863, Box 1, JWP; Diaries, 10 December 1863, Box 3, JWP; and Amy Post to Isaac Post, 10 December 1863, IAPFP. Excerpts from these three sources are woven through the paragraph.

48. Amy Post to Isaac Post, 10 December 1863, IAPFP.

49. Amy Post to Isaac Post, 11 December 1863, IAPFP.

50. Ibid.

51. Ibid.

52. Isaac Post to Amy Post, 10 December 1863, IAPFP.

53. Mary W. Willis to Amy Post, 2 January 1863, IAPFP. Mary Willis notes "little girls," but family records suggest that only one daughter, Jessie, born in 1861, survived the war. If there was a second daughter, she died by 1865 or 1866.

54. Sarah Thayer noted Amy Post's visit to Leah Fox Underhill when she wrote Amy on 6 March 1864, IAPFP.

55. Martha Cary to Willet Post, 1 February 1863, IAPFP; and T. H. Burgess to Willet Post, 1 April 1863, IAPFP. Carey and Burgess were schoolmates of Willet Post.

56. Phebe Hathaway to Amy and Isaac Post, 27 February 1864, IAPFP. The activist's name is illegible.

57. Sallie Holley to Amy Post, 27 March [1864?], IAPFP.

58. Sarah Thayer to Amy Post, 6 March and 30 May 1864, IAPFP.

59. Mary Robbins Post to Amy Post, 22 March [1864?], IAPFP.

60. Lucretia Mott speech is noted in "American Anti-Slavery Society Anniversary Meeting," *Liberator*, 20 May 1864.

61. Washington, *Sojourner Truth's America*, 311–12.

62. See announcement of a lecture by Sojourner Truth, n.d., IAPFP. The description of Truth in the announcement refers to the 1864 lecture. For quotes, see report of Sallie Holley, *NASS*, 6 August 1864; and Washington, *Sojourner Truth's America*, 311–12. Holley, like Stowe, transformed Truth's Dutch accent into a southern dialect, so I have used verbatim quotes sparingly.

63. Diaries, 28 July, 7 August, 4 September, 28 and 29 September, 23 October, and 7 November 1864, Box 3, JWP.

64. The battle over the Thirteenth Amendment involved many players. See Richards, *Who Freed the Slaves?*; Goodwin, *Team of Rivals*, 686–90, 693, 695, 728; and Zaeske, *Signatures of Citizenship*, 167–72. On the Freedmen's Bureau, see Faulkner, *Women's Radical Reconstruction*, chap. 5.

65. Louisa Nell Gray to Amy Post, 27 February and 21 March 1865, IAPFP; and Joseph Post to Isaac Post, 23 February 1865, IAPFP.

66. Amy Post to Esther Titus, 28 March 1865, IAPFP.

67. Ibid. See also Willet Post to Amy Post, 12 February 1865, IAPFP. Willie was in school in Westbury at the time. See also Peter Chudoba, "Great Rochester Flood of 1865," 3 April 2015, https://www.linkedin.com/pulse/great-rochester-flood-1865 -peter-petr-chudoba/.

68. Joseph Post to Isaac Post, 23 February 1865, IAPFP.

69. New York State Census, Rochester, N.Y., 1865, CLC. Mrs. Margaret King had previously boarded with Isaac and Amy Post.

70. Sojourner Truth to Amy Post, 1 October 1865, IAPFP.

71. Josephine Griffing to Amy Post, 10 January 1866, IAPFP; Laura Haviland to Amy Post, 22 February 1866, IAPFP; and Cora Hatch Daniels to Amy Post, 2 January 1866, IAPFP.

72. Laura Haviland to Amy Post, 22 February 1866, IAPFP; and Washington, *Sojourner Truth's America*, 327–28. See also Miles, "'Shall Woman's Voice Be Hushed?,'" 18–19.

73. Washington, *Sojourner Truth's America*, 323, 328–30. Letters to Truth from Josephine Griffing and Laura Haviland were sent to the Posts, as well as those from Edward Ives, Phebe Hart Merritt, and Matilda Gardner, all residents of Battle Creek. See IAPFP letters for 1866 and 1867. On one of Truth's trips from Washington, D.C., to Rochester, see Clipping, *New York World*, 14 June 1867, CLC.

74. Josephine Griffing and Sojourner Truth to Amy Post, 26 March 1867, IAPFP. On establishing the committee, see clipping, *Rochester Evening Times*, 12 March 1917, CLC, which notes the committee organized by Truth fifty years earlier. See also Julia Wilbur, "The Freedmen in Washington" and "To the Public," *Rochester Express*, 13 March 1867, CLC.

75. J. S. Bowen to Sojourner Truth, 25 March 1867; Ruth Andrews to Sojourner Truth, 3 April 1867; A. C. Van Epps to Sojourner Truth, 19 March 1867; and Mrs. James Cavan to Sojourner Truth, 16 March 1867, all in the IAPFP. Mary H. Thomas to Sojourner Truth, 13 May 1867, IAPFP, suggests the difficulties that sometimes accompanied efforts to settle southern freed people in the farm towns of western New York. Along with the letters requesting freed people in the Post Family Papers, there is also a list of potential employers. See Miscellaneous File, n.d., IAPFP.

76. Sojourner Truth to Amy Post, 25 August 1867, IAPFP. It is not clear who wrote this letter for Truth, which was sent from Toledo, Ohio.

77. Josephine Griffing and Sojourner Truth to Amy Post, 26 March 1867, IAPFP; and "Colored Farm Hands from the South," *Rochester Evening Express*, 6 June 1867, CLC.

78. On the lyceum series, see Isaac and Amy Post to Joseph and Mary Robbins Post, 29 November 1866, IAPFP.

79. Washington, *Sojourner Truth's America*, 330–31.

80. Diaries, 17 August 1866, Box 3, JWP.

81. Mary Robbins Post to Amy and Isaac Post, 4 August 1866, IAPFP. On Jacobs's travail in Savannah, see Yellin, *Harriet Jacobs*, 191–201.

82. Isaac and Amy Post to Joseph and Mary Robbins Post, 29 November 1866, IAPFP.

83. Ibid.

84. "Waterloo Yearly Meeting," *NASS*, 16 July 1866.

85. Dudden, *Fighting Chance*, 82–93.

86. "Thirty-Second Anniversary," *Liberator*, 26 May 1865.

87. Amy Post to Aaron Powell, n.d., IAPFP. The letter was sent in spring 1865, before the Friends of Human Progress meeting in June. In it, Post urges Powell to attend, which he does.

88. See Faulkner, *Lucretia Mott's Heresy*, 187, quoting Mott to Wendell Phillips, 17 April 1866, and laying out the issues at the formation of the AERA.

89. This paragraph and the next are based on Dudden, *Fighting Chance*, 80–87.

90. Ibid. See also "Equal Rights Convention," *Rochester Express*, 1 December 1866, CLC; and Harper, *Life and Times*, 1:263–65, on equal rights meetings held in Albany and New York City.

91. Mate Rey, "The Women's Rights Convention," *Ontario Repository and Messenger*, 9 January 1867, CLC.

92. Ibid. See also Harper, *Life and Times*, 1:263–65.

93. See Ginzberg, *Elizabeth Cady Stanton*, 120–31, for a detailed discussion of racism, suffrage, Stanton, and Train in the postwar period.

94. Washington, *Sojourner's Truth's America*, 337–41; and Dudden, *Fighting Chance*, 95–100.

95. William Nell to Amy Post, 23 June 1867, IAPFP.

96. "Proceedings of the Waterloo Yearly Meeting," *NASS*, 22 June 1867; and "Waterloo Yearly Meeting of the Friends of Progress," *Rochester Evening Express*, 6 June 1867, CLC.

97. Stanton, Anthony, and Gage, *HWS*, 2:269–309; for the petition of the Friends of Human Progress, see 282.

98. Abbott, ed., *Post, Albertson, and Hicks*, 1:301, 361–62.

99. Washington, *Sojourner Truth's America*, 343. Many scholars view Stanton as more overtly racist in her appeals for woman suffrage, but Douglass did not, at least at this point, distinguish between her and Anthony. Despite her support for the Fifteenth Amendment, Lucy Stone, too, demeaned blacks and immigrants, though more often in private letters than public pronouncements. Eventually

Douglass, Anthony, and Stanton repaired their relationship, and in the 1870s, Stanton credited Douglass with ensuring approval of the woman suffrage resolution at the Seneca Falls Woman's Rights Convention. See Tetrault, *Myth of Seneca Falls*, 150–52.

100. "Spiritualist Convention," *Albany Express*, 28 August 1868, CLC; and *American Association of Spiritualists*, 1868.

101. "Anniversary of Spiritualism," *Union and Advertiser*, 1 April 1868. Although Post spoke at the 1848 woman's rights conventions in Seneca Falls and Rochester, she more often served on business, nominating, and resolution committees at antislavery and woman's rights meetings. She was never considered a featured speaker before the late 1860s.

102. Amy Post to Aaron Powell, "Letter," *NASS*, 26 December 1868. On Geneva event, see "Emancipation Jubilee," *Geneva Gazette*, 28 August 1868; and "Grand Republican Ratification," *Rochester Evening Express*, 29 August 1868, CLC.

103. Jonathan Walker to Amy Post, 1 January 1869, IAPFP.

104. Eliza Leggett to Amy Post, [1869?], IAPFP. This letter was written during the months that Truth spent in Michigan between Grant's election as president and her 1869 lecture tour.

105. Unitarian Society Records, SpecColUR; and conversations with Amy Foster Post and Nancy Foster Owens, 1995 and 1996.

106. Dudden, *Fighting Chance*, chap. 4; Painter, *Sojourner Truth*, chap. 15; and Faulkner, *Lucretia Mott's Heresy*, 187–89, 195–96, and chap. 12.

107. Dudden, *Fighting Chance*, chap. 7, offers a detailed account of the collapse of the AERA and the emergence of the competing NWSA and AWSA.

108. Amy Post to Lucy Stone, 5 November 1869, IAPFP. For the larger context of this letter, see Braude, *Radical Spirits*, 163–73.

109. "Observes 90th Birthday," *Democrat and Chronicle*, 21 February 1913, on Hallowell's friendship with Anthony; and Susan B. Anthony to Amy Post, 2 December 1866, IAPFP.

110. "Equal Suffrage Association," *Rochester Evening Express*, 9 July 1869 (quote). Little else is known about this association. On the New York State Suffrage Association, see "Woman's Suffrage Convention," *Saratogian*, 22 July 1869, CLC.

111. Lois Waisbrooker to Amy Post, 25 April 1867, IAPFP.

112. Colman, *Reminiscences*, 85, 93.

113. This event was reported in the *New York Tribune*, 23 April 1869. Wilbur also noted the event, and probably informed Rochester friends of her participation. Diaries, 22 April 1869, Box 3, JWP.

114. For an extensive list of women's efforts to register and vote between 1868 and 1873, see Gordon, *Selected Papers*, 2: appendix C.

115. Ibid. On various Washington, D.C., efforts at registration, see Terborg-Penn, *African American Women and the Struggle for the Vote*, chap. 3. On Douglass's involvement, see 40.

116. Susan B. Anthony to Mary Hallowell, 11 April 1867, IAPFP.

117. On Robert Johnston, see Gordon, *Selected Papers*, 2:357. Quote on "sacred text," from Tetrault, *Myth of Seneca Falls*, 71. See *Proceedings of the Rochester Woman's Rights Convention . . . Revised by Amy Post*.

118. Ninth Federal Census of the United States, 1870, Rochester, Monroe County, New York, 1st Ward, 32, CLC.

119. On Isaac Post's illness, see Mary Ann Pitkin to Amy Post, 18 November 1866, IAPFP. Pitkin was then employed in Troy, New York. On Nell, see Wesley and Uzelac, *William Cooper Nell*, 47; and Charles Lenox Remond to Amy Post, 21 February 1872, IAPFP.

120. Isaac Post to Jacob Post, 2 March 1872, IAPFP; and Amy Post to All, c/o Jacob Post, 28 March 1872, IAPFP.

121. Frederick Douglass to Jacob Post, 10 May 1872, IAPFP.

122. Isaac Post to Amy Post, 29 April 1858, IAPFP.

123. McFeeley, *Frederick Douglass*, 275–76; and Frederick Douglass, "Letter," *New National Era*, June 1872.

124. "Women Registering," *Union and Advertiser*, 2 November 1872; and Susan B. Anthony to Elizabeth Cady Stanton, 5 November 1872, in Gordon, *Selected Papers*, 2:524–25. Martha C. Wright to Amy Post, 17 November 1872, IAPFP, in which she thanks Post for her detailed letter about the recent election, but the letter has not been located.

125. Susan B. Anthony to Elizabeth Cady Stanton, 5 November 1872, in Gordon, *Selected Papers*, 2:524–25; and Franklin K. Orvis to Amy Post, 21 November 1872, IAPFP. Orvis had spoken at the 5 July 1869 Equal Rights Association celebration. Post may have been following Douglass's logic in his 5 July 1852 speech when scheduling this event.

126. The full list of women who tried to register is unknown. Most were not allowed to register, and the 1872 Rochester registration lists were destroyed in 1972. Compiling information from a variety of sources indicates that as many as fifty women attempted to register in Rochester. The names of some of the women can be found in "Women Registering," *Democrat and Chronicle*, 1 November 1872; Harper, *Life and Work*, 1:423–24; and Mary Hebard, "Female Suffrage," 1873, Pamphlet Collections, New York State Historical Library, Cooperstown, N.Y. See A. Crum, Chairman Board of Inspectors of the First Ward, to Mrs. [Amy] Post, 1 November 1872, on refusal to let her register, City Clerk's Office, Rochester, New York, CLC.

Chapter Nine

1. Linder, "Susan Anthony Trial (1873)," *Famous Trials*, accessed 10 September 2017, http://www.famous-trials.com/anthony. The quotes from primary sources are from this site, which also contains the complete trial record, Anthony letters and speeches related to the trial, and other documents. See also, Gordon, *Selected Papers*, 2:537–621.

2. On the Women's Taxpayers Association, see Hebard, "Female Suffrage," n.d., likely published shortly after Anthony's 1873 trial. A version of one of the speeches that Anthony gave numerous times while awaiting trial—"Is It a Crime for a U.S. Citizen to Vote?"—appears in Gordon, *Selected Papers*, 2:554–83.

3. Flexner, *Century of Struggle*, 165–68. For a detailed contemporary analysis with documents, see Stanton, Anthony, and Gage, *HWS*, 2:628, 687, 689; and Gordon, *Selected Papers*, 2:524–39, 542–45, 554–83, 612–16. The election inspectors were initially found guilty, fined, and imprisoned until they paid their fine, but President Ulysses S. Grant quietly pardoned them following Anthony's trial. The other women who voted alongside Anthony were never tried.

4. Hebard, "Female Suffrage." On the association's condemnation of Hunt, see Gordon, *Selected Papers*, 2:618–19.

5. Ibid.

6. Tetrault, *Myth of Seneca Falls*, chap. 2.

7. First quote, "Second Decade Celebration," *Revolution*, 27 October 1870; second quote from Stanton reading from Davis's call for the event in Tetrault, *Myth of Seneca Falls*, 41–42.

8. Tetrault, *Myth of Seneca Falls*, 68–73.

9. See Clipping, *Democrat and Chronicle*, 18 October 1873, CLC; and Gordon, *Selected Papers*, 2: appendix C.

10. "Sovereigns of Industry," *Fairport Herald*, 1 May 1874, CLC.

11. "National Anti-Slavery Reunion," *New York Times*, 11 June 1874, CLC; and "Looking Backward—Thirty-Five Years Ago Today," clipping from unnamed Rochester newspaper, 31 August 1909, CLC.

12. William Nell to Amy Post, 10 May 1868 and 26 September 1869, IAPFP. Quote from second letter. See also Wesley and Uzelac, *William Cooper Nell*, 680–81; and Stephen Kantrowitz, *More Than Freedom*, 396–97.

13. Rochester City Directory, 1875.

14. On marriages, see "Announcements," *Union and Advertiser*, 28 April 1875 and 1 July 1876.

15. *Atlas of Rochester, New York, 1875*, Plate 016, Wards 3 and 8, CLC.

16. On personal health and medical treatments, see Amy Post's testimonial for Dr. E. B. Fish in *Hudson Daily Star*, 10 April 1875, CLC. Deaths of local coworkers and friends were recorded in family papers, Friends and church records, and local and reform newspapers.

17. "The Liberal League," *Rochester Evening Express*, 27 October 1877, CLC. For more on its history and membership, see "National Liberal League," Freethought Trail, accessed 5 September 2016, http://www.freethought-trail.org/profile.php?By=Person&Page=30.

18. Wedding and births are noted in Post family genealogies provided by Nancy Foster Owen.

19. *Index*, 27 December 1877.

20. The possibility of meeting in Rochester in July 1878 first appeared in "The National Woman Suffrage Association," *National Citizen and Ballot Box*, April 1878; final arrangements appeared in its June 1878 edition under the title "Thirtieth Anniversary," CLC.

21. The 1878 NWSA meeting and anniversary celebration were covered enthusiastically in "N. W. R. Association," *Union and Advertiser*, 19 July 1848, CLC; and "Woman Suffrage: Meeting of the National Association in Rochester," *National Citizen and Ballot Box*, August 1878. See also Stanton, Anthony, and Gage, *HSW*, 3:117–27. The August 1878 *National Citizen and Ballot Box* drew on reports from the *Union and Advertiser*, the *Sunday Morning Herald*, the *Syracuse Journal*, the *World*, and the *Buffalo Express*.

22. *Union and Advertiser*, 19 July 1878, CLC. On the visit of Truth and Titus to Rochester in summer and early fall 1878, see Washington, *Sojourner Truth's America*, 370.

23. Mott, "Remarks at National Woman Suffrage Association Meeting," in *National Citizen and Ballot Box*, August 1878, reprinted in Densmore et al., *Lucretia Mott Speaks*, 214–15.

24. "Woman Suffrage: Meeting of the National Association in Rochester," *National Citizen and Ballot Box*, August 1878. Tetrault, *Myth of Seneca Falls*, 106, sees this speech as "signal[ing] the shift in mood by 1878." This is a reasonable assumption until you read this speech alongside Post's numerous efforts to sustain a broad women's rights agenda before 1848 and after 1878.

25. "Woman Suffrage: Meeting of the National Association in Rochester," *National Citizen and Ballot Box*, August 1878.

26. Ibid.

27. "National Women's Suffrage Convention," *Brooklyn Daily Eagle*, 10 May 1879, CLC; "National Liberal League," *Boston Investigator*, 24 September 1879, CLC.

28. Amy Post to A. L. Rawson, 9 September 1879, IAPFP.

29. The letter included in Amy Post to A. L. Rawson, 9 September 1879, IAPFP, was to be read at the convention. It was published in slightly edited form in "A Letter From Mrs. Amy Post," *Boston Investigator*, 24 September 1879, CLC.

30. On Amy Post's and Joseph Post's families, see Ninth U.S. Federal Census, 1880, Rochester, Monroe County, New York, CLC. Joseph lists himself as a druggist in Charlotte, New York, in the 1880 census.

31. "Tom Paine," *Union and Advertiser*, 2 February 1880. On Dorus M. and Henrietta (Nettie) Pease Fox, see Larry Wood, "Nettie Pease Fox," *Missouri and Ozarks History*, 9 December 2008, http://ozarks-history.blogspot.com/2008/12/nettie-pease-fox.html. It focuses specifically on their time in Springfield, Missouri. Jay Chaapel's name is spelled in various ways in newspapers and city directories. He was likely related to C. Will Chappell of Ontario, who owned a funeral home and casket company in Rochester; and James Chappell who resided at 55 Plymouth Avenue. Jay's name appears as Chappell in the *Union and Advertiser*, 2 February 1880.

32. "The Right to Vote," *Union and Advertiser*, 23 February 1880, CLC.

33. Ibid.

34. Clipping, *Batavia Daily News*, 28 February 1880, CLC.

35. "Free Love and Spiritualism," *Democrat and Chronicle*, 8 March 1880, CLC.

36. On NWSA 1880 convention, see "Meeting of the National Association," *National Citizen and Ballot Box*, July 1880, CLC; and Gordon, *Selected Papers* 3:527–40.

37. "The Freethinker's National Convention," *Ithaca Daily Journal*, 10 July 1880; and "The Free Thinkers," *Evening Gazette*, 17 July 1880. On Mott's frustration with conflicts among suffragists and her turn to peace activism and free religious meetings, see Faulkner, *Lucretia Mott's Heresy*, 189–96 and chap. 12.

38. "The Famine in Kansas," *Democrat and Chronicle*, 2 July 1880, CLC; and Washington, *Sojourner Truth's America*, 372–73.

39. "The National Liberal League," *Man*, 1 November 1880.

40. Faulkner, *Lucrertia Mott's Heresy*, 210.

41. The signed copy of *Incidents in the Life of a Slave Girl* is held in Special Collections at Pennsylvania State University, State College, Pennsylvania. Kate Culkin brought the book and Chaapel's comments to my attention. It is not clear whether Amy Post and Harriet Jacobs were in touch after 1868, so if Chaapel met Jacobs at Post's home, it was likely when he was a boy. Chaapel mistakenly claims that Jacobs wrote most of the book at 36 Sophia Street.

42. On Edmund Willis, see Peck, *History of Rochester and Monroe County*, 1342; and McIntosh, *History of Monroe County*, 128. On William Hallowell, see Obituaries, *Union and Advertiser*, 14 and 17 June 1882; and McIntosh, *History of Monroe County*, 128.

43. Frederick Douglass Jr. to Amy Post, 8 July 1882, IAPFP; and Frederick Douglass to Amy Post, 14 July 1882 and 21 August 1882, IAPFP. See Fought, *Women in the World of Frederick Douglass*, 225–28; and McFeely, *Frederick Douglass*, 312–14.

44. "Mrs. Post's Eightieth Birthday," *Union and Advertiser*, 9 March 1883. On Cornelia Gardner, see "Indignation Meeting," *Lockport Daily Journal*, 23 October 1878, CLC; and Obituary, *Union and Advertiser*, 30 August 1894. Nancy Foster Owen inherited the Amy Post photograph album and allowed me to view it. Unfortunately, most individuals in the pictures are not identified or identifiable.

45. "The Freethinkers," *Rome Daily Sentinel*, 3 September 1883, CLC.

46. Mary Dale Johnson, Record of Inmates, County Poor House, Monroe County, New York, CLC.

47. On a "hard summer," see Frances Titus to Amy Post, 21 July 1883, IAPFP. See also 1884 edition of Truth, *A Narrative of Sojourner Truth*. Copy inscribed by Amy Post to Willet E. Post, Gilder-Lehrman Collection, Gilder-Lehrman Institute, New York, N.Y., CLC.

48. Frederick Douglass to Amy Post, 27 August 1884, IAPFP. Douglass notes Post's earlier letter sending "congratulations and good wishes." See also Fought, *Women in the World of Frederick Douglass*, 229–30, 243–47.

49. Peck, *Semi-Centennial History of the City of Rochester*, 458–62.

50. Parker, *Rochester: A Story Historical*, 245, 258.

51. Amy Post to Joseph and Mary Robbins Post, 24 March [1884?], IAPFP.

52. Norgren, *Belva Lockwood*, 117–19, 118 (quote).

53. Ibid., 120–21.

54. Amy Post to Joseph and Mary Robbins Post, 24 March [1884?], IAPFP.

55. Ibid.

56. "An Honored Visitor," *Boston Investigator*, 6 August 1884.

57. "The Ballot for Women," *Democrat and Chronicle*, 5 October 1884, CLC; and "Woman Suffrage," *Brooklyn Union*, 10 October 1884, CLC.

58. "Anniversary Meeting," *Democrat and Chronicle*, 29 March 1885, CLC; and "Woman Suffragists," *Democrat and Chronicle*, 2 December 1885, CLC.

59. "The Mother of Modern Spiritualism," *Carrier Dove* (San Francisco), July 1886. Thanks to Ann Braude for sending me this article many years ago.

60. "Free Thinkers Convention," *New York Herald*, 12 September 1885, CLC.

61. The story of her attendance at the 1887 Friends of Human Progress Annual Meeting appeared in "Amy Post at Rest," *Democrat and Chronicle*, 30 January 1889; the spiritualists' incorporation was noted in "Stock Corporation of Spiritualists," *Rochester Express* and quoted in the *Daily Times and Express*, 26 November 1888, CLC.

62. "International Council of Women," *Buffalo Daily Courier* and *New York Herald*, 1 April 1888, CLC. The *Herald* referred to the women as the pioneers of "the woman's suffrage movement" rather than the women's rights movement, despite the myriad topics addressed at the International Council for Women convention. See also *Friends' Intelligencer*, vol. 45, 1888, 238–240, http:/books.google.compg /books?id+ha4Qaaaayaaj.

63. My understanding that the family lost knowledge of its roots in the Society of Friends came from conversations with Amy Post Foster and Nancy Foster Owen—Amy Kirby Post's great-granddaughter and great-great-granddaughter—in the late 1990s.

64. See "Mrs. Amy Post at Rest," *Democrat and Chronicle*, 30 January 1889; "Amy Post Dead," *Union and Advertiser*, 30 January 1889; and "A Good Woman Gone," *Buffalo Courier*, 1 February 1889.

65. See also "Obituaries," *Troy Daily Times*, 30 January 1889; *New York Herald*, 30 January 1889; *Union Springs Advertiser*, 30 January 1889; and *Medina Daily Register*, 7 February 1889, all CLC.

66. "Mourning a Benefactor," *Democrat and Chronicle*, 1 February 1889; and "Laid Forever at Rest," *Democrat and Chronicle*, 2 February 1889.

67. "The Passing of Amy Post," *Union and Advertiser*, 1 February 1889; and "Laid Forever at Rest," *Democrat and Chronicle*, 2 February 1889.

68. "Mrs. Amy Post at Rest," *Democrat and Chronicle*, 30 January 1889; and "Amy Post Dead," *Union and Advertiser*, 30 January 1889.

69. *Rome Daily Sentinel*, 22 November 1894; *Elmira Telegraph*, 3 March 1895; and *Democrat and Chronicle*, 22 February 1896, all CLC.

70. Colman, *Reminiscences*, 85.

71. On Mary Hallowell, see "Whole Life in Fight for Sex," *Democrat and Chronicle*, 8 March 1913, as well as "Early Woman Suffragist Leaves $111,000 Estate," 6 September 1913, on the bequests she left to nieces, nephews, and charitable organizations. On Sarah Willis, see "Mrs. Sarah L. Willis," *Union and Advertiser*, 11 April 1914; and "Death of Mrs. S. L. Willis," *Democrat and Chronicle*, 12 April 1914. See also "Many Share in Estate of $600,000," 2 June 1914, on her bequests to family and charitable organizations. Amy Post left an estate of $20,000 divided among family members. See "The Amy Post Estate," *Union and Advertiser*, 25 February 1889 CLC.

72. "Joseph Post," *Union and Advertiser*, 11 December 1915; and "Joseph Post of Charlotte Dies," *Democrat and Chronicle*, 11 December 1915, both CLC.

73. "Jacob K. Post Dies," *Union and Advertiser*, 1 December 1916; and "Death Removes Jacob K. Post," *Democrat and Chronicle*, 1 December 1916, CLC.

74. "Willet E. Post Dies After Being Long Ill," *Democrat and Chronicle*, 23 July 1917; and "Willet E. Post," *Union and Advertiser*, 23 July 1917, both CLC.

75. "Five Rochesterians Spark 1st Women's Rights Conclave," *Democrat and Chronicle*, 20 July 1948, CLC.

76. "Letters Give a Glimpse into a Way of Life," *Democrat and Chronicle*, 5 January 1979.

77. Abigail Bush to Amy Post, [1853?], IAPFP. Bush wrote from New York City while awaiting the boat to take her and her children to California; Susan Lee Humphrey to Amy Post, 30 May 1857, IAPFP.

78. Amy Post, "Mental Autograph Album," compiled by Josephine Wheeler Post. Copy in author's possession.

Bibliography

Newspapers and Periodicals

Albany (N.Y.) *Express*
American Baptist (New York, N.Y.)
Anti-Slavery Bugle (Salem, Ohio)
Ashtabula (Ohio) *Sentinel*
Auburn Cayuga (N.Y.) *Republican*
Auburn (N.Y.) *Journal and Advertiser*
Batavia (N.Y.) *Daily News*
Boston Investigator
Brooklyn (N.Y.) *Daily Eagle*
Brooklyn (N.Y.) *Union*
Buffalo (N.Y.) *Express*
Carrier Dove (San Francisco)
Circumstance (Rochester, N.Y.)
Daily Advertiser (Rochester, N.Y.)
Daily American (Rochester, N.Y.)
Daily Democrat (Rochester, N.Y.)
Daily Gazette (Utica, N.Y.)
Daily News (Batavia, N.Y.)
Daily Sentinel (Rome, N.Y.)
Daily Times and Express (Oswego, N.Y.)
Daily Union and Advertiser (Rochester, N.Y.)
Democrat and Chronicle (Rochester, N.Y.)
Fairport (N.Y.) *Herald*
Douglass' Monthly (Rochester, N.Y.)
Evening Gazette (Port Jervis, N.Y.)
Frederick Douglass' Paper (Rochester, N.Y.)
Friend of Man (Rochester, N.Y.)
Friends' Intelligencer (Philadelphia)
Geneva (N.Y.) *Courier*
Geneva (N.Y.) *Gazette*
Herald of Progress (New York, N.Y.)

Hudson (N.Y.) *Daily Star*
Index: Devoted to Free Religion (Boston)
Ithaca (N.Y.) *Daily Journal*
Liberator (Boston)
Lily (Seneca Falls, N.Y.)
Livonia (N.Y.) *Gazette*
Long Island Advertiser (Jamaica, N.Y.)
Madison and Onondaga County (N.Y.) *Abolitionist*
Madison County (N.Y.) *Abolitionist*
Man: A Weekly Journal of Progress and Reform (New York, N.Y.)
Medina (N.Y.) *Daily Register*
National Anti-Slavery Standard (New York, N.Y.)
National Citizen and Ballot Box (Syracuse, N.Y.)
National Era (Washington, D.C.)
National Reformer (Rochester, N.Y.)
New York (N.Y.) *Herald*
New York (N.Y.) *Evening Express*
New York (N.Y.) *Morning Express*
North Star (Rochester, N.Y.)
Ontario (N.Y.) *Repository*
Ontario Repository and Messenger (Canandaigua, N.Y.)
Ovid (N.Y.) *Bee*
Pennsylvania Freeman (Philadelphia)
Revolution (New York, N.Y.)
Rights of Man (Rochester, N.Y.)
Rochester (N.Y.) *Democrat and American*
Rochester (N.Y.) *Post-Express*
Rochester (N.Y.) *Republican*

Rome (N.Y.) *Daily Sentinel*
Seneca County (N.Y.) *Courier*
Troy (N.Y.) *Daily Times*

Troy (N.Y.) *Daily Whig*
Union and Advertiser (Rochester, N.Y.)
Union Springs (N.Y.) *Advertiser*

Manuscripts

Ann Arbor, Mich.
    William Clements Library, University of Michigan
        Amy Kirby Papers
        Rochester Ladies' Anti-Slavery Society Papers
Boston, Mass.
    Boston Public Library
        Antislavery Collection
        William Lloyd Garrison Papers
Cambridge, Mass.
    Baker Library, Harvard Business School
        R. G. Dun & Company Credit Report Volumes
Cooperstown, N.Y.
    New York State Historical Library
        Pamphlet Collections
Haverford, Pa.
    Special Collection, Haverford College Library
        Julia Wilbur Papers
Hilton, N.Y.
    Private Collection
        Charles Lenhart Collection
Huntington, Calif.
    Huntington Library
        Ida Husted Harper Collection
Jericho, N.Y.
    Jericho Public Library, Local History Room
        "Long Island Houses"
Lyons, N.Y.
    Wayne County Historian's Office
        Mary Durfee Diary, Transcribed by Marjorie Allen Perez
New Haven, Conn.
    Beineke Library, Yale University Manuscripts and Archives
        Frederick Douglass Papers
New York, N.Y.
    Gilder-Lehrman Institute
        Gilder-Lehrman Collection
    Haviland Records Room
        Society of Friends

Friends of Human Progress
Genesee Yearly Meeting
Genesee Yearly Meeting, Men
Genesee Yearly Meeting, Women
Jericho Monthly Meeting, Men
Jericho Monthly Meeting, Women
Jericho Monthly Meeting, Preparative
Rochester Monthly Meeting
Scipio Monthly Meeting
Yearly Meeting of Congregational Friends
New York Public Library
Rochester Monthly Meeting, "Marriage Intents, 1825–1850," compiled by
John Cox Jr., 1911.
Philadelphia, Pa.
Presbyterian Historical Society
Second (Brick) Presbyterian Church, Rochester, N.Y., Records
Third Presbyterian Church, Rochester, N.Y., Records
Rochester, N.Y.
University of Rochester, Rush Rhees Library, Special Collections and
Preservation Department
Benjamin Fish Family Papers
Hillside Children's Center Papers
Samuel D. and Susan F. Porter Family Papers
Isaac and Amy Post Family Papers
Phebe Post Willis Papers
Unitarian Society of Rochester Records
Central Library of Rochester and Monroe County, Local History Collection
William Farley Peck Scrapbook, 3 vols.
Rochester City Directories
Swarthmore, Pa.
Friends Historical Library, Swarthmore College
Congregational (later Progressive) Friends and Friends of Human Progress,
Yearly Meeting
Hicksite Meeting Minutes, Preparative, Monthly, Quarterly, and Yearly,
Manuscript and Microfilm
Mary and Joseph Post Family Papers
Townsend Family Papers
Syracuse, N.Y.
Syracuse University Library
Gerrit Smith Papers
University Park, Pa.
Pennsylvania State University, Special Collections
First Edition, Harriet Jacobs, *Incidents in the Life of a Slave Girl*

Washington, D.C.
    Library of Congress
        Susan B. Anthony Papers
        Antislavery Petitions
    National Archives
        Antislavery Petitions
Westbury, N.Y.
    Westbury Historical Collection
        Hicks Family Papers
Worcester, Mass.
    American Antiquarian Society
        Abby Kelley Foster Papers

Microfilm Collections

Fifth to Tenth U.S. Federal Census, Washington, D.C.: U.S. Government Printing Office, 1832, 1842, 1852, 1862, 1872, 1882.
Charles Grandison Finney Papers, 1817–1878. Cleveland, Ohio: Recordak, 1958.
New York State Census, 1845, 1855, 1865
Society of Friends, Hicksite, Minutes of Yearly, Quarterly, and Monthly Meetings for New York and Genesee Yearly Meetings. Ames, Iowa: Preservation Microfilm, various years.

Websites

Chudoba, Peter (Petr). "The Great Rochester Flood of 1865," https://www.linkedin.com/pulse/great-rochester-flood-1865-peter-petr-chudoba.
Freethought Trail, http://www.freethoughttrail.org/profile.php?By=Person&Page=30.
Halsey, Dick. "Religious Congregations in Rochester, NY, Formed before 1900," http://mcnygenealogy.com/church1.htm#ame#ame.
History of Jericho, http://ms.jerichoschools.org/about_us/jericho_s_history.
James E. Hazard Index to the Records of New York Yearly Meeting of the Religious Society of Friends, www.swarthmore.edu/Library/friends/hazard/.
Linder, Douglas O. "Susan Anthony Trial (1873)," Famous Trials, http://www.famous-trials.com/anthony.
Lockport, N.Y., Underground Railroad, Circle Association's African American History of Western New York State: 1770 to 1830, http://www.math.buffalo.edu/~sww/ohistory/hwny-ugrragents.html.
Memorial AME Zion Church, https://sites.google.com/site/memorialamezionchurch/church-history.
New York Manumission Society Membership Book, 1787–1827, http://triptych.brynmawr.edu/cdm/compoundobject/collection/HC_QuakSlav/id/4632.

New York Manumission Society: Conscience of the Nation, www
   .americanabolitionists.com/new-york-manumission-society.htm#Officers.
Rheumatic Fever, www.mayoclinic.org/diseases-conditions/rheumatic-fever
   /home/ovc-20261251.
Rochester City Directories, http://www3.libraryweb.org/lh.aspx?id=1105.
Underground Railroad Niagara County, N.Y., http://
   niagarafallsundergroundrailroad.org/history-and-documents/historical
   -resources-survey/#.
The Willets Family of Long Island, http://longislandgenealogy.com/Surname
   _Pages/willets.htm.
Wood, Larry. "Nettie Pease Fox." *Missouri and Ozarks History*, 9 December 2008,
   http://ozarks-history.blogspot.com/2008/12/nettie-pease-fox.html.

Historic Structure and Historic District Reports

Wellman, Judith. "1816 Farmington Quaker Meetinghouse, Farmington, New
   York." Historic Structure Report, Draft, October 2016. Albany, N.Y.: John G.
   Waite Associates, Architects.
———. "The Cayuga County Homes of Susan White Doty and Elias Doty." In
   Following the Freedom Trail in Auburn and Cayuga County. Auburn, N.Y.: City of
   Auburn Historic Resources Review Board and Cayuga County Historian's
   Office, 2005.
———. "Freedom Trail in Syracuse and Onondaga County, New York." Syracuse,
   N.Y.: Preservation Association of Central New York, 2001.
———."North Street Friends Meetinghouse (Brick Meetinghouse)." In *Following the
   Freedom Trail in Auburn and Cayuga County*. Auburn, N.Y.: City of Auburn
   Historic Resources Review Board and Cayuga County Historian's Office, 2005.
———. "Sherwood Equal Rights Historic District." In *Following the Freedom Trail in
   Auburn and Cayuga County*. Auburn, N.Y.: City of Auburn Historic Resources
   Review Board and Cayuga County Historian's Office, 2005.
Wellman, Judith, Marjorie Allen Perez, and Charles Lenhart et al. "Sodus Bay
   Phalanx (Alasa Farms)." In *Uncovering the Underground Railroad, Abolitionism,
   and African American Life in Wayne County, New York, 1820–1880*. Lyons, N.Y.:
   Wayne County Historian's Office, 2008.
Wellman, Judith, and Tanya Warren. "Discovering the Underground Railroad,
   Abolitionism, and African American Life in Seneca County, N.Y." Waterloo,
   N.Y.: Seneca County Historian's Office, 2006.

Published Primary Sources

Abbott, Marjorie Post. *Post, Albertson, and Hicks Family Letter*. 2 vols. Centralia,
   Wash: Gorham Printing, 2009.
*American Association of Spiritualists with the Constitution of the American
   Association of Spiritualists and some of the Resolutions adopted at the Fifth*

National Convention, held at Rochester, N.Y., August 25th to 28th, 1868. Philadelphia: Rawlings and Zeising Printers, 1868.

Atlas of Rochester, New York, 1875. Rochester, N.Y.: G. M. Hopkins, 1875.

Bartlett, Elizabeth Ann, ed., Sarah Grimké: Letters on the Equality of the Sexes and Other Essays. New Haven, Conn.: Yale University Press, 1988.

"Basis of Religious Association, adopted by the Conference Held at Farmington, in the State of New York, On, the Sixth and Seventh of Tenth month, 1848." Appendix to Proceedings of the Yearly Meeting of Congregational Friends, Held at Waterloo, N.Y., From the 3d to the 5th of Sixth month, inclusive, 1850.

Blassingame, John, Richard G. Carlson, Clarence L. Mohr, Julie S. Jones, John R. McKivigan, David R. Roediger, and Jason H. Silverman, eds. Frederick Douglass Papers, Series 1: Speeches, Debates, and Interviews. Vol. 3, 1855–63. New Haven, Conn.: Yale University Press, 1982.

Buckley, Paul. The Essential Elias Hicks. Philadelphia: Inner Light Books, 2013.

Cadwallader, Priscilla. Memoir of Priscilla Cadwallader. Philadelphia: Book Association of Friends and T. Ellwood Zell, 1864.

Case of the Seneca Indians. Philadelphia: Society of Friends, 1840.

Colman, Lucy N. Reminiscences. Buffalo, N.Y.: H. L. Green, 1891.

Cornell, Thomas C. Adam and Anne Mott: Their Ancestors and Their Descendants. Poughkeepsie, N.Y.: A. V. Haight, 1890.

Davis, Paulina Wright, ed. Proceedings of the Worcester Woman's Rights Convention, October 23 and 24, 1851. Boston: Prentiss Sawyer, 1851.

Densmore, Christopher, Carol Faulkner, Nancy Hewitt, and Beverly Wilson Palmer, eds. Lucretia Mott Speaks: The Essential Speeches and Sermons. Urbana: University of Illinois Press, 2017.

Dewey, John, comp. Rochester and the Post Express: A History of the City from the Earliest Times. Rochester, N.Y.: Post Express Printing, 1898.

Douglass, Frederick. Oration, delivered in Corinthian Hall, Rochester, by Frederick Douglass, July 5, 1852, Published by Request. Rochester, N.Y.: Lee, Mann, 1852.

French, J. H. Historical and Statistical Gazeteer of New York State. Syracuse, N.Y.: R. Pearsall Smith, 1860.

Frazier, Charles W., comp. The Old Ship of Zion: Its History and Its People. Rochester, N.Y.: printed for the author, 1995.

Genesee Yearly Meeting, Discipline of the Genesee Yearly Meeting: held at Farmington, in western New York. Revised in the Sixth Month, 1842. Rochester, 1842.

Gordon, Ann D., Susan I. Johns, Oona Schmid, Mary Poole, Veronica A. Wilson, and Stacy Kinlock Sewell, eds. Against an Aristocracy of Sex, 1866 to 1873. Vol. 2 of The Selected Papers of Elizabeth Cady Stanton and Susan B. Anthony. New Brunswick, N.J.: Rutgers University Press, 2000.

Gordon, Ann D., Tamara Gaskill Miller, Stacy Kinlock Sewell, Ann Pfau, and Arlene Kriv, eds. In the School of Anti-Slavery, 1840–1866. Vol. 1 of The Selected

Papers of Elizabeth Cady Stanton and Susan B. Anthony. New Brunswick, N.J.: Rutgers University Press, 1997.

Gordon, Ann D., Allison L. Sneider, Ann Elizabeth Pfau, Kimberly J. Banks, Lesley L. Doig, Meg Meneghel MacDonald, and Margaret Sumner, eds. *National Protection for National Citizens*. Vol. 3 of *The Selected Papers of Elizabeth Cady Stanton and Susan B. Anthony*. New Brunswick, N.J.: Rutgers University Press, 2003.

Gue, Benjamin F. *Diary of Benjamin F. Gue in Rural New York and Pioneer Iowa*. Ames: Iowa State University Press, 1962.

Harper, Ida Husted. *The Life and Work of Susan B. Anthony*. 3 vols. Indianapolis, Ind.: Bowen-Merrill, 1899.

Hicks, Elias. *The Quaker; or, A Series of Sermons*. Vol. 4. Philadelphia, 1828.

History and Commerce of Rochester, Illustrated. New York: A. F. Parsons, 1894.

Jacobs, Harriet. *Incidents in the Life of a Slave Girl: Written by Herself*. Boston: printed for the author, 1861. Reprint with appendix, Jean Fagan Yellin ed. Cambridge, Mass.: Belknap Press of Harvard University Press, 1987.

James, Thomas. *Life of Rev. Thomas James by Himself*. Rochester, N.Y.: Rochester Express Printing, 1886.

Jericho Friends Meeting House, 1788–1988. New York: Algonquin Press, 1988.

Lasser, Carol, and Marlene Diehl Merrill, eds. *Friends and Sisters: Letters between Lucy Stone and Antoinette Brown Blackwell, 1846–1893*. Women in American History Series. Urbana: University of Illinois Press, 1987.

Lay, Benjamin. *All Slave-Keepers that keep the Innocent in Bondage, Apostates. . . .* Philadelphia, 1773.

May, Samuel J. *The Rights and Condition of Women: A Sermon Preached in Syracuse, Nov., 1845*. Syracuse, N.Y.: Stoddard and Babcock, 1846. Reprint, Syracuse, N.Y.: Lathrop's Print, 1853. Citations are to the 1853 edition.

McIntosh, W. H. *History of Monroe County, With Illustrations*. Philadelphia: Everts, Ensign and Everts, 1877.

McClymer, John F., ed. *This High and Holy Moment: The First National Woman's Rights Convention, Worcester, 1850*. Fort Worth, Tex.: Harcourt Brace, 1999.

McKivigan, John R., L. Diane Barnes, Mark G. Emerson, Leigh Fought, Robin L. Condin, Rachel L. Drenovsky, Peter P. Hinks, and Susan Hubert, eds. *Frederick Douglass Papers: Series 3: Correspondence*. Vol. 1, *1842–1852*. New Haven, Conn.: Yale University Press, 2009.

Merrill, Walter M., and Louis Ruchame, eds. *The Letters of William Lloyd Garrison*. 3 vols. Cambridge, Mass: Harvard University Press, 1971–81.

New York Yearly Meeting of Friends, Hicksite. *Discipline*. New York: New York Yearly Meeting of Friends, Hicksite, 1836.

Onderdonk, Henry, Jr., *Documents and Letters Intended to Illustrate the Revolutionary Incidents of Queens County; with connecting narratives, explanatory notes, and additions*. New York: Leavitt, Trow, 1846. Reprint, Harriet Stryker-Rodda, ed. New Orleans, La.: Polyanthos, 1976.

Palmer, Beverly, ed. *The Selected Letters of Lucretia Coffin Mott.* Urbana: University of Illinois Press, 2002.

Parker, Jane Marsh. *Rochester: A Story Historical.* Rochester, N.Y.: Scrantom, Wetmore, 1884.

Peck, William F. *History of Rochester and Monroe County.* Chicago, Ill.: Pioneer, 1908.

———. *Semi-Centennial History of Rochester.* Syracuse, N.Y.: D. Mason, 1884.

Post, Amy. Preface to *Reminiscences,* by Lucy N. Colman, 3. Buffalo, N.Y.: H. L. Green, 1891.

———. "The Underground Railroad in Rochester." In *Semi-Centennial History of Rochester,* by William Peck. Syracuse, N.Y: D. Mason, 1884.

Post, Isaac. *Voices from the Spirit World, Being Communications from Many Spirits, by the hand of Isaac Post, Medium.* Rochester, N.Y.: C. H. McDonell, 1852.

Proceedings of the Annual Meeting of the Friends of Human Progress, Held at Waterloo, Seneca County, N.Y., on the Third, Fourth and Fifth of June, 1859. Rochester, N.Y.: C. W. Hebard, 1859.

Proceedings of the Thirteenth Yearly Meeting of Friends of Human Progress, Held at Waterloo, Seneca Co., N.Y., on the thirty-first day of May and the first and second day of June, 1861. Cortland, N.Y.: VanSlyck and Ford's Power Press Print, 1861.

Proceedings of the Woman's Rights Convention, Held at the Unitarian Church, Rochester, N.Y., August 2, 1848, To Consider the Rights of Woman, Politically, Religiously, and Industrially. Revised by Mrs. Amy Post. New York, N.Y.: Robert J. Johnston, 1870.

Proceedings of the Yearly Meeting of Congregational Friends, Held at Waterloo, N.Y., from the 4th to 6th of Sixth Month, inclusive, 1849. Auburn, N.Y.: Oliphant's Press, 1849.

Proceedings of the Yearly Meeting of Congregational Friends, Held at Waterloo, N.Y., From the 3d to the 5th of Sixth month, inclusive, 1850. Auburn, N.Y.: Henry Oliphant, 1850.

Proceedings of the Yearly Meeting of Congregational Friends, Held at Waterloo, N.Y., on the 6th, 7th and 8th of the 6th month, 1852, With an Appendix. Auburn, N.Y.: Henry Oliphant, 1852.

Proceedings of the Yearly Meeting of the Friends of Human Progress, held the 7th, 8th and 9th of June, 1857, at Junius Meetinghouse, Waterloo, Seneca Co, N.Y. Rochester, N.Y.: Curtis, Butts, 1857.

Report of the Woman's Rights Convention, held at Seneca Falls, N.Y., July 19th and 20th, 1848. Rochester, N.Y.: John Dick, 1848.

Stanton, Elizabeth Cady. *Eighty Years & More: Reminiscences, 1815–1897.* New York: T. Fisher Unwin, 1898. Reprint, New York: Schocken Books, 1971.

Stanton, Elizabeth Cady, Susan B. Anthony, and Matilda Joslyn Gage, eds. *History of Woman Suffrage.* Vol. 1, *1848–1861.* New York: Fowler & Wells, 1881. Reprint, New York: Arno Press & New York Times, 1969.

———. *History of Woman Suffrage.* Vol. 2, *1861–1876.* New York: Fowler & Wells, 1882. Reprint, New York: Arno Press and New York Times, 1969.

Sterling Dorothy, ed. *Turning the World Upside Down: The Anti-Slavery Convention of American Women, Held in New York City, May 9–12, 1837.* New York: Feminist Press, 1993.

Steward, Austin. *Twenty-Two Years a Slave, and Forty a Free Man.* Rochester, N.Y.: William Alling, 1857. Reprint, Syracuse, N.Y.: Syracuse University Press, 2003.

Still, William. *The Underground Railroad: A Record of Authentic Facts, Narratives, Letters, etc.* Philadelphia: Porter and Coates, 1872. Reprint, Medford, N.J.: Plexus, 2005.

Stroke, Elliott G. *History of Cayuga County, New York, with Illustrations and Biographical Sketches, Some of Its Prominent Men and Pioneers.* Syracuse, N.Y.: D. Mason, 1879.

Taylor, Francis R., ed. *Life of William Savery of Philadelphia, 1750–1894.* New York: Macmillan, 1925.

Truth, Sojourner. *A Narrative of the Life of Sojourner Truth.* Edited by Olive Gilbert. Boston: printed for the author, 1850. Reprint, Battle Creek, Mich.: Review and Herald Press, 1884.

Wesley, Dorothy Porter, and Constance Porter Uzelac, eds. *William Cooper Nell, Selected Writings, 1832–1874.* Baltimore: Black Classics Press, 2002.

Woodcock, Thomas S. "Some Account of a Trip to the 'Falls of Niagara.'" In *America Firsthand.* 9th ed. Vol. 1, edited by Anthony Marcus, John M. Giggle, and David Bruner. Boston: Bedford/St.Martin's, 2012.

Yellin, Jean Fagan, Joseph M. Thomas, Kate Culkin, and Scott Korb, eds. *The Harriet Jacobs Papers Project.* 2 vols. Chapel Hill: University of North Carolina Press, 2008.

Secondary Sources

Amory, Thomas C. "The Expedition under General Sullivan in 1779." *Proceedings of the Massachusetts Historical Society* 20 (January 1883): 88–94.

Anderson, Bonnie S. *The Rabbi's Atheist Daughter: Ernestine Rose, International Feminist Pioneer.* New York: Oxford University Press, 2017.

Bacon, Margaret Hope. *Mothers of Feminism: The Story of Quaker Women in America.* San Francisco: Harper and Row, 1986.

Barbour, Hugh, Christopher Densmore, Elizabeth H. Moger, Nancy C. Sorel, Alson D. Van Wagner, and Arthur J. Worrall, eds. *Quaker Crosscurrents: Three Hundred Years of Friends in the New York Yearly Meetings.* Syracuse, N.Y.: Syracuse University Press, 1995.

Berlin, Ira. "The Revolution in Black Life." In *The American Revolution: Explorations in the History of American Radicalism*, edited by Alfred F. Young. DeKalb: Northern Illinois University Press, 1976.

Bradley, A. Day. "Progressive Friends in Michigan and New York." *Quaker History*
52 (1963): 95–103.

Braude, Ann. *Radical Spirits: Spiritualism and Women's Rights in Nineteenth-
Century America*. Boston: Beacon Books, 1999.

Breault, Judith Colucci. *The World of Emily Howland: Odyssey of a Humanitarian*.
Millbrae, Calif.: Les Femmes, 1976.

Brekus, Catherine A. *Strangers and Pilgrims: Female Preaching in America,
1740–1845*. Chapel Hill: University of North Carolina Press, 1998.

Brooke, John L. *Columbia Rising: Civil Life on the Upper Hudson from the Revolution
to the Age of Jackson*. Omohundro Institute of Early American History and
Culture Series. Chapel Hill: University of North Carolina Press, 2010.

———. "Cultures of Nationalism, Movements of Reform, and the Composite-
Federal Polity: From Revolutionary Settlement to Antebellum Crisis." *Journal
of the Early Republic* 29, no. 1(2009): 1–33.

Brooks, Corey M. *Liberty Power: Antislavery Third Parties and the Transformation
of American Politics*. American Beginnings, 1500–1900. Chicago: University of
Chicago Press, 2016.

Brown, Elisabeth Potts, and Susan Mosher Stuard, eds. *Witnesses for Change:
Quaker Women over Three Centuries*. New Brunswick, N.J.: Rutgers University
Press, 1989.

Butler, Jon. "The Dark Ages of American Occultism, 1760–1848." In *The Occult in
America: New Historical Perspectives*, edited by Howard Kerr and Charles Crow,
58–78. Urbana: University of Illinois Press, 1983.

Calarco, Tom. *The Underground Railroad in Upstate New York*. Charleston, S.C.:
History Press, 2014.

Calloway, Colin G. *The American Revolution in Indian Country: Crisis and Diversity
in Native American Communities*. Cambridge, UK: Cambridge University Press,
1995.

Carey, Brycchan, and Geoffrey Plank, eds. *Quakers and Abolition*. Urbana:
University of Illinois Press, 2014.

Chmielewski, Wendy E., "'Binding Themselves Closer to Their Own Peculiar
Duties': Gender and Women's Work for Peace, 1818–1860." *Peace and Change*,
20, no. 4(1995): 466–90.

———. ed. *Guide to Sources on Women in the Swarthmore College Peace Collection*.
Swarthmore, Pa.: Swarthmore College, 1988.

Clinton, Catherine. *Harriet Tubman: The Road to Freedom*. New York: Little,
Brown, 2004.

Colaiaco, James A. *Frederick Douglass and the Fourth of July*. New York: Palgrave
Macmillan, 2007.

Coles, Howard W. *The Cradle of Freedom: A History of the Negro in Rochester,
Western New York and Canada*. New York: Oxford University Press, 1942.

Connolly, Brian. *Domestic Intimacies: Incest and the Liberal Subject in Nineteenth-
Century America*. Philadelphia: University of Pennsylvania Press, 2014.

Cross, Whitney. *The Burned-Over District: The Social and Intellectual History of Enthusiastic Religion in Western New York, 1800–1850.* Ithaca, N.Y.: Cornell University Press, 1950.

Davidoff, Leonore, and Catherine Hall. *Family Fortunes: Men and Women in the English Middle Class, 1780–1850.* 2nd ed. New York: Routledge, 2003.

Davidson, Carlisle G. "A Profile of Hicksite Quakerism in Michigan, 1830–1860." *Friends Historical Association Bulletin* 59 (1970): 106–12.

Decker, William Merrill. *Epistolary Practices: Letter Writing in America before Telecommunications.* Chapel Hill: University of North Carolina Press, 2000.

Densmore, Christopher. "The Dilemma of Quaker Anti-Slavery: The Case of Farmington Quarterly Meeting, 1836–1860," *Quaker History* 82, no. 2 (1993):

———. "Quaker Comeouters and the Seneca Falls Woman's Rights Convention of 1848." Paper presented at the New York History Conference, 4–5 June 1993.

———. "The Quaker Tradition: Sustaining Women's Rights." Paper presented at the National Women's Studies Association Annual Meeting, Oswego, N.Y., 1998. http://ublib.buffalo.edu/libraries/units/archives/urr/.

Diedrich, Maria. *Love across the Color Line: Ottilie Assing and Frederick Douglass.* New York: Hill and Wang, 1999.

Dillon, Merton L. *Benjamin Lundy and the Struggle for Negro Freedom.* Urbana: University of Illinois Press, 1966.

Dorn, Adelaide Elizabeth. "A History of the Antislavery Movement in Rochester and Vicinity." M.A. thesis, University of Buffalo, 1932.

Dorsey, Bruce. "Friends Becoming Enemies: Philadelphia Benevolence and the Neglected Era of Quaker History." *Journal of the Early Republic* 18, no. 3 (Autumn 1998): 395–428.

———. *Reforming Men and Women: Gender in the Antebellum City.* Ithaca, N.Y.: Cornell University Press, 2002.

DuBois, Ellen. *Feminism and Suffrage: The Emergence of an Independent Women's Movement in America, 1848–1869.* Ithaca, N.Y.: Cornell University Press, 1978.

Dudden, Faye. *Fighting Chance: The Struggle over Woman Suffrage and Black Suffrage in Reconstruction America.* New York: Oxford University Press, 2011.

Dunn, Mary Maples. "Latest Light on Women of Light." In Brown and Stuard, *Witnesses for Change,* 71–85.

Faulkner, Carol. *Lucretia Mott's Heresy: Abolition and Women's Rights in Nineteenth-Century America.* Philadelphia: University of Pennsylvania Press, 2011.

———. "The Root of the Evil: Free Produce and Radical Antislavery, 1820–1860," *Journal of the Early Republic* 27 (Fall 2007): 377–405.

———. *Women's Radical Reconstruction: The Freedmen's Aid Movement.* Philadelphia: University of Pennsylvania Press, 2004.

Flexner, Eleanor. *Century of Struggle: The Woman's Rights Movement in the United States.* Cambridge, Mass.: Belknap Press, 1973.

Foner, Eric, *Gateway to Freedom: The Hidden History of the Underground Railroad*. New York: W. W. Norton, 2015.

Foos, Paul. *A Short, Offhand Killing Affair: Soldiers and Social Conflict during the Mexican-American War*. Chapel Hill: University of North Carolina Press, 2002.

Forbush, Bliss. *Elias Hicks: Quaker Liberal*. New York: Columbia University Press, 1956.

Fosl, Catherine. *Subversive Southerner: Anne Braden and the Struggle for Racial Justice in the Cold War South*. Lexington: University of Kentucky Press, 2006.

Fought, Leigh. *Women in the World of Frederick Douglass*. New York: Oxford University Press, 2017.

Ginzberg, Lori D. *Elizabeth Cady Stanton: An American Life*. New York: Hill and Wang, 2009.

——. *Untidy Origins: A Story of Woman's Rights in Antebellum New York*. Chapel Hill: University of North Carolina Press, 2005.

——. *Women in Antebellum Reform*. Wheeling, Ill.: Harlan Davidson, 2000.

Good, Cassandra A. *Founding Friendships: Friendships between Men and Women in the Early American Republic*. New York: Oxford University Press, 2015.

Goodwin, Doris Kearns. *Team of Rivals: The Political Genius of Abraham Lincoln*. New York: Simon and Schuster, 2005.

Gordon, Linda. *Woman's Body, Woman's Right: A Social History of Birth Control in America*. Rev. ed. New York: Penguin, 1977.

Graymont, Barbara. *The Iroquois in the American Revolution*. Syracuse, N.Y.: Syracuse University Press, 1972.

Greenspan, Ezra. *William Wells Brown: An African American Life*. New York: W. W. Norton, 2014.

Gregory, James M. *Frederick Douglass, the Orator*. Springfield, Mass.: Willey, 1983.

Gutknecht, David. "Urban Legend: The Army of the Potomac and the New York Draft Riots." *Gettysburg* 48 (January 2013): 84–93.

Hamm, Thomas D. "George F. White and Hicksite Opposition to the Abolitionist Movement." In Carey and Plank, *Quakers and Abolition*, 43–55.

——. "Quakerism, Ministry, Marriage, and Divorce: The Ordeal of Priscilla Hunt Cadwalader." *Journal of the Early Republic* 28, no. 3 (Fall 2008): 407–31.

Hanmer-Croughton, Amy. "The Rochester Female Charitable Society." Rochester Historical Society, *Publications* 9 (1930): 68–70.

Hartsough, Margaret. Foreword to *Farmington*, by Reginald W. Neale, 6. Charleston, S.C.: Arcadia, 2011.

Hauptman, Lawrence M. *Conspiracy of Interests: Iroquois Dispossession and the Rise of New York State*. Syracuse, N.Y.: Syracuse University Press, 1999.

Hawkes, Andrea Constantine. "The Life of Elizabeth McClintock Phillips, 1821–1896: A Story of Family, Friends, Community, and a Self-Made Woman." Ph.D. diss., University of Maine, 2005.

Haynes, Gretchen. "The Quaker Conflict over Abolition Activism: Will of Man, Will of God." http://www.icelandichorse.info/quakerconflictoverabolitionactiv ism.html.

Herr, Pamela. *Jessie Benton Frémont: American Woman of the 19th Century*. New York: Franklin Watts, 1987.

Hersh, Blanche Glassman. *The Slavery of Sex: Feminist-Abolitionists in America*. Urbana: University of Illinois Press, 1978.

Hershberger, Mary. "Mobilizing Women, Anticipating Abolition: The Struggle Against Indian Removal in the Early 1830s." *Journal of American History* 86 (June 1999): 15–40.

Hewitt, Nancy A. "Feminist Frequencies: Regenerating the Wave Metaphor." *Feminist Studies* 38, no. 3 (Fall 2012): 658–80.

———. "Feminist Friends: Agrarian Quakers and the Emergence of Woman's Rights in America." *Feminist Studies* (Spring 1986): 27–49.

———. "The Fragmentation of Friends: The Consequences for Quaker Women in Antebellum America." In Brown and Stuard, *Witnesses for Change*, 93–108.

———., ed. *No Permanent Waves: Recasting Histories of U.S. Feminism*. New Brunswick, N.J.: Rutgers University Press, 2010.

———. *Women's Activism and Social Change: Rochester, New York, 1822–1872*. Ithaca, N.Y.: Cornell University Press, 1984.

Higby, Gregory J. "Chemistry and the 19th-Century American Pharmacist." *Bulletin of the History of Medicine* 28, no. 1(2003): 9–17.

Ingle, H. Larry. *Quakers in Conflict: The Hicksite Reformation*. Knoxville: University of Tennessee Press, 1986.

Isenberg, Nancy. *Sex and Citizenship in Antebellum America*. Chapel Hill: University of North Carolina Press, 1998.

Jeffrey, Julie Roy. *The Great Silent Army of Abolitionism: Ordinary Women in the Antislavery Movement*. Chapel Hill: University of North Carolina Press, 1998.

Jensen, Joan. *Loosening the Bonds: Mid-Atlantic Farm Women, 1750–1850*. New Haven, Conn.: Yale University Press, 1986.

Johnson, Paul E. *A Shopkeeper's Millennium: Society and Revivals in Rochester, New York, 1815–1837*. New York: Hill and Wang, 1978.

Johnson, Reginald O. *The Liberty Party, 1840–1848: Antislavery Politics in the United States*. Antislavery, Abolition, and the Atlantic World. Baton Rouge, La.: LSU Press, 2009.

Jones, Martha S. *All Bound Up Together: The Woman Question in African American Public Culture, 1830–1900*. John Hope Franklin Series in African American History and Culture. Chapel Hill: University of North Carolina Press, 2007.

———. "Overthrowing the 'Monopoly of the Pulpit': Race and the Rights of Church Women in the Nineteenth-Century United States." In Hewitt, *No Permanent Waves*, 121–43.

Jordan, Ryan P. *Slavery and the Meetinghouse: The Quakers and the Abolitionist Dilemma, 1820–1865.* Bloomington: Indiana University Press, 2007.

Kantrowitz, Stephen. *More Than Freedom: Fighting for Black Citizenship in a White Culture, 1829–1889.* New York: Penguin, 2013.

Kaplan, Temma. *Taking Back the Streets: Women, Youth, and Direct Democracy.* Berkeley: University of California Press, 2003.

Kraditor, Aileen. *Means and Ends in American Abolitionism: Garrison and His Critics on Tactics and Strategy, 1835–1850.* New York: Pantheon Books, 1969.

Larson, Kate Clifford. *Bound for the Promised Land: Harriet Tubman, Portrait of an American Hero.* New York: One World, 2009.

Lavoie, Catherine C. "Historic American Buildings Survey of Friends Meetinghouses within the Region of Philadelphia Yearly Meeting." In *Silent Witness: Quaker Meetinghouses in the Delaware Valley, 1695 to the Present.* Philadelphia: Philadelphia Yearly Meeting of the Religious Society of Friends with support of the Historic American Building Survey, National Park Service, 2003.

Levy, Barry. *Quakers and the American Family: British Settlement in the Delaware Valley.* New York: Oxford University Press, 1988

Malczewski, Paul. "The Heinous High Falls Murder," *Epitaph: The Friends of Mt. Hope Newsletter,* Spring 1999.

Mayer, Henry. *All on Fire: William Lloyd Garrison and the Abolition of Slavery.* New York: W. W. Norton, 2008.

McFeely, William S. *Frederick Douglass.* New York: W. W. Norton, 1991.

McKelvey, Blake. *Rochester: The Water-Power City, 1812–1854.* Cambridge, Mass.: Harvard University Press, 1945.

McKivigan, John R. *The War Against Pro-Slavery Religion: Abolitionism and Northern Churches, 1830–1865.* Ithaca, N.Y.: Cornell University Press, 1984.

McPherson, James. *Battle Cry of Freedom: The Civil War Era.* New York: Oxford University Press, 1988.

Melder, Keith. "Abby Kelley Foster." In *Notable American Women: A Biographical Dictionary,* edited by Edward T. James, Janet Wilson James, and Paul S. Boyer, 1:647–48. Cambridge, Mass.: Belknap Press of Harvard University Press, 1971.

Miles, Tiya. "'Shall Woman's Voice Be Hushed?' Laura Smith Haviland in Abolitionist Women's History." *Michigan Historical Review* 39, no. 2 (Fall 2013): 1–20.

Miller, Marla R. *Betsy Ross and the Making of America.* New York: Henry Holt, 2010.

Million, Joelle. *Woman's Voice, Woman's Place: Lucy Stone and the Birth of the Woman's Rights Movement.* Westport, Conn.: Praeger, 2003.

Murphy, Betsey. *Jericho: The History of a Long Island Hamlet.* Jericho, N.Y.: Jericho Public Library, 2009.

Nash, Gary B. "Forging Freedom: The Emancipation Experience in Northern Seaports, 1775–1820." In *Race, Class and Politics: Essays on Colonial and Revolutionary Society,* edited by Gary B. Nash. Urbana: University of Illinois Press, 1986.

———. "The Hidden History of Quakers and Slavery." In Carey and Plank, *Quakers and Abolition*, 209–24.

Neale, Reginald W. *Farmington.* Charleston, S.C.: Arcadia, 2011.

Norgren, Jill. *Belva Lockwood: The Woman Who Would Be President.* New York: New York University Press, 2007.

Noyes, John Humphrey. *History of American Socialisms.* Philadelphia: J. B. Lippincott, 1870. Reprint, New York: Dover, 1966.

Ogden-Malouf, Susan Marie. "American Revivalism and Temperance Drama: Evangelical Protestant Ritual and Theatre in Rochester, New York, 1830–1845." Ph.D. diss., Northwestern University, 1981.

Painter Nell Irvin, *Sojourner Truth: A Life, a Symbol.* New York: W. W. Norton, 1996.

Pierson, Michael D. *Free Hearts and Free Homes: Gender and American Antislavery Politics.* Chapel Hill: University of North Carolina Press, 2003.

Pope-Levinson, Priscilla. *Turn the Pulpit Loose: Two Centuries of American Women Evangelicals.* New York: Palgrave Macmillan, 2004.

Quarles, Benjamin. "Frederick Douglass and the Woman's Rights Movement." History 2000 Occasional Papers Series, No. 1–1993. Baltimore: Morgan State University Foundation, 1993.

———. *The Negro in the American Revolution.* Chapel Hill: University of North Carolina Press, 1961.

Rediker, Marcus. *The Fearless Benjamin Lay: The Quaker Dwarf Who Became the First Revolutionary Abolitionist.* Boston, Mass.: Beacon Press, 2017.

Resnick-Day, Benjamin. "Debating the 'Inevitable': Cherokees, Senecas, and the Rhetoric of Removal, 1827–1847." Ph.D. diss., Rutgers University, New Brunswick, 2016.

Richards, Leonard. *Who Freed the Slaves? The Fight over the Thirteenth Amendment.* Chicago, Ill.: University of Chicago Press, 2015.

Ricks, Mary Kay. *Escape on the Pearl: The Heroic Bid for Freedom on the Underground Railroad.* New York: William Morrow, 2007.

Robertson, Stacey M. *Hearts Beating for Liberty: Women Abolitionists in the Old Northwest.* Chapel Hill: University of North Carolina Press, 2010.

Robnett, Belinda. "African-American Women in the Civil Rights Movement, 1954–1963: Gender, Leadership and Micromobilization." *American Journal of Sociology* 101, no. 6 (May 1996): 1661–93.

Rosenberg, Charles E. *No Other Gods: Science and American Social Thought.* Rev. ed. Baltimore, Md.: John Hopkins University Press, 2007.

Ruchkin, Judith Polgar, "The Abolition of 'Colored Schools' in Rochester, New York, 1832–1856." *New York History* 51, no. 4 (July 1970): 376–93.

Shorto, Russell. *The Island at the Center of the World: The Epic Story of Dutch Manhattan and the Forgotten Colony That Shaped America.* New York: Vintage Books, 2005.

Sinha, Manisha. *The Slave's Cause: A History of Abolition*. New Haven, Conn.: Yale University Press, 2016.

Smith-Rosenberg, Carroll. "The Cross and the Pedestal: Anti-Ritualism, Liminality, and the Emergence of the American Bourgeosie." In *The Rising Tide of Evangelical Religion*, edited by Leonard I. Sweet, 199–231. Mercer, Ga.: Mercer University Press, 1984.

Soderlund, Jean R. "Women's Authority in Pennsylvania and New Jersey Quaker Meetings, 1680–1760." *William and Mary Quarterly* 44, no. 4 (1987): 722–49.

Spence, Taylor. "Women at the Crossroads: The Legal and Political Fight to Reverse Seneca Indian Removal, 1838–1887." Paper presented at the Organization of American Historians, April 11–14, 2013.

Spicer, R. Barclay. "The Farmington Centenary." *Friends' Intelligencer* 74 (1917): 666–67.

Stansell, Christine. *City of Women: Sex and Class in New York, 1789–1860*. Urbana: University of Illinois Press, 1987.

Stauffer, John. *The Black Hearts of Men: Radical Abolitionists and the Transformation of Race*. Cambridge, Mass.: Harvard University Press, 2002.

Sterling, Dorothy. *Ahead of Her Time: Abby Kelley and the Politics of Slavery*. New York: W. W. Norton, 1991.

Stieb, Ernest W. "A Professional Keeping Shop: The Nineteenth-Century Apothecary." *Material History Bulletin* 22 (1985): 1–10.

Stuart, Nancy Rubin. *The Reluctant Spiritualist: The Life of Maggie Fox*. New York: Harcourt, 2005.

Switala, William J. *Underground Railroad in New York and New Jersey*. Mechanicsburg, Pa.: Stackpole Books, 2006.

Taylor, Alan. *American Colonies: The Settling of North America*. New York: Penguin Books, 2002.

Taylor, Nikki M. *Frontiers of Freedom: Cincinnati's Black Community, 1802–1868*. Athens: Ohio University Press, 2005.

Terborg-Penn, Rosalyn. *African American Women and the Struggle for the Vote*. Bloomington: Indiana University Press, 1999.

Tetrault, Lisa. *The Myth of Seneca Falls: Memory and the Women's Suffrage Movement, 1848–1898*. Chapel Hill: University of North Carolina Press, 2014.

Theodore, Alisse. " 'A Right to Speak on the Subject': The U.S. Women's Antiremoval Petition Campaign, 1829–1831," *Rhetoric and Public Affairs* 5, no. 4 (Winter 2002): 601–23.

Ulrich, Laurel Thatcher. *A Midwife's Tale: The Life of Martha Ballard, Based on Her Diary, 1785–1812*. New York: A. Knopf, 1990.

Van Horn, Patrick. "The Ohio Banking Panic of 1854." Social Science Research Network, posted April 10, 2011, papers.ssrn.com/sol3/papers.cfm?abstract_id =1806523.

Velsor, Kathleen S. *The Underground Railroad on Long Island: Friends in Freedom.* Charleston, S.C.: History Press, 2013.

Wagner, Sally Roesch. *Sisters in Spirit: Haudenosaunee (Iroquois) Influence on Early American Feminists.* Summertown, Tenn.: Native Voices, 2001.

——. *The Untold Story of the Iroquois Influence on Early Feminists.* Aberdeen, S.D.: Sky Carrier Press, 1996.

Washington, Margaret. *Sojourner Truth's America.* Urbana: University of Illinois Press, 2009.

Wellman, Judith. *Brooklyn's Promised Land: The Free Black Community of Weeksville, New York.* New York: New York University Press, 2014.

——. *The Road to Seneca Falls: Elizabeth Cady Stanton and the First Woman's Rights Convention.* Urbana: University of Illinois Press, 2004.

——. "The Seneca Falls Woman's Rights Convention: A Study of Social Movements." *Journal of Women's History* 3 (Spring 1991): 9–37.

——. "Women and Radical Reform in Antebellum Upstate New York." In *Clio Was a Woman: Studies in the History of American Women*, edited by Mabel E. Deutrich and Virginia C. Purdy, 113–27. Washington, D.C.: Howard University Press, 1980.

——. "Women's Rights, Republicanism, and Revolutionary Rhetoric in Antebellum New York State." *New York History* 69, no. 3 (1988): 352–84.

Wellman, Judith, and Stephen Lewandowski. "Farmington Quaker Meetinghouse." Crooked Lake Review, Spring–Summer 2007, http://www.crookedlakereview.com/articles/136_150/142springsummer2007/142lewandowski.html.

Whitaker, Paula. *A Civil Life in an Uncivil Time: Julia Wilbur's Struggle for Purpose.* Lincoln, Neb.: Potomac Books, 2017.

Yellin, Jean Fagan. *Harriet Jacobs: A Life.* New York: Basic Civitas Books, 2004.

Yellin, Jean Fagan, and John C. Van Horne, eds. *The Abolitionist Sisterhood: Women's Political Culture in Antebellum America.* Ithaca, N.Y.: Cornell University Press, 1994.

Zaeske, Susan. *Signatures of Citizenship: Petitioning, Antislavery, and Women's Political Identity.* Chapel Hill: University of North Carolina Press, 2003.

Index

African Americans (cont.)
views about integration, 121; and
women's rights, 130, 134–35, 136–37,
138–39, 179–80, 309n54. *See also*
Abolitionists; African Bethel Church
(Rochester); African Methodist
Episcopal Zion Church (AME Zion,
Rochester); Contrabands/Refugees,
from slavery during the Civil War;
Underground Railroad; Western
New York Anti-Slavery Society
(WNYASS); *and individual black
activists*
African Bethel Church (Rochester), 91,
121, 123, 319n21, 325n2
African Methodist Episcopal Zion
Church (AME Zion), 92, 135
African Methodist Episcopal Zion
Church (AME Zion, Rochester), 64,
69, 107, 121, 123, 135, 198, 213, 227,
318n14; Truth lectures at, 166
Akron (Ohio), woman's rights conven-
tion in, 180
Alexandria (Virginia), 13, 235–36,
238–39, 241, 242–45, 247–48, 250,
292–93. *See also* Contrabands/
Refugees, from slavery during the
Civil War
American and Foreign Anti-Slavery
Society, 86, 92
American Anti-Slavery Society
(AASS), 11, 61, 85, 86, 92; annual
convention of, 83, 111, 149–50, 211,
219, 224, 235; debates over future
of, 256; denounces Lincoln, 232–33;
founding of, 59; and gag rule, 79;
Garrison resigns from, 255; meeting
in Rochester, 171–73, 214; and
partisan politics, 101, 102; protests
against Fugitive Slave Act, 160
American Equal Rights Association
(AERA), 13, 256–57, 258; splits over
Fifteenth Amendment, 259

American Woman Suffrage Association
(AWSA), 13, 269; and Edmunds Law,
283; founding of, 261
Ames, Frances. *See* Nell, Frances Ames
(wife of William C. Nell)
Anneke, Mathilda, 273
Anthony, Asa, 212; broad vision of, 99;
death of, 265; friendship with Posts,
147, 195, 225; and spiritualism, 140;
and Underground Railroad, 107–8
Anthony, Daniel, 147, 170, 195; and
woman's rights, 181
Anthony, Huldah, 212; and antislavery
work, 167; broad vision of, 99; and
friendship with Amy Post, 109, 123,
147, 195, 225; and Underground
Railroad, 108
Anthony, Lucy, 147, 195, 262
Anthony, Mary, 277, 285, 287
Anthony, Susan B., 2, 12, 147–48; and
antislavery activities, 224, 227, 235,
239–40; arrest of, 267, 268, 274,
367n1, 368n3; and Frederick
Douglass, 164, 284; and Friends of
Human Progress, 228; and NWSA,
262; and racism, 365n99; and
temperance, 181, 182; tries to vote,
266–67; votes, 272; and women's
rights, 184, 191, 195, 210, 224,
256–57, 264, 269–70, 273–74, 287;
and women's suffrage, 268–70, 278
Anti-Slavery Bugle, 12, 180
Anti-Slavery Convention of American
Women, 81, 92, 99
Antislavery fairs, 87, 88, 155–56, 205;
and conflicts among women abolitionists, 165–69, 174, 176–77, 209;
with Julia Griffiths, 155–56, 157–58,
159–60, 164–67; and Western New
York Anti-Slavery Society (WNYASS),
95–97, 110, 111, 113–14, 118, 139, 143
Ashley, Mary Jane "Mate" (daughter-
in-law), 148, 162, 196, 251, 258, 261,

Sophia Street, 264, 276; moves to county poorhouse, 281

Daniels, Cora Hatch, 201, 204, 251, 254, 356n41

Davis, Andrew Jackson, 196, 203, 215, 219–20, 246

Davis, Mary Fenn Love, 191, 203, 219–20, 261

Davis, Paulina Wright, 269

Declaration of Sentiments (Seneca Falls), 127–28, 135, 136, 147, 190, 264

DeGarmo, Elias, 58, 60, 62, 76, 86, 107, 131; death of, 272

DeGarmo, Rhoda, 58, 60, 62, 131; activism of, 76, 86, 107, 126; death of, 272, 279; friendship with Posts, 109, 195; joins NWSA, 262; and Progressive Friends, 142; and temperance, 181–82; tries to vote, 266, 267; and women's rights, 129, 275

Delany, Martin, 116, 137

Dickinson, Anna, 237, 239, 246

Dorsey, Bruce, 9

Doty, Elias, 50, 58, 60, 206, 225, 252

Doty, George, 50

Doty, Susan White, 50, 53, 58, 60, 156, 200; death of, 174

Douglass, Anna, 92, 157, 164, 168, 173, 177, 214; death of, 280–81; moves to Rochester, 120–21

Douglass, Frederick, 5, 7, 11–12, 119, 212, 214, 260; 5 July oration of, 175–76; as abolitionist, 91, 92, 102, 107, 116–17, 157, 220, 227; advocates use of black soldiers, 230; attacked in New York City, 160; and black male suffrage, 255; calls Anthony and Stanton racist, 365n99; and Compromise of 1850, 159–60; controversy with Amy Post, 153–54, 168, 170–71, 177, 206–7; criticizes antislavery fair, 158; delivers lectures, 164–65, 225; disappointment with Free Soil Party,

143; emancipation of, 115; escape after John Brown's raid, 221–22; as freethinker, 278; and Friends of Human Progress, 228, 255; friendship with Amy Post, 111, 122, 147, 163, 195, 220, 288; and gender equality, 186; and Griffiths sisters, 153, 154, 155, 159, 163; and Harriet Jacobs, 149; house burns, 266; and international unrest, 124–25; jealousy toward, 150; marries Helen Pitts, 282; moves to farm, 173; and political abolitionism, 147, 152, 163, 167; returns from England, 225; and runaways, 108, 161; sends condolences, 265; settles in Rochester, 117; slighted by Anthony, 284; speaks on Emancipation Day, 130; stays at 36 Sophia Street, 97, 281; supports disunion, 101; supports Freedmen's Bureau, 251; supports Lincoln, 226, 227; tours Europe, 109, 110, 111, 115–16; views on segregation, 121, 137; views on spiritualism, 155; and vigilance committees, 169–70; widowed, 280–81; and women's rights, 127, 128, 133, 137, 191, 263, 273–74, 287, 365–66n99

Douglass, Grace, 79

Douglass, Rosetta, 137, 176, 206–7, 280

Douglass League (Rochester), 288–89

Dred Scott case (1857), 194, 205, 215

Dugdale, Joseph, 106, 203, 220

Dugdale, Ruth, 106, 220

Dun and Bradstreet, 328n55

Edmondson, William, 18

Edmunds Law (1882), 283

Education: and African Americans, 137; and Quakers, 57. See also Colman, Lucy; Douglass, Rosetta

Emancipation Day (Rochester), 1, 68–69, 112, 119, 129–30, 134

Friends' Intelligencer, 62, 84
Friends Joint Committee on Indian
  Affairs, 11, 59, 78, 97–98
Friends of Human Progress, 194, 208,
  211, 287; calls for disunion, 215;
  meetings in Waterloo, 220, 225, 228,
  240, 258, 286; supports equal
  suffrage, 255; universalist vision of,
  215. *See also* Congregational Friends;
  Progressive Friends
Friendship, 6, 11, 66, 76; Post with
  black activists, 120, 122, 147, 148, 149,
  150, 151, 161–62, 163, 177–78, 188,
  194, 195, 197, 201, 208, 216, 220, 222,
  225, 234–35, 258, 265, 275, 288; Post
  with women activists, 107, 109, 122,
  123, 147, 149, 177–78, 185, 188, 194,
  195, 201, 216, 222, 224–25, 257, 265,
  275, 289, 293
Frost, Joseph, 40
Fugitive Slave Act, 159–60, 165–66;
  resistance to, 161, 169, 175, 187, 219
Fugitive Slaves, 85, 107–08, 112, 169,
  228, 334n22; Amy Post as conductor,
  282, 319n21; in central New York, 60,
  62; during Civil War, 232; disagreements about, 7, 331n105; and Frederick Douglass, 225; and Fugitive Slave
  Act, 159–60; and Harriet Jacobs, 161,
  227–28; help from Quakers, 60, 84,
  100, 113, 115; in Jericho, 21, 26, 29;
  and the Posts, 7, 13, 87–88, 89, 100,
  115, 147–48, 159, 163, 173–74, 175,
  177, 188–89, 193, 199; in Rochester,
  68–69, 71, 108, 172–74, 188–90, 199.
  See also Brown, William Wells; Jacobs,
  John S.; Underground Railroad

Gage, Mathilda Joslyn, 273, 287
Gardner, Cornelia, 281
Garnet, Henry Highland, 60, 88
Garrison, William Lloyd, 7, 116, 183,
  227; antislavery work of, 59, 85,

86–87, 92, 214; conflict with
  Frederick Douglass over *North Star*,
  116–17; death of, 279; followers of,
  85–86, 87, 100, 102, 107, 111, 128, 148,
  170, 177, 220; and spiritualism, 155,
  209; stays at Sophia Street, 87,
  204–5, 209; and William Nell, 271;
  and women's rights, 190, 274
Genesee River, 62, 63, 64, 65–66, 291;
  importance for fugitive slaves, 66,
  108
Genesee Yearly Meeting (GYM), 56, 76,
  99; adoption of Discipline, 57;
  antislavery efforts, 78; conflicts over
  abolition, 101–3, 106, 126–27;
  founding of, 55; gender equality in,
  58, 77, 275; and Indians, 58–59, 97;
  and worldly associations, 83
Genius of Universal Emancipation, 59,
  61
German Evangelical United Church
  (Rochester), 272
Gibbons, James S., 84, 199
Gibbs, Isaac, 69, 109, 118
Gibbs, Mary, 69, 70, 109, 118, 123, 130
Gibbs family, 69, 88
Gilbert, Olive, 282
Gladwin, Reverend Albert, 243
Good, Cassandra, 6
Grant, Ulysses S., 250, 368n3; and
  election of 1868, 259
Greeley, Horace, 244; speaks at
  Corinthian Hall, 196
Green Plain (Ohio) Quarterly Meeting,
  106
Greene, Anna, 37, 43, 46, 53; on GYM
  committee, 55
Griffing, Josephine, 248, 251, 252, 253,
  254
Griffiths, Eliza, 150, 153, 155, 157
Griffiths, Julia, 5, 195, 214; and alien-
  ation of Amy Post, 168, 177; conflict
  with Anna Douglass, 177, 214;

Orthodox, 44, 70; traveling Friends, 26–27, 54, 78, 83, 100; and views on utopian communities, 100; and women's rights, 127, 129, 270. *See also* Congregational Friends; Friends of Human Progress; Hicksite Friends; Progressive Friends; Society of Friends

R. G. Dun and Co., 103, 104, 119, 148, 196, 231, 328n55
Radical Abolitionist Party, 226
Ramsdell, Laura, 269
Rawson, A. L., 275, 279
Ray, Charles B., 88
Ray, Reverend David, 113, 130
Raymond, Dr. Aurelia, 273, 279, 363n41
Red Jacket, 58
Red King, Chief, 37
Religious liberty, 13, 215, 272, 293; and other social movements, 14, 117, 118, 119, 146, 181, 184, 284
Reminiscences (Colman), 290
Remond, Charles Lenox, 7, 130, 136, 142, 171, 172, 215, 237, 258, 260; friendship with Amy Post, 151–52, 214, 265; lectures at Corinthian Hall, 198; lectures with Frederick Douglass, 97, 116; universalism of, 258; votes for disunion, 101; and WNYASS, 124, 159; and women's rights, 257
Remond, Sarah, 214
Republican Party: election of 1860, 225–26; election of 1880, 278; emergence of, 194, 205, 212
Revolution, 264
Rights and Condition of Women (May), 113–14, 128
Robbins, Esther Seaman (aunt), 24; antislavery views of, 27
Robbins, Willet (uncle), 24; antislavery views of, 27–28

Robbins family, 24, 28
Robinson, Marius, 180, 190
Robnett, Belinda, 4, 304n7
Rochester, Colonel Nathaniel, 68
Rochester, N.Y., *90*, 212; AERA convention in, 256–57; antislavery activism in, 159, 227; antislavery black women in, 96; antislavery convention in, 224; blacks in, 68, 71, 107, 118, 121, 124; charity in, 67–68; cholera epidemic in, 176, 206; configuration of, 66; demographics of, 68, 70; discrimination in, 113, 159; expansion of, 65–66; major flood in, 249–50; newspapers in, 66; Quaker migration to, 62–63; reform movements in, 182, 193; and refugees in, 253; Stout trial in, 217–18; temperance convention in, 181–82; Truth raises funds in, 252; and women's suffrage, 266–67, 268–69, 277–78, 367n126
Rochester: A Story Historical (Parker), 283
Rochester Anti-Slavery Reading Room, 144, 149, 157, 174
Rochester Anti-Slavery Society, 70
Rochester Female Anti-Slavery Society (RFASS), 70, 76, 80, 167, 322n65; dissolution of, 88, 94
Rochester Female Charitable Society, 67, 76, 291
Rochester Ladies' Anti-Slavery Society (RLASS), 5, 167, 169, 170, 176–77, 189, 192, 193, 195; helps freedmen, 235–36, 254. *See also* Wilbur, Julia
Rochester Monthly Meeting, 91, 101, 103, 131; Posts withdraw from, 105, 162
Rochester Orphan Asylum, 76, 291
Rochester Woman's Rights Convention, 129, 130–36, 145, 147, 264, 270, 281, 282, 286

settlement in North America, 16–17; views on worldly activism, 81, 83. *See also* Friends Joint Committee on Indian Affairs; Quakers; *individual meetings*

Sodus Bay Phalanx, 103, 113, 131

Soldiers' Aid societies, 247, 277

Sophia Street, *90*; black school on, 69; "Circle," 161, 197, 198, 233, 236; Circle helps freedmen, 236; divisions over military service, 233; free meetings at, 106; and fugitive slaves, 188–89; as gathering place, 7, 65, 87, 93, 109, 111, 151, 157, 174, 193, 199, 211, 214, 219, 231, 234, 250, 270, 272, 273, 280, 286, 292; and Post's family nearby, 271–72; Posts move to, 64, 319n20

Sovereigns of Industry (Grange), 13, 270, 272

Spencer, John, 98

Spiritualism, 2, 11, 13, 215, 259–60, 277; embraced by Amy Post, 118, 140–41, 196, 254–55, 284–85, 289; first public demonstration of, 154; and Isaac Post, 140, 145, 149, 151, 154–55, 178; and Liberty League, 273; promotion of, 203–4; and woman's rights, 183. *See also* Post, Amy; Post, Isaac

St. Domingue, 112

Stanton, Elizabeth Cady, 2; and abolition, 239–40; elitist and racist sentiments of, 261, 365n99; family ties of, 329n74; helps organize Seneca Falls convention, 126–28; joins Progressive Friends, 142, 174; and marital property rights, 181; and National Liberal League, 272; and temperance, 182, 186; and woman suffrage, 278; and women's rights, 130, 132, 138, 163, 179, 180, 191, 256–57, 258, 264, 269–70, 273–74, 287

Stebbins, Catherine Fish, 114, 123, 127, 131, 151; joins NWSA, 262; and Progressive Friends, 174, 228; and women's rights, 183, 263, 269, 273, 287

Stebbins, Giles B., 114, 151, 220, 224, 227, 228, 240, 258; as freethinker, 278

Steward, Austin, 60, 68–69, 82, 88, 108

Stone, Lucy, 2, 138, 185, 186, 194, 206; and abolition, 239–40; marriage of, 206, 210; racism of, 365n99; and women's rights, 224, 256, 263, 287

Storrs, William C., 267

Stout, Ira, 217–19

Stowe, Harriet Beecher, 204, 227, 237

Sturges, Maria, 79

Suffrage, 257; black male, 128, 231, 257–58, 328n44; and New Departure, 263; state and territorial, 269; universal, 13, 128–29, 255, 256, 257, 258; women's, 13, 133–34, 263–64, 266–67, 268–69, 274, 277–78, 367n126, 368n3. *See also* Anthony, Susan B.; Women's Taxpayers Association of Monroe County

Sumner, Charles, 212, 244

Supreme Court, U.S., and women's suffrage, 268–69

Syracuse, N.Y., woman's rights convention in, 182–83

Tabor, Frank, 271

Taney, Roger, 205

Tappan, Lewis, 103, 328n55

Taylor, Zachary, 143, 146

Temperance: and issue of divorce, 182; and Quakers, 27, 104; and woman's rights, 181, 182. *See also* Woman's New York State Temperance Society

Texas: and Mexican War, 111; opposition to annexation of, 78–79

Working Women's Protective Union (WWPU)

Women's suffrage, 128, 190, 262, 263–64, 266–67, 268–69, 367n126, 368n3; and Amy Post, 13, 133–34, 224, 262, 266, 274, 277–78, 285; objections to, 133, 224; petitions for, 192, 195, 259, 274

Women's Taxpayers Association of Monroe County, 268–69, 271, 277

Wood, Jethro, 50

Woodcock, Thomas, 63

Woolman, John, 18, 24, 26, 178

Working Women's Protective Union (WWPU), 137–38, 139, 185, 270

Wright, David, 61

Wright, Martha Coffin, 61, 126, 183, 240, 262, 270

Wright, Paulina, 102, 111, 204

Wyoming, 269

MIX
Paper from
responsible sources
FSC® C013483